WITHDRAWN

operations
management

operations management

PRODUCING GOODS & SERVICES
DONALD WATERS

Addison-Wesley Publishing Company

Harlow, England • Reading, Massachusetts • Menlo Park, California
New York • Don Mills, Ontario • Amsterdam • Bonn • Sydney • Singapore
Toyko • Madrid • San Juan • Milan • Mexico City • Seoul • Taipei

To Don and Marjorie

Cover designed by op den Brouw, Design & Illustration, Reading
Typeset by CRB Associates, Norwich
Printed and bound in the United States of America

First printed 1996

ISBN 0–201–42789–3

British Library Cataloguing-in-Publication Data
A catalogue record for this book is available from the British Library.

Library of Congress Cataloging-in-Publication Data applied for

Preface

The subject

Every organization takes a number of inputs and converts them to outputs. Factories take components and raw materials and turn them into finished products; hospitals take sick patients and turn them into healthy ones; power stations convert fuel into electricity; restaurants take food and turn it into meals. All the activities needed for these conversions are called **operations**.

At the heart of every organization – whether it is a manufacturer, service, government, charity, or any other kind of organization – is a set of operations. **Operations management** is concerned with the way these operations are designed, planned, organized, and controlled.

Operations management is used in every organization, and at every level. Because of this, it is often difficult to find general terms which apply to all circumstances. To simplify the terms, this book assumes that every organization makes a **product**. This product might be goods or a service, or a combination of the two – whatever an organization produces is called a product.

Early books on operations management concentrated on manufacturing. But 80% of people in industrialized countries work in the service sector, so this book takes a more general view. It discusses all types of operations, whether they are in primary producers, manufacturers, or any of the services.

In recent years operations management has become increasingly important. There are many reasons for this, including international competition, improved manufacturing processes, more emphasis on product quality, and changing customer expectations. Perhaps the most important influence has been the recognition that an organization can only be successful if it supplies the products that customers want.

Approach of the book

The book gives a broad introduction to operations management. It assumes little previous knowledge from the reader – so it can be used for many introductory courses. Anyone who wants an introduction to operations management will find the book useful.

As the book is designed for people meeting operations management for the first time, it takes a conceptual viewpoint. Ideas are introduced by discussion, examples, and cases. There are a series of management perspectives, interviews, and real case studies to show how these ideas are applied in practice.

Some of the ideas of operations management are based on quantitative reasoning – but this does not mean that operations management is mathematical. We are more interested in the concepts than the detailed arithmetic – we are looking at principles rather than calculations. So quantitative ideas are only included if they are useful – and then they introduced are by worked examples. Most people have access to computers. This book does not assume everyone has a computer, but any calculations can be done easily using standard packages – particularly spreadsheets.

Contents

In this book we follow a logical path through the decisions made in an organization. To make this easier it is divided into five parts. Part I gives an introduction to the subject – it defines operations management and gives examples of the kinds of decisions made.

All organizations make a product, so Part II looks at different aspects of product planning. It describes the aims of product planning, how to maintain high quality, how to forecast demand for products, and the processes which can be used to make products.

Part III looks in more detail at the process used to make a product. It describes the layout of a process, its capacity, and other measures of performance. The last chapter in this part shows how to control the process to give high quality products.

Part IV looks at the hierarchy of planning that is needed for an organization to work effectively. This starts with strategic capacity plans and moves down through aggregate plans, master schedules, materials planning, short-term scheduling, and on to detailed job design.

Part V describes some aspects of materials management through logistics, inventory control, and location decisions.

Appendices give solutions to review questions and Normal distribution tables.

Format of each chapter

To give more examples of the context for the material, each of the five parts has an Interview with a company and a Management Perspective.

Within the parts, each of the 19 chapters follows a consistent format. This starts with a list of the specific Objectives of the chapter followed by the main material of the chapter, divided into sections. Each section of the chapter has a set of Review Questions to make sure readers understand thoroughly the material. The text contains numerous Examples and Case Studies to illustrate points. At the end of each chapter is a Review of the main material, a set of Key Terms, a Case Study, Problems, Discussion Questions, and a list of Selected References.

Other material

There is an Instructor's Manual to accompany the text. If you have any comments or queries about this book the author welcomes your views. Perhaps the easiest way to give these is via email to

dwaters@acs.ucalgary.ca   or   dwaters@mgmt.ucalgary.ca

Acknowledgements

Addison-Wesley Publishers and the Author would like to thank the following for their valuable comments and constructive suggestions:

Dr D.J. Smith	University of Derby
Ian Graham	University of Edinburgh
John Bothams	University of Strathclyde
Lesley Davis	Loughborough University of Technology
Lynne Baxter	Heriott-Watt Business School
Mike Cuming	Thames Valley University
Geoffrey Sykes	Sheffield University Management School
Dr J.L. Huxell	Maastricht School of Management
Dr J.F.H. Nijhuis	University of Limburg
Dr J. Olhager	Linköping University

Special thanks go to David Smith for his constant support of this project and for providing the five excellent Management Perspectives in the book.

The Publisher and the Author would also like express their appreciation and gratitude to the following interviewees and their organizations for their time and contribution:

Graham Ward and Vincent Hammersley	Rover Group
Brian Harris and Tim Cavanagh	THORN Transit Systems International
John Sullivan and Kay Duvall	ICI Chemicals & Polymers Limited
Kevin Whalley and Miranda Aspen	Tesco
Ken Sykes	A to Z Supplies, Essex Commercial Services

Additional thanks to the following people for their help in producing this book: Paula Harris, Editor; Victoria Cook, Editorial Assistant; and Martin Tytler, Production Editor. To those who remain unmentioned thanks are also extended.

C.D.J. Waters
November 1995

Contents

Part III Decisions about the process 243

8 Layout of facilities 247

9 Managing capacity 289

10 Controlling quality 337

Introducing operations management

This book is divided into five parts. Each part describes a different aspect of operations management. This is Part I, which gives an introduction to the subject.

There are three chapters in this first part. Chapter 1 defines **operations** as the activities in an organization that are directly concerned with making a product. This product may be goods, services, or a combination of the two.

Operations are a central part of any organization. But it may be surprising to see that managers in widely differing organizations face similar problems. Chapter 2 looks at the decisions needed to solve these problems, and introduces **operations management**. Chapter 3 shows how different types of decisions lead to an **operations strategy**.

An important point in Part I is that all organizations make a product to satisfy customer demand. Later sections describe the decisions needed to support this product. Part II looks at product planning. Part III discusses the process used to make the product. Part IV looks at the planning and scheduling of resources. Part V describes some aspects of materials management.

Together, these five parts cover the most important decisions made in an organization.

Graham Ward
Rover Group

The Rover Group is split into Business Units which consist of Land Rover, Longbridge and Cowley. The plant at Cowley in Oxford manufactures luxury cars, including the Rover 600 Series, and employs 4,500 people who produce around 500 cars a day. Each of the Rover plants has a Managing Director, to whom seven Directors report, including the Manufacturing Director. Graham Ward is the Manufacturing Director of the Large Cars Business Unit at Cowley.

Q How are your operations structured?

A Our Manufacturing Processes are split into units within the factory. We have different areas or block units for the assembly of different parts of the car. The car starts life in the 'Body and White' area, which is where the raw mould of the car is put together. The raw mould is then taken on to the next stage of the manufacturing process. It will then move on to a new area where the bonnet is added, on to another for painting, and so on until the car is complete. I have overall responsibility for all of the units which are concerned with manufacturing and, as our business is all about manufacturing, other areas of the business influence what I do. There are nine Senior Managers who are responsible for the units involved in manufacturing and they report in to me.

Within each unit we run a cell management system, which is headed by a Production Manager who is responsible for around 80–90 people – mostly assembly staff. The Production Manager requires both people management and technical management skills. We have found that this system works better than the old structure where Service Managers were wholly responsible for individual sections. The old method limited communications and prevented us from working together as a team. Accountability is moving down the line in todays operations within the Rover Group.

Q What operations issues/strategies are involved in the making of your product?

A We work on a Just-in-Time (JIT) basis, and we have a firm understanding of the issues involved with running an effective JIT system. Our JIT system works on an hourly basis – for example, Rover 600 cars are built in batches of 30 per hour. We will produce batches of the same model, colour, specification, and so on (that is, red cars with sunroofs, for example). We now turn 80% of our parts over every hour at Track Side (that is at the production line), which means that we have to have regular deliveries of parts. At present, the parts are delivered to our distribution centre, from there they are brought to the Track Side. We aim in the near future to have all of the parts delivered on an hourly basis from our suppliers directly to the Track Side. This system means that we are now more efficient and have cut down wastage as we no longer have spare stock stored in the factory. Effective materials control and batch control is crucial to attain the high quality that our customers demand, and is a fundamental process of the successful manufacturing of Rover Cars.

Q **What importance do you place on quality issues?**

A We are a lot closer to our suppliers these days than in the past, and we have a much stronger understanding of their systems and techniques. Through our own improved quality systems, we now ensure that our suppliers deliver the product that we want in the way that we want it, and consequently we can ensure that only high quality products are supplied to us.

We no longer employ quality inspection teams, but rely on teamwork to identify any quality problems. We have to assume that there might be quality problems, and this is where the teamwork concept works well. All quality inspection is now undertaken on the line, and all members of the production team are responsible for checking and highlighting any quality issues. Because of the costs involved, the track never stops unless there is a serious quality problem. The cost of stopping the track for just one minute is about £16,000!

Q **How has your operations strategy developed?**

A The turnaround in Rover's success followed the comment of its Chairman, Michael Edwards – 'Gentlemen, my managers are going to manage'. Since then, Rover has undergone a transformation in its industrial relations, and in its processes, which has allowed its managers to do just that – manage.

In 1972, we were producing 5.62 cars per man per year. By 1994, this figure had risen to 33. Meanwhile, the Cowley plant has reduced in size from 104 acres in 1992 to just over 50 acres today. Despite the fact that we have incorporated new systems, this increase in productivity is not purely due to new technology, but owes a lot to our work ethos. Our factory does not have such a high degree of technology as may be found in many of the Japanese car factories for example.

We encourage our staff to participate in the processes, and we believe that effective communication is very important. All our managers are encouraged to listen to their workforce, to understand their problems and concerns, and to develop coaching skills. As a manager, I take time to listen to staffing issues and I spend an hour and a half on the shop floor every day and encourage feedback from the whole workforce, not just the Senior Managers. We follow a policy of upward appraisal, which gives the employees the opportunity to rate their boss in the review process.

When we became the Rover Group the workforce were offered a trade off. They were offered the chance to stay with Rover, and have a 'job for life' in return for their flexibility in the workplace. The Trade Unions accepted this offer, and we now operate on a level of trust and compromise with the Unions. At one time everything went through the Shop Steward, and confrontational situations were common. Now we go straight to the staff, and we have a much more trusting relationship. By giving the management the skills to manage, the communication channels remain open and the need for arguments is negated. With the cooperation of the staff, the emphasis today is placed on managing the process rather than the people.

Q How much emphasis do you place on customer relations?

A At one time our concern with quality used to finish at the end of the production line, but this concern now extends to the customers' response to our cars. We solicit feedback from our customers, which is stored on our database. The collection of customer responses means that the Production Managers have constant feedback on how their processes are working – both positive and negative – which means that the systems can constantly be refined and improved. We encourage better customer relations with our franchise holders, and with the man on the street, who we consider to be our real customer.

Q How will the buy out of Rover by BMW affect your operations?

A Over the last few years Rover has gone from strength to strength. I believe that the partnership between Rover and BMW will be a good one, and that the managers have a lot to learn from each other to maintain the high standards which we boast today.

1   Defining operations

Contents

Objectives

After reading this chapter you should be able to:

- define 'operations'
- understand the aims of operations management
- see how different types of organization can have similar operations
- outline the types of decisions needed in organizations

What are operations?

Every organization makes a product. This product may be goods, services or a combination of the two. **Operations management** is concerned with the way the product is made.

Operations management is important for every organization. It is a complicated subject, so we are going to introduce it in two stages. In this chapter we define **operations**, and give some real examples. In the next chapter we shall add more details and discuss the methods of operations management.

We can start looking at operations by saying again that the purpose of any organization is to make a **product**. This seems reasonable for manufacturers like Rover, Hoover or Dulux which clearly make tangible goods. But it is also true for organizations that provide a service, like the BBC, Prudential Insurance or the Post Office. Anything an organization produces must be a product -- so **all** organizations make a product. This product can be physical goods – such as a computer, washing machine, bottle of beer or car – or intangible services – such as education, insurance, a holiday or television programme.

At the heart of an organization are the activities that make this product. These activities are the **operations**. They form part of a cycle, where customers demand products that are supplied by operations, as shown in Figure 1.1.

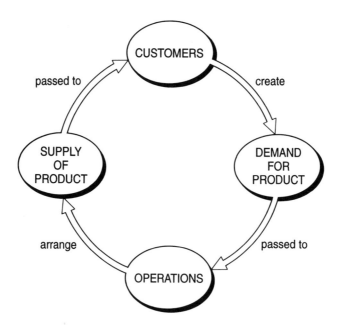

Figure 1.1 Operations make products to satisfy customer demand.

> The **operations** in an organization consist of all the activities that are primarily concerned with making the organization's products. These products may be either goods or services.

To put it simply, operations describe what the organization does. Operations in Ford make cars; in IBM they make and sell computers; in British Rail they run trains; in hospitals they cure sick people; in schools they educate children; in banks they borrow and lend money, on farms they grow food.

When you look at different organizations, it might seem that their operations have little in common. At first sight the operations of ICI, for example, seem completely different to the operations of a self-employed picture framer. But if you look closer there are surprising similarities. Both have to choose the best location for their operations. They both buy raw materials and use these to make products. They sell these products to customers. They forecast demand for their products and then calculate the capacity they need. They organize resources to meet the demand. They are concerned with cash flows and human resources. They want efficient operations and high productivity. They look for reliable suppliers.

So managers in very different organizations actually face similar problems. We can show how they tackle these problems by looking at the operations in some specific organizations. The following example looks at some of the decisions made when Nissan opened a manufacturing plant in the United Kingdom. While you are reading this, think about the operations involved, the decisions being made, and what they are trying to achieve.

ex Example – Nissan Motor Manufacturing (UK) Limited

Nissan was formed in 1911 to manufacture cars in Japan. After the Second World War, it decided to expand into world markets. In particular, it thought its cheap, small, efficient cars would sell in the United States, but General Motors, Ford and Chrysler already dominated the domestic market. So Nissan and the other 50 foreign companies trying to compete did not have much early success. By 1960 Nissan had 18 employees and 60 dealers in the United States and it sold a total of 1640 vehicles.

Nissan continued to develop its international operations, setting up plants in Mexico and Australia. By 1970 it was exporting a million cars a year, and the 240 Z was the leading foreign sports car in the United States. The company was growing to become the world's fourth largest car manufacturer.

During its early expansion Nissan made all its cars in Japan and met overseas demand by direct exports. This policy had obvious drawbacks. The

United States was becoming unhappy about its balance of trade deficit with Japan, and it began to restrict imports. The European Union was now the world's largest car market, and they could encourage domestic manufacturers by restricting foreign imports. Nissan realized that the best way to avoid such problems was to set up local operations, and in 1981 it decided to build a major facility in Europe.

Having decided to make cars in Europe, Nissan now had to choose a location. In 1984 it decided this would be in the United Kingdom, because there is a large domestic market and a site within the European Union would allow free trade with other major markets. The UK was also a technologically advanced country with a history of car production, and had the necessary skills, education and infrastructure.

Nissan considered several sites within the UK, and finally chose Sunderland. This had the advantages of:

- a tradition of engineering and manufacturing that gave a skilled workforce;

- high unemployment, giving a pool of people eager to work for a new employer;

- a very positive attitude of local people and trade unions;

- a large, flat, cheap site on the old Sunderland Airport where building would be easy and quick;

- excellent infrastructure, with the A19 and access to the A1 nearby;

- the deep water port of Teesport nearby;

- government grants for development in an enterprise zone.

In April 1984, Nissan Motor Manufacturing (UK) Limited was established. This had the aim of 'building profitably the highest quality vehicles sold in Europe, to achieve the maximum possible customer satisfaction and thus ensure the prosperity of the company and its staff'.

Now Nissan had a site and could finalize the size of the plant. After looking at projected long-term demand for cars in Britain, Europe and the world, it decided to build a factory that could produce 250,000 cars a year by 1994. This would cost over £3 billion on the site and employ 4250 people (see Table 1.1).

Nissan had to make major decisions about the way the plant was organized. Would it be better, for example, to:

- import components from Japan and assemble them in Sunderland;

- buy components from European suppliers; or

- make its own components in Sunderland or elsewhere?

Table 1.1

Year	Production	Employees	Investment (£m)
1986	5,100	470	50
1987	28,800	1,100	
1988	56,700	1,800	610
1989	77,000	2,500	
1990	76,200	2,700	670
1991	124,500	3,000	
1992	179,000	4,600	900
1993	246,300	4,250	900

There were also questions about manufacturing methods. Could the company use the methods it had developed in Japan, or should it use current European methods? It also had to decide whether to use Japanese managers or European ones.

In the event, Nissan decided to become a European company, using local people and suppliers. But it used many of the manufacturing methods and systems it had developed in Japan. These included automated assembly lines, Total Quality Management, just-in-time operations, flexible manufacturing, and continuous improvement. You will hear about these later in the book, but the important point is that they give high productivity and very high quality products.

The company started making Bluebird cars in 1986. At first it imported parts from Japan, but within a few years developed a network of 200 suppliers so that almost all parts for the new Primera and Micra cars were bought in Europe. The only major components imported from Japan were the transmission and engine block.

Some suppliers built facilities on Nissan's site in Sunderland – including Reydel, Calsonic, Sommer, MKL, Hashimoto, Autrans Europe, Ikeda Hoover and Nissan Yamato. These reduced lead times for parts to hours or even minutes, compared with the weeks needed to ship parts from the Far East. Local suppliers now employ 1000 people on the Nissan site, and a further 2000 in the north-east of England.

Because of this local content, the Society of Motor Manufacturers and Traders has defined cars made in Sunderland since 1991 as 'British' and they can be sold freely in the European Union. Eighty-five per cent of production is exported to over 30 countries (including Japan and Taiwan), and Nissan has become Britain's largest car exporter. It won the Queen's Award for Export Achievement in 1992 and 1993.

Operations in the Sunderland plant can be summarized as 'making cars'. This involves:

• organizing the delivery of raw materials

• using these materials to make parts

- organizing the delivery of other parts from suppliers
- assembling all the components into finished cars.

These assembly operations are in seven stages, as shown in Figure 1.2. There is also a number of other operations, such as research and development, marketing, vehicle testing and human resources.

- **Panel pressing** The panels for car bodies are pressed from steel sheets. Most of Nissan's panels use Durasteel which has a specially developed zinc-nickel coating to improve anti-corrosion, formability, welding and painting. Six high-speed presses with a capacity up to 5000 tonnes gives Sunderland the highest concentration of advanced presses in Europe.

- **Body assembly** After pressing, the body panels are welded together to form the body. This uses a highly automated body assembly plant directly linked to the pressing plant. Eighty per cent of this work is automated, using more than 200 programmable robots.

- **Paint** The finished bodies are painted several times. Painting often gives problems with the emission of solvents. The Sunderland paint plant is an automated, semi-sealed clean air environment with emissions controlled to surpass all likely government regulations. Solvent emissions are reduced by using environmentally friendly water-based paints.

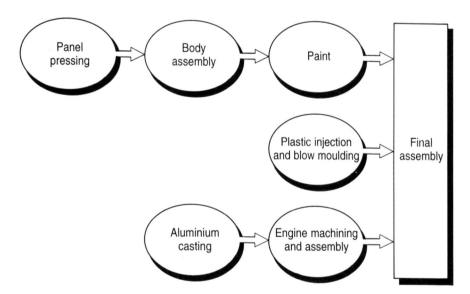

Figure 1.2 Schematic view of Nissan's Sunderland plant.

- **Plastics injection and blow moulding**   Many parts of a car are made of plastic, such as fuel tanks which are sandwiches of polyethylene and nylon. Plastic bumpers, radiator grills and facia parts are also made in this area. Recovery and recycling programmes allow Nissan to use 30% recycled material.

- **Aluminium casting**   Parts for the engine are cast in the foundry and then passed on for machining and assembly. The aluminium casting plant is the most modern in Europe and produces cylinder head castings and inlet manifolds.

- **Engine machining and assembly**   This finishes the different parts of the engine and assembles them into complete units. Machining of inlet manifolds, cylinder heads and camshafts is done by high volume, fully automated lines. Fifty-two variations of engines are made – the largest number on a high volume production line in Europe.

- **Final assembly**   This is the point where all the components are brought together to make finished cars. Final assembly starts when a body shell leaves the painted body store. Then a transponder fitted during body assembly is scanned by the computerized control system. This system prints a 'build sheet' giving the specifications and customer order details for the car. The computer also sends this information to sub-assembly stations and component supply points around the site. Then all parts needed for the final assembly are organized to arrive at the right place at the right time.

As you can imagine, co-ordinating these operations is extremely difficult. Collecting the thousands of parts needed to build a car at one place, in the right order and at the right time would be very complicated, but the plant repeats this continually every few minutes. The high-speed operations leave little room for mistakes. The company does not keep buffer stocks of work in progress – as parts are only delivered to the assembly line when they are needed – so any mistake would cause major problems. This kind of operation is only possible with a combination of computerized control, high levels of automation, completely reliable supplies of components, no defective components, short lead times and a flexible workforce.

Nissan gives strong support to its workforce. Initial training and management was done by Japanese employees, but local people replaced them when they had developed the necessary skills and knowledge. All managers are now British. To achieve this, the company puts a major effort into training, and gives employees an average of nine days off-the-job training and 12 days on-the-job training a year. This is one reason why the Department of Employment gave Nissan an 'Investor in People' award in 1991.

The company clearly states, 'We aim to manufacture the highest quality vehicles sold in Europe. It is the quality of our people that determines the quality of our product ... we believe that high calibre, well-trained and motivated people are the only key to success.' Nissan believes its success depends on mutual trust and co-operation among all people within the company. To help achieve this, everyone has the same terms and conditions of employment – including single status, subsidized canteens, use of a sports centre and social club, voluntary private health insurance, voluntary union membership (with a single union agreement with Amalgamated Engineering and Electrical Union), a company council that promotes effective communication and harmonious relations, no privileged parking, and communications meetings held with all staff every day. Everyone is encouraged to help improve conditions and is rewarded for increasing productivity.

The Nissan factory is one of the largest and most efficient integrated manufacturing facilities in the world. It is the most productive car manufacturer in Europe, and has been so successful that Toyota has opened a factory in Derby and Honda has a plant in Swindon. This success did not come by accident but needed a lot of management effort.

The brief description of Nissan's operations shows some of the decisions it had to make. Should it open factories outside Japan? Which country should it work in, and what site within this country? How many cars will it sell? What kind of cars should it make? What capacity should its factories have? How can it plan for future needs? How can it guarantee a reliable supply of parts and materials? How many parts should it import from Japan? Which local suppliers should it use? What transport will it need? How can it reduce lead times? How should it organize the factory? How can it maintain high productivity and quality? What automation should it use? What planning does it need to make sure components arrive at the assembly line just as they are needed? How can it schedule work? How should it treat its employees? What training should it give?

There are literally thousands of decisions needed to keep the Nissan plant working, and this book will show how operations management tackles them. You may think these decisions are unique to Nissan, but they are typical of the decisions in any organization. To show this, we shall describe the operations in a completely different organization. While you read the next example, again think about the operations, the decisions being made and what they are trying to achieve.

ex Example – Saint Andrew's Maternity Hospital

Saint Andrew's Maternity Hospital provides all the maternity services for a large part of the City of Glasgow. In common with the rest of the health service, it is continuously trying to improve its performance. Saint Andrew's has been affected by a series of health service reforms, and there was a recent reorganization of the regional health authority. This encouraged the hospital managers to make a major review of their operations.

The hospital was built in 1843 to give a central maternity service for the City of Glasgow. Over the years there have been many changes, including:

- the population of Glasgow has declined;

- the number of people living in the city centre has fallen sharply as it changed from a residential area to a commercial one;

- other hospitals opened maternity units in the suburbs;

- Saint Andrew's became a regional specialist unit, dealing with all difficult cases;

- the building is now considered small and old fashioned;

- the site is small, congested and noisy;

- there is no space for expansion, parking or other facilities.

There are three levels of management in the hospital. The National Health Service sets overall policies, guidelines, objectives and provides the funding. The regional health authority sees how the needs of the region – which covers most of the population of Western Scotland – can best be met. Hospital managers are in charge of the day-to-day running of Saint Andrew's.

In the review of its operations, managers at Saint Andrew's started by asking if they should move from the present location. The site is commercially valuable, and selling it could provide enough money for a new hospital at another location, or improved facilities at an existing hospital. The managers thought such a move was inevitable in the long term, but at present the city centre still needs a central maternity hospital. Its location gives a visible, central maternity service for the region and gives expertise, specialized treatment and facilities that are not available anywhere else. At the same time it serves people who live nearby and is convenient for those who rely on public transport.

The decision to stay in the city centre balanced the quality of service offered with the cost of providing it. Hospital managers had a lot of discussions over this balance. They recognized that the hospital's aim was to provide 'first class health care', but had problems when it came to defining exactly what this meant. How can anyone measure the quality of health care actually given, or the quality aimed for? This is a common problem in health services – and one which has yet to be solved.

Saint Andrew's gives five basic services to mothers and babies before, during and after birth:

(1)   *Out-patient checks before birth* Pregnant women visit the hospital several times for tests to make sure their baby is developing normally and there are no complications: minor problems are dealt with in out-patients' clinics.

(2) *Out-patient checks after birth* The hospital does routine tests during a baby's first few months to make sure it is progressing normally: again some minor problems are dealt with, but mothers are normally referred to their doctor.

(3) *Normal in-patient care* This is usually a short stay in hospital for the delivery of the baby and to allow recovery: sometimes longer stays are needed if the mother or baby have problems.

(4) *Emergency out-patients* This is for problems that need fast, but fairly short treatment.

(5) *Emergency in-patient care* This applies when there is a more serious problem.

These services define the operations of the hospital. Managers must plan and organize these operations to meet the demand from patients in the best possible way.

For long-term planning, managers use records of the number of births each year, together with expected changes, to forecast the expected number of births over the next few years. These forecasts give the overall capacity needed in Saint Andrew's. At present there are the equivalent of 160 beds, 140 medical staff and 120 support staff. If there are changes in demand, managers have to adjust these numbers, but this can take a lot of time and effort. A 5% growth in births, for example, means eight more beds and 13 more staff. It would be difficult to find these, or fit them into the building without making major changes.

Medium-term plans look at the use of resources over the next few months. Managers use more detailed forecasts of demand to make minor changes to resources – typically changing beds from non-emergency to emergency use, arranging staff training and holidays, timing expenditure on equipment, and so on.

More detailed plans are based on the number of births expected in the near future. This is known fairly accurately because the hospital has seen most of the mothers in pre-natal clinics. Managers use these numbers to design timetables for doctors, nurses, ancillary staff, porters, and so on, and schedules for beds, consulting rooms, medical equipment, operating rooms, kitchens, medicines and supplies.

As you can imagine, there are several complications in this planning. One problem is the emergencies. There is a widely varying number of mothers and babies who need emergency treatment. The hospital has its own emergency cases, and it receives difficult cases from other hospitals in the region. To deal with these it keeps some spare capacity which can be used at short notice. Unfortunately, spare capacity in the emergency service is very expensive and often has very low use.

A smaller problem comes with seasonal variations in the number of births. There are more births in spring than in autumn, and more on weekdays than at weekends. The hospital must have enough capacity to meet the peak demand, but does not want idle resources at slack times.

This balance of allocating limited resources between competing activities is a constant theme in Saint Andrew's. It is made more difficult by the serious ethical issues. If resources are stretched, how can the hospital balance the needs of 100 non-emergency patients and one emergency patient who has the same costs? What happens if the hospital spends all its grant and then gets new patients? If the hospital put more resources into preventive treatment it could reduce the cost of emergency care, but there are no resources for such investment.

As you can see, there are many operational decisions in the health service that most people never notice. When we make an appointment with the doctor, we assume this only needs an appointment in a diary. We forget that someone has to arrange a building and room for appointments, schedule the clinic, buy necessary supplies, organize the doctor's time, arrange for ancillary staff, keep track of costs and pay bills, arrange tests, update medical records, make reports to the National Health Service, and so on. Then there are a whole range of related operations such as preparing staff and patient meals, running the laundry, cleaning the buildings, arranging transport and training staff.

At Saint Andrew's several computer systems help plan these operations. Patient records are computerized so that managers can check patient details, forecast demands, order drugs, make appointments, design timetables for doctors and nurses, prepare menus for meals, record expenditure, and generally make sure the hospital runs smoothly. Medical staff use the system to record patient details, monitor their progress, make appointments, highlight any problems, record drug use, and so on.

The example above shows some of the decisions made in Saint Andrew's. The hospital has to respond to changing conditions, and organize its operations in the best possible way. Managers must start planning with decisions about their aims, which are to provide first class health care. Then they make decisions about the best location, demand for their services and how this demand can be met. They make sure there is enough capacity for services, and make decisions about a whole range of resources. Some of these decisions are long term, such as building new facilities; some are medium term, such as the recruiting and training of staff; some are short term, such as buying supplies and preparing meals. But again you can see that managing the operations, and making sure everything runs smoothly, is very difficult.

These two examples have described completely different organizations. One is a very large manufacturer of cars; the other is a much smaller, not-for-profit service. One makes tangible goods; the other gives an intangible service. Yet managers in both organizations face similar problems. Where is the best place to locate facilities? What are the objectives of their organizations? How can demand be forecast? Is there enough capacity to meet this demand? How can operations be organized to run smoothly and efficiently? How can productivity be improved and costs reduced? How can high quality be maintained? What suppliers should be used and what stocks should be held? How can resources be scheduled most effectively?

These are some of the problems that operations managers face in every organization. In the following chapters we shall see how to tackle them.

Chapter review

- Operations are the activities that are directly concerned with making a product. This product may be goods, services or a combination of the two.

- Operations management is concerned with the way a product is made.

- Operations managers in different organizations face similar problems. In the rest of this book we shall see how these problems can be tackled.

Key terms

goods	6	product	6
operations	7	services	6
operations management	6		

CS Case study – Godolphin Green General Store

Godolphin Green is a village in the west of Cornwall. It has a population of 380, one pub and a general store. This store has been run for the past seven years by Tim Penhale. It is a traditional small shop in the front of Tim's house, and occupies about 45 square metres. It stocks a range of basic food, newspapers, an off-licence and anything else that villagers may want in a hurry.

Tim had no direct competition in Godolphin Green as the nearest shop is a BP filling station about five miles away. The main shopping centres are seven miles away in Penzance and 10 miles away in Helston.

A major problem for small shops is the high overheads that make them relatively expensive. This means that most villagers do the bulk of their shopping in nearby Helston and Penzance, but use the village store for convenience and to buy small items. Tim noticed a decline in his sales in 1993 after Safeway opened in Penzance, and again in 1995 when Tesco opened in

Helston. These supermarkets could often sell goods cheaper than Tim could buy them from his wholesaler.

Tim is getting increasingly worried by the competition from supermarkets, and is wondering what he can do to improve his position.

Questions

- What are the operations in the village store? What is the product it supplies?

- How might Tim improve his operations?

- Can you give examples of similar decisions in other organizations?

Discussion questions

1.1 What exactly do managers do?

1.2 Do you think the operations in different types of organization are really similar? Give examples to support your view.

1.3 Describe, in detail, the operations of some organizations you are familiar with.

1.4 Can you list some ways that operations have changed over the past 20 years? What changes might there be over the next 20 years?

1.5 In 1975 the biggest car manufacturers in the UK were British Leyland, Ford, Vauxhall (owned by General Motors) and Rootes (owned by Chrysler). In 1995 the biggest manufacturers are Rover (owned by BMW), Ford, Vauxhall, Peugeot-Talbot, Nissan, Honda and Toyota. Do you think that changes in operations might have caused these changes?

2 What is operations management?

Contents

Objectives

After reading this chapter you should be able to:

- define 'operations management'
- show how operations convert inputs to desired outputs
- say why operations management is important to every organization
- see operations management as a central function in an organization
- describe some other views of operations management
- discuss the differences between manufacturing and service organizations

Defining operations management

In the last chapter we saw that every organization makes a **product**. At the heart of an organization is the set of activities directly concerned with making this product. These activities are the **operations**, and are the organization's most important function. **Operations management** is concerned with the way the operations are performed.

> **Operations management** is the management function that is responsible for all the activities directly concerned with making a product. It is responsible for collecting various inputs, and converting them into desired outputs.

You can see from this definition how organizations take a variety of inputs, and perform the operations needed to convert these into desired outputs. The inputs include raw materials, money, people, machines, time, and other resources. Operations include manufacturing, assembly, packing, serving, training, and so on. The outputs include goods, services, staff wages, waste material. To give specific examples:

- A car assembly plant takes inputs of components, materials, energy, robots, people, and so on; it performs operations of pressing, welding, assembly, painting, finishing; the outputs include cars, spare parts, wages.

- A restaurant takes inputs of food, chefs, kitchen, energy, waiters, tables, and so on; it performs operations of food preparation, cooking, serving; outputs include meals and (hopefully) satisfied customers.

- A university takes inputs of students, books, buildings, staff, and so on; it performs operations of teaching, research, administration, service; outputs include better educated people, research findings, new books.

Some more examples of operations are given in Table 2.1.

You can see from the examples in Table 2.1 that operations management works in all kinds of organizations. These can be:

- primary industries – agriculture, mining and quarrying;

- secondary industries – manufacturing and construction; or

- tertiary industries – which are all the services.

It is important to emphasize again that 'products' can be either tangible goods or intangible services, and 'operations' are any activities that produce these.

Table 2.1 Examples of operations.

Organization	Inputs	Operations	Outputs
Farm	seeds, fertiliser, fields, animals, machinery	planting, growing, harvesting, milking, shearing	cereals, milk, wool, meat
Coal mine	miners, coal seam, tools, explosives, transport	extraction, removing waste, cleaning, delivery	coal, waste, wages
Oil refinery	crude oil, chemicals, energy	refining, distribution, processing	petrol, oil, plastics
Computer manufacturer	components, materials, designs, energy, robots, people	assembly, finishing, testing, packing	computers, spare parts, wages
House building	land, bricks, wood, cement, people, capital, equipment, plans	brick laying, carpentry, plastering, plumbing	house, investment, garden
Brewery	hops, water, cans, grain, bottles, skills, experience	preparing, mixing, brewing, canning, bottling	bottled and canned beer
Hospital	patients, staff, beds, medicines, equipment	surgical operations, treatment, monitoring	healthy patients, information
Retail shop	goods, customers, space, servers	selling, marketing, advising, packing	purchases, satisfied customers
Airline	planes, terminals, passengers, agents	booking tickets, flying, entertaining	satisfied passengers, goods moved

We should also describe the work of managers. In general, **managers** make the decisions within an organization. To be more specific, their jobs include:

- **Planning** To establish goals and the means of achieving these.

- **Organizing** Structuring the organization in the best way to achieve its goals.

- **Staffing** Making sure there are suitable employees to do all jobs.

- **Directing** Telling employees the tasks they should be doing.

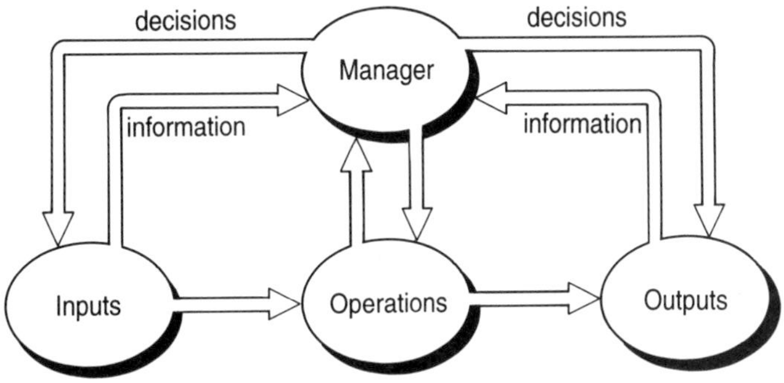

Figure 2.1 Schematic of operations management.

- **Motivating** Encouraging employees to do their jobs well.

- **Allocating** Assigning resources to specific jobs.

- **Monitoring** To check progress towards the goals.

- **Controlling** Taking action to make sure the organization keeps moving towards its goals.

- **Informing** Keeping everyone informed of progress.

Managers can also do other jobs, like being a figurehead and spokesperson, liaising with other organizations, negotiating, handling problems, exercising authority and initiating change.

Now we can bring these ideas together and draw the schematic view of operations management shown in Figure 2.1. Here, managers make the decisions that keep an organization working effectively. Their decisions affect inputs, operations and outputs. Then they use feedback on performance and other relevant information to make further decisions.

Three other elements can be added to Figure 2.1:

(1) customers who receive the outputs, give comments and opinions, create demand etc;

(2) an external environment in which the organization operates, including competitors, government, national priorities, society etc.;

(3) the separation of operations into a series of connected processes rather than a single step.

Adding these elements gives the overall view of operations management shown in Figure 2.2.

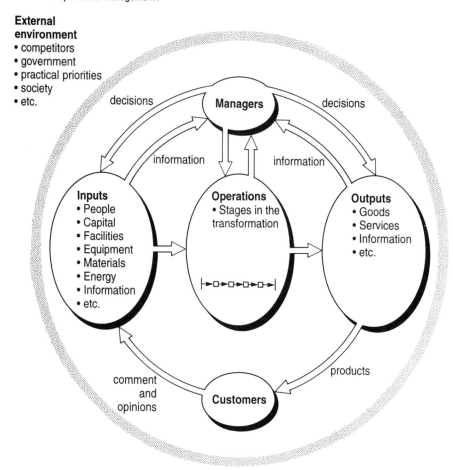

External environment
- competitors
- government
- practical priorities
- society
- etc.

Figure 2.2 Overall schematic of operations management.

ce Case example – Gladstone Community School

The government has overall control of education, designing the national curriculum, setting attainment targets, and so on. Since 1988, however, each school is largely responsible for its own management. The operations managers are now a mixture of school governors and senior teachers. Local authorities also keep some responsibility for functions like building maintenance.

Jane Goodall is chairman of the board of governors of Gladstone Community School. This is a primary school in a socially mixed area of Nottingham. The school is considered successful in a number of ways: it encourages links between local industry and the pupils; it is proud of its academic record; it encourages understanding of different ethnic traditions; its pupils enjoy coming to school; there is low staff turnover; teams are successful in local sports; the facilities are well maintained and volunteers collect large amounts for school funds.

Gladstone has recently opted out of local authority control, so its management is now completely independent. The board of governors and a management team of teachers is responsible for all decisions – acting as operations managers. The governors generally look after finances and other major decisions, like the need for new buildings or more staff or marketing the school to attract more pupils. The management team of teachers consists of the Head, Deputy Head, Head of Infants and Head of Juniors. They make decisions about academic matters and day-to-day running of the school, including the timetable, curriculum, allocation of teaching duties, staff development, organizing cleaning and meals.

One of the school's problems is that none of the governors has any management experience. To overcome this Jane organized a series of weekend discussions about school management. The first of these meetings tried to develop overall aims for the school and asked, 'What are we trying to do in our school?' Unfortunately, the governors could not agree. Some said the school's purpose is to provide a traditional education; others wanted to develop good citizens; others suggested different aims.

Deciding the school's priorities is particularly important, because there was recently a 3% cut in its operating budget. School managers had to decide where this money should come from, remembering that 85% of their costs are staff salaries.

Gladstone faces a surprisingly common problem, where people with no managerial experience are put in charge of an organization. Their main problem is developing the skills, knowledge and experience needed for the job.

Questions

- What do are the products of Gladstone Community School? What are the operations?

- Can you think of other organizations where people with no management experience are put in charge of operations?

- What type of decisions do you think the governors are likely to face at Gladstone?

Review questions

2.1   What are 'operations'?

2.2   Define 'operations management'.

2.3   Look at a number of organizations you are familiar with and list the inputs, operations and outputs.

2.4   What are the main functions of managers?

Growth of operations management

Operations management is not new: it has been around ever since people started working together to achieve common goals. But it has grown most rapidly since the industrial revolution. Throughout the nineteenth century, organizations increased their output and productivity by improving the technology they used. Then, at the turn of the twentieth century, people began to look beyond the technology and consider the way it was managed. They found that:

*   the productivity of an organization depends on both the technology available, and how well this technology is managed;

*   good managers use a variety of knowledge and skills in their decision making, and do not rely on intuition and guesswork.

These findings stimulated the growth of operations management, particularly in the United States. Largely because of this, American companies soon dominated many areas of business. IBM was the world's largest computer manufacturer, General Motors was the largest car maker, ESSO was the largest oil company, American Express was the leading credit card, McDonald's served billions of hamburgers.

But by the 1970s these leading companies seemed to become complacent and did not take advantage of new opportunities. American car manufacturers ignored early demands for smaller, more economical cars, and imported cars soon took a major share of their market. IBM ignored personal computers and continued to work with the shrinking mainframe market. In 1960, seven of the world's 10 largest banks were American, but by 1991 Citicorp – ranked number eight – was the only US bank in the top 10. PanAm and TWA were the world's leading airlines, but neither survived massive reorganizations of the industry.

By the 1980s Japanese companies were leaders in operations management. They concentrated on high quality, customer service and high productivity – and soon dominated industries like motor cycles, consumer electronics, photocopiers, cameras, machine tools, steel, computer chips, shipping, cars and banking. The Japanese share of world car production rose from 3% in 1960 to over 30% in 1990.

Japanese companies did not use any magical formula to achieve their success, but they used sound operations management. As an example, car manufacturers used to hold large stocks of raw materials to make sure their production lines worked without any interruptions. Toyota thought these stocks were a waste of resources, so they spent 20 years developing a **just-in-time** system which still kept production lines busy, but virtually eliminated stocks of raw materials (this is described in Chapter 13). Similarly, Yokogawa-Hewlett-Packard spent five years improving the quality of their goods to meet the high standards demanded by their customers. The result was a tripling of market share and profit, combined with a halving of manufacturing costs.

More evidence that the Japanese success comes from good management appears when they take over existing factories. In 1977 Motorola employed 1000 hourly paid employees and produced about 1000 television sets a day at their Quasar plant in Chicago. Later that year Matsushita bought the plant. Within two years they cut the indirect staff from 600 to 300, reduced assembly repairs by 95%, reduced annual warranty costs from $16 million to $2 million, doubled the production rate to 2000 sets a day, yet still kept the same 1000 hourly paid staff.

Other countries have learnt from Japan's economic success, and are now following their lead, particularly the Pacific Rim countries of South Korea, Taiwan, Singapore and Hong Kong. The economies of India, China and several other countries are developing quickly. At the same time companies in America and Europe are improving their own operations to regain their competitive edge. This has lead to a dramatic increase in world trade and international competition. Such competition can only be met by using good operations management. By emphasizing operations management an organization can compete – ignoring operations will inevitably lead to failure.

Review questions

2.5　Why do you think interest in operations management has increased in recent years?

2.6　What happens if an organization ignores operations management?

Central functions in an organization

We have already shown how an organization takes a variety of inputs and converts these to desired outputs. So we can say:

> The **main purpose** of an organization is to produce goods and services that satisfy customer demand.

From this statement you can identify three central functions that must exist in all organizations.

(1)　*Sales/marketing* This identifies customer demand, stimulates new demand, collects and analyses information on customer needs, organizes advertising, takes orders, makes sure that products are delivered to customers, gives after-sales service, and so on.

(2) *Operations management* This is responsible for actually producing the goods and services.

(3) *Accounting/finance* This raises capital, invests funds, records financial transactions, collects money, pays bills, collects cost information, maintains accounts, and so on.

These central functions are **directly** concerned with the product. You might say that an organization needs many other functions, such as human resources, research and development, catering, computer services, administration and public relations, but these can either be included in one of the central functions, or they are not **directly** concerned with the product. Table 2.2 shows some examples of the central functions in different organizations.

The three central functions work together to achieve the goals of the organization (see Figure 2.3). They exist in all organizations, but the emphasis put on each will vary. A manufacturing company might emphasize operations, but must still market its products and control its finances; a brewery might concentrate on sales and marketing, but still needs efficient operations and control of its accounts; an insurance company might pay particular attention to its financial performance, but still has to deliver products to customers.

Table 2.2 Examples of the central functions in different organizations.

Organization	Sales and marketing	Operations	Accounting and finance
Brewery	advertising, marketing, distribution	brewing, packaging, delivery	attracting investment, recording costs, analysing profits
Car assembly plant	advertising, marketing, running dealerships	assembling cars, making spare parts	controlling investments, paying suppliers
Hospital	publicity, improving public relations	treating patients, doing medical research, training staff	paying staff, checking costs, attracting donations
Retail shop	organizing sales, advertising, purchasing stock	selling, stockholding, delivering	recording costs, paying suppliers, collecting cash
Airline	organizing sales, advertising, forming partnerships	flight operations, ground operations, engineering	collecting fares, paying expenses, buying planes
University	attracting students, getting publicity, recruiting staff	teaching students, research, consulting	paying staff, collecting fees, contingency planning

Figure 2.3 Central functions in an organization.

During the 1970s companies tended to emphasize marketing, while the 1980s saw a move towards stronger financial management. More recently people have realized that the long-term survival of any organization depends on its ability to satisfy customer demand. In other words, the emphasis has moved to operations management. This recognizes the fact that the operations of a typical organization employ the majority of people, use most of the assets and generate all the income.

ce Case example – Consumer Electronics

Consumer Electronics (CE) is a division of a large British conglomerate. It makes a variety of radios, televisions, stereo equipment and video equipment. In common with all companies in this industry, CE has had problems competing with manufacturers from the Far East.

CE was first affected by Japanese imports in 1970, when it made a loss of £17 million. At the time, CE felt the competition could be met by spending more on advertising. By the following year the advertising budget had been tripled, but CE still made a loss of £21 million.

The problem was that Japanese products were 20% cheaper than equivalent ones made by CE. So the company started a severe cost-cutting programme. As part of this, the research and development budget was cut by 65%. Not surprisingly, by 1980 CE's products were outdated and had been overtaken by new ideas from competitors. The market had become even more competitive, with products from other Far East countries arriving in large numbers.

This time CE responded by restructuring. It closed down two plants, sold three others, and bought two medium-sized manufacturers in South America. But in 1990 CE lost £123 million and appointed a new Chairman, who immediately saw that despite cosmetic changes, CE had been making essentially the same products for 20 years, and used the same production methods.

The new Chairman decided that CE could compete by concentrating on its operations. This meant making better products more efficiently. The Chairman got the marketing department to find out exactly what customers wanted. Then he invested in research and development to design products that would satisfy these demands. The next stage was to invest in efficient operations to make the products.

CE built a state-of-the-art manufacturing centre in northern England. This used a lot of automation, but still relied on the skills of a large workforce. CE sent every employee in their new centre on a two week course, followed by on-job training to make sure they made high quality products and gave reliable customer service. By 1994 sales had doubled and CE was making a profit for the first time in 25 years.

The above example shows how one company responded to competition by improving its operations. It tried increasing the marketing effort and changing the financial arrangements, but in the end it only succeeded by improving its products and operations.

Review questions

2.7 What are the central functions in an organization?

2.8 Give some details of the central functions in an organization that you are familiar with.

2.9 Why is human resource management not considered a central function? What about product design?

Other views of operations management

In the last section we described operations management as a central function within an organization. This gives one view, but we could take others, perhaps describing operations management as:

- a profession;

- using a specific approach to tackle management problems; or

- looking at decisions in specific areas.

The rest of this book looks at the way decisions are made in specific areas, so here we shall look at the alternative views.

Operations management as a profession

Most early studies of management looked for ways of improving the efficiency of factories. These studies led to a number of related disciplines, such as **work study**, **management services**, **industrial engineering** and, most commonly, **production management**. Then a typical manufacturing company would have a production manager to look after their operations. Later studies of management looked at service industries, and the equivalent of a production manager became known as an operations manager. So a production manager would run a factory, while an operations manager would run a service. In recent years we have recognized that these two people do the same job, and now use the general title **operations manager**.

This title is not, however, universal. Whenever you look at an organization – whether it is a factory, bank, shop, university, office complex or hospital – there is someone in charge of the operations. These people may not be called operations managers, but that is certainly their job. Their titles may include production manager, plant manager, site manager, materials controller, operations analyst, inventory controller, scheduler, shop manager, matron, postmaster, chef, supervisor, headmaster, transport manager, factory superintendent, maintenance manager, quality assurance engineer, production engineer, management scientist, and so on.

There are so many different kinds of operations that we might not know exactly what a particular operations manager does, but we do know they are involved in managing the central function that makes their organization's products.

ce Case example – Job advertisements

You can see a variety of operations management jobs advertised in many newspapers. The following examples are taken from one edition of *The Sunday Times*.

Operations Director for ice cream/confectionery

The Operations Director will join the company's top management team to take them through the present increase in sales and take an active role in the strategic general management of the company. Quality, customer satisfaction and cost effectiveness are the vital ingredients.

Chief Operating Officer for cable communications

A unique opportunity for a Chief Operating Officer to join the management team of one of the United Kingdom's most successful independent cable telecommunications groups. You will be responsible for expanding the company's service into new geographical areas.

Project Director for power station construction

This is a blue chip company which is recognized as a world class player in the design, engineering and commissioning of major power generation facilities. This job has overall responsibility for constructing a major gas-powered facility in Britain, with future contracts in the Middle East.

Operations Manager in manufacturing

The operations manager is responsible for all manufacturing activities within the division. This is a major division of a US multinational. The facility is truly world class and is now three years old. It supplies an extensive range of short life-cycle durable products, in high volume, to a variety of distributor/retail systems throughout Europe. Both the manufacturing operations and the supply chain are complex, very fast moving and extremely sensitive.

Operational Financial Systems in the food industry

Your role will embrace operational systems and procedures in the plant and at Group level as well as fulfilling a range of financial, auditing and treasury requirements. The key objective is to bring about improvements in the efficiency of the plant from both an economic and a production efficiency perspective.

General Manager in a retail group

As a key member of the executive management team you will have a major impact on the company's ongoing success. Your challenge will be to develop and lead the already strongly positioned multi-branch building supplies and hardware division.

Operations Manager for a transport company

One of the country's leading transport operators requires a manager for its depot in Central Scotland. You will report to the site general manager and be responsible for the day-to-day working of the depot.

Manager Business Processes in financial services

A major international financial institution is looking for a multi-skilled individual to work closely with senior management in the evaluation of business processes, the examination of options for the future and the implementation of change.

Director of Operations and Development for a charity

There are 35,000 members of this organization around the world. We now require a forward looking person with financial and commercial experience who can help us expand, initiate new developments and take responsibility for day-to-day business management of the organization.

Senior Consultant in management consultancy

As one of the UK's leading firms of accountants and management consultants, we deliver tangible business improvements, through multi-functional performance-orientated teams. You will have senior management experience and a demonstrable history of business improvement, preferably in creative, fast-moving, high-technology companies.

The operations management approach to problems

Another view of operations management looks at the way it tackles problems. It does this in four stages:

(1) *Observation* Here, managers realize there is a problem and that something must be done about it. They examine the problem, collect data, set objectives, consider the context and discuss various ideas.

(2) *Formulation* This is where people with appropriate skills review the data, build models of the situation, find solutions to the models, suggest alternative actions.

(3) *Analysis* Here, managers examine the alternatives, give values to parameters, identify the best decisions and make recommendations.

(4) *Implementation* This is where managers make final decisions, implement the solution, monitor actual performance, collect feedback and keep results up to date.

You can see from this approach that operations management often uses a **model** to describe a problem. A model is a simplified view of reality and is sometimes, but not always, quantitative. A typical quantitative model would represent the number of units sold by a variable, N, and the selling price for each unit by another variable, S, so the revenue generated, R, is given by:

revenue = number sold × selling price of each unit
$$R = NS$$

If the average cost of making a unit is C, we can extend the model to show the profit, P:

profit = number sold × profit on each unit
= number sold × (selling price − cost)
$$P = N(S - C)$$

Now we can use such models to predict results without interrupting operations. If the example above has $N = 100$, $S = 8$ and $C = 7$, we can predict the profit as:

$$P = N(S - C) = 100 \times (8 - 7) = 100$$

We can find this without having to change the operations, make actual observations, measure results, or disrupt work in any way. We can also do experiments to find the effects of changing the price to, say, 9.

$$P = N(S - C) = 100 \times (9 - 7) = 200$$

Not all operations management models are quantitative. There are many circumstances where there is no numerical data. When you are describing the quality of restaurants, newspapers or cars, for example, you may feel that one is better than another, but would find it difficult to put a numerical value to this feeling. We must always remember that quantitative analyses do not give the whole answer, but only one view. Although this view may be important, managers should consider **all** available information when making decisions (see Figure 2.4).

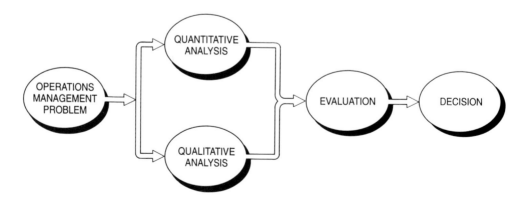

Figure 2.4 Use of both quantitative and qualitative analysis in decisions.

Review questions

2.10 How could you define operations management in four different ways?

2.11 List 10 different titles for 'operations managers'.

2.12 Why does operations management use models?

2.13 'Operations management usually needs quantitative analyses.' Do you think this is true?

Operations in services

We often judge the wealth of a nation by the amount of goods it produces. But in most countries this manufacturing output is only a small part of the gross domestic product (GDP). This is one effect of economic development, which can be considered in three stages.

(1) The first stage is pre-industrial, with economic activity concentrated in the **primary industries** of agriculture, mining, quarrying and forestry.

(2) As an economy develops it becomes industrial with emphasis on the **secondary industries** of manufacturing and construction.

(3) As prosperity continues to grow, economic activity moves to the post-industrial **service sector** of government, education, health, retailing, catering.

Most countries still have economies that are in the first stage. India, China, Brazil, South Africa and other developing countries rely on agriculture, but are developing by encouraging manufacturing. Much of Europe, North America, Japan, and some other developed countries are in the third, post-industrial stage. These have about 5% of the workforce in primary industries, 20% in manufacturing, and the remaining 75% in services.

You have already met the convention that:

• **goods** are physical items, usually made by manufacturers;

• **services** are all the intangible products supplied by the service sector; and

• **products** include both goods and services supplied by any organization.

It is often easier to describe the making of goods than the provision of a service. You can probably imagine a car being built on an assembly line, but how is an insurance policy developed? You have probably seen films of ships being built, but what are the equivalent operations in a merchant bank? This means that when we describe general operations, we may illustrate them by manufacturers making goods. In spite of this, you should always remember that our ideas apply to all kinds of products – operations management is concerned with **all** operations and not just manufacturing.

At this point we should describe some of the differences between services and goods. Table 2.3 is not always true, but it gives some useful guidelines.

After reading the list in Table 2.3 you might get the impression that service organizations are all rather similar. This is not true. There is a range of size from individuals to the United Nations, and a range of activities from saving souls in churches to destroying them in armies. The term 'services' covers a very wide range of activities. We can classify them according to:

- *public services* provided by national and local government such as defence, social services, health and education;

- *retail and wholesale shops*;

- *distribution services* for both goods and information, including transport, mail, libraries and newspapers;

- *non-profit services* such as charities and churches;

- *other services for industry* including finance, legal and a variety of professional services;

- *other services for individuals* including leisure, banking and domestic services.

As we are emphasizing the differences between services and goods, you might imagine that they are completely separate. But this is not true. In reality all products are a combination of goods and services. Consider, for example, a restaurant; this provides a service, but at the same time it makes meals. A television company makes both goods – with video tapes of programmes – and

Table 2.3 Differences between services and goods.

Services	*Goods*
• The product is intangible	• The product is tangible
• Services cannot be kept in stock	• Goods can be kept in stock until needed
• There is simultaneous production and consumption	• There is a delay between production and use
• Products are more likely to be unique and cannot be mass produced	• Products are usually similar and can be mass produced
• There is a lot of contact with the customer	• There is little contact between manufacturers and customers
• Customers participate in the service	• Customers do not help with manufacturing
• Facilities are located near to customers	• Factories are located away from customers
• Services are labour intensive	• Manufacturing is largely automated
• Quality is difficult to measure	• Quality can be easier to measure
• Quality depends largely on the server	• Quality does not depend on one person
• It is difficult to measure the output	• The output can usually be counted

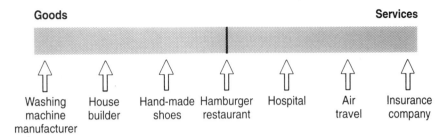

Figure 2.5 A spectrum of goods and services.

services – with transmissions. A company that makes washing machines is clearly a manufacturer, but it also gives an after-sales service.

So there is not really a clear distinction between goods and services. It would be better to describe a spectrum of organizations. At one end of this spectrum are organizations that mainly supply goods, such as Whirlwind which make kitchen equipment. At the other end of the spectrum are organizations that mainly provide services such as Sun Alliance who give insurance. McDonald's hamburger restaurants come in the middle of the spectrum, giving a combination of goods and services (see Figure 2.5).

Looking at all products as a combination of goods and services, you can see why managers in all organizations face similar problems. Regardless of their industry they have to plan products, forecast demand, organize activities, motivate staff, and so on. In the rest of the book we shall see how they do this.

Review questions

2.14   What do you understand by (a) goods (b) services (c) products?

2.15   What stages do national economies usually go through as they develop?

2.16   Most people in industrialized countries work in manufacturing industry. Do you think this is true?

2.17   In what way are service industries fundamentally different from manufacturing ones?

Chapter review

- Operations are the activities that are directly concerned with making a product; they convert a variety of inputs into desired outputs.

- Operations management is the management function responsible for this conversion.

- Developments in the past few years, particularly increased competition, have highlighted the need for skilled operations managers.

- Operations management is a central function in all organizations, along with sales/marketing and accounting/finance.

- Operations management can also be described as a profession, by its approach to solving problems, and by the problem areas it tackles.

- There are some differences between service and manufacturing organizations. But most products are a combination of goods and services. Operations management is relevant to organizations in all sectors of the economy.

Key terms

accounting/finance	26	operations management	19
goods	33	outputs	19
inputs	19	products	19
managers	20	production management	29
model	31	sales/marketing	25
operations	19	services	33

CS Case study – British Telecommunications plc

Until it was privatized in 1984, British Telecommunications (BT) had a virtual monopoly of telecommunications in the UK. After privatization the government wanted to encourage competition and imposed strict regulations on BT's activities. Competition came from other telecommunications companies, such as Mercury Communications, and new companies entering the market, such as the cable television companies and Energis which is owned by National Grid. In 1994 sixty companies submitted applications to start telecommunications networks, including AT&T, the world's biggest telephone company. This combination of regulations and increasing competition means that BT's share of the UK telephone market will probably continue to fall from its current 85%.

To meet the competition, BT is adopting a number of policies in operations, marketing and finance.

- *It aims to give customers a high quality service.* This is measured in many ways, including value for money, reliability, response time, timed appointments for installation and repairs, clarity of communications, use of modern technology, 90 BT shops and 116,000 public payphones around the country, and services for special needs such as typetalk for the deaf.

- *It develops new products.* BT spends over £270 million a year on research and development and has won five Queen's Awards for Technological Achievement. Recent developments include videophones, increased use of optical fibres, high technology digital exchanges, videoconferencing, cellnet, camnet and various features offered on telephones – such as mid-call diversion, call waiting signals, three-way calls and caller display to identify incoming calls.

- *It moves into other markets.* BT is expanding its communications business alongside its core telephone operations. It carries television channels on its networks and transmitters, supplies the sound and vision circuits for live radio and television transmissions, designs trading systems for financial dealers, and so on.

- *It develops international business.* Of BT's total revenue, 98% is generated in the UK. BT is expanding internationally, designing, supplying and managing a range of networks in Europe, Australia and around the world. It has 30 overseas offices and employs 2600 people outside the UK. Expansion into the large US market is difficult, because of the restrictions on foreign ownership. BT bought 17% of McCaw Cellular Communications in America, but later sold this to AT&T for almost $2 billion. Now its most important move is Concert – an alliance with MCI, America's second largest network operator. It also has an alliance with VIAG in Germany.

- *It emphasizes community relations.* This involves a number of activities, such as the emergency 999 service, an environment protection purchasing policy and award for suppliers, charity contributions of £15 million a year, sponsorship of the arts, and special services for the disabled.

These policies aim at increasing the competitiveness of a huge organization which has assets of £20 billion, 140,000 employees, a turnover of £14 billion and a profit of £2 billion a year.

Year	1989	1990	1991	1992	1993	1994	1995
Profit (£m)	1579	1535	2080	2074	1248	1805	1736

Questions

- What are the operations in BT? What are its inputs and outputs?

- What do you think are the main threats facing BT and its main opportunities?

- Could you suggest other changes in BT's operations, marketing or finance?

Discussion questions

2.1   What do you think will happen to a company that does not continuously update its operations?

2.2   How can people be convinced of the importance of operations management?

2.3   What do you think are the most important issues currently facing operations managers?

2.4   All organizations have both primary outputs – their products – and secondary ones, such as taxes, improved technology, waste materials, and so on. Take a factory you are familiar with and describe *all* the outputs and inputs.

2.5   There are three central functions in an organization. Does this mean the other functions are not needed? What are these other functions?

2.6   How has international trade developed in recent years? Has this affected operations?

2.7   Managers make the decisions within a company – but what does this mean?

2.8   The economic development of a country is in three stages. Do you think that progress through these stages is inevitable? Are there alternative routes to development? Does moving to the next stage mean a country can forget the industries developed in the previous stages?

2.9   When a showroom sells a car is it producing goods or providing a service? What about the car manufacturer? Is there really a clear distinction between the suppliers of goods and services?

2.10 In 1982 Peter Blake opened his first ice cream parlour in the Medway Shopping Mall. He served a small selection of snack foods, mainly ice cream, doughnuts, sandwiches and coffee. The main business came from people who wanted a few minutes break while shopping in the mall, and those who had a tea break while working in other shops. Peter's shop was comfortable and clean, he left newspapers and magazines around for his customers to read, and he trained his staff to be cheerful and welcoming. What product do you think Peter is supplying? What are his operations?

Selected references

Many of books on operations management are aimed at the US market and are similar in style, content and presentation. The following list gives some texts of varying quality.

Aquilano N.J. and Chase R.B. (1991). *Fundamentals of Operations Management*. Homewood: Irwin.

Dilworth J.B. (1992). *Operations Management*. New York: McGraw-Hill.

Evans J.R., Anderson D.R., Sweeney D.J. and Williams T.A. (1990). *Applied Production and Operations Management* (3rd edn). St Paul: West Publishing.

Gaither N. (1994). *Production and Operations Management* (6th edn). Chicago: The Dryden Press.

Krajewski L.J. and Ritzman L.P. (1993). *Operations Management* (3rd edn). Reading: Addison-Wesley.

Lee S.M. and Schniederjans M.J. (1994). *Operations Management*. Houghton Mifflin: Boston.

McClain J.O., Thomas L.J. and Mazzola J.B. (1992). *Operations Management* (3rd edn). New Jersey: Prentice-Hall.

Murdick R.G., Render B. and Russell R.S. (1990). *Service Operations Management*. Boston: Allyn and Bacon.

Schroeder R.G. (1993). *Operations Management* (4th edn). New York: McGraw-Hill.

Schmenner R.W. (1990). *Production/Operations Management* (4th edn). New York: MacMillan.

Stevenson W.J. (1993). *Production/Operations Management* (4th edn). Homewood: Irwin.

Vonderembse M.A. and White G.P. (1991). *Operations Management* (2nd edn). St Paul: West Publishing.

3   Operations strategy

Contents

Objectives

After reading this chapter you should be able to:

- describe the different levels of decision making in an organization
- describe strategic, tactical and operational decisions
- discuss an organization's mission and business strategy
- see how these lead to a range of other strategic, tactical and operational decisions
- outline different types of operations management decisions

Making decisions in an organization

The last chapter showed how managers make the decisions within an organization. In this chapter we are going to look at the types of decisions they make.

Some decisions are very important to an organization, with consequences felt over many years. Other decisions are less important, with consequences felt over days or even hours. We can use these levels of importance to classify decisions as either **strategic**, **tactical** or **operational**.

- **Strategic decisions** are made by senior management, they are long term, use many resources and involve high risk.

- **Tactical decisions** are made by middle management, they are medium term, use fewer resources and involve less risk.

- **Operational decisions** are made by junior management, they are short term, use few resources and involve low risk.

A useful analogy compares the organization with a small boat. The captain – representing top management – examines charts to decide where the boat should go; the helmsman – representing middle management – is directed by the captain and steers the boat in the right direction; a crewman – representing junior management – rows the boat to keep it moving.

Every organization makes decisions at all levels.

- For a manufacturer, a decision to build a new factory five or 10 years in the future is strategic; a decision to introduce a new product one or two years in the future is tactical; a decision about the number of units of a product to make next week is operational.

- In a university, deciding whether to concentrate on postgraduate education in the next few years is strategic; whether to offer a particular postgraduate course in one or two years' time is tactical; choosing someone to teach a course next week is operational.

- A research organization could make a strategic decision to continue looking for new knowledge in electronics, a tactical decision to develop a new micro-processor, and an operational decision about scheduling the work to be done in the next few weeks.

- For a railway, deciding whether to continue a passenger service to an area is strategic; whether to structure the fares to attract business or leisure passengers is tactical; designing short-term crew schedules is operational.

- On a farm, a decision to continue growing grain is strategic; choosing the kind of grain and areas to sow next season is tactical; organizing the planting of seeds is operational.

The timescale of decisions varies widely between organizations. A strategic decision for National Power might involve the building of new power stations. This decision looks 20 years or more into the future and involves an expenditure of hundreds of millions of pounds. A strategic decision for Albert Street Corner Shop might look one or two years into the future and involve an expenditure of a few thousand pounds. The important point is that decisions are always needed at different levels (see Table 3.1).

Senior managers make the strategic decisions that set an organization on its course. These decisions are not an end in themselves, but are the beginning of a planning process that filters down through the entire organization. Strategic decisions set the environment in which lower level decisions are made; they are passed down the organization to middle management and give the objectives and constraints for more detailed tactical decisions. These, in turn, are passed down the organization to give the objectives and constraints for the detailed operational decisions made by junior managers. The result is a hierarchy of decisions shown in Figure 3.1.

While decisions are passed downwards through the management hierarchy, information about actual performance and other feedback is passed upwards. This information must be filtered as it passes upwards, or top managers would be swamped by too much detailed, irrelevant information. They need enough detail to be useful, but not so much that overall patterns are hidden.

Table 3.1

Decision	Strategic	Tactical	Operational
Level of manager	senior	middle	junior
Importance	high	medium	low
Resources used	many	some	few
Timescale	long	medium	short
Risk	high	medium	low
Uncertainty	high	medium	low
Amount of detail	very general	moderate	very detailed
Data available	uncertain	some	certain
Structure	unstructured	some	structured
Focus	whole organization	divisions in the organization	individual units

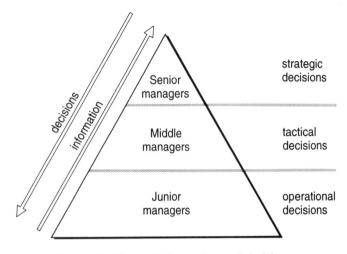

Figure 3.1 Flow of information and decisions.

Although this picture of decision making is generally true, improved information technology is making some important changes. This technology allows senior managers to access all information in the organization, automatically sort it, and present it in the best format. At the same time, organizations are recognizing that the best person to make a decision about an operation is the person most closely involved – and this is often a junior manager. The result is a squeeze on middle managers who are losing their traditional roles. Many organizations are now reorganizing and becoming flatter – with fewer layers of management and most middle managers removed.

ce Case example – Scottish Mutual Assurance plc

This example illustrates some decisions of different types in a large organization.

The Scottish Mutual Assurance Society was founded in Glasgow in 1883. It was founded on the belief that the world of finance could, and should, be used for the good of the individual and the community as a whole. In 1992 the society transferred its business to a proprietary company, Scottish Mutual Assurance plc, which is a wholly-owned subsidiary of Abbey National. By this time it looked after £2300 million of investors' money, mainly in pensions, mortgages, investment and inheritance tax planning.

Strategic decisions, such as the takeover by Abbey National, are made by senior managers at their principal office in Glasgow. Details of these decisions are passed to 24 branch offices around the country which make tactical decisions. Below the branch offices are a network of agents and financial advisors who make operational decisions.

Typically, the principal office makes a strategic decision, perhaps to develop single premium pensions. Details of the policies are settled and passed to branch offices. The branches see how the new product fits into their business, and make plans for the medium term. They might, for example, check the support needed by the new policy over the next two years, and make sure there are enough trained staff to give this support. The branch offices pass details of the pension policy to agents and advisors who make operational decisions about contacting potential customers, and so on. So decisions about the policy are passed down through the organization from the principal office, through branch offices to individual agents.

The agents and advisors talk to potential customers and collect their views on the new policy. These are summarized and passed back to the branch offices. Each branch office reviews the reports from individual agents, summarizes them, and passes the regional view back to the principal office. At the principal office, reports from each branch office are reviewed and summarized to find patterns for the whole country. So information about the product is passed up the organization from agents, through branch offices to senior management.

Questions

- What other decisions might be made at each level of Scottish Mutual Assurance?

- Can you give other examples of this kind of decision making?

You can see that the management of an organization relies on an exchange of information and decisions. These must be consistent so that achievable objectives are set for each part of the organization. In particular, there must be no conflicts between decisions at different levels, or between functions. This is often surprisingly difficult in large organizations that are divided into many parts. On the other hand, small organizations need a less formal approach to decision making. Families, for example, are small organizations that makes strategic, tactical and operational decisions, but they do not usually have a formal decision-making process.

Review questions

3.1 What are the different levels of decision in an organization?

3.2 Tactical decisions are most important to an organization because they concern its day-to-day running. Do you agree with this statement?

3.3   What kind of decision is:
   (a)   finding the best location for a new factory;
   (b)   deciding how many hours of overtime are needed next week;
   (c)   deciding whether to start an air service to South America;
   (d)   deciding whether to publish a proposed textbook?

Mission and business strategy

Mission

The last section showed how decisions are made at various levels within an organization. This section discusses some strategic decisions that set the overall course of an organization.

Many organizations have an overall statement of their purpose, which defines their **mission** or **vision**. This gives the purpose of the organization – its reason for existence. Some examples of missions are:

- *a University*: discovering and disseminating knowledge;

- *a hospital*: providing first class health care;

- *a bank*: safeguarding and increasing the value of customers' investments;

- *a manufacturer*: supplying high quality products to a wide market, while making a reasonable profit;

- *a television network*: entertaining, informing and educating the widest possible audience;

- *Walt Disney*: 'making people happy'.

The mission statement is sometimes very brief. Eastern Electricity, for example, say, 'Our mission is to be the best public electricity supplier in the United Kingdom.' Often the statements are longer and describe the fundamental beliefs and aims of the organization. They answer questions like, 'What is our purpose?', 'What business are we in?' and 'What are our overall objectives?' Sometimes they describe the organizations responsibilities to its shareholders, employees, customers and community – and some missions include views on productivity, markets, technology used, public image, company philosophy, and a range of other topics.

Many organizations do not have a formal statement of their mission. But there are benefits in having a precise statement of overall purpose. This gives a focus to make sure employees are working towards the same aims, that there are no conflicts, and that resources are sensibly shared out. A mission statement is the starting point for all other decisions in the organization – it sets the context that the organization works in.

ce | Case example – Tesco plc

Tesco plc has the following corporate objective.

Tesco is one of Britain's leading food retailers with 430 stores throughout England, Scotland and Wales and an additional 98 stores in France operated by Catteau. We are pleased to serve more than eight million customers every week. Tesco is committed to:

- offering customers the best value for money and the most competitive prices;
- meeting the needs of customers by constantly seeking and acting on their opinions regarding product quality, choice, innovation, store facilities and service;
- providing shareholders with outstanding returns on their investment;
- improving profitability through investment in efficient stores and distribution depots, in productivity improvements and in new technology;
- developing the talents of its people through sound management and training practices, while rewarding them fairly with equal opportunities for all;
- working closely with suppliers to build long-term business relationships based on strict quality and price criteria;
- participating in the formulation of national food industry policies on key issues such as health, nutrition, hygiene, safety and animal welfare;
- supporting the well-being of the community and the protection of the environment.

Task

- Tesco publishes this corporate objective in its annual report. Look through the annual reports of other companies to find other examples of mission statements.

Business strategy

Once the mission has been defined, senior managers can make a series of other strategic decisions. These might design the structure of the organization, where it operates, what its relations are with other organizations, how it treats customers, and so on. These strategic decisions which refer to the whole organization form the **business strategy**. Some other terms are used for this, particularly **corporate strategy**, **organizational strategy** and **long-term plans**. We will use the term business strategy for all types of organization, whether or not they are strictly businesses.

A business strategy is the set of plans that makes sure the mission is achieved. These plans include decisions about:

- **Organizational structure**   This is how the organization is divided, what each division does, who works there.

- **Geographical locations**   This relates to where operations are done, which markets are important, where administration is done.

- **Competitive position**   This describes how the organization stands in relation to its competitors.

- **Amount of diversification**   This describes how wide a range of products the organization makes.

- **Acquisitions policy**   This is how the organization might expand by growing or buying other organizations.

- **Profitability**   This describes the relationship between income generated and costs.

- **Productivity**   The amount of products made in relation to the resources used.

- **Resources used**   The relative amounts of various resources used by the organization.

- **Innovation**   This describes how the organization changes the way it works.

The design of a business strategy is important, as it sets out the way that an organization achieves its mission. This design starts by considering three factors. The first is the mission itself, which sets the overall goals. The second is the environment in which the organization works. The third is the organization's distinctive competence which allows it to succeed in this environment (see Figure 3.2).

The **environment** includes all the factors that affect an organization, but over which it has no, or very little, control. These include:

- *customers*: their expectations, attitudes, demographics;

- *market conditions*: size, location, stability;

- *technology*: current availability, likely developments, rate of innovation;

- *economic conditions*: gross domestic product, rate of growth, inflation;

- *legal restraints*: trade restrictions, liability and employment laws;

- *competitors*: number, ease of entry to the market, strengths;

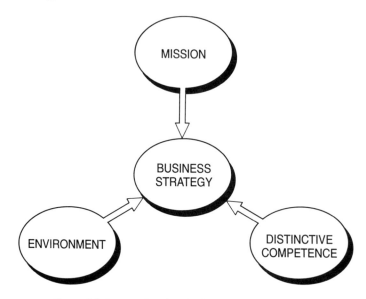

Figure 3.2 Inputs for developing a business strategy.

- *shareholders*: their target return on investments, objectives, profit needed;
- *interest groups*: their objectives, how strong they are, amount of support they have;
- *social conditions*: customers' lifestyles, changing demands, significant trends
- *political conditions*: stability, amount of governmental control, external relations.

All organizations that make competing products are likely to have a similar environment. This means that an organization can only succeed in its environment if it has a **distinctive competence**. This is defined by the factors that are under the control of the organization, and which set it apart from its competitors. A company that can design new products very quickly and has enough resources to market these, could say this ability to innovate is part of its distinctive competence. A bank may develop a very personal and friendly service as its distinctive competence; a hospital may specialize in treating certain diseases; a shop may have expertise with specific types of goods; a management consultant may offer help with a certain type of problem. A distinctive competence develops from an organization's assets, which include:

- **customers**   their demands, loyalty, relationships;
- **employees**   skills, expertise, loyalty;
- **finances**   capital, debt, cash flow;

- **products** quality, reputation, innovations;
- **facilities** capacity, age, value;
- **technology** currently used, plans, special types;
- **suppliers** reliability, service, flexibility;
- **marketing** experience, reputation;
- **resources** patents, ownership.

When managers want to think about their business strategy, a useful way of summarizing ideas is a SWOT analysis. This lists different aspects of the organization according to:

- Strengths: what the organization does well – features it should build on;
- Weaknesses: what problems the organization has – areas it should improve;
- Opportunities: which can help the organization – openings it should seize;
- Threats: which can damage the organizations – hazards it should avoid.

Then IBM could start a SWOT analysis by listing its strengths as market dominance, customer service and large resources; it weaknesses as lack of innovation and high costs; its opportunities as growing demand for computers and new technologies; its threats as manufacturers copying IBM products and low cost competitors. A full SWOT analysis would add many other factors to these lists.

ce Case example – Eastern Electricity

This example suggests some steps in the design of a business strategy for a major service company, starting with a SWOT analysis.

The UK electricity supply industry was privatized in 1990. The 12 regional boards became independent companies, with Eastern Electricity as the largest. It supplies electricity to 3 million customers in a region that stretches from North London to Peterborough, and from Buckinghamshire to the coast of East Anglia. In common with all regional electricity suppliers, it has a virtual monopoly in this area. The company employs 7000 people, has a turnover of £2 billion and makes a profit of £200 million.

The mission of Eastern Electricity is 'to be the best public electricity supplier in the United Kingdom'. This allows managers to develop a business strategy. One way of starting this is a SWOT analysis which could list:

- **Strengths** Experience in the business, existing network of customers and suppliers, a virtual monopoly in the region, financially secure.

- **Weaknesses** Business practices inherited from a nationalized industry, need to upgrade management skills, there is a single product, the company operates in one geographical region.

- **Opportunities** Economically developing region, growing demand for electricity, moves into related businesses.

- **Threats** New competition from other suppliers, tight government regulation, alternative energy sources.

Extending this list would give a more detailed view of Eastern Electricity, and show how to develop a business strategy. For example, among the threats are tight government regulations introduced at the time of privatization. The company could avoid these by moving into related businesses that are less tightly regulated. It has done this by diversifying into wholesale and retail gas supply, electricity generation, combined heat and power systems and contracting services.

Questions

- What else do you think could be included in the SWOT analysis for Eastern Electricity?

- Based on this, what would you expect to see in their business strategy?

Competitive strategy

An important part of an organization's business strategy concerns its ability to compete. All organizations have competitors – both the organizations that already supply similar products, and those that might start making similar products in the future. The part of business strategy that deals with competition is sometimes separated in a **competitive strategy** or **competitive positioning**.

When an organization is developing a competitive strategy it must look at its own strengths and weaknesses in relation to its competitors. If a company is good at making a high quality product, while most of its competitors are aiming for lower quality, its strategy is clear – it should produce the best product available. If there is a trend for very large supermarkets on trading estates, one competitive strategy is to build small corner shops. This illustrates the principle behind a competitive strategy, which searches for a **favourable position** in the industry.

There are basically two ways of finding such favourable positions – cost leadership and product differentiation.

- **Cost leaders** make the same products more cheaply. This means the organization lowers its unit costs by having efficiently operations, often making large numbers of a standard product.

- **Product differentiation** make different products. This means the organization makes products that are significantly different to competitors', and they can charge higher prices.

A computer manufacturer, for example, must decide whether to make a standard computer at a low price, or a computer with features that distinguish it from the competition. Lyons make standard cakes so efficiently that their unit costs are low, while La Patisserie Francaise makes different types of cakes and charges higher prices. Ford makes a large number of similar, inexpensive cars, while Rolls Royce makes a few different, expensive cars.

You might think that some form of compromise would give better results – using some aspects of cost leadership with other aspects of product differentiation. But there is widespread agreement that this approach does not work. Companies with 'average' products and 'average' costs do markedly worse than those that concentrate on either low costs or unique products (see Figure 3.3).

Some people say the way to get a favourable competitive position is to concentrate on the 'four Ps':

- **product**   developing the right product for customers;

- **place**   making sure the product is delivered to customers;

- **promotion**   telling potential customers about the product;

- **price**   setting a price that is acceptable to customers.

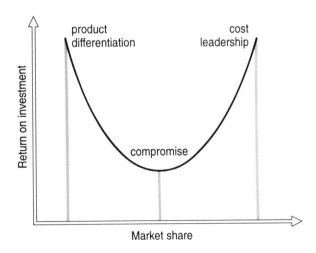

Figure 3.3 Success comes from product differentiation or cost leadership.

A broader view says that an organization can compete with cost, quality, service, reliability, availability, flexibility, delivery speed, location and a number of other features.

The essential point about a competitive strategy is that it compares an organizations' operations with those of its competitors. Then it might ask, who are the competitors? How many competitors are there? What are the competitors' strengths? What are our strengths? What flexibility do we have? What are our future prospects? Who are the customers?

The answers to these questions suggest a range of more detailed questions like, what products should we concentrate on? What volumes should we produce? What quality should we give? Do we supply low or high cost products? Are our products reliable? Do we give fast deliveries? Who are our biggest customers? Do we have adequate financing?

At this stage the decisions are more directly related to functional areas, as they ask specific questions about operations, marketing and finance. The next type of decisions, then, are still strategic, but they are made within the central functions of operations, sales/marketing and accounting/finance, as illustrated in Figure 3.4.

You must remember that these strategic decisions within the functional areas are still made within the context of business strategy. If a business strategy is to make large numbers of a product at low cost, this might lead to a strategic decision within operations to use an automated production line. This in turn will affect other strategic decisions about the product, customers,

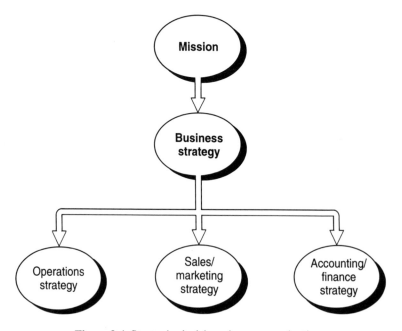

Figure 3.4 Strategic decisions in an organization.

production process, costs, and so on. We shall discuss such strategic decisions within operations in the next section.

Review questions

3.4   What is an organization's 'mission'?

3.5   What is a 'business strategy'?

3.6   What factors should be considered when designing a business strategy?

3.7   What questions are asked when designing a competitive strategy?

Operations management decisions

So far we have seen how strategic decisions in the organization as a whole lead to strategic decisions within the central functions. These strategic decisions in turn lead to tactical and operational decisions, as shown in Figure 3.5. In this section we shall look at the types of decision tackled by operations management.

In Figure 3.5 you can see a problem with the terms used. Unfortunately, there is little alternative but to call decisions at the operational level in the operations function 'operational operations decisions'. Thankfully, this is a term we shall not have to use often.

Strategic decisions within the operations functions form the **operations strategy**. This is developed directly from the business strategy. Then a business strategy to win a large share of some market might lead to an operations strategy of making large numbers of high quality products. The operations strategy is clearly linked to strategic decisions within the other central functions. If the operations strategy is to use a 'mass production' process, the marketing strategy must aim at selling large numbers, and the finance strategy must make a heavy investment in equipment.

The strategies of each function must reinforce each other and work towards the organization's mission. But some organizations find this kind of co-operation difficult. Take one example where a manufacturer aims for high profits. The operations function might see this as a sign to reduce costs by concentrating on a narrow range of products. At the same time, the marketing function might see it as a sign to increase sales by offering a wide range of products. These two contradictory views must somehow be resolved. Although each function has its own objectives, these are secondary, and should not interfere with the overall aims of the organization.

The operations strategy answers questions like:

●   What type of products does the organization make?

●   What types of process does it use to make the products?

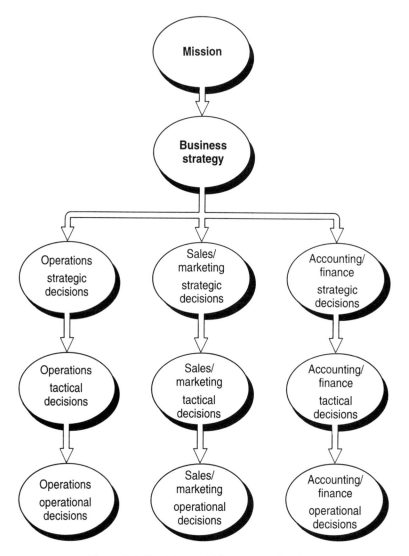

Figure 3.5 Decisions within an organization.

- How does it maintain high quality?
- What geographic areas does it work in?
- How does it plan capacity?
- Does it emphasize the product made or process used?

We will answer these questions in the rest of the book, but should mention the last one here. This asks whether an organization emphasizes its product or process. As we shall see in Chapter 7, the **process** is the method used to make a product – so baking is the main process in making bread, brewing is the process used for making beer, selling is the process in a shop and education is the process in a school. An important question in some organizations is whether they have a product focus and see themselves as making a product, or a process focus and see themselves as using a process.

- A company that sees itself as running a bottling plant has a process focus: one that makes bottled lemonade has a product focus.

- Expensive restaurants have a process focus – they cook foods: hamburger restaurants have a product focus – they sell hamburgers.

- A telephone company has a product focus – it arranges telephone calls: a communications company has a process focus – it arranges suitable communications.

- A general store has a process focus – it sells things: an ice cream shop has a product focus – it sells ice-cream.

This distinction may not be very clear, as all organizations both use a process and supply a product. But the focus asks if the organization sees itself **primarily** as making a product or using a process. This apparently subtle difference can have important effects on operations, which we shall look at again in Chapter 7.

The operations strategy sets the overall direction for operations. Then a series of shorter term tactical decisions can be made about the layout of facilities, process design, capacity planning, make/buy decisions, quality assurance, maintenance plans, recruiting, and so on. These tactical decisions, in turn, lead to short-term operational decisions about resource scheduling, inventory control, reliability, expediting, and so on. Some illustrations of these decisions are shown in Table 3.2.

The distinctions between strategic, tactical and operational decisions are not really as clear as Table 3.2 suggests. Quality, for example, is a strategic issue when a company is planning its competitive strategy, perhaps aiming for a very high quality product. But, it becomes a tactical issue when the organization is deciding how quality can be measured and what quality targets should be set. Then it becomes an operational decision when testing production to see if quality targets are being met. In the same way, inventory may be a strategic issue when deciding whether to build a warehouse for finished goods or ship directly to customers, a tactical issue when deciding how much to invest in stock, or an operational issue when deciding how much of a product to order this week.

All the decisions we have mentioned so far are related to the supply of a product. The long-term survival of any organization depends on its ability to supply products that satisfy customer demand. The supply of these products does not come by chance, but needs good decisions by managers. The rest of this book describes how these decisions are made.

Table 3.2 Types of decisions.

Decision area	Typical operations decisions
Strategic decisions	
Business	What business are we in?
Product	What products are made?
Process	How are products made?
Location	Where are products made?
Capacity	How large should facilities be?
Quality management	How good are the products?
Tactical decisions	
Layout	How should operations be arranged?
Planning	When should a new product be introduced?
Quality assurance	How is planned quality achieved?
Logistics	How should distribution be organized: what transport should be used?
Maintenance	How often should equipment be maintained and replaced?
Staffing	How many people should be employed and what skills do they need?
Technology	What level is most appropriate for planned production?
Make/buy	Is it better to make or buy components?
Operational decisions	
Scheduling	In what order should products be made?
Inventory	How much should be ordered and when should orders be placed?
Reliability	How often does equipment break down: what can be done to improve this?
Maintenance	When can maintenance periods be scheduled?
Quality control	Are products reaching designed quality?
Job design	What is the best way to do an operation?
Work measurement	How long will an operation take?

ce Case example – Sutton Byfleet Council

This example shows how decisions about operations are made at different levels in local government. As you read it, think how similar decisions are made in other organizations.

In common with all local governments, Sutton Byfleet Council has looked for ways of increasing efficiency. A consultant's report suggested an increase in the use of computers – so the council includes computerization as part of its strategic policy. In particular, it plans to reduce paperwork by 50% and increase staff productivity by 80% over the next seven years. This would both reduce costs and improve the service offered.

The council passed this strategic policy to all their functional areas. Operational Services adapted their own plans to include computerization of all administrative functions over the next five years. Managers then made a number of tactical decisions about the system, including the type of computer hardware, software design, suppliers, links between systems, maintenance contracts, training given to staff, and so on. These decisions were effective over the next year or so.

The next decisions aimed at using the new system as efficiently as possible. Supervisors designed schedules to make sure trained people were always available for operations; they changed the layout of desks in the main office; phone calls replaced letters wherever possible, so more phones were installed; clerks recorded their work load to show productivity changes; a suggestions scheme was started; stocks of stationery were removed; clerks found the best way of avoiding problems.

Computerization of the administrative system lead to a series of changes in other areas. For example, records became available to show the real cost of maintaining the council's fleet of vehicles. This was so expensive that a private contractor was given the job and reduced costs by 30%. On the other hand, the number of complaints about the quality of school meals was now recorded, and the council stopped using a catering company and returned to its own cooks.

Two years after Sutton Byfleet Council made its decision to increase computer use, Operational Services had increased productivity by 25% and reduced costs by 15%. At the same time the service offered was maintained, or even improved. The number of complaints from the public – now received on a free 'Tell Us How We Are Doing' telephone line – fell by 60%.

Review questions

3.8   What are the main characteristics of an organization with a product focus?

3.9   What is the difference between business strategy, competitive strategy and operations strategy?

3.10 Which level of operations decision should be made first?

Chapter review

- This chapter discussed the decisions needed within an organization.

- Decisions are made at several levels, and are classified as strategic, tactical or operational.

- Strategic decisions are made by senior management, involve more resources, more risk and a long time-span: tactical decisions are made by middle management, involve less resources, some risk and a medium time-span; operational decisions are made by junior management, involve few resources, little risk and a short time-span.

- An organization's mission describes its overall beliefs and aims. This sets the context for all other decisions.

- The mission allows a series of strategic decisions about the organization as a whole. These define the business strategy. Other strategic decisions are made within functional areas.

- Strategic decisions within the operations function form the operations strategy. This sets the context for a range of operations decisions at tactical and operational levels.

Key terms

CS Case study – University of Rondstat

The University of Rondstat has a Department of Operations Management, which is part of the Business School. For some time the University has felt that certain departments lack direction. To correct this, the University President has asked every department to prepare a mission statement and strategic plan. At the same time the President has asked for the University's mission and all Faculty missions to be updated.

The Department of Operations Management has formed a small committee to consider both its long-term goals, and plans for achieving these goals. As their starting point, this committee looked at the current missions of the University and the Business School.

The mission of the university is rather long and covers several pages. The first paragraph gives the following summary.

> The University of Rondstat is a place of education and scholarly enquiry. Its mission is to seek truth and disseminate knowledge, which we achieve by excellence in research and teaching. We contribute to society directly by research, and by preparing students who carry their knowledge on to future generations. We co-operate enthusiastically with

other parts of the education system, with government at every level, and with all parts of our community. We pursue this mission for the benefit of all humanity and encourage local, national and international communications.

The Business School's mission is considerably shorter.

The mission of the business school is to be internationally recognized as a leader in management education and research. Our goals are:

● to instill leadership and knowledge of management in our students;
● to be a leading contributor to management knowledge through research;
● to employ faculty who achieve excellence in teaching and scholarship;
● to maintain outstanding facilities for management education;
● to remain close to the practice of management within our community.

You have been asked to suggest new mission statements. You might start by asking whether it is reasonable for the University, Business School and Department of Operations Management all to have missions. What features should be included in the updated mission of the University and Business School? What would be a suitable mission statement for the Department of Operations Management? How could the mission lead to a business strategy?

Discussion questions

3.1 'Strategic decisions are less structured than tactical and operational ones.' What exactly does this mean?

3.2 Describe some decisions at different levels in an organization you are familiar with.

3.3 Compare the mission statements published by a number of organizations, and say how these are affected by the type of organization. Why are some mission statements short and others very long?

3.4 Suppose you are about to start a management consultancy. Do a SWOT analysis of your business. What would be your business strategy?

3.5 Explain, giving suitable examples, the differences between business strategy and functional strategies.

3.6 How can a service industry develop a competitive strategy? What happens when the service has a near monopoly, such as health or education?

3.7 Consider a specific organization you are familiar with and design a business strategy for it. How does this lead to tactical and operational decisions?

3.8 There is often inter-departmental rivalry within an organization. Do you think this should be encouraged?

3.9 Markland, Merrit and Anderson is a well-established company specializing in marine insurance. Their mission statement leads to a series of objectives and key values that are shown in the following summary:

> Our mission is to be a leader in the international market for marine insurance. We shall achieve this by using the highest professional standards and integrity to provide our customers with the best possible service. This will allow us to form long-term, mutually beneficial partnerships with our customers, employees and share holders.
>
> To fulfil this mission we must achieve the following objectives:
> - the highest possible level of customer satisfaction;
> - efficient and cost effective operations;
> - high profitability to reward shareholders;
> - knowledgeable, trained and motivated staff;
> - long-term commitment to the industry.
>
> To achieve these objectives we must adopt the following key values:
> - responsiveness to customers;
> - concern for people;
> - teamwork and co-operation;
> - professionalism and expertise;
> - value for money.

How do you think these objectives and key values lead to a business strategy? What would you expect to see in their operations strategy?

3.10 Deming (who we shall meet again in Chapter 5) discussed 'The Seven Deadly Diseases' of managers.

(1) *Lack constancy of purpose* The whole organization must know where it is heading, and aim at improving its performance.

(2) *Emphasis on short-term profits* Organizations are too often judged by their short-term performance, like annual profit and quarterly sales. They should take a longer view and aim for the best results over the long term.

(3) *Evaluation of performance, merit rating, or annual review* Again, this tends to emphasize people's short-term performance, when they should be looking at the long term. Another problem occurs when people do badly in these evaluations, and are left bitter, dejected and unfit for work.

(4) *Mobility of top management* Managers move freely between companies, but such moves leave them with no knowledge or interest in the long-term success of a particular organization. They are often more interested in their own 'market value'.

(5) *Running a company on visible figures alone* Some of an organization's performance can be measured, such as income or profit. There are many aspects of performance which can not be measured, but they should not be ignored.

The last two of Deming's diseases are only relevant to the United States and are:

(6) *Excessive medical costs;*
(7) *Excessive costs of law suits.*

Do you think these diseases can be avoided by defining suitable strategies?

Selected references

Blackburn J.D. (1991). *Time-based Competition*. Homewood, Ill.: Business One Irwin.

Certo S.C. and Peter J.P. (1991). *Strategic Management* (2nd edn). New York: McGraw-Hill.

Hall R. (1987). *Attaining Manufacturing Excellence*. Homewood, Ill.: Dow-Jones Irwin.

Hill T. (1989). *Manufacturing Strategies*. Homewood, Ill.: Richard D. Irwin.

Hill T. (1993). *Manufacturing Strategy*. London: Macmillan.

Irons K. (1994). *Managing Service Companies*. Wokingham, UK: Addison-Wesley.

Mintzberg H. (1993). *The Rise and Fall of Strategic Planning*. New York: The Free Press.

Mintzberg H. and Quinn J.B. (1991). *The Strategy Process* (2nd edn). Englewood Cliffs, NJ: Prentice-Hall.

Porter M.E. (1989). *The Competitive Advantage of Nations*. New York: Free Press.

Tregoe B.B. (1989). *Vision in Action*. New York: Simon & Shuster.

Voss C.A. (1992). *Manufacturing Strategy*. London: Chapman & Hall.

A typical day: operations manager

Estech Ltd is a medium-sized manufacturing company that manufactures and repairs marine seismic equipment used by oil companies engaged in offshore oil exploration. The main activity is the manufacture and repair of 'seismic towed arrays'. These are hydrophonic cables towed by seismic survey ships. Each cable is made up of sections and costs about £500,000. Repair and technical support arrangements are vital given the hostile nature of the marine environment.

Steve Jones is the operations manager for the company's British facility. The plant is divided into two main areas, cable manufacture and repair and technical manufacture and repair. Each area has a manager who is responsible to Steve. He currently has 40 people working for him. Steve is directly responsible to the Managing Director, George Hanson, for all aspects of production, repairs, logistics, quality, site facilities and research and development.

The factory

The main factory starts at 7.30 am and Steve likes to 'get the smell of the place' by walking round the plant for half an hour before the administrative staff begin work at 8.30 am. As he walks from shop to shop, he talks briefly to various people, including John Butler, the filling shop supervisor. The previous day there were problems with one of the machines and Steve wants to check progress.

Steve's office

By 8.00 am Steve is back in his office. Jim Edwards, the quality manager, appears at the office door to report that problems with the delivery of a key component have been sorted. Five minutes later it is the site facilities manager who calls. Steve operates an 'open door' policy and consciously sets this time aside for 'mopping up' problems from the previous day.

Cable and repair manager's office

At 9.00 am Steve joins the daily meeting of the production team in the cable manufacture and repair manager's office. During the night Steve received a telephone call from the MD who had in turn received a call from a 'party chief' on board a survey ship off the coast of Nigeria. A party chief is the leader of a survey ship's seismic team. The party chief had damaged three of his six cables in a collision. He is anxious to get the damaged sections of cable repaired. This morning's meeting has to consider the feasibility of getting the damaged sections repaired within the next two weeks as the MD promised. Steve's task is to assess the situation with all those directly involved and with them arrive at a decision.

The key question is: What is the scope for rescheduling work to fit in the new job for Nigeria? Not only do the team have to consider what is technically possible, they have to think through the consequences of rescheduling work. Fortunately two of the jobs being done this week are routine ones, put into the schedule because there was a gap between two high priority jobs. After much discussion of priorities and careful evaluation of the work planned both for the remainder of this week and next, the consensus is that the Nigerian job can be fitted in. Steve will not have to break bad news to the MD. Production staff are going to have to reschedule their work and there will have to be some overtime, but the client is going to get what he wants.

Steve's office

Within about 45 minutes Steve is back in his office. The next hour and a half are devoted to paperwork. Steve has a number of ongoing projects. These include negotiating the technical requirements of a major new potential customer, the development of a new product and the evaluation of a new supplier.

Reception

Steve goes down to reception to meet two visitors from a potential new customer. After a tour of the plant he joins them in a meeting with the cable repair manager and two technicians.

Canteen

It is then time for lunch and an opportunity to talk to two new members of staff about their training course.

Steve's office

Steve is back in the office at about 2.00 pm. He has some phone calls and faxes to make and a meeting with the management accounts manager. The board has requested that the monthly production report should be available seven days after the month end rather than 14 days as at present. The meeting is to explore what needs to be done in order to meet the request. Once this meeting is over, Steve checks his 'things to do list'. The human resource manager has requested a job specification for a new technical post. It has to be ready the following day.

The factory

The job specification is still not complete. Steve is back on the shop floor to check progress on the Nigerian job. All the schedule revisions have been sorted out and work will start in two days' time when the damaged cables arrive back in the UK.

Steve's office

Steve takes stock of the day. The job specification is still incomplete. He checks the 'things to do list' again. He has an appointment with the R&D manager at 5.00 pm. There are some minor administrative tasks that can be put off to the end of the day. Steve decides to finish the job specification immediately and then put in an hour on his supplier evaluation project.

R&D manager's office

He then attends the meeting with Dr Broadley, the R&D manager. He is working on an enhancement to one of the company's major products and is anxious that a new piece of equipment be purchased to facilitate his work. Steve agrees to take the matter up with the MD.

MD's office

Steve goes to see the MD and report on his supplier evaluation project. This takes about 30 minutes. The two men then review the day's events, particularly their success in fitting in the repair job for Nigeria.

Steve's office

At about 6.00 pm Steve returns to his office and dictates three letters and a couple of memos for the following day. He sorts out the few remaining items left on his desk ready for tomorrow. At 6.30 pm Steve locks up and leaves.

Planning the product

This book is divided into five parts, each of which describes a different aspect of operations management. The first part introduced the subject. This is the second part, which looks at the planning needed to make a product.

There are four chapters in this part. Chapter 4 introduces the subject by describing the type of planning needed for a product. Chapter 5 discusses quality management; Chapter 6 looks at ways of forecasting demand; Chapter 7 outlines different processes that can be used to make a product.

These chapters discuss some of the strategic issues faced by every organization: how to plan products, how to maintain quality, how many units to make, and how to make them.

Chapter 7 forms a link with Part III, which looks in more detail at the process used to make the product. Then Part IV considers the scheduling of resources, and Part V discusses some aspects of materials management.

operations management

Brian Harris
Operations Director

THORN Transit Systems International

THORN Transit Systems International Limited (TTSI) is part of THORN EMI plc, and is based in Wells, Somerset. It operates on a global basis, producing Automatic Fare Collection Systems for the Mass Transit market worldwide. Brian Harris is the Director of the Operations Department with some 40 staff.

Q **What product does TTSI manufacture?**

A We don't actually manufacture a product as, for example, a car manufacturer does. TTSI is a 'Systems House' and our product is an 'Automatic Fare Collection System' (AFCS) for mass transportation networks. A complete system will contain a wide range of equipment and software which includes typically:

- Automatic Ticket Vending Machines and Ticket Office Machines issuing magnetically encoded and printed tickets. The former of these are passenger operated and will include Coin Systems, Bank Note Systems, Printers and Magnetic Encoders.

- Flap and Turnstile Gates for controlling entry and exit of passengers from the stations. These are operated by means of the tickets issued from the vending machines listed above, validated by Magnetic Readers and printed with information for the passenger.

- Computer Systems from the station level equipment through a communications network to a central computer system. This network allows the user to pass fare table information from the central computer to each individual item of equipment on the stations and to receive all transaction details of these items – tickets sold, passenger journeys, revenue taken, and so on.

The key to our business is the provision of an integrated operational system, which includes supply, installation and commissioning; training and support; and maintenance of both the hardware and software elements of the system.

We have supplied Automatic Fare Collection Systems for Light Railways and Metro Systems in Manchester, Stockholm,

Istanbul, Ankara, Hong Kong and Seoul. There are currently major prospects for our systems on the Asia Pacific Rim, and our most recent contract is to supply the Fare Collection System for the new Lantau Airport line in Hong Kong.

Q How do you undertake product planning?

A The TTSI product is a highly customized system, designed to meet very specific requirements of individual clients. We therefore plan in response to our customer needs, supplying a 'turnkey project' – so called because the system is designed, delivered and installed to a customer, and finally put into operational use. We appoint a project manager responsible for all aspects of each new project from cradle to grave.

Our product planning cycle begins when we receive an invitation to tender for the supply of a new system. The invitation will generally come as a result of the activity of our Marketing Department who will arrange for prospective customers to invite us to bid as a result of our previous track record and experience. Our tender takes the form of a proposal drawn up in response to the customer's requirement specification. The proposal will include: a full technical specification; a system design proposal; details of specific items of equipment; definition and description of software and a price quotation. If the tender is successful, we begin detailed planning of the system. The lead times for the design and development of a system are usually long enough to allow us to plan, design and manufacture customized modules in time for their installation and entry into service as part of the overall system.

We have to ensure that our standard modules are up to date with latest applicable technology, responsive to customer needs and with a competitive edge. We operate a process of reliability growth, constantly refining and improving our existing modules, whilst at the same time planning and developing new ones.

Q How do you decide what processes to use to make your product?

A A typical TTSI Fare Collection System will contain a number of proprietary modules such as Coin Systems, Bank Note Validators, Computers, and so on, together with modules designed in-house by TTSI. We plan which elements of the system we can design or manufacture ourselves, and which we need to buy-in according to our key strengths and skills in the area of automatic ticketing systems. Most of our system and software design is done in-house using system and software engineers, although we do use some specialist skills from outside companies. Much of the hardware manufactured for the system is subcontracted, this key activity being the responsibility of the TTSI Procurement Director. We manufacture hardware products ourselves within the Operations Department, but only for prototype development and when small numbers, or very specialized products are required. If we have an overload on our in-house manufacturing unit, we will either subcontract work or take on additional subcontract staff to supplement our core workforce. When choosing our subcontractors, we ensure that they have the necessary skills and ability to manufacture products in accordance with our procurement specifications and quality standards.

Frequently, when we are dealing in overseas territories, we have to include an element of 'in-country' work. This required 'local content' of a country may be met, for example, by having the high technology items made in the UK and shipped to the country for final assembly, testing and installation by local workers.

Q How do you ensure that quality standards are maintained?

A We have a Quality Assurance department headed by a Senior Manager with specific responsibility for ensuring that quality standards are met and maintained. We are an accredited supplier to the British Standard BS5750 and the International Standard ISO900. Award and maintenance of these accreditations is subject to the company's quality system and standards employed satisfying the requirements of the accrediting bodies, with regular audits being performed by them.

When choosing subcontractors, we ensure that they have the necessary capability in management, skills and facilities to manufacture products in accordance with the requirements of our procurement specifications. We therefore either select subcontractors who have internationally recognized quality accreditation, as we ourselves hold, or we thoroughly audit them to ensure they meet our quality criteria as specified in a Quality Plan. We undertake inspection and testing of products at defined stages, where appropriate on our subcontractors' premises. We have documented standards and procedures, which, together with the drawings and specifications, form the complete definition of the product to be manufactured. Any deviations from original specifications that prove necessary are controlled through a formal change/deviation control procedure.

Client approval for the quality of the system is a continuous process throughout the design and manufacture stages. There are generally two formal stages of acceptance:

(1) factory acceptance testing which the customer witnesses at the TTSI factory;

(2) site acceptance testing, following installation and commissioning of the complete system, to the satisfaction of the customer.

Q **How do you forecast demand for your product?**

A We do not forecast demand in the same way that a high volume manufacturing company does. Our Marketing Department maintains details of developments around the world in the fare collection sector of the mass transit industry, in the form of a computer database. Potential new customers who are planning railway systems are approached to ensure that we are invited to tender for the fare collection system. Forecasting then becomes an assessment of how many of these potential contracts we can secure.

Our primary concern when forecasting is to ensure that we have a competitive edge with the quality and price of our products and systems. For example, we are investigating the application of the contactless smart card to our ticketing equipment. A major reduction in the cost of these cards will be needed before their worldwide use in ticketing is possible, as in many of the developing countries, the cost of the smart card is more than the rail fare itself.

While working on current projects, we constantly look for ways to improve, refine and develop our product to ensure our technical superiority. In this way, our position as a market leader is maintained.

4 Product planning

Contents

Objectives

After reading this chapter you should be able to:

- discuss the purpose of product planning
- say why organizations make a range of products
- describe the stages in developing a new product
- use scoring models to compare products
- calculate break-even points
- calculate net present values and internal rates of return
- describe the stages in a typical product life-cycle
- discuss the different operations, costs and profits during a product life-cycle
- outline different entry and exit strategies

Purpose of product planning

What is product planning?

All organizations make products. These products may be goods – like a car, computer, house or clothes – or they may be services – like transport, a holiday, health care or insurance. In Chapter 2 we saw that most products are really a combination of goods and services. So a washing machine manufacturer also gives an after-sales service, and a health service also supplies medicines and other materials.

An organization can only be successful if it makes the products that customers want. So an organization must find the kind of products that customers really demand, and then it must make the products to satisfy this demand. This is the basis of **product planning**. Essentially, product planning makes sure that an organization continues to supply the kinds of products that customers want.

> **Product planning** is concerned with all decisions about the introduction of new products, changes to existing products and withdrawal of old products.

One of the main difficulties with product planning is that the customer demands change over time. In winter we want warm clothing, but in summer we want clothes that keep us cool; 10 years ago we wanted pine cupboards in the kitchen because they were fashionable, but this year we want oak ones; we used to want FAX machines which connect to telephones and computers in our homes, but now we want portable FAX machines; this year we want videophones, but next year we will want some other electronic gadgets that are not yet available. For a variety of reasons, customer demands change over time.

Organizations must respond to these changes by continually offering new products. British Telecom develop new digital exchange equipment, Rover introduce new models of car, and the BBC replace a show whose ratings have fallen.

> The aim of **product planning** is to make sure that an organization continues to supply the products that customers demand.

Range of products offered

Ideally, organizations would like to supply a single product, as this makes their operations very simple. But customers all have slightly different needs. We all buy clothes, for example, but we want different sizes, styles and colours. The overall demand for any product is made up of a large number of individual demands, each of which is slightly different. Organizations allow for these differences by supplying variations of a basic product. Universities offer different courses, construction companies build different types of houses, bakers make different kinds of cake, car makers produce different models, management consultants offer different services, and so on. The result is that most organizations supply a *range* of similar or related products.

But an organization will usually concentrate on one kind of product. The reason for this is obvious, as a company that has experience as a ship builders will have the knowledge, skills and experience to build a new type of ship, but it does not have the expertise to start making perfume. So car makers will bring out a new model of car; insurance companies will introduce new types of policy, ice cream parlours will sell new flavours; universities will offer a new academic course. Any new product must be similar to those they already made, but different enough to create new demand. Then it will both:

- satisfy customer demand;

- fit in with existing products.

When an organization makes a range of variations on a basic product, we can ask how wide this range should be. The decision must balance two factors:

- if the range is narrow, the organization can use standard operations, but some customers will be lost to competitors who offer more products or different ones;

- if the range is wide, the organization can satisfy varied customer demands, but it loses the efficiency that comes from standardization.

So there is always a compromise between producers who would like to make a narrow range of products, and customers who would like a wide range.

From the producer's viewpoint a narrow range of products has the advantages of:

- allowing specialized equipment that can give high productivity;

- allowing long production runs that reduce equipment set-up times;

- making production routine and well-practised;

- increasing employee experience and expertise with the product;

- encouraging long-term improvements to the product;

- making purchasing, inspections and handling routine;

- reducing staff training time;

- lowering stocks of parts and materials.

In spite of these benefits, varying customer demands force almost all organizations to make a range of similar products. In the next section we shall see how these factors are considered in the development of new products.

ce Case example – Microprocessors

Manufacturers of microprocessors work in a highly competitive, rapidly changing market. It is very expensive to develop a new microprocessor, but when the design and tests have been done manufacturing is relatively easy. This means that a company's success depends to a large extent on its ability to develop a continuing series of new products. Companies can only be successful if they are innovative and at the forefront of technology.

In 1993 Intel Corporation was the world's largest manufacturer of microprocessors. It had developed the highly successful 286, 386 and then 486 processors. These had been industry standards for 10 years. Intel was making record profits, and in April 1993 launched its latest Pentium 60/66 MHz processor.

But other companies were trying to break into this profitable market, particularly PowerPC. This is a consortium backed by Motorola, IBM and Apple. In March 1994 PowerPC launched its new 60/66 MHz processor to compete directly with Pentium. Intel responded by rushing through the final stages of its faster Pentium 90 MHz for April 1994 and its Pentium 100 MHz by July 1994. Because they needed to introduce their new chip very quickly, they had supply problems and the first chips were slow to sell. There were more troubles when a bug was found in the early chips which raised questions of their reliability. PowerPC responded to Intel's new products by announcing their own 100 MHz and 160 MHz processors for December 1994. Again Intel responded by announcing its Pentium 150 MHz for Spring 1995.

Competition for microprocessors was giving a stream of new products, with increasing power and significant price reductions. Other manufacturers were also trying to enter the market, including Advanced Micro Devices, Nex-Gen Microproducts and Cyrix Inc.

One interesting feature of this market is the role of IBM. They dominate the computer market, and in 1993 were Intel's biggest customer. But they backed the rival PowerPC system, and in April 1994 announced a deal to use microprocessors from Cyrix which were essentially clones of the Pentium.

Questions

- What effects do you think the speed of developing new products will have on operations?

- Can you think of other examples where there is such a rapidly changing market?

Review questions

4.1   What is a product?

4.2   What is the purpose of product planning?

4.3   Why do most organizations supply a range of products?

Developing new products

Stages in product development

We have now seen how organizations continually change their product range – introducing new products and updating or withdrawing old ones. Introducing a new product is expensive and needs careful planning. Research and development (R&D) for a new computer or car needs huge amounts of money. The development of the Airbus Industrie A3XX, for example, cost £6 billion up to 1995. Ford of America spent $6 billion developing their Mondeo in 1993. In the same year Saab cut costs and developed a model to replace their 900 series for £750 million.

The planning for a new product goes through a number of stages. These start with the generation of ideas, and end when the product is actually sold to customers. The details of the planning depend on the organization and the product, but a common approach has six stages.

(1)   generation of ideas;

(2)   initial screening of ideas;

(3)   initial design, development and testing;

(4)   market and economic analysis;

(5)   final product development;

(6)   launch of product.

Generation of ideas

Most organizations continuously search for new ideas they can exploit. Some of these ideas come from within the organization – a research department may develop a new product, or the operations people may suggest a change to an existing product. Many ideas come from outside the organization – a competitor's product might be adapted to fit into a company's range, customers may demand a product that is not currently available, or new regulations make a new product essential. Initial ideas can come from many sources, including:

●   results from research and development that lead to a new product;

●   sales and marketing reporting changes in customer demand;

- other internal sources, perhaps operations suggesting a change that makes an existing product easier to make;

- competitor's products that can be adapted;

- customers contacting the organization to suggest new products;

- changing government regulations that create demand for a new product, such as sprays which contain no CFCs;

- other external sources.

People used to say, 'Build a better mousetrap and the world will beat a path to your door.' Unfortunately, the inventors of thousands of better mousetraps say that this is misleading. New ideas are easy to find; the difficulty is looking at these ideas, selecting the best and turning them into viable products for which there is a demand.

Initial screening of ideas

All ideas must go through an initial screening to reject those that have obvious flaws. This screening can quickly reject products that:

- are impossible to produce, or are technically too difficult;

- have been tried before without success;

- duplicate an existing product;

- use expertise or skills that the organization does not have;

- do not fit into current operations.

This screening is typically done by a team of people from marketing, finance and operations. It might remove 80% of the original ideas, leaving 20% that have no obvious flaws and can move to the next stages of development (see Figure 4.1).

Initial design, development and testing

This stage gives a technical evaluation of ideas. It sees if the product could be made by the organization and typically asks two types of questions.

(1) *General questions about the concept.* Could the product be made? Is the idea based on sound principles? Is it entirely new, or a variation on old ideas. If it is an old idea, why has the organization not made it before? Are there problems with patents or competitors? Are developments likely to overtake the product?

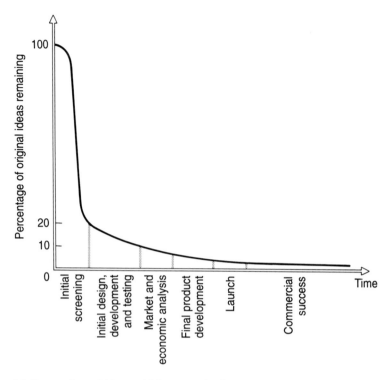

Figure 4.1 Proportion of ideas which are typically lost at each stage of development.

(2)   *More specific questions about the product.* Is the proposed design technically feasible? Can it be made with available technology? Would it fit into current operations? Does the organization have the necessary skills and experience? To answer some of these questions a prototype might be developed and tested.

This stage removes about half the remaining ideas.

Market and economic analysis

If the product passes the technical evaluation it moves on to a commercial evaluation which sees if it will make a profit. This studies the market and financial aspects to see how the product will sell, what competition there is, how much profit it will make, what investment is needed, what returns can be expected, and so on. Market surveys to gauge customer reaction can be done at this stage.

Unfortunately, the commercial evaluation rejects many ideas that are technically good. It is sometimes difficult to accept that an idea which is technically sound may not have enough sales to make a profit. The technical evaluation and commercial analysis together form the **feasibility study**.

Final product development

If the product passes the feasibility study, it moves to final design and testing. This is where the product changes from a prototype or concept model, to the form that will be sold to customers. Lessons from the technical and commercial evaluation are used to finalize the design.

The final design of a product is often the most important stage. This design must be functional (so that it can work efficiently), attractive (so that customers like it) and easy to make (so that production costs are low). It can be difficult to satisfy all three criteria and a team of people from different functions must work towards the best solution. At this stage the product design is finalized, together with the process used to make it. Then production starts and the new product is launched.

Launch of product

At the launch, an organization offers its new product to customers. This is the first chance to see if the planning has worked and the product will actually be a success. Many products are not successful and are quickly withdrawn. Some have been spectacular failures, like the Ford Edsel which lost $350 million in the late 1950s. In the 1970s Joseph Schlitz Brewing Co. in America started 'accelerated batch fermentation' for their beer. Customers did not like this, sales plummeted and the company never recovered from its losses. IBM's PC junior lost $100 million by 1985. In the 1980s Coca-Cola changed its recipe, but customers forced a return of the original 'classic' range.

Very few of the initial ideas, perhaps 1% or 2%, complete all stages of this development process to the point where they are launched on the market. Even fewer become successful products.

The success of a product often depends on the competition. Customers weigh a number of factors when making comparisons, but the most common are:

- **Price** If similar products are competing, the one with the lowest price will usually be most successful. This is not always true and there are many examples ranging from perfumes to luxury cars where it seems better to charge higher prices.

- **Availability** The most obvious aspect of availability is fast delivery. A washing machine that you can take home from a shop will usually be more successful than an identical one that can be delivered in 10 weeks. More people will use a bus if there is a regular service every few minutes than if there is an irregular service with only two or three arrivals a day.

- **Quality** There are two important aspects to quality. The first is designed quality, which shows how good a product is meant to be. A silk shirt, for example, has a higher designed quality than a polyester one, and a luxury hotel has a higher designed quality than a boarding house. The second aspect of quality describes actual achievement. An airline might design its timetables so that 98% of flights arrive on time – if only 30% of flights actually arrive on time the designed quality is high, but achieved quality is low.

- **Flexibility** The ability of an organization to meet specific customer requirements or react to changing circumstances is called flexibility. An organization with more flexibility can meet customer demands more precisely and, therefore, offers better products.

Product design

We said above that the design of a product is very important for its success. Some houses sell badly simply because they are poorly designed; some VCRs do not sell because they are too difficult to work; some buses are not used because they are uncomfortable. We should give some guidelines on how to design good products, but this is very difficult. There is such a wide range of products, and so many different factors, that it is almost impossible to describe what makes a good design. The only thing we can do is make some very general points.

We have already said that there are three main requirements for product design. It must be:

- **Functional** which means the product must be able to do the job it is designed for. You can probably think of many gadgets that look good, but do not work properly – such as new types of cork screw or kitchen aids. These are not functional. The best way to make sure a design is functional is to ask potential customers what they want the product to do, and then form a team of designers to meet the needs. The designs must be tested and adjusted, perhaps using prototypes, before they are finalized.

- **Attractive** which means the product must have an appearance that customers like. This is obviously more important for products like clothes than industrial machines, but designers must usually take some notice of aesthetic values.

- **Easy to make** the cost of a product depends on many factors, but the design is probably the most important. As you can imagine, a product that is made automatically on an assembly line will cost less than one that needs a lot of skilled manual work. Generally, higher costs come from:
  - needing an expensive process to make the product;
  - using non-standard parts and components;
  - using too many, or expensive materials;
  - demanding too high quality;
  - interfering with the production of other items.

You can see from these comments that the design of a product needs teamwork. There are artistic, technical, operational, financial and other aspects to be considered, with important inputs from marketing and customers themselves.

From an operations point of view, an organization should try to simplify and standardize its product designs. **Simplifying** means that unnecessary parts are removed so the product is easier to make. This might mean using moulded plastic parts that snap together rather than metal parts that are bolted together. **Standardizing** uses common components in a range of different products. This allows longer production runs of components and reduces unit costs. Standardization does not necessarily reduce the choice available to customers, as the standard parts can still be used in a wide range of products. Car manufacturers, for example, use standard components, but juggle these to give a wide range of models. So an ideal design for operations would give a product that:

- is made by the cheapest available process;

- has few steps in the process;

- is easy to make with a minimum amount of work;

- contains few varieties or different products;

- uses standardized, interchangeable components and parts;

- uses high quality materials so that scrap and reworking are minimized.

Review questions

4.4   What are typical stages in the introduction of new product?

4.5   What criteria are used to judge a new product?

4.6   The most difficult part of launching a new product is getting new ideas from the research team. Do you agree with this?

Comparing products

In the last section we saw how organizations do a feasibility study on new products. This includes both a technical and commercial evaluation. We can not really make general comments about technical performance, but we can describe some widely used commercial analyses.

Suppose an organization is looking for a new product and has several alternatives that finish initial screening at the same time. Sometimes the organization will have enough resources to develop and market all of these alternatives, but usually resources are limited and one product must be chosen above the others. So we need some way of comparing products and choosing the best. There are several ways of doing this, including:

- scoring models
- break-even point
- net present value
- internal rate of return.

Scoring models

To compare different products we usually have to consider a range of factors, such as quality, cost, size, appearance, performance, and so on. Some of these factors are numerical, in which case comparisons can be fairly straightforward. Other factors are subjective, in which case comparisons are more difficult. Burger King, for example, can not measure the difference in taste between their hamburgers and McDonald's – and it is impossible to put numerical values to the design of competitors' products, the amount of innovation they contain, or its colour, or our experience with similar products.

In general, then, the easiest way of making comparisons is to list the important factors and decide whether or not a product gives satisfactory performance in each. The definitions of satisfactory, and whether or not a product achieves this, must be found by discussion and agreement.

we Worked example

A company lists 10 factors it considers important in a new product. It is considering proposals for four new products, but only has enough resources to develop one of these. After intense discussions, managers have agreed about the performance of each product on the 10 factors. In Table 4.1 a tick shows that a

Table 4.1 The 10 important factors in a new product.

Factor	Product			
	A	B	C	D
Time to develop	✓	✓	✓	✓
Expected useful life	✓		✓	✓
Cost of developing	✓			✓
Fit with other products	✓		✓	✓
Equipment needed	✓			✓
Initial demand	✓	✓	✓	
Stability of demand	✓	✓	✓	
Marketing requirement	✓	✓	✓	
Competition	✓	✓	✓	
Expected profit	✓	✓	✓	✓

product has reached a satisfactory standard. Which product do you think the company should develop? If this product is found to be technically infeasible, which alternative should the company develop?

Solution

The only product that satisfies all 10 factors is A, so this one should be developed.

If product A is infeasible the company has several alternatives. It can say that no product satisfies all the factors, so none of them will be developed. In practice, it is unusual to find an ideal product that satisfies all criteria, so a compromise is needed and the best available one is chosen. In this case the best is clearly not B, as C satisfies all the conditions that B does, as well as some others. So the choice is between C, which performs well in marketing, and D, which performs well in development. The company must arrange further talks before making a final decision.

One problem with simple check lists is that they treat each factor as equally important. **Scoring models** avoid this by giving a different weight to each factor. Expected sales might be twice as important as the equipment needed, so its score is given twice as much weight.

The first step in building a scoring model is, again, to list the important factors. But this time we show their relative importance by giving a maximum possible score to each. We might give a maximum score of 10 to technical factors; marketing is half as important so we give it a maximum score of 5; return on investment is twice as important and we give it a maximum score of 20; and so on. When maximum scores have been given, each product is examined to see how it actually performs. Then each product is given an actual score for each factor, up to the maximum. The scores for each product are added and the product with the highest score is the best.

This procedure can be summarized as follows:

(1)   decide the most important factors in a decision;

(2)   assign a maximum possible score to each factor;

(3)   consider each product in turn and give a score for each factor up to the maximum;

(4)   add the total scores for each product;

(5)   find the best product as the one with the highest total score;

(6)   discuss the result, look at other factors, and make a final decision.

Scoring models allow a numerical view of qualitative data – harsher critics suggest it is a way of building a defence for decisions that may turn out to be wrong.

we Worked example

A television company compares four alternative products using five factors, with the results in Table 4.2. What is the relative importance of the factors? Which product would you recommend? Which product has the best financial performance?

Table 4.2

Factor	Maximum	A	B	C	D
Technical	20	11	15	18	15
Finance	30	28	16	26	12
Market	15	9	13	12	8
Production	25	18	19	20	19
Competition	10	9	7	6	9

Solution

The most important criterion is finance, which is given the highest maximum score. Production is slightly less important (25/30 times as important), then technical (20/30 times as important), market and competition.

Adding the scores for each product gives totals of:

$$A = 75 \qquad B = 70 \qquad C = 82 \qquad D = 63$$

On this evidence, product C is clearly the best.

Product A has the best financial performance, with a score of 28 out of 30. It is interesting that the product with the best performance in the most important factor is not the best overall.

we Worked example

A company is planning a new product and wants to choose the best of three alternatives. A project team has found the important factors, together with maximum scores, shown in the spreadsheet in Figure 4.2. After considerable

FACTOR		SCORES Maximum	A	B	C
Product:					
	Time to develop product	7	7	3	5
	Research and development needed	8	7	4	6
	Experience with similar products	12	11	4	7
	Similarity to existing products	5	4	1	3
	Expected life	12	9	6	8
	Ease of manufacture	18	16	9	14
	Skills needed at various stages	8	8	3	5
	New production equipment needed	4	4	2	3
	Requirements of raw materials	6	4	4	2
sub-totals		80	70	36	53
Finance:					
	Research and development cost	12	11	9	10
	Capital outlay	17	13	8	10
	Return on investment	25	12	14	20
	Net present value	18	10	14	18
	Reduced profit from existing products	11	3	8	6
sub-totals		83	49	53	64
Market:					
	Initial demand	25	21	9	14
	Marketing effort needed	8	6	3	8
	Advertising needed	4	2	1	4
	Current competition	15	5	12	10
	Interactions with existing products	12	3	7	8
	New competition likely	8	5	5	5
	Stability of demand	5	3	2	4
	Market trends	10	4	9	7
sub-totals		87	49	48	60
Totals		250	168	137	177
Rank			2	3	1

Figure 4.2 Spreadsheet used for scoring model.

discussion the team also agreed scores for each product. Which product would you recommend?

Solution

Spreadsheets are very useful for this type of calculation. In this example the total scores show product C is best, but it is not far ahead of A. Product B is some way behind and should probably not be considered. A does well in the product section, while C does better in the finance and market areas. Managers should look at these factors in detail, together with other relevant information, before making a final decision.

Break-even point

Before introducing a new product, an organization must know if demand will be high enough to make a profit. The income generated must cover the cost of producing each unit, but it must also recover the money which was spent on development before the product was launched. This includes the costs of research, tooling, prototypes, market surveys, trial runs, and so on.

We can define the profit from selling a product as:

Profit = income − total costs

In this equation the total costs come from a number of sources and can be classified as:

● **fixed costs**, which are constant regardless of the number of units made, and

● **variable costs**, which depend on the number of units made.

Research and development costs, for example, are fixed regardless of the number of units made. Other fixed costs come from marketing, administration, lighting, heating, rent, debt repayments and a range of overheads. On the other hand, the cost of raw materials, direct labour, maintenance and some other costs are directly affected by output – a doubling of output will double these costs. You have probably met this when running a car. There is a fixed cost of repaying the purchase loan, road tax, insurance, and so on, and a variable cost for each mile travelled for petrol, oil, tyres, depreciation.

Then:

$$\begin{aligned} \text{total costs} &= \text{fixed cost} + \text{variable cost} \\ &= \text{fixed cost} + \text{number of units made} \times \text{cost per unit} \\ &= C_F + nC_U \end{aligned}$$

where:

n = number of units sold
C_F = fixed cost
C_U = variable cost per unit

The income is much simpler and comes from:

$$\begin{aligned} \text{Income} &= \text{number of units sold} \times \text{price charged per unit} \\ &= nP \end{aligned}$$

where:

P = price charged per unit

We now have an income and total costs that both rise linearly with the number of units made, as shown in Figure 4.3. The break-even point occurs when the income equals the total costs, and is the point where these lines cross each other.

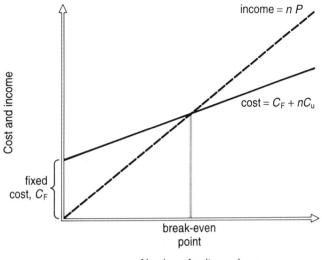

Figure 4.3 Defining the break-even point.

> The **break-even point** is the number of units that must be sold
> before an organization covers all costs and begins to make a profit.

Suppose a new product has £150,000 spent on research and development, tooling and other preparation for production. Other overheads cost £50,000, giving a total fixed cost of £200,000.

During normal production each unit has a variable cost of £300 and is sold for £400. The company will only start to make a profit on this product when the original £200,000 has been recovered. The point when this occurs is the break-even point. Each unit sold contributes £400 − 300 = £100 to the company, so 200,000/100 = 2000 units must be sold to cover the fixed cost. Then:

- the break-even point is 2000 units;

- if less than 2000 units are sold the company will make a loss on the product;

- if more any than 2000 units are sold the company will make a profit on the product.

In general, the break-even point comes when:

income = total costs
$nP \quad = C_F + nC_U$

$$\text{The break-even point} = n = \frac{C_F}{P - C_U}$$

This analysis also shows one reason why organizations can get economies of scale. With higher production the fixed costs are spread over more units, so the average unit cost falls. In general, the average cost per unit is:

$$\text{total costs/number of units} = (nC_U + C_F)/n = C_U + C_F/n$$

In practice, allocating the costs is not always easy and it is particularly difficult to find fixed costs. Suppose a factory makes a number of products and has to assign a reasonable proportion of overheads to each one. If the product mix is constantly changing, the allocation of overheads to each product may also change. In other words, the costs and profits made by each product can change, even though there has been no change in the product itself or the process used to make it.

Break-even analyses are useful for the obvious purpose of seeing how many units must be sold to make a profit, but they also help with choices between alternative products, decisions about buying or leasing equipment, making sure there is enough capacity when buying new equipment, decisions about buying an item or making it within the company, choices of competitive tenders for services, and so on.

we Worked example

Ace Adventure Holiday Company sells an average of 100 holidays a month. The income generated has to cover fixed costs of £63,000 a month. Each holiday sold has travel, accommodation and other variable costs of £500.

(a) Does the company make a profit if the price for its holidays is £1200?

(b) If the price of a holiday is reduced to £1000 and sales increase to 150 a month does the company make a profit?

Solution

(a) We are told that:

$$
\begin{aligned}
\text{fixed cost, } C_F &= 63{,}000 \\
\text{cost per unit, } C_U &= 500 \\
\text{selling price per unit, } P &= 1200 \\
\text{number of units sold} &= 100
\end{aligned}
$$

Then the break-even point is calculated from:

$$n = C_F/(P - C_U) = 63,000/(1200 - 500) = 90$$

The company is actually selling 100 a month. This is more than the break-even point, so it is making a profit. We can calculate the profit from:

income $= nP = 100 \times 1200 = £120,000$ a month

total costs $= C_F + nC_U = 63,000 + 100 \times 500$

$= £113,000$ a month

profit $=$ income $-$ total costs $= 120,000 - 113,000$

$= £7000$ a month

(b) The new break-even point is:

$$n = C_F/(P - C_U) = 63,000/(1000 - 500) = 126$$

Actual sales are 150 so the product is making a profit. This can be calculated from:

income $= nP = 150 \times 1000 = £150,000$ a month

total costs $= C_F + nC_U = 63,000 + 150 \times 500$

$= £138,000$ a month

profit $=$ income $-$ total costs $= 150,000 - 138,000$

$= £12,000$ a month

This shows that an organization can still make a profit with a low selling price, provided sales are high enough.

we Worked example

A company is planning a new product. It must select one product from three available and has estimated the following data:

	Product		
	A	B	C
Expected demand each year	600	900	1200
Unit cost of production	£680	£900	£1200
Unit selling price	£760	£1000	£1290
Fixed cost incurred before production	£200,000	£350,000	£500,000
Expected product life	3 years	5 years	8 years

Which product would you recommend?

Solution

There are several ways of looking at this problem. The break-even points are calculated from:

$$n = C_F/(P - C_U)$$

so, for each product we have:

A: $n = 200{,}000/(760 - 680)$ $= 2500$
B: $n = 350{,}000/(1000 - 900)$ $= 3500$
C: $n = 500{,}000/(1290 - 1200) = 5556$

If the company wants the lowest break-even point it would choose product A. But the company might be more interested in the time taken to break even. This is given by:

time to break even = break-even point/demand

For each product this gives:

A: $2500/600$ $= 4.2$ years
B: $3500/900$ $= 3.9$ years
C: $5556/1200 = 4.6$ years

In this case product B is the first to start making a profit. Another objective might be to maximize long-term profit. Over the expected product lives:

total profit = income − total cost

with:

income   = lifetime × annual demand × unit selling price
total cost = lifetime × annual demand × unit cost + fixed cost

For each product the lifetime profit is:

A: $(3 \times 600 \times 760) - (3 \times 600 \times 680) - 200{,}000$ $= -56{,}000$
B: $(5 \times 900 \times 1000) - (5 \times 900 \times 900) - 350{,}000$ $= 100{,}000$
C: $(8 \times 1200 \times 1290) - (8 \times 1200 \times 1200) - 500{,}000 = 364{,}000$

Product A makes a net loss over its expected life while product C gives the best total profit.

Overall, the best decision depends on the objectives of the company, but product B seems useful.

ce Case example – Jaguar Cars

This example illustrates the cost and time needed to develop a new car. By looking at the fixed development costs, you can get an idea of the break-even point.

Ford bought Jaguar Cars in 1989 for $2.6 billion. At the time Jaguar produced the highly successful XJ6, with smaller sales of the XJS and specialized sports/racing cars. The latest model of the XJ6 was three years old. It takes up to five years to develop a new model, so work was soon started on a replacement. This was the XJR which was launched in 1994.

By this time Ford had invested another $1.4 billion in Jaguar. Part of this was spent replacing the old production process by a more automated version. In particular, they replaced the 40-year old two-track assembly line at Brown's Lane, Coventry by a single-track assembly line which had 25% more capacity. The new line needed fewer skilled workers than the old process – and it needed people with different skills. One result of the change was that the company began to make a profit after selling 35,000 cars a year, rather than the 50,000 needed previously.

Net present value

Break-even analyses assume that the value of money does not change over time. In other words, £100 now has exactly the same value as £100 in 10 years time. In practice this is not true. You can invest money to earn interest and its value increases over time. On the other hand, if you keep money under a mattress it loses value as inflation raises prices. In this section we will look at the changing value of money over time and show how this can be used to compare products.

Suppose you put an amount of money A_P into a bank account and leave it untouched for a year earning interest at a rate I. At the end of the year you will get interest and the amount will have grown to $A_P(1 + I)$. Here the interest rate, I, is a decimal fraction, or proportion, rather than a percentage, so an interest rate of 10% gives $I = 0.1$.

If you leave the money untouched for a second year, it will earn interest not only on the initial amount, but also on the interest earned in the first year. The amount will then grow to:

$$[A_P(1 + I)] \times (1 + I) \quad \text{or} \quad A_P(1 + I)^2$$

The amount of money will grow in this compound way, so that N years in the future the account will contain an amount, A_F, where:

$$A_F = A_P(1 + I)^N$$

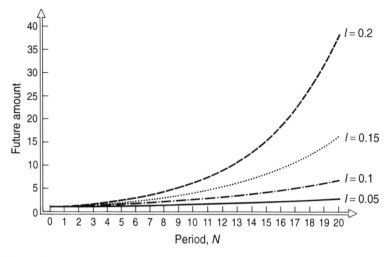

Figure 4.4 Amount N periods in the future which discounts to 1 at present.

Provided consistent units are used, the time period need not be years but can be any convenient period. So turning this equation around, we can say that an amount, A_F, N periods in the future has a present value, A_P, of:

The present value of an amount is: $A_P = \dfrac{A_F}{(1+I)^N}$

Calculating the present value of a specified future amount is called **discounting to present value**. Figure 4.4 shows the amounts N periods in the future that are discounted to £1 at present using different discounting rates. Now you can see how amounts of money available at different times in the future can be compared directly by discounting them all to their present value.

we Worked example

A company is comparing two possible new products, both of which need an initial investment of £100,000. Although the revenues are phased over many years, they can be summarized as:

● Product 1 gives a revenue of £300,000 in five years time

● Product 2 gives a revenue of £500,000 in 10 years time.

Which product should the company introduce if it uses a discounting rate of 20% a year for future revenues?

Solution

To compare amounts of money earned at different times we calculate the present value of each using $A_P = A_F/(1 + I)^N$. Here the discounting rate is 20%, meaning $I = 0.2$.

- *Product 1*: revenue is £300,000 in five years time. This has a present value of:

  $$\text{present value} = 300,000/(1 + 0.2)^5 = 300,000/2.488 = £120,563$$

- *Product 2*: revenue is £500,000 in 10 years time. This has a present value of:

  $$\text{present value} = 500,000/(1 + 0.2)^{10} = 500,000/6.192 = £80,753$$

Product 1 clearly gives a higher present value and should be chosen.

If we subtract the initial investment of £100,000 from these revenues, product 1 makes a net profit of £20,563 at present values, while product 2 makes a net loss of £19,247. So product 2 should not be introduced even if something stops the company from making product 1.

We have compared incomes generated at different times by discounting them to present values. We can do the same discounting for costs. Then we can subtract the present value of all costs from the present value of all incomes to give a **net present value**.

Net present value = sum of discounted incomes − sum of discounted costs

Now we can compare products by calculating their net present values – with the best product having the highest net present value. A negative net present value means the product will make a loss and should not be made.

we Worked example

Three alternative products have the initial development costs and projected net incomes shown below (values are in thousands of pounds).

Product	Initial cost	Income generated in each year				
		1	*2*	*3*	*4*	*5*
A	2000	1000	800	600	400	200
B	1400	100	200	500	600	700
C	800	100	200	300	200	0

The company uses a discounting rate of 10% a year. If it only has enough resources to make one product which would you recommend?

Solution

To compare the products we need to discount all amounts to present values.

Income for product A:
    1000 in year 1 has a present value of $1000/1.1 = 909.09$
    800 in year 2 has a present value of $800/1.1^2 = 661.16$
    600 in year 3 has a present value of $600/1.1^3 = 450.79$

and so on.

Figure 4.5 shows the details of these calculations in a spreadsheet. Subtracting the present value of costs (in this case the single initial project cost) from the present value of income gives the net present value.

Product A has the highest net present value and should, all other things being equal, be developed. Product C has a negative net present value and should be avoided. One other point is that the incomes from A are declining – suggesting the product has a limited lifespan of around five years – while incomes from product B are rising – suggesting a longer potential life. Factors like this should be taken into account before making any final decisions.

Year	Discounting Factor	Product A Income	Present value	Product B Income	Present value	Product C Income	Present value
1	1.10	1000	909.09	100	90.91	100	90.91
2	1.21	800	661.16	200	165.29	200	165.29
3	1.33	600	450.79	500	375.66	300	225.39
4	1.46	400	273.21	600	409.81	200	136.60
5	1.61	200	124.18	700	434.64	0	0.00
Totals	Incomes	3000	2418.43	2100	1476.31	800	618.20
	Costs		2000		1400		800.00
Net Present Value			418.43		76.31		-181.80

Figure 4.5 Calculation of net present values.

CE   Case example – PowerGen/GEC Alsthom

GEC Alsthom is an Anglo-French supplier of equipment for power stations. In 1993 it won an order from PowerGen for a 1440 megawatt power station at Connah's Quay in north Wales. This project was due for completion in 1995. Normally in large construction projects the customer pays 10%–20% of the cost up-front, with progress payments during construction, and a final payment on completion.

But in this case PowerGen paid all the cost of £450 million up-front in exchange for a discount of about 7% from GEC Alsthom. This arrangement gave PowerGen the advantages of a price discount, together with some tax benefits in a year it made pre-tax profits of £470 million. GEC Alsthom had the benefits of cash in hand from the start of the project.

Question

- Do you know of other examples of discounts given for early payment, or penalties for late payment?

Internal rate of return

An obvious problem with finding present values is the choice of a discounting rate which takes into account interest rates, inflation, taxes, opportunity costs, exchange rates and everything else. An alternative approach is to find the discounting rate that leads to a specified net present value. The usual target for these calculations is a net present value of zero, and the discounting rate that gives this is called the **internal rate of return**.

> The **internal rate of return** is the discounting rate that gives a net present value of zero.

Now we have another way of comparing products. We can find the internal rate of return for each, and the product with the highest value is the best. There is no easy formula for calculating the internal rate of return, so you would be sensible to do the arithmetic using a spreadsheet or other software.

we   Worked example

What is the internal rate of return for a product that gives the following net cash flow?

Year	0	1	2	3	4	5	6	7	8
Net cash flow	−2000	−500	−200	800	1800	1600	1500	200	100

Solution

Such calculations are easily done with a computer. In this example the internal rate of return is 20%, as shown in Figure 4.6 (the value of −0.11 is simply due to rounding).

Year	Net Cash Flow	Discounting Factor	Discounted Value
0	-2000	1.00	-2000.00
1	-500	1.20	-416.67
2	-200	1.44	-138.89
3	800	1.73	462.96
4	1800	2.07	868.06
5	1600	2.49	643.00
6	1500	2.99	502.35
7	200	3.58	55.82
8	100	4.30	23.26
Totals	3300		-0.11

Figure 4.6 Calculating the internal rate of return using a spreadsheet.

Review questions

4.7 Why are scoring models used?

4.8 What costs might be included in 'fixed costs'?

4.9 The break-even point for a product is 1000 units. What happens if actual sales are 1200 units?

4.10 Which would you expect to have the highest value: (a) £5000 now (b) £5000 in five years time (c) £5000 in ten years time?

4.11 How could you compare the net benefits from two products, one of which generates income for three years and the other for eight years?

4.12 What is the 'net present value'?

4.13   Three alternative products, A, B and C, have internal rates of return of 10%, 15% and 20% respectively. Which of these gives the best financial returns?

Product life-cycle

Stages in the life-cycle

Earlier in the chapter we described how new products are introduced. But we know that customer demands change over time, so demand for any particular product will eventually fall, and the organization should stop making it. You can see this when cars are replaced by new models, computer software is upgraded, books go out of print, and so on. As a result, almost all products have a limited life-span. Experience shows that demand for most products follows a standard life-cycle. This has five stages, as shown in Figure 4.7.

(1)   **Introduction**   A new product appears on the market and demand is low while people learn about it, try it and see if they like it (for example, colour photocopiers, grass skis and telephone banking).

(2)   **Growth**   New customers buy the product and demand rises quickly (for example, FAX machines, mobile telephones, multi-media computer systems).

(3)   **Maturity**   Most potential customers know about the product and are buying it in steady numbers: demand stabilizes at a constant level (for example, cars, colour television sets, postal service).

(4)   **Decline**   Sales fall as customers start buying new, alternative products that become available (for example, beef, suntan lotion, marathon runs).

(5)   **Withdrawal**   Demand declines to the point where it is no longer worth making the product (for example, black and white television sets, telegrams, three wheel cars).

We can illustrate this life-cycle by looking at related products that are at different stages (see Figure 4.8). There are, for example, several different kinds of printer for personal computers. Some of these are fairly new, such as colour laser printers which are at the introductory stage; ordinary laser printers have become established and as their price falls they are moving through a growth stage; ink jet printers are moving into the maturity stage; dot-matrix printers are at the mature stage and starting to decline; printers based on typewriters are no longer selling and are well into the decline stage.

The exact shape of the life-cycle changes from product to product, but the most important variable is its length. Each edition of a newspaper has a life-cycle of a few hours; clothing fashions and fad computer games have

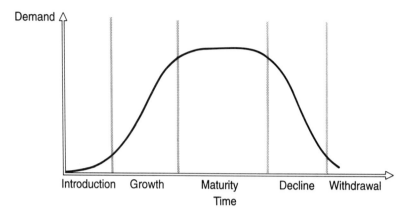

Figure 4.7 Life-cycle of a product.

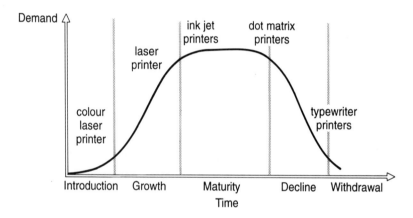

Figure 4.8 Life-cycle of a product.

life-cycles of months or even weeks; consumer durables like washing machines have life-cycles of five or 10 years; some basic commodities like soap and coffee remain in the mature stage for decades. Unfortunately, there are no real guidelines about the length of a life-cycle. Some products have an unexpectedly short life, while others stay at the mature stage for a very long time. Some products, like full cream milk and beer have been at the mature stage for a long time, and are now in a decline.

Organizations can take several years to develop a new product, so they must start planning well before the new product is actually needed. In practice, most organizations keep a range of products at different stages in their life-cycles. This gives long-term stability, with new products being phased-in while older ones are declining and being withdrawn. As a result, overall production is smoothed rather than having wide fluctuations, as shown in Figure 4.9.

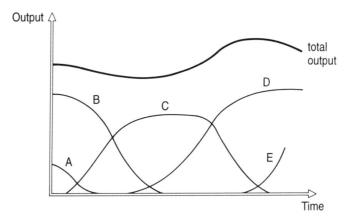

Figure 4.9 Introduction and withdrawal of products (A–E) to maintain stable total output.

ce Case example – Boeing and Airbus

This example shows how the growing market for long range, medium-sized aircraft has encouraged new products and changes to existing ones.

Air travel is forecast to grow at over 5% a year until 2015. To cater for this growth airlines must buy 12,000 new aeroplanes worth $980 billion. Of these 3100 worth $317 billion will be long range aircraft with between 200 and 350 seats. Aircraft manufacturers are competing strongly for this lucrative market.

In 1987 Airbus Industrie launched its four-engined A340 and twin engined A330. These were technologically advanced planes, and by the end of 1990 had won 250 orders. McDonnell Douglas soon introduced the three-engined MD11, and won 175 orders. Boeing was left behind, but eventually announced its B777 which was bigger than the competitors and cheaper to operate. The B777 is 25 cm narrower and 6 m shorter than the ageing B747 which it replaced on many routes.

By the Spring of 1994 Boeing employed 2600 people, working in three shifts, to make the B777. Prototypes were assembled from 4 million components in the world's largest building in Seattle. These were followed by the first production models for British Airways and United Airlines. New engines had been designed and built by Rolls Royce, Pratt & Whitney and General Electric. The cost of getting to this stage was estimated to be $4 billion, and this was still six months before the first B777 was due to fly.

This kind of competition, and the huge costs involved, are common in the aircraft industry. One exception was the very large, jumbo market where Boeing had a monopoly with the B747 for over 25 years. This allowed them an estimated gross profit of 30% on each of the 1000 planes they sold since 1970. But by the 1990s Boeing faced two problems in this market. Despite continual modifications to the B747, giving the B747-400 and B747-500, demand was falling as airlines were looking for newer designs. Some orders were transferred to the new B777 and equivalent aeroplanes, which were much cheaper to operate. A more serious problem came from Airbus Industrie who plan to enter the market from 1996. The A3XX, with a development cost of $8 billion, will have a full length double deck for carrying 600 passengers up to 8000 miles.

Questions

- Is the introduction of new aeroplanes different to other products?

- How do you think aircraft manufacturers will develop their products over the next few years?

Product life-cycles have three important consequences for operations management:

(1)   Organizations emphasize different types of operations at each stage of the life-cycle.

(2)   Costs, revenues and profits vary considerably at each stage.

(3)   Organizations with different expertise start (and later stop) making products at different points in the life-cycle.

Emphasis of operations during the life-cycle

We can illustrate the different emphases of operations during a life-cycle by following a typical manufactured product. Although the terms may vary, the principles are the same for services.

As we saw earlier in the chapter, a new product needs a lot of development work before it can be marketed. This means that operations centre around research and development. At the end of this, the product is launched and offered to customers. Initially, an organization will make small numbers of units, perhaps in a craft environment or with individual units made for specific orders. Operations emphasize the need to meet due dates and specifications, while refining the design and generally giving acceptable quality.

If customers like the new product, the organization will increase production. Then operations look for improvements in the production process. This often means a change from a low volume craft process to a mass-production process which might use some automation. The aim is to make more units while keeping high quality and reducing unit costs. This in turn puts more emphasis on supply and procurement systems which must find reliable sources of parts and materials. At the same time, marketing and distribution networks are built to stimulate and meet customer demand.

If the product's success continues, it moves into the growth stage when demand quickly increases. Operations are now concerned with forecasting future demand and making sure there is enough capacity to meet this. Products are no longer made for specific orders, but are put into a stock of finished goods, from which customer demands are met with short lead times. Production planning becomes important as resources are scheduled to make sure production matches demand.

At some stage the product matures and reaches its steady demand. Forecasting, capacity planning and production planning have now become routine as production has stabilized with little variation. The process may have changed several times, perhaps ending with a high volume process like an assembly line. This could be automated, perhaps giving standard products with fewer options. Increased competition may force the operations to emphasize cost reduction and improved productivity.

During the decline stage, the supplier might change the product design to try and extend its life. When this is no longer worthwhile, termination procedures are designed to stop production.

Costs and profits during the life-cycle

When a new product is introduced, a lot of money has already been spent on research, development, design, planning, testing, tooling, setting up facilities and so on. You saw earlier in the chapter that the development of a new aircraft can cost $8 billion and a new model of car $6 billion. These are part of the fixed costs that have to be recovered from later sales.

In the early stages of the life-cycle, when small numbers are made, the unit costs are high. This is mainly because the low volume production process is expensive. The organization may, however, also try to recover some of the fixed costs from early sales. At this stage the profit on each unit may also be high, as customers are willing to pay a premium to get a new or novel product. Total revenue is limited by small sales as shown in Figure 4.10.

Total revenue begins to rise when the product moves from introduction to the growth stage. At this point the fixed costs may be recovered and the product starts to make an overall profit. The profit per unit can be high, as customers still view the product as new and are willing to pay a reasonably high price, there is little competition, and new production equipment is working efficiently.

Revenue will rise until the product is somewhere in the mature stage. By this time competitors start to make similar products and demand slackens. This reduces both the price charged and the revenue. Continually changing the production process to give higher volumes can reduce unit costs, but over time the profit must decline.

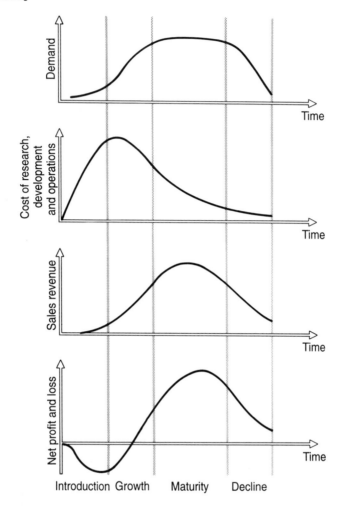

Figure 4.10 Revenue, costs, profit and loss during a typical life-cycle.

Beyond the mature stage profits will decline as excess capacity leads to competition for the smaller demand. Sometimes, improved production methods, experience and higher productivity will offset the decline, but profits will inevitably fall. At some stage demand and profit fall to an unacceptable level and the organization withdraws the product.

It is usually much cheaper to extend the life of an existing product than to introduce a new one. There are several ways of extending the life of a product, including:

● increasing advertising and market support;

● finding new uses for the product and hence new markets;

- modifying the product to make it appear new or different – by redesign, additional features, etc.;

- changing the packaging with new sizes, different emphasis, and so on;

- selling the product in new geographical areas.

The disadvantage of these changes is that they are usually short term and only really give cover until a new product is available.

we Worked example

The revenue and costs of a product over the past 13 months are given below. Where do you think the product is in its life-cycle and what plans would you expect the supplier to be making?

Month	Revenue (£'000s)	Cost (£'000s)
1	12.3	4.2
2	13.0	3.4
3	13.3	2.7
4	13.2	2.4
5	12.9	2.0
6	12.7	1.8
7	12.4	1.6
8	12.0	1.4
9	11.4	1.1
10	10.8	1.0
11	9.7	0.8
12	9.0	0.6
13	8.3	0.5

Solution

Subtracting the cost from the revenue gives the profits shown in the following spreadsheet, which includes a graph of performance. Although we do not know demand, the revenue and profit from the product have started to go down in recent months. This suggests the product has moved from maturity to decline. This decline is quite fast, and the product is clearly approaching the withdrawal stage. The company should have already introduced a replacement product or have one very close to introduction (see Figure 4.11).

Month	Revenue	Cost	Profit
1	12.3	4.2	8.1
2	13	3.4	9.6
3	13.3	2.7	10.6
4	13.2	2.4	10.8
5	12.9	2	10.9
6	12.7	1.8	10.9
7	12.4	1.6	10.8
8	12	1.4	10.6
9	11.4	1.1	10.3
10	10.8	1	9.8
11	9.7	0.8	8.9
12	9	0.6	8.4
13	8.3	0.5	7.8

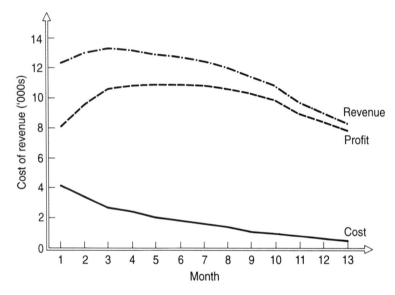

Figure 4.11 Spreadsheet showing results for example.

Entry and exit strategies

Some companies spend a lot of money on research and development. This research looks for new knowledge and can be either:

- *pure research*, which looks for new discoveries; or

- *applied research*, which looks for solutions to particular problems.

Most of this research looks for new products that can be marketed. Some pharmaceutical manufacturers, for example, do research to develop entirely new drugs; building societies offer new types of service; car makers look for new safety features. These companies look for the high profits that come from new products. The obvious disadvantage of this approach is the high cost of research and development. In pharmaceuticals, for example, both Roche and Ciba have annual research budgets of over a billion pounds, or 10–15% of revenue.

Most organizations do not start with basic research to develop entirely new products. Nor do they continue supplying a product through its entire life-cycle until demand dies away. Most companies start their product planning by looking at products that are already being supplied by competitors. They look for existing products which would fit into their range, and make modifications to create their own 'new' product. In other words, they start supplying an existing product that is already some way through its life-cycle. The time when an organization starts – and later stops – making a product defines its **entry and exit strategy**.

The entry and exit strategy used by an organization depends on its overall objectives. Some organizations do basic research and provide the ideas and technology for new developments, but they do not exploit them. They work in the introduction stage and leave the market before the growth stage. Typically, such organizations are very good at innovation, but lack the resources and production skills to manage a growing demand.

Other organizations look for research that has commercial potential and then exploit it during the growth stage. These aim for the high prices available during growth, and exit when profit margins begin to fall. Other organizations can design very efficient operations, so they enter the market at the mature stage and produce large quantities efficiently enough to compete with organizations already in the market. These exit when the product declines and the volume is too low to maintain high production levels.

We can classify these different entry and exit strategies as follows.

- **Research driven**
    - good at research, design and development
    - innovative with constant changes in product
    - high quality and high cost
    - low sales volumes
    - slow delivery

- **New product exploiters**
    - identify new products with wide appeal
    - good at developing new processes for production
    - strong in marketing to create demand
    - high quality with reducing cost
    - moving to high volume

- **Cost reducers**
  - high volume, low cost production
  - low innovation, concentrating on established products
  - low price and fast delivery
  - often automated with production or assembly lines

Review questions

4.14 What are the usual stages in a product life-cycle?

4.15 What would be typical lengths of life-cycles for: (a) model of personal computer; (b) model of car; (c) particular insurance policy; (d) copy of a newspaper?

4.16 As operations are performed throughout the life of a product, the main operational emphasis remains the same. Do you think this is true?

4.17 How do costs and profits vary over a product's life?

4.18 How could you classify organizations based on their entry and exit strategies?

Chapter review

- An organization can only be successful if it supplies products which customers want. The purpose of product planning is to make sure organizations have a continuous supply of suitable products.

- Most organizations supply a range of products so they can meet varied demands and maintain a stable output.

- Customer demands vary over time, so organizations must continually update their range of products, introducing new ones and discarding old ones. There are several stages between the initial idea for a new product and its launch onto the market.

- Products are judged by a combination of features. Scoring models allow a rational view of quantitative and qualitative factors.

- The break-even point is the number of units of a product that must be sold before all costs are recovered and a profit is made.

- An amount of money has a higher value now than the same amount at some point in the future. Discounting takes this into account, and is used in net present value calculations. An alternative approach calculates the internal rate of return.

- The life-cycle of a product has five stages of introduction, growth, maturity, decline and withdrawal. These stages have different operations, costs, revenue and profit.

- Most organizations do not develop entirely new products, but adapt existing ones. The organization's strengths and objectives determine their entry and exit strategies.

Key terms

break-even point	87	internal rate of return	95
competitive advantage	74	life-cycle	97
discounting to present		net present value	93
value	92	product planning	73
entry and exit strategy	105	product range	73
feasibility study	78	scoring model	83
fixed costs	86	variable costs	86

CS Case study – Escential Fragrances

Escential Fragrances is a wholly-owned subsidiary of a major French fashion house. It makes a number of well-known perfumes, which it transfers to the parent company to sell under its own name. Its production is based on two types of perfume:

- 'exclusive' brands that are sold at high prices and in small numbers;

- 'mass' brands that are less expensive and sell in larger quantities.

Production of the exclusive brands give few problems, but the mass brands are more difficult. One problem is their limited lifespan. This means that after some time – usually three or four years, but sometimes only a few months – they are withdrawn from the market to be replaced by new brands.

All marketing is done by the parent company. In one sense this is an advantage for Escential as it concentrates on production and is not worried by short-term fluctuations in its finances. On the other hand, it means it is separated from the market, with production guided by the parent company. If, for example, the parent company is putting some effort into a new 'oriental look', pressure is put on Escential to produce perfumes with an oriental appeal.

As its income is fixed by the internal transfer prices set by the parent company, Escential is not interested in making a profit, but aims to use its facilities to full capacity. Its performance is effectively judged by the number of bottles of perfume it transfers to the parent company.

Escential has enough capacity to make around 5300 bottles of perfume a day. Of this 500 bottles are exclusive brands and the remainder is available for mass brands. This capacity can be varied in the short term by changing working hours or rescheduling, but in the longer term is fixed. The capacity has remained unchanged since the 1920s.

The design of a new perfume is straightforward, and a new brand could be available in a very short time. But before production starts a series of market surveys is done and the parent company must be convinced the new brand fits into its current needs. Suitable bottles and artwork must be designed and manufactured. When this is complete, the parent company runs its marketing effort to launch the new brand. This process increases the time needed to introduce a brand to about nine months. Sometimes the process can be speeded up, but at others times it takes up to two years.

A meeting was recently held to discuss medium-term production plans. In particular, the management of Escential wanted to discuss the withdrawal of some perfumes and the introduction of replacements. It currently makes a range of nine mass perfume brands. Table 4.3 shows the average daily sales over a recent 19-month period.

When these figures were presented to the meeting they caused some concern, particularly with Guy Mignard who is the Marketing Director from the parent company. He said that perfume sales are known to be seasonal and

Table 4.3

	Perfume code number								
Month	*LP4098*	*LP6032*	*LP6275*	*LT3127*	*LT4092*	*MA985*	*LP1075*	*MA247*	*LT2240*
1	120	1170	–	1030	680	–	320	724	403
2	150	1180	–	1040	660	–	286	693	519
3	190	1170	–	1050	610	–	307	751	622
4	250	1170	–	1050	560	–	310	660	540
5	310	1150	–	1060	500	60	324	703	490
6	450	1130	–	1070	410	100	301	691	603
7	600	1080	–	1080	320	150	279	673	397
8	770	1050	–	1090	240	310	292	711	501
9	940	970	50	1200	150	370	314	741	488
10	1000	940	50	1210	110	390	288	687	561
11	1050	930	50	1190	90	380	292	729	473
12	1100	890	60	1200	80	380	301	700	502
13	1150	850	70	1210	70	390	314	691	450
14	1180	840	80	1200	60	370	306	673	423
15	1210	780	90	1210	60	380	285	659	607
16	1230	730	100	1210	60	370	299	712	555
17	1240	670	120	1090	50	360	305	736	487
18	1250	560	160	1000	50	320	289	705	491
19	1250	450	210	860	40	280	310	603	497

yet the figures did not show much variation. The explanation from Marcel Gagnon, who is Escential's Materials Manager, is that the variation in sales is much more pronounced than the variation in production. Although perfume deteriorates over time it can be stored in refrigerators with variations in stock levels to allow a steady production. The figures he provided were movements from production to the refrigerated store.

Guy Mignard suggested that to remain competitive in the perfume market the company needed to appeal to different types of people and should, therefore, expand its range as soon as possible. He suggested rushing an additional perfume onto the market in six months and adding another three brands within the next year.

The opposite view was taken by Marcel Gagnon who said that production was already stretched beyond capacity. When output had peaked in month 17, the company realized it could not continue at this rate for long, and was much more comfortable since average production had fallen. As it is easier to produce large batches of the same brand, he suggested removing the four brands with lowest sales and concentrating on the remaining five. New brands should only be considered when sales of existing brands fall considerably, or when they expand the existing facilities.

A middle view was taken by Jean Pouliot, who is Escential's company secretary. He suggested that recent production levels had been too high for the company to manage and should be cut back to a reasonable level. The implication is that no extra brands should be considered immediately. But sales of three current brands are clearly declining and the company should replace them at some point. He had been talking to the parent company and suggested Escential should consider three new brands. He had done a limited analysis – summarized in Table 4.4. The introduction of these brands at some

Table 4.4

	Code number					
	LP6587		LP7045		LT4950	
Quarter	Costs (£'000s)	Revenue (£'000s)	Costs (£'000s)	Revenue (£'000s)	Costs (£'000s)	Revenue (£'000s)
1	300	20	350	150	150	10
2	100	40	200	200	150	10
3	–	60	100	250	100	10
4	–	80	60	300	100	20
5	100	100	150	300	50	30
6	–	100	100	250	50	50
7	–	100	60	200	50	80
8	–	100	–	150	50	120
9	100	100	100	110	10	160
10	–	100	60	70	10	200
11	–	100	–	30	10	220
12	–	100	–	–	10	220

point would fit into the parent company's objectives over the next five years, but there was no pressure to introduce all three brands, or to introduce them at the same time.

The figures given by Jean Pouliot are not discounted (which would reduce future values by about 5% a quarter) and are based on an average transfer price of £5 a bottle.

Questions

- What would you do if you were a manager of Escential?

- At what stages in their life-cycles are the nine mass perfumes?

- What are likely future sales?

- What should Escential do about withdrawing, replacing or extending its current brands?

- Which of the new products gives the best returns?

- How useful is the data given, and how accurate does it seem?

Problems

4.1   Four products are judged by 10 criteria, with points given to each as shown below. What is the relative importance of the criteria? Which product would you recommend?

Factor	Maximum	A	B	C	D
Resources	10	8	10	8	7
Finance	30	28	27	24	17
Market	35	17	33	22	18
Production	25	18	19	20	19
Competition	20	12	11	16	19
Technical	15	10	9	5	12
Skills	10	9	4	3	9
Compatibility	5	3	3	1	5
Location	10	6	10	7	6
Experience	15	8	6	4	12

4.2   Every week a company makes 100 units of a product which it sells for £100 each. Unit variable costs are £50 and fixed costs amount to £150,000 a year. What is the break-even point for the product, and what profit is the company making? What is the average cost per unit? How much would production have to rise to reduce the average cost per unit by 25%?

4.3 An airline is considering a new service between Paris and Vancouver. Its existing aeroplanes, each of which has a capacity of 240 passengers, could be used for one flight a week with fixed costs of £30,000 and variable costs amounting to 50% of the ticket price. If the airline plans to sell tickets at £200 each, how many passengers will be needed for the airline to break even on the proposed route? Does this seem a reasonable number?

4.4 How much will an initial investment of £1000 earning interest of 8% a year be worth at the end of 20 years?

4.5 Several years ago a couple invested in an endowment insurance policy which is about to mature. They have the option of receiving £10,000 now or £20,000 in 10 years time. Because they are retired and pay no income tax, they could invest the money with a real interest rate expected to remain at 10% a year for the foreseeable future. Which option should they take?

4.6 A product has projected costs and revenues (in thousands of pounds) as follows:

Year	1	2	3	4	5	6
Costs	100	–	–	50	–	–
Incomes	10	20	50	80	60	40

What is its net present value? What is the internal rate of return?

4.7 A company has to choose one of three alternative products. The costs and incomes are shown below. What should the company do?

	Product A		Product B		Product C	
Year	Income (£'000s)	Costs (£'000s)	Income (£'000s)	Costs (£'000s)	Income (£'000s)	Costs (£'000s)
1	10	70	80	30	120	40
2	20	60	90	20	110	40
3	50	45	90	10	100	50
4	100	40	100	20	100	60
5	150	40	100	20	90	60
6	170	40	110	30	90	70
7	180	40	110	30	80	80

4.8 The revenue and costs of supplying a product over the past 11 months are as shown below. Where is the product in its life-cycle and what plans would you expect the supplier to be making?

Month	Income (£'000s)	Cost (£'000s)
1	3.5	7.5
2	4.8	8.7
3	7.0	10.2
4	8.9	10.5
5	10.2	9.8
6	11.9	8.8
7	12.7	7.7
8	13.4	6.8
9	13.7	5.2
10	13.7	3.8
11	13.5	3.0

Discussion questions

4.1 How does an organization decide the number and variety of products to make? Give some examples of product ranges in different organizations.

4.2 Describe a product you would like to market and discuss the steps needed to launch it. What are the major problems you would meet? What time-scale and budget would you need?

4.3 How can an organization make sure it has enough ideas that lead to useful new products?

4.4 Discuss, with examples, some practical difficulties of using scoring models.

4.5 How would you determine a realiztic discounting rate for a company? What are the problems of using this for calculating net present values? What other analyses might you do?

4.6 Design a set of spreadsheets for comparing alternative products. You might design spreadsheets for scoring models, break-even points, net present values and internal rates of return.

4.7 Describe in detail the changes seen as a specific product moved through its life-cycle. You might consider a particular type of computer, fast food, fashion accessory, or any other product you are familiar with.

4.8 Some people say that few products follow the precise life-cycle described in this chapter. Do you think they are right?

4.9 Describe the entry and exit strategies of a number of national companies. Why have they adopted these strategies?

4.10 How could you classify service industries according to their entry and exit strategies?

4.11 The Amantti Foundation is a privately funded think-tank which considers the effects of technological developments on society. A recent study looked at some products that are ready to be marketed and could have a widespread impact. These products include virtual offices, multimedia education, smart money to replace coins and notes, hybrid diesel/electric cars, interactive television, genetic engineering to grow organs for human transplants, and so on. What stage do you think these products are at in their development? Where do such ideas come from? Can you add to this list of products?

Selected references

Dhillan B.S. (1989). *Life Cycle Costing*. New York: Gordon and Breach.

Gause D.C. and Weinberg G.M. (1989). *Exploring Requirements*. New York: Dorset House.

Harrigan K.R. (1984). *Strategic Flexibility*. Lexington, Mass.: Lexington Books.

Hill T. (1989). *Manufacturing Strategy*. Homewood, Ill.: Irwin.

Hollins B. and Pugh S. (1990). *Successful Product Design*. London: Butterworths.

Onkvisit S. and Shaw J.J. (1989). *Product Life Cycles and Product Management*. New York: Quorum Books.

Sachs W.S. and Benson G. (1981). *Product Planning and Management*. Tulsa: Penwell Publishing.

Wheelwright S.C. and Clark K.B. (1992). *Revolutionising Product Development*. New York: Free Press.

Wind Y.J. (1982). *Product Policy: Concepts, Methods and Strategy*. Reading, Mass.: Addison-Wesley.

5

Quality management

Contents

Objectives

After reading this chapter you should be able to:

- appreciate the importance of product quality
- define quality in different ways
- discuss the costs of quality management
- outline recent developments in quality management
- describe the main features of Total Quality Management
- see how quality management is introduced to an organization
- discuss quality management in services

Definitions of quality

Background

The last chapter described product planning. It showed how every organization makes a product, and this product must be designed to satisfy customer demands. But customers judge a product in a variety of ways, particularly looking at its price, availability, quality and flexibility. In this chapter we are going to see how an organization makes sure its products have the high quality demanded by customers.

In recent years a lot of attention has been given to quality management. Ford use the slogan 'Quality is Job 1', and a lot of companies advertise that they are 'Quality companies – registered for BS 5750'. These are not just slogans, but are signs that the organizations are serious about the quality of their products.

But the first problem with talking about quality is defining exactly what we mean. If someone asks you to judge the quality of a novel you can say whether you enjoyed reading it, but would find it difficult to describe its quality. If a survey asked you to describe the present government you could talk about their various policies but could not give a measure of their quality. You can see this problem clearly when sports commentators try to say how good a football match was, or wine tasters compare different vineyards, or enthusiasts discuss a new video game.

Sometimes there are agreed measures for quality, such as the industry standards for concrete, but these are very specific and can not be used for other products. You can see, then, that measuring the quality of any product is likely to be difficult.

As a starting point, we can look at our own experiences, when we think that a ball-point pen has good quality if it writes without smudging. An airline gives a high quality service if it gets you to your destination on time. In other words, we think of products as having high quality if they do the jobs they were designed for. This suggests a general idea that a product's overall quality depends on its ability to meet customer expectations.

> In its broadest sense, **quality** is the ability of a product to meet – and preferably exceed – customer expectations.

This shows the reason why quality is so important. The only way an organization can remain competitive is by making products with the high quality demanded by customers. If it does not do this it will inevitably lose market share and profits. Managers now realize this, and have put a lot of effort into **quality management**.

> **Quality management** is the management function that is concerned
> with all aspects of a product's quality.

Everyone is concerned with the quality of products whether they are a family buying a new house, an electorate voting for a government, a patient having an operation, a company buying a piece of equipment, or an audience watching a play. These concerns have been around for a long time, so you might assume that:

- quality management is an area that organizations have been looking at for a long time;

- all the main problems were solved some time ago.

The first of these may be true, but the second is certainly not. Quality management is an area that is still evolving. In the past few years there have been a whole range of new developments, which some people refer to as the **quality revolution**. These developments happened for three main reasons:

- improved processes for making products can guarantee consistently high quality;

- organizations began to use high quality to gain a competitive advantage;

- consumers have got used to high quality products, and are now unwilling to accept anything less.

Now you can see why organizations **must** make high quality products. Any organization that ignores the demand for high quality will lose out to competitors that can meet customer expectations. Although high quality will not guarantee a product is a success, low quality will certainly guarantee its failure. Some of the benefits an organization can expect from high quality products are:

- enhanced reputation

- increased competitiveness

- reduced marketing effort

- improved sales

- higher productivity

- long-term profitability

- reduced liability for defective products

- reduced costs

Most of these are fairly obvious – if we increase the quality of our products we expect people to recognize this, prefer our products over

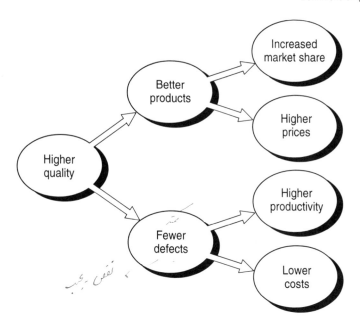

Figure 5.1 Some benefits from higher quality.

competitors', buy them and help make our organization successful. The statement that increasing quality can reduce costs is, however, particularly interesting. This goes against the traditional view that increasing quality can only be bought at increasing cost. It seems obvious that making a higher quality product uses more time, more careful operations, a more skilful workforce, better materials, and so on. But if you look at the wider costs, you can find some costs that actually go down with increasing quality.

Suppose a washing machine is sold with a faulty part. The customer will complain and the manufacturer arranges for the machine to be repaired. The manufacturer could have saved money by finding the fault before the machine left the factory, and it could have saved even more by making a machine that did not have a fault in the first place (as shown in Figure 5.1). We will return to this theme later in the chapter.

ce Case example – Federal Express

Federal Express has grown to become a leader in its field by giving a guaranteed high quality service. This example illustrates one aspect of this service, when a customer enquired about a delivery.

Gill Seymour had sent an important legal document from New York to Turin. It was Friday and she had expected a phone call from Turin to acknowledge receipt of the document. This had not come, so she phoned Federal Express to see if they had delivered the document, bearing in mind their stated policy of, 'Absolutely, Positively, Overnight'. Using Federal Express's free enquiry line she was told by the operator,

> Our Super Tracker computer system shows a complete log of your document's journey. Briefly, our service man, Jim Baxter, picked it up from Martin Pearce in your New York office at 4.30 pm on Wednesday; it was routed through our Superhub in Memphis and was put on our overnight flight to Italy. It arrived in Rome by 1 pm on Thursday, and our delivery van took it to your Turin office at 4.00 pm. Unfortunately, there was a local holiday and the office was closed. We delivered the package again at 9.00 o'clock this morning, where it was signed for by Paulo Carerra. We pointed out the note asking him to phone you and confirm delivery.

The product supplied by Federal Express is an extremely efficient parcel delivery service. They use high technology, efficient operations and many other means of giving a consistently high quality service.

Questions

- How do you think Federal Express could measure the quality of their service?

- Can you find other examples of organizations that use guaranteed quality to compete?

Different views of quality

We said before that a product can only be high quality if it satisfies customer expectations. As individuals, we normally think of quality in terms of engineering excellence, aesthetic value, finish, or some other vague concept. An organization must turn these vague ideas about quality into products that get customer approval. We can start seeing how they do this by looking at specific products that are generally considered to be high quality. A Rolls Royce is probably the highest quality car available; a Wedgwood dinner service has a much higher quality than a plastic equivalent; *Hamlet* is a higher quality play than a television soap opera. But if we try to be more specific about these observations, we come across serious problems. If the purpose of a car is to provide transport between two points, then a cheap car will do this just as well as a Rolls Royce; if the purpose of a dinner service is to provide a surface to rest food on while we eat, a cheap plastic one works just as well as an expensive china one; audience figures show that far more people watch a television soap opera than go to see *Hamlet*.

Faced with these problems, some people simply give up when asked to define quality and say, 'We don't know how to define quality but we recognize it when we see it'. Others make vague statements about inherent values, such as, 'Quality measures innate excellence'. Other people are more specific and say, 'Quality measures the fitness of a product for its intended use'. Others look at the product's design and say, 'Quality measures the degree to which a product conforms to designed specifications'. Yet other people balance the cost and benefit to suggest that quality is related to the ratio of performance to price.

The problem is that quality depends on many factors, only some of which can be measured. Consider, for example, a television set. We might judge its quality by how expensive it is, how attractive the cabinet is, how big it is, how easy it is to operate, how clear the picture is, how accurate the colours are, how often it needs repairing, how long it will last, how many channels it can pick up, how good the sound is, what additional features it has, and so on. The judgement of quality for almost any product would need a similar list, perhaps relating to:

- innate excellence
- fitness for intended use
- performance
- reliability
- durability
- specific features, perhaps for safety or convenience
- technology used
- conformance to design specifications
- uniformity, with small variability
- meets or exceeds customer expectations
- perception of high quality by customers
- convenience of use
- attractive appearance and style
- ratio of performance to cost
- customer service before and during sales
- on-time deliveries
- after-sales service.

Any reasonable view of quality must take into account many such factors, and it would be foolish to judge a product by some factors and ignore others. We can not, for example, judge a doctor's quality by the number of patients they see without considering the treatment given; we can not judge a computer by its performance without knowing how long it will last; we can not judge a government by its defence policy but ignore its handling of the economy. A common practice, then, is to consider a 'cocktail' of factors which, taken together, define high quality.

Some of the factors for judging quality can be measured – such as weight, number of breakdowns a year and guaranteed life – while others can not – such as appearance, comfort of facilities and courtesy of staff. The main problem with quality management is bringing all these factors together in a coherent view. This is particularly difficult as it depends to a large extent on the perspective taken. A school with large classes might be considered high quality by a government which judges efficiency, but low quality by parents who look at educational achievements. With a car, a production engineer might judge it by its conformance to engineering design; a mechanical engineer might be more interested in the power generated per cubic centimetre of engine capacity; a salesman might look at how quickly it sells; an insurance company by how frequently and severely is it damaged in accidents; a mechanic by how easy it is to maintain; a banker by how long it will last and how much it depreciates; a customer by the colour of the paint, and so on.

Two specific views of product quality are:

(1)　An **internal** view of the producer, who defines quality as the closeness of a product's performance to its designed specifications.

(2)　An **external** view of the customer, who defines quality by how well a product does the job it was bought for.

In the past organizations tended to emphasize the internal view, suggesting that a product which meets the standards of the producer should be acceptable to the customers. People who complained to companies were often surprised to get letters back saying, 'We have considered your complaint, but have found that our product was perfectly satisfactory.' More recently, organizations have taken more notice of customer opinions. As we said above, these opinions are based on a range of factors, so customers will not always demand products that have the highest technical quality. They want some balance of attributes that gives an acceptable overall picture. A Rolls Royce car has the highest possible quality of engineering, but most people include price in their judgement and buy a cheaper make. Bearing this in mind, we should really define two types of quality:

(1)　*designed quality*: which determines the quality that a product is designed to have;

(2)　*achieved quality*: which shows how closely a product achieves the designed quality.

An airline which plans to have 98% of its flights to arrive on time has a high designed quality. If only 30% of flights are actually on time, its achieved quality is much lower.

Review questions

5.1   If the price is right people will buy a product regardless of its quality. Do you think this is true?

5.2   Why is quality management important to an organization?

5.3   Why is it difficult to define 'quality'?

Costs of quality management

Types of cost

We suggested earlier that costs can be reduced by increasing the quality of a product. At first this seems strange, but let us consider a specific example where a manufacturer sells products, 5% of which are defective. When these defects are reported by customers the manufacturer replaces them under its warranty. This kind of operation is clearly inefficient. To start with, the manufacturer has to increase production by 5% to cover the defects. It also has to maintain a system for dealing with customer complaints, and an associated system for collecting defective units, inspecting, repairing or replacing them, and returning them to customers. If the defects are eliminated, productivity will rise by 5%, unit costs will fall, there will be no customer complaints so the cost of dealing with them is eliminated, and the whole system for correcting faults becomes unnecessary.

Another consequence of poor quality is the outdated idea of **overage**. If a factory needed 100 components it would buy 110 on the assumption that 10 would be defective. This overage was often doubled, as suppliers who were asked for 110 units would send 120 to make sure 110 were satisfactory. An old example of this is a request for 12 loaves of bread which would be satisfied by a 'baker's dozen'. The use of overage is obviously wasteful and is no longer accepted.

In general, then, we can say that making a product without defects has the benefits of:

●   increased productivity

●   reduced unit cost

●   reduced administration costs for dealing with customer complaints

●   elimination of procedures for correcting defects

- reduced warranty costs

- a range of indirect benefits such as increased customer goodwill and improved reputation.

The conclusion is that organizations can save money by making higher quality products.

We have emphasized the savings that can be made from higher quality, but common sense tells us there are must be some additional costs. Before we move on, we should have a look at the costs in more detail. In the past the costing of quality has often been done badly. This is partly because managers did not fully understand the costs involved as accounting systems did not identify them properly. There was a general feeling that quality costs were 5–10% of sales, but more reliable figures might be 20–30%.

There are four components to the costs of quality:

(1)   design costs

(2)   appraisal costs

(3)   internal failure costs

(4)   external failure costs.

Design costs

The quality of a product is usually set at the design stage. So the best way to get high quality in a product is not by inspections during the production process, but by designing a good product in the first place. In part, this means that the design should be robust enough to allow high quality despite small, unavoidable variations during the production process. It can also include product simplification, which reduces the number of parts in a product and simplifies those that remain.

Design costs include all aspects of quality that are designed into the product. They include direct costs for the product itself, such as the choice of materials, inclusion of certain features, amount of time needed to make the product, and so on. They also include indirect costs, like the ease of production, amount of automation that can be used, skill level needed by the workforce, type of process that can be used, procurement needed, the amount of training needed, and so on. In essence, the design costs are incurred for the planning and design of a product and process to make sure they achieve high quality. Design costs are sometimes called **prevention costs**, as they include all the work done to prevent defects in the final product.

All things being equal, design costs rise with the quality of the product, largely because of the direct costs. But customers will not pay a limitless amount to get products of the highest possible quality. There is a ceiling on the price they will not pass regardless of the quality offered, and this sets the practical limit for designed quality. A rather dated view looked at the difference

Figure 5.2 Optimal value for design quality.

between price and design cost – then the point where this is greatest gives the best designed quality. Typical graphs of costs and prices are shown in Figure 5.2, but you should treat these with caution. We have already said that the relationship between quality and cost is not as clear as this, and most products have to achieve a certain level of quality before they attract any customers at all.

Appraisal costs

These are the costs of making sure the designed quality is actually achieved. As products move through their process, they are inspected to make sure they reach the quality specified in the design. Related costs include sampling, inspecting, testing and all the other elements of quality control (which we shall meet in Chapter 10). Generally, the more effort that is put into quality control, the higher will be the end quality of the product and the higher will be the costs needed to achieve this.

Internal failure costs

As a product goes through the various operations in its production, it may be inspected several times. Any units that do not meet the specified quality are scrapped, returned to an earlier point in the process, repaired, or allowed to continue in the hope that the defect is not important enough to affect the product's value. With the exception of the last, these alternatives involve additional work to bring a unit up to a satisfactory quality. There is also the implication that some work already done has been wasted. The cost of this work forms part of the internal failure cost, which is the total cost of making defective products that are detected somewhere within the process.

The further a product goes through the process, the more money will be spent on it and the more expensive it will be to scrap or rework. Ideally, then, defects should be found as early in the process as possible. This means that the option mentioned above, of allowing a defective unit to continue in the process, is misguided. It involves spending more money on a unit that is known to be defective, and later detection and scrapping will increase the total waste.

Part of the internal failure costs come directly from the loss of material, wasted labour effort, wasted machine time in making the defective item, and so on. Another part comes from the indirect costs of higher stock levels, longer lead times, and extra capacity needed to allow for scrap and rejections.

External failure costs

Suppose a product goes through the entire production process, is delivered to a customer and is then found to be defective. The producer will usually give some kind of guarantee, and is responsible for correcting any faults. This means the product must be brought back from the customer and replaced, reworked or repaired as necessary. The cost of this work is part of the external failure cost, which is the total cost of making defective products that are not detected within the process, but are recognized as faulty by customers.

External failure faults are often the highest costs of quality management and are the ones that should be avoided. In 1982 General Motors found a fault in some of its cars and had to recall 2.1 million vehicles at a cost of over $100 million; in 1994 Ford of America recalled 900,000 vehicles because of a fault in the hand brake. The cost of such failures can be even higher if, say, a defective part in an aeroplane causes a crash that leaves the manufacturer liable for damages. Similarly, the builders of Chernobyl and Three Mile Island power stations must wish they had built higher quality reactors, and those involved with the Challenger Space Shuttle would have preferred more rigorous quality checks.

External failure costs, like internal failure costs, decline with higher quality (see Figure 5.3).

Minimizing the total cost of quality

The total cost of quality is found by adding the four separate components of design, appraisal, internal failure and external failure costs. The result can be surprisingly high, often amounting to 25% of the cost of sales. Traditionally, organizations have tried to minimize this by drawing graphs like that shown in Figure 5.4. In this, the design and appraisal costs increase with quality, while the failure costs decrease. The total quality cost has a clear minimum which shows an optimal level of quality.

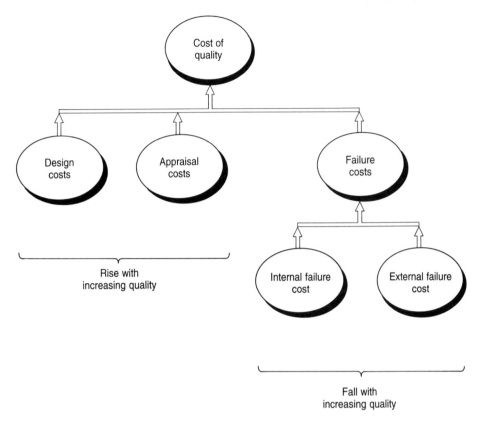

Figure 5.3 The costs of quality.

Unfortunately, such analyses are not very convincing. They set a target number of faults, so the organization accepts poor quality as normal with no incentive for improvement. In effect, the analyses assume – and even encourage – a certain number of defects.

The main weakness of the analyses is that they underestimate the cost of external failures. Customers are now unwilling to accept any defects in products, so low quality usually leads to very low sales. It is also clear that producers are being held more responsible for the consequences of defects in their products – surgeons are liable if their negligence during an operation injures a patient; pharmaceutical manufacturers are responsible for side-effects in their drugs; management consultants are responsible for bad advice, and so on. The resulting high costs of external failure mean that the optimal quality for a product is generally 'perfect quality', where every unit is guaranteed to be free of any faults. This is the idea of **Total Quality Management**, which is described in the rest of this chapter.

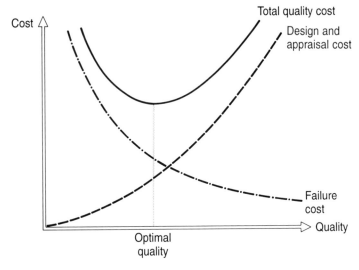

Figure 5.4 Finding the optimal quality.

we Worked example

A company has recorded costs for two years immediately before changing its quality management programme and two years immediately after. How effective do you think the change has been?

Year	−2	−1	+1	+2
Sales value (£'000s)	1247	1186	1456	1775
Costs (£'000s)				
Design	8	9	30	32
Appraisal	17	20	64	65
Internal failure	72	75	24	20
External failure	60	66	23	17

Solution

The easiest way to judge the quality management programme is to calculate the total cost of quality as a percentage of sales.

Year	-2	-1	$+1$	$+2$
Costs (£'000s)				
Design	0.64	0.76	2.06	1.80
Appraisal	1.36	1.69	4.40	3.66
Internal failure	5.77	6.32	1.65	1.13
External failure	4.81	5.56	1.58	0.96
Total (£'000s)	12.58	14.33	9.69	7.55

The new quality management programme has clearly put more emphasis on design and appraisal, and this has reduced the cost of failures. The overall costs decline and sales increase, so the programme must be judged a success.

Review questions

5.4 Higher quality inevitably comes at a higher cost. Do you think this is true?

5.5 What is the total cost of quality?

5.6 Why do internal failure costs decline with increasing quality?

5.7 How would you find the optimal level of quality for a product?

Managing for perfect quality

Total Quality Management

In the last section we suggested that organizations should aim for perfect quality or **zero defects** in their products. As you can imagine, it is very difficult to get perfect quality. If you consider the things you do every day, how often do you achieve perfect quality? So how can large organizations with complex operations get this?

The obvious way to increase quality is to use more rigorous inspections with statistical quality control (which we shall describe in Chapter 10). For many years this was the main tool of quality management. Sometimes quality controllers tested every unit as it passed through its process, but often they only tested a sample. This allowed some defective units to go undetected and move on to customers. Although statistical quality control is still widely used, there has been a significant change of emphasis shown by the phrase that 'you can't inspect quality into a product'.

Quality managers have realized that the best way to improve quality is not to inspect production and discard defective units, but to make sure that no defective units are made in the first place. The term **quality control** is now used for sampling and inspection. The broader management function responsible for all aspects of quality is known as **quality assurance**, **quality engineering**, and the term we use here, **quality management**.

> **Quality management** is a broad function that includes all functions concerned with the quality of an organization's products.
>
> **Quality control** is a more limited function that does statistical sampling and testing to check the quality of a product.

The important point about quality management is that it is not a separate function to be treated in isolation, but is an integral part of all operations. Suppose you go to a tailor and order a suit. You will only be satisfied if the suit is well designed, if it is well made, if there are no faults in the material used, if the price is reasonable, if the salesperson is helpful, if the shop is pleasant, and so on. This means that everyone in the tailor – from the person who designs the suit to the person who sells it, and from the person who owns the organization to the person who keeps it clean – is directly involved in the quality of their product. This is the view taken by **Total Quality Management** (TQM).

> With **Total Quality Management**, the whole organization works together and systematically improves product quality.

TQM was developed by Japanese manufacturers. In the 1940s Japanese industry had been disrupted by wars, its plant and equipment were out of date, productivity was low, and products designed to support their war effort were no longer needed. To start rebuilding its industry, Japan made cheap, low quality imitations of products from other countries. Over time, living standards rose and operating costs became higher. It became increasingly difficult to make cheap products, so Japanese manufacturers began to concentrate on more expensive ones with high added-value. They were obviously successful and by the 1970s dominated world markets in motor cycles, consumer electronics, cars, machine tools, steel, computer equipment, banks, and so on.

The key element in Japan's success was the recognition that they could compete by offering consistently high quality. This emphasis on quality was illustrated by studies in the early 1980s which found that air conditioners made in the United States had 70 times as many defects on the assembly line as those made in Japan, and had 17 times as many breakdowns in the first year of operation. A US manufacturer of television sets had more than 150 defects per 100 completed sets, and was trying to compete with Japanese companies that averaged 0.5 defects per 100 completed sets. US manufacturers of car components had warranty costs 10 times higher than their Japanese counter-parts. In 1977 Hertz reported its fleet of Chevrolets needed 425 repairs per 100 vehicles in the first 12,000 miles of operation, while its Toyotas needed 55 repairs.

An ironic feature of Japan's success is that much of the early work was done by Deming, an American who visited Japan in the late 1940s to help improve productivity and quality. He found a receptive audience in Japan, but was largely ignored in the rest of the world for the next 30 years. Deming gave Americans seminars on quality management, and in 1979 had 15 people attending. By 1984 the movement toward quality had started and 1700 people attended, with 3800 in the following year.

Now we take it for granted that organizations aim for high quality, as Ford use the slogan, 'Quality is Job 1', and IBM say 'We will deliver defect-free competitive products and services on time to our customers'.

Effects on the organization

Traditionally, organizations have used a separate quality control department to inspect the work of production departments. These two functions had different objectives. Production would try to make products as quickly as possible, while quality control inspected products to make sure they met specifications, possibly by slowing down production. This inevitably led to conflicts, with one department seen as benefiting only at the expense of the other. Sometimes this conflict was so intense that departments forgot they really had the same objective – satisfied customers.

Improved production processes can guarantee high quality, so quality management moved its emphasis from inspections at the end of production to focus on:

- operations during the process itself, to make sure no defects are being produced; or

- before production in the planning stages, to make sure the design allows high quality.

Quality management then stopped being a separate function and became an integral part of the process. In effect, production departments took responsibility for their own quality. This meant quality assurance staff could spend less time on inspections, and their job changed from inspecting to facilitating. They work with customers, operations, marketing, engineers, and anyone else involved, to look for ways of ensuring high quality and continual improvements in products and processes (see Figure 5.5).

The transfer of quality management from a separate department to part of the production function does not simply mean that different people do the same inspections. It is part of a fundamental change in an organization's

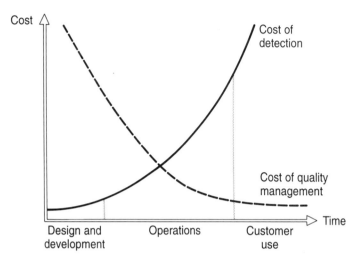

Figure 5.5 Cost of detecting a defect, and managing quality.

attitude towards quality. This is the basis of Total Quality Management, which realizes that quality must be a part of every operation.

You can imagine the effects this has on people working on the production process. Each person becomes responsible for only passing on products that are of perfect quality. This is called **quality at source**, with **job enlargement** for each person who is now responsible for both their previous job and an inherent quality management function. All operators must now be able to understand some statistics, such as bar charts, histograms, and Pareto analyses. These are displayed so that everyone knows how well each operation is working – and any problems are noticed and solved as quickly as possible.

Each person is responsible for passing on products of perfect quality. If someone finds a fault, it means that something has gone wrong. Quality at source programmes give anyone authority to stop the production process and investigate a fault. The reason for the fault is found and suggestions are made for avoiding other faults in the future. This contrasts with traditional operations that only stop the production process as a last resort, and the cause of the fault may then go unnoticed until the problem becomes severe. Moving responsibility down to the workforce means that fewer supervisors are needed and the organization becomes flatter.

TQM also affects the way people are paid. Traditionally people working in production were paid for making high volumes, often regardless of quality. Many people were paid by 'piece work' where their job was simply to make as many units as possible. TQM says that they should also be paid for quality, so they become interested in how well they make the product and are willing to suggest improvements. Managers should collect these comments through suggestion boxes or informal progress meetings.

More regular meetings are arranged through **quality circles**. These are informal, voluntary groups of about 10 people involved at all levels in a part of the process. A typical quality circle meets for an hour once or twice a month to discuss ways of improving their operations. They might identify a problem that is affecting the quality of their product, discuss alternatives for improvements, examine comments put into a suggestions box, suggest modifications to designs, and so on. Their aim is simply to discuss the operation and try to find improvements.

Many companies who use quality circles have immense benefits, but they can only be used when a number of conditions are met. These include:

- a well-educated workforce capable of recognizing, analysing and solving problems;

- people who are able and willing to exchange ideas;

- people who see themselves as working for the good of the organization;

- a management who are willing to share information on costs and operations.

Some of the effects of TQM are illustrated in Figure 5.6, while the differences introduced by TQM are summarized in Table 5.1.

Table 5.1 Differences introduced by TQM.

Criteria	Traditional attitude	New attitude with TQM
Importance	quality is a technical issue	quality is a strategic issue
Cost	high quality costs money	high quality saves money
Responsibility	quality assurance department	everyone in the organization
Defined by	average quality level	zero defects
Emphasis	detecting defects	preventing defects
Attitude	inspect quality in	build quality in
Target	meet specifications	continuous improvement
Defined by	organization	customers

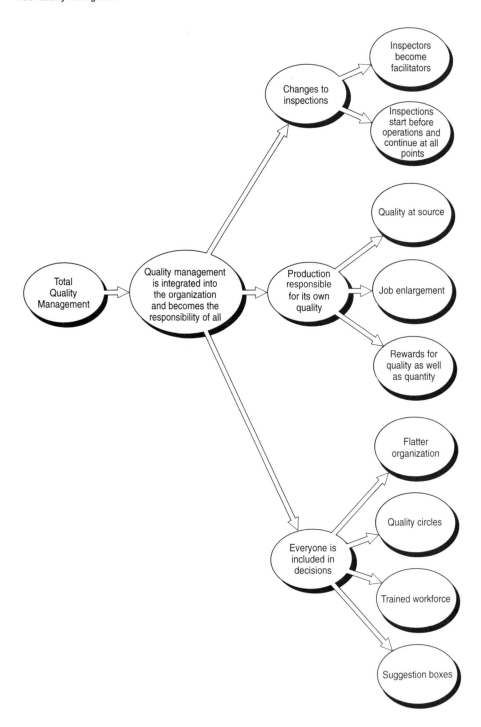

Figure 5.6 Some effects of total quality management.

ce Case example – Total Quality Management

There are many stories about companies which introduced TQM and get substantial benefits. Most of these are anecdotal, as shown in the following examples.

- Japan Steel Work Hiroshima Plant began work on TQM in 1977. Between 1978 and 1981 production rose 50%, the number of employees fell from 2400 to 1900, the accident rate fell from 15.7 per million man-hours to 2.3, the cost of defects fell from 1.57% of sales to 0.4% and the number of suggestions per employee rose from 5.6 a year to 17.6.

- In 1984 Ford of America had been running its 'Quality is Job 1' programme for five years. During this period the number of warranty repairs dropped 45%, faults reported by new owners fell 50%, their share of the US market rose to 19.2%, sales rose 700,000 units in a year to 5.7 million units, pre-tax profits rose to $4.3 billion, annual operating costs fell by $4.5 billion.

- Within one year Hewlett-Packard's Computer Systems Division increased direct labour productivity by 40%, faults with integrated circuits fell from 1950 parts per million to 210, faults with soldering fell from 5200 parts per million to 100, and faults in the final assembly fell from 145 parts per million to 10.

Implementing Total Quality Management

You can see some of the effects of aiming for total quality – reorganized quality management function, lower costs, higher productivity, involved workforce, quality at source, and so on. But achieving these can take several years of effort. Deming spent 40 years developing TQM in Japan. During this time he compiled a list of 14 principles for quality management, which give guidelines on how an organization should implement TQM.

DEMING'S 14 POINTS

(1) Create constancy of purpose towards product quality.

(2) Refuse to accept customary levels of mistakes, delays, defects and errors.

(3) Stop depending on mass inspection, but build quality into the product in the first place.

(4) Stop awarding business on the basis of price only – reduce the number of suppliers and insist on meaningful measures of quality.

(5)   Develop programmes for continuous improvement of costs, quality, productivity and service.

(6)   Institute training for all employees.

(7)   Focus supervision on helping employees to do a better job.

(8)   Drive out fear by encouraging two-way communication.

(9)   Break down barriers between departments and encourage problem solving through team-work.

(10)   Eliminate numerical goals, posters and slogans that demand improvements without saying how these should be achieved.

(11)   Eliminate arbitrary quotas that interfere with quality.

(12)   Remove barriers that stop people having pride in their work.

(13)   Institute vigorous programmes of life-long education, training and self-improvement.

(14)   Put everyone to work on implementing these 14 points.

Deming's 14 points do not form a programme that has a fixed duration, but they give a new way of thinking in organizations. They emphasize the fact that managers are in control of the organization, and are responsible for improving its performance. Conversely, if an organization is performing badly, managers should take the blame. Many people say that workers are responsible for poor quality, but Deming suggests this is unfair. A production process can be divided into two parts:

(1)   the *system* over which managers have control, and which contributes 85% of the variation in quality;

(2)   the *workers* who are under their own control, and who contribute 15% of the variation in quality.

Major improvements in quality come from managers improving the system rather than workers improving their own performance. This is similar to productivity where the best way to find improvements is not to make people work harder but to improve the design of the process. A person digging a hole with a spade can work very hard but still have a lower productivity than a lazy person with a mechanical digger. Similarly, a person working very conscientiously to get high quality in a poor system will get worse results than a less conscientious person in a better system.

Another important point in Deming's list is that everybody should be properly trained for their job. It may seem obvious that people can only do their job if they are well trained, but many organizations overlook this. How many times have you had poor service simply because the server did not really know what they should do? In contrast, Ford of America sent over 6000 people to training courses in two years. They realized that they could only make good products if they had good components, so they also trained 1000 suppliers.

When training their suppliers, Ford gave a clear statement that they would only consider suppliers whose feelings towards quality matched their own. This view became more common as organizations looked for some way of ensuring the quality of materials. Larger organizations followed the example of Ford and gave their suppliers the training they needed. Other organizations moved their inspections of materials to the suppliers' premises, so that faults were found before delivery. But in many cases neither of these options was realistic. There was a growing need for some qualification to show a supplier would give consistent quality. This is the aim of the International Standards Organization (ISO) 9000 family of standards.

Several countries developed their own quality standards, such as the British BS5700, and these were brought together in the ISO 9000 family of standards. Now organizations that achieve certain quality standards can apply for ISO 9000 certification. There are actually five separate standards.

(1) ISO 9000 defines quality and quality characteristics and gives a series of quality standards an organization might aim for;

(2) ISO 9001 deals with the whole range of TQM, from initial product design and development, through to standards for testing final products and services;

(3) ISO 9002 deals with quality management during the actual production process, and how this quality can be documented for ISO certification;

(4) ISO 9003 deals with final product inspection and testing;

(5) ISO 9004 says what should be done within the operations to develop and maintain quality, including management responsibilities.

ISO 9000 and 9004 are guides to be used within the organization for setting up quality management programmes. ISO 9001, 9002 and 9003 describe what a quality management system must achieve to be certified.

These ISO standards can be used in almost any organization. They check the quality management procedures designed by the organization, and then check that these procedures are actually being used. But the standards do not guarantee that quality is high, only that it is consistent. A manufacturer of metal bearings, for example, may specify the tolerance on the diameter of a bearing. ISO certification means that production is within this tolerance, but it does not judge whether the tolerance is good enough for any intended use. For this reason, ISO standards are one part of overall quality management. Organizations that are leaders in quality management might apply for one of the prestigious awards in the area, like the Deming award in Japan, the Malcolm Baldridge award in the United States, or the Swedish Quality Prize.

ISO certification gives an organization a competitive advantage. More importantly in the long term, a growing number of organizations – particularly those who already have certification themselves – will only deal with suppliers who have certification. It must become increasingly difficult for an organization that is not certified to compete.

In practical terms, an organization needs seven steps to implement TQM.

(1) *Get top management commitment* Managers have control of the organization, and they must be convinced that TQM is not another management fad, but a way of thinking that really improves performance.

(2) *Find out what customers want* This goes beyond simply asking for their opinions, and gets them involved in the process, perhaps discussing designs in focus groups.

(3) *Design products with quality in mind* The aim is for products that meet or exceed customer expectations.

(4) *Design the production process with quality in mind* Quality must be considered at all points in the process so that high quality products can be made.

(5) *Build teams of empowered employees* Recognize that employees really are an organization's most valuable asset and make sure they are trained, motivated and able to produce high quality products.

(6) *Keep track of results* Measure progress, use benchmarks to compare performance with other organizations, and strive for continual improvements.

(7) *Extend these ideas to suppliers and distributors.*

These stages may seem straightforward, but they need a considerable effort. Implementing TQM might take five or more years of continuous effort, so it is not surprising that many organizations fail somewhere on this road.

Although we have concentrated on the benefits of TQM, there are disadvantages. The most important of these is the time and commitment needed by everyone in the organization. You might think that this limits the use of TQM to larger companies, but the principles can be used almost anywhere. There is certainly a wide range of organizations that have found the benefits of high quality far outweigh the costs.

Review questions

5.8   What is the difference between quality control and quality management?

5.9   The best way to ensure the quality of a product is to have a lot of inspections to find faults. Do you think this is true?

5.10 TQM means that quality is totally controlled by production departments. Do you agree with this?

5.11 What is meant by 'quality at source'?

5.12 What is a quality circle?

5.13 What are the benefits of TQM?

ce Case example – Standard Aero

This example shows how TQM was used to great advantage in a service company.

Standard Aero Ltd is an engine repair company. When Bob Hamaberg became its president in 1988, the company was very inefficient and heavily dependent on government contracts. By 1991 Hamaberg realized that Standard Aero had to change the way it worked if it was going to survive.

Hamaberg recognized the importance of quality, and knew that Standard Aero did not give a high quality service. So he decided to introduce TQM. For this he chose a team of nine members from various departments. The team decided that TQM should be gradually phased in to the organization, and started with the T56 Allison turboprop engine line. The team's first job was to find out what customers really wanted. They spent two months and £50,000 doing this. To their surprise, customers' major concerns were not cost and quality, but lead times and ease of doing business. Standard Aero decided that it wanted to be twice as good as the perceived best company in the industry, so it set a target of overhauling a T56 in 15 days compared to the industry average of 75 days and the industry best of 35 days.

The team simplified and improved the engine overhauling process. They studied the process, critically analysed it and improved it by cutting 93% of non-chargeable steps and 80% of the distance travelled. They divided the line into eight cells with 20 workers each. These workers spent dozens of hours learning team-building and having training in everything from statistics to running a lathe. As a result the process was reduced from 213 steps to 51.

When Standard Aero bid for a $10 million contract to overhaul some of the gearboxes for the US military, they were 50% below the competition with a much shorter delivery date. The Pentagon would not believe the bid, so they sent a team of 13 senior officers to inspect the company. The team liked what they saw and Standard Aero was awarded the contract. Hamaberg firmly believes they only won because of TQM.

Quality in services

Many products have some specific features which can be measured to judge their quality. We can measure the weight of a sack of coal, or the volume in a bottle of detergent. It is relatively simple to make sure each unit satisfies this measure of quality – but the overall quality of the product still relies on subjective judgements. How clean, for example, is the coal or how pleasantly does the detergent smell?

Even services have some measurable attributes, such as the proportion of trains that arrive on time, or the time it takes to process a mortgage application. The quality of service offered by a bank will include both measures – such as ratio of loans to deposits, interest rates, charges, total deposits – and attributes which can not be measured – such as how secure any investment is, how courteously customers are treated, how competently transactions are processed, how well the offices are decorated, and so on. The problem is that services do not have as many measurable attributes as goods. This means that their quality is largely a matter of opinion. It is difficult to measure the quality of a haircut, but people generally know when they get a bad one. Similarly, restaurants rely on their reputation to attract customers, but it is impossible to measure the quality of their products – how could you measure the taste of a meal, or compare the quality of a waiter who smiles as you approach with one who scowls?

In general, the quality of a service is judged by looking at:

- its reliability
- availability
- responsiveness to customer needs
- competence of staff
- courtesy
- understanding customer requirements
- credibility
- security
- comfort of surroundings for customers
- communication between participants
- associated goods provided with the service.

But how can an organization see if it is meeting customer expectations in these areas? The usual way is to ask customers a series of questions after they have received the service. You often see this in airlines or fast food restaurants. Customers are handed a questionnaire as they are about to leave and asked to evaluate a series of features of the service by giving each a score between 1 (for excellent) through 3 (for average) to 5 (for very poor). The response to these questionnaires shows how closely customer expectations are being met, and what areas need improvement.

A clear result from such surveys, is that training is particularly important for people who come into direct contact with their customers. These people need good personal skills, and these can be improved by training.

we Worked example

A university is trying to measure the quality of teaching in one of its faculties. How can it do this?

Solution

Some aspects of teaching can be measured, so data can be collected on the number of students taught, lectures, tutorials, seminars, and so on given by each faculty member. Judgements about the quality of teaching can be made by the customers who are attending classes. The obvious way of judging teaching is to give each student a questionnaire to complete at the end of courses. This might ask about:

- course content (how relevant it was, how useful, how it fitted in with other courses);
- how good the teaching was (were classes interesting, did the teachers explain things well, how were questions answered);
- teachers' attitudes (how enthusiastic they were, did they encourage discussion, how did they mark exercises);
- how teachers got on with students (how interested they were, how courteous, did they have a sense of humour);
- how the course matched expectations (were the course contents as expected, was the approach to the subject useful, was any important material missing, and so on).

By asking for answers on a five point scale, the responses of entire class can be averaged, and used as a measure of quality.

Customers are particularly sensitive to the quality of services. Many services are tailored to individual needs and are expensive – you can, for example, buy a computer relatively cheaply but it is very expensive to get one repaired. These high costs raise customer expectations, but these expectations are often not met. The problem is the difficulty of defining a good service – which many people use as an excuse for giving a poor one. We can also examine goods before buying them, but services can only be judged after they have been paid for. To be fair, there are a number of reasons why the quality of services may be lower than goods. These include:

- Services are intangible, so it is difficult to define and measure satisfactory quality.

- Services depend on personal contact between customer and supplier. This gives more opportunity for disagreements and ideas about poor service.

- People working in services often see them as short-term jobs. This leads to poor training and lack of dedication.

- Customer expectation is lower for services than goods (based largely on experience).

- Each product is largely customized to individual requirements, so there are more opportunities for errors.

- The spontaneous supply of products means there is less chance to practise and correct mistakes.

ce Case example – Grand & Toy

Grand & Toy (G&T) was founded in 1882 and now runs 68 shops which sell office supplies, business furniture and printed forms. They provide a service package that consists of four parts – goods supplied, facilities, explicit services and implicit services. The quality of service offered by G&T can be judged by their performance in these four areas.

(1) *Goods*, which are bought by customers. G&T sell a range of over 3000 items in each shop, but 10,000 items are kept in central stores and can be delivered within a short time. The company only keep high quality goods in stock, and low quality or damaged goods are immediately discarded. If a customer wants something that is not available, the staff will trace the product and arrange its delivery as soon as possible. This also helps with all aspects of stock control.

(2) *Facilities*, the shops and warehouses. The shops are conveniently located in city centres, often within shopping malls. They are well designed and laid out in a standard pattern with no annoying lights, sights or noises. To get customers' attention, three display units are put at the front with special offers, and all shelves are obviously well stocked. The shops are clean, well-carpeted, attractive, and welcoming, with cleaning done continuously by all staff during quiet periods.

(3) *Explicit services*, benefits that are readily observable and define the essential features of the service. G&T believes that its staff are the most important part of their service package. All staff have on-the-job training, weekly meetings to discuss products, concerns and plans, and

are encouraged to study product development, sales techniques, and so on. G&T aims for a consistent service across its shops, and part of the training describes the service that staff must give to customers. This goes beyond selling, and includes giving information and advice. Staff times are scheduled so that no customer has long to wait for service, even at busy times.

(4)   *Implicit services*, benefits which are not readily observable but which enhance the customer's experience. G&T attract the best employees by offering competitive wages, benefits, opportunities for promotion and an attractive work place. Because of their good conditions the staff are friendly to customers, proud of their company and enthusiastic about their job. Surveys have found a very high level of customer satisfaction with the staff and shops in general.

Review questions

5.14   Measuring the quality of services is totally different from measuring the quality of goods. Do you think this is true?

5.15   How might you measure the quality of a hairdresser?

Chapter review

- Organizations must supply the kind of products that their customers want. As customers are no longer willing to accept poor quality products, organizations must make sure their products have consistently high quality. This is the function of quality management.

- It is difficult to give a general definition of quality. One view says it is the ability to meet customer expectations; a more specific view judges quality by a number of factors and viewpoints.

- The total cost of quality is found by adding the design, appraisal, internal failure and external failure costs. These last two can be particularly high, but decline with increasing quality. This suggests that organizations should aim at perfect quality in their products.

- Quality affects every part of an organization. So quality management has moved away from its traditional role of quality control – doing the inspections to find defects – to a wider role including all aspects of quality.

- Total Quality Management focuses the effort of the entire organization on quality. It encourages features like quality at source and quality circles. Deming has described a number of features needed by organizations using TQM.

- Assuring the quality of services can be particularly difficult, as it relies on opinions about customer satisfaction.

Key terms

appraisal cost   123
design costs   122
external and internal failure
   cost   123–4
ISO 9000   135
job enlargement   130
quality   115

quality at source   130
quality circles   131
quality control   128
quality management   116
Total Quality
   Management   128
zero defects   127

CS Case study – The Great Bake Cake Company

The Great Bake Cake Company is a large supplier of cakes to supermarkets, specialized bakeries, restaurants and company canteens. They provide a range of products that taste reasonably good for their low price.

Two years ago the company narrowly avoided prosecution by the local Consumer Protection Department, when a customer reported a rusty nail in one of their cakes. The company was not prosecuted because of their good past record and their rigorous quality control procedures. Company sales fell for a while after this incident, but recovered within a year, and have been rising ever since.

Quality was checked by the Quality Control Department, which did a series of inspections and tests. Ingredients were brought from national suppliers and caused almost no concern. Nevertheless, they were given a visual inspection before being mixed into batches. There were further tests on each batch after mixing, before baking, after baking, after finishing and after packing. Most of these tests concerned taste and appearance, and made sure the baking staff continued to make a consistent, reasonable product.

Recently the company has been having some difficulties. In particular, the number of customer complaints has risen by 15% over the past two years, and there are now around 150 complaints per million sales. Most of these complain about taste, but occasionally there are foreign bodies or other serious faults. The company responded by employing more inspectors and increasing the rigour of its inspection, so that quality control costs rose by 20%. It was becoming a joke with the baking staff that they now had an inspector constantly looking over each shoulder.

As an experiment, managers of the company introduced 20 faults into cakes as they were passing through the process to see if the quality control inspectors would find them. Only 12 of these were spotted before they were due to leave the bakery.

Questions

The management of The Great Bake Cake Company is understandably concerned about its performance and is looking for advice.

● What would you suggest?

● Could they introduce TQM?

● How should they set about this?

Problems

5.1 A company has had the following costs over the past six years. Describe what has been happening.

Year	1	2	3	4	5	6
Sales value (£'000s)	623	625	626	635	677	810
Costs (£'000s)						
Design	6	8	18	24	37	43
Appraisal	15	17	22	37	45	64
Internal failure	91	77	32	36	17	10
External failure	105	101	83	51	27	16

Discussion questions

5.1 What are the possible consequences of poor quality products? Is it ever really possible to make products of perfect quality?

5.2 How would you explain the shape of the graphs in Figure 5.1.

5.3 Do you think it is reasonable for organizations to aim for perfect quality? Are there some cases where the costs of achieving this are too high?

5.4 Explain, giving suitable examples, the difference between designed quality and achieved quality. Which of these is more important?

5.5 Is Deming's the only view of quality management?

5.6   It is generally felt that the quality of services now causes more concerns than the quality of goods. Why do you think this is? What can be done to alter this?

5.7   Describe the development of quality in a specific product you are familiar with, such as computers, education, health, cars, houses.

5.8   What incentive is there for a monopoly to improve the quality of its product?

5.9   Honda believes that customer satisfaction is the ultimate goal of the company, and to achieve this they aim for exceptional products. They believe they can not make exceptional products by using the same manufacturing processes as other companies, so they design and build almost all their own manufacturing systems. These manufacturing systems are designed for two customers:

(1)   external customers who buy Honda products;
(2)   internal customers who use the systems to make these products.

These two groups have different views and consider different factors important:

(1)   *external customers consider the final products*: they look at attractiveness, quality, price, delivery.
(2)   *internal users consider use of the system*: they look at safety, reliability, the environment, ease of maintenance, types of communications, good service.

Do other organizations have to work with several customers? Could there be conflicts between the two customers? Do you think Honda's approach to quality is good?

5.10 Pinefresh Sprays make a range of products in spray cans, including hair sprays, deodorants and room fresheners. They recently appointed John Kantz as Director of Quality Assurance, with a clear mandate to do whatever is necessary to improve the company's quality. John spent the first few weeks talking to people and trying to get to know the real quality problems at the company.

John found a basic problem was the production department's main aim of meeting production quotas at almost any price. This could be seen with a problem of over-pressurized cans. An inspector had rejected some sprays that were over-filled and asked the operator to set them aside until he could find the cause of the problem. The factory supervisor was concerned about his schedule and told an operator to release a little pressure from the cans and ship them out.

The quality inspector tried to find the cause of the problem and found that the pressure gauge on the filling machine was not working properly, the spray can nozzles delivered by a regular supplier were not up to standard, and the machine operator was new and not fully trained.

What are the quality problems at Pinefresh? Do you think the supervisor was right to ship the defective cans? What should John do to solve the immediate quality problems? What should he do in the long term?

Selected references

Clemmer J. (1992). *Firing on All Cylinders*. Homewood, Ill.: Business One Irwin.

Crosby P.B. (1979). *Quality is Free*. New York: New American Library.

Deming W.E. (1986). *Out of the Crisis*. Cambridge: MIT Press.

Dobyns L. and Crawtrot-Mason C. (1991). *Quality or Else*. Boston: Houghton Mifflin.

Gitlow H.S. (1990). *Planning for Quality, Productivity and Competitive Position*. Homewood, Ill.: Dow Jones-Irwin.

Gitlow H.S., Gitlow S.J., Oppenheim A. and Oppenheim R. (1989). *Tools and Methods for the Improvement of Quality*. Homewood, Ill.: Richard Irwin.

Hutchins D.C. (1992). *Achieve Total Quality*. Cambridge: Director Books.

Ishikawa K. (1985). *What is Total Quality Control?* Englewood Cliffs, NJ: Prentice-Hall.

Juran J.M. (1988). *Juran on Planning for Quality*. New York: Free Press.

Kinlaw D.C. (1992). *Continuous Improvement and Measurement for Total Quality*. San Diego: Pfeiffer.

Munro-Faure L. and Munro-Faure M. (1992). *Implementing Total Quality Management*. London: Pitman.

Oakland J.S. (1989). *Total Quality Management*. New York: Nichols.

Oakland J.S. (1992). *Total Quality Management* (2nd edn). London: Heinemann.

Peters T.J. and Waterman R.H. (1982). *In Search of Excellence*. New York: Warner Books.

Saylar J.H. (1992). *Total Quality Management*. New York: McGraw-Hill.

Townsend P.L. (1992). *Quality in Action*. New York: John Wiley.

6

Forecasting product demand

Contents

Objectives

After reading this chapter you should be able to:

- appreciate the importance of forecasting
- list different methods of forecasting
- describe a variety of judgemental forecasting methods
- define 'time series' and understand their importance
- calculate errors in forecasts
- describe the characteristics of causal forecasts
- find lines of best fit using linear regression
- describe the characteristics of projective forecasting
- forecast using actual averages, moving averages and exponential smoothing
- forecast series with seasonality and trend

ce Case example – Jim Brown of Midway Construction

Jim Brown was in a bad mood. Business had been slack for the past few months, and he now had too many workers on his construction sites. He had just fired 25 people. Unless things picked up, he would have to fire another 40 people before the end of the month.

'This is crazy!', Jim thought. 'This is the sixth time in two years that I've laid-off good, reliable workers. What usually happens next is that business picks-up. Then I desperately look for people with the right skills that I can hire. If I could forecast the amount of work some time in advance, I could smooth the workload and not have to go through these peaks and troughs.'

Jim is right. If he did some forecasting he could plan his workload properly. He could smooth the work and avoid his current 'hire and fire' approach.

Question

● What benefits could Jim get from forecasting his future workload?

Importance of forecasting

Forecasts are needed for almost every management decision. All decisions become effective at some point in the future, so they should be based on circumstances not as they are at present, but as they will be when the decisions become effective. When British Aerospace plans its production, it does not make enough aeroplanes to meet current demand, but enough to meet forecast demand when the planes are ready for sale. In the same way, every decision in an organization must be based on forecasts of future conditions. You can see from this that forecasting is one of the most important jobs that managers do.

Forecasts are used throughout an organization – so they should certainly not be prepared by an isolated group of specialists. Neither should you think that forecasting is a job that is done once and is then finished. Forecasting is continuous and there is no stage at which it is ever finished. As time moves on, actual circumstances are compared with forecasts, original forecasts are updated, plans are modified, decisions are revised, and so on. This process is shown in Figure 6.1.

In this chapter we shall generally talk about 'demand' being forecast, but this is just for convenience. You can think of it as a general term that is not meant to limit the range of things actually being forecast.

We can start by looking at the different methods of forecasting. It would be useful to say that 'much work has been done on forecasting and the best method is ...'. Unfortunately, we cannot do this. Because of the different types

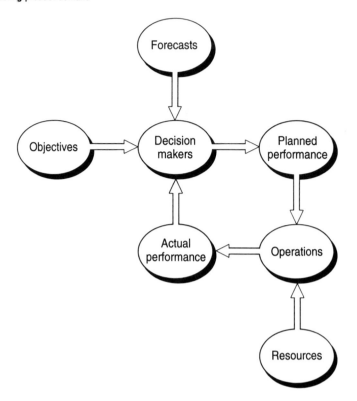

Figure 6.1 The position of forecasting in decisions.

of things to be forecast, and the different situations in which forecasts are needed, there is no single method that is always best. The only thing we can do is look at a variety of methods and see the circumstances in which each can be used.

Forecasting methods can be classified in several ways. The first concerns the time in the future covered by forecasts.

- **Long-term forecasts** look ahead several years – the time typically needed to build a new plant.

- **Medium-term forecasts** look ahead between three months and two years – the time typically needed to replace an old product by a new one.

- **Short-term forecasts** cover the next few weeks – describing the continuing demand for a product.

You can see a clear link here with the different levels of decision making described in Chapter 3. Generally, long-term forecasts are concerned with strategic decisions, medium-term forecasts with tactical decisions, and short-term forecasts with operational decisions.

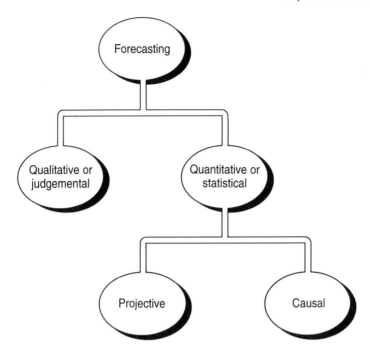

Figure 6.2 Qualitative and quantitative forecasting methods.

The time horizon affects the choice of forecasting method because of the availability of historical data, how relevant this will be for the future, the time available to make the forecast, the cost involved, the seriousness of any errors, the effort considered worthwhile, and so on.

Another classification of forecasting methods shows the difference between qualitative and quantitative approaches (as shown in Figure 6.2).

If an organization is already making a product it will have records of past demand, and will know the factors that affect this. Then it can use a quantitative method for forecasting future demand. There are two ways of doing this:

(1)   *Projective methods* which look at the pattern of past demand and extend this into the future. If demand in the last four weeks has been 10, 20, 30 and 40, we can project this pattern into the future and suggest that demand in the next week will be around 50.

(2)   *Causal methods* which analyse the effects of outside influences and use these to forecast. The productivity of a factory might depend on the bonus rates paid to employees. Then it would be more reliable to use the planned bonus rate to forecast productivity than to project figures achieved in the past few months.

Both of these approaches rely on accurate, numerical data. Suppose, though, that an organization is introducing an entirely new product. There are

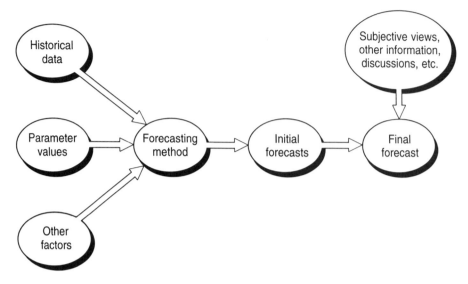

Figure 6.3 Use of managers' views to update forecasts.

obviously no past demand figures the organization can project into the future, and it does not know what outside influences affect demand. This means that a quantitative method can not be used – so the only alternative is a qualitative method. Such methods are generally called **judgemental**, and they rely on subjective views and opinions.

This classification of methods does not mean that each must be used in isolation. Managers should look at all available information and then make the decision they feel best. This means that any forecasts should have a subjective review before they are used (see Figure 6.3).

ce Case example – Euro Disney

Euro Disney runs the major theme park outside Paris. In the early years after it opened, the park had continuous financial problems. By March 1994 it faced permanent closure. At this time its owners, 61 banks and other investors, agreed a rescue package valued at Fr 13 billion.

The basic problem was that Euro Disney's income was not meeting its costs. The capacity of the park, the number of people employed, the number of rides, and almost every other aspect of operations were based on forecasts of the number of visitors. There were no other Disney parks in Europe, so these forecasts were based largely on US experiences. Unfortunately, later results showed that there were significant differences in Europe.

In 1993 Euro Disney attracted nearly 10 million visitors. Despite the considerable effort put into forecasting, this was 13% fewer than expected. At the same time, each visitor spent at least 10% less than forecast. The result was an annual loss of Fr 5.34 billion, which grew worse when 1994 saw less than 9 million visitors.

So all decisions about Euro Disney were based on faulty forecasts. When actual performance became known, the theme park had to make significant changes to operations. They tried to attract more visitors, by cutting prices in the park, reducing hotel costs, seasonal pricing in the Autumn and Winter when only 30% of visitors came, special deals for pensioners, school groups and 'kids-free' packages, more emphasis on short packages, and more promotion in Britain. Several other measures were agreed with Walt Disney, who own 49% of Euro Disney. These include Fr 1.1 billion of extra credit, selling Fr 1.4 billion of assets to Walt Disney and leasing them back at favourable terms, waiving of royalties on entry fees, food and merchandise, and suspending management fees. Other plans included greater cost control, a new shopping mall, multiplex cinema, new restaurants, more convention facilities, high-speed rail link and improved access. These measures aimed at making the park financially secure by 1997.

Questions

● Could Euro Disney have done anything to get better forecasts for their park?

● Do you know of other examples of errors in forecasts having major consequences?

Review questions

6.1 Why is forecasting used in operations management?

6.2 Forecasting is a specialized function that uses mathematical techniques to project historical data. Do you think this is true?

6.3 List three different approaches to forecasting.

Judgemental forecasting

Judgemental forecasting methods are subjective views, often based on the opinions of experts. They are sometimes called **qualitative** or **subjective** forecasts.

Suppose a company like Zenecca is about to market an entirely new product, or a medical team in Papworth Hospital is considering a new organ transplant, or the board of directors of BP is looking at plans for 25 years in the future. There is no relevant historical data they can use for a quantitative forecast. Sometimes there is a complete absence of data, and at other times the data available is unreliable or irrelevant to the future. As quantitative forecasts can not be used, a judgemental method is the only alternative. Five widely used methods are:

(1)   personal insight

(2)   panel consensus

(3)   market surveys

(4)   historical analogy

(5)   Delphi method.

Personal insight

This uses a single person who is familiar with the situation to produce a forecast based on their own judgement. This is the most widely used forecasting method – and is the one that managers should try to avoid. It relies entirely on one person's judgement, as well as their opinions, prejudices and ignorance. It can give good forecasts – but often gives very bad ones. The major weakness of this method is its unreliability.

Comparisons of forecasting methods clearly show that someone who is familiar with a situation, using experience and subjective opinions to forecast, will consistently produce **worse** forecasts than someone who knows nothing about the situation but uses a more formal method.

Panel consensus

One person can easily make a mistake, but collecting together a group of people should give a consensus that is more reliable. If there is no secrecy and the panel talk freely and openly, a genuine consensus may be found. On the other hand, there may be difficulties in combining the views of different people when a consensus can not be found.

Although it is more reliable than one person's insight, panel consensus still has the major weakness that everybody, even experts, can make mistakes. There are also problems of group working, where 'he who shouts loudest gets his way', everyone tries to please the boss, some people do not speak well in groups, and so on. Overall, panel consensus is an improvement on personal insight, but you should be cautious about the results from either method.

Market surveys

Sometimes, even groups of experts do not have enough knowledge to give a reasonable forecast. This happens, for example, with the launch of a new product. Experts can give their views, but more useful information can be collected from potential customers. Market surveys collect data from a sample of customers, analyse their views and make inferences about the population at large.

Market surveys can give useful information but they tend to be expensive and time consuming. They are also prone to errors as they rely on:

- a sample of customers that accurately represents the population

- useful, unbiased questions

- fair and honest answers

- reliable analyses of the answers

- valid conclusions drawn from the analyses.

Historical analogy

Chapter 4 described the life-cycle of a product as having periods of introduction, growth, maturity, decline and withdrawal. If an organization is introducing a new product, it might have a similar product that was launched recently, and assume that demand for the new product will follow the same pattern. Suppose, for example, a publisher is selling a new book – it could forecast demand for this book from the actual demand for a similar book it published earlier.

Historical analogy can only be used if a similar product has been introduced fairly recently. In practice, it is often difficult to find such similar products, or to fit the characteristic life-cycle curve.

Delphi method

This is the most formal of the judgemental methods and has a well-defined procedure. A number of experts are contacted by post and each is given a questionnaire to complete. The replies from these questionnaires are analysed and summaries are passed back to the experts. Each expert is then asked to reconsider their original reply in the light of the summarized replies from others. Each reply is anonymous so that undue influences of status and the pressures of face-to-face discussions are avoided. This process of modifying responses in the light of replies made by the rest of the group is repeated several times – usually between three and six. By this time, the range of opinions should be narrow enough to help with decisions.

We can illustrate the Delphi method by an example from off-shore oil fields. Suppose a company wants to know when underwater inspections on platforms will be done entirely by robots rather than divers. A number of experts are contacted to start the Delphi forecast. These experts come from various backgrounds, including divers, technical staff from oil companies, ships' captains, maintenance engineers and robot designers. The overall problem is explained, and each of the experts is asked when they think robots

Table 6.1 Comparison of methods.

| Method | Accuracy in term | | | Cost |
	Short	Medium	Long	
Personal insight	poor	poor	poor	low
Panel consensus	poor to fair	poor to fair	poor	low
Market survey	very good	good	fair	high
Historical analogy	poor	fair to good	fair to good	medium
Delphi method	fair to very good	fair to very good	fair to very good	medium to high

will replace divers. The initial returns probably give a wide range of dates from, say, 1998 to 2050. These are summarized and passed back to the experts, who are asked if they would like to change their answer in the light of other replies. After repeating this several times, views might converge so that 80% of replies give a date between 2005 and 2015. This is close enough to help planning.

Each of these judgemental methods works best in different circumstances. If a quick reply is needed, personal insight is the fastest and cheapest method. If reliable forecasts are needed it may be worth the time and effort of organizing a market survey or Delphi method. A general comparison of methods is shown in Table 6.1.

Review questions

6.4   What are 'judgemental forecasts'?

6.5   List five types of judgemental forecast.

6.6   What are the main problems with judgemental forecasts?

Time series

Quantitative forecasts often look at **time series**, which are series of observations taken at regular intervals. The number of shifts worked each month, daily cost figures, weekly production, and annual sales are examples of time series.

If you have a time series, you should start by drawing a graph of it. This will show any underlying patterns in the data. The three most common patterns in time series are shown in Figure 6.4 as:

(1)   *constant series*   where values stay roughly the same over time, such as annual rainfall;

(2)   *series with a trend*   which either rise or fall steadily, such as the gross national product per capita;

(3)   *seasonal series*   which have cycles, such as weekly sales of soft drinks.

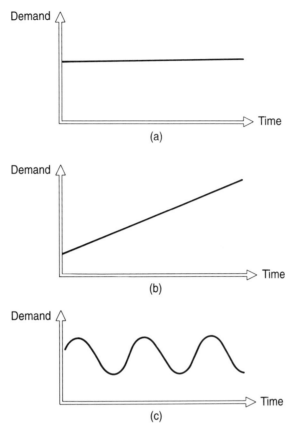

Figure 6.4 Common patterns in time series: (a) constant series; (b) series with trend; (c) seasonal series.

If observations followed such simple patterns there would be no problems with forecasting. Unfortunately, there are almost always differences between actual observations and the underlying pattern. These differences are seen as a random **noise** which is superimposed on the underlying pattern. Then a constant series, for example, does not always have exactly the same value, but is somewhere close. So:

200   205   194   195   208   203   200   193   201   198

is a constant series of 200 with superimposed noise.

Actual value = underlying pattern + random noise

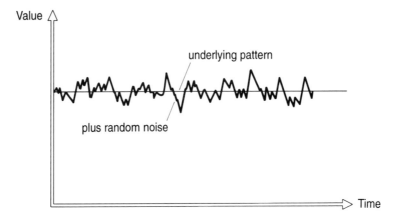

Figure 6.5 Random noise superimposed on an underlying pattern.

The noise is a completely random effect that is caused by many factors, such as variations in demand from customers, hours worked by employees, speed of working, weather conditions, rejection rates at inspections, and so on. It is the noise that makes forecasting difficult. If the noise is relatively small we can get good forecasts – but if there is a lot of noise it hides the underlying pattern and forecasting becomes more difficult (see Figure 6.5).

Because of the noise, there are almost always errors in forecasts. In other words, there is a difference between the forecast and actual values. If we forecast demand in period t to be F_t, and it actually turns out to be D_t, there is an error in our forecast of:

$$E_t = D_t - F_t$$

where:

$\quad t \ = $ time period
$\quad D_t = $ demand in time period t
$\quad F_t \ = $ forecast **for** time t (*not* the forecast made **at** time t)

If this is repeated over a number of periods, n, we can find the average error in each period.

$$\textbf{Mean error} = \frac{\sum E_t}{n} = \frac{\sum (D_t - F_t)}{n}$$

The drawback with the mean error is that positive and negative errors cancel each other, and very poor forecasts can have zero mean error. Look at the following values.

t	1	2	3	4
D_t	100	200	300	400
F_t	0	0	0	1000

The demand pattern is clear, so forecasting should be easy. The forecasts are obviously poor, but if we calculate the mean error it is:

$$(100 + 200 + 300 - 600)/6 = 0$$

This shows that the mean error does not really measure forecast accuracy, but it measures bias. If the mean error has a positive value, the forecast is consistently too low: if it has a negative value, the forecast is consistently too high.

We clearly need an alternative measure of error, and the most useful squares the errors and calculates the mean squared error.

$$\textbf{Mean squared error} = \frac{\sum E_t^2}{n} = \frac{\sum (D_t - F_t)^2}{n}$$

The mean squared error does not have a clear meaning, but it is useful in other ways. We shall meet it again in the next section on linear regression.

we Worked example

The Bayview Hotel makes the following forecasts for rooms needed for a week, and compares these with actual bookings. What are the errors? What do these errors show?

	1	2	3	4	5	6	7
Demand, D_i	20	34	39	35	22	15	11
Forecast, F_i	19	31	43	37	25	16	12

Solution

The error for each week is found from:

$$E_i = D_i - F_i$$

so for the first week:

$$E_1 = D_1 - F_1 = 20 - 19 = 1$$

and so on.

	1	2	3	4	5	6	7
Demand, D_i	20	34	39	35	22	15	11
Forecast, F_i	19	31	43	37	25	16	12
Error, E_i	1	3	-4	-2	-3	-1	-1

Calculating the errors gives:

- mean error $= (1 + 3 - 4 - 2 - 3 - 1 - 1)/7 = -1$

- mean squared error $= (1 + 9 + 16 + 4 + 9 + 1 + 1)/7 = 5.86$

The mean error of -1 shows that the hotel expects one more room to be filled than it actually has. This is reasonably close, but if the mean error were bigger it would mean the hotel brings in more staff than it needs, and it is generally planning for more guests than it actually has. The mean squared error does not have such a specific meaning.

Review questions

6.7 Why do forecasts almost always have errors?

6.8 What is the mean error of a forecast and why is it of limited use?

6.9 How would you compare different forecasting methods?

Causal forecasting

Linear regression

Causal forecasting looks for a cause or relationship that can be used to forecast.

The sales of a product might depend on the price being charged. Then, we can find the relationship between price and sales, and use this to forecast future

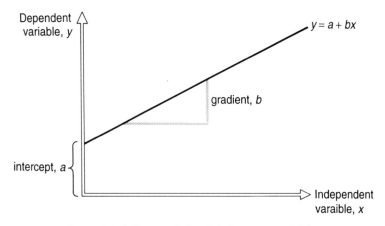

Figure 6.6 A linear relationship between variables.

sales at any particular price. Similar relationships can be found between the speed of a machine and its output, bonus payments and productivity, interest rates and amount of money borrowed, amount of fertilizer used and crop size, and so on. These are examples of true relationships where changes in the first, **independent variable** actually cause changes in the second, **dependent variable**.

We shall illustrate causal forecasting by linear regression. This assumes the dependent variable is linearly related to the independent one, as shown in Figure 6.6.

we Worked example

A factory keeps records of the number of shifts worked each month and the output. If the factory needs 400 units next month, how many shifts should it work?

Month	1	2	3	4	5	6	7	8	9
Shifts worked	50	70	25	55	20	60	40	25	35
Output	352	555	207	508	48	498	310	153	264

Solution

The best thing to do with a set of data like this is to draw a graph. A scatter diagram of shifts worked (the independent variable) and units made (the dependent variable) shows a clear linear relationship (see Figure 6.7).

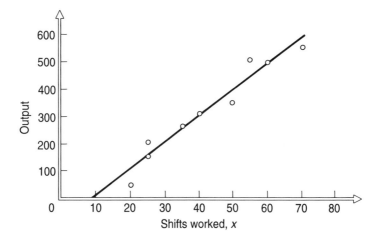

Figure 6.7 Linear relationship in the example.

You can draw by eye a reasonable straight line through the data. This shows that about 50 shifts are needed to make 400 units.

In the worked example above, we drew a scatter diagram, noticed a linear relationship and then drew a line of best fit by eye. This informal approach can work quite well. But we really need a more reliable method that can find the equation of the line of best fit. This means finding values for the constants a and b in the equation:

dependent variable $= a + b \times$ independent variable

or

$$y = a + bx$$

where:
  $x =$ value of independent variable
  $y =$ value of dependent variable
  $a =$ point at which the line crosses the y axis
  $b =$ gradient of the line.

Because of the random noise, even the line of best fit through the data will not be a perfect fit. There is an error in each observation, and we want to find the line that minimizes this error. We saw earlier that simply adding the errors and finding the mean allows positive and negative errors to cancel. To avoid this we will find the line that minimizes the mean squared error. This line is given by the following rather messy-looking equations. You need not worry about these as, in practice, the calculations are always done on a computer.

For linear regression:

$$y = a + bx$$

$$b = \frac{n \sum xy - \sum x \sum y}{n \sum x^2 - (\sum x)^2}$$

$$a = \frac{\sum y}{n} - b \frac{\sum x}{n} = \bar{y} - b\bar{x}$$

where:

  $\bar{x}$ and $\bar{y}$ are the mean values of x and y
  $n =$ the number of observations

we Worked example

A company is about to change the way it inspects one of its products. The company has done experiments with different numbers of inspections, and has found the corresponding numbers of defects.

Inspections	0	1	2	3	4	5	6	7	8	9	10
Defects	92	86	81	72	67	59	53	43	32	24	12

If the company plans to use six inspections, how many defects should it expect? What is the effect of doing 20 inspections?

Solution

The independent variable, x, is the number of inspections and the dependent variable, y, is the corresponding number of defects. The graph (see Figure 6.8) shows a clear linear relationship between these, and we can do the calculations in the following table.

												Totals
x	0	1	2	3	4	5	6	7	8	9	10	$\sum x = 55$
y	92	86	81	72	67	59	53	43	32	24	12	$\sum y = 621$
xy	0	86	162	216	268	295	318	301	256	216	120	$\sum xy = 2238$
x^2	0	1	4	9	16	25	36	49	64	81	100	$\sum x^2 = 385$

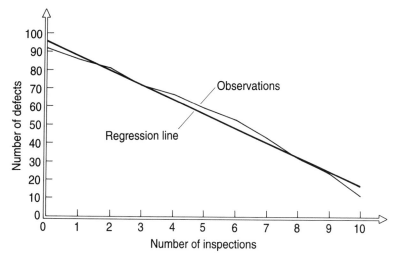

Figure 6.8 Graph of regression from example.

With $n = 11$, substitution gives:

$$b = (n \sum xy - \sum x \sum y)/(n \sum x^2 - \sum x \sum x)$$
$$= (11 \times 2238 - 55 \times 621)/(11 \times 385 - 55 \times 55) = -7.88$$
$$a = (\sum y)/n - b(\sum x)/n$$
$$= 621/11 + 7.88 \times 55/11 = 95.85$$

The line of best fit is:

$$y = 95.85 - 7.88x$$

or

$$\text{Defects} = 95.85 - 7.88 \times \text{Number of inspections}$$

With six inspections the company could forecast $95.85 - 7.88 \times 6 = 48.57$ defects.

With 20 inspections we have to be a bit more careful as substitution gives $95.85 - 7.88 \times 20 = -61.75$. We obviously can not have a negative number of defects, so we simply forecast zero defects.

Coefficient of determination

Now we can calculate the line of best fit through a set of data – but this does not tell us how good the line is. If the errors are small the line is a good fit, but if the errors are large even the best line is not very good. To measure the goodness of fit we use a measure called the **coefficient of determination**.

The coefficient of determination looks at the total variation of independent values from the mean. Some of this variation is explained by the linear relationship – some is unexplained and is random noise. The coefficient of determination is the proportion of the total error that is explained by the linear relationship. It has a value between zero and one. If it is near to 1, most of the variation is explained by the regression and the straight line is a good fit. If the value is near to zero, most of the variation is unexplained and the line is not a good fit.

The easiest way of calculating the coefficient of determination is the very messy looking equation:

$$\text{Coefficient of determination} = \left\{ \frac{n \sum xy - \sum x \sum y}{\sqrt{[n \sum x^2 - (\sum x)^2] \times [n \sum y^2 - (\sum y)^2]}} \right\}^2$$

Again we should say that, in practice, these calculations are always done using a computer.

we Worked example

Calculate the coefficient of determination for the inspection data in the last example.

Solution

Drawing the table of results as before, and adding the values for $\sum y^2$ gives:

												Totals
x	0	1	2	3	4	5	6	7	8	9	10	$\sum x = $ 55
y	92	86	81	72	67	59	53	43	32	24	12	$\sum y = $ 621
xy	0	86	162	216	268	295	318	301	256	216	120	$\sum xy = $ 2238
x^2	0	1	4	9	16	25	36	49	64	81	100	$\sum x^2 = $ 385
y^2	8464	7396	6561	5184	4489	3481	2809	1849	1024	576	144	$\sum y^2 = $ 41,977

We already know the line of best fit through this data is $y = 95.85 - 7.88x$. Now we are seeing how well this line fits the data. The coefficient of determination is calculated as:

$$\text{Coefficient of determination} = \left\{ \frac{n\sum xy - \sum x \sum y}{\sqrt{[n\sum x^2 - (\sum x)^2] \times [n\sum y^2 - (\sum y)^2]}} \right\}^2$$

$$= \left[\frac{11 \times 2238 - 55 \times 621}{\sqrt{(11 \times 385 - 55 \times 55) \times (11 \times 41977 - 621 \times 621)}} \right]^2$$

$$= (-0.9938)^2$$

$$= 0.9877$$

This is very close to 1, so it shows the line is a very good fit. Normally any value for the coefficient of determination above about 0.5 is considered a good fit.

■

Coefficient of correlation

A second useful measure in regression is the coefficient of correlation which asks the question 'are x and y linearly related?'. The coefficients of correlation and determination answer very similar questions, and:

coefficient of determination = (coefficient of correlation)^2

The coefficient of determination is usually called r^2, and the coefficient of correlation is r. This correlation coefficient has a value between $+1$ and -1.

● a value of $r = 1$ shows the two variables have a perfect linear relationship with no noise at all, and as one increases so does the other;

● a low positive value of r shows a weak linear relationship;

● a value of $r = 0$ shows there is no correlation at all between the two variables and no linear relationship;

● a low negative value of r shows a weak linear relationship;

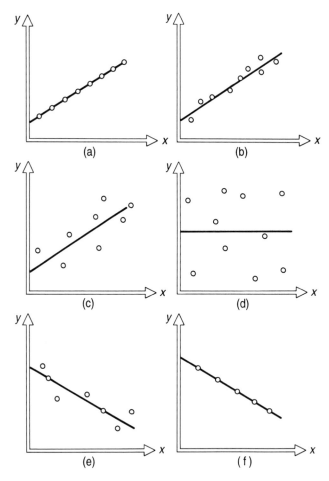

Figure 6.9 Coefficient of correlation: (a) $r = +1$ (perfect positive correlation);
(b) r is close to $+1$ (line is a good fit); (c) r is getting smaller (line is getting worse fit);
(d) $r = 0$ (random points); (e) r is close to -1 (line is a good fit);
(f) $r = -1$ (perfect negative correlation).

- a value of $r = -1$ shows the two variables have a perfect linear relationship and as one increases the other decreases.

With correlation coefficients near to $+1$ or -1 there is a strong linear relationship between the two variables. When r is between 0.7 and -0.7 the coefficient of determination is less than 0.49 and less than half the variation is explained by the regression. So linear regression is only reliable when the coefficient of correlation is between about 0.7 and -0.7 (see Figure 6.9).

we Worked example

The amount of time lost in an intermittent process seems to be related to the number of product changes. Find the coefficients of correlation and determination for the following data, to see if this is true.

Product changes, x	4	17	3	21	10	8	4	9	13	12	2	6	15	8	19
Time lost, y	13	47	24	41	29	33	28	38	46	32	14	22	26	21	50

Solution

Many packages calculate regression, and Figure 6.10 shows the result from a spreadsheet.

Product Changes, x	Time lost, y	Regression value
4	13	21.56
17	47	41.64
3	24	20.01
21	41	47.82
10	29	30.83
8	33	27.74
4	28	21.56
9	38	29.28
13	46	35.46
12	32	33.92
2	14	18.47
6	22	24.65
15	26	38.55
8	21	27.74
19	50	44.73

Regression Output:

Constant	15.38
Std Err of Y Est	7.26
Coeff of Correlation	0.80
Coeff of Determination	0.63
No. of Observations	15.00
Degrees of Freedom	13.00
X Coefficient(s)	1.55
Std Err of Coef.	0.33
Equation	y = 15.376 + 1.545x

Figure 6.10 Spreadsheet showing regression example.

As you can see the:

- line of best fit is $y = 15.38 + 1.55x$
- coefficient of correlation is 0.79
- coefficient of determination is 0.63.

These figures show that line is a good fit to the data. 79% of the variation is explained by the regression, and only 21% is due to random noise.

There are several extensions to the basic linear regression model. One considers multiple linear regression, with a linear relationship between a dependent variable and several independent ones.

$$y = a + b_1 x_1 + b_2 x_2 + b_3 x_3 + b_4 x_4 \ldots$$

The sales of a product might depend on its price, the advertising budget, number of suppliers, local unemployment rate, and so on. The arithmetic in multiple regression is very tedious, and it should only be tackled with a computer. There are many standard packages for this.

Review questions

6.10 What is 'linear regression'?

6.11 What is measured by the coefficient of determination?

Projective forecasting

Causal forecasting is **extrinsic**, as it tries to forecast demand by looking at other variables. Projective forecasting is **intrinsic**, as it examines historical values for demand and uses these to forecast the future. Projective forecasting ignores any external influences and only looks at past values of demand to suggest future values. We will describe four methods of this type:

(1) simple averages

(2) moving averages

(3) exponential smoothing

(4) model for seasonality and trend.

Simple averages

Suppose you are organizing an annual trade show at the National Exhibition Centre and want to know the number of people who will attend. The easiest way of finding this is to look up records for previous years and take an average. If you find the average numbers attending over the past five years, say, you should have a reasonable figure for next year's attendance. This is an example of forecasting using simple averages.

Forecasting with actual averages: $F_{t+1} = \dfrac{\sum D_t}{n}$

where:

n = number of periods of historical data
t = time period
D_t = demand at time t
F_{t+1} = forecast for time $t+1$

we Worked example

Use simple averages to forecast demand for period six of the following time series. How accurate are the forecasts? What are the forecasts for period 24?

Period	t	1	2	3	4	5
Series 1	D_t	98	100	98	104	100
Series 2	D_t	140	66	152	58	84

Solution

- For series 1 $F_6 = \sum D_t/n = 500/5 = 100$

- For series 2 $F_6 = 500/5 = 100$

Although the forecasts are the same, there is clearly less noise in the first series than the second. So you would be more confident in the first forecast and expect the error to be smaller.

Actual averages assume the demand is constant, so the forecasts for period 24 are the same as the forecasts for period for 6 (that is 100).

Using actual averages to forecast demand is easy and can work well for stable demands. But it does not work so well if the demand pattern changes. Older data tends to swamp the latest figures and the forecast does not respond to changes. Suppose demand for an item has been constant at 100 units a week for the past two years. Actual averages would forecast demand for week 105 as 100 units. If the actual demand in week 105 suddenly rises to 200 units, actual averages would give a forecast for week 106 of:

$$F_{106} = (104 \times 100 + 200)/105 = 100.95$$

A rise in demand of 100 gives an increase of 0.95 in the forecast. If demand continues at 200 units a week, the following forecasts are:

$$F_{107} = 101.89 \quad F_{108} = 102.80 \quad F_{109} = 103.70 \quad \text{and so on.}$$

The forecasts are rising but the response is very slow.

Very few time series are stable over long periods, so the restriction that actual averages can only be used for constant series makes it of limited use.

Moving averages

Demand often varies over time, and only a certain amount of historical data is relevant to future forecasts. This means that all observations older than some specified age can be ignored. Then one forecasting method takes the average weekly demand over the past, say, six weeks as a forecast, and any data older than this is ignored. This is the basis of **moving averages**. Instead of taking the average of all historical data, only the latest n periods of data are used.

For moving averages:

F_{t+1} = average of n most recent demands

= latest demand + next latest + ... + n^{th} latest

$$= \frac{D_t + D_{t-1} + \dots D_{t-n+1}}{n}$$

we Worked example

The demand for a product over the past eight months is as follows:

t	1	2	3	4	5	6	7	8
D_t	135	130	125	135	115	80	105	100

The market for this item is unstable, and any data over three months old is unreliable. Use a moving average to forecast demand for the item.

Solution

Only data more recent than three months is useful, so we can use a three month moving average for the forecast. If we look at the situation at the end of month 3, the forecast for month 4 is:

$$F_4 = [D_1 + D_2 + D_3]/3 = (135 + 130 + 125)/3 = 130$$

At the end of month 4, when actual demand is known to be 135, this forecast can be updated to give:

$$F_5 = [D_2 + D_3 + D_4]/3 = (130 + 125 + 135)/3 = 130$$

Similarly,

$$F_6 = [D_3 + D_4 + D_5]/3 = (125 + 135 + 115)/3 = 125$$

$$F_7 = [D_4 + D_5 + D_6]/3 = (135 + 115 + 80)/3 = 110$$

$$F_8 = [D_5 + D_6 + D_7]/3 = (115 + 80 + 105)/3 = 100$$

$$F_9 = [D_6 + D_7 + D_8]/3 = (80 + 105 + 100)/3 = 95$$

In the above example, the forecast is clearly responding to changes, with a high demand moving the forecast upwards, and a low demand moving it downwards. At the same time the forecast is smoothing out variations, so that it does not blindly follow changes in the random noise. The rate at which a forecast responds to changes is called its **sensitivity**.

The sensitivity of moving averages can be adjusted by altering the value of n. A high value for n takes the average of a large number of observations and the forecast is unresponsive – the forecast will smooth out random variations, but may not follow genuine changes in demand. On the other hand, a small value for n will give a responsive forecast that will follow real changes in demand, but may be too sensitive to random fluctuations. A compromise value of n is needed to give reasonable results, and typically a value around six is used.

we Worked example

The following table shows monthly demand for a product over the past year. Use moving averages with $n = 3$, $n = 6$ and $n = 9$ to produce one month ahead forecasts.

Month	1	2	3	4	5	6	7	8	9	10	11	12
Demand	16	14	12	15	18	21	23	24	25	26	37	38

Solution

The earliest forecast we can make using a three period moving average (that is, $n = 3$) is

$$F_4 = [D_1 + D_2 + D_3]/3$$

Similarly the earliest forecast for a six and nine period moving average are F_7 and F_{10} respectively. A computer printout of the results is shown in Figure 6.11.

Plotting a graph of these forecasts, as illustrated in Figure 6.12, shows how the three-month moving average is most sensitive to change and the nine month moving average is least sensitive.

Month	Observation	Moving Average with Period Three	Six	Nine
1	16			
2	14			
3	12			
4	15	14.00		
5	18	13.67		
6	21	15.00		
7	23	18.00	16.00	
8	24	20.67	17.17	
9	25	22.67	18.83	
10	26	24.00	21.00	18.67
11	37	25.00	22.83	19.78
12	38	29.33	26.00	22.33
13		33.67	28.83	25.22

Figure 6.11 Calculation of moving averages.

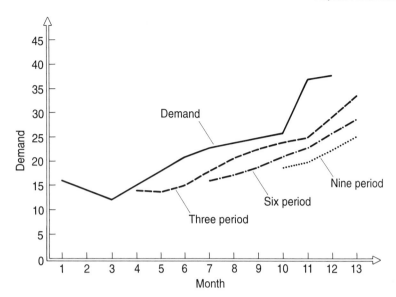

Figure 6.12 Graphs of moving averages.

You can see one useful property of moving averages when they forecast demands that have strong seasonal variations. If n is chosen to equal the number of periods in a season, a moving average will completely deseasonalize the data.

we Worked example

The average share price of J. Oxborough (Holdings) plc over the past 12 months is given below. Use a moving average with 2, 4 and 6 periods to find the one month ahead forecasts of share price.

Month	1	2	3	4	5	6	7	8	9	10	11	12
Price	100	50	20	150	110	55	25	140	95	45	30	145

Solution

This data has a clear seasonal pattern, with a peak every fourth month. Calculating the moving averages gives the results shown in the spreadsheet shown in Figure 6.13. The patterns are shown clearly in Figure 6.14.

Month	Price	Moving Average with Period		
		Two	Four	Six
1	100			
2	50			
3	20	75.00		
4	150	35.00		
5	110	85.00	80.00	
6	55	130.00	82.50	
7	25	82.50	83.75	80.83
8	140	40.00	85.00	68.33
9	95	82.50	82.50	83.33
10	45	117.50	78.75	95.83
11	30	70.00	76.25	78.33
12	145	37.50	77.50	65.00
13		87.50	78.75	80.00

Figure 6.13 Calculation of moving averages.

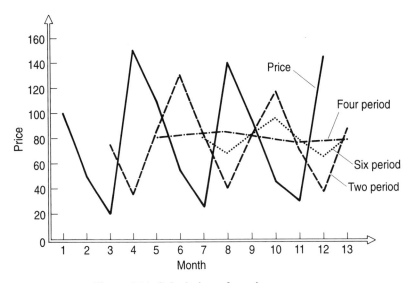

Figure 6.14 Calculation of moving averages.

The moving average with both $n = 2$ and $n = 6$ has responded to the peaks and troughs of demand, but neither has got the timing right – both forecasts lag behind demand. As expected, the two period moving average is much more responsive than the six period one. The most interesting result is the four period moving average that has completely deseasonalized the data.

Although moving averages overcome some of the problems with actual averages, they still have three major defects:

(1)   all historical values are given the same weight;

(2)   the method only works well with constant demand – as we have seen it either removes seasonal factors or gets the timing wrong;

(3)   a large amount of historical data must be stored to allow forecast updates.

These problems are overcome by using exponential smoothing.

Exponential smoothing

Exponential smoothing is the most widely used forecasting method. It is based on the idea that as data gets older it becomes less relevant and should be given less weight. In particular, exponential smoothing gives a declining weight to older data, as shown in Figure 6.15.

We can get this declining weight using only the latest demand figure and the previous forecast. To be specific, a new forecast is calculated from a proportion, α, of the latest demand and a proportion, $1 - \alpha$, of the previous forecast.

For exponential smoothing:
New forecast $= \alpha \times$ latest demand $+ (1 - \alpha) \times$ last forecast
$F_{t+1} = \alpha D_t + (1 - \alpha)F_t$

In this equation, α is the **smoothing constant** which usually takes a value between 0.1 and 0.2.

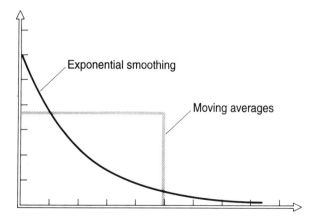

Figure 6.15 Weight given to data.

We can show how exponential smoothing adapts to changes in demand with a simple example. Suppose a forecast was optimistic and suggested a value of 200 for a demand that actually turns out to be 180. Taking a value of $\alpha = 0.2$, the forecast for the next period is:

$$F_{t+1} = \alpha D_t + (1 - \alpha)F_t = 0.2 \times 180 + (1 - 0.2) \times 200 = 196$$

The optimistic forecast is noticed and the value for the next period is adjusted downwards.

we Worked example

Use exponential smoothing with $\alpha = 0.2$ and an initial value of $F_1 = 170$ to give one period ahead forecasts for the following time series:

Month	1	2	3	4	5	6	7	8
Demand	178	180	156	150	162	158	154	132

Solution

We know that $F_1 = 170$ and $\alpha = 0.2$. Substituting these values gives:

$$F_2 = \alpha D_1 + (1 - \alpha)F_1 = 0.2 \times 178 + 0.8 \times 170 = 171.6$$
$$F_3 = \alpha D_2 + (1 - \alpha)F_2 = 0.2 \times 180 + 0.8 \times 171.6 = 173.3$$
$$F_4 = \alpha D_3 + (1 - \alpha)F_3 = 0.2 \times 156 + 0.8 \times 173.3 = 84.2$$

and so on, as shown in the spreadsheet in Figure 6.16.

Month	Demand	Forecast
1	178	170.00
2	180	171.60
3	156	173.28
4	150	169.82
5	162	165.86
6	158	165.09
7	154	163.67
8	132	161.74
9		155.79

Figure 6.16 Forecasts using exponential smoothing.

The value given to the smoothing constant, α, is important in setting the sensitivity of the forecasts. α determines the balance between the last forecast and the latest demand. A high value of α – say 0.3 to 0.35 – gives a responsive forecast: a lower value – say 0.1 to 0.15 – gives a less responsive forecast. A compromise is again needed between having a responsive forecast that might follow random fluctuations, and an unresponsive one that might not follow real patterns.

we Worked example

The following time series has a clear step upwards in demand in month 3. Use an initial forecast of 500 to compare exponential smoothing forecasts with varying values of α.

Period	1	2	3	4	5	6	7	8	9	10	11
Demand	480	500	1500	1450	1550	1500	1480	1520	1500	1490	1500

Solution

Taking values of $\alpha = 0.1$, 0.2, 0.3 and 0.4 gives the results shown in the spreadsheet in Figure 6.17.

Period	Demand	Forecast with varying alpha			
		0.1	0.2	0.3	0.4
1	480	500.00	500.00	500.00	500.00
2	500	498.00	496.00	494.00	492.00
3	1500	498.20	496.80	495.80	495.20
4	1450	598.38	697.44	797.06	897.12
5	1550	683.54	847.95	992.94	1118.27
6	1500	770.19	988.36	1160.06	1290.96
7	1480	843.17	1090.69	1262.04	1374.58
8	1520	906.85	1168.55	1327.43	1416.75
9	1500	968.17	1238.84	1385.20	1458.05
10	1490	1021.35	1291.07	1419.64	1474.83
11	1500	1068.22	1330.86	1440.75	1480.90
12		1111.39	1364.69	1458.52	1488.54

Figure 6.17 Forecasts using exponential smoothing.

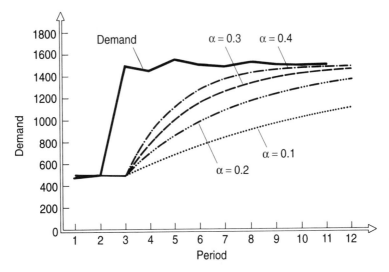

Figure 6.18 Graph of forecasts.

All these forecasts would eventually follow the sharp step and raise forecasts to around 1500. Higher values of α make this adjustment more quickly and give a more responsive forecast, as shown in Figure 6.18.

Model for seasonality and trend

The methods described so far give good results for constant time series, but they must be adjusted to deal with other patterns. In this section we shall develop a model for data that has both **seasonality** and **trend**.

Trend is the amount demand grows between two consecutive periods. If two consecutive periods have demands of 100 and 120, the trend is 20: if two consecutive periods have demands of 100 and 80, the trend is −20. Many types of operations have such trends, such as the long-term decline in beer production, increasing numbers of people getting higher education, and increasing proportion of small car sales.

Seasonality is a regular cyclical pattern, that is not necessarily annual. It is measured by seasonal indices, which are defined as the amounts deseasonalized values must be multiplied by to get seasonal values. Then:

$$\text{Seasonal index} = \frac{\text{Seasonal value}}{\text{Deseasonalized value}}$$

Suppose a newspaper has average daily sales of 1000 copies in a particular area, but this rises to 2000 copies on Saturday and falls to 500 copies on Monday and Tuesday. The deseasonalized value is 1000, the seasonal index for Saturday is $2000/1000 = 2.0$, the seasonal indices for Monday and Tuesday are $500/1000 = 0.5$, and seasonal indices for other days are $1000/1000 = 1.0$. As you can imagine, many products have this kind of seasonal demand, ranging from ice cream to office blocks.

There are several ways of forecasting complex time series, but the easiest is to split observations into separate components, and then forecast each component separately. The final forecast is found by recombining the separate components. To be specific, we shall consider demand to be made up of four components:

(1)   *Underlying value (U)* is the basic demand that must be adjusted for seasonality and trend.

(2)   *Trend (T)* is the long-term direction of a time series. It is typically a steady upward or downward movement.

(3)   *Seasonal index (S)* is the regular variation around the trend. Typically this shows the variation in demand over a year.

(4)   *Noise (N)* is the random noise whose effects can not be explained.

Then the demand is made up of a trend added to the underlying value, and multiplied by the seasonal index, with added noise.

$$D = (U + T)S + N$$

For our calculations it is easier to combine the underlying value and trend into a single figure, T, the underlying trend. As we do not know the noise, N, our forecasts come from:

$$F = TS$$

we Worked example

What value would you forecast for demand if the underlying trend is 20 and seasonal index is 1.25?

Solution

With $T = 20$ and $S = 1.25$, the forecast is:

$$F = TS = 20 \times 1.25 = 25$$

Now for our forecasting we have to:

- deseasonalize the data and find the underlying trend, T

- find the seasonal indices, S

- use the trend and seasonal indices to forecast, $F = TS$.

There are two ways of finding the underlying trend, T, both of which we have already met:

(1)   linear regression with time as the independent variable;

(2)   moving averages with a period equal to the length of a season.

Both of these give good results. If the trend is clearly linear, regression is probably the better approach; if the trend is not clearly linear, moving averages are better. The choice is often a matter of individual preference.

we Worked example

The demand for a product over the past 12 periods is:

Period	1	2	3	4	5	6	7	8	9	10	11	12
Demand	291	320	142	198	389	412	271	305	492	518	363	388

Use linear regression to find the deseasonalized trend. What are the seasonal indices?

Solution

With the values given:

$$n = 12 \quad \textstyle\sum x = 78 \quad \sum y = 4089 \quad \sum x^2 = 650 \quad \sum xy = 29{,}160$$

Substituting these in the standard linear regression equations gives:

$$b = \frac{n\sum(xy) - \sum x \sum y}{n\sum x^2 - (\sum x)^2} = \frac{12 \times 29{,}160 - 78 \times 4089}{12 \times 650 - 78 \times 78}$$

$$= 18.05$$

$$a = (\textstyle\sum y)/n + b(\sum x)/n = 4089/12 - 18.05 \times 78/12$$

$$= 223.41$$

The line of best fit gives the trend as:

$$\text{demand} = 223.41 + 18.05 \times \text{period}$$

The deseasonalized underlying trend for period 1 is $223.41 + 1 \times 18.05 = 241.46$; for period 2 it is $223.41 + 2 \times 18.05 = 259.51$, and so on. These deseasonalized values are shown in the table below.

The seasonal indices are found by dividing the actual demand by the deseasonalized values. Taking a single period, say 4, we have an actual demand of 198. The deseasonalized value from linear regression is 295.61, so the seasonal index $198/295.61 = 0.67$. Repeating this calculation for other periods gives the results shown in Table 6.2.

Now we have a seasonal index calculated for each period, so we can take averages to find more accurate values. We know from the graphs shown in Figure 6.19 that there are four periods in a season, so we need to calculate four seasonal indices.

Taking periods 1, 5 and 9 as the first periods in consecutive seasons gives an average seasonal index for the first period in a season as $(1.21 + 1.24 + 1.28)/3 = 1.24$. Similarly, the average indices for other periods in a season are:

- first period in season $(1.21 + 1.24 + 1.28)/3 = 1.24$

- second period in season $(1.23 + 1.24 + 1.28)/3 = 1.25$

- third period in season $(0.51 + 0.77 + 0.86)/3 = 0.71$

- fourth period in season $(0.67 + 0.83 + 0.88)/3 = 0.79$

Table 6.2

		Linear regression	
Period	Actual demand	Deseasonalized trend value	Seasonal index
1	291	241.46	1.21
2	320	259.51	1.23
3	142	277.56	0.51
4	198	295.61	0.67
5	389	313.66	1.24
6	412	331.71	1.24
7	271	349.76	0.77
8	305	367.81	0.83
9	492	385.86	1.28
10	518	403.91	1.28
11	363	421.96	0.86
12	388	440.01	0.88

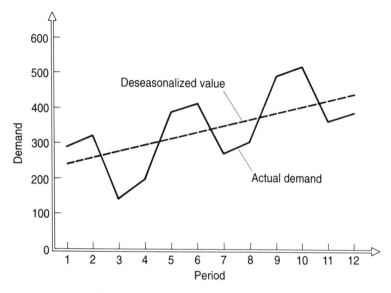

Figure 6.19 Graph of seasonal demand.

Now we know how to find both trend and seasonal index – and can start forecasting. For this we:

●   find the deseasonalized value in the future

●   multiply this by the appropriate seasonal index.

we Worked example

Forecast values for periods 13 to 17 for the time series in the last example.

Solution

The trend was found by linear regression to be:

demand $= 223.41 + 18.05 \times$ period

Now we can substitute 13 to 17 for the period and find the deseasonalized trend for these times. Then we multiply these by the appropriate seasonal index to get the forecasts.

Period 13
> deseasonalized trend $= 223.41 + 18.05 \times 13 = 458.06$
> seasonal index $= 1.24$ (first period in season)
> forecast $= 458.06 \times 1.24 = 568$

Period 14
> deseasonalized trend $= 223.41 + 18.05 \times 14 = 476.11$
> seasonal index $= 1.25$ (second period in season)
> forecast $= 476.11 \times 1.25 = 595$

Period 15
> deseasonalized trend $= 223.41 + 18.05 \times 15 = 494.16$
> seasonal index $= 0.71$ (third period in season)
> forecast $= 494.16 \times 0.71 = 351$

Period 16
> deseasonalized trend $= 223.41 + 18.05 \times 16 = 512.21$
> seasonal index $= 0.79$ (fourth period in season)
> forecast $= 512.21 \times 0.79 = 405$

Period 17
> deseasonalized trend $= 223.41 + 18.05 \times 17 = 530.26$
> seasonal index $= 1.24$ (first period in season)
> forecast $= 530.26 \times 1.24 = 658$

we Worked example

Forecast demand for the next four periods of the following time series.

t	1	2	3	4	5	6	7	8
D	986	1245	902	704	812	1048	706	514

Solution

Looking at the data, you can see that there is a linear trend with a season of four periods. We could confirm this by drawing a graph, but the pattern is already clear. As before, we will use linear regression to deseasonalize the data and then calculate four seasonal indices. A spreadsheet is a convenient way of doing these calculations, and Figure 6.20(a and b) shows one approach.

Period	Demand	Deseasonalised	Seasonal Index	Forecast
1	986	1091.83	0.90	
2	1245	1026.92	1.21	
3	902	962.00	0.94	
4	704	897.08	0.78	
5	812	832.17	0.98	
6	1048	767.25	1.37	
7	706	702.33	1.01	
8	514	637.42	0.81	
9		572.50	0.94	538.15
10		507.58	1.29	654.78
11		442.67	0.97	429.39
12		377.75	0.8	302.20

(a)

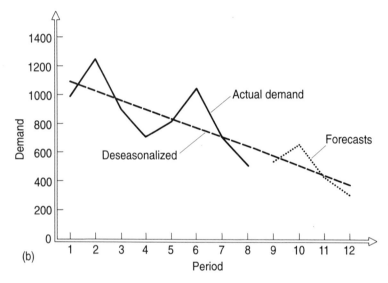

(b)

Figure 6.20 (a) spreadsheet of calculations; (b) graph of demand values.

This finds:

- linear regression equation: $y = 1156.75 - 64.92t$
- average seasonal indices: 0.94, 1.29, 0.97 and 0.80

Then the forecast for period 9 is:

$$(1156.75 - 64.92 \times 9) \times 0.94 = 538$$

Similarly, the forecasts for periods 10, 11 and 12 are:

$$(1156.75 - 64.92 \times 10) \times 1.29 = 654$$
$$(1156.75 - 64.92 \times 11) \times 0.97 = 430$$
$$(1156.75 - 64.92 \times 12) \times 0.80 = 301$$

ce Case example – Generating electricity

Although the principles of forecasting are simple, real circumstances are often complicated and forecasting becomes quite difficult. This case gives an example of how complicated forecasting can be in practice.

One of the most difficult problems of forecasting is the demand for electricity. Electricity can not be stored – except in very small quantities using batteries – so all demand must be exactly matched by the supply from generators in power stations. Shortages of electricity lead to power cuts, which are not accepted by consumers, but excess capacity wastes expensive resources.

The long-term demand for electricity is expected to rise steadily. So enough power stations must be built to meet this long-term demand. Planning and building a nuclear power station can take 20 years and cost billions of pounds. Conventional stations, particularly gas fired ones, can be built faster and cheaper, but they are still based on forecast demand a decade or more in the future.

In the shorter term, demand for electricity follows an annual cycle: generally, demand is heavier in winter when more heating systems are switched on. There may also be short irregular periods when demand is particularly high, perhaps during very cold periods. In addition, there are cycles during the week, with lower demand at the weekends when industry is not working so intensely. On top of this are cycles during the day, with lighter demand during the night when most of us are asleep. Finally, there are irregular peaks during the day, often said to correspond to breaks in television programmes, when people turn on their electric kettles for tea.

Power stations need 'warming up' before they can start supplying electricity. So a stable demand would make operations much easier to manage. Electricity suppliers try to stabilize demand by giving off-peak price incentives, but these do not solve the problems of variable demand. In practice, they must still forecast demands with long-term trends, annual cycles, periods with changes, weekly cycles, daily cycles and short-term fluctuations. Electricity generators must then match their supply to this ever-changing demand from the cheapest possible sources.

ce Case example – McGraw, Finch and Happendon

This example gives a view of the way to plan forecasts, and some common mistakes.

Colin Fairweather has retired as Senior Partner in the Management Consultancy firm of McGraw, Finch and Happendon. Before he left, he collected some ideas in a series of notes for his future replacements. A lot of his work had involved forecasting, and he wrote the following guidelines.

How to do a forecast

(1) Clearly define the purpose of the forecast. This should say what you are trying to forecast, why, how you will use the forecast, when you will need the forecast, how detailed it should be, and so on.

(2) Say what time horizon the forecast must cover – perhaps forecasting demand for the next six months or two years.

(3) Choose a suitable forecasting method – preferably quantitative and often exponential smoothing. This choice will depend on many things, but the availability of historical data is one of the most important.

(4) Collect any historical data needed for your model – and test both the data and the model.

(5) Implement the forecasts and track how good they are over time by comparing the forecast with actual demand. If the errors are too large, change the method or parameters used.

What goes wrong with forecasts

(1) Forecasters do not involve other people. Remember that a good forecast is not just playing with numbers, but depends on many internal and external factors. It is always best to involve knowledgeable people in the forecasting process.

(2) People can have too high expectations of a forecast. Warn them about possible errors, so that if the forecast turns out to be wrong they will not get disillusioned.

(3) Forecasts often give too much detail. This typically happens when demand is forecast for individual items, when it would make more sense to forecast for groups of items.

(4) Always recognize different people's needs. Sales people, for example, often like forecasts to be optimistic, while finance people prefer a more pessimistic view.

Review questions

6.12 Why are actual averages of limited use for forecasting?

6.13 How can moving average forecasts be made more responsive?

6.14 How can data be deseasonalized using moving averages?

6.15   Why is the forecasting method called 'exponential smoothing'?

6.16   How can you make exponential smoothing forecasts more sensitive?

6.17   What is a seasonal index?

Chapter review

- All decisions become effective at some point in the future. This means that managers must make decisions that are not based on present circumstances, but on circumstances as they will be when the decisions become effective. These circumstances must be forecast. So forecasting is an important function in all organizations.

- Despite its importance, progress in many areas of forecasting has been limited. There are many different methods of forecasting, each of which is best in different circumstances.

- There are three basic approaches to forecasting; judgemental, causal and projective.

- When there is no relevant quantitative data, judgemental or qualitative methods must be used. These collect opinions from groups of experts – and range from personal insight to the more formal Delphi method.

- Most quantitative forecasts are concerned with time series, where demand is measured at regular intervals of time. Demand can usually be described by an underlying pattern with a superimposed random noise. This noise can not be forecast and is the reason why forecasts almost always contain errors.

- Causal forecasts looks for relationships between variables. These methods were illustrated by linear regression, which draws the line of best fit through a set of data.

- Projective forecasts look at the patterns in historical data and project these into the future. There are many ways of doing this, and we considered simple averages, moving averages, exponential smoothing and a model for seasonality and trend.

Key terms

actual value   155
causal forecast   158
coefficient of
   correlation   163

coefficient of
   determination   162
Delphi method   153
exponential smoothing   173

CS Case study – Electrotime Manufacturing

Electrotime is a major manufacturer of electronic timers. Its best-selling products are a range of timers used in electrical equipment like washing machines, tumble driers, central heating controls, street lights, radio clocks, and so on. The company also makes more accurate timers that are used at sporting events, and can record times to an accuracy of a thousandth of a second. At the most expensive end of its range are specialized timers, typically used in scientific instruments, which are accurate to at least a hundred thousandth of a second.

Electrotime is part of a diversified engineering group that has manufacturing plants in 37 countries around the world, and sells in over 120 countries. The parent company controls Electrotime fairly loosely and leaves most operating decisions to local managers.

Many of Electrotime's employees are specialized engineers. These are often promoted to management positions, following the company's standard policy of promoting those engineers with longest service. The parent company is now applying pressure to change this policy, as it feels Electrotime needs more commercial skills. In response to this pressure, the Managing Director has recently appointed Susan Walker as a Business Analyst. Susan is a graduate from the City of London School of Business and is the only person in the company, apart from accountants, who has a commercial qualification.

In her first week in the company, Susan reported to the Production Manager, Jim McGovern, who gave her an initial project.

> I normally put new arrivals to work in the design area for a few weeks so they get a feel for the company products and how they work. In your case you wouldn't understand any of this so it would be a waste of time. I thought you could do a bit of forecasting to start with. Every month head office insist we produce forecasts of weekly demand for regular products for the next three months. I normally find someone in the office who has a bit of spare time and ask them to do this, but you can do it this month. It shouldn't take very long.

Susan was keen to make a good impression. She knew about forecasting and felt a good job here would improve her standing in the company. The first thing she did was to find David Hume, who prepared the forecasts last month. He told her: 'I've done the forecasts three or four times over the past few years. This is the sort of job you get if you don't look busy at the right time.'

Susan thought she could do something useful, and looked up some past records. Every week for the past 10 years a clerk had recorded, by hand, the number of units sold of over 2000 products. These, together with other related figures, now filled eight filing cabinets in the administration area. Susan felt that she could not spend too long analysing these without showing some results, so she decided her best plan was to start with one of the best selling products. She collected the weekly sales for this product over the past six years, as shown in Table 6.3.

Table 6.3

Week	Year 1	Year 2	Year 3	Year 4	Year 5	Year 6
1	5312	6683	6987	6993	8460	8661
2	5247	6620	7009	7003	8413	8708
3	5201	6675	6557	6937	8372	8654
4	5188	6682	6418	6988	8312	8555
5	5151	6678	6374	6990	8290	8539
6	5145	6639	6300	7012	8280	8499
7	5161	6642	6230	6887	8256	8597
8	5098	6601	6228	7003	8227	8530
9	5091	6598	6240	6989	8209	8520
10	5083	6500	6241	7015	8192	8487
11	5080	6513	6128	6821	8210	8519
12	5085	6501	6102	7015	8179	8557
13	5089	6488	6091	6999	8215	8599
14	5093	6498	6024	6822	8317	8607
15	5110	6421	5904	7045	8282	8711
16	5110	6375	5902	6994	8298	8779
17	5115	6311	6002	7092	8428	8778
18	5180	6204	5907	7110	8553	8843
19	5181	6198	6001	7230	8584	8854
20	5190	6103	6021	7251	8623	8927
21	5195	6047	6013	7285	8788	9087
22	5220	6052	5902	7304	8775	9218
23	5230	5995	6022	7566	8923	9197
24	5280	5986	5918	7612	8901	9234
25	5301	5900	6089	7700	9081	9309
26	5367	5880	6111	7822	8954	9298
27	5452	5779	6089	7917	9122	9356
28	5500	5873	6124	8033	9207	9397
29	5497	5921	6299	8122	9246	9441
30	5495	5935	6336	8209	9256	9460
31	5689	6001	6474	8307	9267	9465
32	5760	6039	6591	8440	9271	9483
33	5802	6056	6698	8447	9278	9491
34	5801	6109	6780	8556	9260	9503
35	5991	6147	6887	8601	9217	9398
36	6079	6193	6991	8635	9220	9443

Table 6.3 *(cont.)*

Week	Year 1	Year 2	Year 3	Year 4	Year 5	Year 6
37	6080	6233	6986	8670	9200	9461
38	6150	6243	6995	8745	9217	9503
39	6235	6278	7065	8753	9101	9376
40	6355	6339	7092	8695	9117	9372
41	6354	6375	7088	8690	9091	9370
42	6350	6380	6935	8721	9006	9289
43	6480	6435	7043	8596	8929	9234
44	6520	6478	6988	8700	8933	9202
45	6533	6501	7053	8648	8946	9199
46	6520	6492	6934	8632	8817	9206
47	6580	6487	7000	8712	8901	9124
48	6611	6501	6911	8699	8871	9034
49	6643	6543	7010	8677	8800	8999
50	6692	6720	6900	8553	8789	8970
51	6693	6737	6878	8607	8667	8965
52	6689	6888	6945	8487	8657	8824

Questions

- How well do you think Electrotime organizes its forecasting?

- What would they use the forecasts for?

- How could you forecast demand from the data given?

- What would you do if you were Susan?

Problems

6.1 The productivity of a factory has been recorded over a ten-month period, together with forecasts made the previous month by the production manager, the foreman and the Management Services Department. Compare the three sets of forecasts.

Month	1	2	3	4	5	6	7	8	9	10
Productivity	22	24	28	27	23	24	20	18	20	23
Forecasts:										
Production Manager	23	26	32	28	20	26	24	16	21	23
Foreman	22	28	29	29	24	26	21	21	24	25
Management Services	21	25	26	27	24	23	20	20	19	24

6.2 A local amateur dramatic society is staging a play and wants to know how much to spend on advertising. Its aim is to attract as many people as possible, up to the hall's capacity of 300. For the past 11 productions the spending on advertising (in hundreds of pounds) and resulting audience is shown in the following table. How much would you spend on advertising?

Spending	3	5	1	7	2	4	4	2	6	6	4
Audience	200	250	75	425	125	300	225	200	300	400	275

6.3 Ten experiments were done to find the effects of bonus rates paid to employees on output, with the following results.

% Bonus	0	1	2	3	4	5	6	7	8	9
Output ('00s)	3	4	8	10	15	18	20	22	27	28

What is the line of best fit through this data?

6.4 The number of accident-free shifts worked in a company over the past 10 months are shown below. Use linear regression to forecast the number of accident-free shifts for the next six months. How reliable are these figures?

Month	1	2	3	4	5	6	7	8	9	10
Sales	6	21	41	75	98	132	153	189	211	243

6.5 Find the 2, 3 and 4 period moving average for the following time series, and say which gives the best results.

t	1	2	3	4	5	6	7	8
D_t	280	240	360	340	300	220	200	360

6.6 The following figures show the number of road accidents per quarter in a given area. Deseasonalize the data and find the underlying trend.

Quarter	1	2	3	4	5	6	7	8	9	10
Number of accidents	75	30	52	88	32	53	90	30	56	96

6.7 Use exponential smoothing with smoothing constant equal to 0.1, 0.2, 0.3 and 0.4 to produce one period ahead forecasts for the following time series. Use an initial value of $F_1 = 208$ and say which value of α is best.

t	1	2	3	4	5	6	7	8
D_t	212	216	424	486	212	208	208	204

6.8 The demand for a product is shown below. What forecasts would you give for demand in the following year?

Month	Jan	Feb	Mar	Apr	May	June	July	Aug	Sept	Oct	Nov	Dec
Year 1	100	87	86	75	92	107	115	131	120	118	120	142
Year 2	123	101	105	93	121	136	130	155	158	142	147	181

Discussion questions

6.1 Is forecasting really essential for all decisions? Can you give examples where it is not needed?

6.2 How might poor forecasts affect an organization's performance? Give some examples to support your views.

6.3 What factors do you think should be considered when choosing a forecasting method?

6.4 How can forecasting systems be integrated with other operations?

6.5 What are the assumptions of linear regression? Are these generally realistic?

6.6 A lot of forecasting can be done with spreadsheets. Design some spreadsheets for this. Compare the results with standard forecasting programs.

6.7 Can you think of other methods for forecasting demand that has both seasonality and trend? How, for example, could you extend the basic exponential smoothing model?

6.8 Why do forecasts use smoothing? How could you judge the best amount of sensitivity for a forecast?

Table 6.4

	June	July	Aug	Sept	Oct	Nov	Dec	Jan	Feb	Mar	Apr
Daily Telegraph	1012	1017	1028	1008	1011	1032	1008	1033	1015	1001	999
Financial Times	283	288	275	287	288	294	294	284	300	304	299
Guardian	407	403	392	404	403	402	389	406	405	403	397
Independent	339	335	326	332	329	314	302	291	292	277	271
Times	362	360	354	442	445	445	439	456	468	471	478
TOTAL	2403	2403	2375	2474	2475	2487	2433	2470	2481	2455	2445

6.9 One problem with projective forecasting is that it cannot deal with sudden, unexpected changes. In July of 1993, for example, *The Times* had 15% of the quality daily newspaper market in Britain. The owner of *The Times* was Rupert Murdoch's News International, who decided to boost sales and cut the price from 45p a day to 30p.

Average daily sales (thousands of copies) of quality newspapers between June 1993 and April 1994 is shown in Table 6.4.

In June 1994 News International dropped the price of *The Times* from 30p to 20p and said this was now a permanent price.

How do you think newspapers forecast their demands? Would it have been possible to forecast the effects of a sudden drop in price of *The Times*?

Selected references

De Lurgio S.A. and Bhame C.D. (1991). *Forecasting Systems for Operations Management*. New York: John Wiley.

Ellis D. and Nathan J. (1990). *A Managerial Guide to Forecasting*. New York: Graceway Publishing.

Hanke J.E. and Reitsch A.G. (1989). *Business Forecasting* (3rd edn). Boston, Mass.: Allyn and Bacon.

Kress G. (1985). *Practical Techniques of Business Forecasting*. Westport, Conn.: Quorum Books.

Linstone H.A. and Turoff M. (1975). *The Delphi Method: Techniques and Applications*. Reading, Mass.: Addison-Wesley.

Makridakis S., Wheelwright S.C. and McGee V.E. (1983). *Forecasting: Methods and Applications* (2nd edn). New York: John Wiley.

Wheelwright S.C. and Makridakis (1985). *Forecasting Models for Management* (4th edn). New York: John Wiley.

Willis R.E. (1987). *A Guide to Forecasting for Planners and Managers*. Englewood Cliffs, NJ: Prentice-Hall.

7 Designing the process

Contents

Objectives

After reading this chapter you should be able to:

- say why process planning is needed
- describe different types of process
- discuss factors that affect the choice of process
- outline ways of improving the performance of intermittent processes
- describe various levels of automation
- discuss processes within the service sector
- use different types of process charts

Planning for the process

In the past few chapters we have looked at various aspects of product planning: what product to make, what quantities to make, how to get high quality, and so on. In this chapter we are going to look more directly at how to **make** a product. This involves the design of the **process**.

> The **process** describes the detailed operations used to make a product.

In different circumstances, a process might change a product's:

- *physical form* – when manufacturing a product;
- *chemical structure* – such as the processing of oil into chemicals and plastics;
- *owner* – by selling something;
- *location* – when transporting goods;
- *age* – by warehousing until needed;
- *condition* – by repairing faults; or
- *information* – in clerical processes.

Whatever a process does, its purpose is to make a product. Most products can be made by a number of different processes. A table, for example, can be hand-built by craftsmen, it can be assembled from bought-in parts by semi-skilled people, it can be made automatically by machines on an assembly line, it can be formed in one piece from plastic, and so on. The choice of process has a major effect on the efficiency and costs of operations. So it is important for managers to plan the process carefully – they must match the characteristics of the product with the best process for making it. This is the function of **process planning**.

> **Process planning** makes the decisions about a process. It gives a detailed description of the operations needed to make a product. The aim is to design a process that makes the product as efficiently as possible.

Organizations need to make decisions about the process whenever there are significant changes to operations, such as:

- they introduce an entirely new product
- they change an old product

- there are significant changes in demand

- costs of inputs or operations alter

- competitors change their products

- there are changes in the market

- the current performance is unsatisfactory.

ce Case example – van Heugen Fabricators

Van Heugen Fabricators run a number of workshops in the Netherlands. They take customers' designs and can make almost any product in metal. Most of their products are made by one of five processes:

(1) *casting*, where liquid metal is poured into a mould;

(2) *hot forming*, where metal is heated until it can be shaped under pressure;

(3) *cold forming*, where high pressure is used to shape metal without heating;

(4) *machining*, where machines remove metal by drilling, boring, turning, milling, shaping, planing or grinding;

(5) *assembly*, where components are joined together.

When customers submit a design, a production planning team meets to consider the best process to make it. Often they will suggest changes that will improve the quality or reduce the cost of the finished product.

Questions

- What do you think the main processes are at van Heugen?

- Who should decide the best process to use? How might they make such decisions?

Review questions

7.1   What is a 'process'?

7.2   What is process planning and when is it used?

Process design

In this section we describe the different types of process that an organization can use.

Types of process

A useful classification of processes looks at the frequency with which products change. At one extreme are continuous flows like an oil refinery that makes the same product without any changes or interruptions for 24 hours a day. At the other extreme, are single projects like satellite manufacturers who rarely make the same product twice. We can use these differences to define five types of process:

(1)   project

(2)   job shop

(3)   batch processing

(4)   mass production

(5)   continuous flow.

Each of these processes is suited to different circumstances, particularly the variety of products and the quantities made.

Project

This type of process makes a single unit, usually tailored to individual customer specifications. Building a Formula 1 racing car, writing a book and building the Channel Tunnel are projects.

A project makes products that are essentially unique – so the process is characterized by a lot of variety. This means there is little standardization and general purpose equipment must be used. There must be a lot of flexibility in the process to deal with new situations and problems. This needs a skilled and well-trained workforce. The process is controlled by project management methods (which we shall look at in Chapter 16). Although the number of units made is low, each can involve a lot of work. This kind of process usually has very high unit costs.

This is generally the type of process that people like to work with. There is more variety, and the work is interesting. People gain satisfaction from making a significant contribution to an identifiable end result.

Examples include ship building, satellite assembly, building an office block, writing a book, developing software for a new computer system, preparing a management consultant's report.

Job shop

This type of process makes small numbers of a wide variety of products. It is typically used in small engineering works that makes products to customer specifications. If, for example, you need a set of pistons for a vintage car, they would probably be made in a job shop.

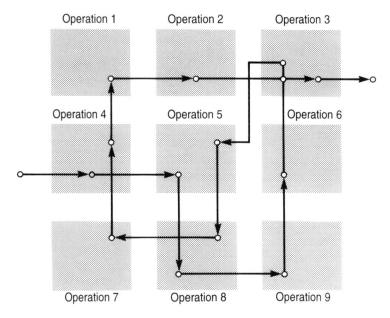

Figure 7.1 Job shop with products moving to equipment as needed.

Job shops make a narrower range of products than projects, but there is still a lot of variety. The process uses general purpose equipment which must be set up and changed every time a new product is started. Each product goes through a different sequence of operations on the equipment (see Figure 7.1). This needs flexibility from equipment and a skilled workforce.

Each product will only use some of the resources available. So a lot of resources are idle at any time – either because of short-term mismatches between capacity and work load, or because of the setups needed between changes of product. The average utilization of resources is low, typically 25% and often as low as 5% or 10%. But at other times there are bottlenecks as some resources are temporarily overloaded. The result is that job shops have low capital costs, but high unit costs. The mix of different products makes scheduling and keeping track of work difficult.

Examples include makers of specialized vehicles, printers, furniture manufacturers, restaurants, travel agents arranging holidays.

Batch processing

This occurs when small batches of similar products are made on the same equipment. In a job shop, every time a new product is started there are costs for setting up the equipment. These costs can be reduced by making more units in each run. Over time, a series of batches are made, with products held in stock until they are needed to meet customer demand. Making more units in each batch reduces the setup cost per unit.

This process is useful for medium volumes of products where customer needs are known in advance. This means there is less product variety and little customizing. Equipment is still fairly general, but there is room for some specialization. The process can have frequent setups and changes, so some skilled workers are needed.

Examples include book publishers, pharmaceuticals and clothing manufacturers, bottling plants, universities organizing courses, insurance companies processing different types of policies.

Mass production

This is typical of an assembly or production line that makes large numbers of a single product. Computers, cars and washing machines are made by mass production. There is very little variety in the product, except small changes to the basic model introduced in the finishing.

Mass production processes rely on a steady, high demand for a product. Then specialized equipment can be used. As the product does not change, there are no disruptions to the process and few management problems. There is, for example, no need to schedule individual pieces of equipment or check the progress of individual units of the product. Once the system has been set up it needs a small workforce to keep it functioning and in extreme cases may be completely automated. Unit costs for mass production are low (see Figure 7.2).

People do not generally like to work on such high volume processes, as they often find the work dull and monotonous. Each person does such a small part of the overall process that they get little job satisfaction.

Examples include cars, computers, consumer electronics such as television sets, domestic appliances such as washing machines, processing photographs, newspaper publishing.

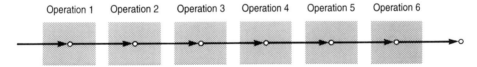

Figure 7.2 Mass production with equipment arranged in a line to make a product.

Continuous flow

These are used for high volumes of a single product or small group of related products, such as bulk chemicals, oil and paper. The process is different to assembly lines as the product emerges as a continuous flow rather than discrete units. Such processes use highly specialized equipment that can work for 24 hours a day with virtually no changes or interruptions. The process is capital intensive, but it needs a very small workforce and the high volume leads to low unit costs.

Examples include petrol refineries, breweries, paper mills, sugar refineries, television broadcasts, police service.

Table 7.1 Differences among process types.

Process type	Volume	Product variation	Frequency of changes
Project	one	one-off	not applicable
Job shop	low	considerable	frequent
Batch processing	medium	some	some
Mass production	very high	little (minor modifications)	none
Continuous flow	continuous	none	none

You can see that these processes are used for different production quantities and variety of products. Project, job shop and batch processes are called **intermittent** – as they make a variety of different products and keep changing between them.

Another important difference between processes is that projects and job shops are make-to-order systems, which wait to receive an order from a customer and then make the product requested. Batch, mass production and continuous flow are make-to-stock systems, which make the product according to some plans and then keep it in stock until customers actually demand it. These differences are summarized in Table 7.1 and Figure 7.3.

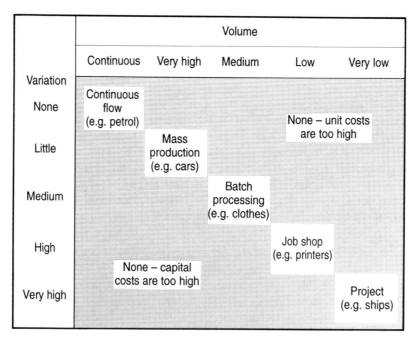

Figure 7.3 Types of process and their product quantities and variation.

Table 7.1 (*cont.*)

Equipment	Number of operators	Skill level	Capital cost	Unit cost
general	large	high	low	high
general	large	high	low	high
some specialized	smaller	medium	medium	medium
specialized	small	low	high	low
specialized	small	low	very high	low

As you can see from the examples given, the terms used are used equally to describe manufacturing and service operations.

ce Case example – Henry Penhaligan Watercolours

This perspective shows the way a process can be changed, and the way this effects the product.

Henry Penhaligan lives in St Ives, Cornwall. Twenty years ago he began to paint watercolours of the local coastline. These sold well to tourists, but he found it difficult to make a comfortable living. His alternatives for increasing his income were to charge higher prices, or to paint more pictures. He ruled out the first option because tourists would not pay much more than his current prices. So he decided to paint more pictures.

Henry realized that the best way to increase his output was to change the process he was using. Originally he used a project process, where each picture was a unique product. Although it meant a fundamental change to his products, he decided to aim for larger sales of mass produced pictures. This meant making standard products – typically a view of the coast with cliffs and a beach – and having different people work quickly on each painting. One person would paint the sky and cloud formations, a second would add the cliffs, a third would paint the sea, a fourth would add the beach in the foreground, and so on. This was equivalent to a job shop process.

Eventually Henry refined the process so it became almost mass production, with paintings moving past a series of artists each of whom added a small part to the picture. Using this method, Henry could get a finished painting in under an hour. The final product is obviously very different from Henry's original paintings, but the output has risen dramatically.

Like all decisions about processes, this one needed to balance several factors. Henry Penhaligan's main aim was to increase his income, so he had to monitor costs and sales very carefully.

Chapter 4 described how the demand for a product changes over its life-cycle. There is a clear link between the stages in the product's life-cycle and the process used to make it. During the product planning stage, small numbers of a product are made on a project basis. These may be prototypes or samples used to test various properties of the product. Later, during the introduction stage, demand is small and several variations may be used to test market reaction. These are made by a job shop process. As the product moves through introduction and into a growth stage, the variety of products is reduced as those versions that customers did not like are removed. The volume of remaining versions increases and batch processing is the most effective. As the product moves to maturity, demand is stable, product variation is reduced further and competition increases. Higher efficiency is needed to produce higher volumes at lower costs, so the process moves toward mass production.

These changes are illustrated in Figure 7.4. It is clear that an organization needs to adjust both the product and the process as they move through the life-cycle. The effort put into such innovation is shown in Figure 7.5. You can see that this is a simplified view, as many products never reach the volumes needed to support batch production, let alone mass production.

Choosing the best type of process

Decisions about the process can have long-term consequences on profitability, production, costs, flexibility, and so on. When a car maker builds an assembly line it can cost hundreds of millions of pounds. If the company then decides that it should not have used an assembly line, correcting the mistake is very expensive. This example shows that there is often disagreement about the best type of process. Ever since Henry Ford started building cars on assembly lines it has been accepted that this is the best process for mass produced cars. But

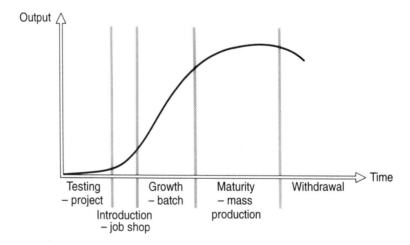

Figure 7.4 Different processes used during the product life-cycle.

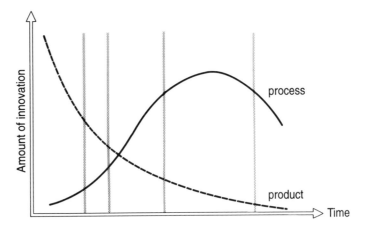

Figure 7.5 Amount of innovation during a product life-cycle.

Volvo built a plant at Uddevalla in Sweden that had small groups of people assembling separate cars in workshops. This had some success and was popular with the workers, but its high costs forced it to close in 1993. The works should re-open in 1996, but this time using a conventional assembly line.

An organization should consider a number of factors before choosing the type of process, including the following.

Product design

The product's design will set the overall type of processes needed. If a tailor designs a very high quality suit to specifications given by a customer, the process is fixed as a hand-made project rather than use a mass production process. But most designs allow a number of alternative processes. A well-designed product should allow an efficient process and give low production costs.

Overall demand

The number of units to be made clearly affects the best type of process. Portraits, for example, can either be painted or photographed – painters use a project process to produce very small numbers, while film processors use mass production to make very large numbers. If demand is high enough, an organization can use mass production to reduce unit costs.

Changes in demand

As well as the total numbers being produced, the changing patterns of demand affect the choice of process. If production changes to meet a highly seasonal demand, it must use a flexible process that can meet peak demands and still work efficiently during slacker times. This is called **demand flexibility**. Hotels, for example, must cater for large numbers of guests in holiday seasons, but still work efficiently with smaller numbers out of season.

Product flexibility

This describes the speed a process can stop making one product and start making another. The combination of demand and product flexibilities allows a process to respond quickly to changes in customer needs.

Human resources

Another aspect of flexibility concerns the workforce. A flexible process relies on operators who are skilled enough to do a variety of different jobs. Different processes need different abilities, so the process affects the workforce skills, management skills, training needed and labour productivity.

Automation

Until recently, automation could only be used for high volume processes. It needed expensive, specialized equipment that gave little flexibility. On the other hand, low volume processes used cheaper, more flexible, general purpose equipment. In the past few years this has changed – and we will discuss some aspects of flexible automation later in the chapter.

Customer involvement

Customers are not usually involved in manufacturing processes. But they can play an active part in service processes. Self-service petrol stations, self-service restaurants and automated banking machines use customers to take over much of the process that was previously done by employees. Those processes with high customer involvement generally give a more personal service.

Product quality

As we saw in Chapter 5, organizations should aim at making products of perfect quality. The traditional means of getting high quality was to employ highly skilled craftspeople to make small numbers of a product. These craft processes are still best for some products, but automated processes give high quality in a wide range of other products. The most reliable computers, for example, are not hand-made but come from completely automated assembly lines.

Finances

Different processes have widely different costs. The choice of process can be affected by the capital available and installation cost. In turn, the process will affect the operating expenses, return on investment and purchase price of the product.

Amount of vertical integration

Logistics is the function that co-ordinates all the movement of products from initial suppliers through to final customer. Vertical integration refers to the amount of the logistics function – or the supply chain – that is owned by one organization. A manufacturer that buys all its components from suppliers and sells all finished products to wholesalers has little vertical integration. Another manufacturer that makes all its own components and sells to customers through its own distributors has a lot of vertical integration.

Vertical integration can affect the process in several ways. There is usually more vertical integration with higher volumes. It also means that large investments are needed in production facilities so the amount of flexibility in a process is reduced.

Improving the performance of intermittent processes

Mass production and continuous flow processes use specialized equipment which, once started, needs little supervision either by management or operators. These processes typically have high capital costs, low unit cost, and utilization of resources that can approach 100%. On the other hand, intermittent processes, like projects and job shops make a variety of products and continually change the mix. They typically have low capital cost, high unit cost, and low utilization of resources.

This means that an organization that wants to increase the utilization of resources should move away from intermittent processes and towards mass production. Unfortunately, many products never have demands that are either high enough or stable enough to justify the capital costs of mass production. These products must continue to use intermittent processes. But there are several ways of improving the performance of intermittent processes.

Reorganize machine operators

Intermittent processes often have one operator assigned to a piece of equipment. We have already said that the utilization of equipment is low, so this means the operator spends a lot of time idle. Productivity could be improved by assigning one operator to a number of machines. This is most useful when machines can operate for some time without direct operator involvement. Often, an operator can be kept busy loading and unloading several machines which actually work without further attention.

Increase batch sizes with group technology

A more imaginative approach uses group technology. In this a number of distinct products that share some characteristic are grouped together to form a single batch. Several different products may, for example, need a three-centimetre hole drilled. These products can all be combined into a single batch for drilling. The equipment setup time is then reduced, and more efficient, automated equipment may be justified by the larger batches.

Use flexible automation

Flexible automation uses high technology equipment to reduce the setup time between products. Numerically controlled machines, for example, can be reprogrammed very quickly between batches, and industrial robots can make a variety of products with very little setup time. This allows small batches to be made with almost the same efficiency as larger batches. We will meet this idea again with flexible manufacturing systems.

we Worked example

A manufacturing company is planning the process for making a new product. Related costs are:

Process	Annual fixed cost	Unit variable cost
Job shop	100,000	50
Batch	250,000	40
Mass production	1,000,000	15

The company has forecast a demand of 25,000 units a year. Which type of process do you think they should choose? Within what range is each type of process best?

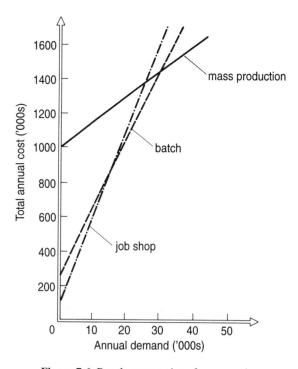

Figure 7.6 Break-even points for example.

Solution

This is an example of a break-even analysis, as shown in Figure 7.6.

●   A job shop process is best for demand, D, from zero until:

$$100,000 + 50D = 250,000 + 40D \quad \text{or} \quad D = 15,000$$

●   A batch process is best for demand from 15,000 until:

$$250,000 + 40D = 1,000,000 + 15D \quad \text{or} \quad D = 30,000$$

●   After this, a mass production process is best.

   With a forecast demand of 25,000 a year the company should look at batch processes.

■

we Worked example

You should always try to do calculations on a computer. An example of a break-even analysis is shown in the spreadsheet and graph in Figures 7.7(a) and (b). This shows a printout for comparing the costs of three processes. Which is best?

Break-even	unit cost calculatons		
	Process		
Production	Manual	Hard automation	Flexible automation
0	20	100	80.00
5	20	90	64.40
10	20	80	50.60
15	20	70	38.60
20	20	60	28.40
25	20	50	20.00
30	20	40	13.40
35	20	30	8.60
40	20	20	5.60
45	20	10	4.40
50	20	0	5.00
Cheapest	0 to 25	25 to 47.75	over 47.75

Figure 7.7(a) Spreadsheet showing unit costs for different production levels.

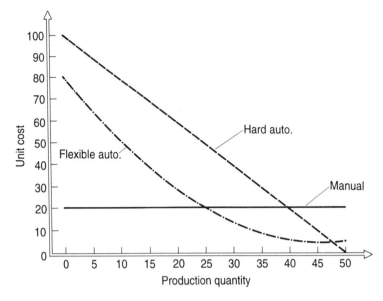

Figure 7.7(b) Graph showing break-even analysis.

Solution

As you can see, the spreadsheet does all the calculations and shows that the manual process is for production up to 25 units, then hard automation is cheapest up to 47.75 units, then flexible automation becomes cheapest.

Review questions

7.3   What factors can be important in process design?

7.4   What are the different types of process?

7.5   Which type of process would be best for:
   (a)   washing machines
   (b)   liquid fertilizer
   (c)   'home baked' cakes
   (d)   specialized limousines
   (e)   printed T-shirts
   (f)   aeroplanes

7.6   How is the choice of process related to the product life-cycle?

7.7   What types of process have highest productivity, and why?

7.8   How can the productivity of intermittent processes be increased?

Process technologies

Classification of technologies

An important question for planning the process is the level of technology to be used. If you look at the way equipment is controlled, this can be described as:

- manual
- mechanized
- automated

Manual systems

In these an operator has full control over the equipment, which needs their continuous attention. The operator loads the equipment, works with it and then unloads it. Driving a bus is an example of a manual process.

Historically, manual processes were developed first and are still widely used. They have the benefits of flexibility, low capital costs and low risk. Their disadvantages are high unit cost, need for a skilled workforce, variable quality and low output. If an organization wants to increase production with a manual process, it employs more people and equipment. But there comes a point when it is cheaper to invest in some mechanized process.

Mechanized systems

In these an operator loads the equipment, but this can work without further intervention until the task is finished, when the operator unloads it. Using a VCR is an example of a mechanized process.

Mechanized processes were developed during the industrial revolution, and were the most advanced technology available until quite recently. Initially, mechanization was based on general purpose machines such as lathes, grinders and drills. Later, more specialized machines were designed for specific products. This step is equivalent to moving from a batch process to mass production. As we have seen, the resulting mechanized processes have the advantages of producing high volumes of uniform products at low unit cost, but the disadvantages of high capital cost and inflexibility.

Mechanized processes still need operators to load the machines, do some of the operations, and help with problems. As technology improved it became clear that human operators often slow down the process, add variability to the quality and increase unit costs. These problems can be overcome by using automated processes.

Automated systems

This is a broad category, in which equipment can perform a number of tasks without any operator involvement. Some details of different types of automation are given in the following section.

You might imagine these different levels of automation with some examples:

- A manual lathe needs an operator to load it and then control the operations; a mechanized lathe is loaded manually but will then operate without further intervention; an automated lathe can operate without any operator intervention at all.

- A manual system for sorting letters in a post office needs people to put letters into appropriate bags; a mechanized system has operators directing equipment to route letters; an automated system has scanners to read the post code and automatically move letters.

- A manual warehouse needs people to put stock on shelves and later remove it for customers; a mechanized warehouse has people operating equipment (such as fork lift trucks) to do this; an automated warehouse has a computer to control automatic equipment for stock movements.

This classification is clearly linked to the process type, with higher levels of automation used for higher volumes of output. Low volume processes are usually manual, medium volume processes are mechanized and high volumes use automation, as shown in Figure 7.8. You might imagine:

- projects and jobs shops with manual processes

- batches made with mechanized processes

- mass production and continuous flows using automation.

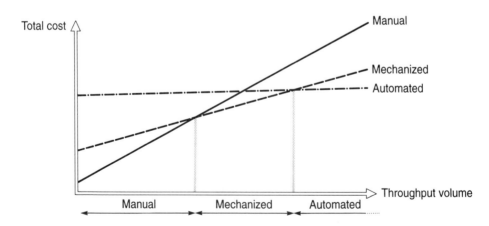

Figure 7.8 Costs of different types of automation.

Types of automation

Traditionally, automation meant using equipment that had been specially designed to make a single product. But this kind of automation is capital intensive and organizations can only justify its use for very large numbers of a single product. These systems are now called **fixed** or **hard automation**. They typically have a conveyor moving units along a fixed path between single-purpose, specialized machines. As the conveyor moves units, they are worked on in turn by the machines. The result can be a highly specialized, efficient operation, but with no flexibility.

More recently, there has been a lot of progress in using high technology for lower volume processes. These systems aim at combining flexibility with efficiency and are called **flexible** or **programmable automation**.

Flexible automation for intermittent processes first became possible with **numerically controlled** (NC) machines. These were originally simple, general purpose machines which were designed to run without the immediate control of humans. In other words, they allowed mechanization rather than automation. Paper tapes were used to control the machines and they could be quickly reprogrammed by simply replacing the tape.

NC machines developed into large machine tools that could follow a series of pre-programmed instructions, perhaps drilling, planing, milling, boring and turning products of many different shapes and sizes. These machines have the advantages of not needing a human operator – except to change the programme or to load the machine – and they give consistently high quality with low unit cost.

Magnetic tapes replaced paper tapes for the control of NC machines, and these, in turn, were replaced by microcomputers. Each machine is now controlled by a microcomputer dedicated to its operation. **Computerized numerically controlled** (CNC) machines do a series of operations without interruption. Readily available programs allow even small production quantities to be made reliably and at low cost. Such systems, where computers assist in the actual manufacturing processes, are called **computer-aided manufacturing** (CAM).

CNC machines were early examples of CAM. Nowadays computer-aided manufacturing often uses industrial robots. Industrial robots were developed in the 1960s, but they have only become common since the 1980s. In essence, they are stationary machines that have reprogrammable 'manipulators' to move materials through a variety of tasks and perform a limited range of activities. A robot can move a spray to paint a car, or a welding torch to assemble panels into car bodies. Car assembly lines were the first major users of robots, but as technology improved the range of jobs they can do has increased. Typically they are used for spot welding, spray painting, testing, automatic inspection and limited assembly. They have obvious uses in reaching places that are difficult for humans to get at, or handling dangerous substances, such as explosives, hot steel ingots or radioactive materials.

The next types of automated production are **flexible manufacturing systems** (FMSs). These combine the computers which control each piece of equipment (CNC or robot) so a number of separate machines are under the control of a central computer. This computer can co-ordinate the operations and find the best overall production schedule. It can also control the flow of goods with an automated transport system, with wire-guided trucks moving between machines. This transport system carries products, components, materials and tools as needed. The link between the transport system and the manufacturing machines is made with automatic loading and unloading stations. So we can list the essential parts of FMS as:

- a central computer to schedule, route, load, and control operations;

- a number of machines under the control of the central computer;

- a computer controlled transport system between machines;

- computer controlled loading and unloading equipment.

As you can see, once a FMS is programmed the system can work with very little human intervention.

FMSs bring a number of advantages:

- They allow faster changes between different products and these changes are cheaper.

- Labour costs are reduced to a minimum.

- The computer takes over the difficult jobs of scheduling and routing.

- Utilization of machines can be very high – up to three times that of conventional machines.

- The computer can also controls inventories, reducing stocks of raw materials and work in progress.

- The output has consistently high quality, without the variation found in less automated processes.

On the other hand, there are some disadvantages of FMSs:

- The equipment is expensive to buy and set up.

- Although the systems can be programmed to make many different products, there are limitations and they lack the flexibility of some other processes.

- The system must match current production, so there may be problems with major changes to products in the future.

- The technology is still being developed and there are often teething troubles.

- FMS works best with families of similar products that need small changes, rather than radically different products.

- The machines still have fixed capacities, tolerances, and so on, so they can not deal with unusual products.

Computer assisted design

Automation is used directly in the production process. But it can also be used in associated operations, like product design. For many years designers have used computers to design products on a screen. They can design, test and change plans very quickly. Initial design time is also cut by having computers store designs of similar products – then rather than designing from scratch, similar designs are recovered and modified as necessary. This approach is called **computer assisted design** (CAD).

The computer can also check the design for obvious faults, do related calculations, print the results, produce sets of blueprints, transmit results to distant sites, and so on. Then CAD:

- reduces initial design time;

- allows very quick changes to existing design;

- enhances basic drawings, showing how the actual product will look, rotating it, showing other perspectives, enlarging sections, and so on;

- does calculations about stresses, strengths and any other engineering factors;

- produces all necessary drawings and blueprints from the master set;

- stores a library of designs;

- estimates costs for products as they are being designed;

- generates bills of material;

- communicates with other computer systems.

In the past, even when designs were drawn with the help of computers, there was a break between the design stage and the manufacturing stage. It soon became obvious that if computers were designing the products (CAD) and controlling the machines (CAM) the two systems could be linked to form a single CAD/CAM system. In these, designs are worked on and finalized in the CAD part, and are then automatically transferred to the CAM part which generates the programs to control machines and actually makes the products.

This kind of FMS is sometimes described as **computer integrated manufacturing** (CIM). Terms in this area are often used rather vaguely, but most people view CIM as a further extension of FMS. Then FMS consists of the actual production machines, while CIM includes design and related systems.

CIM would include product design and production control, and it would also get information from marketing, procurement, maintenance, accounting and logistics. The system now has a common database and allows all functions to work together as an integrated unit.

Integrated systems are now common, and there seems little to prevent the development of an **automated factory**. This would have a product designed with computer assistance, and then computers would take over to do all the following stages automatically. Manufacture would be planned and controlled, parts would be ordered, final products delivered, and bank accounts updated, without any human intervention. No such factories exist at the moment, but the principles have been established and the reality is not far away.

One other type of technology we should mention processes information. Computers are almost universally used for processing information, but there are particularly interesting developments in **artificial intelligence** (AI). This is the branch of computer science that attempts to give computers the ability to understand language, reason, make assumptions, learn and solve problems. In other words, to create computers that can make reasoned decisions in the same way as humans.

One aspect of AI concerns **expert systems** which help in making decisions by recording the skills of experts in the field. Engineers collect experts' knowledge, skills, opinions, decisions and rules in a knowledge base. A user of this knowledge base passes their problem to an inference engine which is the control mechanism. This looks at the problem and the knowledge base and decides which rules to apply to get a solution.

Choosing the level of technology

High technology can increase the productivity of a process, but this does not mean that every organization should immediately replace its current processes by high technology alternatives. Many other factors must be considered – the most obvious being the high capital costs of high technology systems. Unless high volumes are made, the capital costs are spread over too few units and the unit cost becomes too high.

we Worked example

The current manual process for a product has fixed costs of £150,000 a year and variable costs of £40 a unit. The company is considering an automated process that has fixed costs, including capital repayment, of £450,000 a year and variable costs of £20 a unit. What production level would be needed to justify this system?

Solution

The automated process would be justified when its costs are lower. With an annual production of P, this means:

$$(450{,}000 + 20P) < (150{,}000 + 40P) \quad \text{or} \quad P > 15{,}000$$

With annual production up to 15,000 units the manual system would be cheaper, but above this the automated system would be better.

Apart from cost, there are several other factors to consider with decisions about technology. We have already seen that higher levels of automation reduce the flexibility and variability in a system. Another problem may be the barriers created between customers and the final product – which is one reason why people walk past cash dispensing machines to talk to someone in a bank. But perhaps the major criticism of automated systems is that they ignore the skills which people can bring, including:

- pattern recognition
- creativity
- drawing upon varied experiences
- intelligent use of all available information
- use of subjectivity and judgement
- flexibility
- ability to adapt to new and unusual circumstances
- generate entirely new solutions.

On the other hand, machines have the advantages of:

- working with consistent precision
- being very fast and powerful
- doing many tasks at the same time
- storing large amounts of information
- doing calculations quickly
- working continuously without tiring
- being reliable
- being good at monitoring and reacting to signals.

People and machines are better at different jobs, and because automation is better in some circumstances you should not assume that it is better in all circumstances.

ce Case example – Automatic banking machines

This example shows how technology is affecting operations in a major service industry. It also shows how people are often afraid of using new technology, and this must be taken into account when introducing new ideas.

Banks have been increasing their use of automation for many years. Their internal administration is largely computerized, and they encourage customers to get cash from cash dispensing machines. More advanced banking machines allow customers to pay bills, transfer funds, update account information, use credit cards, and so on. Automated banking machines have had a major effect on banking operations. There is obviously less contact with customers, but there is also less paperwork, fewer mistakes, and a lot fewer staff employed.

The next generation of banking machines allow some face-to-face contact, even though it is electronic. The TSB has experimented with an automated branch, where cash machines have video links that allow customers to talk directly to bank staff. All the normal face-to-face operations can be done using the machine, but bank staff do not have to be on the premises. Initial customer reaction was mixed, and some people were so overwhelmed that a bank adviser had to rush out and comfort them.

The Co-operative Bank had similar experiences with a pilot banking kiosk. In theory, customers could use a telephone video link in the unmanned kiosk to talk with bank staff. Trials showed customers did not like the moving video, and were more comfortable when this was replaced by a still photograph.

Such systems are seen as an intermediate step between the current process which use a wide network of branches, and the future aim of banking at home through a multimedia package. Telephone banking is another move in this direction, but again banks have found many customers reluctant to change.

Questions

● Is it fair to say that many people are afraid of using new technology?

● What effects might the answer have on the introduction of high technology processes?

we Worked example

Your company is considering an automated assembly plant that has an initial cost of £12 million, an installation cost of £3 million and maintenance costs of £0.6 million a year. This plant will reduce operating costs by £4 million a year and will have a scrap value of £2 million at the end of its expected life of 5 years. Use a discounting rate of 10% a year to see if the plant would be a reasonable investment.

Solution

The plant will cost £15 million to buy and install. Then it will give net savings of £3.4 million a year for five years. We can calculate the present values for costs and savings using the discounting rate of 10% shown in the spreadsheet in Figure 7.9.

Year	Discount factor	Cost	Present value	Savings	Present value
0	1.00	15	15		
1	1.10			3.40	3.09
2	1.21			3.40	2.81
3	1.33			3.40	2.55
4	1.46			3.40	2.32
5	1.61			5.40	3.35
Totals			15		14.13
NPV			-0.87		

Note:
Calculations in million pounds.

Figure 7.9 Calculations for process using a spreadsheet.

The net present value of the assembly plant is −£0.87, so it does not seem a good investment.

Review questions

7.9   What classification could be used to describe the technologies available for processes?

7.10 What types of automation might you see in a factory?

7.11   What do the following abbreviations stand for?

    (a)   NC   (b)   CNC   (c)   CAM
    (d)   CAD   (e)   FMS   (f)   CIM

7.12   What are the main aims of automated production?

7.13   Rank the following in terms of increasing levels of automation:

              CIM   NC   FMS   CAM   CNC

ce   Case example – Paula Minuetto

Paula Minuetto employs 15 craftsmen to make musical instruments. Most of her products are different kinds of brass instruments, particularly from the trumpet family. The output is small, but quality is very high. Most business comes from successful musicians who want an instrument customized to their needs.

For many years, Japanese companies have been selling mass produced instruments, and Paula has decided to enter this market. She plans to make a range of standard quality instruments for a broader market. Although she will never make very large numbers of instruments, the extra output will use equipment in the assembly area more fully. Paula will also be able to introduce some automation for standard operations. Although some extra people will be hired, most work on the new products will be done by existing staff. Paula is confident they can fit this new work into slack periods of their traditional work.

Questions

- What processes do you think Paula will use for her traditional and new lines of instruments?

- What problems do you think she will face with the new products?

- How do you think her employees will react to the changes?

Processes in service industries

You may think that a lot of the previous section has described processes in manufacturing. If this seems true, it is largely for convenience and exactly the same principles apply to services.

Consider, for example, the service given by a restaurant. There are specialized restaurants where customers phone their orders in advance and the restaurant prepares the meal they request. This is a project. Expensive restaurants have an extensive menu, so the preparation of any meal is like a job shop. Canteens and cafeterias have set meals, which are produced in batches. Busy hamburger restaurants work like mass production assembly lines. Meals are discrete, so it is difficult to describe a continuous flow process, but the coffee or beer served with meals approaches this.

In services there is also the familiar pattern of intermittent processes having more flexibility but higher unit costs, while mass production has less flexibility but lower unit costs. Unfortunately, many services – such as those provided by dentists, lawyers, doctors, accountants, hairdressers, taxis, and so on – are produced either singly or in very small batches. Each customer demands a different product from the service, so it uses a project or job shop process. This inevitably leads to higher costs.

But in recent years automation has become common in many services. The only problem is that services are so diverse it is difficult to describe automation in the same general terms we used for manufacturing. The service offered by a lawyer, for example, has little in common with a postal service. Perhaps, the principles behind automation in services is best illustrated by some specific examples.

Offices

The operations in offices include typing, copying, filing and handling messages. Until fairly recently all of these were done manually, with an electric typewriter as the most sophisticated technology available. Clerical jobs have now been transformed by technology. Wordprocessors and desk top publishers have dramatically increased the productivity of typists; copying is done either by automatic photocopiers or using networked word processors. Filing is done on computerized databases; messages are handled by electronic mail or FAX machines. Longer term developments aim for the paperless office and the virtual elimination of manual clerical jobs.

Banks

Customers in banks used to be served by tellers. These provided a flexible service, but queues seemed inevitable at busy times. To avoid these queues and reduce costs, banks introduced plastic cards and automatic cash dispensing machines. Then, a manual operation was replaced by an automated one, cheques were replaced by machine-readable cards, paperwork was reduced, the customers did some of the work themselves, and banking operations became less expensive. In the future cards and machines will become much more sophisticated, with coins and notes being replaced by machine readable cards.

Supermarkets

Customers in grocery shops used to tell an assistant what they wanted. The assistant would then fetch the goods, weigh and wrap them, and present a bill. Supermarkets introduced a mechanized system, where customers did most of the work and checkout operators added the costs and presented a bill. The next stage is automated, with computer readable shopping lists, automatic materials handling equipment to fetch and deliver goods to a customer and automatic debiting of bank accounts. Beyond this, there will be no need to visit the supermarket, as communications via telephone and television will allow simulated visits with automatic ordering, delivery and accounting.

Post office

Sorting letters was a labour intensive manual process, but now it is largely automated, with the use of post codes. More recently the need to send letters has been reduced by electronic mail and FAX machines. 1993 was the first year when the number of letters sent declined, largely due to the growth of electronic mail.

Warehousing

Traditionally, warehouses had people moving goods to and from racks, with stock movement recorded on cards. Such systems could not cope with high volumes or rapid movements, so mechanized systems were introduced. Later, automated warehouses were developed, where computers not only record stock movements but also control the physical handling of goods.

Reservation systems

Airlines started using on-line reservation systems in the 1960s. They are now considered essential, and similar systems are used by buses and trains, theatres, sporting events, taxis, and so on.

There are many examples of service organizations moving to automated processes. As with manufacturing, the aim is to bring the efficiency of mass production processes to smaller batches. As the average productivity of service industries is low, this area has considerable potential.

ce Case example – Multimedia education

This example outlines the effects of technology on the process used in an important service.

Education has traditionally used a batch process, where a class of children are taught the same things at the same time. The aim of many educators is to move towards a project process, where each child is taught as an individual. At the moment this is too expensive, as pupils would need a lot of individual attention in very small classes. But multimedia CD-ROMs can revolutionize the way children learn. They give students access to vast amounts of information which is presented through sound, text, pictures and videos. Perhaps most importantly, they allow interaction so that students can control the pace, depth and direction of their learning.

Well over two million **CD-ROM** drives will be sold in Europe this year, and the Department for Education is financing thousands of these in schools. Surveys suggest that 80% of parents think they are a good idea for enhancing learning. Traditional teaching methods can appear uninteresting, but CD-ROMs can be so entertaining that the market for 'edutainment' or 'infotainment' discs is likely to expand dramatically.

Review questions

7.14   How could you classify the types of process used in services?

7.15   Services are expensive because the batch size is small and each job is a project. Do you agree with this?

Analysing a process

Process charts

If you want to describe the details of a process, you have to show the sequence of individual operations. **Process charts** are used to show the relationships between each operation in a process.

> **Process charts** show the details of the relationship between the operations in a process.

There are several types of process chart, but they all start by breaking down the process into a number of separate operations. Suppose, for example, we look at the process which a patient goes through when visiting a doctor's surgery. The operations might be described as:

- enter and talk to the receptionist
- sit down and wait until called
- when called, go to the examination room
- discuss problems with the doctor
- when finished, leave the examination room
- talk to the receptionist and leave.

This can be drawn as the informal process chart shown in Figure 7.10. This informal chart gives a general view of the process, but it does not give many details. We really want answers to questions like, 'What operations are

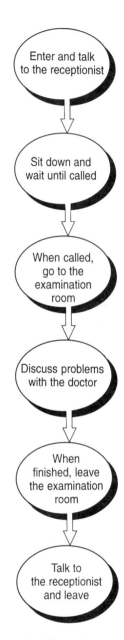

Figure 7.10 Informal process chart.

done?', 'What is the sequence of these?', 'Which operations can not be started until others have finished?', 'How long does each operation take?', 'Is there any idle time?' and 'Are products being moved?'.

The answers to these questions should give a clear picture of the current process. Then we can start asking about potential changes and look for improvements – 'Why are things done like this?', 'How might things be done better?' One approach to this starts by looking at each operation and classifying it as:

- *operation*, where something is actually done;

- *movement*, where products are moved;

- *storage*, where products are put away until they are needed;

- *delay*, where products are held up;

- *inspection*, which tests the quality of the product.

Now we can look at a process and describe it in a chart. The procedure for this has six steps. The first three steps describe the current process, while the last three look for improvements.

(1)   Look at the process and list all the operations in their proper sequence from the start of the process through to the finish.

(2)   Classify each step according to operation, movement, inspection, delay and storage. Find the time taken and distance moved in each step.

(3)   Summarize the process by adding the number of each type of operation, the total time for the process, the rate of doing each operation, and any other relevant information.

These three steps give a detailed description of a process, and an example of the resulting chart is shown in Figure 7.11. Steps 1 and 2 are probably done by observation, while step 3 is a calculation. The next part of the analysis looks for improvements to the process:

(4)   Critically analyse each operation. Ask questions like, 'Can we eliminate this activity?', 'How can we improve this operation?', 'Can we combine operations?'.

(5)   Based on this analysis, revise the process. This should give fewer operations, shorter times, less distance travelled, and so on. Make sure that each operation can still give the output needed by the process. If there are bottlenecks in the process or equipment which is being used inefficiently, adjust the process to give improvements.

(6)   Check the new process, prepare the organization for changes, train staff and implement the changes.

Figure 7.11 shows a process chart, with the time and distances given. Now we can find the maximum output from this process. Operation 1 takes 2.5 minutes, so the maximum output is $60/2.5 = 24$ an hour. Operation 2 takes 2 minutes, so the maximum output is 30 an hour, and so on. The overall output of the process is found from the operation that takes longest. Finishing the product takes 5.5 minutes, so this product can not be made at a rate faster than

Process chart: Part 421/302									
Step number	Description	Operation	Movement	Inspection	Delay	Storage	Time (min)	Distance (metres)	Comment
1	Fetch components		X				2.5	50	
2	Put components on machine	X					2.0		
3	Start machine	X					1.2		
4	Fetch sub-assembly		X				3.0	40	
5	Wait for machine to stop				X		5.2		
6	Unload machine	X					2.0		
7	Inspect result			X			1.5		
8	Join sub-assembly	X					5.0		
9	Move unit to machine		X				2.5	25	
10	Load machine and start	X					2.0		
11	Wait for machine to stop				X		5.0		
12	Unload machine	X					1.4		
13	Carry unit to inspection area		X				2.0	25	
14	Inspect and test			X			5.2		
15	Carry unit to finish area		X				1.4	20	
16	Finish unit	X					5.5		
17	Final inspection			X			3.5		
18	Carry unit to store		X				5.3	45	

Summary		No.	Time		
	Operations	7	19.1	Time:	56.2 min
	Movements	6	16.7	Distance:	205 metres
	Inspections	3	10.2		
	Delays	2	10.2		
	Storage	0	0		
		18	56.2		

Figure 7.11 Example of a typical process chart.

$60/5.5 = 10.9$ units an hour. If forecast demand is higher than this, the process must be changed, perhaps adding more finishers, or changing the way the finishing is done.

The process chart can also suggest areas for improvements. In operations 5 and 11 the machine operator has to wait a total of 10.2 minutes. This might be reduced by better planning. In operations 1, 4, 9, 13, 15 and 18 the product is moved a total of 660 feet, taking 16.7 minutes. This might be reduced by better layouts.

we Worked example

Draw a chart of the process involved when a person goes to a bank and asks for a personal loan.

Solution

Details of the process, and particularly the time, will vary considerably. Figure 7.12 shows an example of a chart.

	Process chart – Personal bank loan								
Step number	Description	Operation	Movement	Inspection	Delay	Storage	Time (min)	Distance (metres)	Comment
1	Customer selects bank and visits		X						
2	Initial screening	X					5		
3	Move to loans office		X				2	15	
4	Wait				X		10		
5	Discuss with loans officer	X					15		
6	Complete application forms	X					15		
7	Carry forms to verifier		X				2	10	
8	Forms are checked			X			2		
9	Wait as credit analysis and verification is done				X		25		
10	Supply further information	X					5		
11	Move back to loans office		X				2	15	
12	Wait				X		20		
13	Forms are checked			X			5		
14	Complete arrangements	X					15		
15	Leave		X						

Summary		No.	Time		
	Operations	5	55	Time:	123 min
	Movements	5	6	Distance:	40 metres
	Inspections	3	7		
	Delays	3	55		
	Storage	0	0		
		15	123		

Figure 7.12 Process chart for example.

ce   **Case example** – Conference registration

At the last conference of the International Management Association 2100 delegates had to register. The process for registration was as follows.

Delegates picked-up registration forms at the information booth. They filled out the forms, walked 20 metres to the hotel reception, and lined up at the front desk. Here a receptionist checked the delegates' details, confirmed their hotel booking and gave them information about their room.

Then the delegates went to a conference administrator who was 80 metres from the front desk. The administrator checked the delegates' forms and saw what sessions and functions they planned to attend. Then delegates walked to the conference registrar's office. Here a clerk calculated the delegates' fees based on their plans for the conference. Then they went to a cashier's window which was 20 metres away to pay their fees.

If delegates wanted car parking at the hotel, they had to go to the parking desk which was 150 metres from the cashier.

On average, the wait at any one of the windows was about 10 minutes and the actual processing time was two minutes.

Questions

• Draw a process chart for delegates who want to register for the conference and pay for their parking.

• Calculate the average time a delegate needs to go through the whole process.

• Can you suggest any improvements to this process?

Precedence diagrams

An alternative form of process chart is a **precedence diagram**. This uses a network of circles and arrows to show the relationships of operations. Suppose a simple process has two operations A and B, and A must be finished before B can start. We can represent the operations by two circles and the relationship by an arrow, as shown in Figure 7.13. The arrow from A to B shows that B must be done after A. We can extend this approach to more complex processes, as shown in the following example.

Figure 7.13 Relationship between operations A and B.

we Worked example

The process in a bottling hall consists of the following five operations:

(1)   clean and inspect the bottle

(2)   fill the bottle

(3)   put a cap on the bottle

(4)   stick a printed label on the bottle

(5)   put the bottle in a box and move it away.

Draw a precedence diagram of this process.

Solution

Some operations must clearly be done before others – as the bottle must be filled before the cap is put on, and so on. We can start by defining all these precedences. Operation 1, cleaning and inspecting the bottle, can be done right at the beginning. Operations 2, filling, and 4, labelling, can both be done immediately after operation 1. Operation 3, capping, can be done after operation 2, while operation 5, putting the bottle in a box, must wait until both operations 3 and 4 are finished. This gives the following list of precedences.

Operation	Must be done after
1	–
2	1
3	2
4	1
5	3, 4

These relationships can be drawn in a precedence diagram. This starts with the earliest operations and moves systematically through the process. So we start by drawing operation 1 at the left, and then add operations 2 and 4.

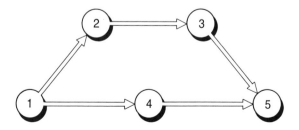

Figure 7.14 Precedence diagram for example.

Operation 3 is added after operation 2. Finally, operation 5 is added, after both operations 3 and 4 are finished. The complete precedence diagram is shown in Figure 7.14.

we Worked example

A product has to go through eleven operations with the precedence shown in the following table:

Operation	Must be done after
1	–
2	1
3	1
4	2, 3
5	4
6	4
7	4
8	5
9	6, 7
10	8, 9
11	10

Draw a precedence diagram of the process.

Solution

To draw the precedence diagram we start with the earliest operations and then systematically work through all other operations. Operation 1 can be done right

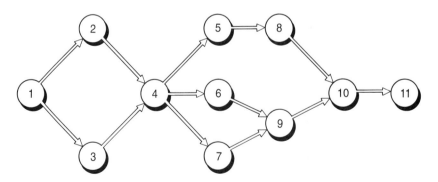

Figure 7.15 Precedence diagram for example.

at the start. When operation 1 is finished both operations 2 and 3 can start. Operation 4 can be done after both operations 2 and 3, and so on. The results are shown in Figure 7.15.

Multiple activity charts

Process charts and precedence diagrams show the relationships between the operations in a process. They are useful in describing and analysing a process, but they do not show what each participant in the process is doing at any time. We may, for example, not only be interested in the total time that an operator is busy during a process, but how this time is distributed. If the operator is idle for long periods we could assign them to other jobs, but we could not do this if the operator is idle for a number of short periods. This kind of analysis is done using a **multiple activity chart**.

A multiple activity chart has a timescale down the side of the diagram, with all the participants listed across the top. Then the time each participant works on the process is blocked-off. Suppose two typists work on word-processors that are connected to a single high quality printer. The participants in the process are the typists, the wordprocessors and the printer. If each typist has a series of documents to type, each of which takes 15 minutes to type and five minutes to print, we could draw the multiple activity chart for their operations during the first hour of a day, shown in Figure 7.16. This

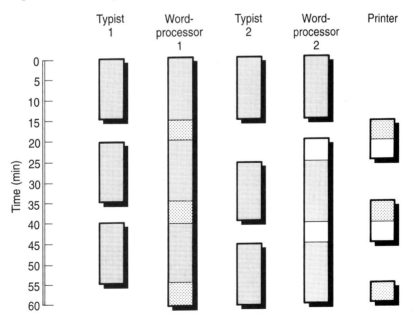

Figure 7.16 Multiple activity chart for typists.

assumes that the two typists start at the same time, that the printer can only print one document at a time, that a wordprocessor can not be used while a document is being printed, and that each document is printed before the next is typed.

This chart shows at a glance what each participant is doing at any time in the process. At the start of the day, both typists use their wordprocessors to type documents. After 15 minutes they both finish. Wordprocessor 1 is connected to the printer, while both typists and wordprocessor 2 wait for the printer to finish. After 20 minutes typist 1 starts their second document, while wordprocessor 2 is connected to the printer, and so on. At the end of the hour, we can see that both typists have been idle for 15 minutes, the wordprocessors are in use all the time after the initial 5 minute wait, and the printer has been used for 25 minutes.

we Worked example

One operator is currently assigned to each of three machines. The machines work a cycle with six minutes for loading, six minutes of operating and four minutes for unloading. An operator is needed for the loading and unloading, but the machines can work without any supervision. The operations manager plans to make savings by using two people to operate the three machines. Draw a multiple activity chart to see if this can be done. What are the utilizations?

Solution

A multiple activity chart for three machines and two operators is shown in Figure 7.17, assuming all people and machines are idle at the start, and we follow the process for the first hour of operation.

The process starts with operators 1 and 2 loading machines A and B respectively. These machines start operating, while operator 1 loads machine C. Machines A and B are unloaded as soon as they are finished, and are then reloaded. Machine C has to wait to be unloaded until an operator is free. This process continues for the 60 minutes. At the end of this time, operator 1 has been idle for 8 minutes, operator 2 has been idle for 8 minutes, and the three machines have been idle for 0, 4 and 10 minutes. Utilizations are 87% for operators and an average of 92% for machines. Some of this idle time was needed at the start of the day, and if we had drawn the chart for longer the average utilization of machines would increase. Overall the new arrangement seems to work.

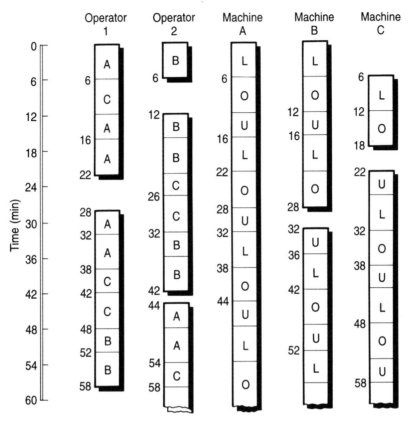

Figure 7.17 Multiple activity chart for example.

Review questions

7.16 What is the purpose of process charts?

7.17 What are precedence diagrams and when are they used?

7.18 What exactly is meant by 'operation A precedes operation B'?

7.19 When are multiple activity charts used?

Chapter review

- The process describes the detailed operations needed to make a product. Process planning finds the best possible process for a product.

- Processes can be classified as project, job shop, batch, mass production or continuous flow. Each of these has different characteristics and is best suited to different types and quantities of products.

- A number of factors are important in choosing the best process, including demand, variation in demand, product mix, capital available, workforce skills, and so on. The choice may also be related to the stage of the product in its life-cycle.

- Intermittent processes have lower productivity than mass production processes. Their productivity can be improved by reorganizing equipment operators, using group technology, or flexible automation.

- Different levels of automation are classified as manual, mechanized or automated. Higher levels of technology generally have higher productivity.

- Several levels of automation were described, ranging from numerically controlled machines to automated factories. The best level of automation should be chosen for any process, but this is not necessarily the highest level that is technically feasible.

- Many ideas in the chapter were introduced by reference to manufacturing. The same principles apply to services. Many services use project or job shop processes, but others are highly automated.

- Process charts describe the details of an existing process and highlight areas where improvements can be made. Several types of charts were described, including process charts, precedence diagrams and multiple activity charts.

Key terms

automation   209
batch processing   196
computer assisted
   design   211
computer aided
   manufacturing   209
computer integrated
   manufacturing   211
continuous flow   197
flexible manufacturing
   system   210

job shop   195
mass production   197
multiple activity chart   227
numerically controlled   209
precedence diagram   224
process   193
process chart   219
project   195
vertical integration   202

CS Case study – Retooling for the FX100A camera

A camera company[†] started making cameras 70 years ago to meet the rapidly growing demand for inexpensive cameras. It was run by the same family until twenty years ago. By then the Board of Directors were all distant relatives of the original founder, but had little interest in the business and few management skills. Despite falling sales, they kept drawing large salaries, and refused to invest money in the business. In 1992 the company made a substantial loss and was only saved from bankruptcy when the banks organized a major restructuring. They appointed a number of directors and insisted the family give up control. At the same time a number of well-known business figures and some senior managers from within the company were invited to join the Board. Among these was Jim Wright, the Production Manager.

At the next Board meeting there would be four managers, who were reasonably competent and had been responsible for the turn around of the company. There would also be four members of the family, who always oppose expenditure and want higher profits distributed among shareholders, three bankers who give cautious support for any sensible investment, and three external directors.

At this Board meeting Jim Wright would give a presentation on the case for retooling the assembly line which made their FX100A camera. This is an expensive semi-automatic camera which is noted for its high quality. It is the company's best selling line, accounting for 30% of sales and 40% of profits. The main customers are professional photographers and keen amateurs, with 80% of production exported primarily to the United States and European Union.

Jim considered the retooling of their best selling product to be an important project. The current process had grown with demand, and there had never been a chance to make fundamental changes. Jim thought this would be a good time to modernize the assembly process by moving away from the manual process and towards a more automated one. To see if this was feasible, he hired a firm of consulting engineers. They wrote a 550-page report which suggested three alternatives:

(1)   improve the present process to increase productivity by 5%

(2)   install hard automation

(3)   install flexible automation.

The Board had to make a decision, and to help with his presentation, Jim made the following notes.

[†] The company and the FX100A camera are fictitious and are used only for example.

Product

FX100A semi-automatic camera

Monthly sales (in hundreds) over the past three years

	Jan	Feb	Mar	Apr	May	Jun	Jul	Aug	Sep	Oct	Nov	Dec
1992	70	40	59	108	127	140	139	127	73	58	99	144
1993	77	43	68	121	143	150	154	136	95	71	116	172
1994	82	51	60	113	137	152	159	144	104	65	128	168

Current operations

- Raw materials and components are bought from 68 suppliers and put in the Materials' Store in the Old Works.

- Some components and sub-assemblies are made in the Old Works.

- The Assembly Plant was built 20 years ago on the back of the Old Works, and all final product assembly is done here.

- Requests for parts and materials are passed from the Assembly Plant to the Materials' Store, and in normal circumstances delivery is guaranteed within half an hour.

- Three parallel assembly lines in the Assembly Plant, working a single eight-hour shift each day for five days a week. The manual assembly is labour intensive. There are 258 separate operations in the process. If all goes well these take a total of an hour and a half for each camera.

- Finished products are moved to the Warehouse which was built five years ago adjacent to the other buildings.

Number, cost and availability of employees

- 168 people work on the assembly line, for a standard 38 hour week and an average of five hours a week overtime.

- 12 supervisors work a standard 38 hour week and an average of seven hours a week overtime.

- One floor manager work a standard 38 hour week, with unpaid overtime as needed.

The company uses a formula for staff costs that takes into account wages, stoppages, subsidized meals, training, and a range of other direct costs. This gives guidelines for the total cost of employing one person for an hour, as:

- *assembly line workers*: £10 an hour normally and £13 an hour for overtime

- *supervisors*: £14 an hour normally and £17 an hour for overtime
- *floor manager*: £18 an hour (with no overtime payments).

Each employee gets 33 days a year paid holiday. Sickness, training and other absences mean that an average of 12.3 assembly line employees are absent in any particular day.

Quality

The FX100A sells well because of its consistently high quality. During assembly there are 24 separate inspections and last year these detected 4749 faults. Most of these were minor and could be corrected, but about 10% meant the camera had to be scrapped. The company received 511 complaints from customers and replaced the camera under a comprehensive warranty.

Main alternatives for retooling

(1) *Adjust current operations* This option left the operations essentially unchanged but made some improvements in planning, scheduling and quality that could increase productivity by about 5%.

(2) *Hard automation* This replaces the manual assembly by machines designed especially to assemble the FX100A automatically.

Capital costs:	planning and design, £1.5 million
	production machines, £6 million
	associated equipment, £1.5 million
	refurbishing plant, £1 million
Operating costs:	maintenance at 6% of cost a year
	depreciation at 17% a year
	capital at 18% a year
Time:	18 months to complete installation
Staff:	20 operators equivalent to current supervisors
	6 maintenance engineers, each with a total cost of £40,000 a year
Savings:	all of current assembly line costs
	£250,000 a year in Old Works by moving assembly to the main plant
Capacity:	1000 units a day

(3) *Flexible automation* This replaces the manual assembly by CNC machines and general purpose robots that could be programmed to automatically assemble the FX100A.

Capital costs:	planning and design, £1 million
	production machines, £5 million
	associated equipment, £1 million
	refurbishing plant, £1 million

Operating costs: maintenance at 8% of cost a year
                                depreciation at 12% a year
                                capital at 18% a year

Time: one year to complete installation

Staff: 30 operators equivalent to current supervisors
                                10 maintenance engineers, each with a total cost of
                                £40,000 a year

Savings: all of current assembly line costs
                                £250,000 a year in Old Works by moving assembly
                                to the main plant

Capacity: 800 units a day

Other points

- Unemployment in the area is generally high, but there are severe shortages of some specific skills.

- Seven trade unions have members within the company.

- The consultants' report listed six feasible alternative for tooling, but Jim had reduced this to two.

- The company make seven different types of camera, all using a similar process, and a range of camera accessories.

- Four of the current Board members are close to retirement.

- The Family still own 35% of the shares in the company.

Problems

7.1   A manufacturing company is considering a new product, but has not yet forecast demand. Experience suggests their costs will depend on the type of process used, as follows.

	Annual fixed cost	Variable cost
Project	100,000	2,000
Job shop	150,000	250
Batch	450,000	150
Mass production	1,500,000	100

Within what range is each process best?

7.2   A factory works two eight-hour shifts a day, five days a week for 50 weeks a year. Welders have the unpleasant job of getting into an awkward, enclosed space to spot weld two parts. For this, they are paid

£7 an hour directly with a further £3 an hour in other costs. The operations manager has suggested that a robot for this job would cost £150,000. This would work virtually non-stop for an expected life of seven to 10 years, and with operating costs of £2 an hour. Do you think this is a reasonable investment?

7.3 A company can use three different processes to make a product, with total unit costs as follows:

- manual process: fixed at £40 a unit
- hard automation: $£200 - 4D$
- flexible automation: $£10,000 - 25D$

where D is the annual demand in hundreds of units. Over what range would each type of process give the lowest unit cost?

7.4 A factory works three eight-hour shifts a day for five days a week. It could save £20 an hour in labour costs by using an industrial robot which costs £250,000. If the factory pays 15% interest on a debt with the bank, and the robot has a life expectancy of seven years, is this a good investment?

7.5 It is suggested that a new machine will generate the following incomes and costs over the next five years. Use a discounting rate of 12% to see if the machine would be a good investment.

Year	Income	Costs
–	–	36,000
1	5,000	–
2	27,000	12,000
3	36,000	–
4	12,000	4,000
5	2,000	–

7.6 Draw two alternative charts to describe the process of getting a mortgage from a building society.

7.7 A product goes through eight operations with the precedences shown in the following table. Draw a precedence diagram of the process.

Operation	Must be done after
1	–
2	1
3	2
4	1
5	4
6	3, 5
7	3, 6
8	5, 6

7.8 A unit of product comes off a production line and a random sample is taken for inspection. The inspection of each unit has three separate elements, each of which uses a different type of machine. There are two machines of each type in the inspection area. Each unit of product takes three minutes on each machine for inspection, and then two minutes on each machine for final adjustment. There are three inspectors working in the area. Draw a process chart for the inspection area. How many units can be inspected each hour?

Discussion questions

7.1 What technological developments do you think have had most effect on operations over the past decade or so? What developments will affect future operations?

7.2 'It is not the process that matters but the final product.' Do you agree with this view?

7.3 Describe the processes used to make a number of products you are familiar with. Why are these processes used? How could the processes be improved?

7.4 Some people suggest that operations can only be automated at the expense of the people working in them. Do you think this is true? Do you think that increasing automation reduces the skills people develop?

7.5 What is meant by the flexibility of a process? What factors would increase the flexibility? Why is it useful to increase flexibility?

7.6 Automation increases productivity and should be introduced as widely as possible. Do you think this is true?

7.7 When people think about automation they often imagine factories and car assembly lines. Most people work in services. Describe some specific areas where automation has affected services. What do you think will happen in the future?

7.8 What information should you be able to get from a process chart? What kinds of chart can be used to get this information (do not restrict yourself to the charts described in this chapter)?

Selected references

Ayres R.U. and Miller S.M. (1983). *Robotics: Applications and Social Implications.* Cambridge, Mass.: Ballinger.

Chang T.C. and Wysk R.A. (1985). *An Introduction to Automated Process Planning Systems*. Englewood Cliffs, NJ: Prentice-Hall.

Collier D.A. (1986). *Service Management: The Automation of Services*. Reston: Reston Publishing.

Doyle L.E., Keyser C.A. *et al*. (1985). *Manufacturing Processes and Materials for Engineers* (3rd edn). Englewood Cliffs, NJ: Prentice-Hall.

Groover M.P. and Zimmers E.W. (1984). *CAD/CAM: Computer Aided Design and Manufacturing*. Englewood Cliffs, NJ: Prentice-Hall.

Gunn T.G. (1987). *Manufacturing for Competitive Advantage*. Cambridge, Mass.: Ballinger.

Hill T. (1985). *Manufacturing Strategy*. Basingstoke: Macmillan.

Horwitch M. (ed.) (1986). *Technology in the Modern Corporation*. New York: Pergamon.

Liebowitz J. (1988). *Introduction to Expert Systems*. Santa Cruz, Ca.: Mitchell Publishing.

The Tay engine

Rolls-Royce

The development of new civil aero engines is both lengthy and expensive. The development cost can exceed £1 billion and because civil aero engines have to satisfy extremely high reliability and efficiency criteria, it can take up to 10 years, from the point at which design work starts, to get an engine into service. These factors account for some of the financial difficulties that Rolls-Royce faced in the early 1970s. However, the engine at the centre of these difficulties, the RB-211, went on to sell in large numbers and proved to be profitable. It also spawned a number of derivatives including the 535 engine that powers the Boeing 757 and the 524 engine that powers the Boeing 747 jumbo jet. This family of engines has enabled the company to enhance its position as one of the 'Big Three' civil engine producers with about a quarter share of the total market.

Although it is probably better known these days for its large engines, the company is also actively involved in the low thrust segment of the market. In the late 1970s this presence centred upon the Spey engine. This engine powered two of the three main British airliners of the 1960s and 1970s – the Trident and the BAC One-Eleven. Development of the Spey began in 1959, went into volume production in the mid-1960s, and was used by a wide range of airlines over the next 20 years. The life of the engine was extended, as is normally the case with civil aero engines, by producing a number of derivatives. These included an 11,500 lbs thrust version for the BAC One-Eleven 300/400 series with 97 seats compared to 79 on the original aircraft and a 12,500 lbs thrust version for the BAC One-Eleven 500 series with 119 seats. Another version of the engine was developed specifically for the Dutch aircraft manufacturer Fokker (now part of Daimler-Benz's Deutsche Aerospace subsidiary), for its F 28 short haul airliner that came into service in the 1970s. The development of a number of versions of the Spey extended the life-cycle of the engine and it was still in volume production in the 1980s.

The problem

By the early 1980s, however, Rolls-Royce faced considerable problems if it was to retain its share of this segment of the civil aero engine market. Among the most significant were:

(1) The introduction of new noise and emission regulations throughout the world, meant the days of the old-fashioned and noisy Spey engine were clearly numbered.

(2) The company was at this time preoccupied with developing a number of major new engines including the RB-211 derived 535 and 524 engines in the high thrust sector of the market and a new '10 tonne' medium-thrust engine, the V2500, being developed in collaboration with Pratt and Whitney.

(3) Plans for new regional airliners to come into service in the late 1980s and early 1990s, like the Fokker 100 and the Gulfstream IV highlighted the need for a new fuel-efficient engine utilizing the latest in aero engine technology.

Rolls-Royce was therefore faced with a major financial outlay if it was to develop a new engine and retain its position in the market. The development of a new engine would tie up some of the company's best engineers and its research and development facilities, precisely at a time when they were required for other projects. Worse still, a completely new engine would take time to develop and would not be on the market until the end of the decade.

The solution

Rolls-Royce got round these difficulties by developing an engine that 'borrowed' components and technologies from other engines in its product range. Designated the Tay, the new

engine retained the established and certificated central high pressure section or core of the Spey engine. Avoiding the development of a totally new core saved not only money but also a great deal of time. It also provided other benefits including longer service life from the start of operation, lower service requirements and spares cost and better reliability. To the established core was added an advanced low pressure system incorporating the latest proven advances in engine technology. These included a wide cord fan derived from the 535-E4 engine and a new intermediate pressure compressor in place of the Spey's low pressure compressor. The new fan was a vital part of the new engine. Derived from the 535 engine, it permitted the use of a much higher bypass ratio of 3:1 compared to the 1:1 ratio of the Spey. This meant that the new engine was similar in structure to the RB-211. More significantly the high bypass ratio meant that the engine was considerably quieter than the earlier Spey. Overall the developments built into the new engine made it capable of producing 25% more power, using 15% less fuel, while generating seven decibels less noise, than the engine it superseded.

The Tay engine made its first flight in a Gulfstream IV in September 1985. The lengthy and time-consuming process of airworthiness certification was greatly shortened and simplified because a major part of the engine was already proven. Certification was completed in 1986 and deliveries began shortly afterwards.

By 1990 more than 500 Tay engines had been sold. With a thrust range between 12,500 lbs and 15,000 lbs the Tay dominated the market for regional airliners and large corporate jets. Not only had the engine sold well in Europe, where customers included British Midland and UK Air, sales had also been strong in the United States where large numbers of Tay engines were bought by American Airlines. As well as the market for new aircraft, the Tay had also carved out a niche market for re-engining existing aircraft, such as the Boeing 727 and the BAC One-Eleven, in order to meet stringent new noise regulations. Among the aircraft re-engined with Tay engines were United Parcel Service's fleet of Boeing 727-100 aircraft.

Sales of the Tay engine are likely to continue well into the next century, by which time it will in turn be superseded by the BR700 engine that Rolls-Royce is currently developing in conjunction with the German car manufacturer BMW.

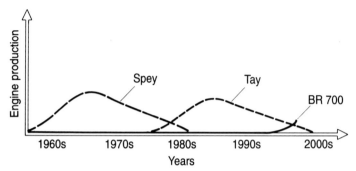

Figure MPII.1 Product life-cycle of low-thrust engines.

Decisions about the process

This book is divided into five parts, each of which describes a different aspect of operations management. Part I introduced the subject. Part II looked at the planning needed for a product. This planning included some of the strategic issues faced by every organization: how to plan products, how to maintain quality, how many units to make, and how to make them.

We saw in Chapter 7 that a specific process is used to make every product. In this third part of the book we will look in more detail at the process.

There are three chapters in Part III. Chapter 8 describes the layout of facilities. This is clearly linked to the type of process used. Chapter 9 looks at the need to match available capacity to forecast demand, and relates this to various measures of performance. Chapter 10 describes ways of controlling quality.

Part II described a number of strategic decisions. In this section we are moving towards tactical decisions. Later in the book, Part IV considers the planning and scheduling of resources, and Part V discusses some aspects of materials management.

John Sullivan
ICI

ICI is divided into a number of large businesses, one of which is ICI Chemicals & Polymers Ltd. One of ICI Chemicals & Polymers large manufacturing sites is Merseyside Operations in Runcorn. Merseyside Operations includes Bulk Chemical and Industrial Chemical Businesses and is made up of a series of sub-units or Strategic Business Units. These Strategic Business units consist of a number of manufacturing assets which make chemicals. The production management responsibility for some of these assets lies with John Sullivan, the Production Area Manager. Merseyside Operations has six production areas – a production area being a number of chemical plants which are integrated and linked to each other.

Q **What processes do you use to make your product?** **A** We use a range of processes to manufacture our products, one of which is 'continuous chemical process' (as opposed to 'batch process'). In this process, raw materials go in at one end, and the product comes out at the other on a continuous basis. There are two basic unit operations comprising this process – Reaction and Separation. Most chemical plants will have these two sections.

We work on a large industrial basis, processing thousands of tonnes of chemical products each year. Our processes include a combination of patented ICI technology and licenced technology.

Q **How does the layout of facilities link to the type of process you use?** **A** The layout of our plant has been directed to a certain extent by its physical environment. Because water is a vital service in the manufacture of chemicals, Merseyside Operations is situated alongside a major river, and on the other side of the plant is a cliff. The site has had to be developed within these physical constraints. Given a greenfield site we would probably design the layout of the plants somewhat differently.

The history of Merseyside Operations goes back many years, and our current layout must be viewed in this historical context.

Our layout follows a continuous flow path via pipelines and tanks. The raw materials supply the process via pipelines which normally feed in to the Reaction Section, on to the Separation stage(s) and then in to storage. We try to always move hazardous material by pipeline around the plants. There are several raw materials used at Merseyside Operations, including two key substances: salt, for the chlorinated products, and fluorspar, for fluorinated products. The layout of our facilities allows for the efficient transportation of these products.

Q **How do you match available capacity to forecast demand?**

A Our processes have been designed to maximize capacity utilization, and the maximum capacity of our assets is normally fixed. We usually aim to run our processes flat out. However, there is some demand on capacity fluctuation influenced by market demands and we will turn up, or turn down production accordingly. In the short term, there is not much change in demand but in the longer term, we have seen large changes in demand. For example, we have closed down three out of four of our Sulphuric Acid Plants because market demand has fallen.

We do have constraints other than market fluctuation on our process capacity manufacture. We are constrained by Health and Safety regulations which put limits on our major hazard inventory. These regulations place restraints on our storage of hazardous materials on site. Therefore, any capacity planning which is undertaken must take account of this constraint.

The fact that we are part of a number of integrated chemical plants also places constraints upon us and affects our internal supply and demand. For example, sulphuric acid is a raw material for hydrofluoric acid, which in turn is a raw material for Arcton 22 which is sold on to another part of ICI to produce PTFE products.

Q **What measures of performance do you use?**

A We have a range of financial and non-financial performance measures:

- *Financial* There are variable costs under which for example raw material would fall, and there are fixed costs. Fixed costs include manpower and maintenance expenses.

- *Non-financial* Our non-financial performance measures include Safety, Health and Environmental measures. These measures are most important as our licence to operate is given on the basis of how well we perform in these areas. ICI is striving to be the World's number one in these areas and we believe that if we are not the best we will not prosper in today's globally competitive environment.

Environmental issues have become more and more important to us in recent years. We are monitored, and have to abide by the requirements of Integrated Pollution Control (IPC). We have to submit a proposal to Her Majesty's Inspectorate of Pollution about how we are going to improve our pollution control. This IPC work has been going on in ICI for the past three or four years. The National Rivers Authority (NRA) has also played an important role in our pollution control measures and with their help much progress has been made. We also have a liaison group which meets with local community representatives to discuss environmental issues. We have good relations with the local community.

Q What quality control measures do you employ?

A We use various analytical techniques to analyse the quality of our products, such as gas liquid chromatography and conductivity tests. Our products are made to a detailed specification. The customer specifies the quality of the product, and we must ensure that the finished product meets these specifications.

We have quality systems which are registered and certified to BS5750, and to ISO9002. We are externally audited annually on our internal systems of quality control. We also have our own internal auditors of quality. We have regular customer visits to audit our processes, and to check our quality procedures. Customers sometimes require Quality Assurance data to be collected in a certain form for their own statistical analysis. Our customers are not just external as we have many internal customers within ICI, who are equally demanding about the quality of products we supply. The quality revolution has been a big part of ICI for the past 10 years. We involve our customers and staff in our quality processes, and we spend time and money to facilitate this.

The Staff Agreement 1991 (implemented in 1994) allows our employees more flexibility. Employees can now undertake any job they are trained, qualified or able to do. People are more involved, can do more, and more of their skills are utilized. The shop-floor is unionized, but we now encourage a co-operative relationship with the unions. There is a high degree of teamwork, and the atmosphere is not adversarial. Our workforce varies in its skill levels at present, and different skills are associated with different processes. Thus, some plant teams are more skilled than others. We expect our operators of the future to be more skilled, and hold at least an HNC or HND qualification. We have a training partnership with Shell and Octel, and many of our staff come already skilled. We are moving towards a multi-skilled and educated workforce. Personal development is encouraged for those who are interested – such as supervisory courses at NVQIII. We run part-time HNC courses in Chemical Engineering and we run a part-time Chemical Engineering degree with Strathclyde University. These courses are open to all employees who are interested. We are committed to employee development.

8 Layout of facilities

Contents

Objectives

After reading this chapter you should be able to:

- discuss the meaning and importance of facility layout
- describe alternative types of layout
- describe process layouts
- design process layouts that minimize movement between areas
- describe product layouts
- use a line balancing algorithm for product layouts
- describe hybrid layouts, particularly work cells
- discuss the characteristics of fixed layouts
- describe some layouts such as warehouses, offices and retail shops

ce Case example – Hart House Restaurant

'It is very simple', said Joe Mellors, owner of the Hart House Restaurant. 'We have a popular bar, and behind this is a restaurant. Last year people would come for a meal in the restaurant. They would walk through the main door into the bar, see the crowds, assume the restaurant was also full and go somewhere else to eat. Often the restaurant was almost empty, but people were leaving to eat next door.'

'To solve this problem I changed the layout. I added a reception area at the front of the building and built a passage through to the restaurant. Now people come through the main door and turn left to go into the bar. People who want the restaurant are met by a receptionist who leads them down the corridor. They know straight away that there is room in the restaurant, and they never even look into the bar. It may seem simple, but changing the layout increased the restaurant's income by 180%.'

This example gives one example of the benefits that come from making the layout of facilities match the operations.

Layouts for different types of process

The last chapter described the different types of process that can be used for making product. In this chapter we shall look in more detail at the way these processes are physically arranged or laid out.

> **Facility layout** is the physical arrangement of equipment, offices, rooms, and so on, within an organization. It describes the location of resources and their relationship to each other.

When you go into a Sainsbury's supermarket you see that goods are arranged in parallel aisles. A lot of thought and experiment has gone into this layout. It is especially designed to encourage customers to buy more goods. Every other organization has to consider the layout of its operations, whether it is a manufacturer, warehouse, office or government debating chamber.

Well laid out facilities are efficient and allow a smooth flow of work through the process: poorly laid out facilities disrupt operations and reduce efficiency. You can see this in, say, libraries – one library is convenient and easy to use, while another is confusing and poorly arranged. In the same way, some airports handle large numbers of people very efficiently, while others have queues, crowds milling around and people wandering around looking lost. The purpose of layout planning is to arrange the facilities so that the process can run as smoothly as possible.

> **Layout design** aims to organize the physical arrangement of facilities so that operations run as efficiently as possible.

Two common objectives of layout design are:

(1) to arrange the facilities needed by a process so that the desired output is achieved using minimum resources; or

(2) to arrange available facilities so that the maximum output is achieved.

These objectives raise a number of related questions about how much space should be given to each operation, how the space should be arranged, what types of equipment should be used, what services are needed in each area, and so on.

Every organization must design its layout to achieve a number of these objectives. At the same time, it must consider the constraints on layout. There is, for example, only a certain amount of space available for operations. Other constraints on the layout come from:

- the product design

- planned capacity

- type of process

- total space available

- other site constraints

- materials handling equipment

- capital available for investment

- need for service areas

- communications and information flows

- safety needs.

In the rest of the chapter we shall see how these factors affect layout design. In particular, we shall describe the five different types of layout:

- process layout

- product layout

- hybrid layout

- fixed position layout

- a series of specialized layouts, such as retail shops and warehouses.

ce Case example – West Marshes Post Office

The purpose-built post office in West Marshes was used since the 1930s. But recent changes in policy have transferred the counter service to a nearby newsagent. A post office counter was opened at the back of the newsagent, with the layout shown in Figure 8.1.

This layout did not work well. People did not know where to queue in front of the counters, it was not clear if there was one queue or several, queues got in the way of people wanting to look at the shelves in the shop, people waiting for the post office noticed that others waiting for the newsagent got served much faster, there was nowhere to fill in forms, people looking at magazines got in the way of those wanting to get to the post office, and so on.

The newsagent changed the details of layout of the shop over the next three years, adding barriers to form a single queue, adding a counter to fill in forms, closing the end of aisles so that newsagent customers were kept more separate from post office customers. These changes certainly improved things,

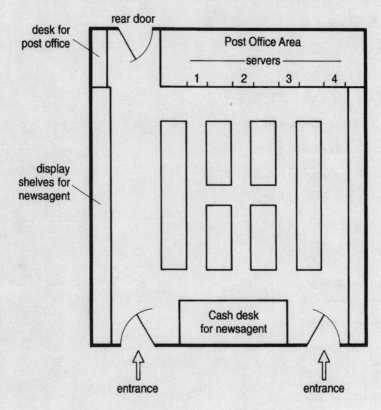

Figure 8.1 West Marshes post office/newsagent.

but there was still a general feeling that the service had declined since the purpose-built post office was closed.

Questions

- Why are there problems with the new post office counter?

- How would you overcome these problems?

Review questions

8.1   What is meant by 'layout' and why is it important?

8.2   What are the objectives of layout design?

8.3   What different types of layout are there?

Process layouts

In a **process layout** all similar pieces of equipment are grouped together. Drilling machines might be put in one area, grinders in another area, sanding machines in a third area, and milling machines in a fourth. Hospitals use a process layout and put all equipment for emergencies in one ward, surgical patients in another, paediatrics in another, and so on. Every product uses a different sequence of operations, so each product will follow a different route through the facilities, as shown in Figure 8.2.

This layout works best when many different products are made on the same equipment. You can imagine this as a job shop which makes small batches of different products. Process layouts have the following advantages and disadvantages.

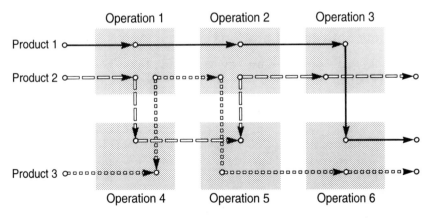

Figure 8.2 Products following different paths through a process layout.

Advantages of process layout

- a variety of products can be made on the same equipment;

- equipment is general purpose and less expensive than specialized equipment used in product layouts;

- operations can continue if some equipment is unavailable because of break-down or planned maintenance;

- it is suitable for low volumes and variable demand;

- products can be made for specific orders;

- people work in cohesive groups and generally enjoy the environment.

Disadvantages of process layout

- small batches give lower utilization of equipment and higher unit costs;

- movement of jobs between operations is complicated, with larger stocks of work in progress;

- scheduling work on equipment is complicated and must be done continuously;

- higher levels of operator skills are needed;

- controlling the work is difficult;

- there is a lot of handling of products and materials.

One feature of process layouts, is that people work in groups according to their skills. So accountants might work in one area, lawyers in another, and so on. These can form cohesive groups that work together well, giving both high morale and productivity. But it becomes difficult to make any changes to layouts, as the group does not want to be split-up.

Movements between operations

In process layouts a product must physically move to the next set of equipment between operations. If there are 10 operations in a process, the product must be moved 10 times. This can give a lot of movement, and one objective in designing layouts is to minimize the overall distance travelled.

There are several ways of reducing the amount of movement, but the most widely used are simple rules of thumb. Suppose there is a lot of movement between two operations, say packing and mailing. It would be sensible to put these operations as close together as possible. Other areas with no movement can be placed far apart.

A common way of organizing this is to draw a plan of the available space and add the most frequent movements. Arrows can be used for this, with the thickness of the arrow showing the number of movements. People are very good at recognizing patterns, and they can quickly look at these plans to get some ideas for layouts. More formally, computer software can simplify the drawing of plans and compare alternate layouts.

we Worked example

A museum has seven main galleries. These have recently been renovated and the number of visitors has risen considerably. A questionnaire was given to visitors to see how they liked the new arrangements. Most comments were favourable, but some people felt they passed the same exhibits several times before visiting all the galleries. To see if this was true, the routes taken by all people visiting the gallery during a typical morning were recorded. The most frequent movements are shown in Figure 8.3. In this diagram the thickness of the arrows shows the number of people following the path. How might the layout of the galleries be improved?

Solution

If you look at the dominant flows in Figure 8.3 you can see that the criticisms are justified. Some improvements to the layout can be made as follows:

- Most people walk through gallery 4 as they move from gallery 5 to gallery 6. On the other hand, gallery 5 is visited twice (after both galleries 1 and 7) but it does not have a central position. An obvious improvement is to exchange galleries 4 and 5, so gallery 5 moves to the centre and gallery 4 moves out of the way.

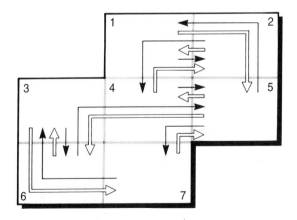

Figure 8.3 Original layout of seven galleries in museum.

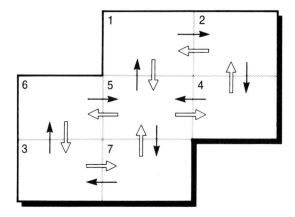

Figure 8.4 Improved layout that reduces movement.

- Most people walk through gallery 3 to get to gallery 6 and then return to gallery 3. These two could also be exchanged.

These simple adjustments give the improved movements shown in Figure 8.4.

Designing process layouts

Informal approaches to layout design work well with small problems, but we need a more rigorous approach for larger problems. One procedure has the following three steps.

- *First*, collect relevant information about:
  - the space needed for each area
  - quantities moved between areas
  - number of trips between areas.

- *Second*, build a general block plan and try to minimize the total movement.

- *Third*, talk to architects, engineers, consultants and other experts to add details to the block plan and give a final layout.

The second step in this procedure designs a general block plan. We can do this using the following procedure.

(1) List the separate areas or departments to be located and find the space needed by each one.

(2) · Build a 'from–to' matrix. This shows the number of trips directly between each pair of areas, and is usually found by observation over some typical period.

(3)   Use sensible arguments to develop an initial layout – perhaps based on the current layout or layout of a similar process.

(4)   Find a cost for this layout. This can be given in terms of total distance moved $(= \sum (\text{movements} \times \text{distance}))$, weight-distance moved $(= \sum (\text{movements} \times \text{distance} \times \text{weight}))$ or some other convenient measure. If this solution is acceptable go to step 6, otherwise continue to step 5.

(5)   Improve the initial layout. This may be done by trial and error, some algorithm, or experience. Go back to step 4.

(6)   Complete the block plan by adding details of cost, other constraints, preferred features, problems, and so on.

we Worked example

The Seminar Block in Meescham College essentially has six rooms of equal size fitted into a rectangular building. Students move between these rooms during the day. During a typical period the following movements were seen between rooms.

		To					
		a	b	c	d	e	f
	a	–	30	10	0	12	0
	b	0	–	10	40	5	0
From	c	0	5	–	60	0	20
	d	0	10	15	–	0	10
	e	60	20	0	0	–	10
	f	0	0	30	5	10	–

Draw a block diagram of a good layout for the building.

Solution

Following the procedure described above:

•   Step 1 has already been done with six rooms, a to f, each needing the same amount of space.

•   Step 2 builds a from–to matrix. Assuming that a journey from a to b is effectively the same as a journey from b to a, we can combine the top and bottom halves of this matrix to give a revised from–to matrix.

		To				
	a	b	c	d	e	f
a	–	30	10	0	72	0
b		–	15	50	25	0
From c			–	75	0	50
d				–	0	15
e					–	20
f						–

- Step 3 uses sensible arguments to develop an initial layout. One approach is to rank the links according to the amount of movement. The busiest link is c–d with a value of 75, next comes a–e with a value of 72, and so on.

Rank	Link	Value
1	c–d	75
2	a–e	72
3	b–d	50
4	c–f	50
5	a–b	30
6	b–e	25
7	e–f	20
8	b–c	15
9	d–f	15
10	a–c	10
11	a–d, a–f, b–f, c–e, d–e	0

Common sense suggests that rooms c and d should be close together as they have most movements, while a and d have no movement and can be far apart. If we concentrate on those rooms that should be close together, and move down the ranking above, we could draw the layout shown in Figure 8.5.

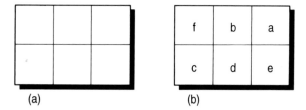

(a)   (b)

Figure 8.5 Initial layouts for example: (a) rectangular building with six areas; (b) trial layout.

- Step 4 finds a cost for this layout. A simple cost can be found by multiplying the movements in the from–to matrix by the distance on each journey. We can simplify the calculations by assuming the rooms are squares with sides one unit long and use rectilinear distances – which are simply the sum of horizontal and vertical distances moved. Then f is 1 unit from c, 2 units from d and 3 units from e, and so on. These distances are given in the following table. We only want to compare the costs of different layouts, so the actual units are not important – so long as they give consistent values.

		To					
		a	b	c	d	e	f
	a	–	1	3	2	1	2
	b		–	2	1	2	1
From	c			–	1	2	1
	d				–	1	2
	e					–	3
	f						–

Multiplying the number of movements by the distance gives the following costs:

		To					
		a	b	c	d	e	f
	a	–	30 × 1	10 × 3	0	72 × 1	0
	b		–	15 × 2	50 × 1	25 × 2	0
From	c			–	75 × 1	0	50 × 1
	d				–	0	15 × 2
	e					–	20 × 3
	f						–

The total cost for this layout is the sum of these individual costs, which is 477. If this is not good enough, we can now adjust the layout and look at an alternative.

- Step 5 looks for improvements to the layout. One weakness is the distance between e and f which contributes 60 to the total cost. This could be reduced by rearranging the rooms as shown in Figure 8.6.

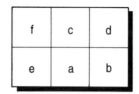

Figure 8.6 Improved layout.

Using the same approach to costs as before gives a total cost of 417. This cost is much lower, but if we wanted a better solution we could continue the procedure:

		a	b	c	*To* d	e	f
	a	–	30 × 1	10 × 1	0	72 × 1	0
	b		–	15 × 2	50 × 1	25 × 2	0
From	c			–	75 × 1	0	50 × 1
	d				–	0	15 × 2
	e					–	20 × 1
	f						–

- Step 6 adds details to this block plan. These details could include the exact size and shape of each room, as well as layout of aisles, stairs, offices and other general purpose areas. Later, details of individual pieces of equipment, furniture and partitions can be added.

An obvious problem with this procedure comes in step 5, where we need to find improvements to layouts. Using common sense works well for small problems, but it is difficult for larger ones. There are more formal methods, but these need a lot of calculations and must be done with a computer. Typically, they take the initial layout and make small adjustments to look for improvements – perhaps exchanging the positions of two or three areas. These adjustments are continued until no further improvement can be found. There are many packages for process layouts and the following example illustrates one of these.

we Worked example

A computer program was used to design a new layout for a process. Figure 8.7 shows the computer printout. This starts by summarizing the data. There are nine departments and those areas of the facility that can not be used are

(a) Input data for problem - layout example

```
Criterion:               Minimize
Number of Departments = 10
Number of rows in the initial layout = 20
Number of columns in the initial layout = 25


Input data   --   Area of each department

Department  1  :   27        not fixed
Department  2  :   15        not fixed
Department  3  :   70        not fixed
Department  4  :   42        not fixed
Department  5  :   24        not fixed
Department  6  :   14        not fixed
Department  7  :   48        not fixed
Department  8  :   35        not fixed
Department  9  :   24        not fixed
Department  A  :  207        fixed


Total               506


Input data   --   Initial layout

        1 2 3 4 5 6 7 8 9 0 1 2 3 4 5 6 1 8 9 0 1 2 3 4 5

1    1 1 1 1 1 1 1 1 1 7 7 7 7 7 7 7 7 7 7 7 7 7 7 7 7
2    1                 1 7                             7
3    1 1 1 1 1 1 1 1 1 7 7 7 7 7 7 7 7 7 7 7 7 7 7 7 7
4    2 2 2 2 2 A A A A A A 8 8 8 8 8 A A A A A A A A A
5    2         2 A             A 8       8 A           A
6    2 2 2 2 2 A             A 8       8 A           A
7    3 3 3 3 3 A             A 8       8 A A A A A A A A
8    3         3 A             A 8       8 9 9 9 9 9 9 9 9
9    3         3 A A A A A A A 8             8 9           9
0    3         3 6 6 6 6 6 6 6 8 8 8 8 8 9 9 9 9 9 9 9 9
1    3         3 6 6 6 6 6 6 6 A A A A A A A A A A A A A
2    3         3 A 5 5 5 5 5 5 A                       A
3    3         3 A 5             5 A                   A
4    3         3 A 5 5 5 5 5 5 5 A                     A
5    3         3 4 4 4 4 4 4 4 4 A                     A
6    3         3 4             4 A                     A
7    3         3 4             4 A                     A
8    3         3 4             4 A                     A
9    3         3 4             4 A                     A
0    3 3 3 3 3 4 4 4 4 4 4 4 4 A A A A A A A A A A A A A
```

Figure 8.7 (a) Printout for example layout.

described as a tenth Department A which occupies a fixed space. The next tables show the current layout and the movements between departments. The computer then iteratively checks for improvements to the layout and prints the results when it finds the best.

(b)   Input data   --   Inter-departmental flows

From :	To:									
1	1:	20	2:	0	3:	0	4:	35	5:	70
	6:	0	7:	0	8:	45	9:	0	A:	0
2	1:	30	2:	0	3:	50	4:	0	5:	20
	6:	0	7:	0	8:	0	9:	10	A:	0
3	1:	10	2:	10	3:	0	4:	0	5:	35
	6:	40	7:	0	8:	0	9:	70	A:	0
4	1:	0	2:	0	3:	0	4:	0	5:	10
	6:	50	7:	40	8:	80	9:	0	A:	0
5	1:	10	2:	0	3:	10	4:	0	5:	0
	6:	0	7:	25	8:	25	9:	50	A:	0
6	1:	25	2:	0	3:	30	4:	45	5:	70
	6:	25	7:	50	8:	20	9:	15	A:	0
7	1:	0	2:	0	3:	0	4:	70	5:	0
	6:	60	7:	0	8:	80	9:	0	A:	0
8	1:	0	2:	0	3:	0	4:	0	5:	0
	6:	120	7:	0	8:	0	9:	0	A:	0
9	1:	0	2:	25	3:	0	4:	35	5:	0
	6:	15	7:	0	8:	10	9:	0	A:	0

```
Optimizing procedure  --   run   --   solution found

Output data   --   Optimal solution

Iterations  =  4
Costs = 15564.53

Output data   --   Optimal layout
          1 2 3 4 5 6 7 8 9 0 1 2 3 4 5 6 7 8 9 0 1 2 3 4 5
1    7 7 7 7 7 7 7 7 7 8 8 8 8 8 8 8 8 8 7 7 7 7 7 7 7
2    7                 7 8             8 7             7
3    7 7 7 7 7 7 7 7 7 8 8 8 8       8 8 7 7 7 7 7 7 7
4    2 2 2 2 2 A A A A A A A 8 8 8 8 8 A A A A A A A A
5    2         2 A           A 8 5 5 5 5 A           A
6    2 2 2 2 2 A           A 8 5       5 A           A
7    3 3 3 3 3 3 A           A 8 5       5 A A A A A A A A
8    3         3 A           A 5 5       5 1 1 1 1 1 1 1 1
9    3         3 A A A A A A A 5 5 5 5 5 1               1
0    3         3 6 6 6 6 6 6 6 6 5 5 1 1 1 1 1 1 1 1 1 1 1
1    3         3 6 6 6 6 6 6 6 6 A A A A A A A A A A A A A
2    3         3 A 4 4 4 4 4 4 A                       A
3    3         3 A 4           4 A                       A
4    3         3 A 4           4 A                       A
5    3         3 4 4 4 4 4 4 4 A                       A
6    3         3 4 4 4 9 9 9 9 A                       A
7    3         3 4 4 9 9       9 A                       A
8    3         3 4 4 9         9 A                       A
9    3         3 4 4 9         9 A                       A
0    3 3 3 3 3 4 4 9 9 9 9 9 9 A A A A A A A A A A A A A
```

Figure 8.7 *(cont.)* (b) Printout for example layout.

Systematic layout planning

The method described above starts by counting the movements between different areas. Sometimes we cannot count these – when, for example, we want a layout for a completely new process. At other times collecting the data may be particularly difficult, or the amount of movement may not be the best measure for layout. Whatever the cause, some alternative method must be used.

A commonly used method is called **systematic layout planning**. This replaces the from–to matrix by subjective views of how close areas should be together. Suppose, for example, a large office block has a Security Group. There may not be many movements between this group and the main reception area, but the group should be put nearby so they can, when necessary, control access to the building. On the other hand, a noisy or dangerous piece of machinery should be put as far as possible from quiet office areas. These subjective views can be formalized into a number of categories, with letters to show how important it is that two areas are close together.

- A – Absolutely essential

- E – Especially important

- I – Important

- O – Ordinary importance

- U – Unimportant

- X – Undesirable.

We can also add a note about the reason for the decision. The most usual reasons for decisions are:

(1)   sharing the same facilities

(2)   sharing the same staff

(3)   ease of supervision

(4)   ease of communications

(5)   sequence of operations in a process

(6)   customer contact

(7)   safety

(8)   unpleasant conditions.

Then A/5 means it is absolutely essential that two operations are adjacent because of the sequence of operations in the process. We can put these codes into a matrix to show both the importance that operations are close together and the reason. The following matrix shows that areas b and d must be close together because they share the same facilities, while c and e must not be close together because of unpleasant conditions, and so on.

		a	b	c	*Area* d	e	
	a	–	U/–	O/3	O/3	X/8	....
Area	b		–	A/5	E/1	U/–	....
	c			–	U/–	X/8	......
	d				–	I/2	....
	e					–	..

Methods of designing layouts with this kind of information are rather informal. The usual approach is to take links in the order of importance. Then we start by finding all the Xs and put them as far apart as possible. Then we find all the As and put them as close together as possible. Then we move on to find the Es and put them close together, and so on.

we Worked example

A new office is about to be opened, with six equally sized areas as shown in Figure 8.8a. The importance that areas are close together is described by the following matrix.

		a	b	c	*Area* d	e	f
	a	–	E/2	U/3	U/2	A/1	I/2
Area	b		–	X/8	O/3	U/–	U/–
	c			–	X/8	I/8	U/–
	d				–	O/5	E/2
	e					–	E/1
	f						–

Suggest a layout for the office.

Solution

Starting with the available space shown in Figure 8.8a we can put the two X links (b–c and c–d) as far apart as possible. Then the A link (a–e) can be added close together. One trial layout for this is shown in Figure 8.8b.

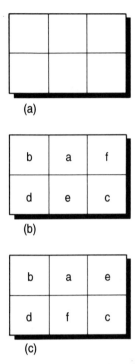

(a)

(b)

(c)

Figure 8.8 Example of systematic layout planning: (a) available areas; (b) trial layout with X and A connections; (c) final layout.

When we move on to the E links (a–b, d–f and e–f), this trial layout only satisfies one of these. An obvious improvement is to exchange e and f, as shown in Figure 8.8c. This still satisfies all the A and X links, but also satisfies two of the E links. This solution seems reasonable, but if we are not happy we could continue making adjustments until we find an improvement.

Review questions

8.4 Product layouts are usually used for intermittent processes like job shops. Do you think this is true?

8.5 Good process layouts can often be found by looking at the pattern of movements. Do you agree with this?

8.6 Why might the number of movements between areas not be a suitable way of judging a layout?

Product layouts

Production lines

A **product layout** groups together all the equipment used to make a particular product. A common form of product layout lines up equipment in the order it is needed, and passes each unit of the product straight down the line. In manufacturing this is the basis of production lines, as shown in Figure 8.9.

The process uses dedicated equipment that is laid out so the product can move through in a steady flow. There is an obvious link between product layouts and mass production processes, and this gives the following advantages and disadvantages.

Advantages of product layout

- a high rate of output can be achieved;

- high equipment utilization leads to low unit costs;

- few operators are needed with increased automation;

- material handling is easy with low stocks of work in progress;

- scheduling and controlling operations is easy;

- high and consistent quality.

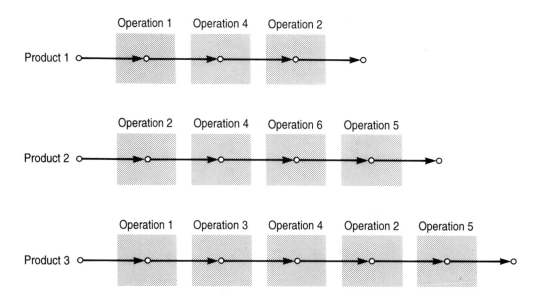

Figure 8.9 Product layouts are like assembly lines.

Disadvantages of product layout

- operations are inflexible, and it is difficult to change the output rate, product or process;

- equipment failure and routine maintenance can disrupt the whole process;

- equipment may be specialized and expensive, needing a high initial investment;

- can not deal with variable demand;

- people often do not like working in process layouts as the repetitive work can be boring.

In principle, product layouts are easy to design, as they consist of a sequence of equipment through which the product moves. The equipment is essentially put into a line and the main problem is to make sure the products can move down this line as smoothly as possible.

Equipment on the line may be divided into a number of distinct **work stations**. A number of operations are done at each work station – so a car moving down an assembly line may have the wheels fitted at one work station, the doors fitted at another, and so on. Then a line consists of discrete work stations, each of which does a number of operations, and products are passed from one work station to the next. A typical product layout is shown in Figure 8.10.

As you can see from Figure 8.10, there are stocks of work in progress between each station. These 'uncouple' adjacent work stations, so that if one breaks down for a short time the other can carry on working normally. But there are disadvantages of such stocks – the main ones being the cost of holding the extra units, and the need for storage space near the line. It is much better to have a balanced line and low stocks of work in progress.

The aim of product layout design is to have a smooth flow of products down the line, with high utilization of all resources. This means the amount of time spent in each work station must be about the same. Then the line is

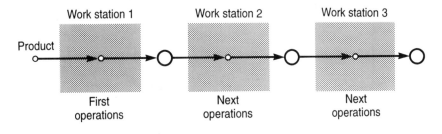

○ stocks of work in process

Figure 8.10 Dividing a product layout into discrete work stations.

balanced. If a line is unbalanced, some parts will finish products quickly, and stock of work in progress will build up in front of the next station which is working more slowly. This in turn leads to bottlenecks that cause delays and low utilization of facilities further down the line.

Imagine a simple line which has two work stations with operations taking one minute in the first and three minutes in the second, as shown in Figure 8.11(a). The output of this line is one unit every three minutes, set by the second work station. Unfortunately, this gives the first work station a utilization of only 33% and the line is unbalanced. An obvious solution is to put three sets of equipment in the second work station. This triples output and gives full utilization. The line is then perfectly balanced, as shown in Figure 8.11(b).

Many product layouts include manual operations. It used to be thought that increasing job-specialization gave high productivity. So organizations used lines where each person did a very small job. This meant that workers needed

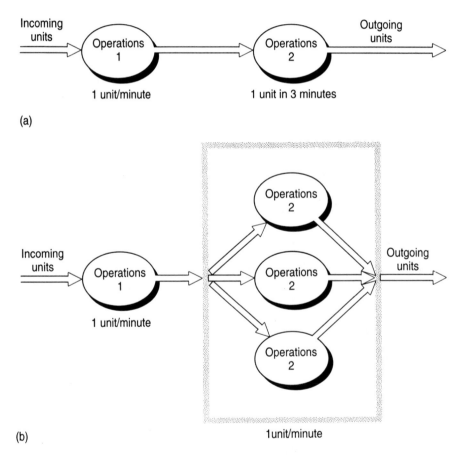

Figure 8.11 Balanced and unbalanced lines: (a) product layout making 1 unit in 3 minutes; (b) product layout making 1 unit a minute.

very little training, and could become very efficient at doing their particular job. But increasing specialization reduces the skills needed, and people get bored. They do not like doing the repetitive work, which becomes dull and tedious. This, in turn, leads to dissatisfaction, lower morale, absenteeism, high employee turnover, and low productivity.

Ways of overcoming such problems include quality circles, job enlargement (which was described in Chapter 5), group working where the group rather than individuals are responsible for operations, and rotating jobs between people.

Line balancing

We have already mentioned that a product layout needs the operations to be balanced. In this section we shall describe a way of doing this.

> **Line balancing** assigns operations to each work station so that the line is balanced, there is a steady flow of products, and equipment has high utilization.

The procedure for line balancing is in three parts:

(1)   Find the **cycle time**, which is the maximum time a station can work on each unit. This is calculated by dividing the planned output by the time available. If, for example, planned production is 60 units an hour, then each operation in the line can last at most one minute. If the operations at any work station take longer than this, there is a bottleneck and the planned output can not be reached.

(2)   Calculate the theoretical minimum number of work stations needed for the entire process. This is found by dividing the total time needed for all operations on a unit by the cycle time. If, for example, it takes a total of five minutes to make a product and the cycle time is one minute, the minimum number of work stations along the line is 5. In practice this can almost never be achieved because of fractional values, the unevenness of work times and the constraints of activity precedence.

(3)   Do the actual line balancing and allocation of operations to each work station. The total time taken for operations in each work station should be as close as possible to the cycle time. An algorithm for this is described below.

The procedure for the third step, actually balancing the line, is best done using a precedence diagram. The steps are then as follows:

(1)   Draw a precedence diagram for the process.

(2)   Take the next unassigned operation and assign it to a new work station.

(3) Starting with the earliest operations (which are normally at the left hand side of the diagram):

- ignore all operations that have already been assigned to work stations;
- ignore all operations whose predecessors have not yet been finished;
- ignore all operations for which there is not enough time left on the current work station.

(4) We now have a set of operations that could be added to the current work station. Use some criterion to rank these, such as the longest operations first.

(5) Add operations in this order to the work station until:

- there are no more operations in the list identified in step 4. If there are still operations that have not been allocated go back to step 2; or
- no more jobs in the list identified in step 4 can be added to the work station without going over the cycle time. If there are still operations that have not been allocated, go back to step 2; or
- all operations have been allocated, in which case the initial design has been completed. Go to step 6.

(6) Calculate the utilization of each work station and make small adjustments to improve the line.

we Worked example

The operations in a product layout are shown in the following table of precedence:

Operation	Time (minutes)	Operation must follow
A	5	–
B	10	A
C	4	B
D	6	B
E	4	C, D
F	2	E
G	4	F
H	5	G
I	3	H
J	2	G
K	5	J
L	8	G
M	4	L
N	2	I, K, M
O	6	N
P	1	O
Q	5	P

The line works an eight-hour day, during which the planned output is 48 units. Design a balanced layout for the process.

Solution

First, we start the procedure by calculating the cycle time.

$$\text{cycle time} = \frac{\text{time available}}{\text{number of units to be made}} = \frac{480}{48} = 10 \text{ minutes}$$

If a work station spends more than 10 minutes on a unit the target output of 48 units a day can not be reached.

Second, we calculate the theoretical minimum number of work stations. This is found by dividing the total time to make one unit of the product by the cycle time. The time to finish all operations on a unit is 76 minutes, so:

$$\frac{\text{theoretical minimum}}{\text{number of stations}} = \frac{\text{total time for a unit}}{\text{cycle time}} = \frac{76}{10} = 7.6$$

This theoretical minimum number of work stations is the ideal, where each station is fully occupied all the time and work flows perfectly smoothly through the line. We can not have a fraction of a work station, so we need at least eight.

Third, we use the algorithm for assigning operations to work stations:

- Step 1 draws the precedence diagram shown in Figure 8.12.

- Step 2 assigns operation A to work station 1.

- Step 3 ignores all activities except B, as their preceding activities have not yet been finished. But B can not be added to work station 1, as the time needed (5 + 10 minutes) is longer than the cycle time.

- Step 4 has no operations that can be added to the current work station.

- Step 5 returns to step 2.

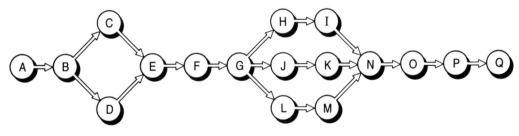

Figure 8.12 Precedence diagram for example.

- Step 2 starts work station 2 with operation B.

- Step 3 ignores all activities except C and D, as their preceding activities have not yet been finished. But neither of these can be added to work station 2 as they give times longer than the cycle time.

- Step 4 has no operations that can be added to the current work station.

- Step 5 returns to step 2.

Returning to step 2, the algorithm assigns operation C to work station 3. Then it considers C and D for adding, and arbitrarily selects D as the longer. This procedure is continued to give the results shown in Table 8.1 and Figure 8.13.

Table 8.1

Work station	Activities	Used time	Spare time	Utilization
1	A	5	5	50%
2	B	10	–	100%
3	C, D	10	–	100%
4	E, F, G	10	–	100%
5	L, J	10	–	100%
6	H, K	10	–	100%
7	M, I, N	9	1	90%
8	O, P	7	3	70%
9	Q	5	5	50%

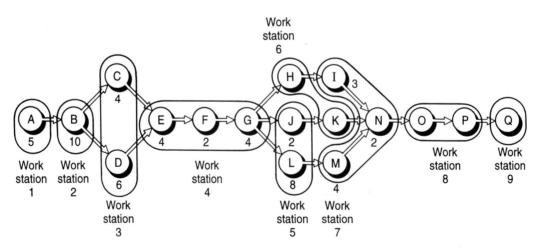

Figure 8.13 Assigning operations to work stations.

Step 6 calculates the overall utilization of the process as:

$$\text{utilization} = \frac{\text{time used in a day}}{\text{number of stations} \times \text{time on each}} = \frac{76 \times 48}{9 \times 480} = 84.4\%$$

Review questions

8.7 Product layouts are generally more capital intensive than process layouts, but give lower unit costs. Do you think this is true?

8.8 What is the purpose of stocks of work in progress between work stations?

8.9 What sets the maximum output from a product layout?

8.10 What is the aim of line balancing?

Hybrid layouts

Often the best layout is not a pure process layout, nor a pure product layout, but is some combination of the two. A product might, for example, be assembled from two components, one of which is made in a job shop, while the other is made on a production line. This arrangement is called a **hybrid layout**.

One common hybrid arrangement is a **work cell**. This is an arrangement with a dominant process layout, but with some operations set aside in a product layout. You can imagine this in a factory where most machines are laid out in a process layout, but a certain sequence of operations is repeated so often that a special area, or work cell, is set aside to deal with them on an assembly line. These work cells form islands of product layout in a sea of process layout, as shown in Figure 8.14.

The aim of work cells is to get the high utilizations of product layouts in a process environment. This type of layout has become more popular with the growth of **group technology** and **flexible manufacturing**. Group technology combines families of products that share some common characteristic, so they can be processed in larger batches. Several products might, for example, each need a 5 cm hole drilled. The products could be combined into bigger batches for the drilling. If these batches get big enough it makes sense to do the common operations using a product layout, even though most other operations use a process layout.

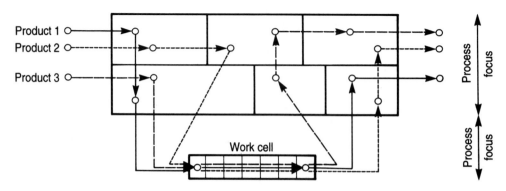

Figure 8.14 Example of a work cell.

We can give several examples of work cells.

- A job shop that gets an order to make a large number of a particular product. It might then keep its overall process layout but could set aside a separate work cell as an assembly line to meet the order.

- An airport passenger terminal has a process layout with separate ticket purchase area, check in area, cafeteria, duty free shops, and so on. Despite this, there are some product layouts such as customs clearance.

- A fast food restaurant has areas of the kitchen set aside for different purposes, but a line which prepares all hamburgers.

- A hospital has wards set aside for different types of illness, but the patient admissions area has a product layout.

Some people suggest there is an important difference between the first of these examples and the others. The arrangement in the job shop is temporary to meet a specific order, while the others are all designed as permanent arrangements. If this distinction is important, we might use the term **work cell** to describe a temporary arrangement and **focused work centre** to describe a permanent arrangement. A car repair workshop, for example, might use a process layout, but if it has a lot of work replacing tyres and exhaust systems it might move some equipment to a separate area to do these on an assembly line. If this arrangement is permanent it would be a focused work centre. Obviously the borderline between work cells and focused work centres is unclear and the distinction is largely artificial.

The idea of a focused work centre can be extended to focused factories. With these, the focused work centre is now moved to another building. Then a focused factory uses a product layout to make a component or product for use in another facility. A factory that uses an assembly line to make windscreen wiper motors for cars is an example of a focused factory.

ce Case example – Dalmuir Knitwear

This example shows why one company chose to use a work cell.

Dalmuir Knitwear makes fairly small numbers of fashion garments. It weaves, knits, dyes, sews, assembles and finishes a range of clothing, mainly for women but with some sportswear for men. Because of the fairly small production quantities, Dalmuir uses a predominantly process layout, with a weaving room, knitting room, finishing room, and so on.

Two years ago it won a large contract to supply garments to Marks & Spencer. This was a major success for the company, which was pleased that it could meet the extremely high standards demanded by Marks & Spencer. Because these standards were higher than its usual operations, Dalmuir set aside a specific area of its factory solely to make the order. This area was completely refurbished and it moved in its latest machines. The machines were arranged for a product process, so that the Marks & Spencer products were moved in a straight line through the factory.

The plant manager at Dalmuir looked after all the operations. He effectively created a production line to meet this one contract. Any spare capacity in the production line was used to make a new range of high quality garments for other customers.

Review questions

8.11   What are hybrid layouts?

8.12   What is a work cell and why are they used?

Fixed position and specialized layouts

The layouts described so far cover many operations. But there are many other types of layout, which are often designed for specific purposes. We can illustrate these specialized layouts by four common examples: fixed layouts, warehouses, offices, and retail shops.

Fixed position layout

In fixed position layouts the product stays still and operations are all done on the same site. This usually happens when a product is too big or heavy to move around. Common examples are shipbuilding, aeroplane assembly and construction sites. The approach is also useful when special environments, such as dust free rooms, are needed.

Fixed layouts have many disadvantages, including:

- all materials and components must be moved to the site;

- all people involved with operations must move to the site;

- there is often limited space at the site;

- a reliable schedule of operations must be maintained;

- disruptions to this schedule might cause delays in completion;

- the intensity of work varies;

- external factors, such as weather conditions, may affect operations.

Because of these disadvantages, fixed position layouts are only used when moving the product is either impossible or very difficult.

One way to partially avoid these disadvantages is to do as much of the work as possible off-site. A road bridge, for example, must be completed on-site, but many of the parts can be prefabricated or assembled off-site and moved for erection.

Warehouses

The purpose of a warehouse is to store goods at some point on their journey between suppliers and customers (see Figure 8.15). The essential elements in a warehouse are:

- an arrival bay, where goods coming from suppliers are delivered and checked;

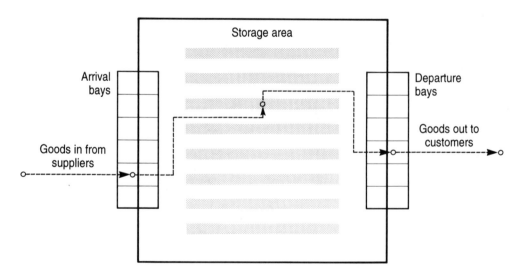

Figure 8.15 Layout of a typical warehouse.

- a storage area, where the goods are kept as stock;

- a departure bay, where customers' orders are assembled and sent out;

- a material handling system, for moving goods around as necessary;

- an information system, which records the location of all goods, arrivals from suppliers, departures to customers, and all other relevant information.

When designing a warehouse the aim is to minimize the total cost. Many of the costs are fixed, such as rent and utilities. Other costs are set by management policy, such as the cost of stock-holding which depends on the amount of stock held. The main variable cost that depends on layout comes from the time spent locating items and either adding them to stock or removing them.

The layout will depend to a large extent on the goods being stored and the handling equipment used. If the goods are small and light, such as boxes of pills, material handling can be done by hand. Then a warehouse should be small enough to walk round, with goods stored in easy reach. If the goods are large and heavy, such as engines, material handling will use fork-lift trucks. Then a warehouse should be big enough for these to manoeuvre. These examples show two approaches to warehousing, which are manual and mechanized. The third level of technology is automated, where materials handling equipment does not need human control. The different levels of technology give warehouses with completely different characteristics.

- **Manual** Warehouses must store light items that are easy to lift. Storage is in shelves that are close together, but can be no higher than two metres. The warehouse must be heated, lit and allow people to work comfortably.

- **Mechanized** Examples are fork-lift trucks, conveyors and tow lines. Some equipment needs wide aisles for manoeuvring, but goods can be stored higher – perhaps up to 12 metres with a fork-lift truck and higher with conveyors. Fork-lift trucks have high costs and are best suited to short journeys around loading and unloading bays. Conveyor systems are cheaper for small items and need less space.

- **Automated** Uses guided vehicles, robots and automated movement to and from storage areas. These systems use narrow aisles and can be very high, allowing computer controlled cranes to reach all items very quickly. As people do not work in the storage areas, money can be saved on heating and lighting.

The layout of the warehouse also depends on the way goods are moved from storage shelves to departure bays. This is called **picking** and we can mention four distinct approaches to this:

- **Out-and-back** where a single item is picked at a time. This is used when demand is low, or with heavy and bulky goods that can only be moved one at a time.

- **Batch picking** where enough units of an item are picked to satisfy a number of customers.

- **Customer picking** where a variety of different items are picked for an order from a given customer.

- **Zone picking** where a picker stays in one area and items are loaded as required onto passing conveyors.

we Worked example

A store has a rack with nine colours of paint in 5 litre tins. At one end of the rack is an issue area where the storekeeper works. Weekly demand for the paint is as follows.

Colour	Red	Blue	White	Black	Brown	Green	Yellow	Grey	Pink
Tins	100	140	860	640	320	120	240	40	60

If all paint is stored in identical sized bins, design a reasonable layout for the rack. What would be a reasonable layout if the size of bins varies with the weekly demand?

Solution

The objective here is to minimize the distance walked by the storekeeper, assuming that each tin of paint needs a separate journey. The paint should be laid out so that colours with highest demand are nearest the issue area. The layout then has paint in order white, black, brown, yellow, blue, green, red, pink and grey (see Figure 8.16). If each bin is one unit wide, this has a total travel distance for the storekeeper of:

$$2 \times [(1 \times 860) + (2 \times 640) + (3 \times 320) + (4 \times 240) + (5 \times 140)$$
$$+ (6 \times 120) + (7 \times 100) + (8 \times 60) + (9 \times 40)]$$
$$= 2 \times 7020$$
$$= 14,040$$

with the factor of 2 allowing for return journeys.

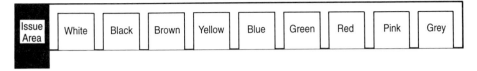

Figure 8.16 The best layout for paint rack.

If the size of the bin is proportional to the weekly demand for paint, and paint is taken from the middle of the bins, it does not matter which order the paint is put in the rack.

Offices

Factories and warehouses which are concerned with the movement of physical goods, but offices are concerned with the movement of information. This can be done:

- face-to-face

- in meetings or groups

- by telephone, intercom or simultaneous computer link

- on paper

- by electronic mail or other computer link.

If all communications were indirect using telephones or some other equipment, the amount of movement in offices would be small. In practice, most efficient communications are done face-to-face, and this needs more planning. Those areas with most personal contacts should clearly be put near to each other, while those with less personal contact can be separated. But this only gives a starting point for office design.

Despite improving technology, most offices need a lot of people, and they must have conditions which are comfortable. Some of their work is best done in private offices, while other jobs are best done in open areas. Discussing private financial arrangements with a customer, for example, is best done in a private office, but processing high volumes of routine paperwork is best done in open areas. Alternative layouts for offices are:

- desks arranged in rows in an open area;

- desks arranged less formally in open areas, with filing cabinets, plants and book cases separating areas;

- desks in open areas separated by moveable partitions which are typically about 2 metres high;

- areas divided into separate offices by semi-permanent floor to ceiling partitions;

- permanent separate offices.

The choice of best layout depends on the type of work being done and how much this varies.

There are a number of other factors that affect office design. These include:

- the amount of face-to-face contact needed will determine the total movements;

- employees within groups usually have a lot of face-to-face contact;

- the type of work determines the best type of office, ranging from open plans to separate offices;

- individual offices usually have different facilities, size, and location depending on the job and status of the occupant;

- areas to be visited by customers often have different needs to those kept for work;

- some special facilities may be needed, such as conference or committee rooms, lecture theatres and board rooms;

- there must be specific areas for lounges, rest rooms, cloak rooms, storage areas, cleaning equipment, and so on;

- aisles should allow all areas to be reached quickly, but without too much traffic past peoples' work places;

- shared facilities, such as photocopiers, files, and coffee machines should be convenient for everyone.

Retail shops

The layout of retail shops is related to that of warehouses. They both have goods brought-in, stored and then taken out to satisfy customer demand. But there is a fundamental difference. A good warehouse design minimizes the total distance travelled to collect goods, so those with highest demands are kept near the issue area. In a shop, the longer a customer walks around the more they will buy – so a good layout maximizes the distance travelled between purchases. You can see this clearly in supermarkets which spreads high demand items of basic food, like bread and milk, around the shop and force customers to pass lots of other goods before finding them all.

Several guidelines have been suggested for shop layouts, including:

- disperse basic goods around the shop, preferably around the outside aisles;

- do not have cross-over aisles as customers should be encouraged to walk the full length of each aisle;

- use the first and last aisle for high-impulse items that have high profit margins;

- set the image for the store near the door – if customers see a lot of special sales here they will assume all prices are low;

- put magazines and chocolates near the checkouts;

- people notice the ends of aisles so these should be used, perhaps for special promotions;

- put goods that are attractive to children within their reach;

ce Case example – Swindon Truck Stop

This example shows that a relatively simple change in layout can bring a lot of benefit. The improved layout needed someone to think about the problem and suggest a sensible alternative.

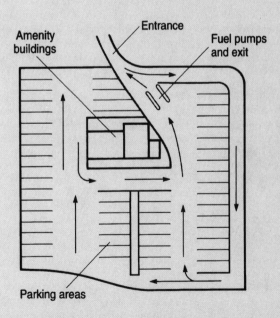

Figure 8.17(a) Original layout of Swindon Truck Stop.

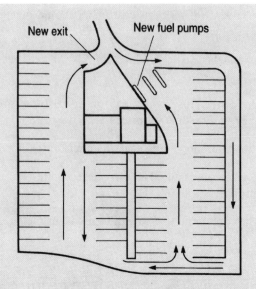

Figure 8.17(b) Modified layout of Swindon Truck Stop.

Swindon Truck Stop is a large service area that is used by long distance lorry drivers. Here they can park, take legally required breaks from driving, rest, have meals, take showers, sleep, check vehicles, fill them with fuel, and so on.

The original layout of the Truck Stop caused some problems. The main area is a fenced enclosure with controlled access. But lorries trying to leave this enclosure at busy times were held up by other vehicles filling up with fuel. In some cases there were delays of 10 or 15 minutes. Obviously this kind of delay was not popular with drivers.

In December 1994 the Truck Stop solved their problem by redesigning the layout. In particular, they built an extra exit, added more fuel pumps, and adjusted the road layout. You may think that these changes, shown in Figure 8.17, are obvious, but they needed a lot of detailed planning by the Truck Stop.

- circulate customers clockwise.

Review questions

8.13 Fixed layouts keep all equipment in fixed locations and move products through these in a specified sequence. Do you think this is true?

8.16   The layout of supermarkets should allow customers to collect their goods as quickly as possible. Do you agree with this?

Chapter review

- Layout is concerned with the way the facilities of a process are physically arranged. The objective of layout design is to find the best arrangement for the operations in a process. A good layout will make sure operations run smoothly, while a poor layout will cause disruptions and other problems.

- There are many types of layout. These can be classified as process, product, hybrid, fixed and specialized. Each of these has different characteristics and is best suited to different circumstances. Some examples are given in Table 8.2.

Table 8.2

Layout type	Examples
Process	job shops, hospitals, kitchens
Product	electronic assembly lines, bottling, production lines
Hybrid	fast food restaurants, airport terminals
Fixed	ship building, road laying, bridge building
Specialized	warehouses, offices, retail shops

- Process layouts group together similar types of facilities. This is typical of the layout in a job shop. The main problem in designing process layouts is to minimize the amount of movement between areas. For small problems this can be done intuitively, but larger problems need more formal methods.

- Product layouts group together the facilities needed to make a product. These are often assembly lines. Product layouts often have a series of work stations, each doing a number of operations in a prescribed sequence. The main problem is to make sure each work station has the same throughput, giving a balanced flow of products.

- Many processes use a mixture of product and process layouts, and these are called hybrid layouts. Work cells are a common type of hybrid layout, where some areas use a product layout, but overall there is a process layout.

- Many layouts can not be labelled as process, product or hybrid. Fixed location layouts, for example, keep the product in a single location where all work is done. There are many types of specialized layout including warehouses, offices and retail shops.

Key terms

CS Case study – Bartholomew's Mail Order

James Bartholomew opened a clothes shop near the centre of Leeds in 1947. His advertisements in local newspapers encouraged people living in remote areas to write for specific items, and he would return these by post. James realized that this side of the business had less competition than the shop and could be organized more efficiently. Over the next few years he developed the postal service and eventually formed the mail order business into a separate operation. By 1968 the business was large enough for him to sell to a national clothing company and retire to the Yorkshire Moors.

Over the years Bartholomew's added many types of product to its mail order business, and now sell almost everything from plants to porcelain figures. Most customers use specialized catalogues, and come from as far away as Australia and Japan. Marketing is reinforced by widespread advertisements.

The company is about to move to a new distribution centre on a trading estate. This centre has a large warehouse with adjacent offices, so most of the company's operations will be done in a single location. The Operations Manager now has to decide how to allocate the space.

The warehouse can be sorted out fairly easily, but allocating office space is more sensitive. A 'relocation team' has been trying to arrange the various departments into new offices. They have asked the 16 main departments how much space they want (in square metres), and have looked up records to get the information shown in Table 8.3.

The space currently used by a department includes corridors and facilities such as photocopiers and coffee machines. Most people work in open areas, so the space needed by each department should generally be related to the number of people who work there. There are some variations for those departments with more equipment or a higher workload. Most departments also have a Manager and one or two others with individual offices.

The new office block is six storeys tall. It is essentially a rectangle with sides 40 metres and 30 metres and at the centre is a 10 metres by 10 metres

Table 8.3

Department	Requested space	Current space	Staff
1	300	220	21
2	350	220	17
3	500	640	44
4	1350	950	60
5	1000	220	10
6	300	400	15
7	1000	800	40
8	600	220	8
9	300	200	37
10	180	40	7
11	1000	400	18
12	200	250	23
13	400	220	21
14	100	100	17
15	400	400	24
16	150	100	9

block of stairs, lifts, washrooms and so on. At the moment the rest of the building is completely empty.

The relocation team looked at the number of movements within departments and between departments. During a typical period they counted the movements shown in Table 8.4.

Table 8.4

	1	2	3	4	5	6	7	8	9	10	11	12	13	14	15	16
1	457	22	47	15	19	125	256	632	87	19	44	86	188	14	223	321
2		31	91	88	28	263	472	103	37	25	137	42	501	23	145	90
3			603	99	421	682	721	284	871	23	656	92	643	57	465	653
4				72	41	132	61	72	12	52	76	65	56	17	87	20
5					128	87	23	68	234	76	451	47	71	19	67	17
6						455	14	35	26	19	109	23	56	22	121	45
7							128	12	32	10	64	61	23	17	209	331
8								78	16	21	69	30	79	32	44	36
9									864	93	237	35	566	60	77	24
10										21	56	31	72	50	69	57
11											683	43	66	23	63	23
12												92	77	20	189	49
13													440	11	445	67
14														67	623	17
15															834	77
16																125

Questions

- If you were a member of the relocation team, how would you set about designing a layout for the new building? What factors would you consider important?

- Draw an initial design for the new building. What are the strengths and weaknesses of your design?

Problems

8.1 A process layout has five identically sized areas in a line. During a normal period, employees made the following movements between areas.

	a	b	c	d	e
a	0	17	12	42	2
b	12	0	1	22	6
c	0	22	0	17	7
d	47	11	3	0	12
e	53	5	6	25	0

What is the best layout for the areas?

8.2 One floor of a building has six office areas, which are all the same size. The current layout is shown in Figure 8.18, but this seems to have a lot of unnecessary movement.

During a normal period records were kept of the number of movements between areas as shown in the following table. How might the layout be improved?

	1	2	3	4	5	6
1	–	–	100	–	35	–
2	120	–	10	20	15	10
3	–	15	–	80	–	75
4	–	55	–	–	75	–
5	–	10	–	125	–	–
6	80	20	–	–	–	–

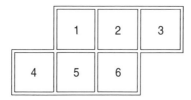

Figure 8.18 Office layout for Problem 8.2.

8.3   Some equipment uses a product layout. The process consists of a
       sequence of 15 operations with the following times.

Operation	1	2	3	4	5	6	7	8	9	10	11	12	13	14	15
Time in minutes	2	6	8	4	10	2	1	15	11	8	2	4	10	7	5

       Find the best allocation of operations to work stations for different levels
       of production.

8.4   An assembly line has seven activities, with times and precedences shown
       in Table 8.5. The forecast demand for bottles is 120 an hour. Find the
       cycle time and minimum number of work stations needed. Balance the
       line by assigning operations to work stations.

Table 8.5

Activity	Description	Time (seconds)	Activity must follow
A	Clean bottle	20	–
B	Inspect bottle	5	A
C	Fill bottle with liquid	20	B
D	Put top on filled bottle	5	C
E	Put label on bottle	5	B
F	Put bottles into boxes	10	D, E
G	Seal boxes and move	5	F

8.5   If each operation described in Figure 8.19 takes 4 minutes, design a line
       that will process six units an hour.

8.6   A warehouse has a single aisle with 12 bins as shown in Figure 8.20. It
       stores six products with the following features. Design a good layout for
       the warehouse.

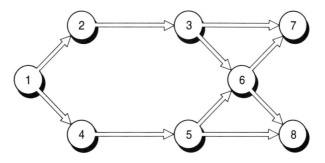

Figure 8.19 Precedence diagram for Problem 8.5.

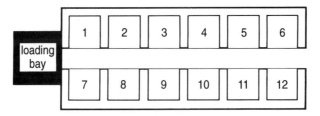

Figure 8.20 Layout for Problem 8.6.

Product	Withdrawals	Bins needed
1	150	1
2	700	3
3	50	1
4	900	3
5	450	2
6	300	2

8.7 If the design in problem 8.6 referred to a supermarket, how would the design differ?

8.8 Confirm the result mentioned in the text that if the storage length of a rack is proportional to demand, and goods are removed from the centre of the racks, the order in which goods are stored does not matter.

Discussion questions

8.1 Do you think that layout design is a strategic issue for an organization? Can it be a tactical issue? Give examples to support your views.

8.2 Describe some successful layouts that you have seen. What makes these successful? Compare them with some unsuccessful layouts for similar operations.

8.3 Layout design should be left to architects and planners. Do you think this would give good results?

8.4 Do you think there is such a thing as an optimal process layout? Do computer packages for designing process layouts give optimal solutions?

8.5 Many computer programs help with layout design. What do you think these should do? Illustrate your answer by describing appropriate software.

8.6 Many people are writing about focused factories at the moment. Why do you think they are writing so much about an old idea?

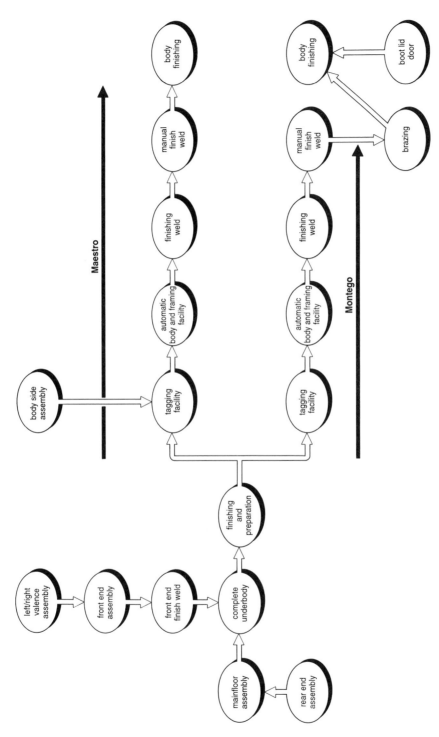

Figure 8.21 Layout of part of Cowley line.

8.7 Describe the features you would expect to see on a production line. What are the major questions for product layout designs?

8.8 If you worked in a factory, which type of process would you like to work with? Why?

8.9 The layout of a supermarket has to balance the convenience of customers with the desire of managers to keep them in the shop as long as possible. Can you think of other services that face similar problems?

8.10 Do you think that offices that customers visit should be more luxurious than others?

8.11 In the 1980s Austin-Rover (which was later re-named Rover) built Maestros and Montegos on their production lines at Cowley. The layout of their underbody and side panel assembly is shown in Figure 8.21. As you can see, parts for both models come down the first part of the line together, but are then separated for the second part. Each model goes down its own, production line for almost identical operations. What problems do you think there might be with this layout? By 1986 Montego sales were twice as high as Maestro. Do you think this is important?

Selected references

Apple J.M. (1977). *Plant Layout and Materials Handling* (3rd edn). New York: Roland Press.

Black J.T. (1991). *The Design of the Factory with a Future*. New York: McGraw-Hill.

Bowersox D.J., Closs D.J. and Helferich O.K. (1986). *Logistical Management* (3rd edn). New York: Macmillan.

Johnson J.C. and Wood D.F. (1990). *Contemporary Logistics* (4th edn). New York: Macmillan.

Luggen W. (1991). *Flexible Manufacturing Cells and Systems*. Englewood Cliffs, NJ: Prentice-Hall.

Murdick R.G., Render B. and Russell R.S. (1990). *Service Operations Management*. Needham Heights, MA: Allyn and Bacon.

Tompkins J.A. and White J.A. (1984). *Facilities Planning*. New York: John Wiley.

9 Managing capacity

Contents

Objectives

After reading this chapter you should be able to:

- describe a number of measures for the performance of an organization
- define and calculate productivity
- define capacity and discuss its measurement
- appreciate the aims of capacity planning
- see how capacity changes over time
- find the best times for maintenance and replacement of equipment
- calculate reliabilities

Measures of performance

The capacity of a process sets the amount of a product that can be made in a specified time. In principle, then, an organization can look at the forecast demand for a product and use this to find the capacity it needs. But in practice things are not this simple. The amount made by a process can vary quite widely – depending on how hard people are working, the number of disruptions, the quality being made, how efficiently equipment is working, and a wide range of other factors.

The output of a process varies. We should really look, therefore, at some measures of performance to see if the process is working well, or if it is having problems. We shall start this chapter by looking at a number of measures of performance.

The basic measure of performance is **capacity**.

> The **capacity** of a process sets the maximum amount of a product that can be made in a specified time.

All organizations make decisions about the capacity of their operations. They should aim to make the capacity of a process match the forecast demand for products. Any mismatch between supply and demand will leave either unsatisfied customers or under-used resources.

- If capacity is less than demand, the organization can not meet all the demand and it loses potential customers.

- If capacity is greater than demand, the organization meets all the demand but it has spare capacity and under-used resources.

When you go into some shops there are not enough people serving and you have to wait. The capacity of the shop is less than demand, and you will probably go to a competitor where the queues are shorter. In other shops there are lots of people waiting to serve you. You do not have to wait, but the cost of paying these under-used people is added to your bill.

Two other measures are directly related to capacity.

- **Utilization** measures the amount of available capacity that is actually used.

- **Productivity** measures the amount of output achieved for each unit of a resource.

Suppose, for example, a process has a capacity of 100 units a week: this is the maximum number of units that can be made. If the process is idle for half the time and actually make 50 units a week its utilization is 50%. If it uses

25 hours of machine time to make these 50 units the productivity is two units per machine hour.

A problem with these measures is that some people use the terms very loosely. The **production** is the total output from a process, but some people confuse this with **productivity**, which is the output achieved for each unit of a resource. So 100 units may be the production while 100 units per machine-day is the productivity. Many people assume that productivity is the number of units made by each person working on the process. But we shall see later that this is only one aspect of productivity.

Another term that causes confusion is **efficiency**. Here we shall use efficiency to describe the percentage of possible output that is actually achieved. Suppose people working in an office can process five forms in an hour, but someone has just spent an hour processing four forms. Their efficiency is $4/5 = 0.8$ or 80%. Sometimes efficiency is confused with **effectiveness**, which measures how well an organization sets and achieves its goals. This is the difference between 'doing the right job and doing the job right'. Opening a walnut with a sledge hammer, for example, would be very effective but it would not be very efficient; building a wall without using cement would be very efficient, as the builder could work very quickly, but it would not be very effective.

Summary

- **Capacity** is the maximum amount of a product that can be made within a specified time.

- **Utilization** measures the proportion of available capacity that is actually used.

- **Production** is the total amount of a product that is made.

- **Productivity** is the amount produced in relation to one or more of the resources used.

- **Efficiency** is the ratio of actual output to possible output.

- **Effectiveness** shows how well an organization sets and achieves its goals.

we Worked example

Two machines are designed to produce 100 units each in a 10-hour shift. During one shift, the machines were actually used for eight hours, and produced a total of 140 units. What measures of performance can you give?

Solution

- Capacity is the maximum amount that could be produced in a given time, which is $2 \times 100 = 200$ units a shift, or 20 units an hour.

- Utilization is the proportion of capacity actually used, which is $140/200 = 0.7$ or 70%.

- Production is the amount actually made, which is 140 units.

- Productivity is the amount produced in relation to resources used, so we can define this as $140/(2 \times 8) = 8.75$ units a machine hour.

- Efficiency is the ratio of actual output to possible output, which is $140/(8 \times 2 \times 10) = 0.875$ or 87.5%.

There are many other measures of performance an organization could use, including:

- flexibility

- quality

- profitability

- return on investment

- market share

- conformance to standards

- morale

- innovation.

Some of these are more difficult to quantify, but are nevertheless important in judging performance. It would, for example, make no sense to aim for high productivity if the quality of products is too low, or if the finished products then sit in a warehouse because there is no demand for them.

we Worked example

The Johnson-Mead Company has ten people making 1000 electric motors a month with direct costs of £125,000. After a small reorganization eleven people make 1200 units a month with direct costs of £156,000. How could you measure the performance of the process? Do you think the reorganization has been useful?

Solution

We have enough information for two useful measures:

- number of units made per person
- direct costs per unit made

Calculating these before the reorganization gives:

- number of units per person $= 1000/10 = 100$
- direct costs per unit $= 125,000/1000 = £125$

After the reorganization:

- number of units per person $= 1200/11 = 109$
- direct costs per unit $= 156,000/1200 = £130$

The number of units per person has improved with reorganization, but the direct cost per unit has also risen. Whether the reorganization is useful depends on the objectives of Johnson-Mead.

The last example shows how different measures of performance can give conflicting views. This is simply because they are measuring different things. When you drive a car faster than usual the time taken for a journey goes down, but the fuel consumption goes up. If an organization reduces the selling price of a product the demand may increase but the profit may decline. If they pay employees poorly the wage bill may go down, but so might productivity. An organization must be careful to use a suitable measure of performance – that is one which shows how well it is achieving its goals. It must not use a measure that is easy to find, or that is chosen simply to show itself in a good light.

Review questions

9.1   What measures can you use to see how well a process is working?

9.2   What is the difference between capacity, utilization, productivity and efficiency?

9.3   Is it possible for the utilization of a process to rise while the productivity declines?

Productivity

Most organizations say they are continually trying to increase their productivity. There are really only four ways of doing this:

- **improve effectiveness** with better decisions;

- **improve efficiency** using fewer inputs to achieve the same outputs;

- **improve performance in some other way** such as higher quality, fewer accidents, less disruption;

- **improve morale** to give more co-operation and incentives.

The old fashioned idea of 'getting people to work harder' has very little to do with productivity. A hard-working person with a spade will be far less productive than a lazy person with a bulldozer. It is generally agreed that 85% of productivity is set by the system which is designed by management. Only 15% is under the control of the individual worker, so productivity does not necessarily measure their effort.

But before we go any further, we should define exactly what we mean by productivity. At the beginning of the chapter we said that productivity is the amount produced in relation to one or more of the resources used. We can expand this definition, by saying **total productivity** is the total output divided by the total input.

$$\textbf{Total productivity} = \frac{\text{total output}}{\text{total input}}$$

This definition has a number of drawbacks. To start with, the input and output must be in consistent units, and this normally means they are translated into pounds. Then the amounts depend on the accounting conventions used and we no longer have an objective measure. Another problem is finding all the inputs and outputs. Some inputs are difficult to evaluate, such as water and sunlight, as are some outputs, such as waste and pollution. Yet all inputs and outputs **should** be included in the measure of total productivity.

Because of these difficulties, most organizations use other measures. These measure **partial productivity**, and are the total output divided by one kind of input. Then the amount produced per machine-hour, or the amount produced per kilowatt-hour of electricity, or the amount produced per pound of investment are examples of partial productivity.

$$\textbf{Partial productivity} = \frac{\text{total output}}{\text{single input}}$$

In practice, the 'total output' is taken as the production and does not include secondary outputs, like waste and scrap. Partial productivity measures are often related to four types of resource:

- **Equipment productivity** such as units of output per machine hour, tonnes made per operating hour, units made per breakdown.

- **Labour productivity** such as units of output per person-hour, tonnes of output per employee, shipments made per pound spent on wages.

- **Capital productivity** such as units made per pound of investment, value of outputs per unit of input.

- **Energy productivity** such as units of output per kilowatt-hour, units of output for each pound spent on electricity, value of output per barrel of oil used.

Whichever measure of productivity is used, its purpose is to assess the performance of the organization. It might be used to:

- compare the current performance of the organization with its performance in the past

- make comparisons with other organizations that have similar operations

- compare different parts of the organization

- measure the effect of change to operations

- help with internal functions, such as wage negotiations.

We usually assume that increasing productivity is a good thing. But you can see from the definitions above that this takes a simplified view. Increasing the use of automation, for example, may increase the labour productivity but reduce the capital productivity.

ce Case example – British Coal

This example shows how one measure of productivity can give a misleading view of an organization's performance.

At the beginning of the century the British coal industry employed over a million miners. In 1947 most of the fragmented industry was nationalized to form the National Coal Board, which later reorganized as British Coal. By the 1980s British Coal employed 250,000 miners. Over the next 12 years improved operations raised reported productivity by a factor of 3, as shown in Figure 9.1.

Superficially, these productivity figures show an industry that has made considerable progress. Certainly British deep mine coal was among the cheapest in the world, and the industry was recognized as among the most efficient. But

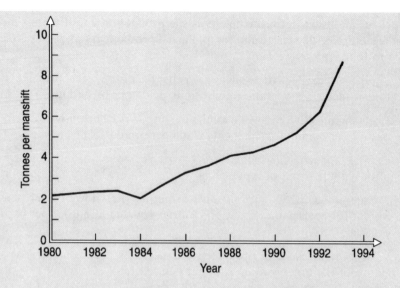

Figure 9.1 Productivity reported by British Coal.

the figures hid the fact that British Coal could not compete with cheap imported coal from open cast mines. By 1994 the government had closed almost all British mines and were selling the remainder. There were now only 15,000 miners, with production and numbers employed shown in Figure 9.2.

Historically it had been important for British Coal to aim for high output. Because of its emphasis on mining operations, and the fact that mining

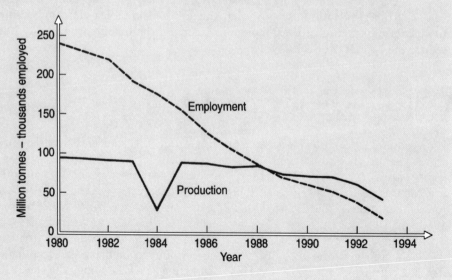

Figure 9.2 Production and employment in British Coal.

Productivity **297**

was labour intensive, productivity had traditionally been measured by the number of tonnes of coal produced per shift. This gives a very limited view of productivity. Now that mining is largely automated it also gives a very misleading view. A much better view includes total production, profit, employees, and a series of other measures. If these other measures were included, the performance of British Coal would be seen as a long-term decline.

You can see from the case of British Coal, that any single measure of productivity gives only one, limited view of the organization. To get a broader, more useful view several measures should be taken which relate to different aspects of operations. But this can be difficult. Consider, for example, the productivity of schools, colleges and universities. Realistically, this is almost impossible to measure as it needs judgements about academic standards, learning skills, teaching quality, and so on. But it is easy to calculate a ratio of students to staff and use this as one measure of productivity. Unfortunately, this one measure is often taken as the only measure, and it is used for major planning decisions. There are some services, such as the police, army and fire service, which would be most successful if they did not work at all – implying there were no crimes, wars or fires.

we Worked example

The following information was collected for a process over two consecutive years:

	1994	1995
Number of units made	1000	1200
Selling price	£100	£100
Raw materials used	5100 kg	5800 kg
Cost of raw materials	£20,500	£25,500
Hours worked	4300	4500
Direct labour costs	£52,000	£58,000
Energy used	10,000 kWh	14,000 kWh
Energy cost	£1000	£1500
Other costs	£10,000	£10,000

How could you describe the productivity?

Solution

We could use several measures of productivity.

- Total productivity in 1994 is:

$$\frac{\text{total output}}{\text{total input}} = \frac{100 \times 1000}{20,500 + 52,000 + 1000 + 10,000} = 1.20$$

By 1995 this had risen to 120,000/95,000 = 1.26, which is a rise of 5%.

- Units of output per kg of raw material in 1994 was 1000/5100 = 0.196. In 1995 this was 1200/5800 = 0.207. This is a rise of 5%

- Some other measures are:

	1994	1995	Percentage increase
Total productivity	1.20	1.26	5
Units/kg of raw material	0.196	0.207	5.6
Units/£ of raw material	0.049	0.047	−4.1
Units/hour	0.233	0.267	14.6
Units/£ of labour	0.019	0.021	10.5
Units/kWh	0.100	0.086	−14.0
Units/£ of energy	1.000	0.800	−20

In general, labour productivity has risen, raw materials productivity has stayed about the same, but energy productivity has fallen.

Review questions

9.4   What is the difference between total and partial productivity?

9.5   Is it possible for some measures of productivity to rise while others are falling?

9.6   Labour productivity is the best measure of an organization's perform-ance. Do you think this is true?

Process capacity

Definition of capacity

We have already defined the capacity of a process as the maximum amount of a product that can be made in a specified time. All operations have some limitation on their capacity: a factory has a maximum output a week, a machine has a maximum throughput an hour, an aeroplane has a maximum number of seats, a hotel has a maximum number of rooms, a lorry has a maximum weight it can carry, and so on. You can see that the first two of these have an explicit reference to time – but the last three also refer indirectly to time. The number of seats on an aeroplane sets the capacity as a maximum number of passengers on a particular flight; the number of rooms in a hotel gives the capacity as a maximum number of guests who can stay each day; the maximum weight of a lorry sets the most it can carry on a single journey. Capacity measures the rate of output, and should always give the relevant time period.

Sometimes the capacity of an operation seems obvious – the number of seats in a theatre, or beds in a hospital, or tables in a restaurant. At other times the capacity is not so clear. How, for example, could you find the capacity of a supermarket, warehouse, university or bank? Because it is particularly difficulty to find the capacity of services, they often use some surrogate measure, such as the number of customers per square metre of floor space. These measures are usually found by discussion and agreement rather than calculation. The maximum size of classes in schools, for example, is an agreed number of pupils rather than some limit set by the building. The maximum number of spectators in a football stadium is set by agreed safety regulations rather than physical limitations of space.

The capacity of a process is its maximum output when working normally. When we design a process, however, we are often thinking of ideal conditions with no disruptions. Then the maximum output of a process under ideal conditions is called the **designed capacity**. As operations rarely work under ideal conditions a more realistic measure is the **effective capacity**. This is the maximum output which can realistically be expected under normal conditions. The difference between designed capacity and effective capacity allows for setup times, breakdowns, stoppages, maintenance periods, and so on. The designed capacity of a ski lift, for example, might be 600 people an hour, but because not all seats are filled, people arrive in groups, and there are disruptions to operations, the effective capacity might only be 400 people an hour.

The actual output will normally be lower than the effective capacity. So we can use these definitions to give a more formal view of efficiency and utilization. Utilization measures the proportion of available capacity that is actually used, so this is the ratio of actual output to designed capacity. Efficiency is the ratio of actual output to effective capacity.

$$\text{Utilization} = \frac{\text{actual output}}{\text{designed capacity}}$$

$$\text{Efficiency} = \frac{\text{actual output}}{\text{effective capacity}}$$

we Worked example

A machine is designed to work for one eight-hour shift a day, five days a week. When working, the machine can produce 100 units an hour, but 10% of its time is needed for maintenance and setups. During one particular week breakdowns, defective output and other problems meant the machine only made 3000 units. What measures can you use to describe these figures?

Solution

- The designed capacity of the machine is the maximum output that could, ideally, be achieved in a week. This ignores the time needed for maintenance and setups.

  Designed capacity = production per hour × number of hours available
  = 100 × 8 × 5 = 4000 units a week

- The effective capacity is the maximum output that could reasonably be expected. This takes into account the time needed for maintenance and setups.

  Effective capacity = production per hour × number of hours that can be used
  = 100 × 8 × 5 × 0.9 = 3600 units a week

- The actual output was 3000 units a week.

- Efficiency is the ratio of actual output to effective capacity.

  Efficiency = 3000/3600 = 0.833 or 83.3%

- Utilization is the ratio of actual output to designed capacity.

  Utilization = 3000/4000 = 0.75 or 75%

we Worked example

A bottling hall has three distinct parts:

(1) Two bottling machines each with a maximum throughput of 100 litres a minute and average maintenance of one hour a day.

(2) Three labelling machines each with a maximum throughput of 3000 bottles an hour and planned stoppages averaging 30 minutes a day.

(3)   A packing area with a maximum throughput of 10,000 cases a day.

The hall is set to fill litre bottles and put them in cases of twelve bottles during a twelve hour working day.

(a)   What is the designed capacity of the hall?

(b)   What is the effective capacity of the hall?

(c)   If the bottling hall works at its effective capacity, what is the utilization of each operation?

(d)   If the line develops a fault which reduces output to 70,000 bottles, what is the efficiency of each operation?

Solution

The bottling hall can be viewed as a production line shown in Figure 9.3.

(a)   All measurements must be in consistent units, and litre bottles a day seems the most convenient. The designed capacities of each stage are:

- *Bottling*: 100 litres/minute on 2 machines = 200 litres a minute = $200 \times 12 \times 60$ bottles a day = 144,000 bottles a day

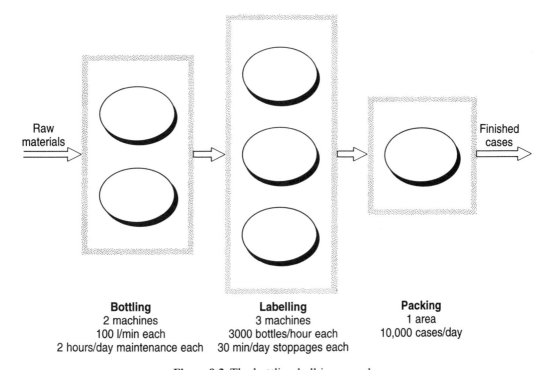

Bottling	Labelling	Packing
2 machines	3 machines	1 area
100 l/min each	3000 bottles/hour each	10,000 cases/day
2 hours/day maintenance each	30 min/day stoppages each	

Figure 9.3 The bottling hall in example.

- *Labelling*: 3000 bottles/hour on 3 machines = $3000 \times 3 \times 12$ bottles a day = 108,000 bottles a day
- *Packing*: 10,000 cases/day = $10,000 \times 12$ bottles a day = 120,000 bottles a day

The designed capacity of the whole process is set by the smallest capacity of any operation, and this is clearly labelling. The maximum throughput of the bottling hall is 108,000 bottles a day, and this is its designed capacity.

(b) The effective capacity of each stage takes into account planned stoppages, so the effective capacity of each stage is:

- *Bottling*: $144,000 \times 11/12 = 132,000$ bottles a day
- *Labelling*: $108,000 \times 11.5/12 = 103,500$ bottles a day
- *Packing*: 120,000 bottles a day

The limiting capacity is still the labelling operation, and effective capacity is 103,500 bottles a day.

(c) If the hall works with a throughput of 103,500 bottles a day, the utilizations of each part of the line are:

- *Bottling*: $103,500/144,000 = 0.719$ or 71.9%
- *Labelling*: $103,500/108,000 = 0.958$ or 95.8%
- *Packing*: $103,500/120,000 = 0.863$ or 86.3%

(d) With an actual output of 70,000 bottles the efficiency of each operation is:

- *Bottling*: $70,000/132,000 = 0.530$ or 53.0%
- *Labelling*: $70,000/103,500 = 0.676$ or 67.6%
- *Packing*: $70,000/120,000 = 0.583$ or 58.3%

Review questions

9.7 Why is the capacity always related to a specific period of time?

9.8 What is the difference between designed capacity and effective capacity?

9.9 What units could you use to measure the capacity of:

(a)	a train	(b)	a cinema
(c)	a squash club	(d)	a social work department

9.10 Which is largest of actual output, designed capacity or effective capacity?

Capacity planning

Alternative policies

Capacity planning aims to match available capacity to forecast demand. If an organization has excess capacity there has been too much investment in facilities and this is both wasteful and expensive. On the other hand, if there is not enough capacity some demand will not be met, giving lost sales and other penalties.

Capacity planning is largely a strategic function. The capacity of a process might be increased by building another facility, or changing the type of process. Excess capacity can be reduced by closing down facilities or using them for other products. Such decisions have long-term consequences. But other aspects of capacity planning are shorter term. Capacity can also be increased by leasing additional space, or working overtime and these are tactical and operational decisions. So we can summarize the objectives of capacity planning as making capacity match forecast demand in the long term, while making adjustments to correct short-term mismatches.

> The aim of **capacity planning** is to match available capacity to forecast demand over the long, medium and short terms.

Capacity planning starts by looking at the forecast demand for a product. Then operations managers have to decide what capacity to allocate to the product. Suppose, for example, an organization is looking at the capacity needed in a set of machines. We have defined utilization as the ratio of actual output to designed capacity, so:

$$\text{Utilization} = \frac{\text{actual output}}{\text{designed capacity}} = \frac{\text{actual output}}{NHSD/T}$$

where:

N = number of machines
H = hours per shift
S = number of shifts worked a day
D = days worked a year
T = time to make one unit in hours

We can turn this equation around to see how many machines are needed to produce a certain number of units. The total machine time available must be greater than, or at least equal to, the total time required. If the forecast demand suggests an annual production target of P, and average utilization of machines is U, we have:

hours of machine time available $\geqslant$ hours of machine time needed

$$NHSDU \geqslant PT$$

or,

number of machines, $N \geqslant \dfrac{PT}{HSDU}$

This example shows how we can set about capacity planning. We need to:

- examine forecast demand and translate this into a capacity requirement;
- calculate the available capacity of present facilities;
- identify mismatches between capacity needs and availability;
- generate alternative plans for overcoming any mismatch;
- compare alternative plans and choose the best.

This process is sometimes called **resource requirement planning**.

we Worked example

A company wants to make 1000 units of a product a week. The product is made on a machine that has a designed capacity of 10 units an hour, but its expected utilization is 80%. The company works a single eight-hour shift five days a week, but could move to double shifts or work at weekends. How many machines does the company need?

Solution

Each week we have production, $P, = 1000$ units, time to make a unit, $T, = 0.1$ hours, hours worked a shift, $H, = 8$ and utilization, $U, = 0.8$. Substituting these values gives the number of machines needed as:

$$N \geqslant \frac{PT}{HSDU} \geqslant \frac{6000}{384 \times SD}$$

- Working a single shift on weekdays has $S = 1$ and $D = 5$ to give:

$$N \geqslant 6000/1920 \geqslant 3.125$$

As machines come in discrete quantities, this number must be rounded up to 4. The utilization of these would be:

$$\text{Utilization} = \frac{PT}{NHSD} = \frac{6000}{4 \times 8 \times 1 \times 5} = 0.625 \text{ or } 62.5\%$$

This low utilization comes from having to buy 4 machines when only 3.125 are actually needed. The company could increase utilization by buying 3 machines and making short-term adjustments to make up the difference.

- If the company moved to a double shift, $S = 2$ and $D = 5$ to give:

    $$N \geqslant 6000/3840 \geqslant 1.56$$

    The company would need two machines, but again utilization is only 62.5%.

- If the company stayed with a single shift but worked at weekends, $S = 1$ and $D = 7$ to give:

    $$N \geqslant 6000/2688 \geqslant 2.23$$

    The company would need 3 machines and utilization is:

    $$U = 6000/10{,}080 = 0.595 \text{ or } 59.5\%$$

The organization now needs to complete its capacity planning by comparing these alternatives and implementing the best. One major consideration is that the first alternative keeps a normal working week, while the other alternatives need people to either work at weekend or on shifts. Neither of these will be popular with employees.

The example above shows one of the problems with matching capacity and demand. While demand comes in small quantities and can take almost any value, capacity often comes in large discrete amounts. Typically, capacity can be increased by building another factory, using another machine, opening another shop, employing another person, using another vehicle, and so on. This makes it very difficult to match capacity exactly to demand.

Suppose that demand for a product rises steadily over time. Capacity should be increased at some point, but the increase will come as a discrete step. This problem can not be avoided, but there are three basic strategies for dealing with it, as illustrated in Figure 9.4:

(1) capacity can be more or less matched to demand, so that sometimes there is excess capacity and sometimes a shortage;

(2) capacity can be made at least equal to demand at all times, which needs more investment in facilities and gives lower utilization;

(3) capacity can be added only when the additional facilities would be fully used, which needs lower investment and gives high utilizations, but restricts output.

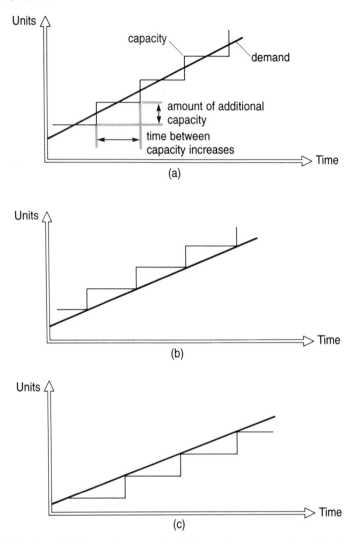

Figure 9.4 Options for increasing capacity: (a) capacity more or less matches demand; (b) capacity is always greater than demand; (c) capacity always lags behind demand.

Each of these strategies is best suited to different circumstances, but there is seldom an ideal solution where all resources reach 100% utilization. Factors that encourage organizations to increase capacity early, as shown in Figure 9.4b are:

- uneven or variable demand

- high profits, perhaps for a new product

- high cost of unmet demand, possibly with lost sales

- continuously changing product mix

- uncertainty in capacity

- variable efficiency

- capacity increases that are relatively small

- low cost of spare capacity – which might be used for other work.

On the other hand, the main factor that makes organizations delay an increase in capacity until the last possible moment, as shown in Figure 9.4c, is the capital cost.

If you think of a large furniture shop, like MFI, most of the capacity to serve customers is set by the number of sales people. Because of the type of demand, the shop is likely to increase capacity early and make sure there are always enough staff to serve all customers. On the other hand, the capacity of airports is set by the number of terminals. Airports usually delay expansions for as long as possible, so that terminals are crowded when they open.

Another question about capacity concerns the size of any planned expansion. Any change in capacity is likely to disrupt operations, so it might be better to have a few large increases than more smaller ones – as shown in Figure 9.5. When an organization builds more offices, for example, it often adds more space than it currently needs to avoid disruptions in the future.

The benefits of large increases include:

- capacity stays ahead of demand for a long time

- sales are unlikely to be lost

- there might be economies of scale

- advantages might be gained over competitors

- there are less frequent disruptions.

On the other hand, the disadvantages include:

- capacity does not match demand so closely

- disruptions may be serious

- there are high capital costs

- utilization will be low

- there is high risk if demand changes

- the policy is less flexible.

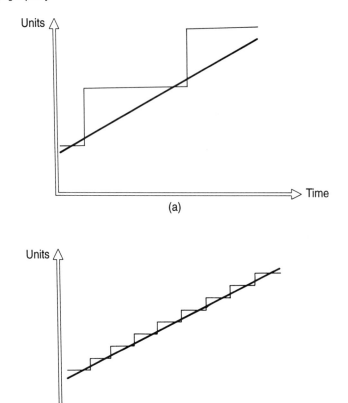

Figure 9.5 Alternatives for increasing capacity: (a) a few large increases; (b) more smaller increases.

we Worked example

One of Excelsior Boat's most profitable products is a set of sails for racing yachts. Excelsior is reviewing its plans for these sails over the next three years. The current annual demand is 100 units, and this is rising by 50 units a year. To meet this demand the company can expand capacity now, or at the beginning of next year, but the capacity can only be increased in discrete steps of 50 units. Each unit of spare capacity has notional costs of £400 a year, while each unit of shortage has costs of £1000 a year. What do you think Excelsior should do about its capacity?

Solution

Excelsior has five alternatives.

● Alternative 1. Do not increase capacity, which gives:

Year	Sales	Spare	Shortage
0	100	0	0
1	100	0	50
2	100	0	100

This has total costs of 0×400 for spare capacity plus 150×1000 for shortages, totalling £150,000 over the three years.

● Alternatives 2 and 3. Increase capacity by either 50 or 100 units now, giving:

	50 increase			100 increase		
Year	Sales	Spare	Shortage	Sales	Spare	Shortage
0	100	50	0	100	100	0
1	150	0	0	150	50	0
2	150	0	50	200	0	0

Increasing capacity by 50 now has total costs of $(50 \times 400) + (50 \times 1000) = £70,000$.
Increasing capacity by 100 now has costs of $(150 \times 400) + (0 \times 1000) = £60,000$.

● Alternatives 4 and 5. Increase capacity by 50 units or 100 units next year, giving:

	50 increase			100 increase		
Year	Sales	Spare	Shortage	Sales	Spare	Shortage
0	100	0	0	100	0	0
1	150	0	0	150	50	0
2	150	0	50	200	0	0

Increasing capacity by 50 next year has total costs of $(0 \times 400) + (50 \times 1000) = £50,000$.
Increasing capacity by 100 next year has costs of $(50 \times 400) + (0 \times 1000) = £20,000$.

The best overall policy is to increase capacity by 100 units next year.

ce Case example – Private Patient Plan

Private Patient Plan (PPP) offers a range of private medical care. It used to rely on written information to attract new customers. PPP would place advertisements in newspapers and magazines. The advertisements included an enquiry form which people could cut out and post back to PPP. When it received the form, PPP would post back details of its services.

In the late 1980s PPP started a free 0800 telephone line. The organization had no previous experience with this type of operation and could not forecast demand. In practice, it underestimated the popularity of the service, and was immediately swamped with enquiries. Perhaps it was too cautious in its capacity plans, but the facilities it set up had nowhere near enough capacity to deal with the actual demand. The telephone operations had to be increased straightaway. Soon, almost all enquiries were handled by telephone rather than post, and this was considered an important factor in doubling PPP's business.

Questions

- How could PPP measure the capacity of its phone system?

- Could you suggest ways of increasing its capacity?

Short-term adjustments to capacity

After an organization has set the long-term capacity for a process, it can still make short-term adjustments to this. Suppose that a local radio station has two people answering telephone calls from the public. This sets the normal capacity. But if the station has a popular phone-in programme they can hire part-time staff to increase capacity during this programme.

Short-term mismatches between supply and demand can be corrected in two ways:

(1) adjust demand to match available capacity, or

(2) adjust capacity to match demand.

Taking the first of these, demand can be adjusted in a number of ways. Many organizations simply change the price – but there are limits here as prices must be high enough to cover all costs and low enough to deal with competition. Ways of adjusting demand include the following:

- vary the price, with increases for products with too little capacity and decreases for products with spare capacity;

- change the marketing effort, with increases for products with spare capacity and reductions for products with insufficient capacity;

- offer incentives, such as free samples of products with spare capacity, or discounts, such as off-peak telephone calls or travel;

- change related products, so that substitution is possible for products in short supply;

- keep spare units in stock to be used later;

- vary the lead time, making customers wait for products in short supply;

- use a reservation or appointment system.

One result of this **demand management** is that business can be actively discouraged at times of high demand. You may think this is strange but it is really quite common. Professional institutions, for example, put up barriers against newcomers wanting to enter; restaurants have queues outside at busy times which discourage people from going there; expensive cars offer long delivery times; artists produce limited editions of prints; perfumes charge very high prices, and so on.

Some of these options show that demand can be managed by changing the time that customers have to wait. Demand is then smoothed by having a continuous queue of customers which gets shorter at times of low demand and longer at times of high demand. Appointment systems are just a formal version of queues, and they are used to smooth demand in almost every profession.

The alternative to demand management is **capacity management**, which looks for short-term adjustments to available capacity. The obvious way of doing this is to change the working time, by working overtime to increase capacity, or short time to reduce it. Other ways of adjusting capacity include:

- changing the total hours worked in any period, by changing the number of shifts or other work patterns;

- employing part-time staff to cover peak demand;

- scheduling work patterns so the total workforce available at any time varies in line with varying demand;

- using outside contractors, or renting extra space;

- adjusting the process, perhaps making larger batches to reduce setup times;

- adjusting equipment and processes to work faster or slower;

- rescheduling maintenance periods;

- making the customer do some work, like using automatic cash dispensing machines in banks or packing their own bags in supermarkets.

You can see that the first four of these adjust designed capacity. The next three adjust effective capacity, and the last one reduces the load put on operations. Such adjustments can not be made too often or too severely. Many of the alternatives affect employees by asking them to work overtime, using part-time staff, and so on. Most people have other arrangements to make, so their work schedules can not be changed every few days. Neither can extra space be rented for a few hours at a time. This means that capacity planning should aim for a stable output. We shall return to this idea in Chapter 11.

Economies of scale

Large increases in capacity can give economies of scale. Then bigger operations are able to produce individual units more cheaply than smaller ones. For example, mass produced cars are much cheaper to make than Rolls-Royce cars; colour supplements to newspapers are cheaper than limited edition prints; ordinary beer is cheaper than real ale, and so on.

These lower costs occur for three reasons:

(1)   fixed costs are spread over a larger number of units;

(2)   more efficient processes can be used, using larger batches and more automation;

(3)   more experience with the product raises efficiency.

The graph shown in Figure 9.6 illustrates this.

Sometimes, rather than give economies, increasing size gives dis-economies of scale. The communications, management and organization structure needed to support large operations get too complex and become less efficient. Some people suggest, for example, that centralized government is inherently inefficient as it is a huge organization that has very complex interactions between large numbers of departments.

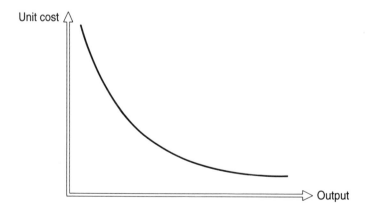

Figure 9.6 Economies of scale giving lower unit costs.

we Worked example

Karen Thorburn runs a tax advisory clinic. She offers help to small companies filing their annual tax returns. Karen employs a number of full-time, part-time and temporary staff. These are usually accountants, but can be 'accounting assistants'. Over the past three years, she has noticed that the number of clients she can help in any period depends on the number of staff employed. Past figures show:

Staff	1	2	3	4	5	6	7
Clients	25	60	110	150	180	205	220

The fixed costs of Karen's operation are £50,000, and each staff member employed costs an average of £25,000. How would you compare the performance of different numbers of staff?

Solution

The spreadsheet in Figure 9.7 shows a table of costs with values in thousands of pounds. The number of clients seen per person is rising for the first three, showing economies of scale. After this it declines as diseconomies appear. Four staff give the highest average output per person. The variable cost per unit is also lowest with four staff. The total cost per unit – which is found by adding variable and fixed costs – is a minimum with five staff. As Karen is probably most concerned with total cost per unit, the best number of employees is five.

Staff	Total clients	Additional clients per staff member	Average clients per staff member	Variable cost	Variable cost per client	Total cost	Total cost per client
1	25	25	25.00	25.00	1.00	75.00	3.00
2	60	35	30.00	50.00	0.83	100.00	1.67
3	110	50	36.67	75.00	0.68	125.00	1.14
4	150	40	37.50	100.00	0.67	150.00	1.00
5	180	30	36.00	125.00	0.69	175.00	0.97
6	205	25	34.17	150.00	0.73	200.00	0.98
7	220	15	31.43	175.00	0.80	225.00	1.02

Figure 9.7 Spreadsheet of calculations for example.

ce Case example – Hospital security

Queen Elizabeth Hospital has a security force of 26 people. These are responsible for the general security of the four hospital buildings and seven hectare site. There are very few serious problems, but a few months ago there were three unrelated incidents which raised concerns. When local newspapers published details of these incidents people started demanding more security. The hospital managers saw this as an operations problem, and passed the demands on to the Facility Operations Manager (FOM).

FOM increased the number of patrols and put more security people in places where they were clearly visible. He also improved the camera surveillance system and experimented with better identity cards for staff and patients. There were no further incidents, but the security people were now working an average of 14 hours a week overtime. After a spell they became tired and morale dropped. FOM knew that the security people could not continue to work at this level, so he put in a request for five more permanent staff, plus an additional six part-time staff to get over the current demand.

Hospital managers were trying to cut overheads, and were reluctant to divert money away from direct medical care. They thought the problem was temporary and would solve itself if they waited a short time.

Questions

- How can you tell if the hospital needs more security people?

- How can you measure the capacity of the current security service? Are there any other useful measures of performance?

- How can the capacity of the security service be increased? Do you think the hospital should hire more security people?

Review questions

9.11   What are the basic steps in capacity planning?

9.12   Why might discrete increases in capacity cause problems?

9.13   What are the two alternatives for dealing with short-term mismatches in demand and capacity?

9.14   Give three reasons for declining unit cost with increasing output.

Changing capacity over time

Capacity planning aims to match available capacity as closely as possible to forecast demand. We have seen that this is made more difficult by factors like discrete capacity and economies of scale. Another major problem is that the capacity of a process changes over time. Even if no changes are made to the process there will be short-term variations due to operator illness, interruptions, breakdowns, and so on. There are also longer-term changes in capacity, which we shall illustrate by learning curves and reducing performance.

Learning curves

We all know that the more often we repeat something, the easier it becomes. Musicians and sportsmen spend a long time practising so they become more skilful and find it easier to perform at a given level. You can see this effect in almost all operations. It means that efficiency increases with the number of units produced. The increased efficiency usually appears as a reduction in the time needed to do an operation, as shown in Figure 9.8. This graph is called a **learning curve**.

A common shape for learning curves has the time taken to do an operation falling by some fixed proportion every time the number of repetitions is doubled. Typically this proportion is about 10%. So the first time an operation is done it takes some time, T; the second time it takes only 90% of this time; the fourth time it takes 90% of the time needed for the second repetition; the eighth time it takes 90% of the time needed for the fourth repetition; the sixteenth time it takes 90% of the time needed for

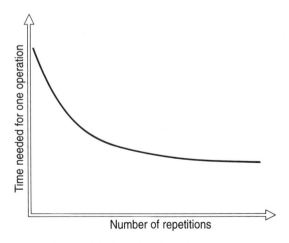

Figure 9.8 A typical learning curve.

the eighth repetition, and so on. This is described as a 90% learning curve, or a learning rate of 0.9. The equation for this curve is:

$$Y = TN^b$$

where:

N = number of repetitions
Y = time taken for the Nth repetition
T = time taken for the first unit
b = log R/log 2
R = learning rate

This may seem an unusual equation, especially the value of b, but it only describes the shape of a common learning curve. You can also see that the value of b is fixed for any particular learning rate.

- For a 90% learning curve, $R = 0.9$, so
  $$b = \log 0.9 / \log 2 = -0.046/0.301 = -0.152.$$

- For an 80% learning curve, $R = 0.8$, so
  $$b = \log 0.8 / \log 2 = -0.097/0.301 = -0.322.$$

- For a 70% learning curve, $R = 0.7$, so
  $$b = \log 0.7 / \log 2 = -0.155/0.301 = -0.515.$$

we Worked example

It takes one hour to produce the first unit of a product. How long will it take to make each of the first eight units with a learning rate of 0.8?

Solution

For an 80% learning curve $b = -0.322$, so the time (in minutes) decreases according to:

$$Y = 60N^{-0.322}$$

Substituting

$N = 1$ gives $Y = 60 \times 1^{-0.322} = 60.0$
$N = 2$ gives $Y = 60 \times 2^{-0.322} = 48.0$
$N = 3$ gives $Y = 60 \times 3^{-0.322} = 42.1$

and so on, giving the following results.

Unit number	1	2	3	4	5	6	7	8
Time to make unit	60	48.0	42.1	38.4	35.7	33.7	32.1	30.7

The total time needed to make eight units is found by adding these eight times, which is 320.7 minutes. The average time for each of the eight units is $320.7/8 = 40.1$ minutes.

Review questions

9.15 What is meant by an 80% learning curve?

9.16 Why does the time taken to do an operation decline over time?

Maintenance of equipment

Learning curves make productivity rise over time, but there are other factors that make productivity fall. The most important of these is the ageing of equipment. As equipment gets older it breaks down more often, develops more faults, gives lower quality output, slows down, and generally wears out. If this goes unchecked, the performance of equipment will decline until it is no longer satisfactory. Sometimes this change is slow – like the fuel consumption of a car which rises over a period of seven or eight years. Sometimes the change is very fast, like a bolt which suddenly breaks. A way of avoiding this decline is to use routine maintenance and replacement.

With routine maintenance, equipment is inspected and vulnerable parts are replaced at regular intervals or after a certain number of hours of use. This happens when you give your car its regular service. By replacing bits that are worn the equipment is restored to give continuing, satisfactory performance.

Now we can ask, 'How often should this maintenance be done?' If it is done too often, the equipment will run efficiently but the maintenance costs will be too high. If it is not done often enough, the maintenance cost will be low but the equipment will still break down. The best answer comes from adding the costs of maintenance and expected failure. If the total cost is plotted against the frequency of maintenance, we get a U-shaped curve that has a minimum. This minimum cost shows the best time between maintenance periods (see Figure 9.9).

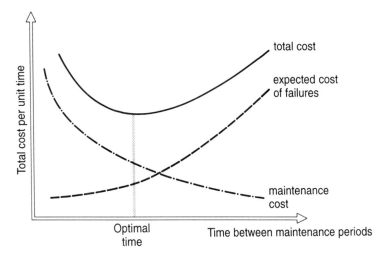

Figure 9.9 Finding the best time interval between maintenance periods.

we Worked example

If a piece of equipment works continuously the expected cost of failure rises each week as shown below. Routine maintenance can be done at a cost of £1000 and this brings the equipment back up to new condition. What is the best time between maintenance periods?

Weeks since maintenance	0	1	2	3	4	5
Cost of breakdowns in week (£)	0	50	150	200	1600	3000

Solution

If the equipment is maintained every week there is no cost for expected breakdowns; if maintenance is done every two weeks the expected cost is £0 in the first week plus £50 in the second week; if maintenance is done every three weeks the expected cost is £0 in the first week, £50 in the second week and £150 in the third week, and so on. Then adding the routine maintenance cost of £1000 gives the costs shown in Table 9.1.

If maintenance is done every four weeks the cumulative cost of breakdowns is £400 and maintenance costs £1000, to give a total cost of £1400. This gives an average of £350 a week, which is the cheapest alternative.

Table 9.1

Weeks between maintenance	Maintenance cost	Cost of break-downs in week	Total cost of breakdowns	Total cost	Cost per week
1	1000	0	0	1000	1000
2	1000	50	50	1050	525
3	1000	150	200	1200	400
4	1000	200	400	1400	350
5	1000	1600	2000	3000	600
6	1000	3000	5000	6000	1000

ce Case example – Trident Submarines

This example shows the clear link between maintenance and capacity. It also shows how back-up equipment is needed to ensure a specified level of capacity. Sometimes the cost of this back-up is very high.

For many years Britain had a fleet of nuclear submarines which carried Polaris missiles. By the 1980s these were getting old and the government decided to replace them with larger submarines which carried Trident missiles. These are being introduced during the 1990s.

An important question was how many of the new submarines should be bought. Each new submarine had considerably more power than the older ones, so the navy would need fewer of them. At the same time, there had been significant political changes, particularly in Eastern Europe, which reduced the need for massive defence expenditure. Most countries were significantly reducing their arms budgets.

The solution adopted by the government was to have a base of four Trident submarines. But at any time only one of these would be on active duty. A second would be getting ready to go on active duty, a third would be in dock for a refit (equivalent to a minor service) and the fourth would be in dock for an overhaul (equivalent to a major service).

This means that one active Trident submarine can provide Britain's perceived capacity for nuclear defence. Making sure this capacity is always available actually takes four submarines – as routine maintenance puts three of the fleet out of action at any time. Initial estimates for the cost of this fleet was £10 billion.

Questions

• How do you think the government decided the best capacity for the Trident fleet?

• Can you think of other operations where maintenance is very expensive?

Organizations do not have to use programmes of routine maintenance. They can simply repair equipment when it breaks down – but this is not generally recommended, as breakdowns can occur at inconvenient times. Routine maintenance can be scheduled for quiet periods at night or weekends, but breakdowns can happen during busy times when important products are being made. A second option is simply to replace equipment when its performance declines to some specified level – but this can give very high capital costs. A third option is to have spare equipment available so that it can take over when there is a breakdown. Most organizations find the cheapest alternative is to use planned maintenance with a periodic replacement policy.

Replacement of equipment

Routine maintenance keeps equipment working efficiently, but there comes a point when maintenance and repairs become too expensive and it is cheaper to buy new equipment. These replacement decisions can be expensive and need

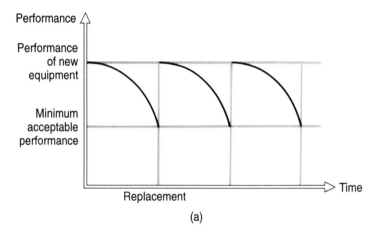

(a)

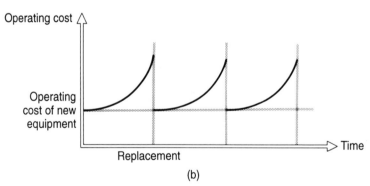

(b)

Figure 9.10 Two approaches for replacement: (a) replacement when performance becomes unacceptable; (b) replacement to minimize operating costs.

careful planning. There are, for example, several nuclear power stations, particularly older Magnox ones, that are being phased out and need replacing. Nobody is really sure of the costs involved because there are still no satisfactory means of dealing with nuclear waste. Other examples of expensive replacement decisions include office blocks, steel mills, ships and aeroplanes.

Figure 9.10 shows two approaches for the timing of replacements. In the first, equipment is replaced when its performance falls so low that it is no longer acceptable – the output may be too low, quality too poor, breakdowns too frequent, and so on. The drawback with this approach is that its response is too late – it comes when the equipment is already unsatisfactory. A better alternative is to analyse costs, and keep the equipment working for the time which minimizes total costs.

A useful way of finding the best age of replacement is to add the cost of operating equipment over a number of years and divide this by the age to give an average annual cost. This calculation will show the best age of replacement.

we Worked example

Every year a company reviews the performance of its production machines so that any replacements can be delivered before the end of the financial year. The cost of replacing each machine is £150,000. Expected resale values at the end of each year, average annual operating costs and maintenance costs are given in the following table. What is the best age to replace the machines?

Age of machine	1	2	3	4	5
Resale value	75,000	45,000	22,500	15,000	7,500
Running cost in previous year	7,500	13,500	22,500	61,500	90,000

Solution

When a machine is sold, the total cost of using it during its life time is in two parts:

(1)   a capital cost equal to the difference between the price of a new machine and the resale value of the old one

(2)   a running cost which is the cumulative cost of maintenance and operation over the machine's life.

If a machine is sold after one year:

- capital cost is $150,000 - 75,000 = £75,000$
- running cost is £7500.

The total cost of using the machine for one year is £82,500.

If the machine is sold after 2 years:

- capital cost is $150,000 - 45,000 = £105,000$
- running cost is 7500 in the first year plus 13,500 in the second year.

The total cost of using the machine for two years is £126,000, which is an average of £63,000 a year.

Repeating these calculations for other ages of replacement gives the following values.

Age of replacement	1	2	3	4	5
Capital cost	75,000	105,000	127,500	135,000	142,500
Running cost	7,500	21,000	43,500	105,000	195,000
Total cost	82,500	126,000	171,000	240,000	337,500
Average cost a year	82,500	63,000	57,000	60,000	67,500

Replacement after three years clearly gives the lowest average annual cost.

These calculations have assumed that the company will buy new machines. In some circumstances it is better to buy secondhand machines. When resale value declines quickly, as it does in this example, secondhand equipment can be bought which is both relatively new and cheap. Obviously the company must consider this option very carefully, as there may be problems with reliability, availability of spare parts, status, use of outdated technology, and so on.

If a machine is bought when it is two years old and used until it is four years old

- capital cost is $45,000 - 15,000 = £30,000$

- running cost is 22,500 in the first year plus 61,500 in the second year.

The total cost over two years is £114,000, or an average of £57,000 a year.

If a machine is bought when it is two years old and used until it is five years old

- capital cost is $45,000 - 7,500 = £37,500$

- running cost is 22,500 in the first year, 61,500 in the second year and 90,000 in the third year.

The total cost over three years is £211,500, or an average of £70,500 a year.

Repeating this calculation for combinations of ages bought and ages sold gives the following table of average annual costs (in thousands of pounds).

		1	2	Age sold 3	4	5
	0	82.5	63	57	60	64.5
	1	–	43.5	44.3	52.5	63.8
Age bought	2	–	–	45	57	70.5
	3	–	–	–	69	83.3
	4	–	–	–	–	97.5

Looking at this you can see that the cheapest option is to buy one year old machines and sell them a year later. A more detailed analysis would discount the costs to give a better comparison.

Reliability of equipment

Maintenance and replacement programmes effect the reliability of equipment. But a lot of the reliability is set by the initial design. If a piece of equipment is poorly designed no amount of maintenance will make it work better.

Suppose we define the **reliability** of something as the probability that it continues to work throughout an entire period. Then a reliability of 90% means there is a probability of 0.9 that it will continue to work normally for a period. To simplify things we will also talk about equipment made up of components. But you should remember that this is just for convenience and does not mean that this is the only application.

The overall reliability of equipment depends on both the reliability of each component and on the way they are arranged. If a single component has a reliability of R, putting two identical components in parallel will increase the overall reliability. The assumption is that the second component will only start to work when the first one fails, and that the equipment can work with only one of the components operating. Adding more components in parallel increases reliability, as the equipment will only fail when **all** components fail.

Consider 2 identical components in parallel with the reliability of each component R, as shown in Figure 9.11. The probability that a component continues to work normally is R, so the probability that it will stop working is $1 - R$. The probability that both components fail is $(1 - R)^2$. The reliability of the equipment is the probability that at least one of the components is operating which is $1 - (1 - R)^2$. Similarly, the probability that n identical components in parallel will all fail is $(1 - R)^n$, and the reliability of the equipment is $1 - (1 - R)^n$. So, putting components in parallel makes the equipment more reliable.

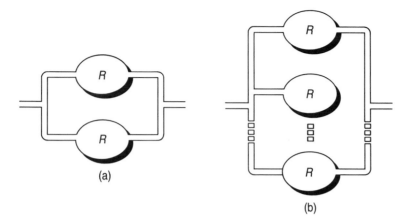

Figure 9.11 Reliability of components in parallel:
(a) reliability of two identical components in parallel is $1 - (1 - R)^2$;
(b) reliability of n identical components in parallel is $1 - (1 - R)^n$.

If components are added in series the reliability of equipment is reduced. This is because equipment with components in series only works if **all** separate components are working. Consider two components in series. If the reliability of each is R, the reliability of the two is the probability that both are working, which is R^2. If there are n components in series their reliability is R^n. So equipment with components in series is less reliable than the individual components (see Figure 9.12).

You can find the reliability of complex systems of components by reducing them to simpler forms, as illustrated in the following worked examples.

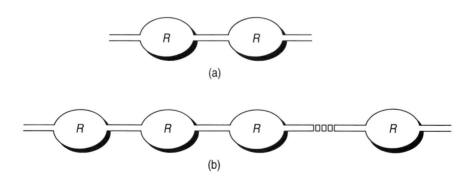

Figure 9.12 Reliability of components in series:
(a) reliability of two identical components in series is R^2;
(b) reliability of n identical components in series is R^n.

we Worked example

Four pieces of equipment on an assembly line can be viewed as the components shown in Figure 9.13. What is the overall reliability of the line?

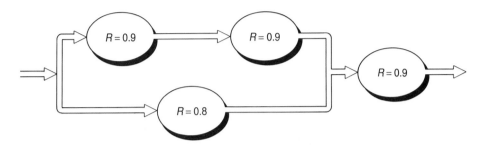

Figure 9.13 Equipment reliability for example.

Solution

The top two components have a combined reliability of $0.9 \times 0.9 = 0.81$. This can be taken as a single component in parallel with the bottom component. The probability of both of these failing is $(1 - 0.81) \times (1 - 0.8) = 0.038$, so the reliability of these two parts is $1 - 0.038 = 0.962$. This is now in series with

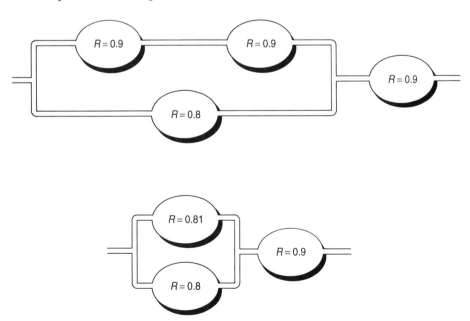

Figure 9.14 Stages in simplifying the assembly line.

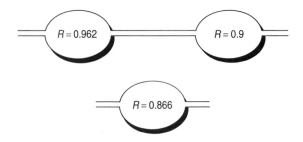

Figure 9.14 *(cont.)* Stages in simplifying the assembly line.

the last component, so the overall reliability is $0.962 \times 0.9 = 0.866$. The stages in this analysis are shown in Figure 9.14.

we Worked example

Figure 9.15 shows the layout of a shop floor in Kaiser Winter Garments. This consists of three parallel production lines A, B and C, whose outputs are 10,000, 12,000 and 20,000 units a week respectively. The diagram shows the reliability of each machine and if a line fails during the week all its production during the week is lost.

(a)   Find the reliability of each line.

(b)   Find the possible outputs from the process and the probability of each.

(c)   What is the expected output of the process?

Solution

(a)   The first step is to simplify the diagram and find the reliability of each line.

If R_i is the probability that machine i continues to work during a week, the reliability of line A is:

$$
\begin{aligned}
R_A &= [1 - (1 - R_1) \times (1 - R_2)] \times R_3 \\
&= [1 - (0.2 \times 0.2)] \times 0.9 \\
&= 0.864
\end{aligned}
$$

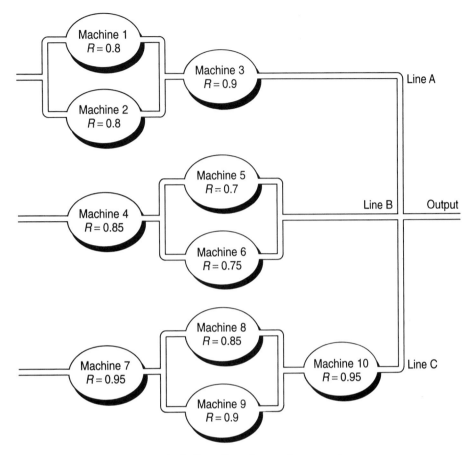

Figure 9.15 Shop floor layout for example.

The reliability of line B is:

$$R_B = R_4 \times [1 - (1 - R_5) \times (1 - R_6)]$$
$$= 0.85 \times [1 - (0.3 \times 0.25)]$$
$$= 0.786$$

The reliability of line C is:

$$R_C = R_7 \times [1 - (1 - R_8) \times (1 - R_9)] \times R_{10}$$
$$= 0.95 \times [1 - (0.15 \times 0.1)] \times 0.95$$
$$= 0.889$$

(b)   The total output is found by taking various combinations of lines failing. If lines A and B fail while line C continues the output will be 20,000. This has a probability of $(1 - R_A) \times (1 - R_B) \times R_C = 0.136 \times 0.214 \times 0.889 = 0.026$. The other possible outputs can be calculated as shown in Table 9.2.

Table 9.2

Output	Probability	
0	$(1 - R_A) \times (1 - R_B) \times (1 - R_C)$	$= 0.003$
10,000	$R_A \times (1 - R_B) \times (1 - R_C)$	$= 0.021$
12,000	$(1 - R_A) \times R_B \times (1 - R_C)$	$= 0.012$
20,000	$(1 - R_A) \times (1 - R_B) \times R_C$	$= 0.026$
22,000	$R_A \times R_B \times (1 - R_C)$	$= 0.075$
30,000	$R_A \times (1 - R_B) \times R_C$	$= 0.164$
32,000	$(1 - R_A) \times R_B \times R_C$	$= 0.095$
42,000	$R_A \times R_B \times R_C$	$= 0.604$

(c)   The expected output is the sum of (probability $\times$ output), so:

$$\text{expected output} = (0 \times 0.003) + (10,000 \times 0.021) +$$
$$(12,000 \times 0.012) + \ldots$$
$$= 35,852$$

ce | Case example – Maintenance of cranes

Maintenance of equipment can have a major affect on its reliability, and therefore the cost of operations. An organization that saves money on maintenance can find itself with high bills for breakdowns and disruptions. Often each organization has to find the best level of maintenance and replacement for its own operations, but sometimes there are agreed maintenance procedures. One international agreement for maintenance concerns the operations of cranes.

ISO TC 96/SC 5 is the international standard for the maintenance of cranes. Case studies at paper mills in Canada, Finland, Sweden and America show that using the procedures described in this standard reduced annual maintenance costs by 33–64%, the number of defects by 46–60% and production failures by 33–97%.

Similar studies in steel mills in Sweden, Canada and America reduced annual maintenance costs by 28–56%, the number of defects declined by 50–83% and the number of production failures by 63–95%.

The improved performance given by the maintenance programmes include benefits to:

- operators who have safer working conditions;

- owners who save money with fewer repairs, production failures, injuries, insurance, and so on;

- manufacturers who get higher quality.

    Once introduced, these standards for crane maintenance can be used in ISO 9000 quality management processes.

Review questions

9.17   What is the purpose of routine maintenance?

9.18   Do you think it likely that maintenance costs for a machine will decline over time?

9.19   When do you think a machine should be replaced?

9.20   What is meant by 'reliability'?

Chapter review

- Several measures can be used for the performance of an organization. These include capacity, utilization, productivity and efficiency.

- Productivity measures the amount of output achieved for a given amount of input. There are several ways of measuring it, the main ones being total and partial productivity.

- Most organizations aim at improving productivity, but the measures they use should relate to overall objectives. Any single measure of productivity gives only one view of performance, so a range of measures must be used to give the overall picture.

- Capacity shows the maximum output in a specified time. This is sometimes obvious, but it often needs calculating or some agreement.

- Designed capacity is the maximum output of a facility in ideal conditions, while effective capacity is the maximum output under normal circumstances.

- The aim of capacity planning is to match available capacity to forecast demand. Important questions in capacity planning are when to change capacity and by how much. These decisions are complicated by factors like the discrete nature of capacity and economies of scale.

- Capacity planning is essentially a strategic function, but it includes both tactical and operational decisions. Short-term mismatches between capacity and demand can be overcome by either demand management or capacity management.

- The capacity of a process changes over time. Two specific causes of this are learning curves and reducing equipment performance.

- Equipment reliability can be increased by good design, planned maintenance and periodic replacement.

Key terms

capacity   290
designed capacity   299
economies of scale   312
effective capacity   299
effectiveness   291
efficiency   291
learning curve   315
maintenance   317

partial productivity   294
production   291
productivity   290
reliability   323
replacement   320
routine maintenance   317
total productivity   294
utilization   290

CS Case study – Ravenstone Hotel

The Ravenstone Hotel was built six years ago on the sea front at Scarborough. It has 105 rooms and attracts people staying both for business and on holiday. During the peak months of June and July it is fully booked and has to turn away potential guests. During quieter months there are a lot of empty rooms and the hotel tries to encourage business.

The hotel has a wide range of rates, depending on the season, the days, length of stay, number of people sharing a room, whether it uses group bookings, conference rates, senior citizens' discounts, weekend specials, and so on. The average number of people in a room is 1.5, and the total income from room bookings in 1995 was £1,290,000. About 60% of this was spent in direct operating costs.

The other main source of income for the hotel is its restaurant. This is open for breakfast, morning coffee, lunch, afternoon tea and dinner. These meals are designed as a service to guests and just cover costs, with the exception of the evening dinner which is very popular and runs at a profit. A small survey suggested that about half the people who stay in the hotel plan to eat dinner in the restaurant. It is often difficult to get a table at a convenient time and guests change their plans, so only about 40% of guests actually eat dinner there. Throughout the year 30% of people eating in the restaurant are guests, and the remaining 70% are visitors. There is a limit to the number of people who can eat dinner in an evening, and this is currently about 160, depending on the composition of parties.

Again, it is difficult to suggest a typical meal cost, but in 1995 the total income from the restaurant was £800,000 from food and £530,000 from the bar service. Roughly 40% of the average bill for food is spent directly on buying and preparing the food, 25% of the average bar bill is spent on buying and preparing drinks, and about 10% of both bills are needed to cover miscellaneous operating costs.

The management of the hotel are now considering expansion, and have collected the figures below and in Table 9.3.

Year	1989	1990	1991	1992	1993	1994
Number of guest nights	10,200	13,100	18,800	24,900	28,800	33,300

Some figures were also collected for a small sample of days to see how many enquiries it had to turn away (Table 9.4). There is no way of saying if these figures are typical.

Three alternative expansions are possible, each of which is largely independent of the others.

(1)   When the hotel was built the top floor was never completed. This could now be finished, making 30 more rooms. The capital cost of these would be £375,000, with additional fixed costs of £65,000. Operating costs would rise by about £55,000 a year.

Table 9.3

Month	Average rooms booked per night		
	1993	1994	1995
January	31	36	42
February	12	17	25
March	23	29	36
April	41	48	61
May	76	85	92
June	105	105	105
July	98	104	105
August	52	78	103
September	43	59	70
October	12	17	24
November	10	14	23
December	39	39	40

Table 9.4

Month	Number turned away per day	
	Hotel	Restaurant
January	1	6
May	3	12
July	30	36
August	24	41
November	2	8

(2)   An additional wing could be added to the hotel, adding 60 more rooms. The capital cost of these would be £850,000, with additional fixed costs of £150,000. Operating costs would rise by about £100,000 a year.

(3)   An extension to the restaurant. This could either be a major extension to add 160 diners a night, or a smaller extension to add 80 diners a night. The larger expansion has total capital costs of £600,000 and additional operating costs of £250,000 a year. The smaller expansion has total capital costs of £450,000 and additional operating costs of £150,000 a year.

Questions

●   What are the capacities of the hotel and dining room? How fully are these being used?

●   What suggestions would you make for matching capacity and demand more closely?

●   Do you think the hotel should expand? Which expansion plan is best?

Problems

9.1   Coffee machines in a works' canteen are designed to serve up to 2000 cups of coffee in a two-hour meal break. During a typical break they were used for 90 minutes and served 1000 cups. How can their performance be measured?

9.2   A family doctor sees patients for an average of 10 minutes each. There is an additional five minutes of paperwork for each visit, so appointments are made at 15 minute intervals. Each surgery lasts for five hours a day, but during one surgery the doctor was called away for an emergency which lasted an hour. Four patients who had appointments during this time were told to come back later. How could the doctor's performance in the surgery be measured?

9.3 A ski lift has pairs of chairs pulled on a continuous wire from the bottom of a ski run to the top. Ordinarily one pair of chairs arrives at the bottom of the slope every five seconds. If the lift works 10 hours a day for 100 days a year, what is its designed capacity? On a typical day 10% of users need help getting on the lift, and they cause average delays of 10 seconds. A further 25% of people using the lift are alone, and only one chair of the pair is used. What is the utilization of the lift?

9.4 In two consecutive years a process had the following characteristics:

	Year 1	Year 2
Number of units made	5000	6500
Raw materials used	15,000 kg	17,500 kg
Cost of raw materials	£40,000	£50,500
Hours worked	1200	1500
Direct labour costs	£12,000	£18,000
Energy used	20,000 kWh	24,000 kWh
Energy cost	£2000	£3000

How has the productivity changed?

9.5 A service organization tries to deal with 100 customers a day. Each person in the organization can see three customers an hour, but has to do associated paperwork which takes an average of 40 minutes a customer. Employees also lose about 20% of their time when they do other things and can not deal with customers' work. The standard working day in the organization is from 0900 to 1600 five days a week, with an hour off for lunch. How many employees should the organization hire, and what is their utilization? One week the organization only dealt with 90 customers. What were the resulting efficiency and utilization?

9.6 The fixed cost of a process is £110,000, and the capacity can be increased by using more machines at a cost of £55,000 each. The total output of the operation, measured in some consistent units, is:

Machines	1	2	3	4	5	6	7	8
Output	55	125	230	310	375	435	460	470

How many machines should be used to give the lowest unit cost?

9.7 It takes 25 minutes to make the first unit of a product. How long will it take to make each of the next nine units with a learning rate of 0.9?

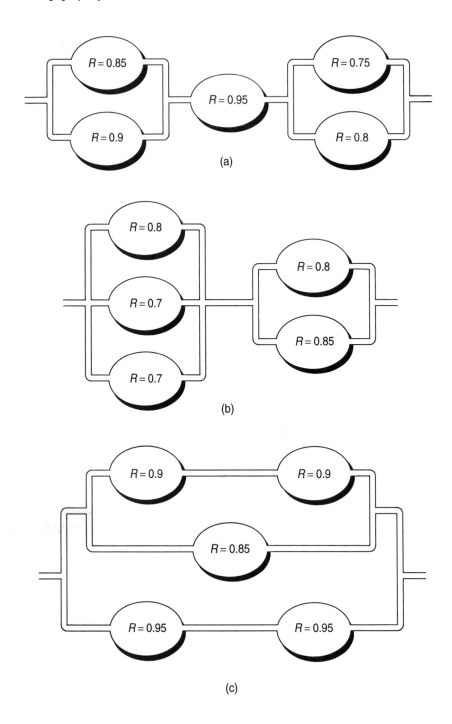

Figure 9.16 Layout of components for Problem 9.9.

9.8 New cars cost a company £12,000 each, with resale values and maintenance costs shown below. What is the best age to replace the cars?

Age of car (years)	1	2	3	4	5	6
Resale value	8000	5000	3000	2000	1200	600
Annual maintenance	1000	1200	1500	2000	3000	8750

9.9 What are the reliabilities of the three sets of components shown in Figure 9.16?

Discussion questions

9.1 Why do you think organizations are so keen to have quantitative measures of performance? How reliable are these likely to be? Does this reduce the emphasis that is put on qualitative factors in performance?

9.2 Employees in a company say that productivity has risen by 20%, so they deserve a pay rise. Employers say that the amount of overtime worked has risen by 20%, raising the wage bill by 30%, so employees should take a pay cut. What do you think of such arguments? Can you find other examples?

9.3 There are so many different meanings of productivity that no-one really knows what it describes. Do you think this is true?

9.4 Organizations are often tempted to find the easiest type of productivity to measure and then concentrate on improving this. What is the consequence of this? Can you give any examples of problems this creates?

9.5 You can often see notices, perhaps at the entrance to a club, which says something like, 'The capacity of this club is 200 people.' What does this really mean?

9.6 Because forecasts contain errors, and the output of a process is variable, capacity planning is very difficult. Say, giving examples, whether you think this is true. Why do organizations not simply get enough capacity to cover all possible demand?

9.7 How can routine maintenance and replacement programmes help increase the efficiency of an organization? Is this equally valid in services and manufacturing?

9.8 Many of the calculations for maintenance and replacement decisions can be done using spreadsheets. Design a spreadsheet that will help in such decisions. How does this compare with standard software you have?

9.9   The Clear Path Club is a group of walkers who meet several times a year to clear public footpaths through the countryside. These paths often get overgrown or blocked, and the Clear Path Club volunteer to keep long sections of footpaths open. How do you think the club could measure their performance?

Selected references

Adam E.E., Hershauer J.G. and Ruch W.A. (1981). *Productivity and Quality: Measurement as a Basis for Improvement*. Englewood Cliffs, NJ: Prentice-Hall.

Chen G.K.C. and McGarrah R.E. (1982). *Productivity Management: Text and Cases*. Orlando, Fl.: The Dryden Press.

Freidenfelds J. (1981). *Capacity Expansions: Analysis of Simple Models with Applications*. New York: Elsevier North-Holland.

Griffin J.M. (1971). *Capacity Measurement in Petroleum Refining*. Lexington: Heath Lexington Books.

Hayes R.H. and Wheelwright S.C. (1984). *Restoring our Competitive Edge: Competing Through Manufacturing*. New York: John Wiley.

Huettner D. (1974). *Plant Size, Technological Change, and Investment Requirements*. New York: Praeger.

Sink D.S. (1985). *Productivity Management: Planning, Evaluation, Control and Improvement*. New York: John Wiley.

Tomkins J.A. and White J.A. (1988). *Facility Planning*. New York: John Wiley.

Wild R. (1980). *Operations Management*. Oxford: Pergamon Press.

10 Controlling quality

Contents

Objectives

After reading this chapter you should be able to:

- describe quality control as part of the broader function of quality management
- know when to do inspections
- say why samples are taken and use sampling distributions
- describe acceptance sampling
- design sampling plans with single samples
- draw operating characteristic curves and do related calculations
- use control charts for process control

Quality management

In Chapter 5 we talked about quality management. In particular we saw how **Total Quality Management** (TQM) has the whole organization focusing its efforts onto making products with perfect quality. Everyone within the organization – from top management to those working directly on the process – must aim for the consistently high quality demanded by customers (see Figure 10.1). Deming was one of the leading advocates of TQM, and we have already mentioned his 'fourteen points'. Many other authors have written about quality management, and a group of the best known are often called the 'gurus' of quality.

Ishikawa adopted Deming's views to the Japanese culture. He originated quality circles and developed cause-and-effect diagrams (which we shall meet later in this chapter).

Juran emphasized three elements of quality management:

(1) *Planning* which sets the product quality level and designs the process to achieve this.

(2) *Control* which uses statistical tests to make sure products are achieving the designed quality.

(3) *Improvement* which focuses on quality problems and continually improves the process to overcome these.

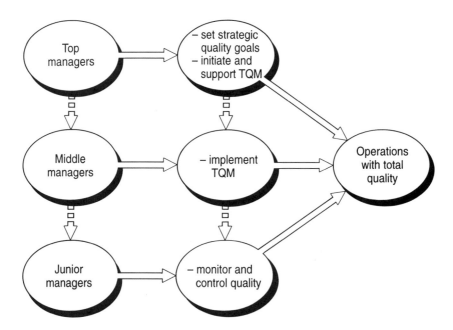

Figure 10.1 The whole organization works towards high quality.

Crosby says that quality starts with conformance to requirements, which is set by managers. This conformance is achieved by using statistical quality control to identify and eliminate problems.

Taguchi looked for both high quality and low costs. He gets this by defining target performance in key areas. Then the process aims not just to be within specified quality limits – in which case being just inside the limits is good enough – but to be near the target value. The organization can then use statistical methods to find the most important factors that set product quality.

As you can see, all the 'gurus' agree about the importance of statistical tests for quality. We already know that high quality is not achieved by inspecting units and discarding defective ones. But quality at source – which makes sure that no defective units are made in the first place – still needs inspections. These are important for giving independent evidence that quality is, in fact, being maintained – that planned quality is actually being achieved. This process of independent inspection and testing is known as **quality control**.

> **Quality control** uses a series of inspections and tests to see that planned quality is actually being achieved.

In the rest of this chapter we shall look at some aspects of quality control.

Review questions

10.1 The best way to get high quality products is to have a lot of inspections to find faults. Do you think this is true?

10.2 What is the difference between quality control and quality management?

Statistical quality control

Inspections

Organizations traditionally maintained quality by a series of inspections. Often these inspections were seen as disrupting the process and were not particularly rigorous. Most effort was put into quality control in the later stages of the process, and many organizations would leave the main inspection until the end of the process, when finished products were about to be delivered to customers. You might think this is sensible, as there is more chance of a product being faulty by the end of the process – so all defects can be found in one big inspection at the end. But it seems obvious that the longer a unit is in a process, the more time and money will be spent on it. It makes more sense, then, to detect faults as early as possible, before any more money is wasted on a defective unit. So rigorous inspections should be done during the process. It would, for example, be cheaper for a baker to detect bad eggs when they arrive at the bakery, rather than use the eggs and scrap the cakes that were made with them. It also makes sense for these inspections to be done by the people most closely involved, who are the people working on the operations. This is one of the key elements in quality management, which we described in Chapter 5.

The major effort in quality control should be put at the beginning of the process, or even earlier. It should start with routine tests of materials sent by suppliers, and there is a strong case for inspections to start within suppliers' own operations. Inspections should then continue all the way from the production of raw materials through to the completion of the final product and its delivery to customers.

If the main effort of inspection is done early enough, very few defects should be found at later stages of the process. Certainly by the time the product gets to the customer it should be as nearly free from defects as possible (see Figure 10.2).

In general, inspections are most useful:

- **for raw materials**
    - during material suppliers' operations
    - on arrival at the organization – for all materials, parts and components

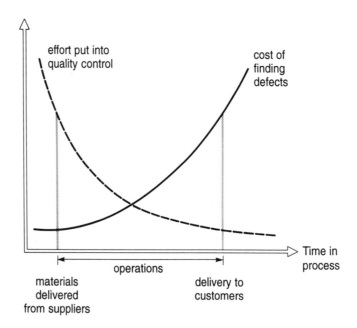

Figure 10.2 Cost of finding defects and effort put into quality control.

- **during the process**
    - at regular intervals during the process
    - before high cost operations
    - before irreversible operations, like firing pottery
    - before operations that might hide defects, like painting

- **for finished products**
    - when production is complete
    - before shipping to customers

Some variation in the output of any process is inevitable, and is beyond the control of even the most stringent checks. An organization must accept this, and design products and processes that reduce the variation as much as possible. Then we can define 'perfect quality' as performing within acceptable limits. Provided a bar of chocolate weighs between, say, 249.99 g and 250.01 g most people do not mind if it is not exactly the advertised 250 g. Only when performance goes outside these limits does a product become defective.

> There is some variation between individual units of every product. Provided the variations remain within acceptable limits a unit has satisfactory quality. When the performance goes outside these limits the unit is defective.

As we said earlier, Taguchi's advice is to aim for a target performance rather than get within some limits. But the random variations in all processes mean we can not always hit the target. When the variations are too large we produce a defect. So a box of soap powder that does not contain the minimum weight, or a journey by a bus that arrives late, or a meat pie that is not cooked properly are examples of defects.

Whenever a defective unit is produced, it is a sign that something has gone wrong with the process. The organization should find the cause of the defect and correct it before any more defects are made. Typical causes of faults are:

- human errors in the operations;

- machine faults, perhaps caused by poor maintenance;

- poor materials;

- faults in operations, such as speed or temperature changes;

- changes in the environment, such as humidity, dust or temperature;

- errors in monitoring equipment, such as errors in measuring tools.

Unfortunately, it is often difficult to find the real cause of a fault. Two diagrams, **cause-and-effect** diagrams and **Pareto Charts**, can help with this.

Cause-and-effect diagrams

A cause and effect diagram is a way of presenting the possible causes of a defect in a simple diagram. Suppose, for example, a customer complains at a hamburger restaurant. The manager may feel the fault is caused by either the raw materials, the cooking, the staff or the facilities. Problems with the raw materials may, in turn, be caused by suppliers, storage, and so on. A cause-and-effect diagram draws these relationships as coming from spines, like a fish bone, as shown in Figure 10.3. These diagrams are usually drawn by a team of people who are familiar with the problem, and can agree the causes. This is typically a quality circle. When the possible causes of faults have been laid out in this form, managers can look at the alternatives, find the problem and correct it.

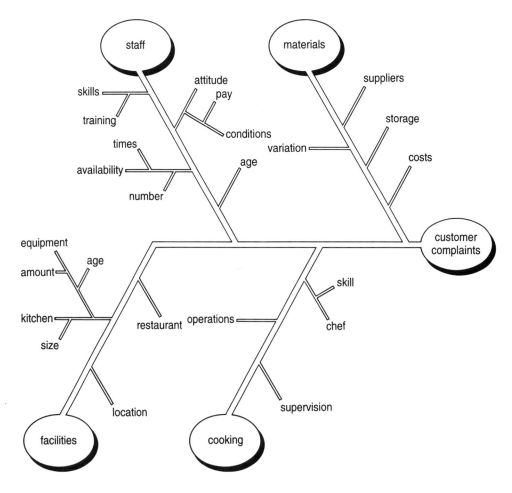

Figure 10.3 A cause-and-effect diagram for a complaint at a hamburger restaurant.

Pareto Charts

These come from the observation that 80% of the problems come from 20% of the causes. So Woolworth's might find that 80% of customer complaints come from 20% of its products. This fact can be used in quality control to add the number of defects for all the possible causes and show these on a bar chart. By simply listing the defects and their causes, we can see the areas that need special attention. If the few main causes of defects are removed, this will have a major effect on quality.

ce | Case example – Freemantle Restaurant

This example shows how a restaurant used a Pareto Chart to improve its service.

The Freemantle Restaurant is a well-established business near the centre of Manchester. It serves a lot of business lunches, and has a healthy demand for its high quality, expensive dinners. Paul Samson is the owner of Freemantle, and looks after all the administration personally. Although there are few complaints from customers, Paul always keeps a record of them. Over the past three years he has collected the figures shown in Table 10.1, and drew the Pareto Chart shown in Figure 10.4.

This clearly shows the main causes of faults. There were almost no complaints about the food, so customers were clearly pleased with what they were eating. Over half of the complaints came from faults in the bill. Paul decided that he could correct these by installing a new computerized cash register.

Sometimes the service was slow. This was usually at busy times when one of the staff was away. Paul contacted an agency who could provide someone to

Table 10.1

Cause	Number of complaints	Percentage of complaints
Faults in the bill	80	51
Slow service	31	20
Smokers too near non-smokers	19	12
Comfort of the chairs	11	7
Wine	5	3
Temperature of the restaurant	5	3
Wait for a table	2	1
Too limited menu	2	1
Food – ingredients used	2	1
Food – cooking	1	1

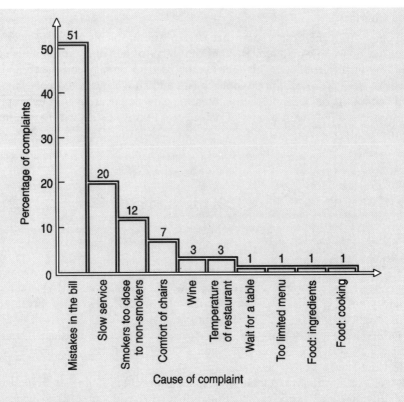

Figure 10.4 Pareto chart for cause of complaint at Freemantle Restaurant.

wait at the tables at very short notice. These two measures alone would deal with almost three-quarters of complaints. When the restaurant needs refurbishment, Paul decided he would get some more comfortable chairs and would increase the size of the non-smoking area. This would deal with another 19% of complaints. By these simple procedures, Paul had dealt with 90% of the complaints.

Statistical sampling

Quality control performs the independent checks that makes sure products are reaching their designed quality. In practice, this means testing their performance in key areas to make sure they are within acceptable limits. This raises a series of questions about the testing. For example, how frequently should it be done? Where should it be done? What sample size should be used? What defines acceptable performance? The answers to these questions rely on statistical analyses, and these are provided by **statistical quality control**.

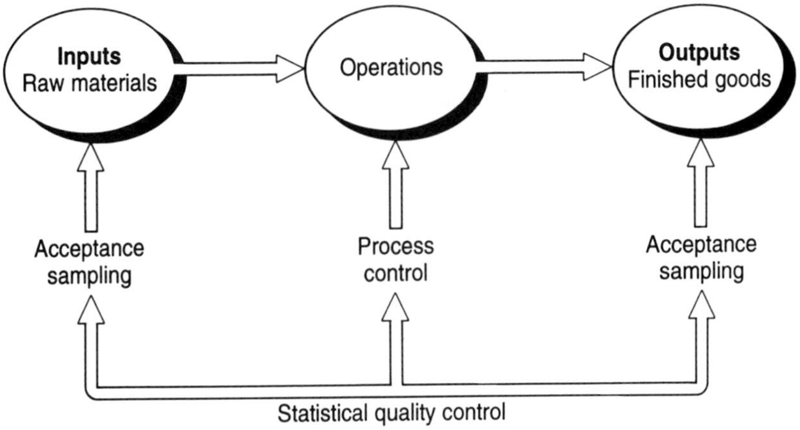

Figure 10.5 Types of statistical quality control.

There are two types of statistical quality control (see Figure 10.5):

- **Acceptance sampling** tests the quality of products. It is done at the beginning and end of an operation. It takes a random sample of products to see whether batches of output should be accepted or rejected.

- **Process control** tests the performance of the process. It is done during operations. It takes a random sample to see if the process is working within acceptable limits or if it needs adjusting.

Acceptance sampling emphasizes the detection of defects – it sees if a batch of products has high enough quality. Process control emphasizes the prevention of defects – it sees if the process is working properly.

Although they look at different things, the general approach of both acceptance sampling and process control is the same. They take a random sample of units from a batch and tests these to see how many of the sample meet designed specifications. If a pre-determined number of the sample reach an acceptable standard, the whole batch is accepted or the process is said to be working properly. If fewer than the pre-determined number reach an acceptable standard the batch is rejected or the process is adjusted.

An obvious question is why use a sample and not test every unit made? There are several reasons for this:

- **Expense** It may cost a lot to test each unit, and if the proportion of defects is small it is a very expensive way of finding the few defects.

- **Time needed** Some tests are so long or complicated that they could not be fitted into normal operations – the time taken to test all units would simply be prohibitive.

- **Destructive testing** Sometimes tests are destructive. If you want to see how long light bulbs last you could test all the production to find the average life – but there would be no bulbs left to sell. Similarly, in bottling plants the only way of guaranteeing every bottle contains the right quantity is to empty the contents into a measuring can – being careful not to lose any of the contents during measurement.

- **Reliability** Testing all the units can give results that are no more reliable than a sample. No inspection is completely reliable, as there are random variations, inspectors become tired or bored, people make mistakes, automatic tests develop faults, subjective judgements are needed, and so on.

- **Feasibility** In some cases there is an infinite number of tests that could be done. To completely test the effectiveness of a medicine it must be given to everybody who might take it, in all possible circumstances. This would give an almost infinite number of possible combinations.

There are many processes where the entire output is tested, but quality control usually relies on a random sample. If this sample performs well, it is assumed that the whole batch has high enough quality: if the sample performs badly, it is assumed that the whole batch should be rejected. Although we talk about 'batches', this is only for convenience and does not mean that we are only concerned with batch production. The output during any particular period can be taken as a batch for quality control.

Unfortunately, sampling is not completely accurate. A test might reject good batch because the sample has an unexpectedly large number of defects. At other times it might accept a bad batch because the sample has an unexpectedly small number of defects. Suppose, for example, a process makes a batch of 1000 units, and each batch has 100 defective units. If we inspected samples of 100 units, we would expect about ten defective ones. But there will be some random variations, and in the extremes we could have a sample with either 100 defective units or none.

we Worked example

Maybole Electrics make light fittings on an assembly line. At one point the electric wiring is fitted, and experience suggests that faults are introduced to 4% of units. An inspection at this point would find 80% of faults, and would cost £0.30 to inspect each light and £0.50 to correct faults. Any fault not found will continue down the line and be detected and corrected later at a cost of £5. Without the inspection after wiring, later tests cost an extra £0.20 a unit and each fault corrected costs £5. Is it worth inspecting all light fittings when the wiring is fitted?

Solution

We can answer this by calculating the expected cost per unit of doing a 100% inspection and of not doing one.

- With 100% inspection after wiring the expected costs per unit are:
  - cost of inspection = £0.30
  - faults detected and corrected after wiring = proportion of faults detected × cost of repair = $0.04 \times 0.8 \times 0.5 = £0.016$
  - faults not found until later = proportion not detected × cost of later repair = $0.04 \times (1 - 0.8) \times 5 = £0.04$

  This gives a total of $0.30 + 0.016 + 0.04 = £0.356$ a unit.

- Without an inspection after wiring the costs per unit are:
  - additional cost of inspection = £0.20
  - faults detected and corrected = proportion with faults × cost of repair = $0.04 \times 5 = £0.20$

  This gives a total of $0.20 + 0.20 = £0.40$ a unit.

It is clearly cheaper to do a 100% inspection when the wire is fitted and correct faults as soon as they are found.

Sampling distributions

Larger samples have higher testing costs than smaller ones, but they give more reliable results. A compromise is needed so that the sample is large enough to be representative of all units in the batch and yet small enough to be reasonable and cost effective.

In statistical terms, all of the production is called the **population**, so we are concerned with taking representative samples from a population. Because of random variations, there will always be some variations from sample to sample. If, for example, boxes of fruit are being packed with an average weight of 25 kg we would not be surprised to find a series of four samples with average weights of 25.2 kg, 24.8 kg and 25.1 kg and 25.0 kg. If we took a longer series of samples, the mean weight would follow a distribution. This is called the **sampling distribution of the mean**.

The sampling distribution of the mean has three useful properties:

(1) If the population is Normally distributed, or if a sample of more than about 30 is used, the sampling distribution of the mean is Normally distributed.

(2) The mean of the sampling distribution of the mean equals the mean of the population, μ.

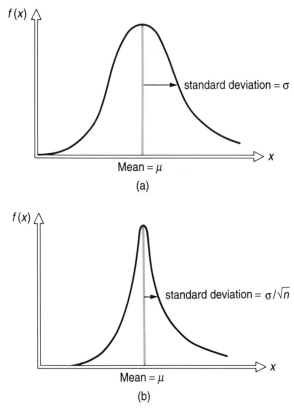

Figure 10.6 Comparison of the population distribution with the sampling distribution of the mean: (a) distribution of population; (b) sampling distribution of the mean.

(3)   The standard deviation of the sampling distribution of the mean is calculated from $\sigma/\sqrt{n}$, where σ is the standard deviation of the population and n is the sample size.

The third property confirms our belief that larger samples give more reliable results (see Figure 10.6).

we Worked example

Midland Steel have a production line that makes pipes with a mean length of 100 cm and a standard deviation of 1 cm. What is the probability that a random sample of 35 pipes has a mean length of less than 99.6 cm?

Solution

With a sample size of 35 the sampling distribution of the mean is Normally distributed with a mean of 100 cm and a standard deviation of $\sigma/\sqrt{n} = 1/\sqrt{35} = 0.169$ cm. So the sampling distribution of the mean is Normally distributed with mean 100 cm and standard deviation 0.169 cm.

The number of standard deviations 99.6 cm is from the mean is:

$$Z = (100 - 99.6)/0.169 = 2.37$$

Normal probability tables (in Appendix B) shows that this corresponds to a probability of 0.0089, as shown in Figure 10.7. So 0.89% of samples will have a mean length of less than 99.6 cm.

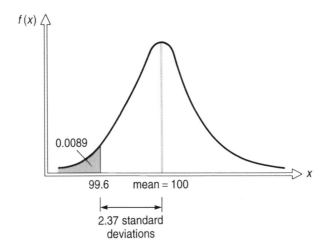

Figure 10.7 Sampling distribution of the mean for example.

Review questions

10.3 Higher quality inevitably comes at a higher price. Do you think this is true?

10.4 When should checks for quality be started in a process?

10.5 What is the difference between acceptance sampling and process control?

10.6 Why are samples used?

10.7 Are the results from statistical sampling completely accurate?

10.8 What is the sampling distribution of the mean?

Acceptance sampling

Sampling by attributes and variables

Acceptance sampling tests the quality of a batch of products. It uses samples to see if the whole batch should be accepted, or whether it should be rejected.

> **Acceptance sampling** tests the quality of a product. It uses a number of units taken from a batch to check that the whole batch meets designed quality.

We can use the results found above for the sampling distribution of the mean to see if a batch should be rejected. This is called **sampling by variables** and involves measuring some continuous property, such as the weight, length or power output of an engine. The average performance of the variable is then compared with some specified acceptable level. For this we can use the standard result given above that a population with mean value for a variable, μ, and standard deviation σ, gives a mean value for samples that is Normally distributed with mean μ and standard deviation of $\sigma/\sqrt{n}$.

we Worked example

Batches of raw materials are delivered to a factory with a guaranteed average weight of 25 kg a unit and standard deviation of 1 kg. A sample of 20 units is taken to test each delivery. Within what range should 95% of the sample means lie?

Solution

The mean weight of samples will be Normally distributed with mean 25 kg and standard deviation $= \sigma/\sqrt{n} = 1/\sqrt{20} = 0.224$ kg. 95% of samples will be within 1.96 standard deviations of the mean, so the range of acceptable sample means is:

$$25 + (1.96 \times 0.224) = 25.44 \text{ kg} \quad \text{to} \quad 25 - (1.96 \times 0.224) = 24.56 \text{ kg}$$

If the company rejects batches with weights outside this range they will be making the right decision 95% of the time.

The alternative to sampling by variables is called **sampling by attributes**. This needs some criterion of quality that allows us to describe a unit as either 'acceptable' or 'defective'. Sometimes this criterion is obvious. If, for example, boxes have to be filled with at least one kilogram of soap powder, we can define a 'defective' box as one containing less than a kilogram and an 'acceptable' one as containing a kilogram or more. Sometimes the criterion relies less on measurement and more on judgement. A piece of furniture made with polished wood, for example, may be rejected because its finish does not look good to an experienced inspector.

A standard result shows that if the proportion of defective units in a population is p, the proportion of defects in samples of size n is:

- Normally distributed

- with mean p, and

- standard deviation $\sqrt{\dfrac{p(1-p)}{n}}$

Then we can use Normal tables to find the numbers of defects which allows us to accept the batch.

we Worked example

Imperial Motor Insurance uses outside contractors to check details of its policies. It insists that the contractors must make errors in less than 4% of policies. One day Imperial receives a large shipment of policies from the contractors. It takes a sample of 200 policies and checks them. What criterion should Imperial use to reject a batch if it wants to be 97.5% sure of not making a mistake?

Solution

Suppose the proportion of errors is 4%, so $p = 0.04$. In samples of size n the proportion of defective units is Normally distributed with mean 0.04 and standard deviation $= \sqrt{p(1-p)/n} = \sqrt{(0.04 \times 0.96/200)} = 0.014$.

95% of sample proportions are within 1.96 standard deviations of the mean, so 95% of samples will have proportions of defects between:

$$0.04 + (1.96 \times 0.014) = 0.067 \quad \text{and} \quad 0.04 - (1.96 \times 0.014) = 0.013$$

With a sample of 200 this means that 95% of batches will have between $200 \times 0.067 = 13.4$ and $200 \times 0.013 = 2.6$ defective units. So only 2.5% of batches will have more than 13.4 defects by chance. If the company rejects batches with more than this they are 97.5% sure of making the right decision (see Figure 10.8).

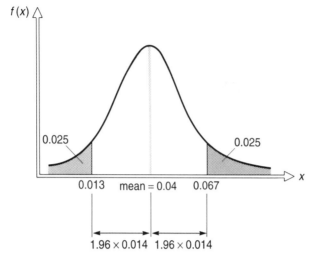

Figure 10.8 Range of accepting a batch in example.

Designing an acceptance sampling plan

The last analysis showed how we can decide whether or not to accept a batch based on the quality of a random sample. We can formalize these results in a **sampling plan**. The simplest form of acceptance sampling plan uses single sampling by attributes. The general procedure for this is:

- specify a sample size, n;

- take a random sample of this size from a batch;

- specify a maximum allowed number of defects in the sample, c;

- test the sample to find the number that are actually defective;

- if the number of defects is greater than this allowed maximum number, c, reject the batch;

- if the number of defects is less than the allowed maximum number, c, accept the batch.

The value of c, the maximum allowed number of defects in a sample, is largely a matter of policy – it relies on opinions about the acceptable level of quality. Four important measures related to this decision are:

- **Acceptance quality level (AQL)** This is the overall percentage of defects that is considered acceptable. Figures around 2% are often quoted for this, but TQM suggests that the real target should be zero.

- **Lot tolerance per cent defective (LTPD)**   This is the upper limit on the percentage of defective units that customers are willing to accept in a single batch. Any batches with more than this percentage of defects are unacceptable.

- **Producer's risk (α)**   This is the probability of rejecting a good batch.

- **Consumer's risk (β)**   This is the probability of accepting a bad batch.

These definitions assume that customers are willing to accept an overall level of quality equal to AQL. As customers are demanding higher quality this is figure is inevitably approaching zero. But we shall assume that customers are willing to accept an overall proportion of defects given by AQL, and they may be willing to accept an occasional batch which is as poor as the LTPD. They will not accept any batches with a higher proportion of defects.

The other two factors are measures of risk. A producer will clearly want to minimize α – the probability of rejecting a good batch. On the other hand, consumers will want them to minimize β – the probability of accepting a bad batch. Typical sampling plans call for values of α equal to 0.05 and β equal to 0.1.

Using these four measures we can find values for n, the sample size, and c, the maximum number of allowed defects. In practice the easiest way of doing this is to use standard tables (such as those in Dodge and Romig listed in the References). An excerpt from these tables is given in Table 10.2.

The procedure is to calculate the ratio of LTPD/AQL and find the entry in Table 10.2 that is equal to, or just greater than, this value. The next column shows an appropriate value for c, and the implied sample size is given in the final column.

Table 10.2

LTPD/AQL	c	n × AQL
44.89	0	0.05
10.95	1	0.36
6.51	2	0.82
4.89	3	1.37
4.06	4	1.97
3.55	5	2.61
3.21	6	3.29
2.96	7	3.98
2.77	8	4.70
2.62	9	5.43
2.50	10	6.17

we Worked example

A company buys components in batches from a supplier. The supplier uses an acceptance quality level of 2% defective, while the company accepts batches with a maximum of 6% defective. What would be appropriate values of n and c?

Solution

The values given are:

$$\text{AQL} = 0.02$$
$$\text{LTPD} = 0.06$$

Then $\text{LTPD/AQL} = 0.06/0.02 = 3$. The value in the table which is equal to or slightly greater than this is 3.21, which corresponds to $c = 6$. The associated value of $n \times \text{AQL}$ is 3.29. We know $\text{AQL} = 0.02$, so $n \times 0.02 = 3.29$, or $n = 3.29/0.02 = 164.5$.

This gives the sampling plan:

- take samples of 165 units

- if 6 or less units are defective accept the batch

- if more than 6 units are defective reject the batch.

```
                       *** QUALITY CONTROL ***
TITLE : INITIAL DATA SET
DATE  : Sunday 03-04-1996
TIME  : 23:53 PM

------------------------------------------------------------------------
                           ANALYSIS FOR
              ATTRIBUTE SAMPLING-DETERMINING THE PLAN
------------------------------------------------------------------------

   DATA ENTERED:
           -------------------------------------------------------
           | Acceptable Quality Level (AQL)    0.02              |
           | Lot Toleran. Perc. Defec.(LTPD)  0.06               |
           | Producer's Risk      (Alpha) .05                    |
           | Consumer's Risk      (Beta) .10                     |
           -------------------------------------------------------

   SUGGESTED PLANS:
           -------------------------------------------------------
           | PLAN NO.      PLAN           ALPHA(a)      BETA(b) |
           | 1       N =  165 C =   6       .051          .137  |
           | 2       N =  176 C =   6       .067          .099  |
           | 3       N =  200 C =   7       .051          .090  |
           | 4       N =  197 C =   7       .048          .098  |
           -------------------------------------------------------
```

Figure 10.9 Example of a package designing sampling plans.

There are many standard programs for doing this sort of analysis. The illustration in Figure 10.9 shows one view of the last example. Notice that this gives four alternative plans based on slightly different values of α and β.

■

Operating characteristics

Setting values for n and c defines an acceptance sampling plan. The purpose of such plans is to separate acceptable batches from those which should be rejected. How well a sampling plan actually separates these is described by its **operating characteristic** (OC) curve. An OC curve shows the probability that a sampling plan will accept batches with different proportions of defects. Each combination of n and c has a distinct curve with the general shape shown in Figure 10.10. The position of two points on this curve are defined first by AQL and α, and secondly by LTPD and β.

We would like a clear distinction between good and bad batches, so the OC curve should be as steep as possible and would ideally be vertical. A vertical OC curve would differentiate perfectly between an acceptable batch (which would have a probability of acceptance of 1) and an unacceptable batch (with a probability of acceptance of 0). The way to get a steep curve is to

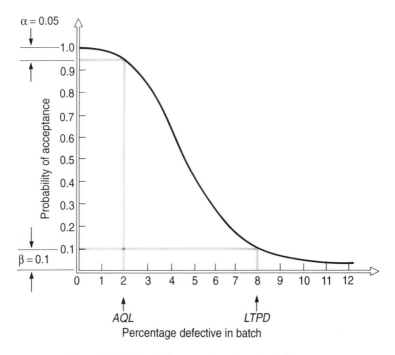

Figure 10.10 Typical operating characteristic curve.

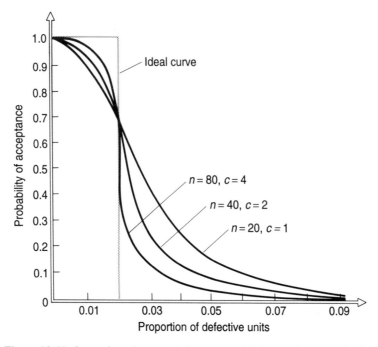

Figure 10.11 Operating characteristic curves with increasing sample size.

take large samples. Even if the proportion of defects remains the same, taking a larger sample will give more reliable results, as shown in Figure 10.11. Unfortunately, larger samples are more expensive and a balance is needed between the costs and benefits.

You can see from the operating characteristic curve how the probability a batch is accepted goes down as the proportion of defective units increases. So poor batches are more likely to be rejected, while good batches are more likely to be accepted. This improves the overall quality of products by selectively rejecting low quality batches. Then we can ask how good the average quality of remaining products is. The answer is defined as the **Average Outgoing Quality** (AOQ).

> The **average outgoing quality** is the expected proportion of defects that pass through a sampling plan.

When the proportion of defective units in the population, p, is small most batches are accepted and AOQ remains low (remembering that AOQ refers to the expected proportion of **defects**). As p increases the AOQ also rises. But as p continues to increase further more batches are rejected and the AOQ begins to fall. With high values of p, most batches are rejected and the AOQ is again low. The result is shown in Figure 10.12.

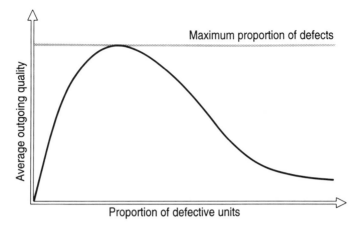

Figure 10.12 Variation of AOQ with proportion of defective units.

Review questions

10.9 What is the purpose of acceptance sampling?

10.10 What is the difference between sampling by attribute and sampling by variable?

10.11 Why would an ideal operating characteristic curve be vertical?

10.12 Average outgoing quality must increase as average product quality increases. Do you think this is true?

ce Case example – Summerview Stoneground Mill

Summerview Stoneground Mill produces wheat and corn flour. Most of its production is put into 25 kg bags and is sold to commercial customers, such as bakeries, hotels and restaurants.

Last week Paula Lam, who is the operations manager, received a couple of complaints from customers. One of the complaints said a recent delivery of bags did not seem very full. The second was more specific, and said that a delivery of 10 bags weighed only 246 kg. Both of these batches came from the same day's production.

Paula checked the procedures for testing the weight of bags with the quality manager, Tim Price. Tim said, 'At the beginning of a run we weigh a few bags, and adjust the machines until they are filling properly. Then the process is largely automatic, so we do not weigh any more samples. We do a visual inspection of all bags to check the seams and stitching. This would also find any bags that do not seem to be properly filled. If the operator thinks the machines are not filling properly he will take some samples and weigh them.'

Questions

- Do you think the quality control procedure at Summerview is good enough?
- How would you improve quality control in Summerview? Would you emphasize acceptance sampling or process control?

Process control

Control charts for attributes

There are two objectives in taking samples: acceptance sampling checks the quality of products, and process control checks that the process is working as planned.

> **Process control** uses a sample of units taken from a batch to check that the process is working properly

There is always some random variation in the performance of a process. **Process control** makes sure that this random variation is within acceptable limits. The way of doing this is to take samples over time to see if there are any noticeable trends. If there is a clear trend the process might need adjusting. This can be seen most clearly in a **process control chart**.

We shall start by describing process control charts for attributes, so we are again considering outcomes that are either acceptable or defective. Then a process control chart takes a series of samples over time and the proportion of defective units in each is plotted. This is sometimes called a **p-chart**.

The proportion of defective units in a sample will usually be around the proportion of defects in the population. Provided it does not vary far from this value, the process is said to be in control. If there is a trend, the proportion of defective units moves away from the mean, and when it reaches some specified limit the process is said to be out of control and needs correcting. To show when a process is out of control we need two limits: an **upper control limit** (UCL) and a **lower control limit** (LCL). Provided the output stays between these two limits the process is in control, but if it moves outside the limits it is out of control (as shown in Figure 10.13).

The key decision in process control is the definition of control limits. For sampling by attributes, this relies on the standard result quoted earlier, that if the proportion of defects in a population is p, the proportion of defective units in a sample of size n is Normally distributed with mean, p, and standard deviation of $\sqrt{(p(1-p)/n)}$. Then we can calculate the control limits from:

- upper control limit = UCL = $\mu + Z \times$ standard deviation
- lower control limit = LCL = $\mu - Z \times$ standard deviation

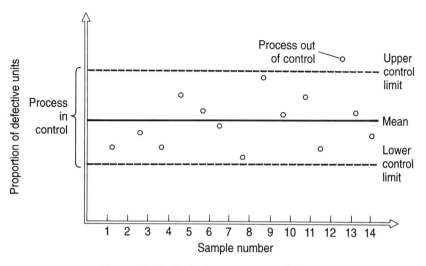

Figure 10.13 Typical process control chart.

where Z is the number of standard deviations of the specified confidence limit. This confidence limit is chosen as part of the designed quality, and it specifies the proportion of samples that would normally be within a range if the process is in control. So a 95% confidence interval (corresponding to $Z = 1.96$) finds the range within which 95% of sample would lie if the process is in control.

we Worked example

June Springwell collected a sample of 500 units of the output from a process for each of 30 working days when it was known to be working normally. She tested these samples and recorded the number of defective units as follows:

Day	Number of defects	Day	Number of defects	Day	Number of defects
1	70	11	45	21	61
2	48	12	40	22	57
3	66	13	53	23	65
4	55	14	51	24	48
5	50	15	60	25	42
6	42	16	57	26	40
7	64	17	55	27	67
8	47	18	62	28	70
9	51	19	45	29	63
10	68	20	48	30	60

Draw a control chart with 95% confidence limits.

Solution

The average proportion of defects is:

$$p = \frac{\text{total number of defects}}{\text{number of observations}} = \frac{1650}{30 \times 500} = 0.11$$

$$\text{standard deviation} = \sqrt{(p(1 - p)/n)} = \sqrt{(0.11 \times 0.89/500)} = 0.014$$

The 95% confidence limits have $Z = 1.96$, so:

- UCL $= p + Z \times$ standard deviation $= 0.11 + (1.96 \times 0.014) = 0.137$

- LCL $= p - Z \times$ standard deviation $= 0.11 - (1.96 \times 0.014) = 0.083$

Now we can assume that if the proportion of defects is between 0.083 and 0.137 the process is under control and differences are simply random variations; if the proportion of defects is outside this range the process is out of control and needs adjusting. With samples of 500 the process is under control when the number of defects is between $0.083 \times 500 = 42$ and $0.137 \times 500 = 69$ (see Figure 10.14).

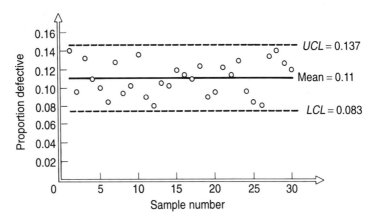

Figure 10.14 Control chart for example.

Notice in the example above that the data for drawing the control charts was collected when the process was known to be working normally. If the process was out of control when the data was collected, the results would be meaningless.

Process control charts will have some observations that lie outside the control limits purely by chance. With a 95% confidence interval, random variations will leave 5% of samples outside the control limits. So every observation suggesting the process is out of control should be carefully checked to see if the process is really out of control, or whether it is actually operating normally.

Control charts can also show a number of other patterns that should be looked into. If, for example, there is a trend, even though the process is in control, it could be a sign that something is going wrong. Patterns which need closer examination are:

- a single reading outside the control limits

- a clear trend

- several consecutive readings near to a control limit

- several consecutive readings on the same side of the mean

- a sudden change in readings

- very erratic observations.

Control charts for variables

Control charts can also be used with variable sampling. The approach is essentially the same as for attribute sampling, with upper and lower control limits specified by a number of standard deviations away from the mean. We can find these limits using the sampling distribution of the mean. Remember that this is Normally distributed with mean the same as the process mean and standard deviation equal to $\sigma/\sqrt{n}$, where σ is the process standard deviation and n is the sample size.

we Worked example

A process makes packaged food with a mean weight of 1 kg and standard deviation of 0.05 kg. Samples of 10 are taken to make sure the process is still in control. Find the control limits which include 99% of sample means if the process is working normally.

Solution

The means of samples will be Normally distributed with

$$\text{mean} = 1\,\text{kg} \quad \text{and} \quad \text{standard deviation} = \sigma/\sqrt{n} = 0.05/\sqrt{10}$$

A confidence interval of 99% corresponds to 2.58 standard deviation. Then:

- $\text{LCL} = \mu - Z \times \sigma/\sqrt{n} = 1 - (2.58 \times 0.05/\sqrt{10}) = 0.959$
- $\text{UCL} = \mu + Z \times \sigma/\sqrt{n} = 1 + (2.58 \times 0.05/\sqrt{10}) = 1.041$

Provided the mean of samples stays within this range the process is in control. If it moves outside the range it is out of control and needs checking.

The approach used in the last example relies on the mean, μ, and standard deviation, σ, of the population – which is all the output – being known. But with sampling we no longer need to test all the output. In other words, these values may not be known. Then we have two alternatives. First, we could use the values from samples to approximate the mean and standard deviation of the whole process. A better alternative is to add a second measure for the range of observations. This gives two charts which are called $\bar{X}$ and R charts, $\bar{X}$ being the sample mean and R the sample range. Then we plot:

- the series of sample means on an $\bar{X}$ chart

- the series of sample ranges on an R chart.

The range is simply the difference between the biggest observation and the smallest. Suppose, for example, a manufacturer takes samples to monitor the weight of a product: an $\bar{X}$ chart monitors the mean weight in the samples and an R chart monitors the ranges found within the samples.

$\bar{X}$ and R charts are drawn in exactly the same way as p-charts for attributes. First, though, we need to define some terms:

$\bar{X}$ = mean value of a sample
$\bar{X}_0$ = overall mean of the sample means
R = range of a sample
R_0 = overall mean of the sample ranges

with m samples this gives:

$$\bar{X}_0 = \frac{\sum \bar{X}}{m} \quad \text{and} \quad R_0 = \frac{\sum R}{m}$$

Now we can find the upper and lower control limits. The easiest way to do this is to use standard tables (such as those in Grant and Leavenworth listed in the references). With these tables, the control limits are:

For $\bar{X}$ charts of means: $\text{LCL} = X_0 - A R_0$ $\text{UCL} = X_0 + A R_0$

For R charts of ranges: $\text{LCL} = D_1 R_0$ $\text{UCL} = D_2 R_0$

Values for A, D_1 and D_2 are given in the tables, an extract of which is shown in Table 10.3.

Table 10.3

Sample size	Factor for $\bar{X}$ chart	Factors for R chart	
	A	D_1	D_2
2	1.88	0	3.27
3	1.02	0	2.57
4	0.73	0	2.28
5	0.58	0	2.11
6	0.48	0	2.00
7	0.42	0.08	1.92
8	0.37	0.14	1.86
9	0.34	0.18	1.82
10	0.31	0.22	1.78
12	0.27	0.28	1.72
15	0.22	0.35	1.65
17	0.20	0.38	1.62
20	0.18	0.41	1.59
25	0.15	0.50	1.54

we Worked example

Samples of 10 units have been taken from a process in each of the past 20 days. Each unit in the sample was weighed. The mean weight in each sample and the range were as follows:

Sample	Mean	Range	Sample	Mean	Range
1	12.2	4.2	11	12.5	3.3
2	13.1	4.6	12	12.3	4.0
3	12.5	3.0	13	12.5	2.9
4	13.3	5.1	14	12.6	2.7
5	12.7	2.9	15	12.8	3.9
6	12.6	3.1	16	12.1	4.2
7	12.5	3.2	17	13.2	4.8
8	13.0	4.6	18	13.0	4.6
9	12.2	4.3	19	13.2	5.0
10	12.0	5.0	20	12.6	3.8
			Totals	252.9	79.2

Draw $\bar{X}$ and R charts for the process.

Solution

The overall mean values for weight and ranges are:

$$\bar{X}_o = 252.9/20 = 12.65 \quad \text{and} \quad R_o = 79.2/20 = 3.96$$

Then we look up the factors for samples of size 10 in the table above and find:

$$A = 0.31, \quad D_1 = 0.22 \quad \text{and} \quad D_2 = 1.78$$

- for an $\bar{X}$ chart of means:
  - LCL $= \bar{X}_o - AR_o = 12.65 - (0.31 \times 3.96) = 11.42$
  - UCL $= \bar{X}_o + AR_o = 12.65 + (0.31 \times 3.96) = 13.88$

- for an R chart of ranges:
  - LCL $= D_1 R_o = 0.22 \times 3.96 = 0.87$
  - UCL $= D_2 R_o = 1.78 \times 3.96 = 7.05$

Provided future samples keep within these ranges the process is in control, but if they move outside these ranges the process is out of control (see Figure 10.15).

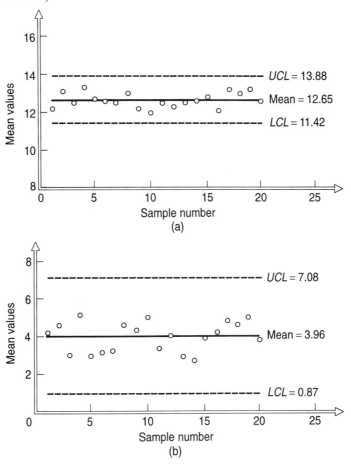

Figure 10.15 (a) $\bar{X}$ chart and (b) R chart for example.

we Worked example

The printout in Figure 10.16 shows the result from using a standard package for drawing process control charts. As you can see, this gives an analysis for process control, and saves a lot of calculation.

```
          ***  QUALITY CONTROL  ***

TITLE : INITIAL DATA SET
DATE  : Sunday 09-04-1996
TIME  : 4:02 AM

-----------------------------------------------------------------
                         ANALYSIS FOR
                   MEAN AND RANGE CHARTS
-----------------------------------------------------------------

DATA ENTERED:
```

OBSERVATION 1	OBSERVATION 2	OBSERVATION 3	OBSERVATION 4
12	8	5	11
15	7	11	15
3	5	7	6

OBSERVATION 5	OBSERVATION 6	OBSERVATION 7	OBSERVATION 8
7	9	13	9
1	10	5	2
10	15	8	3

OBSERVATION 9	OBSERVATION10
3	4
10	12
8	9

Control limits for the Sample Mean	
Upper control limit =	15.773
Center line =	8.100
Lower control limit =	0.428

Control limits for the Sample Range	
Upper control limit =	19.313
Center line =	7.500
Lower control limit =	0.000

Figure 10.16 Example of printout for drawing control charts.

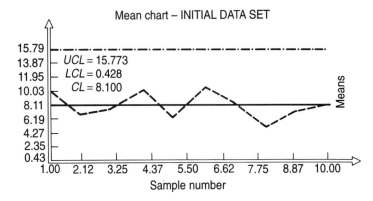

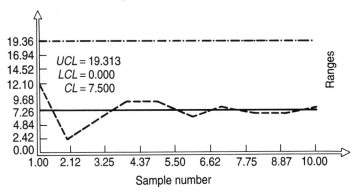

Figure 10.16 *(cont.)* Example of printout for drawing control charts.

ce Case example – Stroh Brewery Company

This perspective gives an example of quality control in practice. Stroh Brewery is one of the biggest in the world and it is very careful about quality. As part of its quality control programme it does 1100 tests on each batch of beer.

The Stroh Brewery Company of Detroit is a major producer of US beer. One of its plants is the Winston-Salem brewery which occupies over 100,000 square metres and makes almost 200 million gallons of beer a year.

Quality control of beer is rigorous and includes many tests. The brewery checks everything from taste to the quantity in each can. For this the Winston-Salem brewery employs 38 people in three separate laboratories for microbiology, brewing and packaging. These people do 1100 separate tests on each batch of beer. If problems are found, the quality control department can stop production at any point and investigate the problem.

A typical test in the brewing laboratory checks the number of yeast cells during fermentation. Beer must have a standard 16 million yeast cells per millilitre of beer. For this test a small sample of beer is taken during fermentation, diluted and the cells are counted through a microscope.

A typical test in the packaging laboratory checks the amount of air in a beer can. Because air can affect the taste, the company allows a maximum of 1 cc of air in a can. This is checked by testing three cans from the production line five times a shift. If a sample is found with more than 1 cc of air, the entire batch is put in 'quarantine' and systematically tested to find the point where the canning goes wrong. As each line fills 1600 cans a minute, this can mean a lot of testing.

You can see from this quick summary that translating the principles of quality control into practice takes a lot of effort. You can imagine the effort that must be needed in companies which make large numbers of goods. When Colgate sample their toothpaste, imagine the variety and number of tests that must be done to make sure everything is still working properly.

Review questions

10.13 What does it mean if an observation is outside the control limits in a process control chart?

10.14 What patterns should be investigated in a control chart?

10.15 Why are R charts used?

Chapter review

- Chapter 5 introduced the ideas of quality management, which is responsible for all aspects of quality in an organization. Several quality 'gurus' have described how to achieve perfect quality.

- Quality control is an important part of quality management. This is concerned with the sampling, inspecting and testing needed to check that planned quality is actually being achieved.

- Statistical sampling uses random samples to test either the quality of products – with acceptance sampling – or the performance of the process – with process control.

- Most quality control uses a series of random inspections. These test the performance of a whole population by looking at a random sample.

- The sampling distribution of the mean relates the means found in samples to the population.

- Acceptance sampling checks that products are reaching designed quality standards. Typically, this takes a single random sample from a batch of products and tests to make sure the number of defects is below a maximum permitted number.

- The other purpose of sampling is process control. The most effective analysis for this uses process control charts. These plot the performance of a series of samples taken over time. A process is in control when the output remains between two control limits. p-charts check the performance of attributes, while $\bar{X}$ and R charts are used to check variables.

Key terms

acceptance sampling   350

average outgoing
   quality   356

cause-and-effect
   diagram   342

operating
   characteristics   355

process control charts   358

quality control   339

sampling by attribute   350

sampling by variable   350

sampling distribution   347

sampling plan   352

statistical quality
   control   339

Total Quality
   Management   338

CS   Case study – West Midland Electronic Car Component Company

David Brown is the Quality Control Manager of West Midland Electronic Car Component Company. He arrived at work at 7.30 one Tuesday morning and was immediately asked to see the General Manager. As David approached, the General Manager threw him a letter that had obviously come in the morning mail. David glimpsed down the letter and saw two sections that the General Manager had circled in red ink.

We have looked at recent figures for the quality of one of the components you supply, AM74021–74222, and find there has been some inconsistency of late. As you will recall, we have an agreement that requires 99.5% of delivered units of this product to be within 5% of target output ratings (as specified in our Technical Report 32/AB/12). While your recent supplies have been achieving this, we are concerned that there has been some inconsistency. We had also hoped that quality would improve so that a renegotiated contract at the end of this year could specify higher quality levels.

As you know we put considerable emphasis on the quality of our own products and think it reasonable to ask suppliers to reach the same standards. We understand that your quality control department is very busy, and would like to discuss ways that we can help with your quality management programme – working together to share ideas.

The General Manager waited for a few minutes and said:

I find it incredible that we are sending poor quality goods to one of our biggest customers. We have a major complaint, and an offer from complete strangers to discuss the quality of our products. They are suggesting that we can't do the job properly, so they will come and show us how to do it. This is clearly your problem, and if you don't come up with some suggestions in the near future we should start looking for someone who can.

The General Manager was clearly in an aggressive mood. This made David rather defensive and his reply was less constructive than normal.

There is absolutely nothing wrong with the quality of the AM74021–74222 unit. We agreed measures for quality and are consistently achieving these. We haven't improved quality because we did not agree to improve it, and any improvement would increase our own costs. In any case, we are making 995 units in a thousand at higher quality than they requested, and the remaining 0.5% are only just below it. To me, this seems a level of quality that almost anyone would be proud of.

The process for making AM74021–74222 is in five stages, each of which is followed by an inspection. The units then have a final inspection before being sent to customers. David saved all historic figures for quality control. He remembered in past years when they were struggling to achieve a defect rate of 2%, and he felt disappointed that now he was being blamed for achieving better than 0.5%. The AM74021–74222 had been in production for 18 months, and this was only the second complaint he had ever received about its quality. The first had been a batch of 500 units shortly after the product had been introduced. By unhappy chance this batch had seven faulty units in it, and the customer refused to accept it. Sorting this out had taken a lot of time and the company had spent about £10,000 repairing customer relations and making sure similar problems did not happen again.

David now considered more 100% inspections, but each manual inspection would cost about £0.60 and the selling price of the unit was only £24.75.

Table 10.4

	A		B		C		D		E		F	
							Inspection					
Week	Inspect	Reject	Inspect	Reject	Inspect	Reject	Inspect	Reject	Inspect	Reject	Inspect	Reject
1	4,125	125	350	56	287	0	101	53	3,910	46	286	0
2	4,086	136	361	0	309	0	180	0	3,854	26	258	0
3	4,833	92	459	60	320	0	194	0	4,651	33	264	0
4	3,297	43	208	0	186	0	201	0	3,243	59	246	0
5	4,501	83	378	0	359	64	224	65	4,321	56	291	0
6	4,772	157	455	124	401	0	250	72	4,410	42	289	0
7	4,309	152	420	87	422	0	266	123	3,998	27	287	64
8	4,654	101	461	0	432	0	278	45	4,505	57	310	0
9	4,901	92	486	0	457	0	287	0	4,822	73	294	0
10	5,122	80	512	0	488	0	301	0	5,019	85	332	0
11	5,143	167	524	132	465	48	290	61	4,659	65	287	0
12	5,119	191	518	0	435	0	256	54	4,879	54	329	0
13	4,990	203	522	83	450	0	264	112	4,610	55	297	0
14	5,231	164	535	63	475	0	276	0	5,002	32	267	0
15	3,900	90	425	56	288	0	198	0	3,820	37	290	58
16	4,277	86	485	109	320	0	229	0	4,109	38	328	0
17	4,433	113	435	0	331	0	265	67	4,259	29	313	0
18	5,009	112	496	0	387	0	198	62	4,821	52	269	0
19	5,266	135	501	65	410	0	299	58	5,007	51	275	64
20	5,197	142	488	0	420	72	301	73	4,912	48	267	0
21	4,932	95	461	0	413	0	266	0	4,856	45	286	0
22	5,557	94	510	0	456	0	160	64	5,400	39	298	61
23	5,106	101	488	74	488	0	204	131	4,795	36	326	0
24	5,220	122	472	0	532	0	277	125	4,989	29	340	56
25	5,191	111	465	0	420	0	245	185	4,927	42	321	0
26	5,620	87	512	45	375	0	223	134	5,357	48	332	0

There was also the problem that manual inspections were only about 80% accurate. Automatic inspections cost only £0.30 and were almost completely reliable, but they could not cover all aspects of quality. At least three inspections had to remain manual. He decided to produce a six-month summary of weekly figures (see Table 10.4) to show that things really had remained in control. During this period there had been few changes in production, and the company continued to work five days a week with two eight-hour shifts a day.

Notes on inspections

For sampling inspections, all production is considered in notional batches of one hour's output. Random samples are taken from each batch and if the quality is too low the whole batch is rejected, checked and reworked as necessary.

• A – automatic inspection of all units: rejects all defects;

• B – manual inspection of 10% of output: rejects batch if more than 1% of batch is defective;

- C – manual inspection of 10% of output: rejects batch if more than 1% of batch is defective;

- D – manual inspection of 5% of output: rejects batch if more than 2% of batch is defective;

- E – automatic inspection of all units: rejects all defects;

- F – manual inspection of 5% of output: rejects batch if more than 1% of batch is defective.

Questions

- Do you think the General Manager's view is reasonable?

- How effective is the quality control at West Midland?

- Do you think the quality needs to be improved? How would you do this?

- What do you think David Brown should do?

Problems

10.1 A part is made on an assembly line. At one point an average of 2% of units are defective. It costs £0.50 to inspect each unit at this point, and the inspection would only find 70% of faults. If the faults are left, all parts will be found and corrected further down the line at a cost of £4. Would it be worthwhile inspecting all units at this point in the line?

10.2 A machine produces parts that have a standard deviation in weight of 1 g. A sample of 100 parts was taken and found to have a mean weight of 2 kg. What is the 95% confidence interval for the true weight of the parts?

10.3 A machine produces parts with a standard deviation in length of 2 cm. A sample of 40 units is taken and found to have a mean length of 148.7 cm. What are the 95% and 99% confidence intervals for the true length of the parts?

10.4 Soft drinks are put into cans that hold a nominal 200 ml, but the filling machines introduce a standard deviation of 10 ml. The cans are put into cartons of 25 and exported to a market that needs the mean weight of cartons to be at least the quantity specified by the manufacturer. To make sure this happens, the canner set the machines to fill cans to 205 ml. What is the probability that a carton chosen at random will not pass the quantity test?

10.5 A company says that its suppliers should send at most 2% defective units. It receives a large shipment and takes a sample of 100 units. The company wants to be 95% sure that a rejected batch is really unsatisfactory. What criteria should it use to reject a batch?

10.6 Batches of raw materials are delivered with a guaranteed average length of 100 cm and standard deviation of 1 cm. A sample of 100 units is taken to test each delivery, and the company want to be 95% sure that its rejected batches are in fact defective. What range of mean weights is acceptable in the sample?

10.7 A component is made in batches and transferred from one part of a plant to another. When it is made an acceptance quality level of 1% of defective is used, but transferred batches are allowed to have a maximum of 4% defective. Limits are imposed to accept a 5% risk of rejecting good batches, and a 10% risk of accepting bad batches. What would be a suitable sampling plan for the component?

10.8 24 samples of 200 units were collected from a process that was known to be working properly. The number of defective units was as shown in Table 10.5. Draw control charts with 95% and 99% confidence limits on the process.

Table 10.5

Day	Number of defects	Day	Number of defects	Day	Number of defects
1	21	9	15	17	20
2	32	10	13	18	19
3	22	11	16	19	25
4	17	12	17	20	16
5	16	13	20	21	15
6	14	14	19	22	13
7	21	15	17	23	24
8	17	16	22	24	25

10.9 A process makes products with a mean length of 75.42 cm and standard deviation of 2.01 cm. Samples of 8 are taken to make sure the process is still in control. Find the control limits that will include 99% of sample means if the process is working normally.

10.10 Thirty samples of size 15 have been taken from a process. The average sample range for the 30 samples is 1.025 kg and the average mean is 19.872 kg. Draw $\bar{X}$ and R control charts for the process.

Discussion questions

10.1 What are the differences between quality management and quality control?

10.2 How do you think the quality 'gurus' view quality control? How has the function of quality control changed in recent years?

10.3 How does acceptance sampling differ from process control? Do these really test different things?

10.4 What are the advantages and problems of using samples rather than complete inspections? Give some examples you are familiar with.

10.5 Is it true that quality control guarantees the quality of products? What is meant by producers' and consumers' risks? Describe exactly how an OC curve works.

10.6 Is it true that statistical sampling assumes a certain number of units are defective? Then, provided there are not too many defects in a batch, operations are satisfactory. How does this fit into the ideas of total quality management?

10.7 What is the purpose of control charts? Describe some operations where they can be used. Are there other ways of getting the same results?

10.8 Discuss some applications of statistical sampling in service industries. Are there any differences between quality control in services and manufacturing?

10.9 Local authorities have a legal obligation to sample milk and make sure it reaches acceptable standards. Because this obligation has been in effect for a long time, most authorities have a well-established procedure for sampling milk. This takes random samples of milk at any point on its journey from cows to final customers. In practice, inspectors take some samples from farmers' milking parlours, shops, delivery vans, and in tankers, but most of the tests are done at dairies. The larger dairies are so careful with their process that there is almost never any problem. The few deficient samples that are found usually come from smaller operations or are caused by mistakes.

In 1993 the operations manager of the Consumer Protection Department in East Yorkshire was looking at the way it sampled milk. In particular it wanted to know if it was doing the right tests, or doing enough of them. At the time the Consumer Protection Department aimed for six tests per thousand population each year. As the population of the area was around 2 million, this meant 12,000 samples a year or about 50 a working day. Last year only 32 of the milk samples had any problems and the council only received 15 complaints about milk from the public.

How can the council set a reasonable number of samples for milk? As it finds so few problems, is the money spent on testing milk being wasted?

Selected references

Banks J. (1989). *Principles of Quality Control*. New York: John Wiley.

Besterfield D.H. (1986). *Quality Control* (2nd edn). Englewood Cliffs, NJ: Prentice-Hall.

Bounds G., Yorks L., Adams M. and Ranney G. (1994). *Beyond Quality Management: Towards the Emerging Paradigm*. Maidenhead: McGraw-Hill.

Crosby P.B. (1979). *Quality is Free*. New York: McGraw-Hill.

Dale B.G. (ed.) (1994). *Managing Quality* (2nd edn). Hemel Hempstead: Prentice-Hall.

Deming W.E. (1986). *Out of the Crisis*. Cambridge, Mass.: MIT Centre for Advanced Engineering Study.

Dodge H.F. and Romig H.G. (1959). *Sampling Inspection Tables – Single and Double Sampling*. New York: John Wiley.

Duncan A.J. (1986). *Quality Control and Industrial Statistics* (5th edn). Homewood, Ill.: Richard D. Irwin.

Evans J.R. and Lindsay W.M. (1993). *The Management and Control of Quality* (2nd edn). St Paul, Minn.: West Publishing.

Feigenbaum A.V. (1986). *Total Quality Control* (3rd edn). New York: McGraw-Hill.

Garrity S.M. (1993). *Basic Quality Improvement*. Englewood Cliffs, NJ: Prentice-Hall.

Garvin D.A. (1988). *Managing Quality*. New York: Free Press.

Gitlow H.S., Gitlow S., Oppenheim A. and Oppenheim R. (1989). *Tools and Methods for the Improvement of Quality*. Homewood, Ill.: Richard Irwin.

Grant E.L. and Leavenworth R.S. (1988). *Statistical Quality Control* (6th edn). New York: McGraw-Hill.

Ishikawa K. (1986). *Guide to Quality Control* (2nd edn). White Plains, New York: Kraus International.

Juran J.M. (1988). *Juran on Planning for Quality*. New York: Free Press/Macmillan.

Montgomery D. (1991). *Introduction to Statistical Quality Control*. New York: John Wiley.

Oakland J.S. and Followell R.F. (1990). *Statistical Process Control – A Practical Guide* (2nd edn). London: Heinemann.

Taguchi G. (1986). *Introduction to Quality Engineering*. Tokyo: Asian Productivity Organization.

Derwent Doors

Derwent Doors began the manufacture of doors two years ago as an offshoot of the firm's main business – a retail showroom that specializes in the sale of door 'furniture', that is brass handles, locks and hinges. Six months ago, Jean Bettison took up the post of operations manager. Today, Jean is taking a friend and former colleague Denis Smith, around the plant to show him the progress made over the last six months.

The product

Jean plans to start the tour in the cutting area where timber is sawn. A typical door is made up of at least 10 pieces. A top, a bottom and two side pieces make up the outer part of the door, together with vertical and horizontal cross-members and at least four panels. Originally, Derwent Doors produced a wide range of door styles that were available in both pine and hardwood. The ratio of pine to hardwood doors was and still is about 3:1. Sales staff prided themselves on meeting each customer's precise requirements with the result that most doors were customized products with variations in size, number of panels, decorative mouldings and the like. Manufacture was organized on a one off, jobbing basis with very little planning.

The process

'When I arrived, the overwhelming impression was of a cramped working area with piles of timber everywhere', says Jean,

> Production begins with the saw operator taking a length of timber from the timber store. In the past he set up the saw to cut the timber to the required length, but instead of cutting just the pieces required, say two sides, he would cut as many as he could get from that length of timber. Those pieces actually required for the door he would take to the assembly area and the excess ones he would pile on the floor.

Cut timber was everywhere and if not used immediately it was unlikely ever to be used because most doors were designed to customers' specific requirements. The saw operator was well meaning, he thought that because the saw had been set up, he was saving time and effort cutting a whole length of timber. He was saving effort on his part, but he was costing us a fortune in work-in-progress. It was 'just-in-case' production rather than 'just-in-time'. To make matters worse the piles of cut timber were constantly getting in the way. Production was slowed down because it was difficult to move around the plant.

Looking at the neatly laid-out cutting area, Jean remarks, 'One of the first things I did was to plan production so that now the saw operator cuts to order, no more and no less. Most production orders are for six doors, so that's what he cuts. The cut timber is built up into a "kit" of parts that goes through to the assembly area. Any unused timber is taken back to the timber store.'

Jean and Denis now move into the assembly area. This consists of six work-benches. On each there is a door under construction. A series of jigs ensures that each door is identical. Two joiners are busy gluing components into place. Jean says:

This part of the plant was just as chaotic. There was only space for two benches. One per joiner. They worked independently, each making a different door. Since most of the doors were customized, jigs were of little use. Instead the pieces were glued in place and held together by a series of large clamps. Because these were heavy, a large 'curing' area was required, where completed doors were left for 48 hours until the glue had dried. I introduced a quick-acting glue and jigs. The jigs made construction easier and permitted the doors to be stacked while curing. The quick-acting glue meant that the doors could be left to cure overnight. We trebled the space available and were able to set up six work-benches instead of two.

From the assembly area Jean and Denis go through a door into the finishing shop. Here excess glue is scraped off, small holes and irregularities are filled and each door is sanded down before being sprayed with up to three coats of varnish. As Jean says:

> We made significant changes here as well. We still have only one spray unit. When we were making doors on a one-off basis, the spray unit had to be thoroughly cleaned several times a day because we use a different varnish depending on whether the door is constructed of pine or hardwood. Having switched to production based on batches of six, we usually only clean the spray unit once or twice a day. This has made life easier for the person who does the spraying and has again helped to increase our capacity.

They enter the packing area. Finished doors sealed in polythene are stacked on pallets. A forklift truck lifts a pallet onto racking that runs from floor to ceiling. At one end of the room a man is operating the packing machine which seals finished doors with a sheet of clear polythene film. Jean comments:

> Now that we have rationalized production to four door styles in either pine or hardwood, packing and distribution is a lot easier. In the past we had difficulty identifying doors because they were all built to different specifications. Sometimes deliveries were late, just because we couldn't find a customer's door. We'd made it, but it hadn't been properly labelled and we didn't know where it was. Now the door packaging is colour coded and doors are easily located.

The options

Reflecting on the changes, Jean remarks,

> You're probably surprised that I keep talking about changes. Well it might not look much, but we have

transformed the way we do things. When I arrived we were short of capacity and could not make enough doors to keep pace with our rising sales. The MD said we could increase capacity by investing in a new plant, investing in new technology, and employing more staff. We could have chosen any one of these options, but we could not go for more than one. In the event I took a long hard look at what we were doing and rejected all three. Instead I chose better management through planning and organization. Now we produce nearly three times as many doors, but with one less person on the payroll.

Planning and scheduling resources

This book is divided into five parts, each of which describes a different aspect of operations management. Part I introduced the subject. It described the types of decision needed in an organization. Part II looked at some strategic issues and discussed various aspects of product planning. Part III talked about the process used to make a product. It described the types of process available, their layout, capacity planning and quality control. This is the fourth part, which looks in more detail at the planning and scheduling of resources.

There are five chapters in this part. Chapter 11 describes a hierarchy of planning decisions. These decisions start with the strategic capacity plans discussed earlier. The chapter continues by talking about higher level aggregate plans. Chapter 12 looks at lower levels of planning and describes materials requirement planning. Chapter 13 continues this theme by looking at just-in-time systems. Chapter 14 discusses more detailed, short-term, scheduling. Chapter 15 looks at job design and work measurement, which are the most detailed levels of planning. Finally, Chapter 16 describes some methods used in the important area of project planning.

Later in the book, Part V will discuss some aspects of materials management.

Kevin Whalley
Tesco

Kevin Whalley is the Branch manager of Tesco's flagship and third largest store at Sandhurst. He manages 600 staff, including 32 middle managers and his senior management team of Customer Service Manager, Personnel Manager, and three Trading Managers.

Q **How are your strategic plans drawn up?**

A Our annual strategic planning begins with the Trading Plan which is drawn up by the main Tesco Board of Directors. This plan covers all aspects of the business, including Retail, Marketing, Distribution, Customer Service and Personnel. Once the plan has been drawn up at Board level, it is filtered down to Regional Managing Directors and Retail Directors from where it is adapted, and local objectives and plans drawn up.

To set local objectives, all the Branch Managers in a region (around 20) attend a three-day meeting to discuss the main objectives of the Trading Plan. At this meeting we sift through the information in the Trading Plan and break down the national objectives into regional objectives. These objectives are unique to each region and set out what we want to achieve in the forthcoming year. The next stage is to break down the regional objectives to decide how they will be implemented at store level. Three Branch Managers and a Personnel Manager from each region get together and devise a regional strategy for each of the four areas: People; Marketing; Customer Service; and Systems/Production. Each store will then come up with a specific action plan detailing how they will put the strategy into practice within their own branch.

Q **How do you implement these plans within your branch?**

A Once the strategic plan has been broken down into a local plan, I sit down for half a day with my senior management team of five people and we decide how to break down the regional plan and make it store specific. We all come up with ideas of how to best achieve the store's goals giving us a unique set of objectives and a plan in which all the senior management team have had an input. This input means that we all have a sense of ownership and a clear understanding of the plan.

We have to demonstrate how we have put the Strategic Plan in to action in our own branch, and our performance is judged on this basis. We therefore ensure that we review our objectives on a regular basis. I undertake a 12-week review with my senior management team to ensure we are still on course with our objectives. This review process works back up the ladder, as I am reviewed on a regular basis by my senior manager, and so on back to the main Board Managers. Forty per cent of our pay award is based on meeting our strategic objectives, and 60% on day-to-day issues.

Q **What kind of planning decisions do you make within your branch?**

A Communication is vital and is the essence of the successful operation of the store. Without good communications the store would not be able to operate. Information is obtained through a variety of sources, and our major communication method is e-mail. We receive communication from Head Office twice a week which includes information such as Stock Control Documents and General Managers Bulletins.

Planning for the week begins on Saturday with communications from Head Office. It is important for the whole team to know what is going on in the store and we therefore hold a Senior Management meeting every Monday morning at which we share information and discuss the forthcoming week. We cover issues such as store performance, waste, trading issues, new ranges, merchandizing changes, etc. I give direction and set the focus for the forthcoming week at these meetings, and what we discuss is passed down the line to the rest of the staff. The Senior Managers feed this information to the section managers who in turn feed it down to the staff. If any major issues arise, we have full team meetings. Tesco in Sandhurst is a 24-hour operation, and it is easy for the Night Team Managers to become alienated. To avoid this, I ensure that these managers are included in the meetings. There is always an hour and a half cross-over of the management teams in the morning, and at this time we have daily meetings to discuss waste and any other day-to-day issues that may arise. These meetings are important as they keep the communication channels open and maintain morale.

We have to be prepared for eventualities for which we cannot always plan, such as a change in the weather. A hot spell, for example, will lead to an increased demand for salad. To help us deal with fluctuating demand, we have a sophisticated stock and order system which accounts for 95% of our stock replenishment. The system re-plans every day and anticipates what stock will sell on a daily basis based on recent trends within the store, and on the stock holding from the previous year. The system also re-plans according to fluctuations in stock demand. For example, the system will 'factor up' by a given amount when a bank holiday is approaching and at Christmas time. We hold waste meetings to see how well the system is working. Product specific reports are produced for a season so that plans can be made for the following year. Straight after Christmas the Senior Management Team meet to discuss these reports, and an order for the following year will be placed at this time and confirmed in October. These orders are pinpointed as closely as possible to expected sales but sometimes we have to order in 'blind' when we have new products.

Q How do you schedule staff resources?

A The effective management of people is one of the most important parts of the success of the store. The planning of staff resources depends on branch turnover and we calculate what the branch will take during the forthcoming week based on the budgets which are set. Staffing levels are worked out individually for each department within the store and involve a calculation of the number of staff needed to operate the department effectively, and the amount of money the department actually takes. The department operates with a combination of fixed and variable hours.

Q How do you set your objectives?

A The key business objectives for a store are a vitally important factor in the success of that store.

To set the business objectives I need to know the direction in which the company is heading. In order to set the objectives in line with Company trends a constant view of company figures against regional and store performance is essential. To ensure the objectives are still realistic and achievable objectives need to be enhanced or added.

The objectives are communicated to the management team at the start of the financial year in order that the objectives can be agreed and put into place. A business plan is then cascaded down to each level of personnel. A regular three-month review is conducted to ensure that we are still on track and at the end of the financial year the management team's performance is reviewed against the objectives. The key is to ensure that all levels of management are financially aware of all trends and able to keep track of their own personal performance.

11 Aggregate planning

Contents

Objectives

After reading this chapter you should be able to:

- describe the different levels of planning decisions
- define capacity plan, aggregate plan, master production schedule and short-term schedules
- discuss the factors which make planning difficult
- describe a general planning procedure
- discuss the purpose of aggregate planning
- use a number of methods for aggregate planning
- understand the purpose of master production schedules
- design a master production schedule

Overall planning process

Chapter 3 described some of the strategic decisions made in an organization. It showed how decisions start with a mission, and this leads a business strategy. This business strategy, in turn, leads to strategic decisions within the central functions of operations, sales/marketing and accounting/finance. These strategic decisions are followed by tactical and operational decisions (see Figure 11.1).

In Chapter 9 we looked in more detail at the decisions needed for capacity planning. This aims to match available capacity to forecast demand. Capacity can be increased by building more facilities, changing the process to use higher technology, increasing capital investment, and so on; reducing capacity might involve closing facilities, laying-off staff, selling equipment, and so forth. So capacity planning is clearly a strategic function with effects in the long term.

Now we are going to look at the next stages of planning. These start with the capacity plans and move to more detailed tactical and operational plans.

We can start by showing roughly how this planning process will work. If you look at a manufacturing company, it will forecast demand for a product, and capacity plans will make sure there is enough capacity to meet this demand. Then the company will design a production plan which says when and where products will be made. This production plan can be expanded to give timetables for employees, equipment, purchases, and operations. So we have moved down the planning process from strategic capacity plans to detailed operational

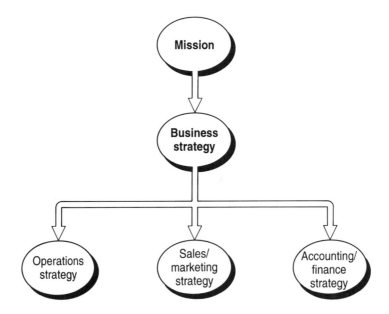

Figure 11.1 Strategic decisions in an organization.

timetables. Although we have outlined this procedure for a manufacturer, the approach is essentially the same for any organization.

Unfortunately, there is some disagreement about the terms used to describe the different levels of planning. We will describe the steps as follows:

- **Capacity plans**   which we have already discussed in Chapter 9.

- **Aggregate plans**   which show the overall production for families of products, typically by month at each location.

- **Master production schedules**   which show a detailed timetable of production for individual products, typically by week.

- **Short-term schedules**   which show detailed timetables and allocation of jobs to equipment, typically by day.

Then we can summarize the overall planning process as follows.

An organization's mission leads to strategic decisions about what products to make, where to make it, how to make it, and so on. These decisions, together with long-term forecasts, lead to capacity plans which match available capacity to forecast demand. The capacity plans give overall production levels in each factory over the next few years. Capacity plans are expanded to give medium-term aggregate plans. These typically show the numbers to make of each family of products each month over the next year or so. These aggregate plans are expanded to give the master production schedule. This

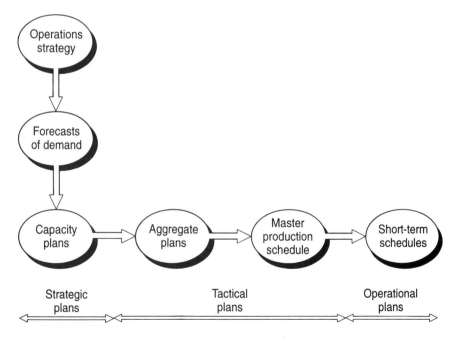

Figure 11.2 Outline of the planning process.

shows a timetable for the production of individual products, perhaps by week. The weekly master production schedule is expanded to give short-term schedules which show daily timetables of machines, operators and other equipment (see Figure 11.2).

ce Case example – Allenby Tools

This example shows the planning decisions made at different levels in a manufacturing company.

Allenby Tools make a variety of garden tools in three factories. One run of their planning procedure can be summarized as follows.

- **Strategic plans** – making the fundamental decisions.
  The Board of Directors, with George Allenby as its Chairman, decides to continue making garden tools of high quality and using appropriate processes. They will continue operations in three factories at Gateshead, Bradford and Exeter.

- **Capacity plans** – examine long-term forecasts of demand and make adjustments to match capacity to these.
  Jane Lucas, the Operations Director, looks at their long-term forecasts. These show demands of 50,000 garden tools a year, which means there is a shortage of capacity of 10,000 tools a year. Jane, along with her Senior Management Team, make a decision to overcome this shortage by increasing the staff in Exeter and working two shifts at Bradford. Then forecast demand can be met by:
  - Gateshead making 10,000 tools a year;
  - Bradford making 20,000 tools a year;
  - Exeter making 20,000 tools a year.

- **Aggregate plan** – breaks down the capacity plans into monthly plans for each location.
  The three Plant Managers get together, look at the capacity plans, and design aggregate plans to meet these.
  - Gateshead makes 1000 tools in January. This needs a staff of 10 and gives 90% utilization of equipment;
  - Bradford makes 2500 tools in January. This needs 20 staff and gives 85% utilization of equipment;
  - and so on.

- **Master production schedule** – breaks down aggregate plans into weekly plans for individual products.
  George Thirkettle, the Plant Manager at Gateshead, passes their aggregate plan to Mary Wilson who produces the master production schedules.

      –   Gateshead
           Week 1 of January
              100 spades
              50 forks
              100 rakes
           Week 2 of January
              50 spades
              250 rakes
           Week 3 of January
              100 spades
              100 rakes
           ... and so on

- **Short-term schedules** – breaks down the master production schedule into daily timetables for individual batches of tools and equipment.
  Mary Wilson passes the master production schedules to her assistants, who design detailed daily schedules.
      –   Gateshead
            Week 1 of January
              Monday morning shift
                10 spades on machines 1 to 4
                10 rakes on machines 5 to 8
                10 forks on machines 1 to 8
              Monday afternoon shift
                20 forks on machines 1 to 8
              Tuesday morning shift
                10 spades on machines 1 to 4
                10 forks on machines 5 to 8
                10 rakes on machines 1 to 8
              ... and so on

As you can see, Allenby Tools have made a series of plans. These start with strategic plans and move down to detailed operational schedules. There is a similar planning process in most organizations.

Review questions

11.1   Capacity planning is a purely strategic function. Do you agree with this?

11.2   What is the usual sequence of planning decisions?

11.3   Which types of plan are likely to refer to:

    (a)   overall production at different locations
    (b)   individual products
    (c)   individual pieces of equipment
    (d)   equipment operators.

Procedure for planning

Overall procedure

In Chapter 9 we described a procedure for capacity planning. This had five steps:

- **Step 1** look at forecast demand and translate this into a capacity needed.

- **Step 2** calculate the capacity of present facilities.

- **Step 3** identify mismatches between the capacity needed and that available.

- **Step 4** suggest alternative plans for overcoming any mismatches.

- **Step 5** compare alternative plans and implement the best.

This is typical of the planning process, and is sometimes referred to as **resource requirement planning**.

we Worked example

A coach operator plans its capacity in terms of 'coach-days'. It classifies its business according to 'full day', which are long distance journeys, or 'half day' which are shorter runs. Forecasts show expected annual demands for the next two years to average 400,000 full day passengers and 750,000 half-day passengers. The company has 61 coaches, each with an effective capacity of 40 passengers a day for 300 days a year. Breakdowns and other unexpected problems reduce efficiency to 90%. The company employs 86 drivers who work an average of 220 days a year, but illness and other absences reduce their efficiency to 85%. If there is a shortage of coaches the company can buy extra ones for £110,000 or hire them for £100 a day. If there is a shortage of drivers they can recruit extra ones at a cost of £20,000 a year, or hire them from an agency for £110 a day. How should the company approach its capacity planning?

Solution

Following the steps listed above:

- *Step 1* starts by translating the forecast demand into capacity requirements. 400,000 full day passengers are equivalent to $400,000/40 = 10,000$ coach days a year, or $10,000/300 = 33.33$ coaches. 750,000 half-day passengers are equivalent to $750,000/(40 \times 300 \times 2) = 31.25$ coaches. So the total demand is 64.58 coaches. Each coach needs $300/220$ drivers, so the company needs a total of 88.06 drivers.

- *Step 2* calculates the capacity of existing resources. The company has 61 coaches, but the efficiency of 90% gives an availability of $61 \times 0.9 = 54.9$ coaches. There are 86 drivers, but an efficiency of 85% reduces this to $86 \times 0.85 = 73.1$ drivers.

- *Step 3* compares the capacity needed and available, and identifies any mismatch. Without details of the timing, we can only take overall figures. There is a total shortage of $64.58 - 54.9 = 9.68$ coaches and $88.06 - 73.1 = 14.96$ drivers.

- *Step 4* suggests alternative plans for overcoming any mismatches. In this case the alternatives are either to buy or hire coaches, and employ or take temporary drivers. The only information we have to evaluate these alternatives are some costs.

- *Step 5* compares the alternatives and implements the best. To buy 10 coaches would cost £1,100,000. To hire coaches to make up the shortage would cost $9.68 \times 300 \times 100 = £290,400$ a year. There is, of course, the alternative of buying some coaches and hiring others. We do not have enough information to make the final decisions, but a reasonable solution would go along the line of buying eight coaches and making up any shortages by hiring.

Similarly, to hire 15 drivers would cost £300,000 a year, while using temporary drivers from an agency would cost $14.96 \times 220 \times 110 = £362,032$ a year. There is also the option of hiring some drivers, say 13, and making up shortages from an agency.

The above example of capacity planning illustrates the general approach of all planning. But this approach has some problems. The most important of these concerns the way that alternatives plans are generated and compared. There is usually a range of competing objectives and non-quantifiable factors, so it can be very difficult to find feasible plans, and then to compare them.

A more realistic view of planning would replace the single procedure described above by an iterative procedure, which keeps modifying proposed plans until a satisfactory one is found. This means that steps 4 and 5 are repeated a number of times. The planning process then becomes as follows:

- *Step 1*: determine the resources needed

- *Step 2*: identify the resources available

- *Step 3*: find mismatches between needs and availability

- *Step 4*: suggest a plan for overcoming these mismatches

- *Step 5*: assess the plan and identify any problems, perhaps broken constraints or objectives not met

- *Step 6*: if the plan needs more revision go to step 4

- ***Step 7***: implement the best plan

This iterative procedure accepts that it is usually impossible to find the 'best' solution. The plans that the marketing department like may be very inefficient for operations; the best plans for operations may not suit personnel; the best plans for personnel may be too expensive for finance. A compromise is always needed between conflicting objectives, subjective evaluation, and so on. This compromise must consider a large number of factors, including the following:

- **Demand**
    - forecast sales
    - sales already made
    - back-orders
    - variation in demand

- **Operations**
    - machine capacity and utilization
    - aim of stable production
    - plans for new equipment
    - use of subcontractors
    - productivity targets

- **Materials**
    - availability of raw materials
    - inventory policies
    - current inventory levels
    - constraints on storage

- **Finance**
    - costs
    - cash flows
    - financing arrangements
    - exchange rates
    - general economic climate

- **Human resources**
    - workforce levels
    - levels of skills and productivity
    - unemployment rates
    - hiring and training policies

- **Marketing**
    - reliability of forecasts
    - competition
    - plans for new products
    - product substitution

Finding a satisfactory balance between these factors is difficult, and the iterative planning procedure may be repeated many times until a plan is finally accepted.

The iterative planning procedure will give plans for a specific period. But the planning process is really continuous and does not end. As plans for one period are finalized and implemented, planning moves on to the next period. So we really need to design a series of plans – one for every period. This actually makes planning easier as plans for one period can be used as the basis of future plans.

The pattern of repeated planning allows organizations to work in cycles. Then in one cycle they might design definite plans the next period and tentative plans for the following period. It is difficult to generalize, but strategic plans might cover the next five years, and be updated annually. Aggregate plans might cover the next six months and be updated every three months. The second half of these plans are more tentative, but the first half are more definite and form the basis of the master production schedules (see Figure 11.3).

Now we can add these cycles to out general planning procedure, as shown in Figure 11.4.

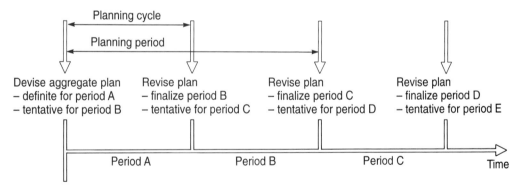

Figure 11.3 Continual updating of plans in cycles.

Updating procedures

You can see that a key element in planning is the updating of previous plans to give new ones. In every planning cycle, an organization does not try to design entirely new plans, but would rather revise the plans for the last cycle. This makes planning easier, and it also gives continuity to operations. We can illustrate this updating by looking at stocks of products.

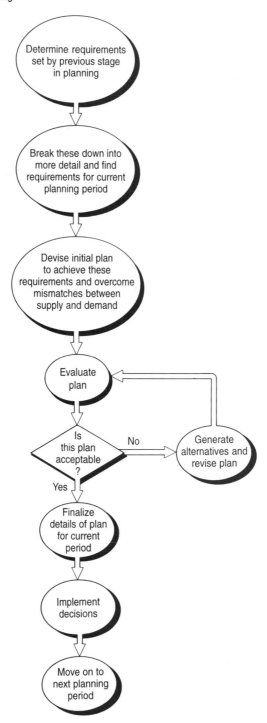

Figure 11.4 Iterative planning process.

Inventories can play an important part in production planning as stocks give a buffer between supply and demand. Then production during a period need not exactly match forecast demand in the period, as demand can be met:

● from stocks already held at the beginning of the period

● from production during the period

● from future production with late delivery.

The best mix of these is the one that minimizes costs, maximizes profit, or meets some other measure of performance.

Suppose we define S_t as the amount of a product held in stock at the end of period t, P_t as the production in period t and D_t as the demand. You can see that:

$$\text{Stock at end of this period} = \text{Stock at end of last period} + \text{Production during this period} - \text{Demand met during this period}$$

or

$$S_t = S_{t-1} + P_t - D_t$$

This assumes there are no back-orders, where some demand in one period is met by production from the following period. If we take this into account we have:

$$S_t = S_{t-1} + P_t - D_t - B_{t-1} + B_t$$

where B_t is the number of back-orders in period t that are met from production in period $t + 1$.

we Worked example

Demand for a product over the next eight months has been forecast as follows.

Month	1	2	3	4	5	6	7	8
Demand	15	25	25	30	40	40	25	20

A minimum of 10 units is kept in stock, and no back orders are allowed. There are currently 35 units in stock and production is in batches of 50, with a very short lead time. Design a production plan to meet the demand.

Solution

We can do the calculations for this in the following table.

Month	1	2	3	4	5	6	7	8	9
Stock at beginning	35	20	45	20	40	50	10	35	15
Demand	15	25	25	30	40	40	25	20	
Production	0	50	0	50	50	0	50	0	
Stock at end	20	45	20	40	50	10	35	15	

At the beginning of the first month there are 35 units in stock and demand during the month is 15. No production is needed and the stock at the end of the month is $35 - 15 = 20$. This stock of 20 is available at the beginning of the second month, when demand is 25. Scheduling production of a batch of 50 units in period 2 gives stock at the end of the month of $20 + 50 - 25 = 45$.

As there must be at least 10 units left in stock, a batch of 50 is made whenever the stock at the beginning of a month minus demand in the month is less than 10. This procedure leads to a plan that makes batches of 50 units in months 2, 4, 5 and 7. This production plan is only one alternative – many others are possible, and they should each be examined before a final choice is made.

This updating procedure can be used for planning other resources. If, for example, we replace stock levels by employees we can do some manpower planning.

Number employed in current month	=	Number employed last month	–	Dismissals and resignations at end of last month	+	New hires at beginning of current month

Review questions

11.4 Where do the initial requirements for a planning period come from?

11.5 A planning process starts of with general plans, and more details are added at each stage of planning. Do you agree with this?

11.6 How do updating planning procedures work?

ce | **Case example** – Kawasaki Heavy Industries

This example describes the levels of planning in a major international manufacturer.

Kawasaki Heavy Industries is probably best known for its motor cycles, which are made in a number of plants around the world. Production planning at these plants has inputs from several sources, including forecasts of local demand and requirements of the main plant in Akashi, Japan. We can outline Kawasaki's current planning process, but it looks for continuous improvements and is always changing this.

- The process starts with a **sales forecast**, which gives the monthly demand for each model of motor cycle for the next year. This is updated every three months.

- The forecasts are consolidated into a **sales plan** which shows the number of each model that must be available for sale each month for the next year. The plan is updated every three months, with the final three months considered firm.

- The sales plan is one input to the **production plan** at plants. This production plan looks up to 18 months ahead and is used for capacity planning and budgeting. The production plan is updated every three months, with the last three months fixed to agree with the sales plan. Scheduled deliveries of parts allow no changes in the last six weeks.

- The production plan is expanded into a **daily production schedule** which is the master production schedule and shows the daily assembly programme. Details of this are added four or five months in advance, and plans are updated every three months to fit into the cycles of the sales and production plans. The last six weeks of this plan are fixed by the production plan, but minor adjustments are made every week.

- The daily production schedule is expanded to give **fabrication schedules** which show the timetable for making components needed for final assembly.

- The fabrication schedules are expanded to find the **purchase orders** needed to get parts and materials from suppliers.

As you can see, Kawasaki has a series of planning decisions. These start with long-term sales and production plans, and end with daily production and other schedules.

Aggregate plans

Introduction

Aggregate plans and master production schedules bridge the gap between strategic capacity plans and operational details. This section considers aggregate plans, and the following section looks at master production schedules.

Aggregate planning takes the forecast demand and capacity, and translates this into production plans for each family of products for, typically, each of the next few months. Aggregate plans only look at production of families of products and are not concerned with individual products. A knitwear manufacturer, for example, produces different styles, colours, and sizes of jumpers and skirts. The aggregate plan only shows the total production of jumpers and the total production of skirts – it does not look in any more detail at the production of a particular style, colour or size. Aggregate plans will look at the total number of barrels of beer to be produced, or books to be printed, but not the number of barrels of each type of beer or the number of copies of each title.

Aggregate planning assumes the long-term demand has been forecast, and that planned capacity can meet this. Now the forecast demand and capacity plan are transformed into an aggregate plan that considers questions like:

- should production be kept at a constant level or changed with demand;

- should stocks be used to meet changing demand, producing for stock during periods of low demand and using stocks during periods of high demand;

- should subcontractors be used for peak demands;

- should the size of the work force change with demand;

- how can work patterns be changed to meet changing demand;

- should prices be changed;

- are shortages allowed, perhaps with late delivery;

- can demand be smoothed.

As you can see, an important question is how much variation should there be in production levels – should production change with demand or should it be more stable? In practice there are three ways you can meet uneven demand.

(1) *Chase demand* where production exactly matches demand (see Figure 11.5). This gives no inventories, but we have to change production every period, hiring or firing workers, changing production levels, and so on. This is the only possible approach for services which can not store their products.

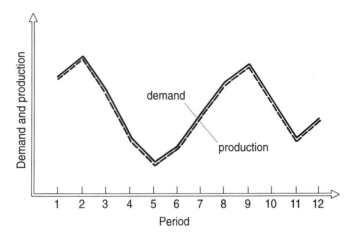

Figure 11.5 Chase demand, where production exactly matches demand.

(2) *Produce at a constant production rate* where production is constant at the average demand for the planning period (see Figure 11.6). Since the production rate is constant and demand is variable, the differences are met by building or using stocks. This means there are always inventory costs and maybe some shortage costs.

(3) *Mixed policy* which is a combination of the first two policies (see Figure 11.7). Here there are some changes in production rate, but not every period. The policy tries to compromise by having a fairly stable production, but reduces the inventory costs by allowing some changes. In practice, this is the most commonly used plan.

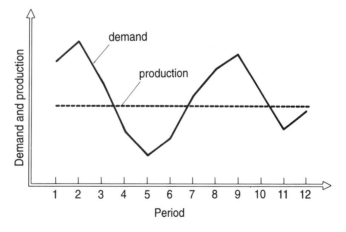

Figure 11.6 Policy of constant production.

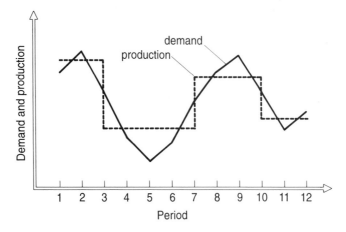

Figure 11.7 A mixed production strategy.

Because of the problems with changing the production rate, organizations generally try to change the production rate as little as possible. There are obvious advantages in having stable production, including:

- planning is easier
- flow of products is smoother
- there are fewer problems with changes
- there is no need to 'hire-and-fire' employees
- employees have regular work patterns
- larger lot sizes reduce costs
- stocks can be reduced as there is less variation
- throughput can be faster
- experience with a product reduces problems.

So we can suggest the following objective for aggregate planning:

The aim of **aggregate planning** is to devise medium-term schedules for families of products that:

- allow all demand to be met
- keep production relatively stable
- keep within the constraints of the capacity plan
- meet any other specific objectives and constraints.

There are four main ways of designing aggregate plans:

(1)   intuitive approaches

(2)   graphical methods

(3)   matrix arithmetic

(4)   mathematical model.

These are described in the following sections.

Intuitive approach

Like most plans, aggregate plans are not usually designed from scratch, but are variations on previous plans: next month's production will be similar to last month's. So the simplest approach to aggregate planning is to get an experienced planner to review the current situation and, in the light of experiences with similar plans, design updated plans for the next period. In practice, this is the most widely used method of planning.

Unfortunately, this intuitive approach gives results that have variable and uncertain quality, they may take a long time to design, may include bias, and so on. The benefits of the approach are that it is convenient and easy to use, the process is well understood, and experts can give results that are trusted by the organization.

we Worked example

Fenmore Enterprises has forecast the following aggregate, monthly demand for a family of products. If this is the only information you have, what production schedule would you suggest for the products?

Month	Jan	Feb	March	April	May	June	July
Aggregate demand	80	70	60	120	180	150	110

Solution

You might suggest that monthly production exactly matches demand. But demand varies quite widely and most organizations would prefer a more stable production.

You could also suggest a steady production equal to the average demand of 110. During the first three months the demand will be less than supply, so stocks will rise, but these will be used during the following months.

Month	Jan	Feb	March	April	May	June	July
Demand	80	70	60	120	180	150	110
Production	110	110	110	110	110	110	110
Stock at month end	30	70	120	110	40	0	0

The stock at the end of each month is found from:

$$\text{Stock at month end} = \text{Stock at end of last month} + \text{Production in month} - \text{Demand in month}$$

An obvious disadvantage of this plan is the high stock levels.

These two policies are a chase policy and constant production. If we had more information about costs, stock holding policies, materials supply, availability of workforce, and so on, we could design a number of mixed policies and compare the results.

As you can imagine, spreadsheets are widely used for this type of intuitive planning. An experienced scheduler can quickly get a good result when they use a spreadsheet for 'what-if' analyses.

Graphical methods

The second approach to aggregate planning uses a graphical method. The most popular format for this has a graph of cumulative demand over some time period. Then an aggregate plan is drawn as a line of cumulative supply. The aim of planners is to get the cumulative supply line nearly straight, giving constant production, and as close as possible to the cumulative demand line. The difference between the two lines shows the mismatch:

- If the cumulative demand line is below the cumulative supply line, production has been too high and the excess has accumulated as stock.

- If the cumulative demand line is above the cumulative supply line, production has been too low and some demand has not been met.

we Worked example

McGrath Holdings has forecast monthly demand for a family of products, as shown below. At the end of each month it assigns a notional holding cost of £10 to every unit held in stock. Any shortages are satisfied by backorders, but each unit of shortage is assigned a notional cost of £100 for lost profit, good-will and future sales. Each time the production rate is changed it costs £10,000. The designed capacity for the products is 400 units a month, but maximum utilization is generally around 75% of this. McGrath Holdings want to spend less than £1900 a month on these activities. Design an aggregate plan for the products.

Month	1	2	3	4	5	6	7	8	9
Aggregate demand	280	320	260	160	120	100	60	100	130

Solution

The designed capacity is 400 units a month, but utilization is generally around 75%, so we should assume a maximum production of $400 \times 0.75 = 300$ a month. McGrath Holdings should aim for stable production as changes are very expensive. A first step, then, is to suggest a constant production equal to the average demand of 170 a month. The cumulative demand and supply for this are shown in Figure 11.8.

Unfortunately, the cumulative demand line is always above the cumulative supply and there are continuous shortages. We can calculate the total cost of these shortages using the spreadsheet shown in Figure 11.9. The total cost of this plan is due to shortages and is found by multiplying the total shortages by £100; that is, $1700 \times 100 = £170,000$. This is considerably above the company target of £1900 a month or a total of £17,100.

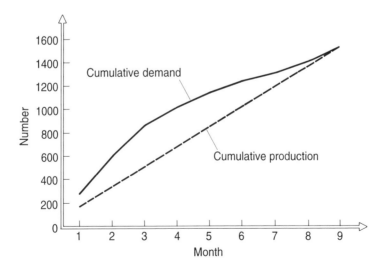

Figure 11.8 Initial aggregate plan for example.

Month	Aggregate Demand	Cumulative Demand	Production	Cumulative Production	Shortage in Month	Stock at End of Month
1	280	280	170	170	110	0
2	320	600	170	340	260	0
3	260	860	170	510	350	0
4	160	1020	170	680	340	0
5	120	1140	170	850	290	0
6	100	1240	170	1020	220	0
7	60	1300	170	1190	110	0
8	100	1400	170	1360	40	0
9	130	1530	170	1530	0	0
Totals					1720	0

Costs	Production changes	0	0
	Shortages	1720	172000
	Storage	0	0
	Total		172000
	Monthly		19111

Figure 11.9 Spreadsheet calculations for example.

Although changing the production rate is expensive, it might be worthwhile to reduce the shortages found in the initial plan. As demand is heavy in the first three months we might try increasing supply by running the process at its maximum output of 300 units a month. The total demand to be met from production in the remaining six months is $[1530 - (3 \times 300)] = 630$,

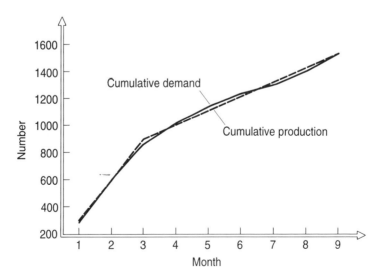

Figure 11.10 Modified aggregate plan for example.

averaging 105 a month. Then a reasonable production plan is 300 for the first three months and 105 for the next six months. The cumulative graph of supply and demand is shown in Figure 11.10 (see also Figure 11.11). There is clearly a close match and we can expect for some cost reductions.

When cumulative supply is greater than cumulative demand, there is stock at the end of the month. When cumulative demand is greater than cumulative supply, there is a shortage in the month. The cost of this plan is found from:

- stock holding $105 \times 10 = 1050$
- shortage $70 \times 100 = 7000$
- production change $1 \times 10,000 = 10,000$

This gives a total cost of £18,050 or over £2000 a month. This is a much better result, but it still does not meet the company target so we must try some more adjustments. Shortages still give high costs, so we could try maintaining production at 300 units for another month. Then the average production in the remaining five months is $[1530 - (4 \times 300)]/5 = 66$ (see Figure 11.12).

With this plan there are no shortages, so costs are:

- stock holding $620 \times 10 = 6200$
- production change $1 \times 10,000 = 10,000$

Month	Aggregate Demand	Cumulative Demand	Production	Cumulative Production	Shortage in Month	Stock at End of Month
1	280	280	300	300	0	20
2	320	600	300	600	0	0
3	260	860	300	900	0	40
4	160	1020	105	1005	15	0
5	120	1140	105	1110	30	0
6	100	1240	105	1215	25	0
7	60	1300	105	1320	0	20
8	100	1400	105	1425	0	25
9	130	1530	105	1530	0	0
Totals					70	105

Costs	Production changes	1	10000
	Shortages	70	7000
	Storage	105	1050
	Total		18050
	Monthly		2006

Figure 11.11 Modified calculations for example.

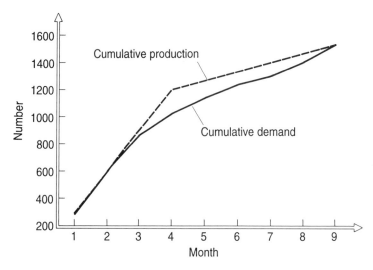

Figure 11.12 Final aggregate plan for example.

This total of £16,200 (or £1800 a month) is within the company target and we could leave this as our final aggregate plan. If necessary, more solutions could be tried, and we could continue adjusting the plan until we find a better result (see Figure 11.13).

Month	Aggregate Demand	Cumulative Demand	Production	Cumulative Production	Shortage in Month	Stock at End of Month
1	280	280	300	300	0	20
2	320	600	300	600	0	0
3	260	860	300	900	0	40
4	160	1020	300	1200	0	180
5	120	1140	66	1266	0	126
6	100	1240	66	1332	0	92
7	60	1300	66	1398	0	98
8	100	1400	66	1464	0	64
9	130	1530	66	1530	0	0
Totals					0	620

Costs			
	Production changes	1	10000
	Shortages	0	0
	Storage	620	6200
	Total		16200
	Monthly		1800

Figure 11.13 Final calculations for example.

Graphical approaches have the advantages that they are easy to use and understand. But they are really only one step better than the intuitive method we described. So they do not guarantee optimal solutions, sometimes give very poor results, may take a long time, and still rely on the skills of a planner.

Matrix calculations

One of the problems with graphs is that they show overall patterns rather than details. If we want to compare a number of alternatives it is often easier to do some calculations using a matrix. The main advantage of this is that planners can use a spreadsheet to do large numbers of calculations very quickly.

The usual approach draws a matrix with the resources to be used down the left-hand side and the time periods across the top. The available capacity for each resource is shown down the right-hand side of the matrix, and the demand is shown across the bottom. The body of the matrix is used for two values, the cost of using resources, and amount of resources used in a period. An example of this is shown in Figure 11.14.

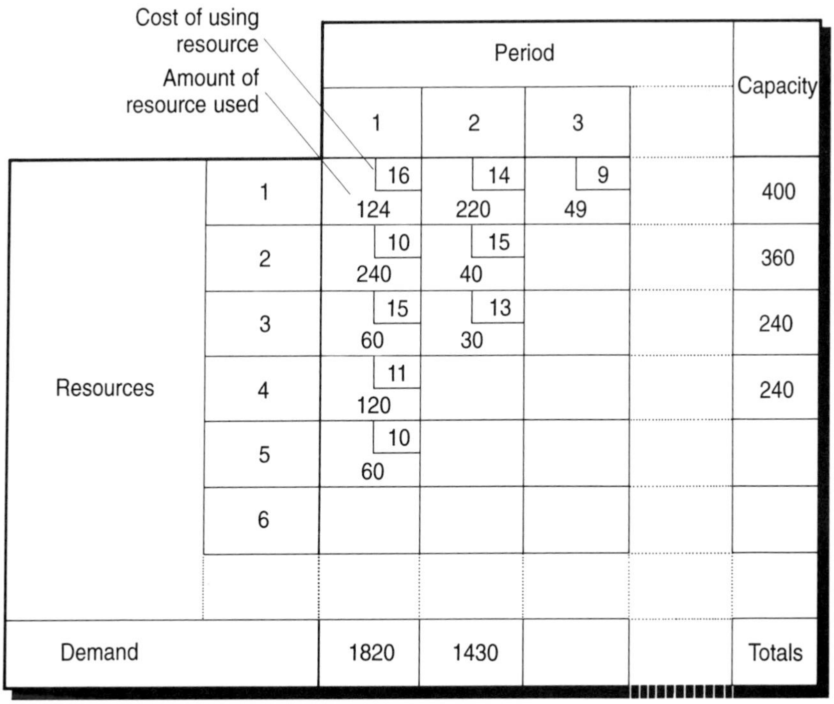

Cost of using resource / Amount of resource used	Period 1	Period 2	Period 3		Capacity
Resources 1	16 / 124	14 / 220	9 / 49		400
Resources 2	10 / 240	15 / 40			360
Resources 3	15 / 60	13 / 30			240
Resources 4	11 / 120				240
Resources 5	10 / 60				
Resources 6					
Demand	1820	1430			Totals

Figure 11.14 Typical matrix for aggregate planning.

Often the resources include the number of units that can be made in regular time, overtime and by subcontractors in each period. Then the costs might include stock holding or back-order costs. This leads to a simple method for designing an aggregate plan as follows.

Procedure for aggregate planning

(1) Take the next time period.

(2) Find the lowest cost in this column.

(3) Assign as much production as possible to the cell with lowest cost, without exceeding either the supply of resources or demand for products.

(4) Subtract the amount assigned from the total capacity to give the spare capacity, and calculate the unmet demand.

(5) If there is unmet demand go to step 2: if all demand has been met, move on to the next period in step 1.

we Worked example

Jim Cooper is the Operations Manager for a small manufacturing company. He forecasts the aggregate demand for a family of products for the next four months as 130, 80, 180 and 140. Normal capacity of the company is 100 units a month, overtime has a capacity of 20 a month and subcontractors have a capacity of 60 units a month. The unit cost is £10 for normal capacity, £12 for overtime and £15 from subcontractors. It costs £1 to stock a unit for a month, and no back orders or shortages are allowed. Jim uses a matrix method to design an aggregate plan for the products. What results does he get?

Solution

The first step is to build a matrix with costs, capacities and demand, as shown in Figure 11.15. The demands and capacities are given directly in the problem. The costs in each cell are a combination of production and stock-holding cost. It costs £10 to make a unit in normal work, but if this is used in a later period holding costs are added and the cost rises to £11 in the following period, £12 in the next period, and so on. No back orders are allowed, so the cells for producing in period 2 for demand in period 1, and so on, are crossed out.

Using the procedure described above, the first step is to look down column 1 to find the lowest cost for the first period. This is the £10 for normal work done in period 1. We make as much there as possible, which is the normal capacity of 100 units, leaving a shortage of 30 units. The next lowest

		Period				Capacity
		1	**2**	**3**	**4**	
Period 1	Normal work	10	11	12	13	100
	Overtime	12	13	14	15	20
	Subcontract	15	16	17	18	60
Period 2	Normal work		10	11	12	100
	Overtime		12	13	14	20
	Subcontract		15	16	17	60
Period 3	Normal work			10	11	100
	Overtime			12	13	20
	Subcontract			15	16	60
Period 4	Normal work				10	100
	Overtime				12	20
	Subcontract				15	60
Demand		130	80	180	140	

Figure 11.15 Initial matrix for example.

cost is £12 for overtime, which has a capacity of 20 units. The shortage is still 10 units, which must be made by subcontracting. These amounts are subtracted from capacities.

Moving to period 2, the lowest cost is the £10 for normal work done in period 2, which can meet all demand.

Moving to period 3, the lowest cost is the £10 for normal work done in period 3. This can meet 100 of the demand. The next lowest cost is £11 for normal work done in period 2. There is still capacity of 20 units here, so this leaves a shortage of 60 units. The next lowest cost with spare capacity is £12 for overtime in period 3. This meets 20 units of demand, but there is still a shortage of 40 units. The next lowest cost is £13 for overtime in period 2. This meets 20 units of demand, but there is still a shortage of 20 units, which can best be met from subcontracting in period 3.

		Period 1	Period 2	Period 3	Period 4	Capacity
Period 1	Normal work	100 │10	— │11	— │12	— │13	0
	Overtime	20 │12	— │13	— │14	— │15	0
	Subcontract	10 │15	│16	│17	│18	50
Period 2	Normal work		80 │10	20 │11	— │12	0
	Overtime		│12	20 │13	— │14	0
	Subcontract		│15	│16	│17	60
Period 3	Normal work			100 │10	— │11	0
	Overtime			20 │12	— │13	0
	Subcontract			20 │15	│16	40
Period 4	Normal work				100 │10	0
	Overtime				20 │12	0
	Subcontract				20 │15	40
Demand		130	80	180	140	

Figure 11.16 Final solution for example.

This process is repeated for period 4, to give the results shown in Figure 11.16.

Mathematical models

The three approaches to aggregate planning we have described so far rely, at least to some extent, on the skills of the planner. We should ask if a more formal, mathematical approach could give better answers. Several methods have been proposed, usually based on linear programming. We can illustrate these by the following example. Do not worry too much about the details of this – we are only using an example to illustrate the approach.

we Worked example

When designing an aggregate plan the important factors are inventory levels, changes in production rate and availability of workers. There are costs for:

- supplying a unit of product

- holding stocks

- every unit of unmet demand

- amount of overtime used

- amount of undertime used (that is, normal working time which is not used)

- increase in production rate

- decrease in production rate.

The objective is to minimize total costs. Formulate this problem as a linear program.

Solution

We can start by defining the costs as:

C_V = variable cost of supplying a unit
C_H = cost of holding a unit of stock for a unit time
C_S = shortage cost per unit of unmet demand
C_O = additional cost per unit made with overtime
C_U = cost per unit of undertime
C_I = cost of increasing the production rate
C_R = cost of reducing the production rate

There are two other constants:

D_t = demand in period t
N_t = normal capacity in period t

Now we can define the variables:

P_t = production in period t
H_t = stock held at the end of period t
S_t = shortage, or unmet demand in period t
O_t = units produced on overtime in period t
U_t = units of undertime in period t
I_t = increase in production rate during period t
R_t = reduction in production rate during period t

With these values we can define the objective function as minimizing the total cost:

$$\text{Minimize} \sum (C_V P_t + C_H H_t + C_S S_t + C_O O_t + C_U U_t + C_I I_t + C_R R_t)$$

There are a number of constraints which hold for every period.

- Supply and demand must be balanced:

$$H_t = H_{t-1} + P_t - D_t + U_t$$

- Total production must equal normal production plus overtime minus undertime:

$$P_t = N_t + O_t - U_t$$

- Changes in production rates are consistent with production in each period:

$$P_t - P_{t-1} = I_t - R_t$$

As you can see, this approach needs some care and experience of linear programming.

Techniques like linear programming have the advantage of finding an optimal solution, in that total costs are minimized or some other objective is achieved. But they have the disadvantages of being complicated, difficult to understand, time consuming, expensive, needing a lot of reliable data, and the model still may not be a good description of the real situation. The example above is a very simple version of a real problem, but for a 12-month period it needs accurate values for seven costs, 24 constants, 84 variables and 36 constraints. Problems of this size are easy to tackle with suitable packages, but when other constraints and variables are added to make the model more realistic, it soon becomes unwieldy.

If you are thinking of using linear programming for an aggregate plan, you must balance the costs against the benefits. In oil companies and many other organizations, small variations from optimal plans give much higher costs so linear programming is always used for aggregate planning. In most other organizations small variations from optimal plans add relatively little extra cost. Then aggregate planning usually relies on intuitive, graphical or matrix methods.

ce Case example – Stevenson (Major Products) plc

Every month the Operations Manager of Stevenson (Major Products) plc, designs an aggregate plan to cover the next six months. This month she has the following information.

Period	1	2	3	4	5	6
Forecast	80	100	125	130	150	75

Costs are:

- Stock holding = £10 a unit held at the month end
- Shortage/back order cost = £100 a unit a month
- Cost of moving an employee to this product from other jobs = £400 per employee
- Cost of moving an employee from this product to other jobs = £300 per employee

Beginning inventory = 0
Beginning number of employees = 16
An average employee can produce 5 units per month.

Using these figures the operations manager did the calculations shown in Tables 11.1–11.3.

Table 11.1 Chase demand.

No	Period	1	2	3	4	5	6	Total
1	Aggregate demand	80	100	125	130	150	75	660
2	Cumulative aggregate demand	80	180	305	435	585	660	660
3	Production rate	80	100	125	130	150	75	660
4	Cumulative production	80	180	305	435	585	660	660
5	Ending inventory	0	0	0	0	0	0	0
6	Stockout/back order	0	0	0	0	0	0	
7	Inventory carrying cost (line 5 × £10)	0	0	0	0	0	0	0
8	Stockout cost (line 6 × £100)	0	0	0	0	0	0	0
9	No. of employees	16	20	25	26	30	15	
10	Cost of moving employees	0	1600	2000	400	1600	4500	10100
11	Total cost (line 7 + line 8 + line 10)	0	1600	2000	400	1600	4500	10100

Table 11.2 Constant production rate.

No	Description	1	2	3	4	5	6	Total
1	Forecasted demand	80	100	125	130	150	75	660
2	Cumulative forecasted demand	80	180	305	435	585	660	660
3	Production rate	110	110	110	110	110	110	660
4	Cumulative production	110	220	330	440	550	660	660
5	Ending inventory	30	40	25	5	0	0	100
6	Stockout/back order	0	0	0	0	35	0	35
7	Inventory carrying cost (line 5 × £10)	300	400	250	50	0	0	1000
8	Stockout cost (line 6 × £100)	0	0	0	0	3500	0	3500
9	Number of employees	22	22	22	22	22	22	
10	Cost of moving employees	2400	0	0	0	0	0	2400
11	Total cost (line 7 + line 8 + line 10)	2700	400	250	50	3500	0	6900

Table 11.3 Mixed policy – initial plan.

No	Description	1	2	3	4	5	6	Total
1	Forecasted demand	80	100	125	130	150	75	660
2	Cumulative forecasted demand	80	180	305	435	585	660	660
3	Production rate	90	90	130	130	130	90	660
4	Cumulative production	90	180	310	440	570	660	660
5	Ending inventory	10	0	5	5	0	0	20
6	Stockout/back order	0	0	0	0	15	0	15
7	Inventory carrying cost (line 5 × £10)	100	0	50	50	0	0	200
8	Stockout costs (line 6 × £100)	0	0	0	0	1500	0	1500
9	Number of employees	18	18	26	26	26	18	
10	Cost of moving employees	800	0	3200	0	0	2400	6400
11	Total cost	900	0	3250	50	1500	2400	8100

Questions

● Are the calculations the operations manager has done correct?

● Which of these three policies do you think is best?

● Can you suggest another policy that would be better?

Review questions

11.7 What period would a typical aggregate plan cover?

11.8 Aggregate plans show detailed production by individual product. Do you think this is true?

11.9 What is the main output of aggregate planning?

11.10 What are the benefits of intuitive aggregate planning?

11.11 How can a good aggregate plan be recognized from a graph?

11.12 What are the benefits of using a matrix method for aggregate planning?

11.13 What is the main benefit of using linear programming for aggregate planning?

Master production schedule

The aggregate plan shows the overall production of families of products. Once this aggregate plan is accepted, it is expanded to give more detail, which is shown in the **master production schedule**. The master production schedule 'disaggregates' the aggregate plan and shows the number of individual products to be made in, typically, each week. This gives a detailed timetable of planned output for each product, and is the first time due dates are put against individual products. An aggregate plan may show 1000 radiators being made next month, while the master production schedule gives details for each product with, say, 50 super radiators, 100 medium radiators and 25 cheaper radiators in week 1, 100 super radiators and 25 medium radiators in week 2, and so on.

The master production schedule is derived from the aggregate plan. So the overall production in the master production schedule must equal the production specified in the aggregate plan. There may be some differences to allow for short-term variations, incorrect forecasts, capacity constraints and so on, but these should be small.

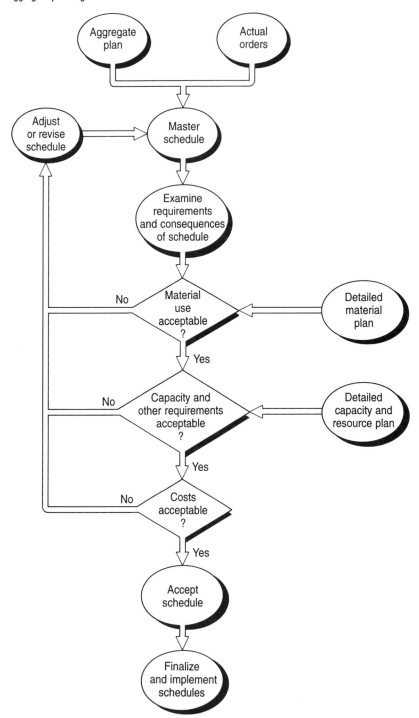

Figure 11.17 Procedure for designing master schedule.

The **master production schedule** gives a detailed timetable for making individual products. This timetable should allow the aggregate plan to be achieved as efficiently as possible.

In principle, designing the master production schedule is similar to designing an aggregate plan. But it deals with more detail, often down to individual customer orders, so it can be much more difficult. Because of the complications and subjective decisions needed, the usual way of designing master production schedules is to use skilled schedulers. They can expand the aggregate plan, probably using spreadsheets, and use their experience to modify previous plans to get good results.

Designing a master production schedule starts by looking at short-term demand as the higher of:

- production specified by the aggregate plan;

- actual customer orders booked for the period.

We know that forecasts are not totally accurate, so this gives the first chance to compare actual customer orders with forecast demand. Most organizations want to avoid shortages so the demand is set at the higher of these two. Some of this demand can be met from stock, so current stock levels and production capacities are compared and a schedule is designed to make up any differences. As before, an iterative approach is used, as shown in Figure 11.17. This iterative procedure can take place up to, say, three weeks before the master production schedule is implemented. As it is the final plan that is used for scheduling operations, the plan must be fixed at some point with no further changes allowed.

we Worked example

Comark Bicycles produce two basic types of bicycle, women's and men's. The aggregate plan has 8000 bicycles made next month, and 6400 the month after. Current stocks are 500 men's and 300 women's, and the factory has a capacity of 2200 bicycles a week. Men's bicycles usually account for 60% of sales, and actual orders have been received for the following deliveries:

Week	1	2	3	4	5	6
Men's	1400	1200	1000	700	300	–
Women's	2000	800	400	100	–	–

Design a master production schedule for the next eight weeks.

Solution

There are unexpectedly high sales for women's bicycles in the first two weeks. As there are 300 in stock, 1700 have to be made to meet orders in the first week. Even using the full capacity of 2200 bicycles a week, this leaves only enough capacity for 500 men's bicycles. These, together with current stocks of 500, still leave a shortage of 400 men's bicycles which must be met by back orders.

In the second week, the back orders for 400 men's bicycles can be cleared together with the 1200 actually ordered. This leaves only capacity for 600 women's bicycles, so 200 must be back-ordered to meet the 800 orders.

The aggregate plan calls for 8000 bicycles the first month. 4400 were made in the first two weeks, so an additional 1800 should be made in each of the last two weeks. In week 3 the back orders for 200 women's can be cleared, plus the 1400 ordered (both men's and women's), and an additional 200 for stock (say 100 men's and 100 women's). In week 4 dividing the 1800 into 1080 men's and 720 women's (to match the expected 60:40 ratio) covers all orders and adds spare units to stock.

In weeks 5 to 8, the planned production of 6400 can be divided into weekly production of 1600 (960 men's and 640 women's). So far there are only orders for 300 units in this period, so the rest are added to stock.

The whole process gives the master production schedule shown in Table 11.4.

The build-up of stock in later weeks shows that this production has not yet been allocated to customers and shows the stock levels if no more orders are received.

This is, of course, only one of many feasible schedules. It has the advantages of meeting the aggregate plan and keeping production at a stable level, but iterative improvements could now be made. This is where spread-sheets are particularly useful.

Table 11.4

Week	1	2	3	4	5	6	7	8
Men's								
Actual orders	1400	1200	1000	700	300	–	–	–
Opening stock	500	−400	0	100	480	1140	2100	3060
Production	500	1600	1100	1080	960	960	960	960
Women's								
Actual orders	2000	800	400	100	–	–	–	–
Opening stock	300	0	−200	100	720	1360	2000	2640
Production	1700	600	700	720	640	640	640	640
Total production	2200	2200	1800	1800	1600	1600	1600	1600
Aggregate plan	←	8000		→	←	6400		→

You can see from this example that schedulers must have a number of skills. They must be able to:

- identify all known demands – forecasts, actual sales, internal transfers

- keep within the aggregate plan

- ensure existing customer orders are met

- balance the needs of production, marketing, finance and all other functions

- identify problems and resolve them

- communicate well with all functions.

These skills are scarce and can take a long time to develop.

At this stage of planning we have a detailed production plan for each product. But this is not the end of planning. Now we have to take this plan and see what resources it needs, how these resources should be scheduled, what people are needed, when we need to buy raw materials, and so on. This next stage of planning, then, takes the tactical master production schedule and uses it to design short-term schedules. There are several ways of doing this. Some of these use material requirements planning; others use just-in-time systems; others look for specific approaches to short-term scheduling. We will describe some of these in the following chapters.

Review questions

11.15 What is the main purpose of the master production schedule?

11.16 What constraints are put on the master production schedule?

ce Case example – Amunsen Classical Furniture

Amunsen Classical Furniture makes a range of reproduction antique furniture at its factory outside Stockholm. It has three product lines – for tables, chairs and other items. Its planning can be outlined as follows.

The Mission is an agreed statement of the Directors, which states the overall aim of the company. The Business Strategy is prepared by the Directors, and shows what the company plans to do over the next five to 10 years.

The Managing Director of the company designs a business plan for the next year. This business plan is based on projected sales and available capacity, and gives an overall view of the company's operations. Target figures are found for each month, as illustrated in Table 11.5.

Table 11.5 Summarized business plan (with values in pounds).

	January	February	March	April	...	...	...	Dec.
Sales	1,500,000	1,250,000	1,100,000	...	...	...	...	
Cost of sales	550,000	500,000	400,000	...	...	...		
Other costs	900,000	650,000	650,000	...	...			
Profit	50,000	100,000	150,000	...				
Assets employed	...	...	...	...				

The Production Manager designs the aggregate plan to show planned production over the next 12 months. The inputs to the aggregate plan include the business plan, machine capacities, workforce size and so on. These plans are updated monthly (see Table 11.6).

Table 11.6 Summarized aggregate plan (in units).

Product line	January	February	March	April	...	...	Dec.
1. Tables	100	110	180	...	...		
2. Chairs	690	750	400	...			
3. Others	850	850	600	...			

The Master Scheduler produces the master production schedule to give production of each type of furniture over the next three months. The inputs to the master production plan include the aggregate production plan, actual production, customer orders, available machine capacities. This is updated weekly (see Table 11.7).

Table 11.7 Summarized master production schedule (in units).

Product	Week 1	Week 2	Week 3	Week 4	5	6	7	8	9	10
Table A10	25									
Table B20		30	30							
Table C30				15						
Chair K11	250									
Chair L22		1000	1000							
Chair M33				2400						
Quilt stand X19		250								
Magazine rack Y29			400							
Book case Z39	200									

Questions

• Does Amunsen's approach to planning seem reasonable?

• Can you give examples of other companies' planning?

Chapter review

• Planning starts with the mission and business strategy. This leads to a series of other strategic plans, including operations strategy.

• Capacity planning is essentially a strategic function that matches available capacity to forecast demand. Typically, capacity plans set the output of each facility over the next few years. This is the first step in a hierarchy of decisions about resource planning.

• The next stage adds details to the capacity plans to gives aggregate plans. Aggregate planning takes the forecast demand and capacity plans and translates these into schedules for each family of products, typically for each of the next few months. The main aims of aggregate planning are to meet demand while keeping production stable.

• Four methods were suggested for aggregate planning, based on intuition, a graphical method, a matrix method and linear programming.

• Details are added to the aggregate plans to give the master production schedules. This gives production of individual products per week. Designing a master production schedule is similar in principle to designing an aggregate plan, but the increased details can make it more complicated.

• In following chapters we shall see how the master production schedule is used to give short-term schedules. Then the whole planning process is summarized in Figure 11.18.

• There is a general procedure for planning. This starts by finding the requirements set by the previous stage of planning. These requirements are broken down into more detail, and alternative plans are designed to meet them. The alternatives plans are compared and the best is implemented.

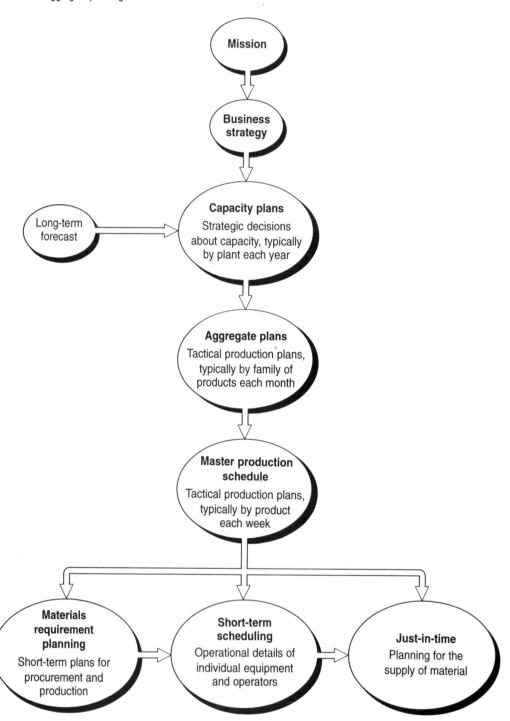

Figure 11.18 Summary of the planning process.

Key terms

CS Case study – Natural Home Brewers

In 1932 James Galloway founded Natural Home Brewers in Port Merdoch on the East coast of Scotland. At the time, all the local pubs were owned by three national brewers, but a small number of independent clubs sold speciality beer, mainly imported from Scandinavia and Germany. James founded Natural Home Brewers to sell his locally brewed beer to these clubs.

The local government encouraged new industries in the area and gave James a grant. He used this, together with a personal loan from the bank, to start his company. He did most of the work himself, with help from his brother and wife.

There was a clear demand for their beers, but James was more interested in traditional brewing for the local market, than making large profits. By 1945 the company was brewing 1500 gallons a week and employed six people. Then there was a sudden surge in demand as new clubs opened in the area, and a number of pubs began selling Natural Home Brew as a special attraction. By 1955 Natural Home Brewers was employing 120 people. At this point a national brewery made a generous offer and bought the company.

The new owners were keen to maintain the image of Natural Home Brewers and kept the name and brands. They started selling the products in their own pubs, as well as maintaining the original markets. By 1990 Natural Home Brewers employed 1500 people. During various expansions the brewing had been largely automated and although customers thought they were buying from a local brewery, they were buying a standard product that was little different to any other.

The brewery was now having trouble with its planning. Several of its most experienced production planners had retired in the same year, and the current planning often seemed haphazard. In particular, there were times when it had trouble meeting demand. Management felt it was time to change their planning procedures, and find some way of guaranteeing reasonable plans. The description of these procedures was the first step in computerizing the whole planning process.

Table 11.8

Month	Demand	Month	Demand
January	9,000	May	6,000
February	8,000	June	8,000
March	6,000	July	10,000
April	4,000	August	10,000

A sample of data was collected for an eight-month period, and agreement was reached about a range of variables. Forecast demand for this period was found, in barrels, as shown in Table 11.8.

Costs and manpower requirement were agreed. Although these were not necessarily exact figures they could be used for comparing plans. These included:

- production cost of £200 a barrel

- storage cost of 1.5% of production cost a month

- shortage cost of £10 a barrel a month

- 5 man-hours to produce a barrel

- direct labour force of 225

- standard wage rate of £8 an hour

- overtime wage rate of 1.5 times standard rate

- a standard working week of five days

- hiring and training cost of £400 a person

- lay-off cost of £500 a person

- subcontractors can be used at an additional cost of £5 a barrel

- opening stock is 2000 barrels

- a reserve stock is kept of 25% of forecast monthly demand

- all shortages are back-ordered

- the three main products are lager, bitter and mild which generally account for 50%, 40% and 10% of sales respectively.

Question

The management of Natural Home Brewers now want you to design:

- a set of alternative aggregate plans for the eight-month period

- a comparison of costs for these plans

- a recommendation for the best plan

- a procedure for developing reliable aggregate plans in the future

- a suggested master production schedule

- a procedure for developing reliable master production schedules in the future.

Problems

11.1 A machine makes two different products A and B. The machine works for 250 days a year, with two eight-hour shifts a day and a utilization of 95%. Other information is as follows.

	A	B
Forecast annual demand	2100	5600
Time to make one unit (hours)	2.0	1.5
Batch size	50	100
Setup time per batch (hours)	5	6

If the company currently has three identical machines, how could it start capacity planning?

11.2 The monthly demand for a family of products is shown below. Use intuitive reasoning to suggest an aggregate production schedule for the products.

Month	1	2	3	4	5	6	7
Aggregate demand	90	120	100	120	180	270	225

11.3 The forecast monthly demand for a family of products is shown below. At the end of each month a notional holding cost of £20 is assigned to every unit held in stock. If there are shortages 20% of orders are lost with a cost of £200 a unit, and the rest are met by back orders, with a cost of £50 a unit. Each time the production rate is changed it costs £15,000. Designed capacity of the system is 400 units a month, but utilization seldom reaches 80%. Use a graphical method to design an aggregate plan for the products.

Month	1	2	3	4	5	6	7	8
Aggregate demand	310	280	260	300	360	250	160	100

11.4   The aggregate demand for a family of products for the next five months is 190, 120, 270, 200 and 140. Normal capacity is 150 units a month, overtime has a capacity of 10 a month and subcontractors can handle any amount of production. The unit cost is £100 for normal capacity, £125 for overtime and £140 from subcontractors. It costs £15 to stock a unit for a month, while back orders have a penalty cost of £100 a month. Use a matrix method to design an aggregate plan for the products.

11.5   The aggregate plan of a manufacturer has 12,000, 10,000 and 10,000 units made in the next three months. A master production schedule is needed for the two products, A and B. Current stocks are 700 of A and 500 of B, and the factory has a capacity of 3000 units a week. Sales of A are usually twice as large as sales of B, and actual orders have been received for deliveries of:

Week	1	2	3	4	5	6	7
A	2100	1800	1600	1100	800	200	–
B	3000	1400	700	400	100	–	–

Design a master production schedule for the next 12 weeks.

Discussion questions

11.1   Where would you start the planning process? What results would you want? What inputs are needed?

11.2   Planning for services is particularly difficult. As there are no stocks of services, production must exactly match demand. How can long-term planning be done?

11.3   What hierarchy of decisions are needed in planning? Do you think this hierarchy will exist in every organization?

11.4   How far ahead does each stage of planning look? Give specific examples to show the variation in this.

11.5   What are planning cycles? How frequently should aggregate plans and master production schedules be updated?

11.6   What costs should be considered in aggregate plans?

11.7   Why is planning so difficult? Do you think that computers could replace human schedulers?

11.8   Spreadsheets are widely used in planning. Why? Design a spreadsheet that could be used for designing a master production schedule.

Selected references

Berry W.L., Vollmann T.E. and Whybark D.C. (1979). *Master Production Scheduling: Principles and Practice*. Falls Church, Va.: American Production and Inventory Control Society.

Buffa E.S. and Miller J.G. (1979). *Production-Inventory Systems: Planning and Control* (3rd edn). Homewood, Ill.: Richard Irwin.

Freeland J. and Landel R. (1984). *Aggregate Production Planning: Text and Cases*. Reston: Reston Publishing.

Glueck W.F. and Jauch L.R. (1984). *Business Policy and Strategic Planning*. New York: McGraw-Hill.

McLeavey D. and Narasimhan S.L. (1985). *Production Planning and Inventory Control*. Boston: Allyn and Bacon.

Salvendy G. (ed.) (1982). *Handbook of Industrial Engineering*. New York: John Wiley.

Vollman T.E., Berry W.L. and Whybark D.C. (1988). *Manufacturing Planning and Control Systems* (2nd edn). Homewood, Ill.: Richard Irwin.

12 Materials requirements planning

Contents

Objectives

After reading this chapter you should be able to:

- describe material requirements planning (MRP)
- say when MRP can be used
- use MRP to timetable orders and operations
- discuss the advantages and disadvantages of MRP
- use a batching rule for MRP orders
- outline ways in which MRP can be extended

Material requirements planning approach

In the last chapter we looked at tactical planning. This uses strategic plans to get aggregate plans and master production schedules. These schedules typically show the amount of each product to make in each week.

In the next four chapters we shall look at the remaining stages of planning. These move from the master production schedule down to detailed operational timetables. There are several ways of getting these short-term schedules. In this chapter we shall look at the planning of materials needed to support operations. This is the basis of **material requirements planning**. In the next chapter we shall see an alternative view of scheduling which gives **just-in-time** operations. In Chapter 14 we shall look at **short-term scheduling** for other resources. Then Chapter 15 describes the most detailed level of planning in **job design**. A summary of the planning process is shown in Figure 12.1.

Materials requirement planning (MRP) expands the master production schedule to give a detailed timetable for the delivery of material needed to support operations.

> **Material requirements planning** uses the master schedule to plan the supply of materials. It expands the master schedule so that materials can be scheduled to arrive when they are needed.

MRP uses planned production to get a timetable for material orders. So the resulting stocks of materials depend directly on the known demand. This kind of system is called a **dependent demand inventory system** – the inventory depends on known demand.

The alternative to MRP is to keep stocks of materials that are high enough to cover any likely demand. These stocks are not directly related to the demand shown in a master production schedule, but are forecast from historical figures. The result is an **independent demand inventory system** (which we shall describe in Chapter 18). You can see the differences in the way a chef plans the ingredients for a week's meals. The MRP approach looks at the meals to be cooked each day, uses this to find the ingredients needed, and then makes sure these are delivered in time. An independent demand system sees what ingredients were used in previous weeks and make sure there is enough of these in stock to cover likely demand.

An important difference between the two approaches is the pattern of material stocks. With MRP, stocks are generally low but rise as orders are delivered just before production starts. The stock is then used during production and declines to its normal, low level. This pattern is shown in Figure 12.2(a). With independent demand systems, the stocks are not related to production plans so they must be higher. Stocks are reduced during

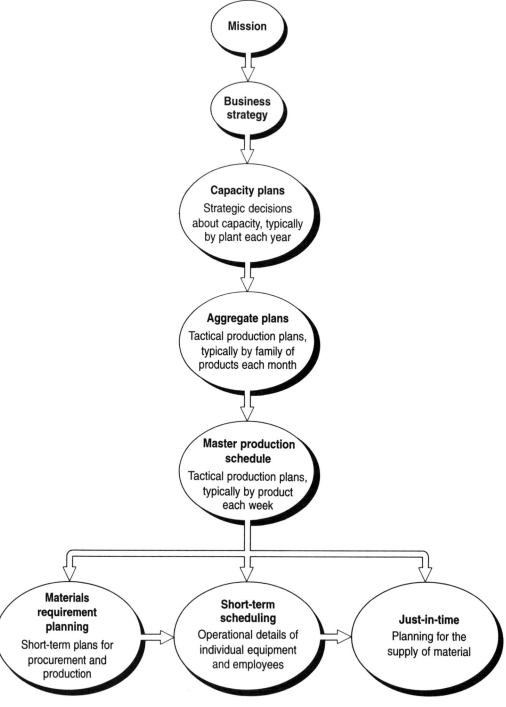

Figure 12.1 Summary of the planning process.

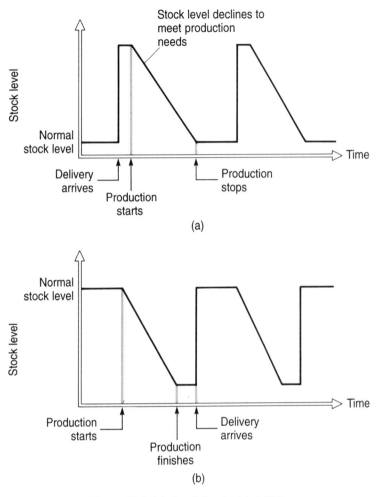

Figure 12.2 (a) Stock level with MRP;
(b) stock level with independent demand system.

production, but they are replenished as soon as possible to give the pattern shown in Figure 12.2(b).

Dependent demand inventory systems are most often used for raw materials. Independent demand inventory systems are most often used for finished goods. MRP has many calculations, and in the past organizations have tried to avoid these by using independent demand systems to control stocks of raw materials – with mixed success. If a company makes bicycles then the numbers of pedals, saddles and wheels it needs are directly related to the number of bicycles it makes. If you are going to make 1000 bicycles next month, you will need 2000 pedals, 1000 saddles, 2000 wheels, and so on. The demand for these parts clearly depends on the production of bicycles – so it should be found from the production schedule and not from forecasts.

MRP was originally designed for manufacturing industries. It is still used most widely used in mass production processes, but it has been adopted by many other industries. For convenience, we shall often use the original terms, which includes talk of components being delivered to make products.

Review questions

12.1   What is MRP?

12.2   What are the important differences between dependent demand inventory systems and independent demand systems?

The MRP procedure

MRP needs a lot of information about products so, in practice, it is always computerized. Its main inputs come from three data files:

- master production schedule
- bill of materials
- inventory records.

The MRP procedure starts with the master production schedule. This gives the number of every product to be made in every period. Then MRP 'explodes' the master production schedule using a **bill of materials** to give details of the materials needed.

A bill of materials is an ordered list of all parts that are needed to make a particular product. It shows not only the materials, parts and components needed, but also the order in which they are used. Suppose, for example, a table is made from a top and four legs. The bill of materials is shown in Figure 12.3,

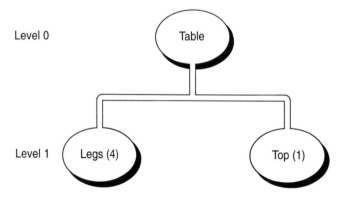

Figure 12.3 Bill of materials for a table.

where the figures in brackets show the numbers needed to make each unit. You can see from this diagram that every item is given a 'level' number that shows where it fits into the process. The finished product is level 0; level 1 items are used directly to make the level 0 item; level 2 items are used to make the level 1 items, and so on.

If we look at the table in more detail we might see that each top is made from a wood kit and hardware, and that the wood kit has four oak planks which are 2 m long, 30 cm wide and 2.5 cm thick, and so on. Part of this more detailed bill of materials is shown in Figure 12.4. Every product has a bill of materials that is prepared either by the designers of the product, or production engineers.

We can use this example of a table to show the overall approach of MRP. Suppose the master production schedule has 10 tables to be made in February. This means we need 10 tops and 40 legs ready to be assembled at the beginning of February.

In practice this gives us the **gross requirements** for parts. Not all the gross requirements need to be ordered, as there may be some stocks already

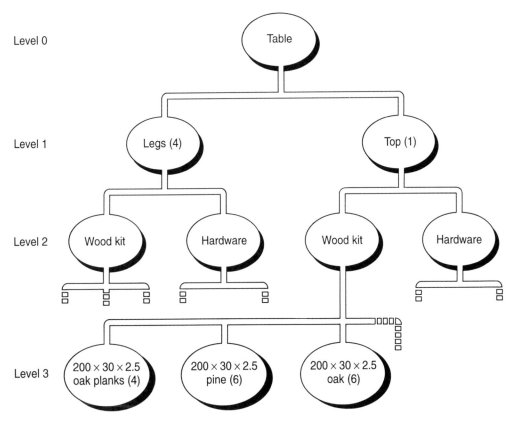

Figure 12.4 Partial bill of materials for a table.

available and orders that have been placed and are due to arrive shortly. If we subtract these from the gross requirements we find the net requirements for materials:

Net requirements = gross requirement − current stock − stock on order

Now we have the quantities to order, and when these orders should arrive. The next step is to find the time the orders must be placed. For this we need to know the lead times so that orders can be placed this lead time before the materials are actually needed. Finding the time to place orders in this way is called **time shifting**. If we buy the table tops and legs from suppliers who give a lead time of four weeks, we need to place orders at the beginning of January. These orders will arrive by the end of January just before assembly is due to start.

Finally, we may have to consider some other information about orders, such as minimum quantities, discounts, and so on. When all this is taken into

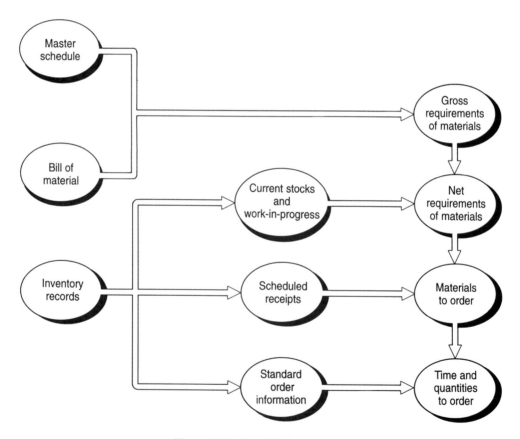

Figure 12.5 The MRP procedure.

account we can design the detailed timetable for orders. This procedure is summarized in Figure 12.5.

The MRP procedure

(1) Use the master schedule to find the gross requirements of level 0 items.

(2) Subtract any stock on hand to give the net requirements of level 0 items, and schedule production to start so these net requirements can be made in time.

(3) If there are any more levels of materials, use the bill of materials to translate the net requirements from the last level into gross requirements for the next level. If there are no more levels go to step 5.

(4) Take each of the materials in turn and:
- subtract the stock on hand and scheduled deliveries to find the quantities of materials to order
- use the lead time and any other relevant information to find the time of orders

Go to step 3.

(5) When there are no more levels of materials, finalize the timetable.

we Worked example

Johnson's Furniture assembles dining room tables using bought-in parts of four legs and a top. These have lead times of two and three weeks respectively, and assembly takes a week. The company receive orders for 20 tables to be delivered in week 5 of a planning period and 40 tables in week 7. It has current stocks of 2 complete tables, 40 legs and 22 tops. When should it order parts?

Solution

Johnson's production schedule for dining room tables is shown below. This gives the gross requirements for level 0 items – which are tables. Subtracting the stocks of finished tables gives the net requirements. Then allowing a week for assembly gives the start times shown in the following assembly plan.

Week		*Level 0 – dining room tables*					
	1	2	3	4	5	6	7
Gross requirements					20		40
Opening stock	2	2	2	2	2		
Net requirements					18		40
Start assembly				18		40	
Scheduled receipts					18		40

The 'scheduled receipts' show the number of units that become available in a week, which is the number started the lead time previously.

The bill of materials for this problem has already been shown in Figure 12.3. This can be used with the assembly plans to find gross requirements for level 1 items (legs and tops). In week 4 there is a net requirement of 18 tables, which translates into a gross requirement of 72 legs and 18 tops. Similarly, the gross requirements for other parts are:

- legs: $18 \times 4 = 72$ in week 4 and $40 \times 4 = 160$ in week 6

- tops: 18 in week 4 and 40 in week 6.

Subtracting stock on hand from these gross requirements gives the net requirements. To make sure the parts arrive on time, they must be ordered the lead time in advance – that is 2 weeks for legs and 3 weeks for tops.

Week		*Level 1 – legs*					
	1	2	3	4	5	6	7
Gross requirements				72		160	
Opening stock	40	40	40	40			
Net requirements				32		160	
Place order		32		160			
Scheduled receipts				32		160	

Week		*Level 1 – tops*					
	1	2	3	4	5	6	7
Gross requirements				18		40	
Opening stock	22	22	22	22	4	4	
Net requirements						36	
Place order			36				
Scheduled receipts						36	

There are no more levels of materials, so we can finalize the time table of events:

- week 2: order 32 legs

- week 3: order 36 tops

- week 4: order 160 legs and assemble 18 tables

- week 6: assemble 40 tables.

we Worked example

A production schedule needs 45 units of a product in week 9 of a cycle, 60 units in week 10 and 40 units in week 13. There are currently 10 units of the product in stock, but the company always keeps 5 units in reserve to cover emergency orders. Each unit of the product takes two weeks to assemble from 2 units of part B and 3 units of part C. Each unit of part B is made in one week from 1 unit of material D and three units of material E. Part C is assembled in 2 weeks from two units of component F. Lead times for D, E and F are 1, 2 and 3 weeks respectively. Current stocks are 50 units of B, 100 of C, 40 of D, 360 of E and 100 of F. The company keeps minimum stocks of 20 units of D, 100 of E and 50 of F. The minimum order size for E is 300 units, while F can only be ordered in discrete batches of 100 units. Orders already placed for 10 units of D will arrive in week 6; 300 units of E will arrive in week 7; 20 units of F will arrive in week 6; and 20 units of C will arive in week 8. Design a timetable of activities for the company.

Solution

As you can see, even a simple MRP problem needs a lot of calculations and gets very complicated. In practice a computer is always used. The printout shown in Figure 12.6 from a simple program shows the results for this problem.

The program starts at level 0, with production of the final product, A. The company keeps a minimum stock of 5 units of A, so this reserved stock must be remembered when calculating the net requirements. Then it moves on to level 1 materials and expands the assembly plan for A into gross requirements for components B and C. The 40 units of A assembled in week 7 is expanded into gross requirements of 80 units of part B and 120 units of part C. The 60 units of A assembled in week 8 is expanded into gross requirements of 120 units of B and 180 units of C, and so on.

Gross requirements for B and C can be partly met from opening stocks, with the shortfall shown as net requirements. We must also remember the

```
                        Material Requirements Planning

   Number of Time Periods :          13
   Bill of Materials

                                         End Item
                                            |
      ---------------------------------
      |               |
      X               X
      |               |
-------         -------
|   |           |
X   X           X
```

```
Level 0 - End Item
 Item Number: Part-0                      Beginning Inventory:      10
 Description: Product A                   Lead Time:                 2
                                          Safety Stock:              5
                                          Lot Size:                  1
```

	Week 6	Week 7	Week 8	Week 9	Week 10	Week 11	Week 12	Week 13
Gross Requirements :	0	0	0	45	60	0	0	40
Available :	10	10	10	10	5	5	5	5
Net Requirements :	0	0	0	40	60	0	0	40
Receipts :	0	0	0	40	60	0	0	40
Requests :	0	40	60	0	0	40	0	0

```
Level 1 - Comp 1
 Item Number: Part-1                      Beginning Inventory:      50
 Description: Part-B                      Lead Time:                 1
 Bill of Materials: 2                     Safety Stock:              0
                                          Lot Size:                  1
```

	Week 6	Week 7	Week 8	Week 9	Week 10	Week 11	Week 12	Week 13
Gross Requirements :	0	80	120	0	0	80	0	0
Available :	50	50	0	0	0	0	0	0
Net Requirements :	0	30	120	0	0	80	0	0
Receipts :	0	30	120	0	0	80	0	0
Requests :	30	120	0	0	80	0	0	0

```
Level 2 - Comp 1-1
 Item Number: Part-2                      Beginning Inventory:      40
 Description: Material-D                  Lead Time:                 1
 Bill of Materials: 1                     Safety Stock:             20
                                          Lot Size:                  1
```

	Week 6	Week 7	Week 8	Week 9	Week 10	Week 11	Week 12	Week 13
Gross Requirements :	30	120	0	0	80	0	0	0
Available :	40	20	20	20	20	20	20	20
Net Requirements :	10	120	0	0	80	0	0	0
Receipts :	10	120	0	0	80	0	0	0
Requests :	120	0	0	80	0	0	0	0

Figure 12.6 Computer printout for Worked example.

Level 2 - Comp 1-2
```
Item Number: Part-3                    Beginning Inventory:        360
Description: Material-E                 Lead Time:                    2
Bill of Materials: 3                   Safety Stock:               100
                                       Lot Size:                   300
```

	Week 6	Week 7	Week 8	Week 9	Week 10	Week 11	Week 12	Week 13
Gross Requirements :	90	360	0	0	240	0	0	0
Available :	360	270	210	210	210	270	270	270
Net Requirements :	0	190	0	0	130	0	0	0
Receipts :	0	300	0	0	300	0	0	0
Requests :	0	0	300	0	0	0	0	0

Level 1 - Comp 2
```
Item Number: Part-4                    Beginning Inventory:        100
Description: Part-C                     Lead Time:                    2
Bill of Materials: 3                   Safety Stock:                 0
                                       Lot Size:                     1
```

	Week 6	Week 7	Week 8	Week 9	Week 10	Week 11	Week 12	Week 13
Gross Requirements :	0	120	180	0	0	120	0	0
Available :	100	100	0	0	0	0	0	0
Net Requirements :	0	20	180	0	0	120	0	0
Receipts :	0	20	180	0	0	120	0	0
Requests :	180	0	0	120	0	0	0	0

Level 2 - Comp 2-1
```
Item Number: Part-5                    Beginning Inventory:        100
Description: ComponentF                Lead Time:                    3
Bill of Materials: 2                   Safety Stock:                50
                                       Lot Size:                   100
```

	Week 6	Week 7	Week 8	Week 9	Week 10	Week 11	Week 12	Week 13
Gross Requirements :	360	0	0	240	0	0	0	0
Available :	100	140	140	140	100	100	100	100
Net Requirements :	310	0	0	150	0	0	0	0
Receipts :	400	0	0	200	0	0	0	0
Requests :	200	0	0	0	0	0	0	0

Figure 12.6 *(cont.)* Computer printout for Worked example.

planned delivery of 20 units of part C in week 7. This schedule for level 1 parts can now be expanded to give the timetable for level 2 items.

The gross requirements for materials D and E are found from the assembly plans for part B. 30 units of B are started in week 6 and this expands into gross requirements for 30 units of D and 90 units of E, and so on. One complication here is the minimum order size of 300 units of E. In week 7 there is a gross requirement of 360 for material E, 170 of which can be met from free stock (keeping the reserve stock of 100). The net requirement is 190, but 300 have to be ordered with the spare 110 added to stock.

Finally, the gross requirements for component F can be found from the assembly plan for part C. 180 units of C are started in week 6 so this expands into a gross requirement of 360 units of F, and so on. Orders must be in discrete batches of 100 units, so they are rounded to the nearest hundred above net requirements.

- **Week 6** start making 30 of B and 180 of C
  place orders for 120 units of D and 200 units of F
  orders arrive for 10 units of D and 400 units of F

- **Week 7** start making 40 of A and 120 of B
  finish 30 units of B
  orders arrive for 20 units of C, 120 units of D and 300 units of E

- **Week 8** start making 60 of A
  finish 120 units of B and 180 units of C
  place order for 300 units of E

- **Week 9** finish making 40 units of A
  start making 120 of C
  place order for 80 units of D
  order arrives for 200 units of F

- **Week 10** finish 60 units of A
  start making 80 units of B
  orders arrive for 80 units of D and 300 units of E

- **Week 11** start making 40 units of A
  finish 80 units of B and 120 units of C

- **Week 13** finish 40 units of A.

Review questions

12.3   MRP is only used by manufacturers. Do you think this is true?

12.4   What information is needed for MRP?

12.5   How is the net requirement for a material found in MRP?

Benefits and disadvantages of MRP

Traditional independent demand inventory systems use forecasts to find likely demand and then hold stocks that are high enough to meet these.

Unfortunately, we know that there are almost always unavoidable errors in forecasts. To allow for these errors, organizations hold more stocks than they really need to give extra safety – but the inventory costs also rise. MRP avoids these costs by relating the supply of materials directly to demand. The result is much lower stocks and associated costs. We can list some direct benefits of MRP as:

- lower stock levels, with savings in capital, space, warehousing

- higher stock turn-over

- better customer service – with fewer delays caused by shortages of materials

- more reliable and faster delivery times

- higher utilization of facilities – as materials are always available when needed

- less time spent on expediting and emergency orders

- encourages better planning

- MRP schedules can be used for short-term planning

- assigns priorities for jobs on the shop floor.

As MRP is based on a master production schedule, organizations are more likely to design a reliable plan and stick to it. The result is better planning. The MRP analyses can also give early warning of potential problems and shortages. If necessary, expediting can be used to speed up deliveries, or production plans can be changed. In this way MRP improves the wider performance of the organization, measured in terms of equipment utilization, productivity, customer service, response to market conditions, and so on.

Another broader benefit from MRP comes from its detailed analyses which can highlight problems that have previously been hidden. If, for example, a supplier is unreliable this may not be noticed – as any problems are avoided by keeping higher stocks. This effectively hides the problem, but increases costs. It would be better to recognize the problem and take steps to solve it, either by changing the supplier or discussing ways of improving their reliability.

In contrast to these advantages, there are also some disadvantages with MRP. The most obvious disadvantage is the information that is needed before MRP can be used. The process starts with a detailed master production schedule that must be designed some time in advance, so MRP can not be used if:

- there is no master production schedule

- the master production schedule is inaccurate

- plans are frequently changed

- plans are not made far enough in advance.

We have also seen the other requirements of MRP, which include a bill of materials, information about current stocks, orders outstanding, lead times, and other information about suppliers.

Many organizations simply do not have this information. Other organizations find their information does not have enough detail or the right format for MRP. Yet other organizations find their data is not accurate enough. Inventory files, for example, are updated with every transaction, but this gives a lot of chances for errors. Ordinarily small errors might not be important, but when the production depends on the results, even small errors become important.

Even when all the information is available, the complexity of MRP systems can give difficulties. You can see from the examples above that very simple situations can give a lot of data manipulation. This means that MRP can only be used when all related systems are computerized. MRP is not a new idea, but it has only become practical with cheap computing.

We have already described the inputs of an MRP system. Now we can look at the outputs, which include:

- **Timetable** of orders and other operations.

- **Planned orders** to implement the proposed timetable.

- **Changes to previous plans** whenever the master production schedule is revised, or any other changes are made, the MRP schedules are updated – giving changes to order quantities, cancelled or changed orders, and changes of due dates.

- **Exceptions** the system may note exceptions that need management action, including late orders, excessive scrap, requests for non-existent parts, and so on.

- **Performance reports** which show how well the system is working and might include measures for investment in stocks, inventory turn-over, and number of stockouts.

- **Planning reports** which can be used in longer term planning decisions.

- **Records of inventory transactions** allowing the system to maintain accurate records of current stock and to check on progress.

These elements of a computerized MRP system are summarized in Figure 12.7.

One problem you can see with MRP systems is that they can generate a huge quantity of reports. This must be summarized so that it does not

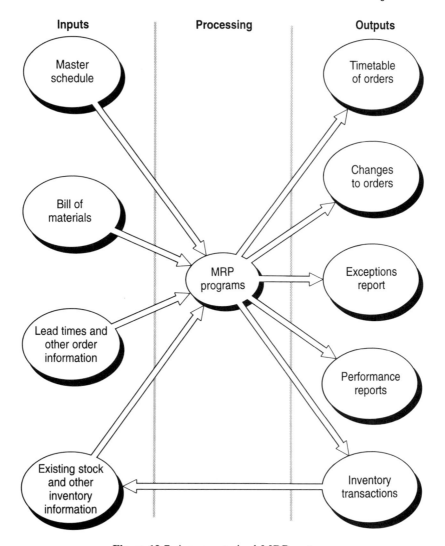

| Inputs | Processing | Outputs |

Figure 12.7 A computerized MRP system.

swamp managers, especially as MRP programs are usually run every week. You can see why some people say that MRP stands for More Reams of Paper.

The limited conditions where MRP can be used and the amount of data manipulation are the main disadvantage with MRP, but there are others. It might, for example, reduce flexibility in responding to changes. Stocks are expensive, but they allow plans to be changed at short notice. With MRP the only materials that are available are those which are needed for the specified master production schedule. Other disadvantages are:

- MRP assumes lead times are constant and independent of the quantities ordered;

- in practice materials are made in a different order to that specified in the bill of materials;

- if MRP is used to schedule the production of parts this may give poor schedules;

- MRP may not recognize capacity and other constraints;

- it can be expensive and time consuming (typically 18 to 24 months) to implement.

Review questions

12.6 What is the main advantage of MRP?

12.7 What is the main problem with using MRP?

12.8 What are typical outputs from an MRP system?

CE **Case example** – Alco Office Supplies

Alco Office Supplies makes a range of desks, filing cabinets and other office furniture. In 1979 it introduced MRP for the manufacture of standard filing cabinets. The manufacturing process was simple, and with the help of a consultant, a new system was working in slightly less than a year at a cost of £80,000. By the end of the second year the system was judged a success and was extended to other products.

Alco's move to MRP illustrates the amount of information needed. Although it had integrated computer systems, these had to be thoroughly checked and overhauled before they were reliable enough for MRP. The biggest single job was getting data in a suitable form. Some of the old systems updated data records overnight. These had to be replaced with real-time systems, with all data files consolidated into a company-wide database.

Alco's experience also shows the complexity of real MRP systems. Its standard four-drawer filing cabinet is assembled from 162 different parts. Many of these are small and duplicated, but exploding the master production schedule needed a lot of calculations. It makes 24 variations on this basic filing cabinet, and a total of 3500 different products. Each of these needed a separate MRP run, and then common parts were combined into larger orders.

On its first trial run of the MRP system, the weekly report was over 8000 pages long. Needless to say, when the system became operational this was trimmed to 200 pages. You can get a feel for this report from the simplified printout in Figure 12.8.

```
--------------------------------------------------------------------------------
                   ***** ALCO OFFICE SUPPLIES - MRP SYSTEM *****


TITLE : DEMONSTRATION
DATE  : Sunday 09-03-1995
TIME  : 10:36 PM


--------------------------------------------------------------------------------

ANALYSIS REQUESTED - DEMONSTRATION

Product (488 available) - DR-45672 - Four Drawer Filing Cabinet
Product Options (24 available) - vertical, sizes, green, locks, fittings.
Components (162 available) - all level 1, first 4 level 2
Weeks (104 available) - first 5
Continuity - no
Report Formats (34 available) - 1, 2, 3
Details (62 pages available) - Summary 2 pages
Options - off


Report 1 - Bill of Materials

Level 0           DR-45672
                  |-----------------------------------------------
                  |             |             |             |
Level 1           DR-46831     FN-53762      FN-62534      FN-26374
                  |
                  |
                  |-------------------------------------------------------others
                  |             |             |             |
Level 2           FN-63541     PR-3645       PR-7495       PR-1135


Report 2 - Inventory

          -----------------------------------------------------------
          |         # OF      # PER   INVENTORY  LEAD        LOT  |
          | NAME    SUBCOMP   PARENT  ON   HAND  TIME        SIZE |
          | DR-45572    4        -         125    1           50  |
          | DR-46831    8        4         487    2         1250  |
          | FN-53762   16        4         257    2         1200  |
          | FN-62534   16        4        1253    2         2000  |
          | FN-26374   16        4         566    3         2000  |
          | FN-63541    8        4         124    4         1000  |
          | PR-3645     4        2         255    1         1500  |
          | PR-7495     4        2         458    1         1500  |
          | PR-1135     4        2        1087    1         2500  |
          |                                                       |
          -----------------------------------------------------------
```

Figure 12.8 Example of a simplified MRP printout.

Report 3 - Master Production Schedule

```
---------------------------------------
|      The Master Production Schedule  |
|--------------------------------------|
| PRODUCT NAME : DR-45672              |
| NUMBER OF SUBCOMPONENTS :   4        |
| ON HAND INVENTORY :   125            |
| LEAD TIME (WEEKS):  1                |
|======================================|
|    WEEK          REQUIRED QUANTITY   |
|     1                     175        |
|     2                     250        |
|     3                     250        |
|     4                     175        |
|     5                     175        |
---------------------------------------
```

Item: DR-45672			Level: 0	
Parent:NONE			Lead Time: 1	
Week	Gross Required	On hand Inventory	Net Required	Planned Receipts	Planned Releases
1	175	125	50	50	250
2	250	-------	250	250	250
3	250	-------	250	250	175
4	175	-------	175	175	175
5	175	-------	175	175	------

Item: DR-46831			Level: 1	
Parent:DR-45672			Lead Time: 2	
Week	Gross Required	On hand Inventory	Net Required	Planned Receipts	Planned Releases
1	1000	487	513	1250	-------
2	1000	737	263	1250	-------
3	700	987	------	-------	1250
4	700	287	413	1250	1250
5	-------	837	-------	-------	-------

Item: FN-53762			Level: 1	
Parent:DR-45672			Lead Time: 2	
Week	Gross Required	On hand Inventory	Net Required	Planned Receipts	Planned Releases
1	1000	257	743	1200	-------
2	1000	457	543	1200	-------
3	700	657	43	1200	1200
4	700	1157	-------	-------	1200
5	-------	257	-------	-------	1200

Figure 12.8 *(cont.)* Example of a simplified MRP printout.

Batching MRP orders

One problem with the MRP procedure we have described is that it may suggest a series of small orders that are placed every week or so. Such frequent orders are inconvenient and can have high administration and delivery costs. If several small orders are combined into fewer, larger batches the costs may be reduced. This is called **batching** or **lot sizing**. There are several ways of finding the best lot size, including:

- **Lot-for-lot** where you order exactly what the net requirement is for each period. This is a very simple method which minimizes inventory carrying costs but can give high ordering or setup costs.

- **Fixed order quantity** where you find an order size that is convenient to use and always order this same amount. This might, for example, be a truck load or a container load or some other convenient size. The organization may calculate an economic order quantity for this (which we shall describe in Chapter 18). This method ignores much of the planning of MRP, but it might allow for other factors, such as price discounts on larger orders.

- **Period order quantity** which combines the net requirements over some fixed period, and places regular orders for different quantities. This tries to reduce both the ordering costs and carrying costs, and is often the most successful approach.

- **A batching rule** which calculates the best order quantity in any particular circumstances. In practice it is difficult to find the best order quantity, so simple rules are usually used to get reasonable results.

We can illustrate one batching rule that generally gives good results. This looks for some optimal number of the period's demand that should be combined into a single batch. If orders are placed more frequently than this, the administration and delivery charges rise and give higher costs: if orders are placed less frequently, stock levels rise and again give higher costs. This means there is a cost curve with a distinct minimum, as shown in Figure 12.9.

We can add all the costs of placing and receiving an order into the single figure R_c, the reorder cost. In the same way, we can add all the costs of holding a unit of stock for a unit of time to give the single figure H_c, the holding cost. Then, if enough stock is bought to cover all orders for the next n periods, we can calculate a total cost based on these. Our object is to find the value of n that minimizes this cost.

One way of finding the best value for n is to start by taking short stock cycles at the left-hand side of the graph in Figure 12.9. Then increasing n will follow the graph downward until costs start to rise, at which point the optimum has been found. This procedure can be described as follows:

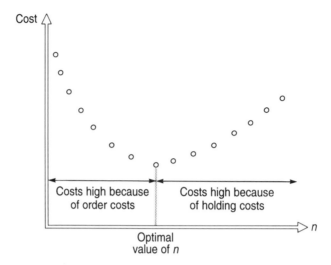

Figure 12.9 Variations in costs with number of periods combined into a single order.

● First calculate the cost of buying for a single period and compare this with the cost of buying for two periods. If it is cheaper to buy for two periods than for one, we are going down the left-hand side of the graph in Figure 12.9 and the cost is going down as the value of n is increasing.

● Next compare the cost of buying for two periods with the cost of buying for three periods. If it is cheaper to buy for three periods we are still on the declining part of the graph and have not yet reached the point of minimum cost.

● Continue this procedure, comparing the cost of buying for three periods with the cost of buying for four periods, and so on. In general, we will always compare the cost of buying for the next n periods with the cost of buying for the next $n + 1$ periods.

● The procedure is continued until at some point it becomes cheaper to buy for n periods than for $n + 1$ periods. At this point we have reached the bottom of the graph and found the point of minimal cost. Any further increases in n would increase costs as we climb up the right-hand side of the graph.

Fortunately, there is a short cut to the arithmetic that removes most of the work. We will not bother with the derivation of this, but the result is:

$$n(n + 1)D_{n+1} > 2R_c/H_c$$

where:

R_c = cost of placing an order
H_c = cost of holding a unit in stock for a period
D_{n+1} = demand in the $(n + 1)^{\text{th}}$ period

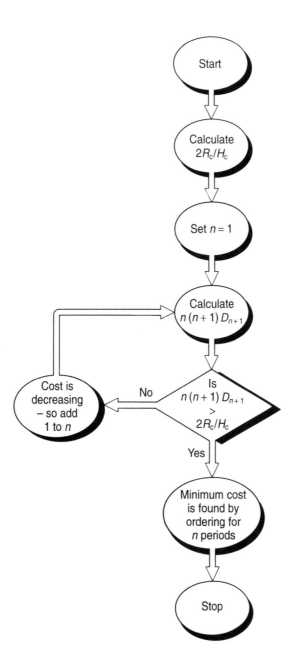

Figure 12.10 Procedure for lot sizing.

If this inequality is **not true** it is cheaper to order for $n+1$ periods than for n, so we are on the left-hand side of the graph of costs in Figure 12.9. If we increase n until the inequality becomes **true** it is cheaper to order for n periods than $n+1$, and we are on the right-hand side of the cost graph. This suggests a procedure where n is set to 1 and the inequality is checked. If it is not true, n is increased to 2 and the inequality is checked again. Then we keep on increasing n, until eventually the inequality becomes true. This means that we are at the bottom of the cost curve and an optimal value for n has been found. The procedure then stops. A flow diagram of this procedure is shown in Figure 12.10.

Several batching rules can be used, but the one described usually gives good results. It does not guarantee optimal solutions because of the assumptions made, such as fixed and known costs, fixed demand, an optimal solution that occurs as soon as costs begin to rise, and so on. Although it seems a little complicated, the procedure is quite straightforward and can be done very easily with a spreadsheet.

we Worked example

The procurement manager of Associated Services knows that the total cost of placing an order and having it delivered is £90. The holding cost of an item is £4 a month. If MRP shows the following demand for the item, find an ordering policy that will give reasonable costs.

Month	1	2	3	4	5	6	7	8	9	10	11	12
Demand	1	3	5	8	8	5	2	1	1	5	7	9

Solution

Following the procedure shown in Figure 12.10, with $R_c = 90$ and $H_c = 4$:

$$2R_c/H_c = 2 \times 90/4 = 45$$

- Then, starting with $n = 1$, $n+1 = 2$ and $D_2 = 3$ we calculate:

$$n(n+1)D_{n+1} = 1 \times 2 \times 3 = 6$$

As this is less than 45 the inequality is not true and we have not reached the minimum.

- Next taking $n = 2$, $n+1 = 3$ and $D_3 = 5$ we calculate:

$$n(n+1)D_{n+1} = 2 \times 3 \times 5 = 30$$

This is less than 45 so the inequality is still not true and we have not reached the minimum.

● Next taking $n = 3$, $n + 1 = 4$ and $D_4 = 8$ we calculate:

$$n(n + 1)D_{n+1} = 3 \times 4 \times 8 = 96$$

This is more than 45 so the inequality is true and we have found the minimum cost with $n = 3$.

This means we order enough at the beginning of month 1 to last for the first three months (that is, $1 + 3 + 5 = 9$) and schedule this to arrive before the beginning of month 1.

It is easier to do these calculations in a table, as shown below.

Month, i	1	2	3	4
Demand, D_i	1	3	5	8
n	1	2	3	
$n(n + 1)D_{n+1}$	6	30	96	
Delivery	9			

We can continue the analysis for the next months. The only thing we have to remember is that every time a new calculation is started the value of n returns to 1.

Month, i	1	2	3	4	5	6	7	8	9	10	11	12
Demand, D_i	1	3	5	8	8	5	2	1	1	5	7	9
n	1	2	3	1	2	3	4	5	6	1	2	1
$n(n + 1)D_{n+1}$	6	30	96	16	30	24	20	30	210	14	54	
Delivery	9			25						12		

A good ordering policy would make sure 9 units arrive by month 1, 25 by month 4 and 12 by month 10.

Review questions

12.9 Why might several small orders be combined into a single larger one?

12.10 What is a batching rule?

12.11 Why does the batching rule described only give a good rather than an optimal solution?

Ce Case example – Mokkelbost Maintenance Division

Mokkelbost Maintenance Division is a medium-sized company based in Copenhagen. Its main business is the maintenance of industrial and commercial heating systems. On a regular basis, the company inspects, tests, repairs and maintains the heating systems installed in buildings. Mokkelbost currently have contracts with 800 companies occupying 3500 buildings.

In recent months Mokkelbost has had a lot of problems. It has been late visiting many companies and has very high overtime costs. On several occasions, it has started work on a system, has scheduled overtime so it can close a system down at a convenient time for their customers, and has then found it does not have the materials to finish the job. Even with 50 million Krona of inventories it has frequent stockouts of parts.

Per Svensen, Vice President of Operations, sent the following memo to Helena Maestriani, Manager of Production Planning and Inventory Control.

Memorandum

To: Helena Maestriani, Manager PP&IC
From: Per Svensen, VP Operations

Our customer service level, measured as on-time services of customer equipment, has been showing a steady downward trend. Our objective is 95%, but, for the last six months, we have been averaging 85%.

I have talked to the president about your suggestion that we consider an MRP system to solve our planning and stockout problems. He likes the idea but would like some more details.

Please prepare a brief report about MRP, explain what it is, what it will do for us and how you would go about implementing it. I will take up your report in the next management committee.

Questions

- Do you think MRP can work in this kind of service environment?

- Prepare the report on MRP that Helena Maestriani could submit to Per Svensen.

Extensions to MRP

Because of its dependence on computers and the need to link several systems, organizations have only really been able to use MRP since the early 1970s. Since then it has been widely adopted in manufacturing industry. But services also need schedules for materials, labour and other resources. The first extensions of MRP, therefore, used it in other types of organization.

It is more difficult to use MRP in services because it needs detailed and accurate master production schedules. But some organizations, such as hospitals, restaurants and universities, have successfully used it.

- In a university, the finished product is graduating students. The master production schedule shows the number of students who will be graduating from each programme in each term. The bill of materials is the courses the students need to take in a term, based on their programme. Then we can use MRP to find the materials needed – which are the number of teachers, classrooms, laboratories, and so on.

- A hospital can use MRP to schedule surgical operations and make sure that supplies and equipment are ready when needed. The master production schedule gives the planned surgical operations in any period. The bill of material contains information about the equipment and resources needed for each type of surgery. The inventory file contains information about surgical instruments, disposable materials, reusable instruments, sterilized materials, and so on.

- A restaurant can use MRP to schedule its food and equipment. The master production schedule gives the meals the restaurant plans to prepare each meal time. The recipes for each meal give the bill of material.

MRP has proved so successful in many organizations, that it is not surprising the basic system has been extended in several ways. The first extensions improved the procedures for dealing with variable supply, supplier reliability, wastage, defective quality, variable demand and variable lead times. Several different batching rules were developed to deal with different circumstances.

Other extensions to MRP added feedback to help with planning decisions. Two main types of feedback are:

(1) if proposed plans would break capacity constraints this is detected by MRP and early rescheduling is done – MRP is taking part in capacity planning;

(2) if actual performance is interrupted the master production schedule can be revised quickly with inputs from the MRP system.

Systems with this kind of feedback are called **closed-loop MRP**. They allow the results from MRP to be used more widely in capacity planning, updating master production schedules and so on (see Figure 12.11).

The next major extension to MRP is **manufacturing resources planning**, or **MRP II**. By the early 1980s organizations realized that the MRP approach of exploding a master production schedule to find material needs could be extended to other functions. Ordering and purchasing were included in MRP, but why not extend the analyses to dispatching, distribution, production

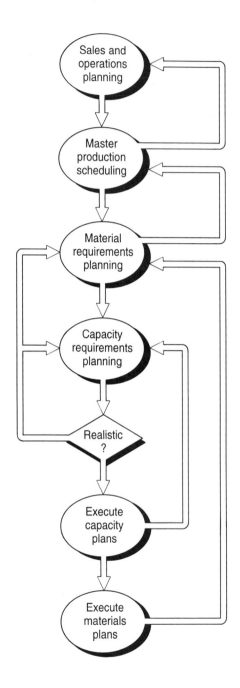

Figure 12.11 Closed-loop MRP diagram.

processes and even marketing and finance? A master production schedule could, for example, show the amount of machinery and equipment needed in each period. This in turn would set levels for manning and other resources. Eventually the master production schedule could form the basis for planning most of the resources used in a process. This was the intention of MRP II.

The original aim of MRP II was to give an integrated system, with all parts linked back to a production plan. But such complete integration usually proved so difficult that it was impractical. This meant that many organizations did not use full MRP II, but used parts of the system, often with different names:

- **Distribution resources planning** schedules transport and other logistics functions needed for the delivery and storage of raw materials and finished goods.

- **Capacity requirements planning** is the part of the system that goes back from the master production schedule to make sure there is enough capacity available to deal with planned production.

- **Resource requirements planning** is sometimes used to mean the same as MRP II, and sometimes used in a wider sense to include all planning decisions.

All such systems rely heavily on computing, and the installation of working systems can be very complicated and expensive.

Review questions

12.12 What is meant by MRP II?

12.13 Distribution resources planning relies on the use of computer systems. Do you think this is true?

Chapter review

- Tactical planning takes the strategic plans and expands these to give master production schedules. In the next stages of planning, organizations add more details to the master production schedules, to give more detailed operational schedules.

- There are several ways of getting these operational schedules. Material requirements planning (MRP) expands the master production schedule to develop timetables for the supply of materials.

- MRP is a dependent demand inventory system, where stocks are matched directly to production plans.

- MRP 'explodes' a master production schedule using a bill of materials to give detailed materials requirements. Orders for materials and operations are then timetabled so the master production schedule can be achieved.

- MRP needs a lot of information before it can be used. This often limits its use to manufacturers, but it is becoming more widely used in services.

- The main benefit of MRP is its ability to match the supply of materials to known demands. This reduces stock levels and associated costs.

- The basic MRP calculations would give frequent, small orders which are inconvenient and expensive to administer. Costs can be reduced by batching several small orders into a single larger one.

- MRP only became possible with cheap computing. It is now widely used and several extension have been designed. The most important extension is MRP II.

Key terms

CS Case study – Schmidt Machine Works

Sityuen Feng and Helmut Bayer work for Schmidt Machine Works. This company is a leading manufacturer of parts for knitting and sewing machines, based in Basel, but with manufacturing facilities in Austria and Germany.

For several weeks Sityuen and Helmut had been talking about MRP. At last, they decided to do an experiment to see if it was worth considering MRP in more detail. To help in this decision, they talked to Pieter Keller from the Production Section, who said:

> The principles of MRP are very easy, but it is difficult to implement. I suggest we pick a couple of products at random and see if MRP

would give any savings. We currently make around 2500 different products so this experiment would simply lay the foundations for a more detailed study. I have chosen two products, and as I couldn't get all the information about these I just made up some typical figures. The real process is so complicated that I made a number of simplifications.

Pieter also explained the present inventory system. This has stock levels reviewed at the end of each fortnight, with orders placed to bring stocks up to specified target levels. This level is set by a formula where each item is classified as A, B or C. Then the target stock levels are:

- A: 1.2 times expected demand in lead time plus two weeks.

- B: 1.4 times expected demand in lead time plus three weeks.

- C: 1.6 times expected demand in lead time plus four weeks.

The figures suggested by Pieter related to two products with codes AP4072 and FL7341. The expected production of AP4072 will remain steady at around 100 units a week for the next two years. FL7341 varies a little more, and monthly production is estimated as shown in Table 12.1.

Holding costs are 0.2% of unit cost a week with shortage costs of 10% of unit cost a week. If stocks of an item are about to run out, it is possible to request urgent deliveries, which cost about twice as much as normal deliveries. Much of Schmidt's production is sold to Germany, so it is common to quote prices in Deutschmarks. Times are quoted in weeks and other details are given in Table 12.2.

Table 12.1

	Year 1		Year 2
Month	Production	Month	Production
1	24	1	60
2	20	2	56
3	18	3	45
4	25	4	65
5	31	5	93
6	45	6	110
7	56	7	132
8	50	8	124
9	46	9	117
10	40	10	110
11	38	11	98
12	56	12	136

Table 12.2

Product code	Unit cost	Reorder cost	Category	Current stock	Lead time	Assembly time	Made from code (units)
AP4072	–	–	–	6	–	2	LF3281 (4)
							LF3282 (1)
LF3281	–	–	–	10	–	1	SF3822 (25)
							TG4071 (5)
SF3822	4	80	A	200	2	–	–
TG4071	20	120	B	75	3	–	–
LF3282	–	–	–	16	–	2	AX0012 (50)
							AX1012 (50)
							LX6734 (4)
AX0012	10	50	A	1000	2	–	–
AX1012	20	50	A	625	2	–	–
LX6734	–	–	–	104	–	1	LK0039 (10)
							LK0040 (10)
LK0039	5	120	A	240	3	–	–
LK0040	6	180	A	360	2	–	–
FL7341	–	–	–	14	–	3	CD4055 (2)
							CD5988 (4)
							CE0993 (1)
CD4055	–	–	–	83	–	2	ML8001 (1)
							MK0126 (2)
							MK0288 (4)
CD5988	–	–	–	122	–	3	LY4021 (10)
							LY4022 (20)
							LY4023 (10)
CE0993	–	–	–	96	–	2	NY0032 (6)
							NX9774 (3)
							NX0312 (12)
ML8001	–	–	–	50	–	1	ML0082 (20)
							ML0083 (10)
MK0126	–	–	–	122	–	2	FY0017 (6)
							NP4021 (24)
							LF7031 (12)
MK0288	–	–	–	124	–	1	ML0082 (40)
							ML0094 (10)
ML0082	–	–	–	250	–	1	BP0174 (4)
							BR3051 (1)
ML0083	–	–	–	220	–	1	BQ7441 (4)
							BQ7442 (8)
FY0017	4	80	B	86	4	–	–
NP4021	2	160	A	450	2	–	–
LF7031	6	120	B	265	3	–	–
ML0094	–	–	–	150	–	1	PX1570 (5)
							PX1571 (5)
							PX1572 (1)
LY4021	–	–	–	200	–	3	ML0083 (6)
							BQ6399 (2)
LY4022	–	–	–	122	–	4	ML0094 (12)
							LF7031 (12)
							LF7032 (2)
							LF7033 (1)
							LF7034 (12)
LY4023	–	–	–	60	–	1	LF7033 (1)
							LF7939 (60)
NY0032	–	–	–	24	–	1	ML0083 (10)
							ML8001 (1)

Table 12.2 *(cont.)*

Product code	Unit cost	Reorder cost	Category	Current stock	Lead time	Assembly time	Made from code (units)
NX9774	–	–	–	36	–	1	LF7032 (2) LF7034 (12) BQ7742 (8)
NX0312	–	–	–	240	–	1	ML0094 (12) LF7031 (12) AP7031 (1)
BQ6399	43	220	B	33	3	–	–
LF7033	86	380	C	40	1	–	–
LF7939	75	420	A	120	2	–	–
ML8001	118	420	B	22	2	–	–
LF7032	66	120	B	145	4	–	–
LF7034	–	–	–	850	–	2	PX4971 (12) PX3055 (2)
BP0174	8	40	A	85	2	–	–
BR3051	6	80	A	155	2	–	–
BQ7441	–	–	–	360	–	1	FY0017 (6) FZ0149 (1)
BQ7442	24	40	B	86	3	–	–
LF7031	6	120	A	780	4	–	–
AP7031	–	–	–	66	–	2	PX1571 (10) PX1420 (2) PX3055 (1)
FZ0149	120	420	C	260	5	–	–
PX1420	69	120	B	857	3	–	–
PX1570	12	40	A	1250	2	–	–
PX1571	8	40	A	2450	3	–	–
PX1572	86	80	B	475	2	–	–
PX3055	57	80	B	125	1	–	–
PX4971	15	80	A	750	2	–	–

Questions

• Would a trial, like the one suggested, give useful information?

• For the products chosen, how well do you think the present inventory control system works?

• Would MRP bring any benefits for these products?

• What would be the next step for introducing MRP in Schmidt Machine Works?

Problems

12.1 A company that makes a final product, A, receives orders for 40 units for delivery in week 16 of a production cycle, 60 units in week 13 and 50 units in week 12. It takes one unit of component B and two units of component C to make each unit of A, and assembly takes two weeks. Components of B and C are bought from suppliers with lead times of three and two weeks respectively. Current stocks of A, B and C are 5, 10 and 20 units respectively and an order for 40 units of C is due to arrive in week 7. Design a production and order plan for the company.

12.2 Each unit of product AF43 is made from 12 units of BL19, 10 units of CX23 and 20 units of DY33. Each unit of BL19 is made from 2 units of EM08, 2 units of FF87 and 2 units of GO95. Each unit of both EM08 and DY33 is made from six units of HX22. A master production schedule needs 60 units of AF43 to be ready by week 8 of a planning cycle and 50 units by week 10. There are minimum order sizes of 2000 units for HX22, and 500 units of both FF87 and GO95. Information about stocks and lead times in weeks (either for assembly or orders) is shown in Table 12.3. Design an order schedule for the materials.

Table 12.3

	Current stocks	Minimum stocks	Lead time (weeks)
AF43	20	10	2
BL19	230	50	3
CX23	340	100	1
DY33	410	100	3
EM08	360	200	2
FF87	620	200	2
GO95	830	200	2
HX22	1200	200	4

12.3 It costs £0.125 to store a unit of an item for one month. The total cost of placing an order for the item, including delivery, is £100. An MRP analysis has found the following demands for the item.

Month	1	2	3	4	5	6	7	8	9	10	11	12	13
Demand	100	50	60	60	100	100	80	60	40	70	80	100	140

Find a good ordering policy for the item.

12.4 It costs £1 to hold one unit of an item in stock for one month, and each order costs a total of £60. There are currently no stocks of the item. MRP has suggested the following demands. Find a good ordering policy for the item.

Month	1	2	3	4	5	6	7	8	9	10	11	12
Demand	40	39	60	81	238	722	998	1096	921	161	0	40

Do you think this is the best ordering policy available?

Discussion questions

12.1 When can MRP be used most effectively? What happens when it can not be used?

12.2 Why do you think that MRP has only been widely adopted in the past few years? Where do you think it has been most widely adopted? Why?

12.3 How can MRP be used in services? Give some specific examples to support your views.

12.4 What extensions can be made to basic MRP systems?

12.5 What features would you expect to see in a commercial MRP computer package?

12.6 MRP is often placed at the end of the planning process. Is this the best place for it? Could it play a more active part in planning?

12.7 Many organizations have had difficulties implementing MRP, and there have been many failures. Why is this?

12.8 How do you think MRP II systems work? What are the difficulties of implementing MRP II and other extensions to MRP? How can these difficulties be overcome?

Selected references

APICS (1971). *Special Report: Materials Requirement Planning by Computer*. Falls Church, Va.: American Production and Inventory Control Society.

Lee S.M. and Schwendiman G. (eds) (1983). *Management by Japanese Systems*. New York: Praeger.

Orlicky J. (1975). *Material Requirements Planning*. New York: McGraw-Hill.

Smolik D.P. (1983). *Material Requirements of Manufacturing*. New York: Van Nostrand Reinhold.

Vollmann T.E., Berry W.L. and Whybark D.C. (1988). *Manufacturing Planning and Control Systems* (2nd edn). Homewood, Ill.: Richard D. Irwin.

Waters C.D.J. (1992). *Inventory Control and Management*. Chichester: John Wiley.

Wight O.W. (1974). *Production and Inventory Management in the Computer Age*. Boston: Cahners Publishing.

Wight O.W. (1982). *The Executive's Guide to Successful MRP II*. Williston, Vermont: Oliver Wight Publications.

Wight O.W. (1983). *MRP II*. Williston, Vermont: Oliver Wight Publications.

13 Just-in-time operations

Contents

Objectives

After reading this chapter you should be able to:

- describe the principles of just-in-time (JIT) operations
- list the circumstances in which JIT can be used
- describe Kanban systems for controlling JIT
- discuss the relationships that JIT needs with suppliers and employees
- list the benefits and disadvantages of JIT

Principles of just-in-time

Definition

In the past few years organizations have given a lot of attention to **just-in-time** or **JIT**. In essence, JIT organizes all operations so they occur just at the time they are needed. This means, for example, that if materials are needed for production, they are not bought some time in advance and kept in stock, but are delivered directly to the production process just as they are needed. The result is that stocks of materials are virtually eliminated. You can think of it as an extension of MRP.

One reason why people have looked so closely at JIT is the success of Japanese manufacturing. Since the 1950s Japan has continuously increased its share of world trade, and is now the dominant manufacturing economy. JIT was developed in Japan. A lot of the original work was done by Toyota, and JIT is now widely used in many industries. If JIT has played even a small part in Japan's success, people concluded that it could bring benefits elsewhere.

Many organizations around the world have adopted JIT, and have had dramatic improvements in their performance. When it can be used, JIT can bring many benefits. The problem is that JIT, like MRP, can only be used in certain circumstances. Even when it can be used, there are many practical difficulties and the benefits only appear after a lot of effort.

JIT is not a new idea. In the 1920s iron ore arriving at Ford's plant in Detroit was turned into steel within a day and into finished cars a few days later. This was a very efficient way of using resources and reducing stocks of work in progress – but few organizations followed Ford's example. Even today, most organizations feel they need stocks of work in progress to make sure they have smooth operations. These stocks allow operations to continue when there are problems with the process. If, for example, some equipment breaks down or material arrives late, most operations can still work normally using the stock of work in progress.

The view that inventories are essential for smooth operations made managers ask the question 'How can we provide stocks at lowest cost?' But during the past few years some organizations changed their view and started asking another question, 'How can we eliminate stocks?' The answer to this laid the foundations of just-in-time. By 1988 an estimated 25% of European manufacturers used some form of JIT, and this had risen to over 50% by the early 1990s.

Effects of JIT operations

We can start describing JIT by looking at its effect on inventories. This is only one aspect of just-in-time operations, but it gives a useful starting point. The main purpose of stock is to allow for short-term mismatches between supply and demand. Independent demand inventory system (which we shall describe in Chapter 18) allow for this mismatch by making sure stocks are high enough to cover any expected demand. Sometimes, particularly with the widely varying demand met in batch production, independent demand systems can give very high stocks. MRP overcomes this problem by using the master schedule to match the supply of materials more closely to demand. The more closely we can match supply to demand, the smaller are the stocks we need to cover any differences. Then if the mismatch can be completely eliminated, so can stocks. This is the basis of just-in-time systems (see Figure 13.1).

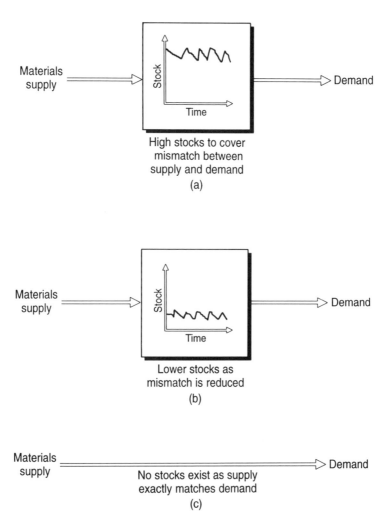

Figure 13.1 Stock levels with different materials planning methods:
(a) conventional system; (b) MRP system; (c) JIT system.

> **Just-in-time** systems organize operations so that they occur just as they are needed. If materials arrive just as they are needed, stocks of work in progress can be eliminated.

You have an example of this when you buy fuel for your lawnmower. If you have a petrol engine there is a mismatch between the fuel supply which you buy from a garage, and demand when you actually mow the lawn. So you have to keep stocks of fuel in the petrol tank and spare can. If you have an electric motor the supply of electricity exactly matches demand and you do not need any stocks. The petrol engine uses an independent demand inventory system, while the electric motor uses a JIT system.

You can imagine JIT in practice by thinking about a car assembly line. Just as the chassis moves down the line to a work station, an engine arrives at the same point and is fitted. This is repeated for all parts. As the car body arrives at another work station, four doors also arrive and are added. All the way down the line materials arrive just at the time they are needed, so the car is assembled in one smooth process.

You can see that JIT is really a simple idea, and we can summarize its main argument about inventories as follows:

- Stocks are held in an organization to cover short-term variation and uncertainty in supply and demand.

- JIT assumes these stocks serve no useful purpose. They only exist because poor co-ordination does not match the supply of materials to demand.

- As long as stocks are held, managers will not try to improve their co-ordination.

- This means that operations will continue to be poorly managed, with many problems hidden by the stocks.

- The proper thing for an organization to do is improve its management, find the reasons why there are differences between supply and demand, and then take whatever action is needed to overcome them.

Now you can begin to see the wider role of JIT. Although we have introduced JIT as a way of reducing stock levels, it is much more than this. JIT really involves a change in the way an organization looks at its operations. Its supporters described it as 'a way of eliminating waste', or, 'a way of enforced problem solving'. It starts with an aim of eliminating all waste from an organization.

JIT believes that stock is only held for negative reasons. In other words it is used to allow for poor co-ordination and management. JIT sees an organization as having a series of problems that hinder efficient operations.

These problems include long equipment setup times, unbalanced operations, constrained capacity, machine breakdowns, defective materials, interrupted operations, unreliable suppliers, poor quality, too much paperwork and too many changes. Stock is held to avoid the effects of these problems and effectively hide them from sight. A much more constructive approach would be to identify the problems and solve them. This approach leads to a number of changes in viewpoint.

- **Stocks** As we have seen, organizations hold stocks to cover short-term differences between supply and demand. JIT systems assume these stocks are actually being used to hide problems. If nothing is done these problems will keep on happening. Organizations should try to find the reasons why there are differences between supply and demand, and then take whatever action is needed to remove them.

- **Reliability** When a machine on a production process breaks down most organizations transfer production to another process or start making another product. The JIT approach does not allow this kind of flexibility, as it is based on continuous, uninterrupted production. Managers are forced to recognize there is a problem with the reliability of the machine, they examine the reason why it broke down, and they take actions to make sure it does not break down in the future.

- **Quality** Organizations have traditionally given acceptable levels of quality for their products. They used to define some arbitrary figure like '2 defective units in 100 means the supply is acceptable'. JIT recognizes that all defects have costs, and it is really cheaper to prevent these from ever happening than to correct them later. This reinforces the principles of total quality management we met in Chapter 5.

- **Suppliers** Many people feel that suppliers and customers are in some sort of conflict, where one can only benefit at the expense of the other. JIT systems rely totally on their suppliers, so they can not allow this kind of friction. Instead they show that customers and suppliers are partners with a common objective – so they should work closely together.

- **Employees** Some organizations have a friction between 'managers' and 'workers'. JIT recognizes that this is a meaningless distinction. The welfare of all employees depends on the success of the organization, so all employees are treated with equal respect.

Now you can see JIT not just as a mean of minimizing inventories, but as a whole way of viewing operations. Its overall aim is to minimize waste by identifying and solving any problems found. This view of operations is known by different names, including 'zero inventory', 'stockless production', 'lean production', 'Toyota system', 'Japanese manufacturing', 'world class manufacturing' and 'continuous flow manufacturing'.

ce Case example – Just-in-time at Guy La Rochelle International

Guy La Rochelle International is one of Europe's leading manufacturers of cosmetics and toiletries. It has a major production plant near Lyon which employs 900 people.

One of the problems with La Rochelle's market is the speed that customers' tastes change, and the resulting changes in demand. To maintain its market share and meet these changing demands, La Rochelle emphasizes its product variety. This means it makes small batches in short production runs.

Over time, La Rochelle has been changing its processes, and is introducing just-in-time manufacturing. This gives smaller batch sizes, less inventory, better service and fast response to changing customers' tastes. Customers are less likely to get stale products that have been sitting on a shelf.

The inventory holding cost is 25%, so when La Rochelle reduced its stock of lipstick by $1 million it saved $250,000 a year. Its Baby Soft bath oil has changed from a production run of 60,000 units every 30 days, to 10,000 units every 5 days; the run of 200,000 units of lipstick every 65 days has changed to 60,000 units every 20 days.

The conversion to JIT is well-supported and liked by La Rochelle employees. Every worker now has a variety of skills, and they work in teams rather than as individuals. Shortening the length of production runs from two days to three hours means that equipment setups have to be fast, and the work is more interesting.

Simplicity of JIT operations

An important point of JIT is the view that the effort put into administrations is an overhead that is largely wasted. So JIT tries to simplify operations and systems so the effort needed to control them is minimized. JIT systems are largely manual, with little paperwork, and most decisions are made on the shop floor. This is in marked contrast to MRP systems which are computerized, expensive to control, and have decisions made by planners who are some distance away.

This aim of simplicity means that the methods used by JIT are all practical and based largely on common sense. Plant layouts are simplified, routine maintenance of equipment is scheduled to avoid breakdowns, everyone is trained in quality management to reduce the number of defects, simpler designs are used to reduce processing time, setup procedures are changed to reduce their time, reorder costs are reduced to allow smaller deliveries, suppliers are encouraged to make more frequent deliveries, and so on. These changes have major effects on operations. They can not be introduced in one go, but evolve with small continuous improvements over a long period. It is said that Toyota made continuous improvements in its operations for 25 years before it had a reasonable JIT system.

Now you can see one reason why there is misunderstanding about JIT. It is based on simple ideas, but these simple ideas are very difficult to implement. Getting materials to arrive just as they are needed is a simple idea, but is very difficult to achieve. Avoiding disruptions by making sure materials have perfect quality is a simple idea, but it is very difficult to achieve.

ce | Case example – Japanese motor cycles

In the 1960s many countries had local manufacturers of motor cycles who met most of the domestic demand. These included Harley-Davidson in America, BSA in Britain and BMW in Germany. But the industry changed dramatically, and many well-established companies went bankrupt. Their problem was the sudden new competition from the Japanese companies of Honda, Yamaha, Suzuki and Kawasaki.

These four companies could supply motor cycles anywhere in the world with higher quality and lower cost than competitors. In 1978 Harley-Davidson in the United States tried, but failed, to prove that the Japanese companies were dumping motor cycles on the market at less than the cost of manufacture. During these hearings it was shown that the Japanese companies had operating costs that were 30% lower than Harley-Davidson's. One of the main reasons for this was their use of JIT manufacturing.

Harley-Davidson recognized that it could only compete by using the same methods, and adopted JIT in 1982. Despite initial problems, it stuck to its 'materials as needed' programme and is once again succeeding in a very competitive market. In a five year period Harley-Davidson reduced machine setup times by 75%, warranty and scrap costs by 60%, and work in progress stocks by $22 million. During the same period productivity rose by 30%.

Key elements in JIT systems

JIT can only be used in certain types of organization. We said that MRP was only really effective in batch manufacturing industries. JIT is even more specialized and can only really be used in large-scale assembly. At present, the most successful users of JIT are car assembly plants which make large numbers of identical products in a continuous process.

The operations within an organization must have several characteristics before JIT can be considered.

- Every time that production is changed from one item to another there are delays, disruptions and costs. JIT says that these changes waste resources and should be eliminated. This means that JIT needs a stable environment where production of an item remains at a fixed level for some time. Standard products are made with few variations.

- This stable environment allows costs to be reduced by using specialized automation. The fixed costs of this can be recovered with high production volumes. This means that JIT works best with high volume, mass production operations.

- The specified production level must allow a smooth and continuous flow of products through the process. Each part of the process must be fully utilized and not leave resources under-used. In other words, careful planning is needed to make sure the assembly line is balanced.

- Deliveries of materials are made at just the time they are needed. So suppliers must be able to adapt to this kind of operation. It would be impractical to bring each individual unit from suppliers, so the next best thing is to use very small batches.

- If small batches are used, reorder costs must be reduced as much as possible or the frequent deliveries will be too expensive. Other inventory control systems assume the reorder cost is fixed, while JIT looks at the problem of supplying small batches and finds ways of reducing the costs. This might include flexible manufacturing.

- Lead times and setup times must be short or the delay in answering a request for materials is too long. Traditional inventory control systems assume that lead times are fixed – JIT sees long lead times as a problem that must be solved. This means working closely with suppliers and having them build facilities, perhaps focused factories, that are physically close.

- Materials arrive just as they are needed. As there are no stocks to give safety cover, any defects would disrupt production. So suppliers must be totally reliable and provide materials which are free from defects.

- If something goes wrong and there is a disruption to the process, the workforce must be able to find out what went wrong. They must take the action needed to correct the fault, and make sure that it does not happen again. This needs a skilled and flexible workforce that is committed to the success of the organization.

If we continue arguing in this way we can list the key elements in JIT operations. These include:

- a stable environment

- standard products with few variations

- continuous production at fixed levels

- automated, high volume operations

- a balanced process which uses resources fully

- reliable production equipment

- minimum stocks

- small batches of materials

- short lead times for materials

- low setup and delivery costs

- efficient materials handling

- reliable suppliers

- consistently high quality of materials

- flexible workforce

- fair treatment and rewards for employees

- ability to solve any problems

- an efficient method of control.

Although it is a simple idea, it is clear that JIT has widespread effects in an organization. Everything is changed, from the way that goods are ordered to the role of people working on the shop floor. Introducing JIT is a major step that needs total commitment from the workforce at all levels.

Review questions

13.1 How are the basic questions asked by JIT fundamentally different from those asked by other inventory control systems?

13.2 What is the main characteristic of a JIT system?

13.3 How does JIT view stocks?

13.4 What type of process is JIT most suited to?

13.5 JIT principles can not be used for small service operations. Do you agree with this?

Ce Case example – Hungry Harry's Burger Bar

Juan Ridellos runs a chain of fast food restaurants in Southern Europe. He is a leading member of his local Institute of Management. Last Summer he went to one of their talks, where a manufacturer of motor components was describing their new just-in-time system.

At the end of this talk, Juan was not impressed. 'I do that all the time', he said to a colleague. 'My hamburger restaurants buy bread from the local baker, we get meat from the local butcher and vegetables from the local market. We can get any supplies within a few minutes. Then we cook exactly what the customer wants and deliver it a few minutes later. We have been using just-in-time for years, but nobody congratulates us on our new management methods. Do the same thing with motor components and you are a hero!'

Questions

- Do fast food restaurants really use just-in-time systems?

- To what extent is JIT used in other services?

- Are there any major differences between just-in-time manufacturing and services?

Achieving just-in-time operations

Controlling operations

So far we have said:

> **Just-in-time** systems try to eliminate all waste within an organization. Their aim is to meet production targets using the minimum amount of materials, with the minimum amount of equipment, the smallest number of operators, and so on. They do this by making sure all operations are done at just the time they are needed.

Now, having have described the foundations of JIT, we need to ask how these aims are achieved. Having said, for example, that JIT systems organize materials to arrive just as they are needed, we must show how this can be done.

One approach uses **Kanbans**. 'Kanban' is the Japanese word for card, or visible record. Here, operations are controlled by having Kanbans 'pull' materials through a process.

In traditional operations, each work station is given a timetable of work that it must finish in a given time. Finished items are then 'pushed' through to form a stock of work in progress in front of the next work station. This ignores what the next station is actually doing – it might be working on something completely different or be waiting for a different item to arrive. At best, the second work station must finish its current job before it can start working on the new material just passed to it. The result is delays and increased stock of work in progress.

JIT uses a 'pull' approach, where a work station finishes its operations, and then requests materials from the preceding work station. The preceding work station only starts making the requested materials when it gets this request, so that stocks of work in progress are eliminated. In practice, there must be some lead time, so requests for materials are passed backwards before they are actually needed. Materials will also be delivered in small batches rather than continuous amounts. So JIT still has some stocks of work in progress, but these are much lower than for 'push' systems. It would, though, be fairer to say that JIT minimizes stocks rather than eliminates them.

One obvious problem is that operations must be perfectly balanced, with the output from each work station exactly matching the demands from following stations. If there is any imbalance some equipment will remain idle until it gets a message to start producing, and the utilization of this equipment will be low. In practice, this problem occurs in all operations and is by no means unique to JIT. But just-in-time would consider any imbalance to be a waste and will find ways of eliminating it.

Kanban systems

Kanban systems use cards to control the flow of materials for JIT operations. There are several ways of using Kanbans, with the simplest one as follows (see Figure 13.2).

- All material is stored and moved in standard containers, with different sizes of container for each material. A container can only be moved when it has a Kanban attached to it.

- When a work station needs more materials – that is when its stock of materials falls to a reorder level – a Kanban is attached to an empty container and this is taken to the preceding work station. The Kanban is then attached to a full container, which is returned to the work station.

- The empty container is a signal for the preceding work station to start work on this material, and it produces just enough to refill the container.

You can see that the main features of this single Kanban system are:

- A message is passed *backwards* to the preceding work station to start production, and it only makes enough to fill a container.

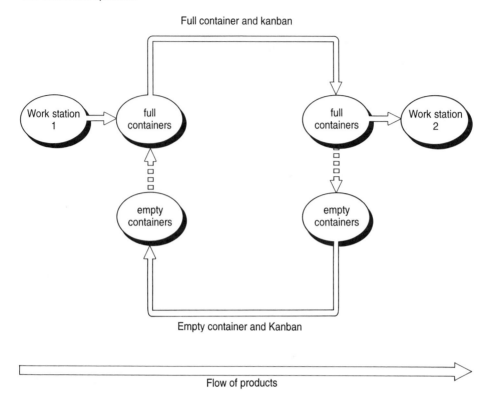

Figure 13.2 Simple Kanban system.

- Standard containers are used which hold a specific amount. This amount is usually quite small, and is typically 10% of a day's needs.

- The size of each container is the smallest reasonable batch that can be made, and there are usually only one or two full containers at any point.

- A specific number of containers and/or Kanbans is used.

- The stock of work in progress can be controlled by limiting the size of containers and the number of Kanbans.

- Materials can only be moved in containers, and containers can only be moved when they have a Kanban attached. This gives a rigid means of controlling the amount of materials produced and time they are moved.

- While it is simple to administer, this system makes sure that stocks of work in progress can not accumulate.

A more usual Kanban system is slightly more complicated and uses two distinct types of card: a production Kanban and a movement Kanban.

- When a work station needs more materials a movement Kanban is put on an empty container. This gives permission to take the container to the area where stocks of work in progress is kept.

- A full container is then found, which has a production Kanban attached.

- The production Kanban is removed and put on a post. This gives a signal for the preceding work station to make enough to replace the container of materials.

- A movement Kanban is put on the full container, giving permission to take it back to the work station.

This process is shown in Figure 13.3.

Although this system has a stock of work in progress, this stock is small. When a full container is removed, it is usually the only container in stock – and the parts are not replaced until the previous work station makes them. The description of moving to the store of work in progress is also misleading. JIT operations almost always use a product layout, such as an assembly line, so that movements of materials are minimized. The small stocks of work in progress are kept as part of the line, and there is no actual movement.

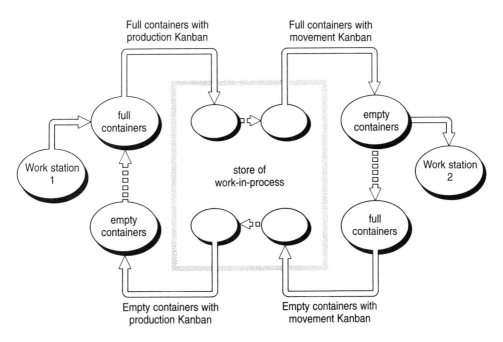

Figure 13.3 A common two-card Kanban system.

As each container has a Kanban attached to it, the number of Kanbans effectively fixes the amount of work in progress. Suppose, for example, there is only one production Kanban. Then the stock of work in progress is limited to at most one container of items. On the other hand, if there is a large number of Kanbans there can be quite high stocks. When a new JIT system is installed, an organization may keep some flexibility by having a fairly large number of Kanbans. But JIT will look for continuous improvements, and will steadily reduce the number of Kanbans. When the system is working properly, the number of Kanbans should be as small as possible.

There are many different ways of using Kanbans. Some systems use different Kanbans for emergency requests, high priority needs, materials requested from suppliers, signals for batch processes to start, and so on. Whatever the differences in detail, each system has a signal between one stage in a process and the previous stage to show when it is time to start making a part.

There is another part of control that comes into play when things go wrong. JIT often uses a system called **Andon**. This has three signals, often coloured lights, above each work station:

- a green signal shows that the station is working as planned;

- an amber signal shows the work station is falling a bit behind;

- a red signal shows a serious problem.

Everyone can see where problems are growing, and can look for ways of solving them.

Relations with suppliers

Traditionally, there has been some friction between suppliers and customers. Because customers pay money directly to suppliers, many people think that one can only benefit at the expense of the other. Suppliers are often rigid in their conditions and, as there is little customer loyalty, they try to make as much profit as possible from each sale. Customers on the other hand shop around to make sure they get the best deal, and remind suppliers of the competition. They are only concerned with their own objectives and will, when convenient to them, change specifications and conditions at short notice. The result is uncertainty among suppliers about items being ordered, the size of likely orders, the time when orders will be placed, and the possibility of repeat orders.

JIT recognizes that customers and suppliers have the same objective, which is a mutually beneficial trading arrangement. The best approach, then, is for an organization to find a single supplier who can best meet their conditions, and develop a long-term relationship. These trading conditions can be quite demanding and include items of perfect quality, with small, frequent deliveries and at reasonable cost. In return for meeting these conditions organizations with JIT use **single sourcing**. This means they buy each item exclusively from one supplier and agree long-term contracts to give stability. At one time, after Toyota had introduced JIT it was using 250 suppliers, while General Motors, who had not yet introduced JIT, was using 4000.

JIT recognizes the importance of stability to a supplier. It knows that they are geared to work with present operations and any changes will cause disruptions. But each supplier has its own suppliers who are, in turn, affected by changes, and so on down the supply chain. A small change in the finished product can have major effects on earlier suppliers. JIT sees such changes as inefficient, so it makes a product that does not change during long production runs.

The stability of these production runs give considerable benefits to suppliers. They allow suppliers to specialize in one type of item, and may reduce the product range and number of customers. Many suppliers to JIT operations build focused factories. As we saw in Chapter 7, a focused factory is a small plant that concentrates almost entirely on making one product, but aims to make this very well and very efficiently.

JIT aims for closer co-operation between a customer and its suppliers. This co-operation can help suppliers adapt to JIT, and even install JIT in their own operations. It also allows suppliers to make suggestions for improvements to customers, without the fear that their future profits will be reduced. Ideally, suppliers become a part of an extended JIT system (see Figure 13.4).

Whenever the customer needs some material it sends a vehicle with containers and Kanbans to the supplier. The vehicle delivers empty containers and exchanges them for full ones from the supplier's stock of finished goods. The Kanbans are then transferred to the full containers, which are delivered to

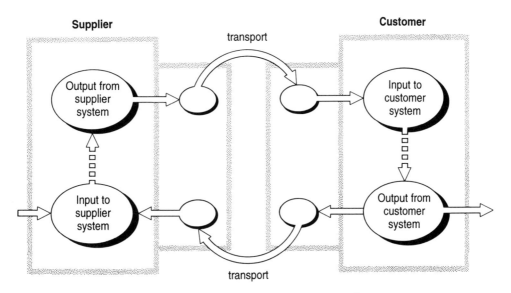

Figure 13.4 Integrating supplier and customer Kanban systems.

the customer. The supplier now has empty containers, which give a signal that it is time to replace the contents.

Despite the close relationships that JIT wants with suppliers, this can be very difficult. Most suppliers still have to keep a number of different customers with different types of operation. In practice, therefore, some compromise is needed on both sides to avoid disagreements.

Jidoka – quality at source

JIT can only work if materials are delivered with perfect quality. As materials are only delivered when they are needed, any defect will disrupt the process. There are two ways of avoiding this.

(1)   The organization could accept the possibility of defects and check the quality of all items as they arrive. But this is wasteful and destroys many of the benefits JIT is aiming for.

(2)   The alternative is to make sure that all items arriving are of perfect quality. This is clearly the better alternative, as we saw when discussing total quality management in Chapter 5.

Even low defective rates are not good enough for JIT operations, so total quality management is essential.

Respect for employees

Japanese companies generally offer their employees a job for life. In return, employees are expected to stay with the same organization for their entire working lives. This is typical of Japanese organizations, which see employees as their most important resource and the most important part of their operations.

This respect for employees is particularly important for JIT, where it has a number of effects. There has traditionally been some friction between 'managers' and 'workers' in an organization. This is largely caused by their different aims. Managers are judged by the performance of the organization and this performance is often measured by profit. On the other hand, workers are not rewarded for performance, but their wages are seen as a drain on profits. JIT says that all employees should be concerned with the success of their organization – and they should all be treated equally. As part of this, all employees are rewarded for the organization's performance by making sure they all have a share in profits.

Another aspect of JIT's respect for employees is the approach to improving a process. In many organizations managers look for improvements while they work in isolation away from the details of the process. Often they employ consultants who have little knowledge of the operations. JIT says that the best people to suggest improvements are those who actually work on the process. So JIT inevitably has suggestion boxes, with rewards for people offering good ideas. A more formal approach for getting suggestions is to use quality circles. As we saw in Chapter 5, a quality circle is an informal group of people who are involved in a particular operation. They meet once or twice a month to discuss ways of improving their operations.

JIT's use of automation can also be seen as a sign of their respect for employees – although some people disagree about this. One view says that JIT encourages automation because it is more reliable and cheaper for the high volume processes used. Another view is that some jobs are so boring, repetitive and unsatisfying that they should not be done by humans if there is any alternative. Robots and computer controlled machines can do most of the tedious work in assembly lines, and this should be automated as a matter of principle.

In return for their respect, organizations using JIT demand more from their employees. When, for example, operators are given authority to stop a process, they must be able to solve the problem that led to the stoppage. We have already seen how quality at source gives everyone responsibility for the quality of their own work. So some responsibility moves from managers working at a distance, to people working on the shop floor.

JIT also needs people to be flexible enough to do a variety of jobs. They must adapt to new practices, possess relevant skills and knowledge, participate actively in the running of the organization, be interested in its success, and so on.

One problem with JIT which is only recently getting attention is the increased stress it can put on the workforce. There is some evidence that employees who work on JIT assembly lines have higher levels of stress than those who work on traditional lines. More work is needed in this area, but even a suggestion of dissatisfaction in the workforce goes against JIT principles.

Review questions

13.6   What is the purpose of a Kanban?

13.7   How is the amount of work in progress limited using Kanbans?

13.8   What is JIT's view of the relationship between customers and suppliers?

13.9   Why might JIT systems be supplied by focused factories?

13.10 Because JIT relies on automated processes, it puts less emphasis on the skills of individuals. Do you think this is true?

Benefits and disadvantages of JIT

When we looked at JIT as a way of controlling stocks, its major advantage was the dramatic reduction of stocks of raw materials and work in progress. Some organizations have reduced these by more than 75%. This gives a number of other advantages, such as reductions in space needed, lower warehousing costs, less investment in stocks, and so on. Other benefits of JIT come from the reorganization needed to get a working system. Several of these have already been mentioned, including:

- reduced lead times

- shorter time needed to make a product

- higher productivity

- higher equipment utilization

- simplified planning and scheduling

- less paperwork

- improved quality of materials and products

- less scrap and wastage

- better morale in the workforce

- better relations with suppliers

- emphasis on solving problems in the process.

Some of these benefits can only be bought at a high price. Making high quality products with few interruptions by breakdowns, for example, usually means that better equipment must be used. Reduced setup times usually need more sophisticated equipment. This equipment must respond quickly to changing demands, so there must be more capacity. So JIT can only work if organizations buy better and higher capacity equipment. Many smaller organizations have found this costs too much, particularly if the costs of training all employees is added. Although the long-term rewards may be high, the short-term costs of JIT can be too high for many organizations to consider.

In addition to the benefits there are some disadvantages with JIT. We have just mentioned that it may be expensive to implement and involve many years of slow progress. Its inflexibility is another weakness. It is difficult to change product design, mix or demand levels – so it does not work well with irregular demand, small production numbers, or specially ordered material. There can also be problems with seasonal variations in demand. There are four ways of overcoming these.

(1) Stocks of finished goods can be built up when demand is low and used when demand is high. This option is, of course, contrary to JIT principles.

(2) Production can be changed to match demand. Again these changes are contrary to JIT principles.

(3) Demand can be smoothed out by pricing policies. In particular, discounts or other offers can be given during periods of low demands.

(4) The delivery time promised to customers can be adjusted. Customers can be asked to wait longer for deliveries when demand is high, with the back-log cleared when demand falls.

None of these options is entirely satisfactory, so JIT systems must be flexible enough to deal with some variation in demand.

Some of the benefits of JIT may also be seen as disadvantages. Having frequent setups and small batches, for example, is essential for JIT – but unless an organization is careful this can give high reorder costs. Similarly, JIT needs decisions to be made on the shop floor. Such devolved decision making, with responsibility given to lower levels in the workforce, may be an advantage or a disadvantage depending on your viewpoint.

Some specific problems listed by JIT users include:

- the initial investment and cost of implementation

- time needed to get improvements

- reliance on perfect quality of materials from suppliers

- problems with maintaining product quality

- inability of suppliers to adapt to JIT methods

- need for stable production

- changing customer schedules

- variable demand from customers

- demand for a range of options with products

- reduces flexibility to change products

- difficulty of reducing setup times

- lack of commitment within the organization

- lack of co-operation and trust between employees

- problems linking to existing information systems

- need to change layout of facilities

- increased stress in workforce.

Perhaps one disadvantage of JIT is its deceptive simplicity. This has led many organizations to try and use JIT without any understanding of its underlying principles. Some companies have tried to add elements of JIT into an existing operation. In extreme cases a note has been circulated simply stating that 'The company is adopting JIT principles by eliminating stocks of work in progress over the next two months. Please change your practices accordingly.' You must remember that JIT is an approach that needs a complete change of attitudes and operations within an organization. It is likely to take several years of careful planning and controlled implementation to introduce it successfully.

Comparisons with MRP systems

There are obvious similarities between JIT and MRP systems. They are, for example, both dependent demand systems – where demand for materials is found directly from production schedules. But there are a number of contrasts:

- JIT is a manual system, while MRP relies on computers.

- JIT is purely a 'pull' system while MRP allows a 'push' system on the shop floor.

- JIT emphasizes physical operations, while MRP is largely an information system.

- JIT allows the actual process to control work using Kanbans, while MRP uses predefined schedules.

- JIT puts overall control of the process on the shop floor, while MRP gives control to planners.

- JIT works with a minimum amount of data, while MRP tries to collect all possible data.

- JIT reduces the amount of clerical effort, while MRP increases it.

- JIT needs a constant rate of production, while MRP can work with varying production.

- JIT has reducing setup cost as a priority, while MRP considers this to be fixed.

- JIT can be easily understood by everyone using it, while MRP is more difficult to understand.

- MRP uses batching rules to set batch sizes, while JIT does not.

- MRP typically carries days' worth of stock of materials, while JIT typically carries hours' worth.

You should not read this list and imagine that JIT and MRP are completely different systems. Despite the comments, the two approaches aim for the same thing – which is an efficient way of controlling operations, and particularly the material supply. The two systems are not necessarily independent. Many organizations now use MRP for overall planning, and JIT for sequencing and process control.

Review questions

13.11 JIT is a system for controlling stocks. Do you think this is true?

13.12 What do you think are the three main advantages of JIT?

13.13 Would it be a good idea to introduce JIT in part of a process to see how it works?

Chapter review

- Just-in-time systems aim at eliminating waste from an organization. They do this by organizing the operations so that they occur just as they are needed. This requires a new way of thinking, which solves problems rather than hides them.

- JIT can only be used in certain types of organization. In particular, it needs a stable environment, small batches, short lead times, total quality, and so on.

- JIT matches the supply of materials to the demand by 'pulling' materials through the process, rather than 'pushing them'.

- In practice, JIT needs a simple control system. This is given by Kanbans.

- An important part of JIT is its emphasis on good relations with suppliers and employees. JIT realizes that co-operation is more productive than conflict.

- JIT can bring substantial benefits to an organization – but there can also be disadvantages.

Key terms

Andon 476	pull system 473
jidoka 478	single sourcing 476
JIT 466	total quality
just-in-time 466	management 467
Kanban 472	

CS Case study – JIT at Pentagon Plastics

Pentagon Plastics make small injection moulded parts for a number of other manufacturers. A few years ago, it was faced by a new problem. One of its best selling parts was used by an instrument maker, and eventually was put into Ford cars. When Ford expanded its quality management programme all its suppliers, including those who were several steps down the supply chain, had to change their habits. In particular, they had to introduce total quality management and just-in-time operations.

Jaydeep Julami was the production manager at Pentagon, and he was wondering how to meet the new demands on his production. Their current production planning was based on a six-week cycle. There were 30 main products, and 120 minor ones. The plant worked a single shift of five days a week. So there was a regular cycle, with the first 15 days spent making the main products, and the next 15 days making the minor products. This schedule gave little disruption with batch setups. These usually took less than an hour, but could take up to four hours if things went wrong.

A dashboard instrument panel was typical of Pentagon's main products. This was made in batches of 25,000 and sent to a store of finished goods. When customers ordered the panel there was a minimum order quantity of 4000. Most orders were met from stock, but if Pentagon did not have enough stock to meet an order, it would reschedule production. This might give a week's delay, as well as upsetting the schedules of other products.

Transport was arranged with a local company. They picked the parts up from Pentagon and delivered them directly to customers, usually within two weeks.

Jaydeep was reading an article about Hewlett-Packard's introduction of JIT. This said that they introduced JIT in seven stages:

(1) design an efficient mass production process

(2) implement total quality management

(3) stabilize production quantities

(4) introduce Kanbans

(5) work with suppliers

(6) continually reduce stocks

(7) improve product designs.

Jaydeep thought about how he could use Hewlett-Packard's experience in his own plant. He knew roughly what was involved, but was still not confident they could make JIT work.

Questions

- Describe in detail the steps that Hewlett-Packard went through when introducing JIT.

- Do you think that JIT could work in Pentagon Plastics? How could it set about introducing it?

- What benefits do you think Pentagon could get from JIT?

Discussion questions

13.1 Is JIT really just an extension of MRP?

13.2 Describe some applications in services where JIT can be used.

13.3 What happens if an organization finds its suppliers can not cope with JIT principles?

13.4 JIT reduces waste in an organization. What is meant by waste in this sense, and how can it occur?

13.5 Suppose a manufacturer only has enough demand to work for seven hours in an eight-hour shift. Would it be more wasteful to leave all operations idle for an hour, or to make extra units and put them into stock?

13.6 What factors are important for the successful implementation of JIT?

13.7 JIT reduces the amount of paperwork for operations. Does this have any consequences for accounting procedures? How can costs be found for operations?

13.8 To what extent is JIT dependent on high technology, such as focused factories, work cells and flexible manufacturing systems?

Selected references

Fucini J. and Fucini S. (1990). *Working for the Japanese*. New York: Free Press.

Goldratt E. and Cox J. (1986). *The Goal*. New York: North River Press.

Hall R. (1983). *Zero Inventories*. Homewood, Ill.: Dow Jones-Irwin.

Hall R. (1987). *Attaining Manufacturing Excellence*. Homewood, Ill.: Dow Jones-Irwin.

Lee S.M. and Schwendiman G. (eds) (1983). *Management by Japanese Systems*. New York: Praeger.

Monden Y. (1983). *Toyota Production System: Practical Approach to Production Management*. Atlanta, Ga.: Industrial Engineering and Management Press.

O'Grady P.J. (1988). *Putting the Just-in-Time Philosophy into Practice*. New York: Nichols.

Ohno T. and Mito S. (1988). *Just-in-Time for Today and Tomorrow*. Cambridge: Productivity Press.

Schonberger R.J. (1982). *Japanese Productivity Techniques: Nine Hidden Lessons in Simplicity*. New York: Free Press.

Schonberger R.J. (1986). *World Class Manufacturing*. London: Collier Macmillan.

Shingo S. (1985). *A Revolution in Manufacturing*. Cambridge: Productivity Press.

Waters C.D.J. (1992). *Inventory Control and Management*. Chichester: John Wiley.

Womack J.P. and Jones D.T. (1990). *The Machine that Changed the World*. New York: Rawson Associates.

14 Short-term scheduling

Contents

Objectives

After reading this chapter you should be able to:

- see how short-term scheduling fits in with other planning
- understand the aims of short-term scheduling
- use a variety of scheduling rules for job shops
- extend these rules to flow shops and employees
- discuss the control of schedules

Purpose of scheduling

In the last few chapters we have been developing some ideas about planning. We have seen how an organization starts with strategic plans and expand these to give shorter term plans. Chapter 11 talked about tactical aggregate plans and master schedules. At this stage an organization has a timetable for the production of individual products. In the last two chapters we described how these timetables can be used to give short-term operational schedules.

We said that there are three ways of getting these operational schedules. In the last two chapters we described **materials requirement planning** and **just-in-time**. These are most directly concerned with materials management. In this chapter we shall describe **short-term scheduling**. This makes decisions about equipment, operators, raw materials, and so on. A summary of the planning process is shown in Figure 14.1.

> **Short-term schedules** give detailed timetables for jobs, people and equipment. They show what any part of the process is doing at any time.

Some specific examples of short-term schedules are:

- university schedules for classes, rooms, instructors and students;

- airline schedules for aeroplanes, pilots, flight attendants and food;

- hospital schedules for patients, nurses, beds and operating theatres;

- manufacturers' schedules for customer orders, employees, machines, material purchases and shipping of completed orders.

The overall aim of short-term scheduling is to achieve the master production schedule, while giving low costs and high utilization of equipment. Although this may seem easy, short-term scheduling is surprisingly difficult. Schedules have to balance a lot of different factors, and many alternative plans must be compared. For this, schedulers will do a range of activities, including:

- allocating jobs to work centres;

- allocating equipment and staff to these work centres;

- setting the sequence of jobs in each work centre;

- controlling the work, including checking progress and expediting late jobs;

- revising schedules for late changes.

Many of the examples we shall use talk about 'jobs' being processed on 'machines'. This is just for convenience. In reality scheduling is one of the most

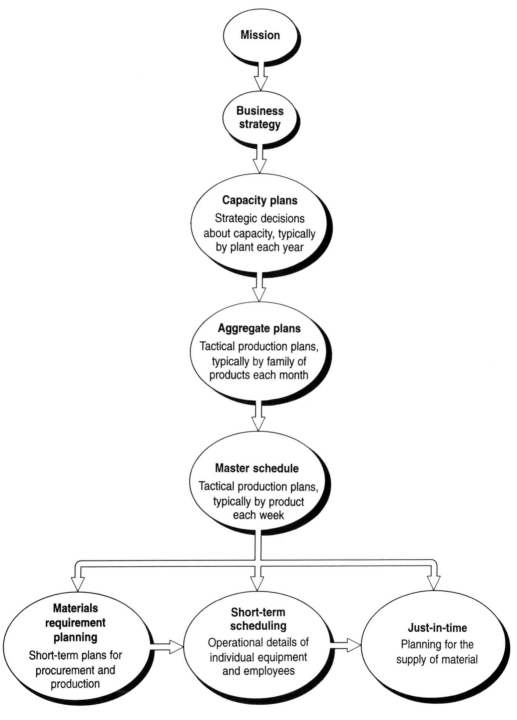

Figure 14.1 Summary of the planning process.

common problems in any organization. Buses and trains work to schedules, delivery vehicles use drop-lists that show when to visit customers, classes are scheduled into rooms, and doctors have appointment books. When describing jobs on machines we are using one type of process to illustrate an approach to a very widely occurring problem.

ce Case example – Scheduling at Sentinel Taxis

Sentinel Taxis has a fleet of 120 cars that work around Madrid. It employs 150 full-time drivers, each of whom works around 40 hours a week. Sentinel also employs a varying number of part-time drivers. Usually there are around 100 of these, but during busy periods there are up to 200. This means the taxis are in use almost 24 hours a day.

The taxis are maintained in the company's garage. This has four bays, six full-time mechanics, two part-time mechanics and four apprentices.

Sentinel also employs 12 controllers. These take telephone calls from customers, schedule the work, and pass instructions on to taxis. The controllers keep a continuous check on the location and work of each taxi.

You can already see that Sentinel must do a range of scheduling. It must schedule the hours worked by cars, so that there are always enough to meet demand from customers. It must also schedule the drivers who do not work the same times as the cars. The controllers add each customer who telephones into the taxis' schedules. This needs to find a car that is near to the customer, with enough free time to do the job. The controllers must also schedule the customers that booked taxis some time in advance and their regular customers. Slightly longer-term schedules are needed for the maintenance of cars and driver holidays.

Questions

- Can you think of any other types of scheduling that might be done at Sentinel?

- How could it do this scheduling? What factors would be important in its decisions?

Review questions

14.1   What is the purpose of short-term scheduling?

14.2   What factors have to be considered in short-term scheduling?

Job shop scheduling

Scheduling rules

In Chapter 7 we described a job shop. This has different types of equipment, and each job goes through these in a different order. As you can imagine, it can be difficult to arrange the jobs so that all equipment is fully used. In this section we shall look at ways of scheduling a job shop.

Job shop scheduling assumes there are a number of jobs, or batches of products, waiting to use equipment (see Figure 14.2). We want to arrange these jobs so the work is done as efficiently as possible – perhaps minimizing the waiting time, minimizing the total processing time, keeping stocks low, reducing the maximum lateness, achieving high utilization of equipment, or some other objective. The problem is effectively one of finding the best sequences of jobs on equipment.

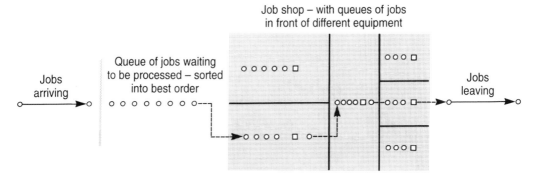

Figure 14.2 Scheduling for a job shop.

A job shop often has jobs that are made for specific customer orders. So the scheduling must take into account the date when the customer needs the product. There are two methods of doing this.

(1)   *Forward scheduling*   where the scheduler knows the start date for the first operation. Then the scheduler can work through all operations needed for a job and can find the date when it will be finished (see Figure 14.3).

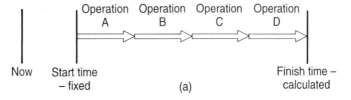

Figure 14.3 Setting times in schedules: (a) forward scheduling;
(b) backward scheduling.

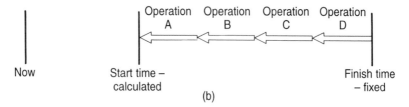

Figure 14.3 *(cont.)* Setting times in schedules: (a) forward scheduling;
(b) backward scheduling.

(2)   *Backward scheduling*   where the customer gives a due date. This due date
is the finish date for the last operation, so the scheduler must work back
through the operations to find the date when the job must be started.

ce Case example – Marc's Car Bodies

For many years Marc West worked for a local Ford dealer in Birmingham. He
had a lot of experience with car body repairs, and was noted for the high
quality of his work. When he decided to start his own car body shop, he knew
that it would be difficult. Although he knew about cars, he did not have any
experience of managing a business.

Now he has to do his own planning. He knows that scheduling
customers' jobs is very important, as customers like their cars back quickly
and at the promised time.

At 8:00 am one Monday morning, a customer brought in a car for
repairs. It needed a lot of body repairs, including welding, finishing and
painting. Marc thought that it would take 1 hour for welding, 2 hours for
finishing and 1.5 hours for painting. The customer wanted to pick up the car at
5:00 pm the same day.

Questions

- Design a forward schedule and a backward schedule for this car repair.

- Suppose a second car arrives at 9:00 am and it needs 1.5 hours of work in
each of the three areas. Design a new forward schedule for Marc.

- What would happen if a third car arrived at 12.00 am for one hour of
emergency work in each area?

You may think these sequencing problems are easy to solve, but in
practice they are notoriously difficult. Many methods have tried to get optimal
solutions, but these are so complicated that they can rarely be used for real

problems of any size. The difficulty is that real scheduling problems are very complicated. The variables include:

- patterns of job arrivals

- amount and type of equipment to be used

- number and skills of operators

- patterns of work flow through equipment

- priority rules for jobs

- disruptions caused by customer changes, breakdowns, and so on, and

- methods of evaluating schedules.

Despite man-centuries spent searching for better methods, the most effective way of scheduling is still to use simple rules. These **scheduling rules** are heuristic procedures that usually give good results.

Suppose there is a number of jobs waiting to use a single machine. If we assume that the setup time for each job is constant, regardless of the job that was worked on previously, the total time for processing is the same for all sequences of jobs. But the order of taking jobs does change other measures of performance. We can see this by considering four standard scheduling rules:

(1) *First-come-first-served* This is the most obvious scheduling rule and simply takes jobs in the order they arrive. It assumes no priority, no urgency, or any other measure of relative importance. The drawback with this rule is that urgent or important jobs may be delayed while less urgent or important ones are being processed. The benefits are simplicity, ease of use and a clear equity. Many queues are based on this system, and when we wait to be served at a supermarket check-out it seems only fair that everyone is treated the same.

(2) *Most urgent job first* This rule assigns an importance, or urgency, to each job and they are processed in order of decreasing urgency. Emergency departments in hospitals, for example, will treat those who are most seriously in need first. There are many other situations where some jobs are more urgent than others. A manufacturer might see when current stocks of parts will run out. Then the most urgent jobs are the ones that replenish parts that will run out first. The benefit of this rule is that jobs which are more important are given higher priority. Unfortunately, those jobs that have low priority may get stuck at the end of a queue for a very long time. Having part-finished jobs waiting a long time for processing is generally a sign of poor planning.

(3) *Shortest job first* A useful objective would be to minimize the average time spent in the system, where:

$$\text{time in the system} = \text{processing time} + \text{waiting time}$$

If a job needs two days of processing but it waits in the queue for three days, its time in the system is five days. Taking the jobs in order of increasing duration minimizes the average time spent in the system. It allows those jobs that can be done quickly to move on through the system, while longer jobs are left until nearer the end. The overall effect is that the average time in the system is minimized. The disadvantage is that long jobs can spend a long time waiting to be done.

(4) *Earliest due date first* For this rule the queue of jobs is sorted in order of delivery date. Those which are expected first are then processed first. This has the benefit of minimizing the maximum lateness of jobs, but again some jobs may have to wait a long time.

Each of these rules is useful in particular circumstances. Students doing coursework often use such rules, usually without stating them explicitly. Some students do work in the order it is set, using first-come-first-served; a more common approach is to do coursework in the order it is due to be finished (most urgent first, which in this case is the same as earliest due date first). If students develop a backlog of coursework they may do the shortest first. This clears their desk quickly, but minimizing the time coursework is in the system may be a strange objective.

we Worked example

The following six jobs must be scheduled on a piece of equipment. Each job fully occupies the equipment for the duration specified.

Job	A	B	C	D	E	F
Duration in days	6	4	2	8	1	5

(a) How long would it take to finish all jobs if they are scheduled in order of arrival?

(b) What schedule would minimize average time in the system?

(c) Suppose each job makes a batch of products which is put into stock. If the demand for these products and current stock levels are as follows, what schedule would you suggest?

Job	A	B	C	D	E	F
Demand	10	15	40	2	5	80
Current stock	260	195	880	20	75	1280

(d) Returning to the basic problem, suppose each job has been promised to customers by the following dates. What schedule of jobs would minimize the maximum lateness?

Job	A	B	C	D	E	F
Due date	6	20	22	24	2	10

Solution

(a) Using the rule first-come-first-served gives the sequence:

Job	Duration	Start	Finish
A	6	0	6
B	4	6	10
C	2	10	12
D	8	12	20
E	1	20	21
F	5	21	26

Then all jobs will be finished by day 26. The sequence of jobs does not change this overall duration, so different sequences try to achieve some other objective.

(b) The average time in the system is minimized by taking jobs in order shortest first. This gives the following schedule:

Job	Duration	Start	Finish
E	1	0	1
C	2	1	3
B	4	3	7
F	5	7	12
A	6	12	18
D	8	18	26

The average time in the system is found from the average finishing date, which is $67/6 = 11.2$ (compared with 15.8 days for first-come-first-served). By day 18 we have finished five jobs with this schedule, while the previous schedule had only finished three.

(c) It would be sensible to schedule the jobs in order of urgency, where urgency is measured by the number of days of remaining stock. This is found from the current stock divided by the demand.

Job	A	B	C	D	E	F
Stock remaining	260	195	880	20	75	1280
Demand	10	15	40	2	5	80
Day's stock remaining	26	13	22	10	15	16
Order of urgency	6	2	5	1	3	4

This gives the following schedule:

Job	Day's stock remaining	Duration	Start	Finish
D	10	8	0	8
B	13	4	8	12
E	15	1	12	13
F	16	5	13	18
C	22	2	18	20
A	26	6	20	26

All jobs are finished before the products are due to run out, except product 6 where stocks run out two days before the job is finished.

(d)   Maximum lateness is minimized by taking jobs in order of due date. This gives the following schedule:

Job	Duration	Start	Finish	Due date	Lateness
E	1	0	1	2	0
A	6	1	7	6	1
F	5	7	12	10	2
B	4	12	16	20	0
C	2	16	18	22	0
D	8	18	26	24	2

This has a maximum lateness of 2 days for jobs 4 and 6, and an average lateness of $5/6 = 0.8$ days (see Figure 14.4).

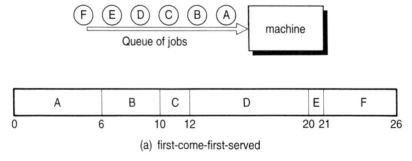

(a) first-come-first-served

Figure 14.4 Results for different scheduling rules.

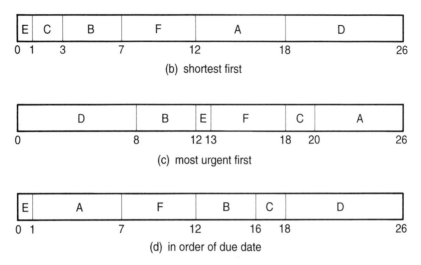

Figure 14.4 *(cont.)* Results for different scheduling rules.

Other scheduling rules

We have only described four scheduling rules, but there are many other rules for different purposes. We could, for example, schedule jobs in the order of least work remaining, or fewest operations remaining. We might have a look at the operations following and look at the combined times for two or three of these. We could look at the **slack**, which is the time remaining until the job is due minus the time needed for processing it.

A useful rule schedules jobs in order of the **critical ratio**. The critical ratio is the time remaining until the job is due divided by the time needed to complete it.

$$\text{Critical ratio} = \frac{\text{due date} - \text{today's date}}{\text{time needed for the job}}$$

If this ratio is low, the time to complete the job is short compared with the time available and the job becomes urgent. If the ratio is high, there is plenty of time left and the job is less urgent. In particular, if the critical ratio is:

- less than zero the job is already late;

- between zero and one the job is behind schedule, but not yet late;

- equal to one the job is exactly on schedule;

- greater than one the job is ahead of schedule.

The critical ratio changes as jobs move through the process, so priorities also change.

We could suggest many other rules, with common objectives of:

- making sure the job is finished when the customer wants it;
- minimizing the time in the system;
- minimizing stocks of work in progress;
- minimizing the idle time of equipment or operators;
- minimizing costs.

ce Case example – Wrightson Duplication

Wrightson Duplication reproduces any kind of document. Most of its customers are businesses who deliver documents during the working day and want copies within 24 hours. These jobs might need typesetting, scanning, graphics work, printing, photocopying, collating, stapling, binding, folding, putting in envelopes, or a range of other operations. Wrightson's has a range of paper handling machines that are organized as a job shop.

When a job arrives at Wrightson, a receptionist puts it in a standard box, together with a form describing the work to be done, and hence the route through the various machines. The box is put into a queue in front of the first machine it needs and waits for the machine to become free. When the job is finished on one machine, the operator checks it, and passes it to the queue in front of the next machine it needs. This is repeated until the job is sent to a 'finished work' area, where it is checked, costed and left until the customer picks it up.

When Wrightson first opened, the boxes were taken first-come-first-served. This lead to complaints from some customers, especially those with short, urgent jobs that had to wait behind longer, less-urgent ones. Wrightson quickly added an order code, based on length and urgency, to each job description. Then the jobs were taken in order of this code. This reduced complaints, but the flow of work was sometimes erratic and jobs were often left waiting for several days.

Eventually, Wrightson bought a computerized scheduling system from a local consultant. This scans the job description form for all new jobs and finds the requirements, length, urgency, customer, and so on. Then it compares the new job with existing schedules and automatically revises the schedules, adding the job where appropriate. It does this using a hierarchy of scheduling rules that were originally developed in a local factory. Whenever a job leaves one of the machines an operator updates the computer – which then signals the next job to be done.

This scheduling system virtually eliminated all customer complaints. It also gives a variety of data to managers who feel it is largely responsible for an increase of 200% in workload over the past three years. The computer system cost £40,000 to install and it paid for itself within six months.

Scheduling of services

Scheduling jobs in services is essentially the same as scheduling in manufacturing. But there are some differences. First, the customer is directly involved in the process. This means that customers often form queues, so waiting times are particularly important. Secondly, services have to be provided when they are needed and cannot be held in stock. This means that capacity must be set to meet peak demands. Wide variations in demand give low utilization of resources – and difficult scheduling problems. Service organizations can deal with uneven demand in several ways.

(1)   *Appointment systems*   where the organization asks customers to set up appointments in advance. This is widely used by doctors, lawyers, counsellors and other professions. Appointment systems increase the utilization of resources and improves customer service. On the other hand they have the drawbacks of making customers wait for a fixed – often long – time, and if the customer makes a late cancellation of an appointment that time is wasted.

(2)   *Fixed schedule system*   where a service is given to many customers at the same, fixed time. Examples of this are a bus or airline schedule, or times of football matches. The schedules are published and known by customers some time in advance.

(3)   *Delayed delivery*   where the service is delayed so that an organization can balance its capacity and work load. This is used when delays do not cause much inconvenience to customers, such as repair shops. If you want your television set mended you take it to a repair shop, and go back later to collect it.

(4)   *First-come-first-served*   which is the most common schedule in services. Customers are simply dealt with in the order they arrive. Examples of this are customers waiting in a bank, fast food restaurants, and the checkout counters of supermarkets.

Review questions

14.3   What is a scheduling rule?

14.4   Which scheduling rules might you use for:
    (a)   hospital admission
    (b)   selling fresh cream cakes
    (c)   telephone calls
    (d)   writing reports for consulting clients

14.5   Are the scheduling rules described the only ones available?

14.6   How does scheduling in services differ from scheduling in manufacturing?

Flow shop scheduling

In the last section we looked at job shop scheduling. This usually involves problems where a queue of jobs has to be processed on a single machine. We should now look at more complicated problems where there is a variety of different machines and other features. Unfortunately, this is rather difficult. When we go beyond simple problems it is almost impossible to find any reasonable scheduling rules that achieve a stated objective.

One problem we can look at is scheduling a **flow shop**, where jobs are processed on the same set of machines in the same order. When there are only two machines in a flow shop – so jobs are processed on machine 1 followed by machine 2 – we have the situation shown in Figure 14.5.

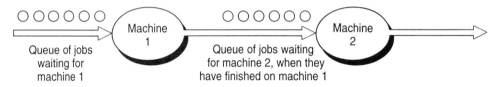

Figure 14.5 A two machine flow shop.

To solve this we can use **Johnson's Rule**. This finds the minimum **make-span**, which is the time between starting the first job and finishing the last job. Johnson's Rule has four steps:

(1)   List the jobs and their processing time on each machine.

(2)   Find the job with the next shortest processing time on either machine.

(3)   If this processing time is on machine 1, schedule the job as early as possible without moving jobs already scheduled: if the processing time is on machine 2, schedule the job as late as possible without moving any jobs already scheduled.

(4)   Do not consider the job just scheduled again, and repeat steps 2 and 3 (working inwards from the ends of the sequence) until all jobs have been scheduled.

we Worked example

A series of four jobs has to be processed on machine 1 followed by machine 2. If the hours needed on each machine are as follows, design a schedule that minimizes the make-span.

Job	A	B	C	D
Time on machine 1	30	20	60	80
Time on machine 2	50	40	10	70

Solution

- *Step 1*. The first step of Johnson's Rule has been done, and we now have a list of jobs and their processing times.

- *Step 2* finds the shortest processing time as job C on machine 2.

- *Step 3* recognizes that this is on machine 2, so the job is scheduled as late as possible. This gives a sequence which is currently:

    C

- *Step 4* now ignores job C and returns to step 2.

- *Step 2* finds the shortest remaining processing time (from jobs A, B and D) as job B on machine 1.

- *Step 3* recognizes this is on machine 1, so the job is scheduled as early as possible to give the sequence:

    B C

Now also ignoring job B the shortest remaining processing time (for jobs A and D) is job A on machine 1. This is scheduled as early as possible to give the sequence:

    B   A C

Now also ignoring job A the shortest remaining processing time (for job D) is job D on machine 2. This is scheduled as late as possible to give the final sequence:

    B   A   D   C

Then the finished schedule, assuming a notional starting time of 0, is:

Job	Machine 1 Duration	Start	Finish	Machine 2 Duration	Start	Finish
B	2	0	2	4	2	6
A	3	2	5	5	6	11
D	8	5	13	7	13	20
C	6	13	19	1	20	21

In this table you can see that jobs can only be started on machine 2 when they have finished on machine 1 and when the previous job on machine 2 has finished. So job B has to wait until job A is finished before it can start, while job D is only held up by the time it takes on machine 1.

The make-span with this solution is 21 days. You can compare this with a make-span of 26 days for the first-come-first-served rule.

	Machine 1			Machine 2		
Job	Duration	Start	Finish	Duration	Start	Finish
A	2	0	2	4	2	6
B	3	2	5	5	6	11
C	6	5	11	1	11	12
D	8	11	19	7	19	26

Bar charts for the schedule are shown in Figure 14.6.

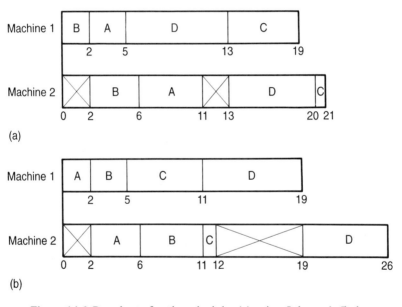

(a)

(b)

Figure 14.6 Bar charts for the schedule: (a) using Johnson's Rule; (b) using first-come-first-served.

Review questions

14.7   What is a flow shop?

14.8   When is Johnson's Rule used?

ce Case example – Satellite Communications

Long-distance television, radio, telephone and data communications are routinely transmitted via satellite networks. Each satellite, like INTELSAT and EUTELSAT, is shared by dozens of earth stations. The signals to and from each of these must be kept separate to avoid interference.

Each earth station digitizes incoming data and stores it in buffers. These buffers are emptied in bursts of high speed transmission to the satellite. Each burst of transmission lasts about 2 milliseconds, and such transmissions are made in cycles to give Time Division Multiple Access.

A communication satellite consists of transmit and receive antennae which cover fixed geographical spots, and a set of repeaters which connect these. The satellite receives a burst of signal from an earth station, routes it through a repeater and transmits the burst to an area on earth, where it is picked up by a receiving station.

The satellite operators face a standard scheduling problem. They have a limited resource – which is the capacity of the satellite. There are a large number of jobs to be processed – these are the messages from earth stations. These jobs must be scheduled so the satellite can handle as much work as possible. A number of algorithms have been developed for this. Even when there are hundreds of millions of pounds worth of equipment to consider, the most useful algorithms use fairly simple procedures that aim for good solutions with a reasonable amount of computing, rather than optimal solutions.

Scheduling employees

So far we have looked at the way equipment is scheduled. Another problem in short-term scheduling looks at the people needed for operations – in other words it designs staff schedules. If the same operators are always assigned to the same equipment, the equipment schedule effectively fixes the staff schedule. But usually this does not happen, and one operator can work on several pieces of equipment. Then we could use some assignment rule that is similar to a scheduling rule, perhaps assigning operators to the equipment that:

- has the most jobs waiting to be processed

- has the job with the earliest due date

- has the job which has been waiting longest.

Again, there are many simple rules we could use. One slightly more complicated approach designs a timetable that gives each person two consecutive days off a week:

Operator scheduling:

(1)   Find the minimum number of operators needed each day of the week.

(2)   Identify the two adjacent days with smallest needs. This means finding the day with smallest needs, then the day with next smallest, then the next smallest, and so on until two adjacent days have been identified.

(3)   Give the next operator these two days off (perhaps giving priority to weekends off if there are ties).

(4)   Reduce the needs by one for those five days when this operator works.

(5)   If there are still more operators needed go to step 2, otherwise a schedule has been found.

we Worked example

Jane Schultz wants to schedule operators for a process. She knows the numbers needed each day are as follows. Each operator has two consecutive days off. What schedule can Jane use?

Day	Mon	Tues	Wed	Thurs	Fri	Sat	Sun
Operators	1	2	3	3	4	4	0

Solution

- *Step 1* is already done with the figures given.

- *Step 2* finds the two adjacent days with smallest numbers of operators. Assuming the schedule is continuous, this is Sunday and Monday.

- *Step 3* gives the first operator these two days off.

- *Step 4* reduces the needs for Tuesday to Saturday by one, and we return to step 2.

Day	Mon	Tues	Wed	Thurs	Fri	Sat	Sun
Still needed	1	1	2	2	3	3	0

The next cycle again finds Sunday and Monday as the adjacent days with lowest demand, so the second operator also works Tuesday to Saturday. Repeating this another three times gives the following results.

		Day						
		Mon	Tues	Wed	Thurs	Fri	Sat	Sun
Cycle 1	Operators	1	2	3	3	4	4	0
Cycle 2	Still needed	1	1	2	2	3	3	0
Cycle 3	Still needed	1	0	1	1	2	2	0
Cycle 4	Still needed	0	0	1	0	1	1	0
Cycle 5	Still needed	0	0	0	0	0	0	0

This completes the schedule, with all demand met by four operators, as follows.

	Day						
	Mon	Tues	Wed	Thurs	Fri	Sat	Sun
Operators needed	1	2	3	3	4	4	0
Operators off	3	2	1	0	0	0	2
Operators available	1	2	3	4	4	4	2
Spare operators	0	0	0	1	0	0	2

Review questions

14.9   When does scheduling operators become a problem?

14.10 Most schedules for employees are designed using simple scheduling rules. Do you think this is true?

Control of schedules

Short-term scheduling gives detailed plans that show what each job, piece of equipment and person should be doing at any time. But there is a difference between designing plans and making sure they are implemented. The next thing we should consider, then, is the control of schedules.

Controlling the schedules makes sure they are accurate, up to date and show what is actually happening. Controls, therefore, check performance to make sure it matches plans and reports any discrepancies. This control of schedules is in two parts:

(1)   The first part records the progress of jobs and gives information back to managers. At regular intervals in the process, details of the jobs' progress are checked and times, efficiency, productivity, utilization and other measures reported.

(2)   The second part of the control occurs when circumstances change or there is some disruption which means that schedules have to be revised.

Both of these feed back information to managers so they know how operations are going, and can take any necessary action. To be more specific, the purposes of a control system are:

●   to make sure jobs are scheduled according to the plans;

●   to warn of problems with resources, delivery dates, and so on;

●   to make sure the materials, equipment and operators are available for each job;

●   to assign jobs to specific orders and set delivery times;

●   to check progress as jobs move through the process;

●   to make small adjustments as necessary to plans;

●   to allow rescheduling if there is a major disruption to plans;

●   to give information on current activities;

●   to give feedback on performance.

An important input to a control system is a **dispatch list**. This shows the short-term schedules as an ordered, daily list of the jobs to be done, their importance and how long each will take. Other inputs might include inventory records, bills of materials, routing through the machines, and orders for jobs to be done. The main outputs from a control system are status and exception reports. Other outputs might include the release of job orders, dispatch of finished jobs and schedule receipts.

Some organizations link the control system to an **input/output report**, which keeps a check on the units entering an operation and those leaving. Obviously these should match, or work is accumulating somewhere. Figure 14.7 shows a section from an input/output report, and you can see that output is well below plans. As the inputs are also below plans there must be a hold-up in some previous operation.

Control systems can become complex, need access to large amounts of information, and yet have to make decisions quickly. This is the type of problem that expert systems might deal with. The argument says that control system usually require humans to access many computer files and programs, and then extract information needed to adjust plans. In some circumstances an expert system could be designed to follow a set of rules and give equivalent results much faster.

Assembly operation 14			Manual assembly	Week 17	Day 4	Operator 2	Tolerance ±10
Week	11	12	13	14	15	16	17
Inputs							
Planned	240	240	200	200	200	240	240
Actual	215	210	200	180	165	200	210
Difference	−25	−30	0	−20	−35	−40	−30
Cumulative Difference	−25	−55	−55	−75	−110	−150	−180
Outputs							
Planned	220	220	220	200	200	200	220
Actual	205	200	195	195	180	190	190
Difference	−15	−20	−25	−5	−20	−10	−30
Cumulative Difference	−15	−35	−60	−65	−85	−95	−125

Figure 14.7 A section from an input-output report.

Review questions

14.11 What is the purpose of a control system for schedules?

14.12 The control of schedules is only important when something goes wrong. Do you agree with this?

Chapter review

- Strategic capacity planning is the first step in a hierarchy of planning decisions. Later decisions give aggregate plans and master production schedules. These in turn lead to short-term scheduling.

- Short-term scheduling expands the master production schedule to give details of operations. It shows detailed timetables for jobs, people, materials and equipment.

- It is very difficult to design good schedules. The most common approach uses heuristic scheduling rules. Many rules have been suggested for job shop scheduling, ranging from first-come-first-served to more complex ones.

- The rules used in job shops can be extended to deal with flow shops and staff schedules.

- A control system is needed to make sure planned production is actually achieved, and report any differences.

Key terms

control system   506
critical ratio   497
flow shop   500
job   488
job shop scheduling   491
Johnson's Rule   500

make-span   500
scheduling   488
scheduling rule   493
short-term schedule   488
slack   497

CS Case study – Bangor Production Consultants

Bangor Production Consultants is a partnership of 34 people. It produces computer software for a range of general management problems. At the moment, its best selling packages prepare payrolls in small companies, control stocks in warehouses, organize vehicle fleet maintenance, and forecast sales. Its usual approach is to prepare a general package, and then tailor this to meet individual customer's needs.

It has been approached by several local companies who have scheduling problems. As a result, Bangor is planning a new set of packages that look at various aspects of planning and scheduling. This is not its first step in this direction. For some time it has had a spreadsheet program that helps with aggregate planning. This connects to a program for generating master production schedules, and there is a separate program for materials requirement planning. Bangor now aims to design a new program for various aspects of short-term scheduling, and then integrate its programs into a comprehensive planning and scheduling system.

The product development group is now making the general designs for this proposed system.

Questions

- What features do you think Bangor should include in its package?

- Who do you think will be its major customers?

Problems

14.1 Eight jobs are to be processed on a single machine, with processing times as follows:

Job	A	B	C	D	E	F	G	H
Processing time	2	5	3	8	4	7	2	3

Use a number of different scheduling rules, and compare the results.

14.2 What order should the jobs in the last problem be scheduled if they have the following due dates?

Job	A	B	C	D	E	F	G	H
Due date	13	7	8	30	14	20	2	36

14.3 Seven jobs are to be processed on machine 1 followed by machine 2. The time needed by each job on each machine is as follows:

Job	A	B	C	D	E	F	G
Machine 1	4	10	20	16	8	24	18
Machine 2	28	14	6	20	10	12	12

What sequence of jobs would maximize the machine utilization?

14.4 Compucash Services has to prepare the payrolls of six factories at the end of each week. This needs the following times for computing and printing:

Factory	1	2	3	4	5	6
Computing time	10	20	20	35	10	15
Printing time	20	15	40	50	15	30

What schedules would you recommend?

14.5 A small museum needs the following numbers of guides:

Day	Mon	Tues	Wed	Thurs	Fri	Sat	Sun
Guides	4	6	8	8	10	14	12

Design a schedule that gives each guide two consecutive days off.

Discussion questions

14.1 What is short-term scheduling and when is it used? Describe some different approaches to short-term scheduling.

14.2 How does short-term scheduling fit in with other planning decisions?

14.3 Why is scheduling such a difficult problem? Give real examples to support your views.

14.4 What scheduling rules would be best for a hamburger restaurant? Would different rules be better for a doctor's surgery? What other examples can you give where different rules are used?

14.5 How do you think spreadsheets can help with short term scheduling? Design a spreadsheet that would help with scheduling.

14.6 The effects of different scheduling rules can be found using computer simulation. What does this mean?

14.7 How do you think control systems could use expert systems?

Selected references

Baker K.R. (1984). *Introduction to Sequencing and Scheduling*. New York: John Wiley.

Fitzsimmons J.A. and Fitzsimmons M.J. (1994). *Service Management for Competitive Advantage*. New York: McGraw-Hill.

Fogarty D.W. and Hoffman T.R. (1983). *Production and Inventory Management*. Cincinnati, Oh.: South-Western Publishing.

Goldratt E. and Cox J. (1984). *The Goal*. New York: North River Press.

Green J.H. (1987). *Production and Inventory Control Handbook* (2nd edn). New York: McGraw-Hill.

Lockyer K. and Gordon J. (1991). *Critical Path Analysis and Other Project Network Techniques* (5th edn). London: Pitman.

McLeavey D. and Narasimhan S.L. (1985). *Production Planning and Inventory Control*. Boston, Ma.: Allyn and Bacon.

Vollman T.E., Berry W.L. and Whybark D.C. (1992). *Manufacturing Planning and Control Systems* (3rd edn). Homewood, Ill.: Richard Irwin.

15 Job design and work measurement

Contents

Objectives

After reading this chapter you should be able to:

- see how job design is a part of planning
- understand the aims of job design
- outline ways of motivating and rewarding employees
- discuss the aims of work measurement
- find how long a job should take
- calculate standard times for jobs

Introduction

The last chapter looked at the scheduling of jobs, equipment, materials and people. For this we assumed that each operation takes a fixed time. But you know from experience that the time needed to do a job can change – it is affected by the layout, process design, convenience of tools and equipment, physical environment, motivation, rewards given, and a whole range of other factors. In this chapter we shall look in more detail at the time needed for a job. In particular we shall consider:

- the best way of doing a job, which is **job design** and

- how long the job will take, which is **work measurement**.

In this context, the aim of an organization is to make its employees as productive as possible. In Chapter 9 we met the definition of labour productivity:

Labour productivity = output/labour input

If a worker makes 40 units in an eight-hour shift, the labour productivity is $40/8 = 5$ units an hour. So increasing labour productivity means raising the number of units that are made in an hour. There are several ways of doing this. So far we have taken a broader view and emphasized ways of improving productivity by designing a better process.

Productivity, however, can also be improved by motivating people to work faster and more efficiently. Later in the chapter we shall talk about incentives and motivation. We can also take a detailed view of each operation that makes up the process, and change the way these are done. This could allow the same job to be done in a better way – perhaps by using better methods, tools, materials or techniques. This is the aim of job design, which we shall describe in the following sections.

At this point you should remember the old saying that 'an organization's most valuable assets are its employees'. This recognizes that the performance of all organizations depends on the employees. So the most effective way of improving output, productivity, and so on, is to create the conditions that allow employees to work more effectively. Dofasco, a Canadian steel company, recognizes this by saying, 'Our product is steel, but our strength is people'.

Review questions

15.1 'Happy people are productive people.' Do you believe this?

15.2 What is the purpose of job design?

15.3 What is the difference between job design and work measurement?

Job design

Aims of job design

In this context, a **job** is the basic set of tasks that a person does for their work. At their work most people repeat the same job many times. Perhaps they talk to customers and arrange insurance, or they drive trains, or make films, or put out fires, or prepare meals. During the working day, a job is repeated many times – perhaps thousands of times. This means that employees can save a lot of time and effort if they use the best possible method for doing the job. Finding this best method is the purpose of **job design**.

> **Job design** describes the tasks, methods, responsibilities and environment used by individuals to do their work. It aims to find the best possible way of doing a job.

There are two groups of people concerned with job design – and we will follow the usual habit of calling them 'managers' and 'workers'. Job design must satisfy the needs of both of these, even though their needs are completely different. Managers want the workers to be productive so they meet production, quality and service targets at low costs. So managers' needs are basically economic and technical. Their main concern is that the value added by the workers is greater than the wages paid to them.

On the other hand, the needs of workers are social and psychological. People want to interact with other people, to be recognized, appreciated and properly rewarded. So there are two main objectives in job design:

(1)   to meet the productivity, quality and other goals of the organization;

(2)   to make the job safe, satisfying and rewarding for the individual.

Until fairly recently the first of these was given far more attention than the second. Traditionally, managers did not give any weight to their workers' feelings and saw any investment in their welfare as an extra cost that had no returns. More recently we have learnt that this view is mistaken. Although it is a simplification to say that 'a happy worker is a productive worker', there is some justification in this. Certainly people give higher productivity when their work is rewarding. So money spent in properly designing a job should be seen as an investment and not a cost.

You can see this change of view with assembly lines. At the beginning of the century Henry Ford found he could get high productivity by having people working on an assembly line. Each person on the line had a simple job that they repeated many times – perhaps thousands of times – a day. The pace of the work was set by the assembly line so that high output could be almost guaranteed. Assembly lines had several advantages for the organization, which could:

- employ unskilled or low skilled people

- train them quickly to do the simple jobs

- pay low wages

- get high output

- control the flow of work.

Unfortunately, this division of labour, where each person endlessly repeats a small job, has clear disadvantages. The main one is that people find the work boring, tiring and unsatisfying. They have no chance of showing initiative, getting promotion, communicating with colleagues or having control over their work. The result is a workforce that has no motivation and low morale. This in turn leads to low productivity, absenteeism, grievances and high staff turnover. So the high productivity these lines were supposed to guarantee was not achieved. This is one reason why manual production lines are far less common than they used to be. Many assembly line jobs have been automated, and others have been redesigned.

Although we know many of the factors that make workers dissatisfied – and so less productive – it is difficult to find the factors they find rewarding, to make them more productive. Some people like work that pays a lot, other like challenges, other like the opportunity to socialize, other like to be left alone. Many studies have tried to analyse the needs of workers, with two important ones done by Maslow and Hertzberg.

(1) *Maslow's Hierarchy of Needs* This suggests that workers have a hierarchy of needs they want to fulfil. This hierarchy starts with physiological or survival needs, which include food, shelter and clothing. Once these survival needs are met, there is another level of needs for security. When security needs are met, there is another level of social needs, and so on. This hierarchy is shown in Figure 15.1.

(2) *Hertzberg's Two Factor Theory* Hertzberg studied over 200 engineers and accountants to see what motivates people in their workplace. He found two sets of factors:

- *Hygiene factors* – without which employees are unhappy. Examples are wages, job security, working conditions, relationship with supervisor, company policies.
- *Motivators* – which motivate employees to work. Examples are recognition, promotion, responsibility, sense of achievement, pleasure in the work itself.

These ideas let us look in more detail at ideas of motivation and rewards.

High order
needs

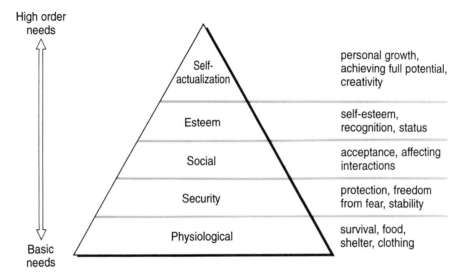

Basic
needs

Figure 15.1 Maslow's hierarchy of needs.

Motivating and rewarding employees

We have already said that job design must satisfy both the management's economic and technical needs, and the workers' behavioural, social and psychological needs. So we really aim for workers who are both productive and happy with their working conditions. To find how to achieve this we can start by looking at employees' needs, and asking, 'Why do people work?' McGregor suggested two answers for this, which he called Theory X and Theory Y.

- **Theory X** assumes that people are essentially lazy, dislike work, lack ambition and avoid responsibility. They will only work because they have to. This means that organizations can only get people to work by using close supervision, threats, punishments, incentives, and so on. But this theory does not explain why people work beyond their retirement age, do voluntary work, work after they have won the lottery, or actually work harder than they need to.

- **Theory Y** assumes that people work because they like to – so work is as natural as rest or play. This means that organizations only have to supply the right conditions and people will work as effectively as they can.

Both of these views are partly right, but you know from experience that neither view gives the whole story. Sometimes a person will work because they have to, and sometimes the same person will work because they want to. In other words, the amount they work depends on their **motivation**.

> **Motivation** is difficult to define, but we generally say that a person is motivated if they keep working hard to achieve an appropriate goal.

You can see from this that there are three aspects to motivation. The first is the effort that a person puts into a job – a motivated person will work hard. The second is the perseverance of the effort – a motivated person will continue their efforts for as long as needed. The third is effectiveness – a motivated person will work towards an appropriate goal. These three factors affect motivation and resulting performance (see Figure 15.2).

So we can summarize this, by saying that managers should design jobs that motivate their workers. This can be done in many ways, including:

- treat people as the most important part of the organization, not as part of the machinery;

- give people broad training for multi-skilled jobs;

- widen work responsibilities to include quality;

- form worker councils and other means of participating in management;

- form work teams with authority to make decisions about operations;

- automate dull or dangerous jobs;

- remove artificial barriers between trades, levels;

- form self-directed work teams.

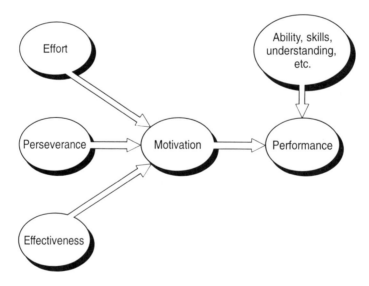

Figure 15.2 Motivation and performance.

Self-directed work teams are one way of using employees' skills and knowledge, and giving satisfying jobs. They are groups of people who have day-to-day responsibility for managing themselves and the process they work with. Instead of being instructed by supervisors, self-directed work teams take the work to be done, and then schedule their time to achieve this most effectively. This approach needs a variety of skills within the team, but many organizations have used it to both increase productivity and reduce costs. Perhaps the most obvious benefit is the increase in employee motivation and morale that comes from giving them challenging work.

You may already see that a common theme from studies on worker needs and motivation is the importance of fair and reasonable treatment of employees. One aspect of such fair treatment is payment. But it is misleading to say that motivation depends on the amount an organization pays its employees. There are many examples of organizations where pay is high, but the workforce is not motivated and gives low productivity. Some people say there are many examples of this in governments. On the other hand, there are many examples of organizations where pay is low, but a well-motivated workforce give high productivity. This is often found in charities and non-profit organizations such as health and education services. But successful organizations usually give good basic wages and other incentives, such as employee discounts, profit sharing and share ownership schemes.

Employee wages can be set in two different ways – **time-based** and **output-based**. In time-based systems, employees are paid for the amount of time spend at work. This includes all hourly-paid and most salaried employees. It is simple to use and control.

Output-based systems are also called incentive plans, where employees are paid for the amount they actually produce. There are many types of incentive plans, including the following:

- **Piece rate or commission** where an organization pays an employee an agreed amount for each unit of output.

- **Basic pay plus bonus** which gives a basic wage that is paid for a basic amount of work, but anyone producing more than this is paid a bonus for each additional unit.

- **Standard-hour plans** where an organization sets a standard time to do a job and the worker is paid for this regardless of how long it actually takes. For example, the standard time for a job might be one hour. If an employee produced nine units in a given day he is paid for nine hours of work, regardless of how long he actually took.

There are several disadvantages of these individual incentive plans. They do not encourage co-operation and team work among employees, some people will try to make extra money by working faster but ignoring quality, different people work at different paces so it is difficult to balance work flows, and so on. Some of these disadvantages can be overcome by group incentive schemes.

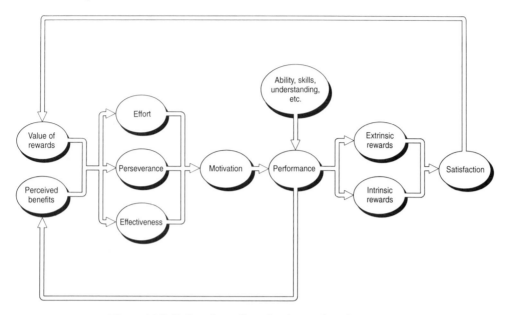

Figure 15.3 Fuller view of motivation and performance.

- *Group incentive systems*, share any gains among all employees. In some circumstances, like assembly lines, no single worker can really affect the output. So any bonuses should be shared between all the workers on the line. This encourages co-operation and teamwork. There are many different types of group plans. Some of the most popular are 'Scanlon plans', where any profits from productivity gains are shared between the workers and the company.

Now we can add such factors as rewards and satisfaction to the earlier diagram, to get a fuller picture, as shown in Figure 15.3.

ce Case example – The Magna Employee's Charter

Magna International Inc. is a global supplier of high technology systems, assemblies and components. In 1994 it had sales of £1.7 billion and a net profit of £110 million. Frank Stronach, the chairman of Magna, believes in fairness and concern for his employees. He has created The Magna Employee's Charter, which has the following points.

- *Job security*
  Being competitive by making a better product for a better price is the best way to enhance job security. Magna is committed to working together with you to help protect your job. To assist you Magna will provide: job counselling, training and employee assistance programmes.

- *A safe and healthy workplace*
  Magna strives to provide you with a working environment which is safe and healthy.

- *Fair treatment*
  Magna offers equal employment opportunities based on an individual's qualifications and performance, free from discrimination or favouritism.

- *Competitive wages and benefits*
  Magna will provide you with information which will enable you to compare your wages and benefits with those earned by employees of your competitors, as well as with other plants in your community. If your total compensation is found not to be competitive, then your wages will be adjusted.

- *Employee equity and profit participation*
  Magna believes that every employee should own a portion of the company.

- *Communication and information*
  Through regular monthly meetings between management and employees and through publications, Magna will provide you with information so that you will know what is going on in your company and within the industry.

Magna has a hotline to register any complaint if an employee feels that these principles are not being met. It also has an Employee Relations Advisory Board to monitor, advise and make sure that Magna operates within the spirit of the Employee's Charter. Magna's Corporate Constitution allocates ten percent of pre-tax profit to employees.

Elements in job design

Now we have some ideas of the needs of an organization – which are mainly technical and economic – and of the employees – which are mainly social and psychological. The next step is to design a job that satisfies both of these. For this we need to look at three main elements:

(1)   *Physical environment*, where the job is done;

(2)   *Social environment*, which affects the worker's psychological condition;

(3)   *Work methods*, which describe how the job is done.

Physical environment

This concerns the place where the job is done, its layout, the tools used, equipment available, and so on. If these are badly organized the environment can be distracting, put heavy burdens on a worker, and even be dangerous. Work on the physical environment is part of **ergonomics**, which designs tools, machines, workplaces, layouts, and so on, to take into account the physical capabilities of people.

Typical questions to be asked about the environment are:

- who will use the workplace

- how will the work be done

- what must the user see

- what must the user hear

- where must the user reach.

Suppose, for example, a person has to repeatedly lean forward to adjust a lever. We know from data banks of body measurements that 75% of people can remain sitting and reach forward a distance of 53 cm or more. But this leaves 25% of people who can not reach this far. The job design would have to ask if the same person will always be doing the job, whether they will be sitting, how much they will have to move, if there is anything in the way, how much time is available for the adjustment, could the lever be moved and is the adjustment necessary?

A lot of early studies of the physical environment looked at operators of manufacturing machines. Nowadays, more emphasis is put on white collar jobs, particularly 'knowledge workers'. Designers now consider the layout of an office, the height of chairs and tables, the position and size of keyboards, and a series of other factors. You can see the effect of this with telephones, which have become lighter, easier to use, with more functions, and connecting to computer systems and other equipment.

Other aspects of the work environment concern:

- **Light** in general jobs which need higher speed and accuracy need more light. The type of light is also important, so we must consider the colour, contrast and direction.

- **Temperature and humidity** most people work at their best in temperatures around 18 to 22 degrees; if the temperature in an office is too high people get sleepy and slow down; if the temperature in a warehouse is too low people spend more time trying to keep warm.

- **Noise and vibrations** noise can be annoying, but it can also damage hearing. There are limits on the time a person can work with loud noise.

- **Air pollution** pollution or fumes can be irritating, but they can also be dangerous. This pollution need not be exotic chemicals, but can be as simple as dust or petrol fumes.

- **Safety** people must always be given working conditions that are safe, and they must be protected from any possible dangers.

Social environment

The design of a job must also take into account the psychological well-being of the people doing it. So an organization must start by giving employees:

- adequate training for the job

- adequate supervision and help

- knowledge of the organization's policies, rules and regulations

- a clear statement of what is expected from each person

- credit for good work.

This aspect of job design is largely concerned with motivation, which we have already mentioned. When designing a job, six important factors for motivation are:

(1) *Task significance* the extent to which employees feel the job has a substantial impact on the organization or the world.

(2) *Task identity* the extent to which employees can see the job as a whole, single piece of work from start to finish.

(3) *Task variety* the extent to which a job contains a variety of different tasks.

(4) *Skill variety* the extent to which workers use a variety of skills and talents.

(5) *Autonomy* the extent to which the worker has freedom, independence and personal control over the work.

(6) *Feedback from the job* the extent to which clear, timely information about individual performance is available.

An organization's most likely way of getting a motivated workforce is to design jobs which are significant, make identifiable products, involve a variety of tasks, use a variety of skills, give workers autonomy and clear feedback.

Work methods

Work methods look at the details of how a task should actually be done. These look at the design of individual tasks, and can be viewed as the most detailed level of planning.

The usual approach of work methods starts by looking at the way a job is done at present. Then it breaks the job into very small parts. A men's hairdresser, for example, spends a lot of time cutting hair. This involves a series of standard tasks such as washing hair, giving an initial cut with scissors, tidying loose ends, trimming with shears, drying hair, and so on. Each of these tasks can be broken down into **micro-elements**, such as reaching out, picking up a hair drier, moving the hair dryer back to the customer's head, and so on. In other words, a whole job can be broken down into a series of very small micro-elements.

The micro-elements can be analysed to find the most efficient way of doing the whole job. The hairdresser, for example, might spend too long reaching for various thing, so the job could be improved by moving them nearer the customer. In general, a series of questions is asked, like: Why is this done? How is it done? Why is it done this way? Could the step be missed out? Could it be done at another time? Could it be done automatically? How could the layout of the workplace be improved? Would different tools help? The answers to these questions lead to better ways of doing the job.

Several different types of diagram can help describe a job through its micro-elements. Process charts of the type described in Chapter 7 are often used for this. Multiple activity charts can look in so much detail that an operator's left and right hand are taken as working separately (see Figure 15.4). Slow-motion videos are widely used to pin-point inefficient movements.

Although such detailed analyses of jobs can be very important, the design of individual tasks is usually less important than the overall view of the job. Some broader views of work methods to consider include:

Operation: assembly
Standard Time: 30 seconds
Equipment: punch, die, press, holder

Left hand	Right hand
Reach for casing	Put last assembly into bin
Pick up casing	
Put casing into holder	Put casing into holder
Reach for washers	Reach for insert
Pick up washers	Pick up insert
	Fit insert to casing
Add washers to insert	Hold casing
Hold casing	Reach for punch
	Pick up punch
Adjust punch and press	Adjust punch and press
	Operate press
Remove assembly	Remove assembly

Figure 15.4 Example of an activity chart for two hands.

- **Job rotation** where the job each person does is rotated, perhaps daily, so they do not get bored. Some organizations have found this only gives a temporary improvement as people soon feel they are being switched around a series of equally boring jobs.

- **Job enlargement** which combines several simple jobs into a larger one. Again some organizations find this is a temporary improvement as it replaces a short boring job by a longer boring job.

- **Job enrichment** which adds more responsibility to the job, and makes it inherently more interesting. This has been mentioned with quality management, where everyone becomes responsible for the quality of their own work.

Review questions

15.4 How do the needs of employees and employers differ?

15.5 Who are the main people concerned with job design?

15.6 People will work hard if they know they can be fired at any time. Do you think this is true?

15.7 Why is job design important?

15.8 What are the main elements in job design?

15.9 What factors will generally improve morale in an organization?

ce Case example – Moorhead Stamping Works

Moorhead Stamping Works is a medium-sized company that supplies stamped parts for consumer appliance industries. Its process starts with coils of sheet metal. These coils are cut into smaller strips using shearing machines. The strips are passed to stamping presses which form the products. Other processes used at the shop are welding, painting, plating and assembly.

The working conditions in the plant are far from pleasant. The plant is noisy and cluttered. It does not have a good heating and ventilation system. There is not a good production planning system, so customer orders are always being expedited, and rush work is quite common. This puts a lot of pressure of workers. Sometimes the machines are operated in unsafe conditions and often by poorly trained workers. Government safety and welfare offices are aware of working conditions, and have often sent inspectors.

There is poor communication between managers and the workers. Mike Peterson, one of the long-time employees, can not remember a single occasion when a manager has shown any appreciation of the job done by a worker. But, he noticed that managers are always complaining about increased costs and low profits. Mike is not surprised that the company has high employee turnover, poor quality, and a series of other problems.

Questions

- Describe some of the problems facing the Moorhead Stamping Works.

- Will a proper job design help the company? How?

- What should be done to improve the quality and profitability of the company?

Work measurement

Purpose of work measurement

The last section discussed the design of jobs. In this section we are going to see how well the jobs are actually done. In particular, we are going to see how long it takes to do a job. This is the function of **work measurement**.

> **Work measurement** finds the standard time needed to do a job.

Work measurement tells us how long a job should take, that is its **standard time**. When we know how long a job will take we can use this for a variety of purposes including:

- capacity planning

- estimating the size of workforce needed

- finding the cost of operations

- designing wage incentive schemes

- monitoring worker performance

- scheduling production.

You may think it is easy to find out how long a job will take, but there are several complications. You know from experience that different people take different times to do a job. You also know that if the same person does a job several times, each repetition will take a different time (we discussed one reason for this with the learning curve in Chapter 9). These variations simply show that humans have different abilities and each individual has some inconsistency in performance. To get around this we try to find the basic work content of a task.

The basic work content of any task gives the minimum time theoretically needed to complete it. This is the time needed if the design of the product is perfect, the ideal process is used, no time is lost, materials are delivered on time, and everything works smoothly. Actual job time will be greater than the basic time, because of:

- **Work added by poor design of the product**
  - the product design may not allow the best process to be used
  - it may need additional or complex tasks
  - there may be no standardization, so small batches are made
  - quality standards may not be set properly
  - it may use too many materials

- **Work added by inefficient operations**
  - using the wrong type or size of machinery
  - not operating the process properly
  - having a poor layout
  - using poor methods that give extra work

- **Ineffective time caused by poor management**
  - making too wide a variety of products
  - having too many design changes
  - poor materials flow from suppliers and on to customers
  - poor maintenance of plant and equipment
  - poor working conditions, morale

- **Ineffective time within the control of the operator**
  - absenteeism, lateness, idling
  - careless workmanship
  - unsafe behaviour causing accidents.

The standard time avoids these complications by giving the basic time that is needed for a particular job. Then we can add whatever allowances are needed for actual circumstances.

Standard times

The International Labour Organization gives the definition:

> **Work measurement** is the application of techniques designed to establish the time for a qualified operator to carry out a specific job at a defined level of performance.

This definition uses a 'qualified operator', which assumes they are:

- properly prepared and qualified for the job

- properly trained and experienced to do the job

- physically and mentally capable of doing the job.

The definition also refers to a 'specific job' – and this means defining the job, the method to be used, and the conditions in which the job is done.

This gives information about the operator and the job, but we still need some way of finding a standard time. Obviously we could time someone doing the job, but individuals do the same job in slightly different ways and take different times. So we should define a standard rate of work that we can use for timings. This can be defined as follows.

> The **standard rate** of work is the average rate that qualified workers will naturally achieve without overdue exertion over their working day – provided they know and adhere to the specified method and provided that they are motivated to apply themselves to the work.

Now we can use this standard rate to find standard times – essentially we can time people doing a job, and compare their work rates with a standard rate. This comparison is called **rating**. In practice, rating relies on judgement and experience. The person measuring the rate of work must know what a standard rate is, and then compare the worker's performance to this standard. This may seem difficult, we do it informally all the time. When you see someone walking down the street, you can easily tell if they are hurrying or strolling casually. With experience, work measurement analysts can do the same thing for a wide range of operations.

Now we can use the work rating to look at three different times for doing a job – actual time, normal time and standard time.

- **Actual time**   This is the time taken by an operator to finish the essential parts of a job. These elements exclude avoidable delays that should not occur (such as dropping tools or looking for something that has been misplaced) and unavoidable delays that are part of natural events but are not part of the job (such as waiting for material, coffee breaks and getting instructions from a supervisor).

- **Normal time**   This is the time needed to do the job at standard rate – it is the time an average worker will need for the job. It follows that:

$$\text{normal time} = \text{actual time} \times \text{rating}$$

The actual time and normal time only consider the essential parts of a job. But there are many other factors that are not part of the job, but still have to be considered – such as tea breaks and interruptions to supplies. These can be classified as:

–   *Personal allowances*, which are the time allowances needed to meet the normal needs of the operator during the working day – tea breaks, lavatory breaks, rest, meals. The time for these allowances varies widely. In an office the personal allowances may be little more than tea breaks. In a steel mill or cold storage depot people will get too tired unless they have frequent breaks. These breaks might take as much as 20 minutes in an hour.

–   *Contingencies*, which are used to cover the random event outside the control of the operator. These include getting instructions, filling in record sheets, in-process inspections, and any other interruptions.

The allowances are usually given as a percentage of normal time, like 10%. Then we can define the third time.

● **Standard time**   This is the total time that should be allowed for a job.

standard time = normal time × (1 + allowance factor)

we Worked example

The times taken by five workers to finish the same job are 3.8, 5.2, 4.6, 4.1 and 4.3 minutes. What is the normal time for the job and the rating of each worker?

Solution

The actual time is the average of the observations, which is $(3.8 + 5.2 + 4.6 + 4.1 + 4.3)/5 = 4.4$ minutes. Then the rating of the first worker is:

rating = normal time/actual time = 4.4/3.8 = 1.16 or 116%

This means the first worker is working 16% faster than the standard rate. The other workers have ratings of 84.6%, 95.7%, 107.3% and 102.3%.

we Worked example

A person doing a job takes five minutes with a rating of 120%. Allowances are 10%. What does this tell you?

Solution

- actual time = 5 minutes, which is the actual time a person took to do the job. The rating of 120% shows they were working hard, at 20% faster than normal

- normal time = 5 × 1.2 = 6 minutes, which is the time taken for the basic job in ideal conditions

- standard time = 6 × (1 + 0.1) = 6.6 minutes, which is the time that should be allowed to complete the job.

Standard time is the basis of all planning, scheduling and control decisions. Although this is based on judgements and opinions it is the best we can manage.

Finding normal times

So far we have assumed that actual times can be found from direct observation. But sometimes this is not possible, when, for example, we are considering a new task that is only going to be done once. So direct observation gives one way of finding actual times, but there are alternatives – historical data, estimation or a time study.

- **Historical data** When a job has been done many times before, the easiest way of finding how long it will take is to see how long it took in the past. But work conditions change, as do the quality of materials, skill of people, condition of equipment, environment, and methods used. Although historical data can give very quick results, these changes mean that it is, perhaps surprisingly, not very reliable.

- **Estimation** This method is used when there is no historical data and it is based on experience. The time needed to complete a job is estimated, based on the analysts experience with similar jobs. You will often meet this with tradesmen. When you take your car into a garage for repairs the garage will give an estimate of costs based on their experience with similar repairs. This method has the usual drawbacks of personal opinions, but is widely used in small organizations, it can be fairly reliable, and is the only approach for projects or one-off jobs.

- **Time study** The most common way of finding the standard time for a job is to use a time study. There are four different ways of doing a time study:

  (1) stop-watch studies
  (2) internal standard data

(3)   predetermined motion–time standards
(4)   work sampling.

Stop-watch studies

This is the most common method of finding actual times, and uses direct observation. An analyst watches an operator and times a number of repetitions, or cycles, of the job. At the same time the operator is rated. In more detail, the analyst must:

- gain the confidence and co-operation of the operators and their supervisors. The analyst must explain that they are looking for a standard time and are not trying to judge the operator;

- be sure the correct methods are being used for the job;

- set the number of cycles to time and choose the workers to study;

- break the job into tasks which have a distinct beginning and end, and can be easily timed;

- time each task and rate the operator's performance over the number of cycles;

- find the actual time for the whole job, usually from the average of cycles;

- adjust the actual time by the rating to give the normal time;

- find the allowances and calculate the standard time.

Internal standard data

Results from stop watch studies can be saved, and eventually the organization will have a database of times for various operations. These can be used to set times for similar jobs, perhaps using regression to find relationships between types of jobs and time needed.

Predetermined motion–time standards

These are similar to internal standard data, except the times for tasks are not found from the organization's experience, but from other organizations. Experience over many years has led to standard times for certain basic movements, such as reaching, grasping, turning and applying pressure, and releasing. These can be combined to give an overall time for the job. Most of these standards were developed in the 1940s and have been refined ever since. The main problem with this approach used to be the large effort needed to get results. But computers can now analyse video recordings of jobs and automatically calculate standard times.

Work sampling

Many jobs, such as cooking meals, answering telephones and interviewing customers are too variable for standard times to be used. But managers still need some way of finding the time people spend on each activity. A receptionist may, for example, answer telephones, talk to customers, write letters, file paperwork, and do other administration work. There are no standard jobs, but managers still need to know how long the receptionist spends on each type of activity. This can be done by work sampling.

With work sampling an analyst uses random visits to operators to record what they are doing. Over many visits a general picture of the operator's work can be built up – typically finding the proportion of time a person spends doing particular activities, or the utilization of equipment. It depends on:

● a clear definition of the type of activities to be studied

● random visits to operators

● a long enough period of visits to allow for work cycles

● a large number of observations

● an analyst who is a skilful observer.

Review questions

15.10 What is the purpose of work measurement?

15.11 What is the difference between actual, normal and standard times?

15.12 How could you find the normal time for a job?

15.13 What time would you use to schedule resources?

Chapter review

● Job design and work measurement look in detail at the jobs actually done by employees. They can be viewed as the most detailed level of planning.

● Job design looks for the best way of doing a job. It usually breaks jobs into very small tasks, analyses these, and sees how the tasks can be done more efficiently.

● There are two parties in job design: employers and employees. These have different aims, but both must be considered.

● Labour productivity is increased by motivating employees. There are several factors in motivation. Some of these include treating employees fairly and reasonably.

● Three important elements in job design are the physical environment, social environment and work methods.

● Work measurement finds the time needed to do a job.

- There are three times for a job: actual time, normal time and standard time. The standard time is the total time needed for a job, and is used in all planning decisions.

- The times can be found from historical data, estimation or time studies. Time studies are the most reliable of these.

Key terms

hierarchy of needs   514
job   513
job design   513
micro-elements   522
motivation   516
normal time   526
rating   526

self-directed work
  teams   517
standard rate   526
standard time   527
time studies   528
work measurement   524

CS Case study – Moncton Welding and Fabrication

Workers in the welding department at Moncton Welding and Fabrication are worried. They heard from their supervisor, Karim Ahmed, that the new production manager is about to implement time standards in the department. There is a general feeling that this is really a way of reducing pay and making working conditions much less pleasant.

Moncton recently hired Cedric Paxton as the production manager. The senior managers at Moncton gave him clear instructions to reduce the company's costs and make it more profitable. Cedric has a long record of successfully doing this with his previous employers.

Moncton makes a standard range of heat exchanger for the chemical industry. There are five different models of heat exchangers, each of which needs a lot of welding. The welding department has seven experienced welders and a supervisor. The quality of their work is very good, but Cedric is concerned that each welder uses his or her own method of working. He feels that better results would come by using standard methods.

One morning, to the surprise of Karim and the welders, Cedric showed up in the welding department with a stopwatch. He started to time a welder working on the tubes of a model XL1-50 heat exchanger. Cedric had taken seven readings when he was interrupted by the supervisor from the cutting department who had some urgent business. Cedric stopped his study to take care of the matter.

Later in the day, Cedric mentioned to Karim the results of his stopwatch study and asked for his opinion. Cedric had set the standard time of 10.5 minutes for welding the tubes in the XL1-50 heat exchanger. He had calculated this from five good readings he had taken earlier in the day. Karim knew from experience that it was an unrealistic standard, and the welders would not accept it.

Questions

• What do you think of Cedric's stopwatch study? What did he do wrong?

• What should Karim tell Cedric?

• What should Cedric do next?

Problems

15.1 An analyst times ten people doing a job. The times they take, in minutes, are:

       14.3   12.8   13.9   16.2   14.8   15.2   13.6   15.8   14.4   14.0

What is the normal time for the job and the rating of each worker who was timed? What is the standard time if allowances of 20% are given?

Discussion questions

15.1 Why is job design important? What factors do you think are most important in designing a job?

15.2 Why is job design viewed as the most detailed level of planning? Is it really a part of the planning process?

15.3 Describe some of the special needs knowledge workers have in their workplaces.

15.4 How has the emphasis of job design changed over time?

15.5 What methods can be used to improve morale and motivation in an organization? Which of these work best in different types of organization?

15.6 How could you design a fair scheme for paying employees?

15.7 What is the purpose of work measurement?

15.8 Do you think that work measurement is becoming less useful with increasing automation?

15.9 How realistic are the standard times used in work measurement? Do you think they are accurate enough to be useful? Is it fair to time workers so closely?

Selected references

Grensing L. (1991). *Motivating Today's Workforce*. North Vancouver: Self-Counsel Press.

Herzberg F. (1966). *Work and the Nature of Man*. Cleveland, Oh.: World Publishing.

Johns G. (1988). *Organizational Behaviour* (2nd edn). Glenview, Ill.: Scott, Foresman and Co.

Kanz S. (1983). *Work Design: Industrial Ergonomics* (2nd edn). New York: John Wiley.

Lamming R. (1993). *Beyond Partnership*. Hemel Hempstead: Prentice-Hall.

Landel R.D. (1986). *Managing Productivity Through People*. Englewood Cliffs, NJ: Prentice Hall.

Maslow A.H. (1970). *Motivation and Personality* (2nd edn). New York: Harper and Row.

McGregor D. (1960). *The Human Side of Enterprise*. New York: McGraw-Hill.

16 Project management

Contents

Objectives

After reading this chapter you should be able to:

- appreciate the need for planning complex projects
- list the aims of project management
- represent projects as networks of connected activities and events
- analyse the timing of projects
- find the critical activities and overall project duration
- extend these analyses to PERT networks
- change the times of activities to achieve different objectives
- minimize the total cost of a project
- draw Gantt charts
- find the resources needed during a project and reschedule activities to smooth these

Projects and their management

Definitions

In Chapter 7, we described different types of processes as project, job shop, batch, mass production and continuous flow. In the last few chapters we have been looking at different aspects of planning and scheduling needed for these. But the methods we have described so far can be difficult to use for projects. There are some basic differences between projects and other processes, and these differences mean that project planning really needs a different approach. This chapter describes the most common methods of project planning.

We can start by defining a project:

> A **project** is a unique job that makes a one-off product. It has a distinct start and finish, and all operations must be co-ordinated within this timeframe.

You can see from this definition that each of us does a number of small projects every day – such as preparing a meal, writing a report, building a fence, or organizing a party. We do these small projects with almost no formal planning – and a little thought is enough to make sure they run smoothly. Projects, however, can be very large and expensive. The installation of a new computer system, building a nuclear power station, organizing the Olympic Games and building the Channel tunnel are examples of large projects which have very high costs. We would only expect such large projects to be successful if there had been a considerable amount of planning. This planning is the function of project management.

> **Project management** deals with all aspects of planning, organizing, staffing and controlling a project. The operations manager in this case is called a **project manager**.

Aspects of project management

All projects have two phases:

- A **planning phase** during which the project is defined, its feasibility tested, goals are set, detailed design work done, resources allocated, times agreed, management and work organized.
- An **execution phase** during which materials are purchased and delivered, the work is done, finished products are handed over to customers, initial operations are tested.

You can imagine these phases with building a house. In the planning phase an architect draws plans, a site is found, approval is given by local authorities, a building company is chosen, and all arrangements are finalized. In the execution phase, the site and foundations are prepared, walls are built, electrical and plumbing work is done, and the house is actually built. You can see from this example, that projects bring together people with a range of knowledge and skills. Most of these work on the project for some time, and then move on to other jobs.

Project managers are central figures in these operations. It is their job to bring together all the resources and make sure the project is a success. This is a notoriously difficult job. Project managers have to work with different kinds of people, in situations where there is a lot of uncertainty, using many resources, keeping within tight constraints on budgets and schedules – and they still have to give a product that satisfies the customer. Project managers are often generalist rather than specialists, and they need wide experience in different operations.

A project manager's job is not necessarily to supervise and direct but to facilitate. In other words, they make sure conditions are right for other people to do their jobs. This means they must manage the relationships between the project team, the rest of the organization, customers, and anyone else involved. So a project manager needs skills in four areas – getting jobs finished, administration, interpersonal relations, and leadership.

As you can see, the choice of a project manager is a key factor in a project's success. The management of larger projects is done by a team under the control of the projects manager. This team typically uses a **matrix organization**, where staff from different functions are brought together into a team for the specific project (see Figure 16.1). Each person is still within their functional area, but they have another responsibility to the project manager.

The aim of project management is to complete the project successfully – giving the customer the product they want, keeping within the specified time, and within the budget. When a project can take many years to complete and use a lot of resources, you can see that timing becomes very important. The project completion date actually becomes part of the product. A construction company that can build a bridge within 18 months offers a better product than a competitor taking two years to build the same bridge. Of course, decisions are not usually this simple, and the company that takes longer may offer a lower price or different specifications.

Projects often need this kind of compromise between costs, time and resources. If a project gets behind schedule, is it better to increase costs by using more resources? If a project gets ahead of schedule is it better to finish it quickly and free-up all the resources early, or slow down and transfer some resources to other projects? If some resources are not available when they are needed should they pay more for alternatives, or allow the project to get behind schedule?

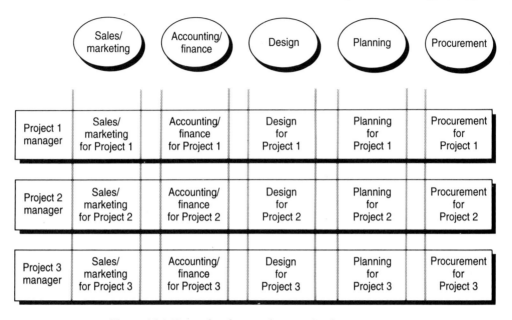

Figure 16.1 Example of a matrix organization structure.

These decisions form a part of every project manager's job. We can list the general main functions of this job as:

(1) identifying all the activities in the project, together with the order in which these activities have to be done;

(2) estimating the time of each activity, the total length of the project, and the time when each activity must be finished;

(3) finding how much flexibility there is in the times of activities, and which activities are most critical to the completion time;

(4) estimating costs and scheduling activities so that overall cost is minimized;

(5) allocating resources and scheduling these so the project can be completed as efficiently as possible;

(6) monitoring the progress of the project, reacting quickly to any deviations from plans, and adjusting schedules as required;

(7) anticipating problems and take any actions needed to avoid them;

(8) giving regular reports on progress.

The first five of these are concerned with scheduling the project and are done in the planning phase. The last three are concerned with control of the project in the execution phase.

ce Case example – Major construction projects

In December 1990 Transmanche Link, a consortium of ten British and French companies, finished the first continuous tunnel under the English Channel. The main tunnels were opened in 1994, and handed over to Eurotunnel to start operations. This was a significant step in a huge project.

The Channel tunnel is the world's biggest privately funded construction project. It is funded by the largest banking syndicate ever put together. By 1994 the cost of the tunnel was £8400 million, with an estimated final cost of £10,000 million, British Rail was investing £1400 million in rolling stock and infrastructure and French Rail had made a similar investment. At its peak, the project employed 14,500 people and cost over £3 million a day.

In 1802 Albert Mathieu, one of Napoleon's engineers, drew a crude plan for a tunnel underneath the Channel: the idea of a tunnel under the Channel is not new, and several trial tunnels have been dug at different times. This project had clearly been developing for a very long time, and it was carried out by some very successful and experienced companies. By all accounts, the tunnel was a triumph of construction and the project was voted a great success. Nevertheless, its costs were several times the original estimates of £4500 million, the consortium was continually looking for additional funding, the opening date was delayed so much that extra interest charges, bankers' and lawyers' fees amounted £1000 million, and the legal battles between participants are likely to last for many years.

By definition, each project is unique so there is little prior experience and no chance to use a learning curve. There is also a lot of uncertainty in projects – inflation raises costs, difficult conditions are met, activities take longer than expected, specifications change, and so on. As a result, major projects often overrun their schedule and budget. There are many examples of this, including the development of the RB-211 jet engine, building Canary Wharf, Nimrod early warning system, the M25, health service computerization, almost any project in the nuclear electricity industry, the Space Shuttle. In 1994 the British Library was half built after 12 years, the cost had tripled to £450 million and a House of Commons Committee reported, 'no one – ministers, library staff, building contractors, anyone at all – has more than the faintest idea when the building will be completed, when it will be open for use, or how much it will cost'.

By 1995 Denver International Airport had cost $4.9 billion rather than the originally estimated $2 billion, and it was still not finished 18 months behind schedule.

There are, of course, many examples of projects that go very well. But the failures show us how important it is to have good project management. In a study of 1449 projects by the Association of Project Managers 12 came in on time and under budget.

Review questions

16.1   What is a project?

16.2   What is the purpose of project management?

16.3   Project management is only concerned with major capital projects. Do you think this is true?

16.4   What are the two main phases of a project?

Project networks

The management of a project starts with a **statement of work**. This is a description of the goals of the projects, the work to be done, a proposed start and finish date, budget, and a list of milestones to check progress. With building a house the statement of work might start by giving the aim of the project – which is the completion of a house; the work involved – which is designing the house, clearing the ground, building the foundations, and so on; the proposed time – perhaps starting on 1 January and finishing by 1 September; the budget – perhaps £100,000; a list of milestones – prepare plans by 1 February, clear ground by 1 July, finish roof by 1 August, and so on.

If the project is very large, it can be broken down into smaller parts. This is done in a **work breakdown structure** which shows the different parts of a project that must be finished by different times. The next level of detail, after work breakdown, describes the whole project as a series of **activities**. These activities are the basic elements in a project, and are used for all the detailed planning. To help with this, project managers use **project network analysis**.

Project network analysis was developed independently by two groups working in the late 1950s. The first group worked on the Polaris missile project for the United States Department of Defense. At that time the US government was worried because its missile systems were being developed so slowly. The Polaris project involved over 3000 contractors, and to help with control they developed a technique called **PERT – project evaluation and review technique**. This reduced the overall length of the project by two years.

The second group worked for Du Pont and developed **CPM – critical path method** – for planning maintenance programmes in chemical plants. PERT and CPM were always very similar, and any differences in the original ideas have disappeared over time. The one difference which still remains is that PERT uses probabilistic durations of activities while CPM assumes durations are fixed.

Drawing networks

To draw a project network we start with a list of **activities** that make up the project. Then we can represent the project by a network of these activities. A

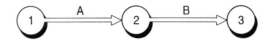

Figure 16.2 Part of a project network.

project network consists of a series of circles, or nodes, connected by arrows. Each activity is represented by an arrow and each node represents the point when activities start and finish. The nodes are called **events** and a network consists of alternating activities and events.

Figure 16.2 shows part of a project network. This has two activities A and B, and three events. Event 1 is the start of activity A, event 2 is the finish of activity A and the start of activity B, and event 3 is the finish of activity B.

These networks are called **activity on arrow networks**. There is another format which has nodes representing activities and the arrows showing the relationships. The choice between these is largely a matter of personal preference. Because some of the calculations are easier with activity on arrow networks, we will stick to this notation.

we Worked example

A gardener is building a greenhouse from a kit. The instructions show that this is a project with three parts:

- A, preparing the base which will take 3 days;

- B, building the frame which will take 2 days;

- C, fixing the glass which will take 1 day.

Draw a network for the project.

Solution

The project has three activities which must be done in a fixed order; building the frame must be done after preparing the base and before fixing the glass. This order can be described by a **dependence table** (Table 16.1). Here each activity is listed along with those activities that immediately precede it.

Table 16.1

Activity	Duration (days)	Description	Immediate predecessor
A	3	prepare base	–
B	2	build frame	A
C	1	fix glass	B

Figure 16.3 Network for building a greenhouse.

Labelling the activities A, B and C is a convenient shorthand and allows us to describe activity B having activity A as its immediate predecessor. This is normally stated as 'B depends on A'. In this table only **immediate** predecessors are given. The fact that C depends on A as well as B need not be stated separately – it follows from the other dependencies. Activity A has no immediate predecessors and can start whenever convenient.

Now we can draw a network from the dependence table, as shown in Figure 16.3.

■

The directions of the arrows in a project network shows precedence – each preceding activity must be finished before the following one is started – and following activities can start as soon as preceding ones are finished. In the example above, preparing the base must be done first, and as soon this is finished the frame can be built. The glass can then be fixed as soon as the frame is built.

After drawing the basic network for the project we can look at its timing. We shall take a notional starting time of 0 for the project, and then we can find the start and finish times of each activity.

we Worked example

Find the times for each activity in the last example. What happens if the base takes more than three days, or the glass is delayed, or the frame takes less than two days?

Solution

If we take a starting time of 0, preparing the base can be finished by the end of day 3. Then we can start building the frame. This takes two days, so we can finish by the end of day 5. Then we can start fixing the glass. This takes one day, so we can finish by the end of day 6.

If the concrete of the base takes more than three days to set, or the glass is not delivered by day 5 the project will be delayed. If building the frame takes less than two days the project will be finished early.

■

Now we have a timetable for the project showing when each activity starts and finishes, and we can use this to schedule resources. This quick example shows the major stages of project network analysis. We can summarize these as:

- define the separate activities

- find the dependence and duration of each activity

- draw a network

- analyse the timing of the project

- schedule resources.

Larger networks

We can draw larger networks in exactly the same as the small example above. Drawing networks from dependence tables is a matter of practice. But a useful approach is to start on the left hand side with the activities that do not depend on any others. Then activities that only depend on these first activities can be added; then activities that only depend on the latest activities added, and so on. The network is expanded systematically, working from left to right, until you have added all the activities and the network is complete. When drawing a network there are two main rules to remember:

- before an activity can begin, all preceding activities must be finished;

- the arrows representing activities only show precedence and neither the length nor orientation is significant.

There are also, by convention, two other rules:

- a network has only one starting and finishing event;

- any two events can only be connected by one activity.

This last rule is only for convenience, so we can refer to 'the activity between events i and j' and know exactly which one we are talking about. Using these rules we can draw networks of almost any size.

we Worked example

Allied Commercial is opening a new office. This is a project with the following activities and dependencies:

Activity	Description	Depends on
A	find office location	–
B	recruit new staff	–
C	make office alterations	A
D	order equipment needed	A
E	install new equipment	D
F	train staff	B
G	start operations	C, E, F

Draw a network of this project.

Solution

Activities A and B have no predecessors and can start as soon as convenient. As soon as activity A is finished both C and D can start: E can start as soon as D is finished and F can start as soon as B is finished. G can only start when C, E and F have all finished. The resulting network is shown in Figure 16.4.

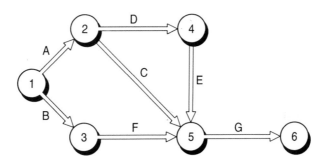

Figure 16.4 Network for opening a new office.

You can see from this network that the project can start with activities A and B. But this does not mean that these **must** start at the same time – only that they can start as soon as convenient and must be finished before any following activity can start. On the other hand, event 5 is the point where C, E and F are finished. But this does not mean that they must finish at the same time – only that they must all be finished before G can start.

Dummy activities

There are two situations that complicate networks. The first is illustrated by the following dependence table:

Activity	Depends on
A	–
B	A
C	A
D	B, C

You may be tempted to draw this as shown in Figure 16.5(a). But this would break one of the rules above which says, 'any two events can only be connected by one activity'. The way around this is to define a **dummy activity**. This is not a part of the project, has zero duration and uses no resources – it is simply there to allow a proper network. In this case the dummy makes sure that only one activity goes between two events and is called a **uniqueness dummy**. In Figure 16.5(b) the dummy activity is shown as the broken line, X.

A second situation that needs a dummy activity is shown in the part of a dependence table shown below:

Activity	Depends on
D	not given
E	not given
F	D, E
G	D

You may be tempted to draw this part of the network as shown in Figure 16.6(a), but the dependence is clearly wrong. Activity F is shown as depending on D and E, which is correct, but G is shown as having the same dependence. The dependence table shows that G can start as soon as D is finished but in the network it also has to wait for E to finish. The way around this is to separate

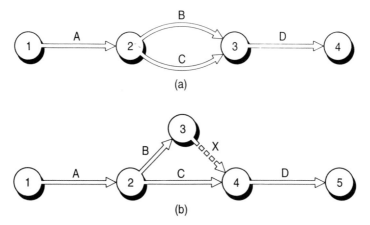

(a)

(b)

Figure 16.5 Uniqueness dummy, X: (a) wrong network; (b) right network with dummy.

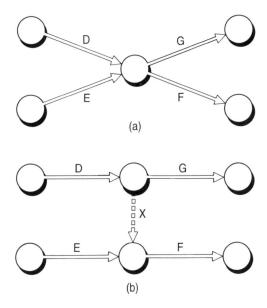

Figure 16.6 Logical dummy, X: (a) wrong network; (b) right network with dummy.

the dependencies by introducing a dummy activity, as show in Figure 16.6(b). The dependence of F on D is shown through the dummy activity X. In effect the dummy can not start until D has finished and then F can not start until the dummy and E are finished. As the dummy activity has zero duration this does not add any time to the project. This type of dummy is called a **logical dummy**.

we Worked example

A project is described by the following dependence table. Draw a network of the project.

Activity	Depends on	Activity	Depends on
A	J	I	J
B	C,G	J	–
C	A	K	B
D	F, K, N	L	I
E	J	M	I
F	B, H, L	N	M
G	A, E, I	O	M
H	G	P	O

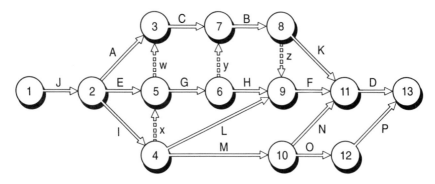

Figure 16.7 Network for example.

Solution

This may seem a difficult network, but the steps are fairly straightforward. Activity J is the only one that does not depend on anything else, so this starts the network Then activities A, E and I, which only depend on J, can be added. Then activities which depend on A, E and I can be added. Continuing this systematic addition of activities leads to the network shown in Figure 16.7. As you can see this includes four dummy activities.

You can see from the above example that networks with a lot of activities can take a long time to draw. In the initial example of building a greenhouse, the project was divided into three activities. It could have been divided into a lot more – such as choose a location, clear vegetation, level and prepare the ground, dig the foundations, lay hardcore, mix concrete and lay concrete base. Then the complexity of the network increases and the importance of each activity declines. A balance must be drawn between using too few activities and reducing its usefulness as a planning aid, and using too many activities and needlessly increasing the complexity.

If the number of activities gets above about 20 it is probably best to use a computer package. If the number of activities is very large the network will be complicated, cover many pages, and difficult to follow. For large projects we can start with a general, master network showing the major activities of the project. Then we can expand each of these major activities into a separate, more detailed network. For very large projects we can go further and break down the more detailed networks into yet smaller parts. This approach is particularly useful when a number of contractors and subcontractors work on a single project. Then the owner of the project may draw a master network, each contractor can be given a network covering their own work, and any major subcontractors can be given separate networks of their parts of the work. At each stage the networks cover less of the overall project but show more detail.

ce | **Case example** – Loch Moraigh Distillery

The managers of Loch Moraigh whisky distillery examined the inventory control system to see how stock levels could be set to meet forecast demand. They concluded that an expanded computer system was needed. This would extrapolate past demand patterns and use these to set appropriate stock levels. These stock levels are then be passed to a production control module that varies the quantities bottled.

The first part of this proposed system was called DFS (Demand Forecasting System) while the second part was ICS (Inventory Control System). The introduction of these systems took about 18 months, including linking to the production control module which was already working. The introduction of DFS and ICS was a self-contained project with the activities shown in Table 16.2.

Table 16.2

Activity	Description
A	examine existing system and environment of ICS
B	collect costs and other data relevant to ICS
C	construct and test models for ICS
D	write and test computer programs for ICS models
E	design and print data input forms for ICS data
F	document ICS programs and monitoring procedures
G	examine sources of demand data and its collection
H	construct and test models for DFS
I	organize past demand data
J	write and test computer programs for DFS models
K	design and print data input forms for DFS data
L	document DFS programs and monitoring procedures
M	train staff in the use of DFS and ICS
N	initialize data for ICS programs (ICS staff)
P	initialize data for DFS programs (DFS staff)
Q	create base files for DFS
R	run system for trial period
S	implement final system

A computer program was used to give the results shown in Figure 16.8.

```
PROBLEM: DISTILLERY                                      Date: 09-09-1995
--------------------------------------------------------------------------
                           ORIGINAL NETWORK DATA

                                               Letter Code for Immediately
        Letter                  Expected          Preceding Activities
No.  Code          Name      Completion Time   1   2   3   4   5   6   7
--------------------------------------------------------------------------
  1   A      Examine system        2.00
  2   B      Collect ICS data      1.00        A
  3   C      Test ICS models       2.00        A
  4   D      Program ICS           4.00        C
  5   E      Design ICS forms      1.00        C
  6   F      Document ICS          2.00        D   E
  7   G      Examine demand        2.00
  8   H      Test DFS models       4.00        A   G
  9   I      Organize data         2.00        G
 10   J      Program DFS           6.00        H   K
 11   K      Design DFS forms      2.00        A   G
 12   L      Document DFS          3.00        J
 13   M      Train staff           2.00        F   L
 14   N      Initialize ICS        1.00        B   M
 15   P      Initialize DFS        1.00        I   M
 16   Q      Create DFS files      1.00        P
 17   R      Trial period          4.00        N   Q
 18   S      Implement             2.00        R
 19   D*1    Dummy--1              0.00
 20   D*2    Dummy--2              0.00
 21   D*3    Dummy--3              0.00
 22   D*4    Dummy--4              0.00
 23   D*5    Dummy--5              0.00
 24   D*6    Dummy--6              0.00


                           ACTIVITY REPORT
     Activity              Events                  Planning Times
--------------------     --------   ---------------------------------------
 No Code     Name       Beg. End.  Exp. t  ES    LS    EF    LF    Slack
--------------------------------------------------------------------------
  1  A    Examine sys    1    2     2.0    0.0   0.0   2.0   2.0   0.0
  2  B    Collect ICS    2   12     1.0    2.0  17.0   3.0  18.0  15.0
  3  C    Test ICS mo    2    4     2.0    2.0   7.0   4.0   9.0   5.0
  4  D    Program ICS    4    5     4.0    4.0   9.0   8.0  13.0   5.0
  5  E    Design ICS     4    5     1.0    4.0  12.0   5.0  13.0   8.0
  6  F    Document IC    5   10     2.0    8.0  13.0  10.0  15.0   5.0
  7  G    Examine dem    1    3     2.0    0.0   0.0   2.0   2.0   0.0
  8  H    Test DFS mo    6    8     4.0    2.0   2.0   6.0   6.0   0.0
  9  I    Organize da    3   13     2.0    2.0  15.0   4.0  17.0  13.0
 10  J    Program DFS    8    9     6.0    6.0   6.0  12.0  12.0   0.0
 11  K    Design DFS     7    8     2.0    2.0   4.0   4.0   6.0   2.0
 12  L    Document DF    9   10     3.0   12.0  12.0  15.0  15.0   0.0
 13  M    Train staff   10   11     2.0   15.0  15.0  17.0  17.0   0.0
 14  N    Initialize    12   15     1.0   17.0  18.0  18.0  19.0   1.0
 15  P    Initialize    13   14     1.0   17.0  17.0  18.0  18.0   0.0
 16  Q    Create DFS    14   15     1.0   18.0  18.0  19.0  19.0   0.0
 17  R    Trial perio   15   16     4.0   19.0  19.0  23.0  23.0   0.0
 18  S    Implement     16   17     2.0   23.0  23.0  25.0  25.0   0.0
 19  D*1  Dummy--1       3    6     0.0    2.0   2.0   2.0   2.0   0.0
 20  D*2  Dummy--2       2    6     0.0    2.0   2.0   2.0   2.0   0.0
 21  D*3  Dummy--3       2    7     0.0    2.0   4.0   2.0   4.0   2.0
 22  D*4  Dummy--4       3    7     0.0    2.0   4.0   2.0   4.0   2.0
 23  D*5  Dummy--5      11   13     0.0   17.0  17.0  17.0  17.0   0.0
 24  D*6  Dummy--6      11   12     0.0   17.0  18.0  17.0  18.0   1.0

Expected Project Duration: 25
The following path(s) are critical.

A    D*2  H      J      L      M    D*5  P      Q      R      S
G    D*1  H      J      L      M    D*5  P      Q      R      S
```

Figure 16.8 Printout for distillery example.

```
                         NETWORK EVENT MILESTONE REPORT
            Event Connections              Times            Activity Connections
      --------------------------    -------------------    ---------------------
 Event  Predecessors  Successors     TE    TL   Slack       Ending      Starting
------------------------------------------------------------------------------------
   1   : none        : 2  3  --  :   0.0   0.0   0.0  : none        : A    G
   2   : 1  -- --    : 12 4  6   :   2.0   2.0   0.0  : A    ----   : B    C
       :             : 7  -- --  :                    :             : D*2  D*3
   3   : 1  -- --    : 13 6  7   :   2.0   2.0   0.0  : G    ----   : I    D*1
       :             :           :                    :             : D*4  ----
   4   : 2  -- --    : 5  5  --  :   4.0   9.0   5.0  : C    ----   : D    E
   5   : 4  4  --    : 10 -- --  :   8.0  13.0   5.0  : D    E      : F    ----
   6   : 3  2  --    : 8  -- --  :   2.0   2.0   0.0  : D*1  D*2    : H    ----
   7   : 2  3  --    : 8  -- --  :   2.0   4.0   2.0  : D*3  D*4    : K    ----
   8   : 6  7  --    : 9  -- --  :   6.0   6.0   0.0  : H    K      : J    ----
   9   : 8  -- --    : 10 -- --  :  12.0  12.0   0.0  : J    ----   : L    ----
  10   : 5  9  --    : 11 -- --  :  15.0  15.0   0.0  : F    L      : M    ----
  11   : 10 -- --    : 13 12 --  :  17.0  17.0   0.0  : M    ----   : D*5  D*6
  12   : 2  11 --    : 15 -- --  :  17.0  18.0   1.0  : B    D*6    : N    ----
  13   : 3  11 --    : 14 -- --  :  17.0  17.0   0.0  : I    D*5    : P    ----
  14   : 13 -- --    : 15 -- --  :  18.0  18.0   0.0  : P    ----   : Q    ----
  15   : 12 14 --    : 16 -- --  :  19.0  19.0   0.0  : N    Q      : R    ----
  16   : 15 -- --    : 17 -- --  :  23.0  23.0   0.0  : R    ----   : S    ----
  17   : 16 -- --    : none      :  25.0  25.0   0.0  : S    ----   : none

Expected Project Duration: 25

The following path(s) are critical.
   1  2  6  8  9 10 11 13 14 15 16 17
   1  3  6  8  9 10 11 13 14 15 16 17
```

Figure 16.8 *(cont.)* Printout for distillery example.

Review questions

16.5 In the networks we have drawn, what is represented by the nodes and arrows?

16.6 What information is needed to draw a project network?

16.7 What are the main rules of drawing a project network?

16.8 When are dummy activities used?

Timing of projects

At the beginning of the chapter we said that the only real difference between critical path method (CPM) and project evaluation and review technique (PERT) is in the timing. In particular, CPM assumes that each activity has a fixed duration that is known exactly, while PERT assumes the duration can vary according to a known distribution. The basic analyses are identical for each of these, so we will illustrate them by CPM and then move on to PERT.

Event analysis

For the timing of events we want to find the earliest and latest times they can occur. It is easiest to show the calculations for this in an example. Suppose a project has the dependencies shown in Table 16.3, where a duration (in weeks) has been added. This project is represented by the network shown in Figure 16.9, where durations have been noted under the activities.

Table 16.3

Activity	Duration	Depends on
A	3	–
B	2	–
C	2	A
D	4	A
E	1	C
F	3	D
G	3	B
H	4	G
I	5	E, F

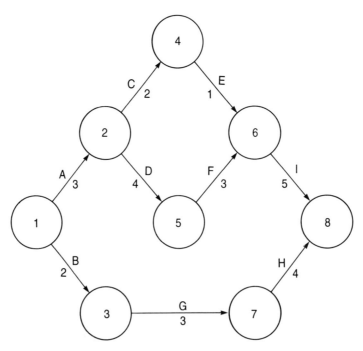

Figure 16.9 Network with activity durations.

The analysis of times starts by finding the earliest possible time for each event, assuming a notional start time of zero for the project as a whole. The earliest time for event 1 is clearly 0. The earliest time for event 2 is when activity A finishes, which is three weeks after its earliest start at 0: the earliest time for event 4 is the time when C finishes, which is two weeks after its earliest start at 3 (that is, week 5). Similarly, the earliest time for event 5 is $4 + 3 = 7$, for event 3 is 2 and for event 7 is $2 + 3 = 5$.

When several activities have to finish before an event, the earliest time for the event is the earliest time by which **all** preceding activities can be finished. The earliest time for event 6 is when both E and F are finished. E can finish 1 week after its earliest start at 5 (that is, week 6); F can finish three weeks after its earliest start at 7 (that is, week 10). So the earliest time when both of these can be finished is week 10. Similarly, event 8 must wait until both activities H and I are finished. Activity H can be finished by week $5 + 4 = 9$ while activity I can be finished by week $10 + 5 = 15$. The earliest time for event 8 is the later of these which is week 15. This gives the overall duration of the project as 15 weeks. Figure 16.10 shows the earliest times for each event added to the network.

Having gone through the network and found the earliest time for each event we can do a similar analysis to find the latest time for each. Then we can see which events need strict control and which have some slack.

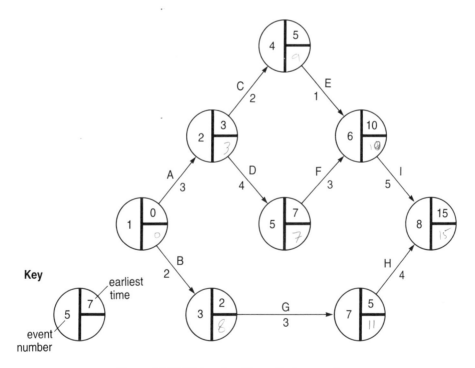

Figure 16.10 Network with earliest event time.

The procedure for finding the latest times is almost the reverse of the procedure for finding the earliest times. Starting at the end of the project with event 8, this has a latest time for completion of week 15. To allow activity I to be finished by week 15 it must be started five weeks before this, so the latest time for event 6 is week $15 - 5 = 10$. The latest H can finish is week 15, so the latest time it can start is four weeks before this and the latest time for event 7 is week $15 - 4 = 11$. Similarly the latest time for event 3 is $11 - 3 = 8$, for event 5 is $10 - 3 = 7$ and for event 4 is $10 - 1 = 9$.

For events that have more than one following activity, the latest time must allow all following activities to be finished on time. Event 2 is followed by activities C and D; C must be finished by week 9 so it must be started two weeks before this (that is, week 7), while D must be finished by week 7 so it must be started four weeks before this (that is, week 3). The latest time for event 2 that allows both C and D to start on time is the earlier of these, which is week 3.

Similarly, the latest time for event 1 must allow both A and B to finish on time. The latest start time for B is $8 - 2 = 6$ and the latest start time for A is $3 - 3 = 0$. The latest time for event 1 must allow both of these to start on time and this means a latest time of 0. Figure 16.11 shows the network with latest times added for each event.

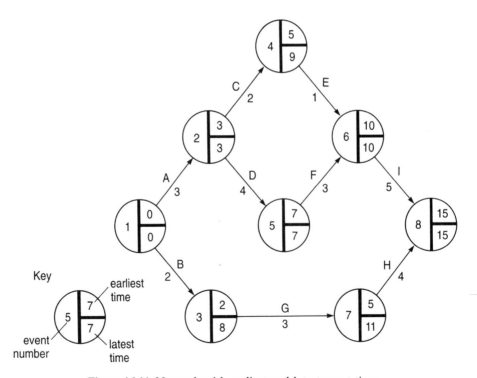

Figure 16.11 Network with earliest and latest event times.

Activity analysis

We can extend the analysis of project times to activities. Then we want to find earliest and latest start times (and corresponding earliest and latest finish times).

The earliest start time for an activity is the earliest time of the preceding event. The earliest finish time is the earliest start time plus the duration. Looking at one specific activity in Figure 16.12, say G, the earliest start time is week 2, so the earliest finish time is week $2 + 3 = 5$.

The latest start and finish time for an activity can be found using similar reasoning, but working backwards. The latest finish time for each activity is the latest time of the following event: the latest start time is the latest finish time minus the duration. For activity G the latest finish is week 11 and the latest start is week $11 - 3 = 8$. Repeating these calculations for all activities in the project gives the results shown in Table 16.4.

You can see in Table 16.4 that some activities have flexibility in time: activity G can start as early as week 2 or as late as week 8, while activity C can start as early as week 3 or as late as week 7. On the other hand, some others activities have no flexibility at all: activities A, D, F, and I have no freedom and their latest start time is the same as their earliest start time. The activities have to be done at a fixed time are called the **critical activities**.

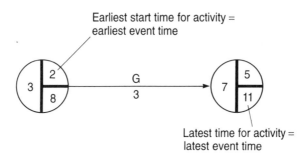

Figure 16.12 Finding activity times.

Table 16.4

Activity	Duration	Earliest start	Earliest finish	Latest start	Latest finish
A	3	0	3	0	3
B	2	0	2	6	8
C	2	3	5	7	9
D	4	3	7	3	7
E	1	5	6	9	10
F	3	7	10	7	10
G	3	2	5	8	11
H	4	5	9	11	15
I	5	10	15	10	15

> The activities that have to be done at a fixed time are called the **critical activities**. They form a continuous path through the network, called the **critical path**.

The length of the critical path sets the overall project duration. If one of the critical activities is extended by a certain amount the overall project duration is extended by this amount: if one of the critical activities is delayed by some time the overall project duration is again extended by the time of the delay. On the other hand, if one of the critical activities is made shorter the overall project duration may be reduced by this amount.

The activities that have some flexibility in timing are the **non-critical activities** and these may be delayed or extended without necessarily affecting the overall project duration. But there is a limit to the expansion and this is measured by the float. The **total float** is the difference between the maximum amount of time available for an activity and the time actually used:

Total float = latest finish time − earliest start time − duration

The total float is zero for critical activities and has some positive value for non-critical activities. It measures the maximum amount the duration of an activity can increase without affecting the completion date of the project.

Calculating the total float for activity G in the example above has:

- earliest start = earliest time of preceding event = 2
- latest finish = latest time of following event = 11
- duration = 3

So

- total float = latest finish time − earliest start time − duration = 11 − 2 − 3 = 6

Repeating the calculations for other activities in the example gives the results shown in Table 16.5.

Table 16.5

Activity	Duration	Earliest time Start	Earliest time Finish	Latest time Start	Latest time Finish	Total float
A	3	0	3	0	3	0
B	2	0	2	6	8	6
C	2	3	5	7	9	4
D	4	3	7	3	7	0
E	1	5	6	9	10	4
F	3	7	10	7	10	0
G	3	2	5	8	11	6
H	4	5	9	11	15	6
I	5	10	15	10	15	0

As the total float measures the amount an activity can expand without affecting the duration of the project, we know that activity E, for example, can expand by up to four weeks without affecting the finish date of the project.

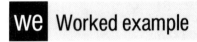 Worked example

A small telephone exchange is planned as a project with 10 main activities. Estimated durations (in days) and dependencies are shown in Table 16.6. Draw the network for this project, find its duration and calculate the total float of each activity.

Table 16.6

Activity	Description	Duration	Depends on
A	design internal equipment	10	–
B	design exchange building	5	A
C	order parts for equipment	3	A
D	order material for building	2	B
E	wait for equipment parts	15	C
F	wait for building material	10	D
G	employ equipment assemblers	5	A
H	employ building workers	4	B
I	install equipment	20	E, G, J
J	complete building	30	F, H

Solution

The network for this is shown in Figure 16.13 and repeating the calculations described above gives the results shown in Table 16.7.

Table 16.7

Activity	Duration	Earliest time Start	Earliest time Finish	Latest time Start	Latest time Finish	Total float
A	10	0	10	0	10	0*
B	5	10	15	10	15	0*
C	3	10	13	39	42	29
D	2	15	17	15	17	0*
E	15	13	28	42	57	29
F	10	17	27	17	27	0*
G	5	10	15	52	57	42
H	4	15	19	23	27	8
I	20	57	77	57	77	0*
J	30	27	57	27	57	0*

* Activities on the critical path.

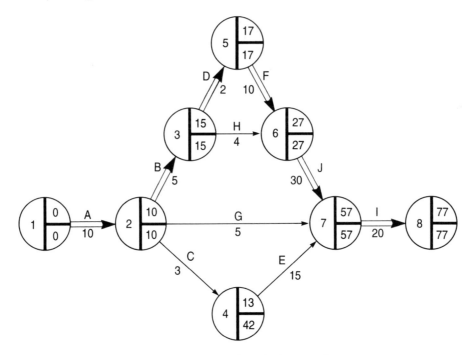

Figure 16.13 Network for telephone exchange.

The duration of the project is 77 days, defined by the critical path A, B, D, F, I and J.

Review questions

16.9   How are the earliest and latest times for an event calculated?

16.10 What is the total float of an activity?

16.11 How big is the total float of a critical activity?

16.12 What is the significance of the critical path?

Project evaluation and review technique

The method we have used so far is the critical path method (CPM) where each activity has a fixed duration. But you know from experience that the time needed for any job can vary quite widely. So a useful extension to CPM adds some uncertainty to activity durations. This extension is the main difference between CPM and PERT (project evaluation and review technique).

Experience shows that the duration of an activity can usually be described by a beta distribution. This looks something like a skewed Normal distribution and has one very useful property – the mean and variance can be found from three estimates of duration. In particular it needs:

- An **optimistic duration** (O) which is the shortest time an activity will take if everything goes smoothly and without any difficulties.

- A **most likely duration** (M) which is the duration of the activity under normal conditions.

- A **pessimistic duration** (P) which is the time needed if there are significant problems and delays.

The expected activity duration and variance are then calculated from the **rule of sixths**:

$$\text{Expected duration} = \frac{O + 4M + P}{6}$$

$$\text{Variance} = \frac{(O - P)^2}{36}$$

Suppose an activity has an optimistic duration of four days, a most likely duration of five days and a pessimistic duration of 12 days. Assuming a beta distribution for the duration:

$$\begin{aligned}
\text{Expected duration} &= (O + 4M + P)/6 \\
&= (4 + 4 \times 5 + 12)/6 = 6
\end{aligned}$$

$$\begin{aligned}
\text{Variance} \quad &= (P - O)^2/36 \\
&= (12 - 4)^2/36 = 1.78
\end{aligned}$$

Now these expected durations can be used for analysing project timing in the same way as the single estimate of CPM.

we Worked example

A project has nine activities with dependencies and estimated activity durations shown in Table 16.8. Draw the network, identify the critical path and estimate the overall duration of the project.

Table 16.8

Activity	Depends on	Optimistic	Duration Most likely	Pessimistic
A	–	2	3	10
B	–	4	5	12
C	–	8	10	12
D	A, G	4	4	4
E	B	3	6	15
F	B	2	5	8
G	B	6	6	6
H	C, F	5	7	15
I	D, E	6	8	10

Solution

Using the rule of sixths for the duration of activity A:

$$\text{Expected duration} = (2 + 4 \times 3 + 10)/6$$
$$= 4$$

$$\text{Variance} = (10 - 2)^2/36$$
$$= 1.78$$

Repeating these calculations for the other activities gives the results shown in Table 16.9.

Table 16.9

Activity	Expected duration	Variance
A	4	1.78
B	6	1.78
C	10	0.44
D	4	0
E	7	4.00
F	5	1.00
G	6	0
H	8	2.78
I	8	0.44

The network for this problem is drawn in Figure 16.14. The critical path for the project is B, G, D and I which has an expected duration of 24. The analysis of activity times gives Table 16.10.

Table 16.10

Activity	Expected duration	Earliest		Latest		Total float
		Start	Finish	Start	Finish	
A	4	0	4	8	12	8
B	6	0	6	0	6	0*
C	10	0	10	6	16	6
D	4	12	16	12	16	0*
E	7	6	13	9	16	3
F	5	6	11	11	16	5
G	6	6	12	6	12	0*
H	8	11	19	16	24	5
I	8	16	24	16	24	0*

* Activities on the critical path.

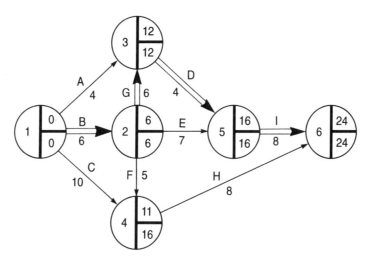

Figure 16.14 Network for example.

The duration of the critical path is the sum of the durations of activities making up that path. If there is a large number of activities on the path, and if the duration of each activity is independent of the others, the overall duration of the project follows a Normal distribution. This distribution has:

● a mean equal to the sum of the expected durations of activities on the critical path;

● a variance equal to the sum of the variances of activities on the critical path.

These values can be used to find the probability that a project will be completed by any particular time.

WE Worked example

What are the probabilities that the project described in the last example will be finished before: (a) day 26 (b) day 20?

Solution

The critical path has been identified as activities B, G, D and I with expected durations of 6, 6, 4 and 8 respectively and variances of 1.78, 0, 0 and 0.44 respectively. Although the number of activities on the critical path is small, we can assume the overall duration of the project is Normally distributed. The expected duration then has mean $6 + 6 + 4 + 8 = 24$. The variance is $1.78 + 0 + 0 + 0.44 = 2.22$, so the standard deviation is $\sqrt{2.22} = 1.49$ (see Figure 16.15).

(a)   The probability that it will not be finished before day 26 can be found using Normal distribution tables. Z is the number of standard deviations the point of interest is away from the mean:

$$Z = (26 - 24)/1.49 = 1.34 \text{ standard deviations.}$$

Tables (in Appendix B) show this corresponds to a probability of $= 0.0901$ so the probability that the project will be finished is $1 - 0.0901 = 0.9099$ or almost 91%.

(b)   Similarly the probability it will be finished before 20 is:

$$Z = (24 - 20)/1.49 = 2.68$$
$$\text{probability} = 0.0037.$$

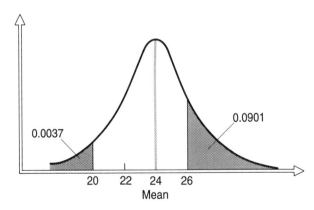

Figure 16.15 Normal distribution of project duration.

Review questions

16.13 What is the difference between CPM and PERT?

16.14 What is the 'rule of sixths' and when is it used?

16.15 How could you calculate the expected duration of a project and its variance?

Resource planning

In this section we shall look at ways of adjusting project plans. We shall start by looking at changes to the duration. There are two main reasons for changing the duration of a project:

- when a network is analysed the timing is found to be unacceptable – it may, for example, take longer than the organization has available;

- during the execution of a project an activity might take a different time to that originally planned.

Reducing the length of a project

If initial plans show the length of a project will be too long, we have to look for ways of shortening it. The first thing we must remember is that the duration of a project is set by the critical path. So we can only reduce the overall duration by reducing the durations of critical activities. Reducing the duration of non-critical activities will have no effect on the overall project duration.

We must also consider is what happens when a critical path is shortened. Small reductions will be alright, but if we keep reducing the duration of the critical path there must come a point when some other path through the network becomes critical. This point can be found from the total float on paths parallel to the critical path. Each activity on a parallel path has the same total float, and when the critical path is reduced by more than this, the parallel path becomes critical.

we Worked example

The project network shown in Figure 16.16 has a duration of 14 with A, B and C as the critical path.

If each activity can be reduced by up to 50% of the original duration, how would you reduce the overall duration to: (a) 13 weeks (b) 11 weeks (c) 9 weeks?

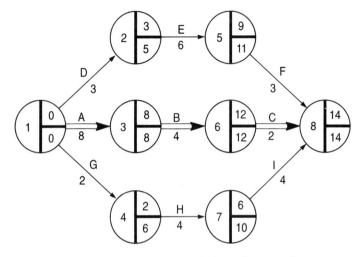

Figure 16.16 Initial network times for example.

If reductions cost an average of £1000 per week what would be the cost of finishing the project by week 9?

Solution

The analysis of activity times for this project is as shown in Table 16.11.

The amount the critical path can be reduced without affecting any parallel path is found from the total float of parallel paths. In this network there are three parallel paths, A–B–C, D–E–F and G–H–I. The total float of activities on these paths are 0, 2 and 4 respectively. This means that we can reduce the critical path A–B–C by up to 2, but if we reduce it any more the

Table 16.11

Activity	Duration	Earliest		Latest		Total float
		Start	Finish	Start	Finish	
A	8	0	8	0	8	0*
B	4	8	12	8	12	0*
C	2	12	14	12	14	0*
D	3	0	3	2	5	2
E	6	3	9	5	11	2
F	3	9	12	11	14	2
G	2	0	2	4	6	4
H	4	2	6	6	10	4
I	4	6	10	10	14	4

* Activities on the critical path.

path D–E–F becomes critical. If we reduce the critical path by more than 4, the path G–H–I also becomes critical.

- To finish in 13 weeks we need a reduction of one week in the critical path. Reducing the longest activity – as it is usually easier to find savings in longer activities – gives A a duration of seven weeks and the project is finished by week 13.

- To finish in 11 weeks needs a further reduction of two weeks in the critical path. We can also remove this from A. Unfortunately the path D–E–F has now become critical with a duration of 12 weeks. One week must be removed from E – again chosen as the longest activity in the critical path.

- To finish in nine weeks would need five weeks removed from the path A–B–C (say four from A and one from B), three weeks removed from the path D–E–F (say from E) and one week removed from the path G–H–I (say from H).

To get a five-week reduction in the project duration we have reduced the durations of individual activities by a total of $5 + 3 + 1 = 9$ weeks. This gives a total cost of $9 \times 1000 = £9000$.

Minimizing costs

The total cost of a project is made up of direct costs such as labour and materials, indirect costs such as management and financing, and penalty costs if the project is not finished by a specified date.

Total cost = Direct costs + Indirect costs + Penalty costs

All of these are affected by the duration of the project. There are no penalty costs if the project is finished on time, but this might need more resources and so increase the direct costs. Sometimes a bonus is paid if a project is finished early, but this again might need extra resources and increase direct costs. Overall, some kind of balance is needed between project duration and total cost. Some useful calculations for this are based on two figures:

(1) *Normal time* is the expected time to complete the activity and this has associated **normal costs**.

(2) *Crashed time* is the shortest possible time to complete the activity and this has the higher **crashed costs**.

To simplify the analysis, we shall assume that the cost of completing an activity in any particular time is a linear combination of these costs. Then the cost of crashing an activity by a unit of time is:

$$\text{Cost of crashing by one time unit} = \frac{\text{Crashed cost} - \text{Normal cost}}{\text{Normal time} - \text{Crashed time}}$$

Now we can suggest an approach to minimizing the total cost of a project. This starts by analysing a project with all activities done at their normal time and cost. Then the duration of critical activities is systematically reduced. Initially, the cost of the project may decline as its duration is reduced, but there comes a point when the cost starts to rise. When this happens the minimum cost has been found. The procedure for this is as follows:

(1)   Draw a project network – then analyse the cost and timings assuming all activities take their normal times.

(2)   Find the critical activity with the lowest cost of crashing per unit time. If there is more than one critical path they must all be considered at the same time.

(3)   Reduce the time for this activity until either:

- it can not be reduced any further
- another path becomes critical
- the cost of the project begins to rise.

(4)   Repeat steps 2 and 3 until the cost of the project begins to rise.

we Worked example

A project is described by Table 16.12, where times are in weeks and costs are in thousands of pounds.

Table 16.12

Activity	Depends on	Normal Time	Normal Cost	Crashed Time	Crashed Cost
A	–	3	13	2	15
B	A	7	25	4	28
C	B	5	16	4	19
D	C	5	12	3	24
E	–	8	32	5	38
F	E	6	20	4	30
G	F	8	30	6	35
H	–	12	41	7	45
I	H	6	25	3	30
J	D, G, I	2	7	1	14

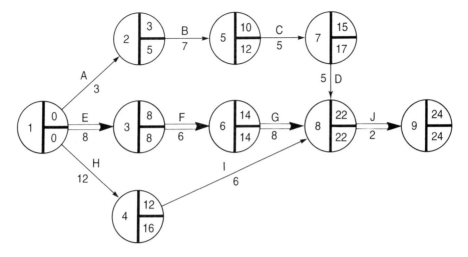

Figure 16.17 Initial times for crashing example.

There is a penalty cost of £3500 for every week the project finishes after week 18. By what week should the project be finished to minimize costs?

Solution

Using the procedure described above:

- *Step 1*. The network for this project is shown in Figure 16.17, with times based on normal durations. The critical path is E–F–G–J which has a duration of 24 weeks, and the total cost is found by adding the normal costs of each activity (£221,000) to the $24 - 18 = 6$ days of penalty costs (£21,000) to give a total of £242,000.

  The cost of crashing each activity (in £1000 a week) is as shown in Table 16.13. The total float of activities on the parallel path A–B–C–D

Table 16.13

Activity	A	B	C	D	E	F	G	H	I	J
Normal time	3	7	5	5	8	6	8	12	6	2
Crashed time	2	4	4	3	5	4	6	7	3	1
Reduction in weeks	1	3	1	2	3	2	2	5	3	1
Crashed cost	15	28	19	24	38	30	35	45	30	14
Normal cost	13	25	16	12	32	20	30	41	25	7
Cost of reduction	2	3	3	12	6	10	5	4	5	7
Cost per week	2	1	3	6	2	5	2.5	0.8	1.7	7

is 2, so if the critical path is reduced by this amount A–B–C–D becomes critical.

● *Step 2* finds the activity on the critical path (E–F–G–J) with lowest cost of crashing, and this is E at £2000 a week.

● *Step 3* reduces the time for activity E by 2 weeks, as beyond this the path A–B–C–D–J becomes critical.

– Total cost of crashing by 2 weeks = 2 × 2000 = £4000
– Total savings = 2 × 3500 = £7000

This step has reduced the penalty cost by more than the crashing cost, so we look for more savings.

● *Step 2* finds the lowest costs in the critical paths as E in E–F–G–J and B in A–B–C–D–J.

● *Step 3* reduces the time of these activities by 1 week, as E is then reduced by the maximum allowed.

– Total cost of crashing by 1 week = 2000 + 1000 = £3000
– Total savings = £3500

Again the overall cost has been reduced, so we look for more savings.

● *Step 2* identifies the lowest costs in the critical paths as B in A–B–C–D–J and G in E–F–G–J.

– Total cost of crashing by 1 week = 1000 + 2500 = £3500
– Total savings = £3500

At this point the savings exactly match the cost, and a minimum total cost has been found. If any more activities were crashed, the cost would be more than the savings from reduced penalties.

The overall duration of the project is now 20 days, with cost of £221,000 for normal activities, £10,500 for crashing and £7000 for penalties to give a total of £238,500.

∎

Gantt charts and resource levelling

When a project is in the execution phase – so the work is actually being done – progress must be constantly monitored to make sure the activities are done at the right times. These times are not always clear from a network. It is much easier to monitor progress using a **Gantt chart**.

A Gantt chart is simply another way of representing a project, which emphasizes the timing of activities. The chart has a time-scale across the bottom, activities are listed down the left-hand side and times when activities should be done are blocked-off in the body of the chart.

we Worked example

Draw a Gantt chart for the original data in the last example ass
activity starts as early as possible.

Solution

The activity analysis for this example was as shown in Table 16.14.

Table 16.14

		Earliest		Latest		
Activity	Duration	Start	Finish	Start	Finish	Total float
A	8	0	8	0	8	0*
B	4	8	12	8	12	0*
C	2	12	14	12	14	0*
D	3	0	3	2	5	2
E	6	3	9	5	11	2
F	3	9	12	11	14	2
G	2	0	2	4	6	4
H	4	2	6	6	10	4
I	4	6	10	10	14	4

* Activities on the critical path.

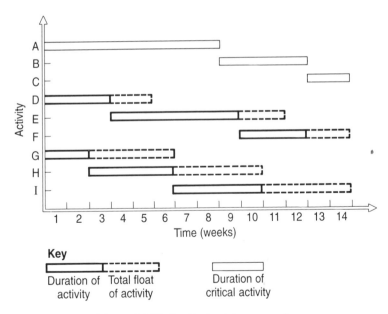

Figure 16.18 Gantt chart for example.

If each activity starts as early as possible, the time needed is shown by the blocked-off areas in Figure 16.18. The total float of each activity is added afterwards as a broken line. The total float is the maximum amount an activity can expand without delaying the project. So provided an activity is finished before the end of the broken line there should be no problem keeping to the planned schedule.

The main benefit of Gantt charts is that they show clearly the state of each activity at any point in the project. They show which activities should be in hand, as well as those which should be finished, and those about to start.

Gantt charts are also useful for planning and allocating resources. Consider the chart shown in Figure 16.18 and assume, for simplicity, that each activity uses one unit of a particular resource – perhaps one team of

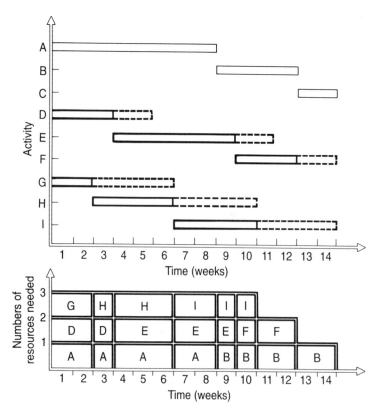

Figure 16.19 Resource use during the project.

workers. If all activities start as soon as possible, we can draw a vertical bar chart to show the resources needed at any time. The project starts with activities A, D and G so three teams are needed. At the end of week 2 one team can move from G to H, but three teams are still needed. Continuing these allocations gives the graph of resources shown in Figure 16.19.

In this example, the use of resources is steady for most of the project and only begins to fall near the end. It is rare to get such a smooth pattern of resource use, and usually there is a series of peaks and troughs which should be levelled. As critical activities are at fixed times this levelling must be done by rescheduling non-critical activities, and in particular by delaying those activities with large total floats.

we Worked example

The network shown in Figure 16.20 shows a project with 11 activities over a period of 19 months. If each activity uses one work team, how many teams will

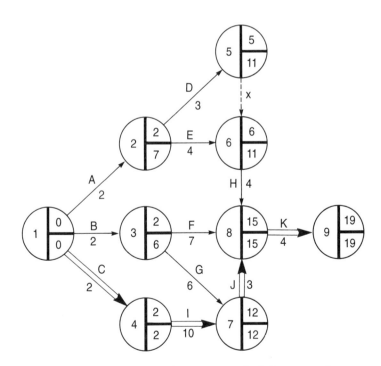

Figure 16.20 Network for resource scheduling example.

be needed at each stage of the project? Would it be possible to schedule the activities so that a maximum of three work teams are used at any time?

Solution

Figure 16.21 shows a Gantt chart for this project with the assumption that all activities start as early as possible. This uses a maximum of five work teams during months 3 to 5.

    If the number of work teams is to be smoothed, activities with large floats should be delayed. One schedule would delay the start of D until month 7, the start of F until 9 and the start of H until 10. This rescheduling reduces the maximum number of work teams needed to 3 and gives a smoother workload, as shown in Figure 16.22.

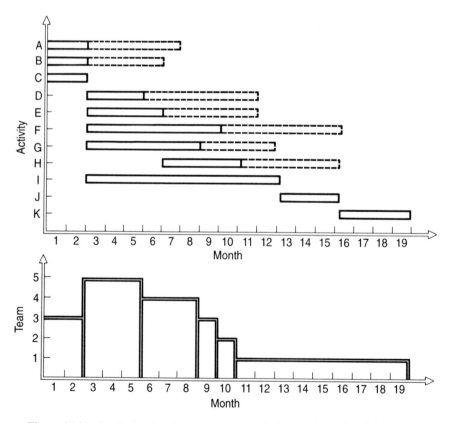

Figure 16.21 Gantt chart and work teams needed assuming all activities start as early as possible.

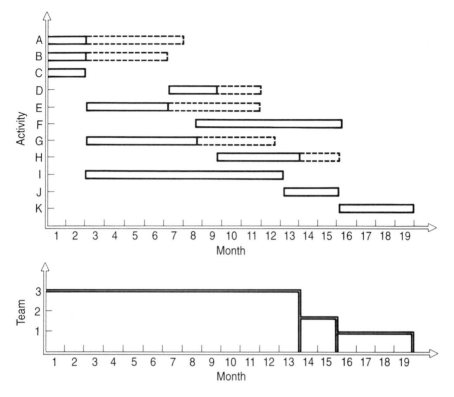

Figure 16.22 Revised schedule with smoother resource use.

Review questions

16.16 Which activities must be shortened to reduce the overall duration of a project?

16.17 By how much can a critical path usefully be shortened?

16.18 By how much can a non-critical activity be expanded without affecting the project duration?

16.19 What is the crashed time of an activity?

16.20 Penalty costs, labour costs, financing costs, and so on, all decline with project duration, so the total cost of a project must decline with its duration. Do you agree with this?

16.21 What are the main benefits of Gantt charts?

16.22 How can the use of resources be smoothed during a project?

ce Case example – Planning term projects

Students are often given projects as part of their coursework. Many of these are group projects, where several students work together to solve a problem. This teaches students how to work in groups, the importance of team work, how to handle large jobs, and a range of planning and organizational skills. But many students find it difficult to co-ordinate the work needed by the group.

Imagine that you have been given a project to complete. This is a group project where four students work together to do a literature search, conduct interviews and surveys, analyse the findings, and write a report. The final report is due 10 weeks from today.

Now suppose that you have five similar projects to do over the next 10 weeks. Each of these projects is similar in principle, but deals with different subjects. The groups have different members for each project.

Questions

- List the main activities needed for the project.
- Draw a network and Gantt chart of the project.
- How would you organize a number of projects in parallel? What specific problems would there be in co-ordinating resources?

Chapter review

- A project is a unique piece of work with a distinct start and finish. It consists of those activities needed to make a one-off product. Projects often use many resources and take a long time, so their management is particularly important.

- Because projects are different in several ways to other processes, we need a different approach to their planning.

- An important factor in the success of a project is the choice of a good project manager and management team.

- Project networks are widely used for managing projects. The relationships between activities is shown in a dependence table. This can be translated into a network of alternating activities and events.

- When the network is complete the timing of the project can be analysed. The critical path identifies the activities that set the duration of the project and need particular attention. Event analyses find the earliest and latest times for events; activity analyses find the earliest and latest start and finish times for activities. The total float measures the amount an activity can expand without affecting the project duration.

- Critical path method (CPM) assumes each activity has a fixed duration. Project evaluation and review technique (PERT) introduces some uncertainty.

- A project can be finished earlier by reducing the durations of critical activities. But if these reductions are too large, parallel paths become critical.

- The costs of a project change with its duration, and a method was described for minimizing total costs.

- Gantt charts allow the progress of a project to be monitored and can also be used for resource planning.

Key terms

CS **Case study** – Mediterranean Orange

Manhattan Incorporated Softdrinks is a conglomerate company which owns over 350 subsidiaries around the world. One of these subsidiaries is European Softdrinks and Equipment Supply (ESES) which has headquarters in London. This company is expanding its business in Southern Europe and has recently acquired Mediterranean Orange. This should markedly increase its sales in Italy, but the next plan is to open a distribution centre on the South coast of Spain.

David Peacock is a planner in the headquarters of ESES. Recently, he was invited to visit Norman Millar, who is the Associate Director of European Operations. It was rare for a relatively junior planner to be called to the Director's suite, but Norman Millar soon explained the problem.

You know that we are expanding operations around the coast of Spain and have recently acquired Mediterranean Orange. You may know its Villa Marbella distribution centre is in the late stages of planning. Last month Mr Solstice (President of the Manhattan parent company) contacted Mr Jones (Managing Director of ESES) asking for details of when this centre will be ready. Mr Jones, in turn, asked the managers of Mediterranean Orange, who sent one of its planner's reports. The only problem is the report consists of a table of figures without any explanation. This means absolutely nothing to any of us. We can't go back to Mediterranean Orange – as our relations are still forming and we want to tread carefully. We also need some figures that we can pass on to Mr Solstice fairly quickly. The only thing I know for certain is that we have about 40 weeks to open the centre, and beyond that our costs start rising at 2% a week. Can you look at the table and give us some information before the end of the week?

David Peacock looked at the information shown in Table 16.15 and said he might manage something within a few days.

Table 16.15

Act	O	M	P	DO	Manning ('000)	NC ('000)	CT	CC
AA	3	3	6	BW	14	8	2	10
AB	3	4	7	AG	7	7	3	9
AC	4	4	6	AB, AE, AY	12	12	3	15
AD	2	3	4	AA	3	2	1	4
AE	3	3	3	AD	2	2	3	2
AF	6	8	14	AD	6	12	4	16
AG	2	2	2	BZ	2	1	2	1
AH	6	8	14	AC, AF	10	20	5	35
AI	6	8	14	AF	12	24	6	36
AJ	7	8	11	AH, AK	12	24	5	42
AK	10	14	20	BQ, BY	22	66	6	85
AL	4	5	7	AK	8	10	2	12
AM	3	3	5	AL	4	3	2	4
AN	5	6	9	AJ	6	9	3	13
AO	8	10	12	AZ	24	60	5	72
AP	4	5	6	BQ	8	10	1	12
AQ	8	10	16	BO, BP	9	23	4	25
AR	3	3	3	BE	11	8	3	8
AS	4	5	6	AP, AQ, AR	3	4	3	6
AT	8	10	15	BT, BV	7	18	7	20
AU	5	6	7	AT	15	23	5	25
AV	4	6	8	AS	18	28	4	30
AW	4	5	9	AM, AN, AO	19	24	3	26
AX	4	4	4	BJ	3	3	3	3
AY	1	1	1	BY	2	1	1	2

Table 16.15 *(cont.)*

Act	O	M	P	DO	Manning ('000)	NC ('000)	CT	CC
AZ	4	5	6	AI	8	10	2	14
BA	1	1	1	–	7	2	1	2
BB	4	5	6	BK	21	27	4	30
BC	4	4	4	BJ	23	24	4	24
BD	5	7	9	AX	17	29	4	35
BE	2	2	2	BN	4	2	1	5
BF	3	5	9	BH	9	11	1	14
BG	2	2	2	BH	6	3	2	3
BH	2	4	6	–	7	7	1	9
BI	1	2	3	–	8	4	1	6
BJ	3	3	3	BK	2	2	3	2
BK	2	2	2	BA	10	5	2	5
BL	2	3	4	BA	15	11	2	15
BM	1	1	1	BI, BL	8	2	1	2
BN	2	4	8	BG, BM	12	12	2	14
BO	6	8	10	BG, BM	22	44	4	60
BP	5	7	11	BF	26	44	3	58
BQ	3	3	3	BF	15	11	3	11
BR	3	6	9	BC	15	38	3	48
BS	4	4	4	BD, BR	7	7	4	7
BT	3	4	8	BS	11	11	3	16
BU	2	2	2	BD	13	7	2	7
BV	2	2	2	BU	5	3	2	3
BW	2	3	3	–	6	5	1	12
BX	5	7	7	BW	8	14	3	18
BY	8	10	15	BX	15	38	4	42
BZ	4	5	8	BW	13	16	2	24

Question

● If you were David Peacock what would you report to the Directors of the London office?

Problems

16.1 A project has the activities shown in the following dependence table:

Activity	Depends on	Activity	Depends on	Activity	Depends on
A	–	E	C	I	E, F
B	–	F	B, D	J	H, I
C	A	G	B	K	E, F
D	A	H	G	L	K

Draw the network for this project.

16.2 (a) An amateur dramatic society is planning its annual production and is interested in using a network to co-ordinate the various activities. What activities do you think should be included in the network?

(b) If discussions lead to the following activities, what would the network look like?

- assess resources and select play
- prepare scripts
- select actors and cast parts
- rehearse
- design and organize advertisements
- prepare stage, lights and sound
- build scenery
- sell tickets
- final arrangements for opening

16.3 Draw a network for the following dependence table:

Activity	Depends on	Activity	Depends on
A	H	I	F
B	H	J	I
C	K	K	L
D	I, M, N	L	F
E	F	M	O
F	–	N	H
G	E, L	O	A, B
H	E	P	N

16.4 If each activity in Problem 16.3 has a duration of one week, find the earliest and latest times for each event. Calculate the earliest and latest start and finish times for each activity and the corresponding total floats.

16.5 Draw the network represented by the following dependence table and calculate the total float for each activity.

Activity	Duration (weeks)	Depends on
A	5	–
B	3	–
C	3	B
D	7	A
E	10	B
F	14	A, C
G	7	D, E
H	4	E
I	5	D

If each activity can be reduced by up to two weeks, what is the shortest duration of the project and which activities are reduced?

16.6 A project is represented by the following table which shows the dependency of activities and three estimates of durations.

- What is the probability that the project will be completed before 17?
- By what time is there a probability of 0.95 that the project will be finished?

		Duration		
Activity	Depends on	Optimistic	Most likely	Pessimistic
A	–	1	2	3
B	A	1	3	6
C	B	4	6	10
D	A	1	1	1
E	D	1	2	2
F	E	3	4	8
G	F	2	3	5
H	D	7	9	11
I	A	0	1	4
J	I	2	3	4
K	H, J	3	4	7
L	C, G, K	1	2	7

16.7 A project consists of 10 activities with estimated durations (in weeks) and dependencies shown in the following table. What are the estimated duration of the project and the earliest and latest times for activities?

Activity	Depends on	Duration	Activity	Depends on	Duration
A	–	8	F	C, D	10
B	A	6	G	B, E, F	5
C	–	10	H	F	8
D	–	6	I	G, H, J	6
E	C	2	J	A	4

If activity B needs special equipment to be hired, when should this be scheduled? A check on the project at week 12 shows that activity F is running 2 weeks late, that activity J would now take six weeks, and that the equipment for B would not arrive until week 18. What affect does this have on the overall project duration?

16.8 Draw a Gantt chart for the project described in problem 16.5. If each activity uses one team of men, draw a graph of the manpower needed assuming each activity starts as soon as possible. How might these needs be smoothed?

16.9 Analyse the times and resource requirements of the project described by the following data:

Activity	Depends on	Duration	Resources
A	–	4	1
B	A	4	2
C	A	3	4
D	B	5	4
E	C	2	2
F	D, E	6	3
G	–	3	3
H	G	7	1
I	G	6	5
J	H	2	3
K	I	4	4
L	J, K	8	2

16.10 In the project described in Problem 16.9 it costs £1000 to reduce the duration of an activity by 1. If there is £12,000 available to reduce the overall duration of the project how should this be allocated and what is the shortest time in which the project can be completed? What are the minimum resources needed by the revised schedule?

Discussion questions

16.1 What do you think are the main elements in a project? Why is managing a project so different to managing other types of process?

16.2 Why is the management of projects so difficult? Illustrate your answer with examples of projects that have had difficulties.

16.3 Describe the matrix management structure usually found in a project. What are the advantages and drawbacks of this?

16.4 What specific skills should a project manager have?

16.5 What information is needed for project network analysis? What can you do if this information is not available?

16.6 How can the timings of activities be found? How accurate are these likely to be?

16.7 How is the control of a project linked to the planning stages?

16.8 Computers are always used for project network analysis. What feature would you expect to see in a good project management package?

Selected references

Original reports:

Kelley J.E. and Walker M.R. (1959). Critical Path Planning and Scheduling, *Proceedings of the Eastern Joint Computer Conference*, Boston, pp. 160–73.

Special Projects Office, Department of the Navy (1958). *PERT, Program Evaluation Research Task*, Phase 1, Summary Report, pp. 646–69.

Other references:

Cleland D.I. (1994). *Project Management* (2nd edn). New York: McGraw-Hill.

Goodman L.J. and Love R.N. (1980). *Project Planning and Management: An Integrated Approach*. New York: Pergamon Press.

Kerzner H. (1984). *Project Management for Executives*. New York: Van Nostrand Reinhold.

Kerzner H. and Thamhain H. (1984). *Project Management for Small and Medium-Sized Business*. New York: Van Nostrand Reinhold.

Lock D. (1992). *Project Management* (5th edn). Aldershot: Gower Publishing.

Ludwig E.E. (1988). *Applied Project Engineering and Management* (2nd edn). Houston, Tx.: Gulf Publishing Co.

Meredith J.R. and Mantel S.J. (1995). *Project Management* (3rd edn). New York: John Wiley.

Shtub A., Bard J.F. and Globerson S. (1994). *Project Management*. Englewood Cliffs, NJ: Prentice-Hall.

Weist J.D. and Levy F.K. (1977). *A Management Guide to PERT/CPM* (2nd edn). Englewood Cliffs, NJ: Prentice-Hall.

Witham Park

The Park

Witham Park is a large area of privately owned woodland that has been open to the public for many years. Located just a short car ride away from a major city, it is popular with walkers, joggers, cyclists, bird watchers and families with young children who use it for picnics. The park is part of a very large private estate. The woodland is managed on a commercial basis, so that the timber is cut and replanted regularly. However the park's owners are keen to encourage recreational access to the woodland as part of a policy of conservation. The estate manager, Jim Longland, has proposed constructing a visitor's centre.

Visitor's centre

Built with timber from the woodland, the visitor's centre will comprise shop, restaurant, toilets and a large exhibition area. The complex will also include a large purpose-built car park to replace the existing informal parking arrangements. In line with the policy of conservation, it is planned that the new facilities will restrict car movements within the woodland and provide scope for directing the public into areas where land use has been carefully planned.

Construction work is to be carried out by workers from the estate, with subcontractors taking on the more specialized tasks such as laying the car park and recruiting and training staff. The visitors centre has to be ready by 1 April, in time for the start of the summer season, when Witham Park is at its busiest.

Jim has prepared a detailed plan for the whole project (see Figure MPIV.1). With a fixed finishing point and a number of organizations and many individuals involved, the plan comprises a detailed schedule of when the various activities will take place. Jim regards the plan as an essential element in his planning and the most effective means of co-ordinating the various interests.

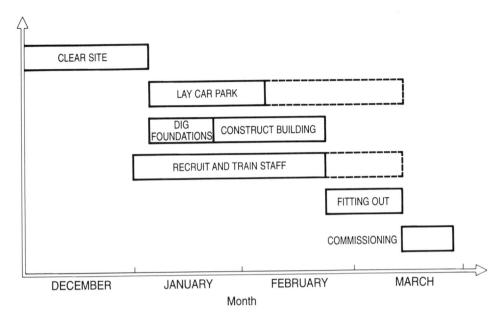

Figure MPIV.1 Plan for visitor's centre project.

The weather intervenes

Work on the visitor's centre gets underway as planned at the end of November. All goes well until a series of gales in early January bring down many trees within the park, including three that fall across the construction site itself. Fortunately, building work was about to start when the gales struck so there is little damage, but it will take at least two weeks to clear the site and repair the foundations.

Getting the project back on course

Jim carefully considers his options. He has to identify the critical activities that still have to be completed and determine the scope for shortening or 'crashing' them, so that the project can get back on schedule. The remaining 'critical' activities are building construction, fitting out and commissioning. Fitting out is in the hands of an external subcontractor who will have serious problems rescheduling the work and commissioning only takes a few days anyway. There are various ways in which building work could be speeded up to re-coup the two weeks that will be lost while the site is cleared of fallen trees:

- overtime working

- diverting workers from other parts of the estate to construction work

- taking on additional temporary construction workers

- subcontracting all building work.

Jim, as project manager for the visitor's centre, has to carefully consider the impact of each option. He can choose between additional costs, poorer quality (caused by rushing the tasks and bringing in inexperienced staff) and the problems caused by putting the opening date back by two weeks.

Materials management

This book is divided into five parts, each of which describes a different aspect of operations management. Part I introduced the subject. Part II looked at some of the strategic issues faced by every organization, particularly the planning needed for a product. Part III discussed the process used to make the product. Part IV looked in more detail at the planning and scheduling of resources. This is the fifth part, which describes some aspects of materials management.

There are three chapters in this part. Chapter 17 gives an introduction to logistics by describing the supply chain. It defines the subject and the various functions involved. In essence, logistics controls the flow of materials through an organization. Chapter 18 looks at inventory control. In particular it describes independent demand inventory systems. We have already mentioned this in Chapters 12 and 13 when we described the dependent demand inventory systems of material requirements planning and just-in-time systems. Finally, Chapter 19 looks at some aspects of location.

Ken Sykes
A to Z Supplies
Essex Commercial Services

Essex Commercial Services is a department of the County Council and is its Centre of Purchasing and Commercial expertise. The Essex Commercial Services Board and Management provide the goods and services required by the County Council through nine businesses. The largest of these by turnover is A to Z Supplies, which has sales in excess of £55 million and employs 200 people. The customer base of A to Z Supplies is largely Education and Social Services and is spread throughout Essex and the neighbouring London boroughs. Ken Sykes is the Operations Manager at A to Z Supplies.

Q **Please describe the supply chain at Essex Commercial Services.**

A We provide our service by three means: delivered from stock held in our warehouse; direct purchase of any goods not held in stock; through contractual arrangements. My area of responsibility is the operational side of the business, that is the delivery of stock held in the warehouse. My area has an annual turnover of £27.5 million, half of which is food.

We operate along the lines of a mail order business, generating sales via a catalogue. Orders are obtained by telephone, fax, post, EDI and are also returned with our drivers who deliver food products. Some 8900 product lines are held in our 120,000 sq ft warehouse, covering a wide range of goods from food to furniture and cleaning products to musical instruments. These goods are delivered by our distribution fleet which comprises 40 vehicles.

Q **What are the controls on the flow of materials through your organization?**

A The floor of the warehouse is broken down into distinct picking areas so that no one person is responsible for the picking of a total order. The picking locations are identified by a five-digit alphanumeric code. Each product is identified by a six-digit numeric code. The picking notes have been designed to give the selectors detailed information presented in a compact and clear format:

- Location
- Catalogue number

- General description
- Quantity

The selectors initial the picking note and, at the confirmation stage, the initials are entered into the computer to create an audit trail. When a picking note is confirmed as completed, the invoice is automatically raised. When a customer's order is received, the computer automatically computes items onto separate picking notes for the different sections, then within each area into an optimum picking schedule taking into account location codes. To avoid the crushing of products, the picking sequence of each section starts with the heaviest items. A high proportion of throughput is broken-case picking (that is, a case is broken open to supply a smaller number of items to a customer) which significantly increases the number of times a picking face is accessed on a daily basis. Our unit of issue is invariably one, that is one bottle of Tipp-Ex, one packet of biscuits:

- Average orders per week: 4,500
- Average pickings per week: 60,000
- Number of customers: 5,845
- Number of delivery points: 9,506.

Q Describe your materials requirement planning. **A** Materials requirement planning is serviced by the Provisioning section which operates within the purchasing groups. Our material requirements is the stock in the warehouse, and the Provisioning section has the responsibility for ensuring correct levels of stock holding within the guidelines of stock availability and the value of stock holding. Our published stock availability figure is 98 per cent. We never slip below this figure and on average achieve 99.3 per cent for food and 98.6 per cent for general products.

A computer generated provisioning report is produced on a weekly basis and contains the following data: product code; description of product; unit of purchase and product usage; stock on hand; buffer stock quantity; maximum stock holding; lead time and order frequency. This information is provided against a 19-week period along with current and previous year's sales data for each product line. Additional information includes highest weekly sales year to date, total requisitions, unit price order, multiple and minimum order quantity. Average lead time for non-food orders is 20 working days with stock holding quantities set at four to six weeks.

Using the above constants, a mathematical calculation will indicate the order quantity. However, a judgement must then be made with regard to seasonal demand. For example, approximately 80 per cent of A to Z Supplies business is in the education sector and, therefore, stock holdings follow seasonal trends.

Once an order has been placed with a supplier, the Operations department starts to take over responsibility. Once goods arrive at Receipts they become my responsibility and are entered onto the warehouse management system. The goods are allocated a bulk storage position and although bulk is stored at random, the system allocates the available position that is nearest to the picking location.

When the picking face requires replenishment, a computer-generated stock movement sheet is produced, stating the product code, bulk pallet position and picking face location. As stated earlier, picking notes are initialled, thereby completing the audit trail to despatch. Journey sheets are produced for each route and the driver signs the journey sheet, with each customer signing for their delivery. The audit trail is then complete.

The link between planning and material management obviously starts at the front end of our supply chain. As we are a purchasing and distribution organization, we do not manufacture anything and, therefore, our stock is the life blood of the organization.

Q **Describe your inventory control systems. How important is inventory control to your operations?**

A Inventory control is crucial to the business and is carried out at various levels at varying intervals of time. The section supervisors monitor fast-moving stock on a daily basis, with particular emphasis on food to ensure correct stock levels, stock rotation and sufficient shelf life. The Stock Accounting section includes the Stock Takers who report to the Finance Manager. Each section of the warehouse has a full stock take once a year with partial stock takes taking place at random throughout the year. These controls are very effective and meets the dual criterion of stock availability and security.

Our annual resource plan is based on estimated sales forecasts. Weekly and daily planning decisions are made with the help of computer-generated data which takes account of total pickings per section per day.

17 Managing the supply chain

Contents

Objectives

After reading this chapter you should be able to:

- say what is meant by 'logistics'
- describe a supply chain and its management
- describe the different functions that make up logistics
- outline the aims of procurement
- discuss the purchasing cycle
- describe a physical distribution system

Logistics

Definitions

Materials are the physical items that are needed for producing goods and services. Materials can be raw materials, components, sub-assemblies, parts, tools, consumables, services or any other types of item. Materials are one of the main inputs to a process, and typically account for 60% of costs. This chapter describes the way they are moved during operations. Managing this movement is the function of logistics.

> **Logistics** is responsible for the physical movement of all materials through an organization.

Logistics really looks at three types of movement:

- **Movement of raw materials** where materials are moved from supplies *into* the organization. Here logistics is concerned with purchasing, inward transport, receiving, storage and retrieval of goods.

- **Movement of work-in-process** where materials are used *within* the organization. Here logistics looks at handling, movement and storage of goods during operations.

- **Movement of finished goods** where materials are moved from the organization *out* to their customers. Here logistics looks at packaging, storage and retrieval from warehouses, shipping and distribution to customers.

Sometimes it is convenient to break the logistics function into parts. Then **materials management** is responsible for the first two of these – movement of materials into and within the organization. **Physical distribution** is responsible for the third – the movement of finished goods out to customers. Unfortunately, there is some confusion in these terms as many people use the terms 'logistics', 'physical distribution' and 'materials management' to mean the same general function.

Logistics controls the flow of materials through an organization on their journey from suppliers, through operations, and on to customers. But the final product of one organization is the raw material of another. For example, petrol is a final product of BP, but a raw material for Pickfords Removals. So materials are actually moved through a series of organizations. This is called a **supply chain**, as shown in Figure 17.1.

This movement of materials can be very complicated. If you think of even a simple product, like a cotton shirt, it has a long and difficult journey

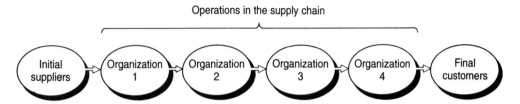

Figure 17.1 Elements in a supply chain.

from the farm growing cotton to the final customer. The supply chain for even a sheet of paper, can involve many organizations. These include loggers, chemical companies, paper makers, transport operators, wholesalers, retailers, and many others (as shown in Figure 17.2).

This journey does not happen by chance, but needs careful planning and co-ordination – which is the function of **logistics**.

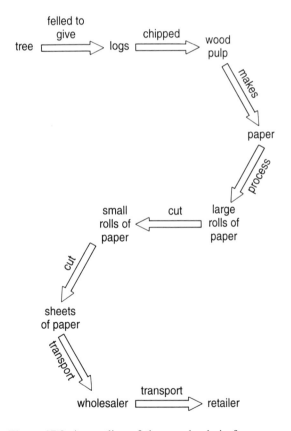

Figure 17.2 An outline of the supply chain for paper.

Aims of logistics

Every part of an organization is affected in some way by the movement of materials. Figure 17.3 shows some of these effects in a simple manufacturing company.

Managing the flow of materials starts with the production plans. These set the raw materials that are needed. Production departments describe the materials needed in a purchase request. A purchasing department actually buys the materials by issuing a purchase order. The materials move into the organization, through receiving and into stores. As the materials are needed, they are removed for use in the production process. Finally, finished goods are sent out to customers.

In principle, logistics is responsible for all these movements. But in many organizations other functions control different parts of the material flow. A procurement department may organize the purchasing of materials and their initial storage, a production department might look after its own stocks of work in progress, and a marketing department might control the stocks of finished goods and movements out to customers. Unfortunately, dividing logistics in this way gives artificial boundaries – with different functions controlling different parts of the materials flow. You might think this does not matter, but it can lead to real inefficiencies. Each department builds up its own administration for logistics, with duplication and redundancy. In extreme

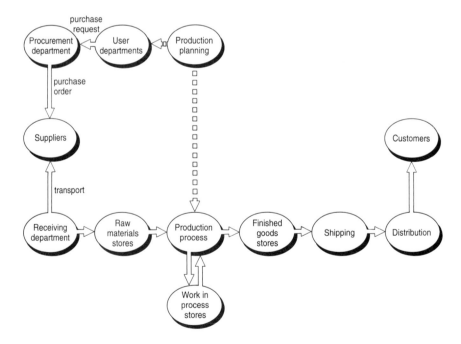

Figure 17.3 Material flow in a manufacturing company.

cases there could be several systems for controlling stocks, none of which are compatible or use the same standards. More importantly, the separate views of logistics have different objectives and this can lead to conflicts. You can imagine some conflicts from the following short list of objectives within an manufacturer.

- *Marketing want*
    - high stocks of finished goods to satisfy customer demands quickly
    - a wide variety of finished goods always held in stocks close to customers
    - an extensive distribution network so products can be moved quickly to customers
    - production to respond to orders from marketing

- *Production want*
    - little variety of products to give long production runs
    - high stocks of raw materials and work in progress
    - efficient movement of materials through operations
    - marketing to respond to output from operations

- *Finance want*
    - low stocks everywhere
    - few plants and warehouses
    - large quantities to reduce costs in long production runs
    - make-to-order operations.

With such conflicting objectives, compromise is clearly needed. The main problem is that each function is trying to satisfy its own needs, often ignoring those of the whole organization. The best way of overcoming this is to have one function in charge of all the material movement. This function can then balance the objectives to get good results for the organization as a whole.

So we can suggest an aim for the integrated logistics function of moving all materials into, through and out of an organization, while making the best use of available resources, and guaranteeing customer service. This is summarized in the aim of supplying, 'the right materials, to the right place, at the right time, from the right source, with the right quality, at the right price'. These general aims lead to a more detailed set of objectives, which:

- give uninterrupted flows of materials into the organization

- find and develop reliable suppliers

- make purchases at lowest long-term cost

- have efficient movement of work in progress

- give efficient movements of finished goods out to customers

- minimize costs of holding stocks

- maintain high quality

- maintain good relations with suppliers and customers.

Functions of logistics

If you think of the integrated logistics function we have been describing, it includes a number of other functions. These include:

- **Procurement or purchasing** which is responsible for buying the raw materials from suppliers.

- **Traffic and transport** which moves the raw materials from suppliers to the organization's receiving area.

- **Receiving** which unloads the trucks bringing in raw materials, inspects the goods for any damage, and checks the goods delivered are the same as those ordered.

- **Warehousing or stores** which stores materials until they are needed, and takes care of them.

- **Inventory control** which deals with the replenishment of stocks and controls inventory levels.

- **Material handling** which moves the materials needed for operations during the process.

- **Shipping** which takes finished products, checks them and loads them onto, say, trucks for delivery to customers.

- **Distribution** which delivers finished products to customers.

- **Location** which decides how many warehouses should be built, and where they should be.

- **Communication** which keeps all records for the logistics system.

If you want to reduce the cost of logistics, you have to look at all of these functions. Trying to reduce each cost separately might actually increase the overall cost. This is because many of the costs need a balance. For example, purchasing could reduce the unit cost of a raw material by buying large quantities, but this increases the cost of inventories. Or traffic might reduce the cost of inward transport by using local suppliers, but this might increase the purchase price.

We can look at some of these functions of logistics in a little more detail. In the following sections we will discuss procurement and physical distribution.

ce Case example – Warehousing for Cadbury

Every year Cadbury sell £1 billion of chocolate in the United Kingdom. In 1994 they closed 13 rented warehouses, and opened a major warehouse on the north-east edge of Birmingham. This location had the advantages of being at the heart of the motorway network, and only 10 miles from Bournville where most of their chocolate is made.

The Cadbury Warehouse covers almost 36,000 square metres – more than 9 football pitches. It has 36 aisles of storage racks which are 106 metres long and 16 metres high, holding a total of 93,000 pallets. There are 19 bays for trucks which allow 120 vehicles a day. The warehouse is fully automated, with all movements controlled by a central computer using bar codes on each pallet. The automation means that only 50 employees are needed.

There are peaks in the sales of chocolate at Christmas and Easter. So the warehouse is designed to work in two distinct ways. During quiet periods delivery vehicles slowly build up stocks; then in the busy periods there are large numbers of movements, and the stocks are quickly depleted. These two modes need different organization and, for example, the automatic guided vehicles that normally move pallets are supplemented by conventional fork-lift trucks.

Questions

• What costs do you think Cadbury considered when building this warehouse?

• Why are there such large economies of scale in warehouses?

Review questions

17.1   What are materials?

17.2   What does logistics do?

17.3   Managing materials is best left to the people most closely involved with them. Do you agree?

17.4   What jobs are usually considered part of logistics?

Procurement

Aims of procurement

> **Procurement** describes the range of activities that are responsible for buying the materials needed by an organization. It is generally responsible for getting materials from suppliers into the organization.

Many organizations use the terms **purchasing** and **procurement** to mean the same thing. Generally, though, purchasing refers to the actual buying of materials. Procurement has a broader meaning and can include purchasing, contracting, expediting, materials handling, transport, warehousing and receiving goods from suppliers.

The purpose of procurement is to make sure that materials needed to support operations are available at the time they are needed. Obviously, if a process does not have the materials it needs, it can not work properly. Perhaps operations are interrupted, customer demand is not met, costs are too high, deliveries are delayed, or productivity is reduced.

How procurement works

When you buy something expensive, like a car, you generally go through a number of steps, looking at different products, comparing different suppliers, and so on. The procurement function in an organization does exactly the same. In particular, procurement aims to:

(1)   buy the materials that are needed for operations

(2)   make sure these materials have reliably high quality

(3)   find good suppliers, work closely with them and develop good relations

(4)   negotiate good prices from suppliers

(5)   keep inventory levels low, by buying standard materials

(6)   expedite deliveries when necessary

(7)   work closely with user departments, understand their needs, and get the materials they need at the right times

(8)   keep informed about price increases, scarcities.

We can look in more detail at the work done in procurement, by considering a typical **purchase cycle**. There are many variations on the basic model, but they usually have the following steps.

(1)   *User department*:

- the person needing the materials makes a request to the department head
- this is checked against budgets within the department
- a purchase request is prepared and sent to procurement

(2)   *Then procurement*:

- receive and analyse the purchase request
- verify and check the request
- check current stocks, alternative products, and so on
- make a short list of possible suppliers, either from regular suppliers or those who are known to be reliable
- send a request for quotations to this short list

(3)   *Then the supplier*:

- examines the request for quotations
- sees how it could best satisfy such an order
- sends an offer back to the organization, with prices, conditions, and so on

(4)   *Then procurement*:

- choose the best supplier, based on their product, delivery, price, and so on
- discuss, and finalize any details with the supplier
- issue a purchase order

(5)   *Then the supplier*:

- receives and processes the purchase order
- makes or assembles the order
- ships the order and sends an invoice

(6)   *Then procurement*:

- do any necessary follow-up to make sure the materials are delivered
- receive, inspect and accept the items
- update inventory records, notify the purchasing department
- approve the supplier's invoice for payment.

A purchase request originates with the person who will be the ultimate user. This person gets authorization to buy the item, perhaps from their department head who checks the request against budgets and agrees the purchase. The request is then sent to the procurement department who process a purchase order.

Procurement check the purchase order to make sure the item is clearly defined, the budget is agreed, the item is not already in stock, it can not be replaced by an alternative, standard item, and so on. When the details of the item are cleared, procurement look for a supplier. Most procurement departments have a list of suppliers for standard items. If there is no acceptable supplier on file, they will search for one. If the item is low value a supplier can probably be found in a journal, catalogue or through business contacts. More expensive items need a more thorough search of industry suppliers.

Normally, an organization will now make a short list of five or six potential suppliers and start negotiating with these. It may not bother with these negotiations if:

- the item is low value

- there is only one possible supplier

- there is already a successful arrangement with a supplier

- there is not enough time for extended negotiations

- the organization has a policy of internal supply.

When necessary, negotiations start with the organization sending out a request for quotations. These are written enquiries which give details of the items needed, and asking potential suppliers to give their prices and conditions. When these quotations are returned, procurement analyse them for specifications, conditions of sale, price, delivery and payment terms. One important point is that the lowest price is not necessarily the best quotation. The right price is the one that is best for all concerned – buyer, supplier, customers, public, and everyone else. It is certainly not in an organization's long-term interest to force the lowest price it can, or use unethical practices in negotiations. The supplier must make a reasonable profit, or they will go out of business and not be there next time the item is needed.

When the quotations have been compared and any difficulties cleared up, the organization can select the best supplier and place an order. A purchase order is a legal offer to purchase the item on agreed conditions. Once accepted by the supplier, it is a binding contract for delivery of the items.

Sometimes, after agreeing conditions in the purchase order, an organization will become concerned over delivery. It might, for example, find that the agreed delivery is actually too late and ask for adjustments, or the supplier might find it difficult to meet the agreed date. Whatever the cause, procurement may decide to take follow-up action. This can be as little as an informal telephone call to suppliers. At other times it can involve further negotiations to revise conditions, expediting transport, finding alternative suppliers, working with the supplier to solve their problems, rescheduling production or taking legal action.

Assuming everything has gone well, procurement must now receive and accept the delivered items. This often involves an inspection on arrival, and comparison of the delivery with the purchase order. Goods might be sent to quality control inspections, and then to the originating department or put into inventory.

Now, having seen what procurement does, we can see why it is important:

- it is essential for the smooth running of operations – all materials are purchased, so poor procurement can lead to poor quality, interrupted operations, late deliveries, wrong quantities, high costs, poor customer service, and so on;

- a typical organization spends 60% of its income on purchases – with a profit margin of 10%, a 1% reduction in the cost of purchased goods can increase profits by 6%.

we Worked example

Last year Zetafile Limited had a total sales of £108 million. Their direct costs were £58 million for materials, £27 million for employees and £12 million for overheads and other costs. What would have been the effects on profits if the cost of materials had dropped by 1%?

Solution

The actual profit last year was $= 108 - (58 + 27 + 12) = £11$ million. This was 10.19% of sales value. If the cost of materials had dropped by 1%, to £57.42 million the profit would have risen to £11.58 million. This is 10.72% of sales value. A 1% decrease in materials costs would have increased profits by 5.2%.

Trends in procurement

The role of procurement has changed significantly in recent years. It used to be little more than a clerical job, buying materials as they were requested. Now it is a profession, and managers expect purchasers to take an active part in planning. General Motors spends over $50 billion a year in purchasing materials, so it is not surprising that this is a senior management role.

One development in procurement is **value analysis**. This is a way of improving product quality and performance, while reducing material cost. In effect, value analysis finds substitute materials that are lower in price but equally as good as the original. Value analysis uses a team of people from different functional areas who critically review a product design. Both purchasing departments and their suppliers are involved early in this review, and generally in product design. The organization and its suppliers then become partners. They can both achieve their common aim – a long-term business relationship that is profitable for both sides.

Such partnerships have encouraged **single sourcing**, which we met with total quality management. In the past purchasing departments had no loyalty to suppliers, and companies used competitive bidding to choose their suppliers. Then contracts were awarded for the short term – typically up to a year.

Organizations thought this gave them good prices as suppliers would compete fiercely to get business. With single sourcing, companies are able to use single suppliers for a given item, with a long contract – typically three to five years. This creates goodwill with the suppliers, who are now prepared to pay attention to orders, and become involved in improvements to product design.

ce Case example – Accounts Payable at Ford

In 1988 Ford of America was looking for increased productivity in its Accounts Payable Department. This employed 500 people who worked a standard accounting system, where:

- the purchase department sent a purchase order to the vendor and a copy to accounts payable;

- the vendor shipped the goods ordered;

- when the goods arrived at Ford, a clerk at the receiving dock checked them, completed a form describing the goods and sent it to Accounts Payable;

- the vendor sent an invoice to Accounts Payable;

- Accounts Payable now had three descriptions of the goods – from the purchase order, receipt form and invoice. If these matched the invoice was paid, but in a few cases there were discrepancies. These often took weeks to trace and clear up.

Ford thought that it could save perhaps 25% of staffing costs by redesigning the system. Then it looked at Mazda, who was running its accounts payable with a fraction of the Ford staff. In the end Ford did a radical redesign of the system. In its revised system:

- the purchase department sends a purchase order to a vendor, and enters details on a database;

- the vendor ships the goods;

- when the goods arrive at Ford, a clerk at the receiving dock uses the database to check them and see if they correspond to an outstanding order. If they do, the clerk updates the database to show the goods have arrived and the computer automatically sends a cheque to the supplier. If there are discrepancies the clerk will refuse to accept the delivery and send it back to the supplier.

The 'we pay when we receive the invoice' has changed to 'we pay when we receive the goods'. The new system takes 125 people to operate, giving a 400% increase in productivity.

Review questions

17.4 What is the main aim of procurement?

17.5 Is there any difference between procurement and purchasing?

17.6 What are the stages in a typical purchasing cycle?

17.7 What trends have there been in procurement?

Physical distribution

Procurement is mainly concerned with moving materials from suppliers into the organization. At the other end of the operations, is **physical distribution** which is concerned with moving finished goods from the organizations and out to customers. Distribution is sometimes described as giving the final link in a supply cycle, as shown in Figure 17.4.

In a typical distribution system, finished goods are moved from operations and stored in warehouses until they are distributed to customers, as shown

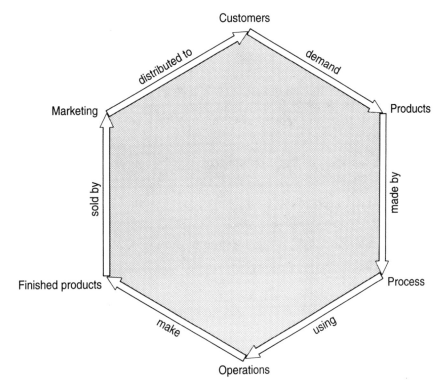

Figure 17.4 Distribution in a supply cycle.

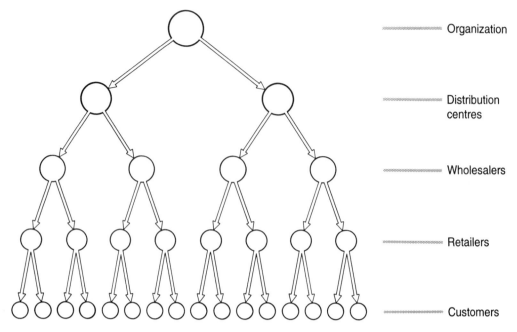

Figure 17.5 A typical distribution system.

in Figure 17.5. Such systems have developed because many operations are done best in locations that are some distance from both customers or suppliers. The best locations for power stations, for example, are some distance from cities and they may also be away from fuel supplies.

There are several advantages in this type of distribution system, including:

- production can achieve economies of scale by concentrating operations in central locations;

- wholesalers keep stocks from many suppliers, allowing retailers a choice of goods;

- wholesalers are near to retailers and have short lead times;

- production facilities do not need to keep large stocks of finished goods;

- retailers can carry less stock as wholesalers offer reliable delivery times;

- wholesalers can place large orders and reduce unit prices;

- distribution costs are reduced as large orders are moved from production facilities to wholesalers, rather than moving small orders directly to retailers or customers.

You probably imagine that this kind of distribution system is used by manufacturers, but it is also used by services. Airlines use a similar system for moving passengers from pick-up points, through feeder services to major 'hub' airports, and back out to destinations. Banks collect all cheques in central clearing houses before sending them back to branches and customers. Blood banks have regional centres that act as wholesalers.

You can see that there are many important decisions needed in logistics. These have the overall aims of:

- an efficient flow of materials through the distribution system

- reliable delivery to customers

- appropriate transport

- low cost storage and high stock turnover

- consistent quality of distribution

- low administration costs

- accurate records.

Each of these leads to a range of other decisions. If, for example, we consider transportation we have to consider the mode of transport. There are essentially five modes of transport; road, rail, air, water and pipeline. The best in any particular circumstances depends on the type of goods to be moved, the distance, value and a whole range of other things. Road transport is the most flexible, as it can usually move goods from door-to-door. But it is not so good for very long distances or high volumes. Rail is better at high volumes, but it can be slower and need transfers at rail terminals. Air transport is fastest, but is expensive and can only take limited weights. Ships can carry big loads, but can only operate between ports. Pipelines can carry large quantities cheaply, but can only carry gas, liquid or slurry over certain areas. The best transport may use more than one mode, perhaps road to a rail terminal, then train to a dock, and so.

ce Case example – Wal-Mart

Sam Walton founded Wal-Mart in Bentonville, Arkansas in 1962. In 1993 it had 2100 stores and sales of $67 billion. The whole organization is considered a model of efficient operations.

The company operates 18 regional distribution centres, with another 15 speciality centres for clothes and hobbies. The largest of these centres covers more than 100,000 square metres and can handle 200 truck deliveries and 250,000 cartons every day. It employs 2500 drivers and runs 2100 articulated tractors and 13,000 trailers. Each store is within 250 miles of its nearest distribution centre, and the allocation of stores to centres is checked twice a year to look for improvements.

In 1988 Wal-Mart opened a chain of Sam's warehouse outlets, and needed greater flexibility than it had with its existing distribution network. It decided to use third party operators, and currently 14 of its 16 centres are run by third party operators. In 1994, when Wal-Mart bought a large part of Woolco in Canada, it decided to expand its third party contacts and use Tibbett & Britten to provide distribution in Canada.

All organizations rely on the movement of goods. This is an expensive function, and one where considerable savings can be made. So we can say that distribution is important to an organization because it:

- is essential
- is expensive
- directly affects profitability
- provides a link between suppliers and customers
- influences lead time, service levels, and so on
- gives public exposure with trucks, and so on
- can be risky, with safety considerations
- determines the size and location of facilities
- may prohibit some operations – such as moving excessive loads
- can encourage development of other organizations.

Review questions

17.7 What is the difference between logistics, physical distribution and materials management?

17.8 What functions does logistics cover?

17.9 What modes of transport can be used?

Chapter review

- Logistics is concerned with the flow of materials from suppliers, through operations and on to final customers. The aim of logistics is to have a smooth flow of materials through the supply chain.

- Logistics interacts with every other function in an organization. For this reason it is often fragmented. There are considerable benefits in having a single integrated logistics function to organize the movement of all materials.

- The complete function of logistics consists of a number of related jobs, including procurement, materials management, warehousing, transport, and inventory control.

- Procurement makes sure an organization has the materials it needs for its operations. It aims to get the right materials, with the right quality, at the right time, to the right place from the right supplier, at the right price.

- There are several steps in procurement. These centre on a purchasing cycle.

- Physical distribution is concerned with moving finished products from operations out to final customers. This is the final link in the supply chain.

Key terms

inventories   588

logistics   588

materials   588

materials management   588

physical distribution   599

procurement   594

purchasing   594

purchase cycle   595

supply chain   588

value analysis   597

CS Case study – Jergensen and Company

Henry Jergensen is worried. Recently his company has been late delivering some important orders. The marketing manager is also upset because his promised deliveries to customers have not been made.

When Henry asked the production manager for an explanation, he found that the shipments were late because shortages of raw materials had interrupted operations. 'But that's impossible', said Henry. 'Inventory levels have been climbing for the past six months, and they were at an all time high last month.'

The inventory controller had an explanation for this. Inventory levels were high because purchasing had been buying some items in large quantities. This gave high stocks for most items, but there were still shortages of other materials. The warehousing budget was being stretched by the current high stocks.

Henry then checked with the purchasing manager, Peter Schmidt. He said, 'Can I remind you that eight months ago you instructed me to reduce materials costs? I am doing this by taking advantage of quantity discounts offered by suppliers.'

Unfortunately, buying large volumes of raw materials, together with the express shipping services used to bring in urgent supplies of materials in short supply, had made the transport supervisor exceed his freight budget for the past three months.

Henry now thought that he knew the problems facing his company. Then the company accountant visited to say, 'The company's inventory costs are so high that we are short of cash. We shall have to borrow money to pay the suppliers next month.' Later that day Henry also found that the late customer deliveries that had started his investigation, were actually caused by poor sales forecasts by the marketing department. They had seriously underestimated monthly demand, so the planned production could not meet actual demand.

Henry knew that all his employees were trying to do their best. But somehow things were going wrong.

Questions

- Why did the inventory levels go up? Why did freight and other costs rise?

- What are the basic problems in Jergensen and Company?

- Would forming a single logistics function help these problems?

- What would you recommend the company do?

Discussion questions

17.1 Describe a supply chain and show how it is used to get complex products to customers.

17.2 What activities are part of logistics? What new issues are facing the function?

17.3 Describe the material flow in an organization you are familiar with. How could this flow be improved?

17.4 Do you think there are real differences between logistics, materials management and physical distribution?

17.5 What are the benefits of an integrated logistics function? Are these inevitable? Could it be better to break logistics into several smaller units?

17.6 What are the main objectives of purchasing?

17.7 Do you think an organization should always negotiate hard with suppliers to get the cheapest prices and best conditions it can?

17.8 Why do you think the amount of goods travelling by rail has been steadily decreasing in recent years?

17.9 How much does logistics cost a typical organization? Do you think this is too much?

Selected references

Bowersox D.J., Closs D.J. and Helferich O.K. (1986). *Logistical Management* (3rd edn). New York: Macmillan Publishing.

Cooper J. (1994). *Logistics and Distribution Planning* (2nd edn). London: Kogan Page.

Coyle J.J., Bardi E.J. and Langley C.J. (1988). *The Management of Business Logistics* (4th edn). St Paul, Mn.: West Publishing.

Johnson J.C. and Wood D.F. (1990). *Contemporary Logistics* (4th edn). New York: Macmillan.

Leenders M.R., Fearon H.E. and England W.B. (1980). *Purchasing and Materials Management* (7th edn). Homewood, Ill.: Richard D. Irwin.

Stock J.R. and Lambert D.M. (1987). *Strategic Logistics Management* (2nd edn). Homewood, Ill.: Richard D. Irwin.

18 Independent demand inventory systems

Contents

Objectives

After reading this chapter you should be able to:

- discuss the costs of holding stocks
- list the main questions asked for inventory control
- calculate economic order quantities
- calculate lead times, costs and cycle lengths
- understand the need for safety stock
- define 'service level' and do related calculations
- describe periodic review systems and calculate target stock levels
- find the optimal number of purchases to cover a single period
- do ABC analyses of inventories

Background to stock holdings

Reasons for holding stocks

Chapter 12 described how material requirements planning controlled stocks of parts and materials. This is an example of a **dependent demand system**, where the demand for an item is found directly from a master production schedule. The alternative approach to stock control is an **independent demand system**. This uses forecasts to find the expected demand for an item. In this chapter we shall describe some aspects of independent demand inventory systems.

> **Stocks** are supplies of goods and materials that are held by an organization. They are formed whenever the organization's inputs or outputs are not used at the time they become available.

All organizations hold stocks of some kind. When a filling station gets a delivery of petrol from a tanker, it is held as stock until sold to a customer; when a factory moves finished goods to a warehouse, they are put into stock; when a restaurant buys vegetables, they join the inventory until delivered with a meal. As there are always costs of holding stocks – to cover warehouse operations, tied-up capital, deterioration, insurance, and so on – an obvious question is, 'Why do organizations hold stock?' There are several answers to this, but the usual one is, 'To give a buffer between supply and demand'.

Think of the raw materials being delivered to a factory. These are usually delivered in large quantities, perhaps a truckload at a time. But they are used in smaller quantities. The result is a stock of raw materials that is replenished with every delivery, and is reduced over time to meet demand. The stock of raw materials gives a cushion against unexpected variations in supply – they allow operations to continue when delivery vehicles are delayed, poor quality materials are rejected, or there is some disruption at the supplier.

At the other end of production are stocks of finished goods. These accumulate at the end of the process until there is enough to meet an order, or to form a load for sending to a distribution centre. These stocks of finished goods allow an organization to meet unexpected demands from customers.

A third type of stock is work-in-progress. This separates the stages in a production process so that each can work at its most efficient rate. If two consecutive operations in a process work most efficiently at different rates, they can be separated or 'decoupled' by having a stock of work-in-progress between them. This grows when the first process works faster than the second, and is reduced when the second process catches up.

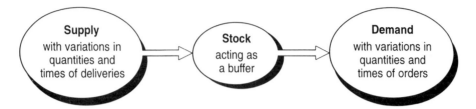

Figure 18.1 Stock acts as a buffer between variable supply and demand.

Then Figure 18.1 shows that:

> The main **purpose of stocks** is to act as a buffer between supply and demand. They allow operations to continue smoothly and avoid disruptions.

A more detailed list of reasons for holding stocks includes:

- to act as a buffer between different operations
- to allow for demands that are larger than expected, or at unexpected times
- to allow for deliveries that are delayed or too small
- to take advantage of price discounts on large orders
- to buy items when the price is low and expected to rise
- to buy items that are going out of production or are difficult to find
- to make full loads and reduce transport costs
- to give cover for emergencies.

Just about everything is held as stock somewhere, whether it is raw materials in a factory, finished goods in a shop or tins of baked beans in a pantry. These stocks are generally classified as:

- **Raw materials** the materials, parts and components that have been delivered to an organization, but are not yet being used.
- **Work-in-progress** materials that have started, but not yet finished their journey through the production process.
- **Finished goods** finished goods that have finished the process and are waiting to be shipped out to customers.

This is a fairly arbitrary classification, as one company's finished goods are another company's raw materials. Some organizations, notably retailers and wholesalers, have stocks of finished goods only, while others, like

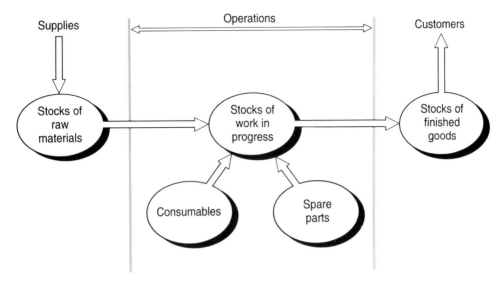

Figure 18.2 Types of stock holdings.

manufacturers, have all three types in different proportions (see Figure 18.2). Nationally, around 30% of stocks are raw materials, 40% work in progress and 30% finished goods. Some stock items do not fall easily into these categories, and two additional types can be defined as:

- **Spare parts** for machinery, equipment, and so on.

- **Consumables** such as oil, fuel, paper, and so on.

ce **Case example** – Stock holding

Tesco

Tesco is one of the largest food retailers in Britain, where it has over 11% of the market. It also operates in France and Hungary. Its 1995 annual report gave the following figures:

Total sales	£10,877 million
Fixed assets	£5210 million
Number of stores	519
Total sales area	12.6 million square feet
Annual growth of sales	15.8%
Stocks	£415 million

ICI

In 1993 ICI had total assets of £9 billion, a turnover of £8.4 billion and a trading profit of £325 million. It is one of the world's leading chemical companies, with five divisions for paints, materials, explosives, industrial chemicals and regional businesses. As you would expect, ICI has huge stocks around the world. These were valued at £1.2 billion – including £396 million of raw materials and consumables, £84 million of work in progress and £719 million of finished goods.

L.T. Francis

L.T. Francis is a manufacturer of pre-cast concrete fittings for the building trade. Its 1995 annual report gave the following figures:

Sales	£15 million
Total assets	£3.8 million
Stock	£2.8 million

As you can see, these organizations hold large stocks. In Tesco the stock is around 4% of sales, in ICI it is 14%, and in L.T. Francis it is 19%. Many organizations have very high stocks, and it is not unusual for manufacturers to hold 25% of annual sales.

Costs of carrying stock

The total cost of holding stock is typically around 25% of its value a year. This is a considerable investment and, not surprisingly, organizations are looking for ways of reducing the costs. Some people think that minimizing costs is the same as minimizing stocks. But this is usually not true. If a shop holds no stock at all, it certainly has no inventory costs, but it also has no sales – and so incurs the cost of losing customers. You can see that there are several types of costs associated with inventories, and we shall define four separate ones:

- unit cost
- reorder cost
- holding cost
- shortage cost.

Unit cost

This is the price of the item charged by the supplier, or the cost to the organization of acquiring one unit of the item. It may be fairly easy to find values by looking at quotations or recent invoices from suppliers. But it is more difficult when there are several suppliers offering slightly different products or offering different purchase conditions. If a company makes the item itself, it may be difficult to give a reliable production cost or set a transfer price.

Reorder cost

This is the cost of placing a repeat order for an item. It might include allowances for drawing-up an order (with checking, signing, clearance, distribution and filing), computer costs, correspondence and telephone costs, receiving (with unloading, checking and testing), supervision, use of equipment and follow-up. Sometimes, costs such as quality control, transport, sorting and movement of received goods are included in the reorder cost.

The reorder cost should be for repeat orders and not first orders – which might have extra allowances for searching for suitable suppliers, checking reliability and quality, and negotiations with alternative suppliers. In practice, the best estimate for a reorder cost is often found by dividing the total annual cost of the purchasing department by the number of orders it sends out.

A special case of the reorder cost occurs when the company makes the item itself. Here the reorder cost is a batch setup cost and might include production documentation costs, allowance for production lost while resetting machines, idle time of operators, material spoilt in test runs, time of specialist tool setters, and so on.

Holding cost

This is the cost of holding one unit of an item in stock for a unit period of time. It might, for example, be the cost of holding a spare engine in stock for a year. The obvious cost is for tied-up money. This money is either borrowed – in which case interest is paid – or it is cash that the organization could put to other use – in which case there are opportunity costs. Other holding costs are due to storage space (supplying a warehouse, rent, rates, heat, light), loss (due to damage, deterioration, obsolescence and pilferage), handling (including special packaging, refrigeration, putting on pallets), administration (stock checks, computer updates) and insurance. Typical annual values for these, as percentages of unit cost, are:

	% of unit cost
Cost of money	10–20
Storage space	2–5
Loss	4–6
Handling	1–2
Administration	1–2
Insurance	1–5
Total	19–40

Shortage cost

This occurs when an item is needed but it can not be supplied from stock. In the simplest case a retailer may lose direct profit from a sale. But the effects of shortages are usually much more widespread and include lost goodwill, loss of reputation, and loss of potential future sales. Shortages of raw materials for a production process can cause disruption and force rescheduling of production, re-timing of maintenance periods, and laying off employees.

Shortage costs might also include payments for positive action to remedy the shortage, such as expediting orders, sending out emergency orders, paying for special deliveries, storing partly finished goods or using alternative, more expensive suppliers.

Shortage costs are always difficult to find, but they can be very high. Now we can look at the purpose of stocks again and say, 'the cost of shortages can be very high and to avoid these organizations are willing to pay the relatively lower costs of carrying stock'.

we Worked example

Overton Travel Group employ a purchasing clerk who earns £12,000 a year. He places an average of 100 orders a month and has a budget of £4800 for the telephone, stationery and postage. Inspections of supplies arriving cost $30 an order. The cost of borrowing money is 15%, the obsolescence rate is 5% and insurance and other costs average 3%. What are the reorder and holding costs for Overton?

Solution

The total number of orders a year is $12 \times 100 = 1200$ orders.

The reorder cost includes all costs that occur for an order. These are:

- salary $= £12,000/1200 = £10$ an order
- expenses $= £4800/1200 = £4$ an order
- inspection $= £15$ an order

So the reorder cost is $10 + 4 + 15 = £29$ an order.

Holding costs include all costs that occur for holding stock. These are:

- borrowing $= 15\%$
- obsolescence $= 5\%$
- insurance and taxes $= 3\%$

So the holding cost is 23% of inventory value a year.

Approaches to inventory control

An important point about inventory costs is that some rise with the amount of stock held, and others fall. The holding cost will be higher when there is more stock, but the shortage cost will be lower. Inventory control must balance these competing costs and suggest policies that give the lowest overall costs. To do this it must answer three basic questions.

What items should be stocked?

No item, however cheap, should be stocked without considering the costs and benefits. This means that an organization should stop unnecessary, new items being added to stock, and it should make regular searches to remove obsolete or dead stock.

When should an order be placed?

This depends on the inventory control system used, type of demand (high or low, steady or erratic, known exactly or estimated), value of the item, lead time between placing an order and receiving it into stock, supplier reliability, and a number of other factors.

How much should be ordered?

If large, infrequent orders are placed the average stock level is high but the costs of placing and administering orders is low. If small, frequent orders are placed the average stock level is low but the costs of placing and administering orders is high.

We shall see how to answer these questions in the following section.

Review questions

18.1   What is the main reason for holding stock?

18.2   How might stock holdings be classified?

18.3   List four types of cost associated with stock holdings.

18.4   How do these costs vary with stock holdings?

18.5   What are the basic questions for inventory control systems?

Economic order quantity

The **economic order quantity** is the basic analysis of scientific inventory control. It has been used since the 1920s. It is often attributed to Harris or Wilson, but has been developed independently several times. The results are very widely used and form the basis of most inventory control systems.

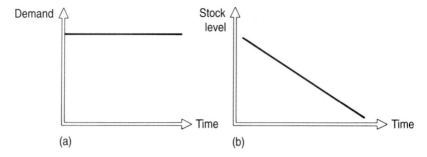

Figure 18.3 Constant demand and resulting stock level: (a) constant demand; (b) steady fall in stock level.

We shall start by considering a single item, where we know the demand is constant at D per unit time. Then the amount of stock falls at a uniform rate, as shown in Figure 18.3. The item is bought from a supplier in batches, and when a batch arrives it can all be used immediately. We shall also assume that unit cost (U_c), reorder cost (R_c) and holding cost (H_c) are all known exactly, while the shortage cost (S_c) is so high that all demands must be met and no shortages are allowed.

We are going to find the best order size, so that orders are always placed for the same quantity, Q. We shall also assume that the lead time between placing an order and having it arrive is known, so we can time orders to arrive exactly when existing stock runs out. Then the stock level follows the saw-tooth pattern shown in Figure 18.4.

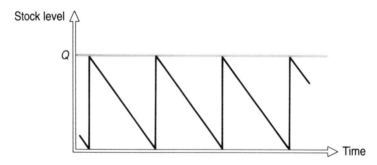

Figure 18.4 Saw-tooth pattern of stock holdings.

The overall approach of this analysis is to find costs for a single stock cycle. Dividing this by the cycle length gives a cost per unit time. Then we can minimize this cost per unit time to find an optimal order quantity.

Calculating the economic order quantity

Consider one cycle of the saw-tooth pattern shown in Figure 18.5.

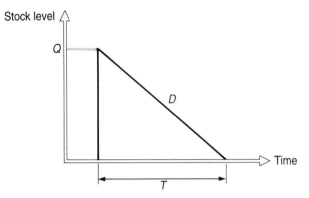

Figure 18.5 A single stock cycle.

At some point an order of size Q arrives. This is used at a constant rate, D, until no stock is left. The resulting stock cycle has length T and we know:

amount entering stock in the cycle = amount leaving stock in the cycle

so:

$$Q = DT$$

We also know that the stock level varies between Q and 0, so the average level is $(Q + 0)/2 = Q/2$.

The total cost for the cycle is found by adding the four components of cost – unit, reorder, holding and shortage. But we know that no shortages are allowed so we can ignore these. We also know that the cost of buying goods is constant regardless of the ordering policy. So we can also leave this out of the calculations.

Then the variable cost for the cycle is:

- total reorder cost: = number of orders(1) × reorder cost$(R_c) = R_c$

- total holding cost: = average stock level$(Q/2)$ × time held(T)
  $$\times \text{ holding cost}(H_c)$$
  $$= H_c QT/2$$

Adding these two gives the variable cost for the cycle, and if we divide this by the cycle length, T, we get the variable cost per unit time, C_T, as:

$$C_T = (R_c + H_c QT/2)/T = R_c/T + H_c Q/2$$

But we know that $Q = DT$, and substituting this gives:

$$C_T = R_c D/Q + H_c Q/2$$

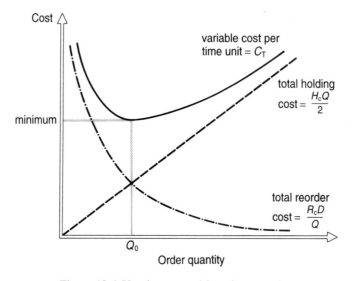

Figure 18.6 Varying cost with order quantity.

We can plot the two parts on the right-hand side of this equation separately against Q, as shown in Figure 18.6.

From this graph you can see that:

●   the total holding cost, $H_c Q/2$, rises linearly with Q;

●   the total reorder cost, $R_c D/Q$, falls as Q increases;

●   large infrequent orders (to the right of the graph) give high total holding costs and low total reorder costs; small frequent orders (to the left of the graph) give low total holding costs and high total reorder costs;

●   adding the two costs gives a total cost curve that is an asymmetric 'U' shape with a distinct minimum. This minimum cost shows the optimal order size.

The optimal order quantity, Q_o, is called the **economic order quantity**, (EOQ). We can find a value for this by differentiating the equation for variable cost with respect to Q, and setting the result equal to zero.

$$0 = -R_c D/Q_o^2 + H_c/2$$

or

$$\text{Economic order quantity, } Q_o = \sqrt{\frac{2R_c D}{H_c}}$$

we Worked example

John Pritchard buys stationery for Penwynn Motors. The demand for printed forms is constant at 20 boxes a month. Each box of forms costs £50, the cost of processing an order and arranging delivery is £60, and holding cost is £18 a box a year. What are the economic order quantity, cycle length and costs?

Solution

Listing the values we know in consistent units:

$$D = 20 \times 12 = 240 \text{ units a year}$$
$$U_c = £50 \text{ a unit}$$
$$R_c = £60 \text{ an order}$$
$$H_c = £18 \text{ a unit a year.}$$

We can substitute these values to give:

$$Q_o = \sqrt{\frac{2R_c D}{H_c}} = \sqrt{\frac{2 \times 60 \times 240}{18}} = 40 \text{ units}$$

Now we can find the variable cost from:

$$C_T = R_c D/Q + H_c Q/2 = 60 \times 240/40 + 18 \times 40/2 = £720 \text{ a year}$$

There is also the fixed cost of buying the boxes. This is the number of boxes bought a year, D, times the cost of each box, U_c. Adding this to the variable cost above gives the total stock cost:

$$\text{total cost} = U_c D + C_T = 50 \times 240 + 720 = £12,720 \text{ a year}$$

The cycle length is found from $Q = DT$, or $T = Q/D$:

$$T = Q/D = 40/240 = 1/6 \text{ years or 2 months.}$$

The best policy – with total costs of £12,720 a year – is to order 40 boxes of paper every 2 months.

You can see an interesting result in the last example if you look at the total reorder cost and total holding cost when Q_o is ordered:

- Total holding cost $= H_c Q_o/2 = 18 \times 40/2 = £360$

- Total reorder cost $= R_c D/Q_o = 60 \times 240/40 = £360$

It is not a coincidence that these two costs are the same. When orders are placed for the economic order quantity, the total reorder cost is always the same as the total holding cost. This gives a short cut for calculating the variable cost of multiplying the total holding cost by 2, to give $H_c Q_o$.

Reorder level

The economic order quantity answers the question of how much to order, but we still need to know when to place an order. This is found from the **reorder level**.

When buying goods, there is a **lead time** between placing the order and having the goods arrive in stock. This is the time taken to prepare an order, send it to the supplier, allow the supplier to assemble the goods and prepare them for shipment, ship the goods back to the customer, allow the customer to receive and check the goods and put them into stock. Depending on circumstances, this lead time can vary between a few minutes and months or even years.

Figure 18.4 shows an inventory level, rising when a delivery is made and falling slowly back to zero to meet demand. Suppose the lead time, L, is constant. To make sure a delivery arrives just as stock is running out, we must place an order a time L earlier. The easiest way of finding this point is to look at the current stock and place an order when there is just enough left to last the lead time. With constant demand, D, an order is placed when the stock level falls to LD and this point is called the **reorder level** (see Figure 18.7).

> **Reorder level** $=$ Lead time demand
> $ROL = LD$

One way of finding when stock falls to the reorder level is to keep a continuous record of the stock level. This has traditionally been done using stock cards, but is now almost always computerized. The computer keeps a record of all transactions and sends a message when it is time to place an order.

Sometimes it is easier to use a **two-bin system**. This keeps, stock in two bins – the first bin holds the reorder level and the second bin holds all the rest of the stock. Demand is met from the second bin until it is empty. At this point the stock level has fallen to the reorder level and it is time to place an order. When the order arrives, the first bin is filled to the reorder level, and all the rest of the delivery is put in the second bin.

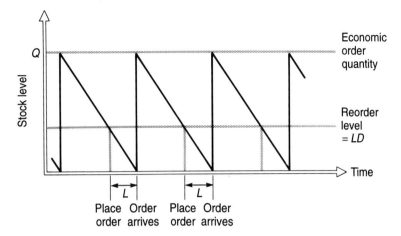

Figure 18.7 Place order when the stock falls to the reorder level.

we Worked example

Demand for an item is constant at 20 units a week, the reorder cost is £125 an order and holding cost is £2 an unit a week. If suppliers guarantee delivery within two weeks what is the best ordering policy for the item?

Solution

Listing the variables in consistent units:

$$
\begin{aligned}
D &= 20 \text{ units a week} \\
R_c &= £125 \text{ an order} \\
H_c &= £2 \text{ a unit a week} \\
L &= 2 \text{ weeks}
\end{aligned}
$$

Substituting these gives:

$$
Q_o = \sqrt{\frac{2R_c D}{H_c}} = \sqrt{\frac{2 \times 125 \times 20}{2}} = 50 \text{ units}
$$

Reorder level $= LD = 2 \times 20 = 40$ units

The best policy is to place an order for 50 units whenever stock falls to 40 units.

The above calculation works well provided the lead time is less than the length of a stock cycle. In the last example the lead time was two weeks and the stock cycle was two and a half weeks. Suppose the lead time is raised to three weeks. The calculation for reorder level then becomes:

$$\text{Reorder level} = LD = 3 \times 20 = 60 \text{ units}$$

The problem is that the stock level never actually rises to 60 units, but varies between 0 and 50 units.

The way around this problem is to recognize that the calculated reorder level refers to both stock on hand and stock on order. Then the reorder level equals lead time demand minus any stock that is already on order.

$$\text{Reorder level} = \text{lead time demand} - \text{stock on order}$$

In the example above, the order quantity is 50 units, so a lead time of three weeks would have one order of 50 units outstanding when it is time to place another order. Then:

$$\text{Reorder level} = 3 \times 20 - 50 = 10 \text{ units}$$

An order for 50 units should be placed whenever actual stock declines to 10 units.

Because the lead time is longer than the stock cycle, there will always be at least one order outstanding, as shown in Figure 18.8.

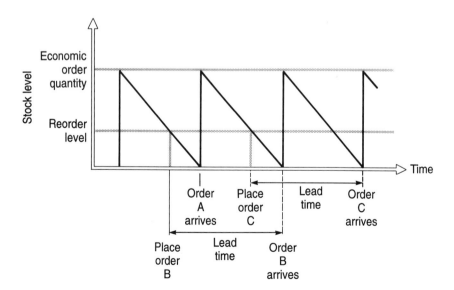

Figure 18.8 Orders when lead time is longer than stock cycle.

Sensitivity analysis

One problem with the economic order quantity (EOQ) is that it can give awkward order quantities. It might, for example, suggest buying 127.6 kg of cement, when we can only buy cement in 50 kg bags. The EOQ might suggest buying 88.39 tyres. We could automatically round this to 88 tyres, but would prefer to order 90 or even 100. We really need to know whether this rounding has much effect on overall costs.

In practice, the cost curve is very shallow around the economic order quantity. The amount we order can be increased to 156% of the optimal value or reduced to 64% and only raise variable costs by 10%. Similarly, the order quantity can be increased to 186% of Q_o or reduced to 54% and only raise variable costs by 20%. This is one reason why the EOQ analysis is so widely used – although the calculation is based on a series of assumptions and approximations, the total cost rises slowly around the optimal. So the EOQ generally gives a good guideline for order size (see Figure 18.9).

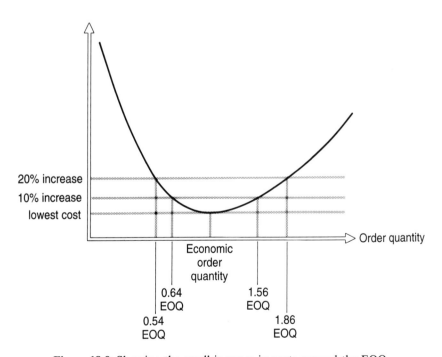

Figure 18.9 Showing the small increase in costs around the EOQ.

we Worked example

Demand for an item is constant at 500 units a month. Unit cost is £100 and shortage costs are known to be very high. The purchasing department sends out an average of 3000 orders a year, and the company's total operating costs are £180,000. Any stocks have capital financing charges of 15%, warehouse charges of 7% and other overheads of 8% a year. The lead time is constant at one week.

● Find an ordering policy for the item.

● What is the reorder level if the lead time increases to 3 weeks?

● What range of order size keeps variable costs within 10% of optimal?

● What is the variable cost if orders are placed for 200 units at a time?

Solution

Listing the values we know and making sure the units are consistent:

$D = 500 \times 12 = 6000$ units a year

$U_c = £100$ a unit

$R_c = \dfrac{\text{annual cost of purchasing department}}{\text{number of orders a year}} = \dfrac{180,000}{3000} = £60$ an order

$H_c = (15\% + 7\% + 8\%)$ of unit cost a year
$= (0.3) \times U_c = £30$ a unit a year

$L = 1$ week

● We can find the best ordering policy by substituting these values into the equations:

-   order quantity,

$$Q_o = \sqrt{\frac{2R_c D}{H_c}} = \sqrt{\frac{2 \times 60 \times 6000}{30}} = 154.9 \text{ units}$$

-   cycle length, $T = Q/D = 154.9/6000 = 0.026$ years or 1.3 weeks
-   variable cost a year $= H_c Q = 30 \times 154.9 = £4647$ a year
-   total cost a year $= U_c D + $ variable cost
$= 100 \times 6000 + 4647 = £604,647$ a year

The lead time is less than the stock cycle, so:

Reorder level $= LD = 1 \times 6000/52 = 115.4$ units

The optimal policy is to order 154.9 units whenever stock declines to 115.4 units.

- If the lead time increases to 3 weeks, there will be two orders outstanding when it is time to place another. Then:

$$\begin{aligned} \text{Reorder level} &= LD - 2Q_o \\ &= 3 \times 6000/52 - 2 \times 154.9 \\ &= 36.4 \text{ units} \end{aligned}$$

- To keep variable costs within 10% of optimal, the quantity ordered can vary between 64% of Q_o, which is 99.1 units, and 156% of Q_o, which is 241.6 units.

- If fixed order sizes of 200 units are used the variable costs will be:

$$\begin{aligned} C_T &= R_c D/Q + H_c Q/2 \\ &= 60 \times 6000/200 + 30 \times 200/2 \\ &= \pounds 4800 \text{ a year.} \end{aligned}$$

Review questions

18.6 What are the main assumptions of the EOQ analysis?

18.7 What is meant by the economic order quantity?

18.8 How does placing small, frequent orders (rather than large, infrequent ones) affect inventory costs?

18.9 What exactly is the reorder level?

18.10 How is the reorder level calculated?

18.11 It is important to order exactly the economic order quantity, as even small differences will give much higher costs. Do you agree with this?

ce Case example – Montague Electrical Engineering

Montague Electrical Engineering (MEE) is a small electric motor manufacturer with annual sales of £8 million. Robert Hellier is the operations manager. He had just read the monthly inventory report and was surprised to find the total inventory had jumped from £2.2 million to £2.6 million in the past month.

Robert noticed there were very high stocks of part number XCT45, which is a 3 cm diameter bearing. MEE uses these steadily, at a rate around 200 a week. The bearings cost £5 each and Robert has been buying 2500 units at a time. There were many such items in the report, and Robert realized that he has been ordering parts without taking any notice of the inventory costs. He remembered that the accountant had calculated the cost of inventory as 30% a year and the ordering costs were about £15 an order.

Uncertain demand and safety stock

The model we have described so far assumes that demand is constant and known exactly. In practice demand can vary widely and have a lot of uncertainty. A company producing a new CD, for example, does not know how many copies will sell in advance, or how sales will vary over time. When the variation is small, the basic EOQ model still gives useful results. But results are not so good when the demand varies more widely.

There are several approaches to variable and uncertain demand. We shall illustrate one of these for Normally distributed demand. If demand is normal, you can easily see why the EOQ will not give good results. The reorder level is the mean lead-time demand, LD. But when demand in the lead time is greater than average, stock will run out and there will be shortages. Unfortunately, the lead time demand will be above the mean in 50% of cycles – and most organizations would view shortages in 50% of cycles as a very poor level of service.

In principle, we should be able to calculate the cost of stock-outs and balance them with the cost of holding stock. It is difficult to find accurate costs for stock-outs, but they are usually high compared with holding costs. This means that organizations are willing to hold additional stocks, above their expected needs, to add a margin of safety. So they increase holding costs to avoid possible shortage costs. These **safety stocks** are available if the normal working stock runs out.

Suppose a computer supplier sells an average of 10 machines a week, and places an order for 20 machines every two weeks. With our previous analyses we would assume that the stocks of computers will fall to zero at the end of the second week, and at this point a new delivery will arrive. But demand may vary, so the supplier keeps an extra five units as a safety stock. With the expected demand these units will not be used, but if there is a sudden increase in demand, it can be met from the safety stock (see Figure 18.10).

The safety stock has no effect on the reorder quantity, which is still defined by the EOQ. But it does effect the time when an order is placed. In particular, the reorder level is raised by the amount of the safety stock to give:

reorder level = lead time demand + safety stock
reorder level = LD + safety stock

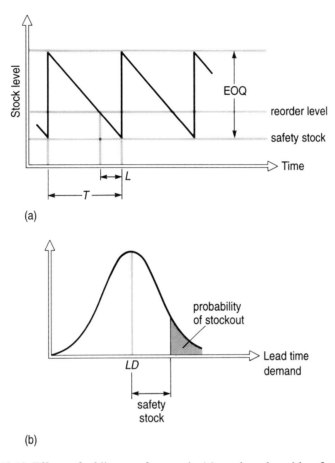

(a)

(b)

Figure 18.10 Effects of adding a safety stock: (a) stock cycles with safety stock; (b) probability of stock-out with safety stock.

The larger the safety stock, the greater the cushion against unexpectedly high demand, and the greater the customer service. Of course, the costs of holding larger stocks are also higher. The question we should now ask is, 'How much safety stock should we hold?'

Because stock-out costs are difficult to find and are often little more than guesses, analyses based on them are notoriously unreliable. An alternative approach relies more directly on the judgement of management to define a **service level**. This is the probability that a demand is met directly from stock. An organization will typically give a service level of 95%. This means that it meets 95% of orders from stock – and accepts that 5% of orders can not be met from stock. The service level needs a positive decision by managers, based on their experience, objectives, and knowledge of customer expectations.

There are several different ways of defining service level, including percentage of orders met from stock, percentage of units met from stock, percentage of periods without stock-outs, percentage of stock cycles without stock-outs, and percentage of time there is stock available. In the remainder of this analysis we will use the probability of not running out of stock in a stock cycle. This is sometimes called the **cycle-service level**.

Suppose that demand for an item is Normally distributed with a mean of D per unit time and standard deviation of σ. If the lead time is constant at L, the lead time demand is Normally distributed with mean of LD. The lead time demand has a variance of $\sigma^2 L$ and standard deviation of $\sigma\sqrt{L}$. This result comes from the fact that variances can be added (but standard deviations can not). If

- demand in a single period has mean D and variance σ^2, then

- demand in two periods has mean $2D$ and variance $2\sigma^2$,

- demand in three periods has mean $3D$ and variance $3\sigma^2$, and so on, so that

- demand in L periods has mean LD and variance $L\sigma^2$.

The size of the safety stock depends on the service level. If an organization has a high service level the safety stock must also be high. To be specific, when lead time demand is Normally distributed the calculation of safety stock becomes:

safety stock $= Z \times$ standard deviation of lead time demand
$$= Z\sigma\sqrt{L}$$

As usual, Z is the number of standard deviations away from the mean, and probabilities can be found from Normal probability tables (see Appendix B). To give some examples,

$Z = 1$ gives a stock-out in 15.9% of stock cycles;
$Z = 2$ gives stock-outs in 2.3% of stock cycles;
$Z = 3$ gives stock-outs in 0.1% of stock cycles.

If demand varies widely, the standard deviation of lead time demand is high – so very high safety stocks are needed to give a service level near to 100%. This is usually too expensive and organizations set a lower level, typically around 95%. Sometimes it is better to give items different service levels depending on their importance. Then very important items have service levels close to 100%, while less important ones are around 85%.

we Worked example

Associated Kitchen Furnishings runs a retail shop to sell a range of kitchen cabinets. Its demand for cabinets is Normally distributed with a mean of 200 units a week and a standard deviation of 40 units. The reorder cost, including delivery, is £200, holding cost is £6 a unit a year and lead time is fixed at three weeks. Describe an ordering policy that will give the shop a 95% cycle-service level. What is the cost of holding the safety stock in this case? How much would the costs rise if the service level is raised to 97%?

Solution

Listing the values we know:

$$D = 200 \text{ units a week} = 10{,}400 \text{ units a year}$$
$$\sigma = 40 \text{ units}$$
$$R_c = £200 \text{ an order}$$
$$H_c = £6 \text{ a unit a year}$$
$$L = 3 \text{ weeks}$$

- Substituting these gives:

$$Q_o = \sqrt{(2R_c D/H_c)} = \sqrt{(2 \times 200 \times 200 \times 52/6)}$$
$$= 833 \text{ (to the nearest integer)}$$

Reorder level $= LD +$ safety stock $= 600 +$ safety stock

For a 95% service level $Z = 1.64$ standard deviations from the mean. Then:

$$\text{safety stock} = Z\sigma\sqrt{L} = 1.64 \times 40 \times \sqrt{3}$$
$$= 114 \text{ (to the nearest integer)}$$

The best policy is to order 833 units whenever stock falls to $600 + 114 = 714$ units. On average orders will arrive when there are 114 units left.

- The safety stock is not usually used, so the holding cost is simply:

$$= \text{safety stock} \times \text{holding cost} = 114 \times 6 = £684 \text{ a year}$$

- If the service level is raised to 97%, Z becomes 1.88 and:

$$\text{safety stock} = Z\sigma\sqrt{L} = 1.88 \times 40 \times \sqrt{3} = 130$$

The cost of holding this is:

$$= \text{safety stock} \times \text{holding cost} = 130 \times 6 = £780 \text{ a year.}$$

Review questions

18.12 What is a service level?

18.13 What is the purpose of safety stock?

18.14 How might the service level be increased?

Periodic review systems

So far we have described models for inventory control that use a **fixed order quantity**. But there is an alternative **periodic review** approach (see Figure 18.11).

- **Fixed order quantity** methods have an order of fixed size placed whenever stock falls to a certain level. A central heating plant, for example, may order 25,000 litres of oil whenever the amount in the tank falls to 2500 litres. Such systems need continuous monitoring of stock levels and are best suited to low, irregular demand for relatively expensive items.

- **Periodic review methods** order varying amounts at regular intervals to raise the stock level to a specified value. Supermarket shelves, for example, may be refilled every evening to replace whatever was sold during the day. The operating cost of this system is generally lower and it is better suited to high, regular demand of low value items.

If the demand is constant these two systems are the same. Differences only appear when demand varies. So we can extend the last analysis, and look

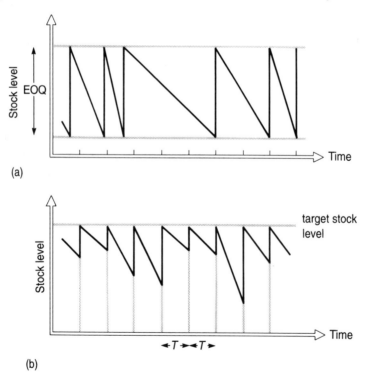

(a)

(b)

Figure 18.11 Alternative inventory control policies: (a) fixed order quantity system; (b) periodic review system.

at a periodic review system where demand is Normally distributed. Then we look for answers to two basic questions:

(1)   How long should the interval between orders be?

(2)   What should the target stock level be?

The order interval, T, can be any convenient period. It might, for example, be easiest to place an order at the end of every week, or every morning, or at the end of a month. If there is no obvious cycle we might aim for a certain number of orders a year or some average order size. One approach would be to calculate an economic order quantity, and then find the period that gives orders of about this size. The final decision is largely a matter for management judgement.

Whatever interval is chosen we need to find a **target stock level**. The system works by looking at the amount of stock on hand when an order is placed, and ordering the amount that brings this up to the target stock level, TSL.

For a periodic review system:

order quantity = target stock level − stock on hand

Suppose the lead time is constant at L. When an order is placed, the stock on hand plus this order must be enough to last until the next order arrives, which is $T + L$ away (as shown in Figure 18.12). The target stock level should be high enough to cover mean demand over this period so it must be at

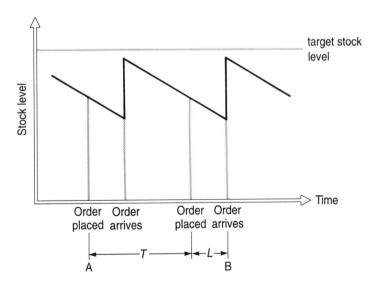

Figure 18.12 An order placed at A must cover all demand until B.

least $D(T+L)$. As demand is Normally distributed, some safety stock is needed to allow for the 50% of cycles when demand is higher than average. Assuming both the cycle length and lead time are constant, the demand over $T+L$ is Normally distributed with mean of $D(T+L)$, variance of $\sigma^2(T+L)$ and standard deviation of $\sigma\sqrt{(T+L)}$. A safety stock can then be defined as:

$$\text{safety stock} = Z \times \text{standard deviation of demand over } T+L$$
$$= Z\sigma\sqrt{(T+L)}$$

So:

$$\textbf{target stock level} = \text{demand over } T+L + \text{safety stock}$$
$$= D(T+L) + Z\sigma\sqrt{(T+L)}$$

we Worked example

Demand for an item has a mean of 200 units a week and standard deviation of 40 units. Stock is checked every four weeks and lead time is constant at two weeks. Describe a policy that will give a 95% service level. If the holding cost is £2 a unit a week, what is the cost of the safety stock with this policy? What is the effect of a 98% service level?

Solution

The variables are:

$$\begin{aligned} D &= 200 \text{ units} \\ \sigma &= 40 \text{ units} \\ H_c &= \text{£2 a unit a week} \\ T &= 4 \text{ weeks} \\ L &= 2 \text{ weeks} \end{aligned}$$

- For a 95% safety stock Z can be found from Normal distribution tables to be 1.64. Then:

$$\text{safety stock} = Z\sigma\sqrt{(T+L)}$$
$$= 1.64 \times 40 \times \sqrt{6} = 161 \text{ (to the nearest integer)}$$
$$\text{target stock level} = D(T+L) + \text{safety stock}$$
$$= 200 \times (6) + 161 = 1361$$

When it is time to place an order, the policy is to find the stock on hand, and place an order for:

$$\text{order size} = 1361 - \text{stock on hand}$$

If, for example, there were 200 units in stock, the order would be for 1161 units.

- The cost of holding the safety stock is $161 \times 2 = £322$ a week.

- If the service level is increased to 98%, $Z = 2.05$ and

  $$\text{safety stock} = 2.05 \times 40 \times \sqrt{6} = 201$$

  The target stock level is then 1401 units and the cost of the safety stock is $201 \times 2 = £402$ a week.

■

Review questions

18.15 How is the order size calculated for a periodic review system?

18.16 Will the safety stock be higher for a fixed order quantity system or a periodic review system?

Single period models

Sometimes managers need an inventory policy for the short term, rather than the long term. This often happens with seasonal goods. A stock of Christmas cards, for example, should satisfy all demand in December, but any remaining cards will have no value in January. In this case, inventory control must try to minimize costs during December. There are many examples of this type, where managers look at the stocks over a single cycle.

A classic example of this is phrased in terms of a newsboy who sells papers on a street corner. The demand is uncertain, and the newsboy must decide how many papers to buy from his supplier. If he buys too many papers he is left with unsold stock that has no value at the end of the day; if he buys too few papers he has unsatisfied demand that could have given a higher profit. Because of this example, single period problems of this type are usually called 'newsboy problems'.

The analysis assumes that customer demand follows a known probability distribution, so we know the probability of selling each number of newspapers. If we also know the profit on each paper sold, S, and the loss on each paper bought but not sold, N, we can suggest an optimal policy.

Suppose the newsboy buys n newspapers. His expected profit on the nth is SP_n where P_n is the probability he sells the nth paper. Alternatively, we could say that the expected loss on the nth paper is $N(1 - P_n)$, where $(1 - P_n)$ is the probability he does not sell the nth paper. As P_n is the probability that the nth paper is sold, it is really the cumulative probability that the demand is greater than or equal to n. The newsboy will only buy n papers if his expected profit is greater than his expected loss. In other words:

$$SP_n \geqslant N(1 - P_n)$$

or

$$P_n \geqslant \frac{N}{S+N}$$

The newsboy's profit continues to rise with n while the inequality remains valid, but at some point the inequality will become invalid and his profit begins to fall. This point identifies the best policy – he should buy the largest value of n for which the inequality is still valid.

we Worked example

In mid-December the owner of a conifer plantation hires a contractor to cut enough trees to meet the expected demand for Christmas trees. He supplies these to a local wholesaler in batches of 100. Over the past few years the demand has been as follows.

Batches	0	1	2	3	4	5	6	7	8	9
Probability	0.0	0.05	0.1	0.15	0.2	0.2	0.15	0.1	0.05	0

If it costs £8 to cut and trim a tree which sells for £12, how many trees should he cut?

Solution

S is the profit on a batch of 100 trees sold,
which is $100 \times (12 - 8) = £400$.

N is the loss on a batch of trees not sold,
which is $100 \times 8 = £800$.

So we want the highest value of n for which the inequality is still valid:

$$P_n \geqslant N/(S+N) \geqslant 800/(400+800) \geqslant 0.67$$

The cumulative probabilities of selling at least n trees are:

n	1	2	3	4	5	6	7	8	9
P_n	1.0	0.95	0.85	0.70	0.5	0.3	0.15	0.05	0

So the largest value of n for which the inequality is valid is 4. The plantation owner should cut 400 trees.

we Worked example

A tour operator wants to book a number of hotel rooms for anticipated future bookings of holidays. The number of holidays actually booked is equally likely to be any number between 0 and 99 (for convenience rather than reality). Each hotel room booked costs the operator £150, and she charges holiday makers £250. How many rooms should she book?

Solution

Here $N = 150$ and $S = (250 - 150) = 100$.

We want $P_n \geqslant N/(S+N) \geqslant 150/(100 + 150) \geqslant 0.6$.

As each number of bookings is equally likely, the probability of each number, n, is 0.01 for all values of n from 0 to 99. So the cumulative probabilities are:

n	0	1	2	3	4	...	39	40	41	...
P_n	1.0	0.99	0.98	0.97	0.96	...	0.61	0.60	0.61	...

The largest value of n for which the inequality is valid is 40.

Review questions

18.17 What is meant by a single period model?

18.18 What is the meaning of P_n in the newsboy problem?

18.19 Why must the inequality $P_n \geqslant N/(S+N)$ remain valid?

ABC analysis of inventories

It takes a lot of effort to make sure an inventory control system runs smoothly and efficiently. Most inventory control systems are computerized, but they still need manual effort to input data, check values, update supplier details, confirm orders, and do other routine jobs. For some items, especially cheap ones, this effort is not be worthwhile. Very few organizations, for example, include routine stationery or nuts and bolts in their computerized stock system. At the other end of the scale are very expensive items that need special care above the routine calculations. An aircraft engine, for example, can cost several million pounds, so airlines look very carefully at their stocks of spare engines.

An ABC analysis puts items into categories that show the amount of effort worth spending on inventory control. This kind of analysis is sometimes called a Pareto analysis or the 'rule of 80/20'. This suggests that 20% of inventory items need 80% of the attention, while the remaining 80% of items need only 20% of the attention. ABC analyses define:

- A items as expensive and needing special care;
- B items as ordinary ones needing standard care;
- C items as cheap and needing little care.

Typically an organization might use an automated system to deal with all B items. The computer system might make some suggestions for A items, but final decisions are made by managers after reviewing all the circumstances. Some C items might be included in the automatic system, but the very cheap ones may be left out, and dealt with using ad hoc procedures.

An ABC analysis starts by calculating the total annual use of items in terms of value. This is found by multiplying the number of units used in a year by the unit cost. Usually, a few expensive items account for a lot of use, while many cheap ones account for little use. If we list the items in order of decreasing annual use by value, A items are at the top of the list, B items are in the middle and C items are at the bottom. We might typically find:

Category	% of items	Cumulative % of items	% of use by value	Cumulative % of use by value
A	10	10	70	70
B	30	40	20	90
C	60	100	10	100

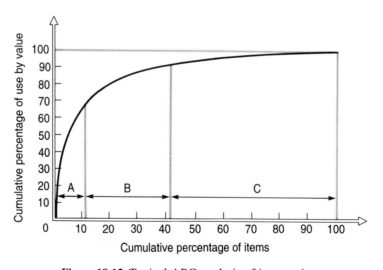

Figure 18.13 Typical ABC analysis of inventories.

Plotting the cumulative percentage of annual use against the cumulative percentage of items gives a graph of the type shown in Figure 18.13.

we Worked example

A small store has 10 categories of product with the following costs and annual demands:

Product	P1	P2	P3	P4	P5	P6	P7	P8	P9	P0
Unit cost (£)	20	10	20	50	10	50	5	20	100	1
Annual demand ('00s)	2.5	50	20	66	15	6	10	5	1	50

Do an ABC analysis of these items. If resources for inventory control are limited, which items should be given least attention?

Solution

The annual use of P1 in terms of value is $20 \times 250 = £5000$. If this calculation is repeated for the other items we get:

Item	P1	P2	P3	P4	P5	P6	P7	P8	P9	P0
% of items	10	10	10	10	10	10	10	10	10	10
Annual use (£'000s)	5	50	40	330	15	30	5	10	10	5

Sorting these into order of decreasing annual use we get the results shown in Table 18.1.

Table 18.1

Product	P4	P2	P3	P6	P5	P8	P9	P1	P7	P0
Cumulative % of items	10	20	30	40	50	60	70	80	90	100
Annual use (£'000s)	330	50	40	30	15	10	10	5	5	5
Cumulative annual use	330	380	420	450	465	475	485	490	495	500
Cumulative % annual use	66	76	84	90	93	95	97	98	99	100
Category	A	← B →		←			C			→

The boundaries between categories of items are sometimes unclear, but in this case P4 is clearly an A item, P2, P3 and P6 are B items and the rest are C items.

The C items account for only 10% of annual use by value. If resources are limited, these should be given least attention.

Review questions

18.20 What is the purpose of an ABC analysis of inventories?

18.21 Which items can best be dealt with by routine, automated control procedures?

Chapter review

- This chapter has described some ways of controlling stocks. It examined independent demand systems which are based on forecasts of future demand.

- The main purpose of stocks is to provide a buffer between supply and demand. There are often uncertainties in both supply and demand, and stocks are the only way of allowing operations to continue smoothly.

- There are several types of stock including finished goods, raw materials, work in progress, spare parts and consumables. These stocks have associated costs that can be very high.

- Inventory control systems aim at minimizing costs by answering three basic questions: what to stock, when to place orders, and how much to order.

- The economic order quantity is the order size that minimizes costs for a simple inventory system. The reorder level shows the times to place orders.

- If demand varies widely another approach should be used. This may use a safety stock to set a customer service level. This is useful when, say, demand is Normally distributed.

- Periodic review systems place regular orders to bring stocks up to a target level.

- One special analysis considered stocks of items that are only kept for a single period before being scrapped.

- ABC analyses show the amount of effort worth spending on controlling items of different types.

Key terms

CS Case study – Congleton Lead Refinery

Congleton Lead Refinery is one of several refineries owned by Meridian Metals. It imports a silver–lead–zinc ore – which is mined by other Meridian companies in Australia and Southern Africa – and refines it into pure metals. Its profitability varies with the market price for refined metals, and recent weaknesses in the price of lead has made it look for ways of reducing operating costs.

A team of management consultants has been advising the Congleton refinery on ways to improve productivity. Their study was drawing to a close when the project manager from the consultancy, Nigel Chatterton, was asked to visit Congleton's Vice President of Operations, Beatrix de Witte. Beatrix explained the purpose of the visit.

> Thank you for all your work on improving the productivity of the refinery. Your suggestions for rescheduling operations lets us reduce the amount of plant and equipment, and still meet expected demands.

> Can you do a small final study for us? Because we will be working with less back-up equipment it is important that the equipment we have continues to work. This in turn depends on our stocks of spare parts. We keep about 25,000 items in the stores and would like some suggestions for improving its effectiveness.

Nigel Chatterton assured Beatrix that the consultancy had a lot of experience with inventory systems, and their final report was already suggesting a study. He then went to talk with Laurens van Hooste who was the Supplies Manager for Congleton.

Laurens van Hooste described the present inventory control system as follows.

> We have 25,000 different items which vary from paper clips to 15 tonne buckets for ore movers. There is no such thing as a typical item. Demand ranges from zero to 100,000 units a year. Current stocks range from one (we carry a few spare engines and big earth movers) to several hundred thousand (like iron balls used in the ore crushers). Lead times vary from 10 minutes for things bought in a local shop, to almost two years for imported furnace bricks. The unit price ranges from almost nothing to £100,000. The reorder price varies from almost nothing for things we buy regularly from local suppliers, to very large amounts when we need a specialized piece of equipment designed and delivered. Shortage costs range from almost nothing to very large sums for things that we absolutely must keep in stock.
>
> The present system was installed about 10 years ago, and has been constantly updated ever since. I am sure you can make some improvements. We are very keen to improve efficiency, and will help your investigations in any way we can.

Nigel found a description of the current system, which is very well documented. Since the original system was installed it has been completely revised twice and has many smaller adjustments. The system categorizes items in a number of ways and deals with each category differently. First, the system considers the importance of the items:

- 5% of items are essential and have to be kept in stock whatever the cost;

- 20% of items are important and have a notional service level of 97%;

- 50% are ordinary items with a notional service level of 93%;

- 25% are low priority items with a notional service level of 80%.

A second classification of items looks at how long they had been stocked:

- New items have their expected demand suggested either by the department requesting the item or by suppliers.

- When an item has been in stock for four months a short history of demand is developing, and forecasts for future demand are made from average values over these four months.

- After nine months, more historic data is available, and forecasting is switched to exponential smoothing. The parameters used for forecasting are monitored and revised every month.

A third classification of items refers to their use:

- Stocks of heavily used items are reviewed at the end of every working day.

- Stocks of normally used items are reviewed at the end of every week.

- Stocks of lightly used items are reviewed at the end of every month.

- Stocks of sporadically used items are reviewed every time there is a withdrawal.

- Stocks of items that have no recorded movement in the past year are considered for removal from stock.

About 20% of items are in each of these categories.

The whole inventory control system is computerized, with records of all transactions and frequent reports on performance and action to be taken. At the end of every working day, for example, the computer lists the heavily used items that have fallen to their reorder levels and sends suggested purchases to the Procurement Section. These show the economic order quantity, actual quantities to be ordered, preferred supplier, supplier reliability rating, lead time, historic quality of deliveries, alternative suppliers, special conditions, probability of shortages if no action is taken, and a range of related information. The Procurement Section examines the suggested orders for the following day, makes any modifications they feel are needed, and confirms arrangements with the computer. The computer then prints orders, arranges payments, makes any other arrangements necessary, and updates its records.

At the end of every week the computer monitors the inventory performance. Forecasts, for example, are compared with actual demand. If there are small differences no action is taken, but items with larger differences are listed, together with suggestions for changing parameters in the forecasting models. If the differences are severe a report is printed and more radical action suggested. All final decisions are under the direct control of the Supplies Department.

Nigel saw that the system appears to be working well. It is based on sound principles and the stocks seem to give little trouble, considering the complexity of a system containing £15 million worth of stock. His immediate problem is to prepare a proposal for an investigation of the system. This would have to include details of the work needed and potential benefits. He thinks that this report should be finished within a week.

Questions

- Describe, in detail, the current inventory control system.

- What information does this system need?

- Are there any obvious weaknesses in the current system?

- In what areas would you look for improvements to the system?

- What additional information would you need to assess the system?

- What should Nigel Chatterton suggest in his proposal?

Problems

18.1 The demand for an item is constant at 100 units a year. The unit cost is £50, the cost of processing an order is £20 and the holding cost is £10 per unit per annum. What are the economic order quantity, corresponding cycle length and costs?

18.2 A company works 50 weeks a year and has demand for an item that is constant at 100 units a week. The cost of each unit is £20 and the company aims for a return of 20% on capital invested. Annual warehouse costs are 5% of the value of goods stored. The purchasing department costs £45,000 a year and sends out an average of 2000 orders. Find the optimal order quantity for the item, the optimal time between orders and the minimum cost of stocking the item.

18.3 Demand for an item is steady at 20 units a week and the economic order quantity has been calculated at 50 units. What is the reorder level when the lead time is: (a) one week (b) three weeks (c) five weeks (d) seven weeks?

18.4 A manufacturer forecasts demand for components to average 18 a day over a 200-day working year. If there are any shortages, production will be disrupted with very high costs. The holding cost for the component is £40 a unit a year and the cost of placing an order is £80 an order. Find the economic order quantity, the optimal number of orders a year and the total annual cost of operating the system if the interest rate is 25% a year.

18.5 A company advertises a 95% cycle-service level for all stock items. Stock is replenished from a single supplier who guarantees a lead time of four weeks. What reorder level should the company adopt for an item that has a Normally distributed demand with mean 1000 units a week and standard deviation of 100 units? What is the reorder level if a 98% cycle-service level is used?

18.6 An item of inventory has a unit cost of £40, reorder cost of £50 and holding cost of £1 a unit a week. Demand for the item has a mean of 100 a week with standard deviation 10. Lead time is constant at three weeks. Design an inventory policy for the item to give a service level of 95%. How would you change this to give a 90% service level? What are the costs of these two policies?

18.7 Describe a periodic review system with interval of two weeks for the company described in Problem 18.5.

18.8 A small store has of 10 categories of product with the following costs and annual demands:

Product	X1	X2	X3	Y1	Y2	Y3	Z1	Z2	Z3	Z4
Unit cost (£)	20	25	30	1	4	6	10	15	20	22
Annual demand ('00s)	3	2	2	10	8	7	30	20	6	4

Do an ABC analysis of these items.

18.9 Annual demand for an item is 2000 units, each order costs £10 to place and the annual holding cost is 40% of the unit cost. The unit cost depends on the quantity ordered as follows:

● for quantities less than 500 unit cost is £1
● for quantities between 500 and 1000 unit cost is £0.80
● for quantities of 1000 or more unit cost is £0.60

What is the optimal ordering policy for the item?

Discussion questions

18.1 Some organizations try to reduce their stocks by making to order, or guaranteeing delivery within a specified period. Do these systems really reduce inventory costs?

18.2 What costs are incurred by holding stock? How can these be found? Why are shortage costs so difficult to find?

18.3 What factors in real inventory control are not included in the economic order quantity model? Why can we still use the EOQ even if these real factors are omitted?

18.4 What is a service level? How can an appropriate service level be set for an item?

18.5 We have now seen how stocks can be controlled by MRP, JIT and independent demand systems. When is each of these most appropriate?

18.6 What features would you expect to see in a computerized inventory control system?

Selected references

Early work:

Harris F. (1915). *Operations and Cost*. Chicago, Ill.: A. Shaw & Co.

Raymond F.E. (1931). *Quantity and Economy in Manufacture*. Chicago, Ill.: McGraw-Hill.

Wilson R.H. (1934). A Scientific Routine for Stock Control. *Harvard Business Review*, No. XIII.

Later work:

Fogarty D.W. and Hoffmann T.R. (1983). *Production and Inventory Management*. Cincinnati, Oh.: South-Western Publishing.

Hadley G. and Whitin T.M. (1963). *Analysis of Inventory Systems*. Englewood Cliffs, NJ: Prentice-Hall.

Lewis C.D. (1970). *Scientific Inventory Control*. London: Butterworths.

Lewis C.D. (1975). *Demand Analysis and Inventory Control*. London: Saxon-House.

Love S.F. (1979). *Inventory Control*. New York: McGraw-Hill.

Plossl G. and Welch W.E. (1979). *The Role of Top Management in the Control of Inventory*. Reston, Va.: Reston Publishing.

Tersine R.J. (1987). *Principles of Inventory and Materials Management* (3rd edn). New York: Elsevier North-Holland.

Silver E.A. and Peterson R. (1985). *Decision Systems for Inventory Management and Production Planning* (2nd edn). New York: John Wiley.

Waters C.D.J. (1992). *Inventory Control and Management*. Chichester: John Wiley.

Waters C.D.J. (1989). *A Practical Introduction to Management Science*. Wokingham: Addison-Wesley.

19 Facilities location

Contents

Objectives

After reading this chapter you should be able to:

- appreciate the importance of location decisions
- discuss factors that affect location decisions
- compare locations using costing models
- compare locations using scoring models
- describe the centre of gravity method

Decisions about location

When are location decisions needed?

Whenever an organization wants a new factory, warehouse, shop, office block or other facility it has to make a decision about the location. When Nissan or Toyota build a new factory, or John Lewis open a new store, or Wimpy open a new hamburger restaurant they have to make a strategic decision about the best location. This is an important decision that can affect the organization's performance for many years. If Nissan opened a factory in a poor location it might find that productivity of the workforce is low, the quality of its cars is poor, and all its costs are high. But it could not simply close down the factory and move. It costs hundreds of millions of pounds to open a new factory, and the costs of moving might be too high. If the John Lewis or Wimpy opened in the wrong location would have low sales could not make a profit.

> **Facilities location** aims at finding the best possible geographic location for an organization's operations.

There are many reasons for an organization to find a new location for its facilities. These include:

- the end of a lease on their existing premises
- they want to expand to new geographic areas
- changes in the location of customers or suppliers
- significant changes in operations so they need a different type of location – such as an electricity company changing from coal generators to gas
- upgrading of facilities – perhaps to introduce new technology
- changes to the logistics system – such as changing from rail transport to road
- changes in the transport network – such as the new bridge across the River Severn or the Channel tunnel.

Commercial estate agents often say, 'The three most important things for a successful business are location, location and location.' Certainly, the decisions about location are some of the most important an organization has to make. A discotheque, for example, is unlikely to do well in an area where most people are retired; a manufacturer with major markets in Western Europe would be unwise to locate outside the European Union; busy art galleries and museums are found at the centre of large cities; small shops cluster around shopping centres. Decisions about locations can determine the success or failure of an organization, and there are many examples of organizations that have located in the wrong place and gone out of business.

ce **Case example** – Canary Wharf

Olympia and York is a property company that has large office developments in many countries. In the late 1980s it decided to build in the Isle of Dogs in East London. This was the largest office development ever undertaken in Britain and among the biggest in Europe.

The Isle of Dogs was the old dock area of London. When the docks closed, they left a large, run-down area near the centre of London. This had obvious attractions for Olympia and York, particularly as the government gave incentives to promote development. Unfortunately, there were also drawbacks with the location and the timing of the development.

Canary Wharf tried to attract companies that wanted office space in the centre of London. But it was not actually in the City – which is the main financial centre. Canary Wharf found it difficult to attract companies away from the City to a more distant, less convenient site, that had poor transport and few facilities. Competing developers opened less prestigious – but more convenient – buildings nearer the City, and the office vacancy rate rose to 17%. This had an effect on average rents which fell by 30%. At the same time Britain was struggling through its worst recession since the 1930s, and most companies were looking for survival rather than expansion into new premises.

By March 1992 Olympia and York had serious financial difficulties, and its debts rose to $20 billion.

Questions

- Was Canary Wharf a good choice for location?

- What could Olympia and York have done differently?

Location decisions are strategic, with consequences felt over a long time. Once an organization chooses a location it usually has to stay there for years or even decades. A factory or a power station built in the wrong place can not simply pack up and move. Even if warehouse or shop space is rented, it is a major undertaking to close down and move to another area. This means that location decisions should consider the long term. Many organizations ignore this and are tempted to make decisions because of short-term opportunities – such as the availability of development grants or a site that becomes vacant. This can be a serious error.

Location decisions can be very complicated. If you think about buying a house, you may find it difficult to choose a location. But this is trivial compared with a decision about where to open a new factory, logistics centre, hospital, university, amusement park or any other major facility. Before making its decision an organization must examine operating costs, wage rates, taxes, international exchange rates, competition, current locations, exchange regulations, availability of grants, reliability of supplies, and a whole range of other factors. Many of these can be measured in some way, but the organization must also consider less tangible factors. These include the attitude of the workforce, political situation, international relations, hidden costs, the legal system, future developments of the economy, and so on. We shall consider these factors later in the chapter, but first will ask if there are alternatives to finding new locations.

Alternatives to locating new facilities

An organization has to make location decisions when it expands, contracts, or there is some other significant change in operations – such as a new process, changing customers or new products. New facilities are inevitably expensive and many organizations prefer to look for alternatives. Suppose, for example, a company decides to sell its goods in a new market. It can do this in five distinct ways. These are listed below in order of increasing investment.

(1) *Licensing/franchising* Local operators are allowed to make and supply the company's products in return for a share of the profits.

(2) *Exporting* The company makes the product in its existing facilities and sells it to a distributor operating in the new market.

(3) *Local warehousing and sales* The company makes the product in its existing facilities, but sets up its own warehouses and sales force to handle distribution in the new market.

(4) *Local assembly/finishing* The company makes most of the product in existing facilities, but opens limited facilities in the new market to finish or assemble the final product.

(5) *Full local production* The company opens complete facilities in the new market.

An organization's choice from these options depends on many factors, such as the capital available, risk the organization will accept, target return on investment, existing operations, timescale, local knowledge, transport costs, tariffs, trade restrictions and available workers. The advantages of local facilities include greater control over products, higher profits, avoidance of import tariffs and quotas, easier transportation, reduced costs and closer links with local customers. These must be balanced against the more complex and uncertain operations.

ce **Case example** – Hudson's Bay Company

Hudson's Bay Company (HBC) is Canada's oldest and largest chain of retail stores. In February 1994 it was considering various options for expansion. These included opening a different style of retail shop such as warehouses, opening speciality retail stores, diversification into non-retail businesses, expansion into the United States, and opening businesses outside North America. It eventually decided to look at the opportunities for opening department stores in China. The plan was to open a store in Beijing or Shanghai in early 1996.

The reasons for this decision were the large market with 1.2 billion consumers, the economic growth of China which averaged 9% a year throughout the 1980s, the increased disposable income and savings of citizens, their enthusiasm for foreign products, and the lack of competition from North American retailers. HBC had existing trade links in the area as it had bought goods from China since the early 1980s. It now bought 25% of its stock from Asia and opened an office in Hong Kong in 1988.

There were several drawbacks with this move. These included the need to form a joint venture with a large Asian company, possibly based in Hong Kong. Other drawbacks included the difficulty of finding suitable locations for a large retail development, the distance from current operations in Canada, the difficulty of repatriating profits, the need to train Canadian executives about the Chinese market, the need to train Chinese employees about HBC's operations, and the need to develop relationships with new customers.

Questions

- What are the benefits and difficulties of the Hudson's Bay Company's planned expansion.

- Do you think it should make this move?

You might think that one way of avoiding the problem of locating new facilities is simply to alter existing ones. But this is still a location decision, as it assumes the current site is the best available. In practice, when an organization wants to change its facilities – either expand, move or contract – it has three alternatives:

(1) expand or change existing facilities at the present site;

(2) use additional, new facilities at another site while keeping all existing facilities;

(3) close down existing operations and relocate.

Surveys suggest around 45% of companies choose on-site expansion, a similar number open additional new facilities, and 10% close down existing operations and relocate.

Economies of scale are important in such decisions, as larger facilities are usually more efficient than smaller ones. This often encourages organizations to expand existing facilities. But if you look more closely at the costs you get a different view. We can show this by looking at the location of warehouses. Some warehouse costs are reduced with fewer, large warehouses, while other costs rise.

- **Operating costs** Larger warehouses are generally more efficient than smaller ones. This means the operating cost is minimized with a few, large warehouses, and it rises with more smaller warehouses.

- **Stock-holding costs** With fewer warehouses there is little duplication of stock, so these costs will be low. As the number of warehouses increases, the amount of stock duplication rises leading to higher inventory costs.

- **Inward transport costs** These are the costs of delivering from suppliers to warehouses. If there are few warehouses, large deliveries are made to a few locations and costs are low. As the number of warehouses rises, smaller deliveries are made to more destinations and the inward transport costs rise.

- **Outward transport costs** These are the costs of moving goods from warehouses to customers. If there are many warehouses they will, on average, be close to customers so the local delivery costs are low. On the other hand, if there are few warehouses customers will, on average, be further away and the costs of local delivery are high.

Plotting these four costs gives the graph shown in Figure 19.1. This shows the total cost has a clear minimum which corresponds to the optimal number of warehouses. In practice, before we make a decision, we should include many other factors, such as management costs, communications, fixed costs, employment effects, customer service, and data processing.

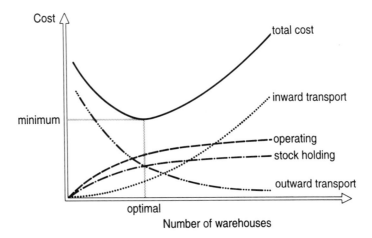

Figure 19.1 Variation in costs with number of warehouses.

we Worked example

Semantic Services is looking at five options for expansion (see Table 19.1). Each of these has a fixed annual payment (for rent, electricity, and other overheads) and a variable cost that depends on production (handling, depreciation, staffing, and so on). Over what range of production is each alternative most attractive?

Table 19.1

Alternative		Fixed cost	Variable cost (per unit)
A	Open new medium-sized facility	£40,000	£45
B	Open two new small facilities	£120,000	£35
C	Expand current facility	£450,000	£26
D	Build large new facility and close old one	£400,000	£18
E	Build large new facility and keep old one	£600,000	£22

Solution

This is an extension of the break even analysis. You can see from the figures that alternatives C and E will never be cheapest, as they are always more expensive than D. This leaves a choice between alternatives A, B and D. The costs for various production levels are shown in Figure 19.2.

- Alternative A is the cheapest for production, X, from 0 until:

$$40,000 + 45X = 120,000 + 35X \quad \text{or} \quad X = 8000$$

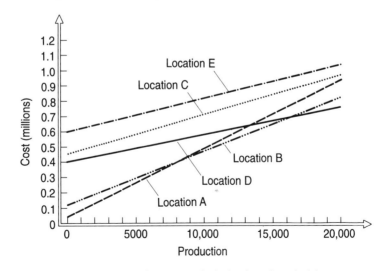

Figure 19.2 Break-even analysis for location decision.

- After this alternative B is cheapest until:
$$120,000 + 35X = 400,000 + 18X \quad \text{or} \quad X = 16,471$$
- After this point D remains the cheapest.

Review questions

19.1 Why are location decisions important?

19.2 If a company wants to start supplying products to a new market, does it have to open new facilities there?

19.3 What are the three basic alternatives if an organization wants to expand its facilities?

19.4 Economies of scale mean that it is always cheaper to operate a single large warehouse than a number of smaller ones. Do you think this is true?

Selecting the geographic region

When an organization decides it must look for a new location, it must make a hierarchy of decisions. This starts with wide view, looking at the attractions of different countries or geographic regions. Then it takes a more local view and considers alternative areas within this region. Then it moves on and looks more closely at alternative towns and cities within this area. Finally it looks at different sites within a preferred town.

At the top of this hierarchy, an organization may take a decision about the country of operation. If its long-term forecasts show continuing demand for a product in a particular country the organization may decide to open facilities there. As we have seen before, this can be avoided by exporting or licensing, but the organization then loses control over its products.

In recent years many organizations open facilities in new countries not to be near their customers, but to take advantage of lower costs. Low wage rates in developing countries have encouraged many manufacturers to open factories in the Far East, South America and Eastern Europe. Often these facilities provide a convenient base for international trade, so that a Japanese company might open a factory in Taiwan to supply goods to Europe. Sometimes the trade is more focused, when, for example, a German company moves one of its plants to Spain, and then imports the products back to Germany. Such arrangements have high transport costs, but reduced operating costs can more than compensate for this.

But you should not assume that low wage rates automatically mean low costs. In many parts of the world low wage rates are accompanied by very low productivity. Perhaps more importantly, manufacturing processes have changed so that labour costs often form a very small part of overall costs. Most organizations now prefer to locate in areas that are near markets, have reliable suppliers, good infrastructure, high productivity, guaranteed quality and skilled work force – even if they also have high labour costs.

In 1980 Tandy Corporation decided to move production of its latest computer to South Korea. But rising shipping costs, the long sea voyage to the US, changing value of the dollar and a redesign of the product to allow more automated production made this location less attractive. In 1987 Tandy moved their production back to Fort Worth in Texas and reduced costs by 7.5%. Steel gives another example of such changes. Steel mills were traditionally located near to sources of coal and iron ore. Then countries like Taiwan and South Korea found they could reduce operating costs by opening large, new mills. These relied on imported coal and ore – and in the long term the transport costs often made their products too expensive.

The location of sites in international markets depends on a number of factors. Some of these are commercial, but experience suggests three other factors are important.

- **Culture** It is easier to expand into an area that has a similar language, culture, laws and costs, than to expand into a completely foreign area. So a company currently operating in Belgium would find it easier to expand in France than in, say, Korea. The decision to build DisneyLand Europe near Paris gives one example where moving a successful operation to a different culture has met with limited success.

- **Organization** If operations expand overseas, there are basically two ways they can be organized. A company may choose to operate internationally or multinationally. An international organization maintains its headquarters in the 'home' country and runs its worldwide activities from there. A multinational organization opens subsidiary headquarters around the world so that each area is largely independent.

- **Operations** Another concern is whether it is better to use the same operations around the world or to adapt to the local environment. McDonald's hamburger restaurants use almost identical operations in all countries they work in. Other organizations blend into the local environment and adapt their operations so they are more familiar to their host countries.

ce Case example – McDonald's in Moscow

The world's largest McDonald's hamburger restaurant is in Moscow. This is operated jointly by McDonald's of Canada who own 49% and a local Russian company who own 51%.

McDonald's has opened branches throughout the world, but this was one of the most difficult to set up. Negotiations started with the Soviet Union 20 years before the restaurant finally opened.

The inside of the restaurant is exactly as you would expect, with the standard menu, colour scheme and decor, staff training, levels of cleanliness and cooking. Everything follows the standard McDonald's pattern. But this was only achieved with considerable effort and could only be done when conditions in Russia changed. As well as the obvious political problems there were significant practical problems. Beef in Moscow is not readily available and the quality is poor. McDonald's had to import breeding cattle and start a beef farm to supply the restaurant. Potatoes are plentiful, but they are the wrong type to make McDonald's fries. Seed potatoes were imported and grown. Russian cheese was not suitable for cheeseburgers, so a dairy plant was opened to make processed cheese.

Although the restaurant is very popular, the initial setup cost was so high that the restaurant does not expect to make a profit in the foreseeable future.

Review questions

19.6   Low wage rates would make a country an attractive location for industry. Do you think this is true?

19.7   Name three non-economic factors that play an important part in the success of an international development.

19.8   If jobs are created in one country, they must inevitably be lost in another. Do you think this is true?

Costing alternative locations

Once a decision has been made about the country or geographical region, more detailed decisions are needed about areas, towns, cities and individual sites. There are several ways an organizations can approach these decisions, and the best depends on specific circumstances. One approach that is *not* recommended is personal preference. There are many examples of poor locations where the decision maker simply chose a site they like – perhaps in the town they live or grew up in, or the area they spend their holidays.

There are several ways of making rational location decisions. These use two distinct approaches.

(1)   *Feasible set approach*   where there are only a small number of feasible sites and the best has to be selected.

(2)   *Infinite set approach*   which uses geometric arguments to show where the best site would be if there were no restrictions on site availability.

A feasible set approach compares sites that are currently vacant and choose the best, while an infinite set approach finds the best location in principle and then look for a site nearby.

We will start by looking at feasible set approaches. An obvious way of comparing locations is to look at the total costs. Many costs can be included, but we shall simplify the calculations by considering only transport costs – both inwards and outwards – and operating costs.

- **Inward transport cost** The cost of moving goods and services into the facility from suppliers. Typically this includes the cost of transporting raw materials and components.

- **Outward transport cost** The cost of moving finished goods and services out to customers.

- **Operating cost** The total cost of running the facility.

These costs will obviously vary with location. In particular, sites near to suppliers will have low costs for inward transport, but high costs of outward transport. On the other hand, sites near to customers will have low costs for outward transport, but high costs for inward transport, as shown in Figure 19.3. We can get a direct comparison of sites by adding these three costs:

$$\text{Total cost of facility} = \text{Operating cost} + \text{Inward transport cost} + \text{Outward transport cost}$$

Operating costs depend on a number of factors such as wage rates, local taxes, reliability of local suppliers and weather conditions. In practice, there is

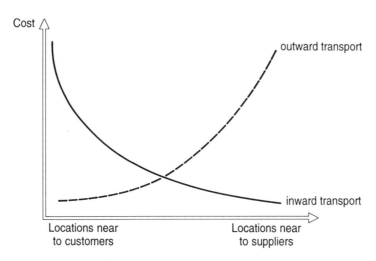

Figure 19.3 Variation in transport cost with location.

often little difference in operating costs between nearby locations, so these can be removed from the equation.

An obvious problem with this approach is that costs are not known with certainty in advance. How, for example, could an organization know accurate costs to outward transport when the customers and demands are not known before opening? Even if the costs are known, they are likely to change and the analysis will become outdated. So the calculated costs are useful for comparisons, but they are not necessarily the costs that will actually be incurred.

If the costs only give comparisons rather than actual values, we can simplify the calculations. It may be difficult to find the exact cost of delivering products to a particular customers, but we can assume transport costs are proportional to the straight line distance from the facility to the customer. Here we are using straight line distance simply because it is easy to find from a map. Then we can approximate the transport cost by:

$$\text{Cost} = dFWP$$

where:

d = straight line map distance between facility and customer

F = a constant factor to convert the straight line map distance into an actual road distance

W = the expected weight of goods to be moved between the facility and the customer

P = the price of moving unit weight a unit distance

This equation gives a measure of the cost of delivering to one customer, so repeating the calculation for all potential customers and adding the results gives an overall cost for outward transport. A similar calculation gives the total cost for inward transport from suppliers.

These surrogate cost figures are only valid for comparison, so any consistent convention for calculations can be used. But you must remember that these are only notional costs and should not be used in other cost calculations.

we Worked example

A warehouse is located at co-ordinates (12, 16) and makes regular deliveries to a customer that is located at (15, 20). Experience suggests that a straight line map distance of 1 unit on the map corresponds to 1.6 kilometres of actual road distance. It costs an average of 20 pence per tonne-kilometre to move goods. What is the annual cost of outward transport if forecast demands from the customer is 8 tonnes a week?

Solution

The straight line distances between the warehouse and customer can be found using Pythagoras's theorem. Distance from warehouse to the customer is:

$$\sqrt{[(x_0 - x_1)^2 + (y_0 - y_1)^2]} = \sqrt{[(15 - 12)^2 + (20 - 16)^2]} = \sqrt{25} = 5$$

We know that the factor, F, $= 1.6$ and price, P, $= 0.2$. So the expected weekly cost of transport to the customer is:

$$\text{COST} = dFWP = 5 \times 10 \times 1.6 \times 8 \times 0.2 = £128 \text{ a week}$$

■

In the above example the cost is only a consistent measure and will not be the actual amount paid for transport. This will vary with factors like the vehicles used, frequency of journeys, routes taken, organization of drivers, and actual orders placed. If we just want to compare different sites we could simplify the calculations even more. The factor, F, for example, could be set as 1, and distance, d, replaced by the simpler rectilinear distance, which is defined as:

$$\text{Rectilinear distance} = \frac{\text{Difference in}}{\text{X co-ordinates}} + \frac{\text{Difference in}}{\text{Y co-ordinates}}$$

we Worked example

Rondacorp Industries wants to build a depot to serve five major customers located at co-ordinates $(120, 120)$, $(220, 120)$, $(180, 180)$, $(140, 160)$ and $(180, 120)$. Average weekly demands, in vehicle loads, are 20, 5, 8, 12 and 8 respectively. Two alternative locations are available at $(140, 120)$ and $(180, 140)$. Which of these is better if operating costs and inward transport costs are the same for each location?

Solution

A map for this problem is shown in Figure 19.4.

As operating costs and transport inward costs are the same for both locations, all we need is a means of comparing the costs of local deliveries from each location, A and B. We will take the distance, d, as the rectilinear distance, and the factor, F, as 1 to give the costs. Then the distance from A to customer 1 is:

difference in X co-ordinate + difference in Y co-ordinate
$= (140 - 120) + (120 - 120)$
$= 20$

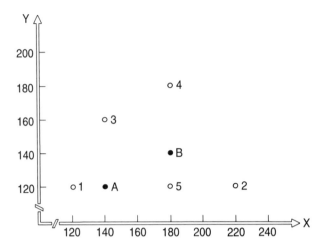

Figure 19.4 Locations for Rondacorp Industries.

All the calculations for this problem are given in the spreadsheet given in Figure 19.5, which shows that location A is clearly better.

Customer		Load	A Distance	Distance Load	B Distance	Distance Load
	1	20	20	400	80	1600
	2	5	80	400	60	300
	3	8	100	800	40	320
	4	12	40	480	60	720
	5	8	40	320	20	160
Totals				2400		3100

Figure 19.5 Calculations for Rondacorp Industries.

Costing models can give very useful comparisons, but they have some weaknesses, including:

● accurate costs are difficult to find

● data depends on accounting conventions

● costs will vary over time

● customer locations may not be known in advance

- customer demands may not be known exactly

- there are many factors that can not be costed.

Because of these weaknesses, other methods – particularly scoring models – are often used to get another viewpoint.

Review questions

19.9　What is the difference between a feasible set approach and an infinite set approach to facility location?

19.10　What costs might be included in a costing model?

19.11　What is the difference between inward transport and outward transport?

Scoring models

Costing models can not deal with some factors that may be important in a location decision. How, for example, can you put a cost to an attractive lifestyle? This would certainly benefit employees, reduce employee turnover and assist in recruiting, but it would be difficult to give a realistic cost. Other factors that may be important, but which are difficult to quantify, include:

(1)　*Country and region:*

- availability and quality of workforce
- climate
- local and national government policies
- availability of development grants
- attractiveness of locations
- quality of life – including health, education, welfare and culture
- reliability of local suppliers
- infrastructure – particularly transport and communications
- economic stability of area

(2)　*City or location:*

- nearness to customers and suppliers
- location of competitors
- potential for expansion
- local restrictions on operations
- community feelings.

One way of considering such non-quantifiable factors is to use a scoring model. We have already described these in Chapter 4 to compare different products, and the procedure for location decisions is exactly the same:

- decide the relevant factors in a decision;

- give each factor a maximum possible score that shows its importance;

- consider each location in turn and give an actual score for each factor;

- add the total score for each location and find the highest;

- discuss the result and make a final decision.

The important factors and relative importance will obviously change with circumstances. Decisions about the location of a new factory are dominated by factors like:

- availability of a labour force with appropriate skills;

- labour relations and community attitudes;

- environment and quality of life for employees;

- closeness of suppliers and services;

- quality of infrastructure;

- government policies toward industry.

On the other hand, decisions about the location of a service put more weight on factors like:

- population density;

- socio-economic characteristics of the nearby population;

- location of competitors and other services;

- location of retail shops and other attractions;

- convenience for passing traffic and public transport;

- ease of access and convenient parking;

- visibility of site.

These lists reinforces the obvious point that manufacturers have different location objectives to service industries. In general, manufacturers try to gain economies of scale by building large facilities that may be near raw materials. They will typically look for a site where costs are low, there is a skilled workforce, and suppliers are nearby. But services must be near to their customers. They can not keep stocks of their services, so they must meet any demand as soon as it arises. These differences are the reason why town centres have shops, but no factories, while industrial estates have factories but no shops.

we Worked example

Jim Bowen is considering four alternative locations for a new electronics warehouse. After a lot of discussions he made a list of important factors, their relative weights, and scores for each site (see Table 19.2). What is the relative importance of each factor? Which site would you recommend?

Table 19.2

Factor	Maximum score	A	B	C	D
Climate	10	8	6	9	7
Infrastructure	20	12	16	15	8
Accessibility	10	6	8	7	9
Construction cost	5	3	1	4	2
Community attitude	10	6	8	7	4
Government views	5	2	2	3	4
Closeness to suppliers	15	10	10	13	13
Closeness to customers	20	12	10	15	17
Availability of workers	5	1	2	4	5

Solution

The most important factors are the available infrastructure and closeness to customers. Jim has assigned up to 20 points each for these. The closeness of suppliers is a bit less important with up to 15 points, and then come climate, accessibility and community attitude with up to 10 points each. Construction cost, government views and availability of workers are least important.

Adding the scores for each location gives:

Location	A	B	C	D
Total scores	60	63	77	69

These scores suggest that location C is the best. Jim must now consider all other relevant information before coming to a final decision.

Review questions

19.12 What are the benefits of using scoring models for location decisions?

19.13 Are the same factors important for locating a factory as locating a retail shop?

19.14 What factors might be important in locating a professional service, such as a doctor's surgery?

ce Case example – Hamburg Double Glazed Windows

Hamburg Double Glazed Windows (HDGW) is one of Europe's largest manufacturers of high quality PVCu windows. It was originally based around Hamburg, where it ran three plants. The first plant was a plastics works where the PVCu was made and the contours for window frames were extruded. The second plant was a glassworks where the windows were made. The third plant was an assembly works, where windows were made, either for individual orders or in standard sizes.

The first two of these plants were capital intensive, using large machines to make either the materials for the frames or the glass. These were largely automated with little manual work. The third part of the process was actually making the windows. This cut the glass and frames into various shapes and sizes and assembled them into finished units. This part of the process used little automation and was very labour intensive.

In 1985 the assembly works was plagued with labour problems. These came to a head with a long strike by workers. After the strike was settled, the average wage rate in the plant was over twice the industrial average for Germany. HDGW had now become a high cost operation and was much less competitive. This, together with the rising value of the Deutschmark, made HDGW lose market share to its rivals.

HDGW then did a study to see how it could reduce its costs and regain its market share. One of the recommendations of this study was moving the assembly works to an economically less developed region. This would have much lower wage rates. After a long search, largely in the Southern part of the European Union, the company picked a site just outside Barcelona. The two main reasons for selecting this site were:

(1)   the Spanish Government and European Union gave generous incentives;

(2)   Barcelona had a lot of cheap, unskilled labour.

The study showed that HDGW would save 10 million Deutschmarks a year by this move.

The company started preparing for the move. This meant moving all the assembly machines from Hamburg to Barcelona. HDGW estimated this move would take six months to complete, with another six months to iron out any production problems. The company lost most of its experienced employees when they accepted an early retirement package rather than move. Of the remaining 100 managers and supervisors, only 20 moved to Barcelona and the rest left the company. All the hourly paid workers in the Hamburg assembly works were laid off.

HDGW hired 200 people in Barcelona with wages about a quarter of the German equivalent. Then its problems began. These unskilled workers spoke only Spanish, while the company's instructions and procedure manuals were all in German. The managers who moved spoke little Spanish. The resulting language barrier created serious problems with supervision, training and keeping efficient operations. These problems reduced productivity and caused labour costs to rise.

There were also technical problems, as some of the assembly machines were damaged in the move. As a result, the last phase of transfer from Hamburg to Barcelona was stopped rather than risk more damage. The cost of transporting materials from the two plants in Hamburg to the assembly works in Barcelona was also higher than expected because of increased petrol prices.

Two years after the start of the relocation project there was still no end in sight to the company's problems. Costs seemed to be getting higher. The marketing department was concerned because its market share was again falling.

Questions

- Did it seem sensible to move from Hamburg to Barcelona?

- What went wrong with the move?

- Why did it have so many production problems at Barcelona?

- What should HDGW do now?

Geometric models

The last two sections described cost and scoring models. These are examples of feasible set approaches for comparing locations. In this section we shall see how an infinite set approach works.

Many location models are based on the geographic layout of customers and suppliers. These models assume that facilities should be located near the centre of potential demands and supplies. One way of finding the centre is to calculate the **centre of gravity** of demand. This uses an analogy from engineering, with the demand at each customer replacing the weight.

The coordinates of the centre of gravity are:

$$X_0 = \frac{\sum X_i W_i}{\sum W_i} \qquad Y_0 = \frac{\sum Y_i W_i}{\sum W_i}$$

where:

X_0, Y_0 are the co-ordinates of the centre of gravity, that is the facility location

X_i, Y_i are co-ordinates of each customer and supplier, i

W_i is expected demand at customer i, or expected supply from source i

As usual, you need not worry too much about the details of these calculations as they are best done with a computer.

we Worked example

Amstead Industries is planning an assembly plant to take components from three suppliers, and send finished goods to six regional warehouses. The locations of these and the amounts supplied or demanded are shown in Table 19.3. Where would you start looking for a site for the assembly plant?

Solution

The calculations for this are shown in the printout shown in Figure 19.6.

As you can see, the centre of gravity is $X_0 = 45.5$ and $Y_0 = 50.3$. This is calculated from:

$$X_0 = \frac{\sum X_i W_i}{\sum W_i} = \frac{16,380}{360} = 45.5 \qquad Y_0 = \frac{\sum Y_i W_i}{\sum W_i} = \frac{18,108}{360} = 50.3$$

Table 19.3

Location	X, Y co-ordinates	Supply/demand
Supplier 1	91, 8	40
Supplier 2	93, 35	60
Supplier 3	3, 86	80
Warehouse 1	83, 26	24
Warehouse 2	89, 54	16
Warehouse 3	63, 87	22
Warehouse 4	11, 85	38
Warehouse 5	9, 16	52
Warehouse 6	44, 48	28

		X	Y	Weight	X*Weight	Y*Weight
Supplier						
	1	91	8	40	3640	320
	2	93	35	60	5580	2100
	3	3	86	80	240	6880
Warehouse						
	1	83	26	24	1992	624
	2	89	54	16	1424	864
	3	63	87	22	1386	1914
	4	11	85	38	418	3230
	5	9	16	52	468	832
	6	44	48	28	1232	1344
Totals				360	16380	18108

Centre of	X =	45.50
Gravity	Y =	50.30

Figure 19.6 Calculation of centre of gravity.

A good place to start looking for locations is around $(45.5, 50.3)$ as shown in Figure 19.7. As this is very close to warehouse 6 it might be better to expand on this site rather than look for an entirely new location.

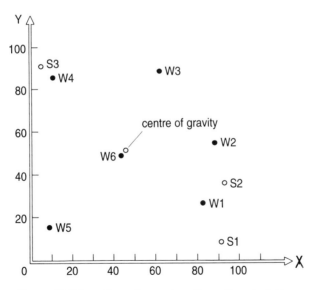

Figure 19.7 Locations for centre of gravity calculation.

The centre of gravity can give a reasonably good location, but it is only a starting point. There may, for example, be no site available anywhere near the centre of gravity, or available sites may be too expensive; it might be a long way from roads, in an area with no workforce, or even in a river. For this reason the centre of gravity it is most useful for cutting down the area of search for a location. Then we can use a finite set approach for comparing locations within this smaller area.

We now have a useful approach to location decisions. This:

- uses the centre of gravity to find a reasonable location for facilities;

- searches near this location to find a feasible set of alternative locations;

- uses a costing method to compare these alternatives;

- adds costs and other information to a scoring model;

- discusses all available information and comes to a final decision.

ce Case example – Kohl Transport

Kohl Transport delivers goods around Western Europe, but most of its work comes from a manufacturer who operates two plants and wants regular deliveries within Germany. A simplified view of the transportation problem is shown in the following table, which shows plant capacities, demands and unit transport costs.

	Berlin	Cologne	Dresden	Hamburg	Munich	Stuttgart	Capacity
Plant A	5.5	5.5	4.5	6.0	1.0	1.5	350
Plant B	1.5	6.5	3.25	2.0	6.5	7.5	400
	22600	4400	9000	8400	13200	7400	

The company decided to use a quantitative model to help with their planning. A linear programming model was developed with the results given in Figure 19.8. This shows the allocation of customers to plants, best plant sizes and distribution costs. The result shown was the first they looked at, and by adjusting this Kohl could see the effect of alternative plans. Eventually they decided to close down plant A and consolidate operations in an expanded plant B.

```
================================================================================
                        TRANSPORTATION PROBLEM SOLUTION
--------------------------------------------------------------------------------
PROBLEM: Kohl Transport                                         Date: 09-04-1995
                                                                        fig19-8

                            ORIGINAL PROBLEM DATA
================================================================================
 From  :                   To Destination                    :
 Source :    Berlin   Cologne   Dresden   Hamburg   Munich    : Capacity
================================================================================
 A     :      5.50      5.50      4.50      6.00      1.00     :    35000
 B     :      1.50      6.50      3.25      2.00      6.50     :    40000
================================================================================
 Demand :    22600      4400      9000      8400     13200     :    75000
================================================================================


================================================================================
 From  :                   To Destination                    :
 Source :  Stuttgart *Spare*                                  : Capacity
================================================================================
 A     :      1.50      0.00                                  :    35000
 B     :      7.50      0.00                                  :    40000
================================================================================
 Demand :     7400     10000                                  :    75000
================================================================================

                            OPTIMAL SOLUTION

                 Source  Destination   Quantity
                 ------------------------------------
                   A        Cologne       4400
                   A        Munich       13200
                   A        Stuttgart     7400
                   A        *Spare*      10000      Used Capacity = 25000
                   B        Berlin       22600
                   B        Dresden       9000
                   B        Hamburg       8400      Used Capacity = 40000

                 Minimum cost is C =   128450
--------------------------------------------------------------------------------
```

Figure 19.8 Results for Kohl Transport.

Review questions

19.15 What exactly is the centre of gravity of customer demand?

19.16 The centre of gravity finds the optimal location for a facility. Do you think this is true?

Chapter review

- Organizations often face decisions about the best locations for facilities. These are important, strategic decisions that can have long-term effects on the organization's success.

- A location decision is needed whenever an organization expands, contracts, or makes major changes to its operations. Organizations often make such changes by opening new facilities. But there are several alternatives to opening new facilities, such as licensing and exporting.

- Choosing the best location involves a hierarchy of decisions. These start with a decision about the region or country to locate in, move through decisions about the best area, town and eventually specific site.

- There are two approaches to location decisions. The first compares a limited number of feasible locations and selects the best. The second uses geometric arguments to suggest where the best location would be in principle, regardless of site availability.

- We illustrated feasible set approaches by costing and scoring models and infeasible set approaches by the centre of gravity method. Often these methods can be used together, so that a centre of gravity method gives a starting point for finding a feasible set of locations.

Key terms

CS   Case study – Authwaite Auto Sales

Richard Authwaite worked for the same car sales firm for over 25 years before starting his own business. He saw an advertisement from an East European car manufacturer who wanted to start selling in Britain. Richard answered the advertisement and spent a year negotiating with the manufacturer.

The manufacturer was impressed by Richard, but was not keen to have all its distribution done by a new and untried company. In the end Richard agreed to set up a company called Authwaite Auto Sales, and the manufacturers agreed to give him exclusive rights to distribute its cars throughout Britain for two years. The agreement would be reviewed after a year and renegotiated after two years.

Richard invited three other directors to join the company. These four are now setting up their dealership and their first problem is to find a location for their head office and main showroom. In the long term the company plan to open a series of facilities around Britain, but now they need a location for their first 'flagship' site. The directors realize that their future success depends on how well this first facility operates. Unfortunately, they are finding it difficult to agree on a location.

At one point they decided to pass the problem to a firm of management consultants, but one of the directors reported the likely costs of this exercise. Firms in similar circumstances have paid up to £50,000 for an initial report while a more detailed analysis could cost £125,000. The directors decided they could not afford this and they would have to solve the problem themselves. The following summary gives an idea of their discussions.

- Gordon Mikaluk left school at 16 to become a car mechanic. He worked as a mechanic for many years until he was promoted to Service Manager. He is now 50 years old and is looking for an opportunity to make some money for his retirement.

  Gordon argues that the location should be in Manchester. The cars could be shipped by sea to Liverpool and then brought to Manchester by train. There are good handling facilities in Manchester and the transport would be easy and efficient. In addition, Manchester is a large city that could meet the large potential market in the North of the country. The four directors have all lived in Manchester and they understand local conditions.

- Sarah Precik has a degree in Mechanical Engineering. She worked in the oil industry for many years before becoming a mining consultant in eastern Europe. She speaks fluent Hungarian and Polish, with some Russian. During her travels she became interested in the car industry and when she returned to Britain she worked on manufacturing and design problems for Ford.

  Sarah is critical of Gordon's approach as being old fashioned and relying more on where he feels at home than on any business criterion. She says they should put their decision making on a sensible footing and not be governed by emotion. The sale of cars is likely to depend on the population so they should look at a map of Britain, see where the main centres of population are, see how many cars they expect to sell in each of these, and then do some fairly straightforward analyses to find the best location.

- Dennis MacGregor worked in banking and insurance where he handled various aspects of car financing. He is now 30 years old and is ambitiously looking for a long-term career that is both challenging and financially rewarding.

  Dennis does not like the idea of opening a single location to see if it works, but suggests they set up a comprehensive distribution network as quickly as possible. This would include head offices – perhaps in London, Edinburgh, Birmingham or some other convenient city – a central receiving area near to a rail terminal, and showrooms around Britain. The fastest way of doing this is to take over an existing dealer, or several dealers, to give coverage throughout the country.

- Richard Authwaite says that Dennis MacGregor's scheme is too ambitious, while the other two put the convenience of the company above the customers. He says there is only one way to sell cars and that is to give customers a product they want in a location they can get to. Richard's idea is to see where other distributors have their showrooms and open up nearby. In particular, he would look for a large dominating location that customers can see from a long way off, that they pass frequently, where they would go to buy cars, and where other distributors have traditionally been able to sell.

     The time is now getting short for a decision. The directors are concerned that if they delay any longer the manufacturer will consider them indecisive, and they will not have time to give a good showing at their first year's review. To build entirely new premises could take a year. Alternatively they could find existing premises that are empty, or they could rent temporary premises until the company finds more suitable, permanent premises.

     Richard has told the other three directors that they have one week to summarize their views and produce a report. After a further week for examination, comment and discussion they will make a decision.

Questions

- If you were a director of Authwaite Auto Sales, what report would you write?

- What factors will be important in its location decision?

- What location would you recommend?

Problems

19.1 A company manufactures a total of 60 tonnes of goods a week in factory A and 40 tonnes a week in factory B. The map co-ordinates of these factories are $(8, 9)$ and $(52, 47)$ respectively. These goods are delivered to 12 main customers whose average weekly requirements and co-ordinates are shown in Table 19.4. The company wants to improve its customer service and decides to open a distribution centre. There are four possible locations, each with the same operating costs, located at $(20, 8)$, $(61, 19)$, $(29, 32)$ and $(50, 22)$. Which of these locations is best?

Table 19.4

Customer	Average	Co-ordinates	Customer	Demand	Co-ordinates
1	4	(11, 16)	7	16	(12, 69)
2	11	(30, 9)	8	2	(27, 38)
3	8	(43, 27)	9	4	(51, 6)
4	7	(54, 52)	10	6	(43, 16)
5	17	(29, 62)	11	3	(54, 16)
6	10	(11, 51)	12	12	(12, 60)

19.2 A new electronics factory is planned in an area that is encouraging industrial growth. There are five alternative sites. A management team is considering these sites and has suggested the important factors and relative weights shown in Table 19.5. They also gave scores to each of the sites. What is the relative importance of each factor? Which site appears best?

Table 19.5

Factor	Maximum score	Scores for sites				
		A	B	C	D	E
Government grants	10	2	4	8	8	5
Community attitude	12	8	7	5	10	5
Availability of engineers	15	10	8	8	10	5
Experienced workforce	20	20	15	15	10	15
Nearby suppliers	8	4	3	6	3	2
Education centres	5	5	4	1	1	5
Housing	5	2	3	5	3	2

19.3 Find the centre of gravity of the data in Question 19.1. What would be the cost of transport for a distribution centre located there?

19.4 An assembly plant is planned to take components from four suppliers and send finished goods to eight regional warehouses. The locations of these and the amounts supplied or demanded are shown in Table 19.6. Where would you start looking for a site for the assembly plant?

Table 19.6

Location	X, Y co-ordinates	Supply/demand
Supplier 1	7, 80	140
Supplier 2	85, 35	80
Supplier 3	9, 81	120
Supplier 4	11, 62	70

Table 19.6 *(cont.)*

Location	X, Y co-ordinates	Supply/demand
Warehouse 1	12, 42	45
Warehouse 2	60, 9	65
Warehouse 3	92, 94	25
Warehouse 4	8, 79	45
Warehouse 5	10, 83	60
Warehouse 6	59, 91	35
Warehouse 7	83, 49	50
Warehouse 8	85, 30	85

Discussion questions

19.1 Do you think that an organization should consider its location as a strategic issue? Give examples to support your view.

19.2 Which areas of the world do you think will develop most quickly over the next decade or so? What effects will this have on the world economy?

19.3 What costs do you think should be considered in a location decision? What other factors should be considered?

19.4 What factors are most likely to affect a manufacturer's decision to locate a factory? Are there different factors for a service?

19.5 Give some examples of location decisions you are familiar with. How successful have these been?

19.6 Compare the location of facilities for a typical manufacturer and an airline. What are the main differences?

19.7 What computer software do you have that could help with location decisions? How could this be used in practice? What problems would there be?

Selected references

Ballou R.H. (1985). *Business Logistics Management* (2nd edn). Englewood Cliffs, NJ: Prentice-Hall.

Bowersox D.J., Closs D.J. and Helferich O.K. (1986). *Logistical Management* (3rd edn). Basingstoke: Macmillan.

Cooper J. (ed.) (1994). *Logistics and Distribution Planning* (2nd edn). London: Kogan Page.

Coyle J.J., Bardi E.J. and Langley C.J. (1988). *The Management of Business Logistics* (4th edn). St Paul, Mn.: West.

Francis R.L. and White J.A. (1987). *Facilities Layout and Location: An Analytical Approach*. Englewood Cliffs, NJ: Prentice-Hall.

Johnson J.C. and Wood D.F. (1986). *Contemporary Physical Distribution and Logistics* (3rd edn). New York: Macmillan.

Lambert D.M. and Stock J.R. (1987). *Strategic Physical Distribution Management* (2nd edn). Homewood, Ill.: Irwin.

Schmenner R.W. (1982). *Making Business Location Decisions*. Englewood Cliffs, NJ: Prentice-Hall.

Shapiro R.D. and Heskett J.L. (1985). *Logistics Strategy*. St Paul, Mn.: West.

Tompkins J.A. and White J.A. (1984). *Facilities Planning*. New York: John Wiley.

Voss C., Armistead C., Johnston B. and Morris B. (1985). *Operations Management in Service Industries and the Public Sector*. Chichester: John Wiley.

Williams Polishes Ltd

The product

Williams Polishes Ltd manufacture a range of well-known polishes that are used both in the home and in industry. Production takes place at a modern manufacturing plant based in Manchester.

The company's product range is divided into consumer products and industrial products. The former are sold both through supermarkets and specialist outlets such as shoe shops, shoe repairers and hardware stores. The industrial products are used in a wide range of industries including car and furniture manufacturing.

Distribution of finished products is organized on a traditional basis through a series of warehouses. The company operates four warehouses. One, the main warehouse, is attached to the manufacturing plant in Manchester. The others are located in London, Glasgow and Bristol. The main warehouse handles the distribution of both categories of polish to industrial and retail outlets, as well as all sales to supermarket chains. The regional warehouses serve Southern England, Wales and the South West and Scotland respectively. The operation of the warehouses comes within the purchasing department. The warehouses are serviced by the company's own fleet of lorries, which are run by a separate transport section.

Changing customer requirements

The company finds that it is faced by increasingly demanding customers. This is especially true of the supermarket chains, who now represent 40% of the company's sales of consumer polishes compared to only 25% a decade ago. They demand not only the lowest possible prices, but deliveries of small quantities, frequent deliveries and deliveries at shorter notice in order to reduce their own inventory costs. Aided by massive investments in computer systems and scanning technology, they are anxious to operate on a 'just-in-time' basis.

Lower costs and better service

These changing customer requirements, especially those associated with delivery arrangements, are proving difficult for the company to meet, not least because the various activities are handled by different departments. Concerned about these demands and the ever increasing costs of warehousing, distribution and transport, the company's senior management team have decided to consider a number of options designed to both lower costs and improve the quality of service:

(1)   *A 'logistics' solution.* This would involve a major internal reorganization, with all the activities surrounding the distribution of finished products being integrated within one function, termed the logistics department.

(2)   *A 'hi-tech' solution.* The regional warehouses would be closed and a new fully automated warehouse costing several million pounds would be built in Manchester. The company's fleet of lorries would be dispensed with and all transportation requirements would be sub-contracted to a haulage contractor.

(3)   *A 'contract out' solution.* The company would adopt a 'logistics' approach but subcontract the whole function to a specialist firm able to provide a full logistics service.

In deciding which option to select Williams's senior managers have not only to weigh potential costs against benefits, they also have to consider whether or not the company has the necessary expertise to adopt a 'logistics' approach. Would it fit within the company? Would it distract attention from the company's core business – manufacturing polishes? Or would they do better to 'stick to the knitting'?

Conclusion

This book has given an introduction to operations management. It started by showing how operations management is a central function in all organizations. Then we saw how to make decisions in a series of areas that are critical to the success of an organization.

In several ways, the book has balanced different viewpoints. It has emphasized that 'operations management' is not the same as 'production management'. Operations are not limited to manufacturing, but are used in every organization. About 75% of us work in the services; another 5% work in primary industries; the remaining 20% work in manufacturing. Almost half of the population does not go out to formal work – usually because they are too young, retired, ill or looking after relatives. About 10% of the potential workforce is unemployed. But we are all concerned with operations. We all belong to, and use, organizations that have different types of operations – whether they are companies, governments, charities, cricket clubs or families.

This book is based on the idea that decisions are needed for all these operations. If good decisions are made, resources are used effectively and there is little waste. If poor decisions are made, resources are wasted. This waste could mean that too many materials are used, people waste their time, money is wasted, and so on. You have probably passed a building site and seen the amount of bricks and other materials that are thrown away; or been asked to fill in a form with information that has no possible use; or had to wait a long time to be served in a shop; or visited an office and been passed from one person to another; or bought something that broke as soon as you started using it. These are a few of the many examples of poor operations you can find every day. Have a look around and see how often you can find organizations that could easily improve their operations.

Operations management looks for good ways of running an organization. Often a little thought is all it takes, but nobody has been able or willing to do this. How often have you looked at an operation and thought, 'Why do they do this – and not this'?

Usually problems are more complicated and need some rational analyses. This is the job of managers – to analyse situations and make decisions. This might involve some quantitative analysis, but any arithmetic is done by computer. There is no point in a manager doing arithmetic by hand; it just wastes time and is inaccurate.

In this book we have met a number of different types of problem that occur in every organization. For convenience these are divided into five parts.

Part I gave an introduction to operations management. It defined the subject and gave some examples of operations. We saw how decisions could be strategic, tactical and operational. In the rest of the book we looked at all levels of decision, but have emphasized strategic choices.

The purpose of every organization is to make a product. This might be goods or services, but is generally a combination of the two. So Part II looked at the ways of planning this product. This part started by looking at product planning and quality management. Then it showed how to forecast demand for the product and design a process to make it.

Now we have described the product, the next part looked in more detail at the process used to make it. Part III started by describing the types of process available and when each can be used. Then it considered the capacity needed, measurements of performance, how to control quality, and design of layout.

Part IV looked at the planning and scheduling of resources. This has a hierarchy of plans, which starts with the organization's mission and moves down to operational detail. In this part we saw how strategic decisions lead to the tactical aggregate plans, and these lead to master production schedules. The master production schedules, in turn, lead to a series of short-term decisions.

Operational schedules can be designed in several ways. Decisions about materials can be made through materials requirement planning or just-in-time systems. We also saw how short-term scheduling can give timetables for other resources. To schedule individual jobs we needed to look at job design and work measurement. Finally, this part looked at the planning of projects.

Part V, the final part, described some aspects of materials management. It described the role of logistics, and linked this to inventory control and location decisions.

We have described some major decisions that are made in every organization. You should now have some clear ideas about the best ways of managing operations. If you think about any organization, its competitiveness depends on its operations. It will only be successful in the long term if it manages its operations properly. So you, as an operations manager, have a direct impact on the success of your organization – and on its long-term survival.

On a wider front, the wealth, standard of living and quality of life in a country depend on the success of its organizations. When you practise good operations management, your effect is wider than you might, at first, imagine. We shall all benefit from your work – so will end by wishing you good fortune.

Appendix

A Answers to review questions

Chapter 2

2.1 All the activities that are directly concerned with making a product.

2.2 The management function that is responsible for all aspects of operations.

2.3 You can give many examples here.

2.4 Planning, organizing, staffing, directing, motivating, allocating, monitoring, controlling, and informing.

2.5 There are many reasons, but many refer to increased competition.

2.6 Its performance declines and it becomes less competitive.

2.7 Operations, accounting/finance, sales/marketing.

2.8 You can give many examples here.

2.9 Human resource management is not *directly* concerned with making the product – and when it is it becomes part of operations management. Product design is part of operations management.

2.10 As a central function in an organization, as a profession, by its approach to problems, or by the problems tackled.

2.11 You can give many alternatives here.

2.12 Because it is easier, cheaper, more convenient and less risky than experimenting with real operations.

2.13 No.

2.14 (a) tangible manufactured objects (b) intangible benefits (c) both goods and services.

2.15 Primary industry (agriculture and extraction), secondary industry (manufacturing and construction) and tertiary industry (services).

2.16 No.

2.17 They are not fundamentally different in any way.

Chapter 3

3.1 Strategic, tactical and operational.

3.2 No; operational decisions concern day to day running. All decisions are important.

3.3 (a) strategic (b) operational (c) strategic (d) tactical.

3.4 A statement of its fundamental beliefs and aims.

3.5 The set of strategic decisions about the organization as a whole.

3.6 The organization's environment and its specific competence.

3.7 What is our industry like?, What are the future prospects?, What are our strengths?, Who are the competitors?, What are the competitors' strengths?, and so on.

3.8 It sees itself as making a product rather than using a process.

3.9 Business strategy refers to the whole organization; competitive strategy is the part of business strategy specifically concerned with how the organization competes; operations strategy is within the operations function.

3.10 Strategic ones.

Chapter 4

4.1 Any goods or services that satisfy customer demand.

4.2 To make sure that an organization continues to supply products that satisfy customer demand.

4.3 Because customers have different needs.

4.4 Generation of ideas, initial screening of ideas, initial design, development and testing, market and economic analysis, final product development, launch of product.

4.5 There are many possible criteria, based on how well the product meets customer expectations and how well it fits into existing operations.

4.6 No.

4.7 To compare alternatives when there is a combination of qualitative and quantitative information.

4.8 Overheads, administration, marketing, research, development, testing, tooling and any other cost that does not depend on the number of units produced.

4.9 The product is making a profit.

4.10 £5000 now.

4.11 By discounting the benefits of both products to their present values.

4.12 The present value of an amount that is available at some time in the future – the sum of discounted income minus the sum of discounted costs.

4.13 C.

4.14 Introduction, growth, maturity, decline and withdrawal.

4.15 Reasonable values are about: (a) 1 year (b) 5 years (c) 10 years (d) 1 day.

4.16 No.

4.17 Costs are higher near the beginning of the life-cycle and decline over time. Revenue is highest around the maturity stage. High profits can be made in the growth stage, but these generally peak with maturity.

4.18 Research driven, new product exploiters, cost reducers.

Chapter 5

5.1 No.

5.2 Because it has implications for survival, reputation, marketing effort needed, market share, prices charged, profits, costs, liability for defects, and almost every other aspect of an organization's operations.

5.3 Because there are so many opinions, viewpoints and possible measures.

5.4 No.

5.5 The sum of design, appraisal, internal failure and external failure costs.

5.6 Fewer defects are produced and these are found earlier, so less effort is wasted making faulty products.

5.7 By minimizing the total quality cost. This is usually done by perfect quality.

5.8 Quality control inspects products to make sure they conform to designed quality; quality management is a wider function that is involved with all aspects of product quality.

5.9 No.

5.10 No.

5.11 Everyone is responsible for passing on products of perfect quality to following operations.

5.12 A small group of people working in an area who meet informally to discuss ways of improving quality and efficiency.

5.13 Survival, high quality products, increased productivity, low costs, reduced conflict, focused organization, and so on.

5.14 No.

5.15 By asking customers how satisfied they are.

Chapter 6

6.1 All plans and decisions are effective at some point in the future. They need relevant information about prevailing circumstances, and this must be forecast.

6.2 No.

6.3 Judgemental, projective and causal forecasting.

6.4 Subjective views based on opinions and intuition rather than quantitative analysis.

6.5 Personal insight, panel consensus, market surveys, historical analogy and Delphi method.

6.6 Unreliability, conflicting views from experts, cost of data collection, lack of available expertise, and so on.

6.7 Forecasting methods look at underlying pattern, but they cannot deal with short-term, random noise.

6.8 The mean error is defined as $1/n \times \sum E(t)$. Positive and negative errors cancel each other, so the mean error should have a value around zero unless the forecasts are biased.

6.9 Use alternative methods for a typical time series and calculate the mean error, mean absolute deviation, and mean squared error for each. All other things being equal, the best method is the one that gives smallest errors.

6.10 Linear regression finds the line of best fit (measured by the sum of squared errors) relating a dependent variable to an independent one.

6.11 The proportion of the total sum of squared error that is explained by the regression.

6.12 Because older data tends to swamp more recent and more relevant data.

6.13 By using a lower value of n.

6.14 By choosing a value of n equal to the cycle length.

6.15 Because the weight given to data declines exponentially with the age of the data, and the method smooths the effects of noise.

6.16 By choosing a higher value of α.

6.17 The amount a deseasonalized value must be multiplied by to allow for seasonal variations.

Chapter 7

7.1 The method used to make a product.

7.2 Process planning aims at making each product by the most efficient method. It is used whenever a new product is introduced, or whenever there is a significant change in operations.

7.3 Many factors can be important including demand pattern, flexibility, vertical integration, customer involvement and product quality.

7.4 Project, job shop, batch mass, production and continuous flow.

7.5 Reasonable answers are: (a) mass production (b) continuous flow (c) batch (d) project (e) job shop (f) any depending on the number produced, and so on.

7.6 A simplified view: planning uses project, introduction uses job shop, growth uses batch, maturity uses mass production.

7.7 Continuous flow and mass production. The process have no time lost for setups, they are largely automated, use more advanced technology and specialized equipment, planning is easier, and so on.

7.8 There are several ways including, reorganization of equipment operators, group technology and flexible automation.

7.9 Manual, mechanized and automated.

7.10 Numerically controlled machines, robots, flexible manufacturing systems and automated factories, all with computer aided design.

7.11 (a) numerically controlled (b) computerized numerically controlled (c) computer aided manufacturing (d) computer aided design (e) flexible manufacturing system (f) computer integrated manufacturing.

7.12 To improve productivity, reduce unit costs and obtain consistent high quality.

7.13 Generally NC, CNC, CAM, FMS and CIM.

7.14 The same as manufacturing: project, job shop, batch, mass production and continuous flow.

7.15 No. Many services are not expensive and some have extensive automation.

7.16 To describe the details of a process and highlight those areas where improvements might be made.

7.17 They show the relationships between individual operations and are used for analysing and describing processes.

7.18 Operation A must be finished before operation B starts, and B can start as soon as A is finished.

7.19 When managers want to see what each participant in the process is doing at any time.

Chapter 8

8.1 Layout is the physical arrangement of facilities in a process. A well laid out process will be efficient and work smoothly: a badly laid out process will reduce efficiency, effective capacity and utilization.

8.2 To make sure the process works as well as possible.

8.3 Process, product, hybrid, fixed and specialized.

8.4 No.

8.5 Yes.

8.6 Because such measures may not be available (particularly for new layouts), the data may be too difficult to collect, or other factors are considered more important.

8.7 Yes.

8.8 To separate consecutive work stations so that a short disruption to one does not interfere with the other.

8.9 The smallest output of any work station along the line.

8.10 To ensure a smooth flow of products through the layout, with all resources used as fully as possible.

8.11 A layout that is neither totally process nor product.

8.12 An arrangement with a dominant process layout, but some operations are taken aside in a product layout. They are used to obtain the high utilizations and other advantages of product processes in a process environment.

8.13 No – the product is in a fixed location not the equipment.

8.14 All materials, components and people must be moved to the site, there may be limited space, scheduling is difficult, the intensity of work varies, external factors affect operations, and so on.

8.15 The size and weight of goods being stored, value of goods, demand patterns, capital available,

operating costs, space available, and so on.

8.16 No.

Chapter 9

9.1 Capacity, productivity, utilization, efficiency, and so on.

9.2 Capacity is the maximum amount of a product that can be processed within a specified time; utilization measures the proportion of available capacity that is actually used; productivity is the amount produced in relation to one or more of the resources used; efficiency is the ratio of actual output to effective capacity.

9.3 Yes, if the efficiency decreases.

9.4 Total productivity measures the ratio of total output to total input; partial factor productivity measures the output for a single input.

9.5 Yes.

9.6 No.

9.7 Because the capacity measures the rate of output. The output has no meaning unless it is related to a period of time.

9.8 Designed capacity is the maximum output in ideal circumstances; effective capacity is the maximum output that can be expected under normal circumstances.

9.9 (a) passengers per trip
(b) customers per performance
(c) games per day (d) cases per week.

9.10 In decreasing order, they are designed capacity, effective capacity and actual output.

9.11 Examine forecast demand and translate this into a capacity requirement, calculate available capacity, identify mismatches between capacity required and available, generate alternative plans for overcoming any mismatch, evaluate these plans and select the best.

9.12 Capacity must be closely matched to demand to give high utilization. This can not be done when demand is continuous, but capacity is discrete.

9.13 Demand management and capacity management.

9.14 Fixed costs are spread over more units, more efficient processes are used and there is more experience with the product.

9.15 If the first operation takes T, the second takes $0.8T$, the fourth takes $0.8^2 T$, the eighth takes $0.8^3 T$ and so on.

9.16 Experience and practice make jobs easier, short cuts are found, skills increase, routines are known, and so on.

9.17 To stop the performance of equipment falling below an acceptable level.

9.18 No.

9.19 After the period that minimizes the total cost per unit time.

9.20 The probability that a part continues to operate throughout a period.

Chapter 10

10.1 No.

10.2 Quality control inspects products to make sure they conform to designed quality; quality management is a wider function that is involved with all aspects of quality.

10.3 No

10.4 As early as possible, preferably at the product design stage, and with suppliers.

10.5 Acceptance sampling sees if products are conforming to design quality; process control sees if the process is working properly.

10.6 Because inspecting all the products may be expensive, destructive or infeasible.

10.7 No; there are always random variations.

10.8 The distribution of means found in samples from the population.

10.9 To see if a batch of products should be accepted as having high enough quality.

10.10 Sampling by attribute classifies units as either acceptable or defective; sampling by variable measure some continuous value.

10.11 Because this would indicate perfect differentiation between good batches (where the probability of acceptance is 1) and bad batches (where the probability of acceptance is 0).

10.12 No; different numbers of defects may be identified and rejected.

10.13 The process is out of control and needs adjusting, but check for random fluctuations before doing this.

10.14 A single reading outside the control limits, a clear trend, several consecutive readings near to a control limit, several consecutive readings on the same side of the mean, a sudden change in apparent mean levels, very erratic observations.

10.15 Because X charts give mean values but they do not show the variation in these means.

Chapter 11

11.1 No; it is largely strategic but there are both tactical and operational decisions.

11.2 Strategic plans lead to capacity plans, then aggregate plans, master schedules and short-term schedules.

11.3 (a) aggregate plans (b) master schedule (c) short-term schedule (d) short-term schedule.

11.4 A number of sources, including forecasts, plans for previous periods, decisions at higher levels of planning, and so on.

11.5 Yes.

11.6 They find the resources available this period, by taking the resources last period, adding any new arrivals and subtracting any deletions.

11.7 Monthly production over the next few months.

11.8 No.

11.9 A schedule of monthly production for each family of products.

11.10 It is easy to use, convenient, the results can be good, the process is well understood and trusted, and experienced planner has credibility in the organization.

11.11 The cumulative supply line should be close to the cumulative demand line, and it should not change gradient frequently.

11.12 It is easy to understand and use, it is convenient and can be done on a spreadsheet.

11.13 It finds an optimal solution and does not rely on the skill of planners.

11.14 To add details to the aggregate plan, and give a timetable for making individual products.

11.15 These mainly come from the aggregate plan, available capacity, actual customer orders and available resources.

Chapter 12

12.1 Material requirements planning – a procedure in which the master schedule is used to plan the arrival of materials, components, parts, and so on.

12.2 Dependent demand systems find requirements from known production plans; independent demand systems forecast demand, usually from historic figures.

12.3 No – although MRP was originally developed for manufacturing companies, any organization that can meet its requirements can use MRP.

12.4 A master schedule, bill of materials, information about current stocks and lead times.

12.5 By subtracting current stock and scheduled receipts from gross requirements.

12.6 It relates demand for materials directly to a master schedule.

12.7 The requirements which limit its applicability, and the amount of data manipulation.

12.8 Timetable of orders, changes to orders, exceptions report, performance reports and inventory transactions.

12.9 Because small orders have high administration and delivery costs.

12.10 A rule to suggest how many separate orders should be combined into a single larger order.

12.11 Because it uses approximations for the average stock level and costs, demands are assumed to be discrete and occurring at fixed points, and we have assumed that an optimal solution occurs as soon as cost begins to rise.

12.12 Manufacturing resources planning, which extends the MRP approach to a wide range of functions.

12.13 Yes; in common with all approaches of this type.

Chapter 13

13.1 Other systems assume that stocks are essential and ask 'How can costs be minimized?'; JIT assumes that stocks are not necessary and asks the question 'How can stocks be eliminated?'

13.2 Operations are organized so they occur just as they are needed, with materials delivered just as they are to be used, and so on.

13.3 They are a waste of resources and should be eliminated; they hide problems which should be tackled and solved.

13.4 An organization with a stable environment, standard products with few variations, a balanced process that uses resources fully, reliable production equipment, small batches of materials, short lead times for materials, efficient materials handling, reliable suppliers, and so on.

13.5 No.

13.6 To control the flow of materials in a JIT system.

13.7 Each container has a Kanban, so the number of Kanbans sets the number of containers and hence the amount of work in progress.

13.8 They are long-term partners who co-operate and have a mutually beneficial trading arrangement.

13.9 Focused factories specialize in making one item very efficiently. They can use specialized equipment in the long production runs guaranteed by JIT systems.

13.10 No.

13.11 No; just-in-time controls stocks but this is only one of its functions.

13.12 There are many advantages to choose from including reduced stocks, easier planning, higher quality, better control, lower costs, and so on.

13.13 No; just-in-time needs a change of attitudes, plans, procedures and operations. It can not be tried as a small experiment.

Chapter 14

14.1 To give detailed timetables for jobs, equipment and people.

14.2 Resources needed and available, the master schedule, costs, and so on.

14.3 A simple heuristic rule that experience has found to give good solutions.

14.4 Useful rules would be (a) most urgent first (b) earliest due date first (c) first-come-first-served (d) shortest first.

14.5 No.

14.6 In principle there is no difference.

14.7 A process where jobs use the same machines in the same order.

14.8 To minimize the make-span in a flow shop with two machines.

14.9 When operators are not permanently assigned to a piece of equipment, and when they are in short supply.

14.10 Yes.

14.11 To monitor progress, make sure planned schedules are actually being achieved, warning of problems, making minor adjustments to schedules, giving feedback, and so on.

14.13 No.

Chapter 15

15.1 To some extent.

15.2 Finding the best way of doing a job.

15.3 Job design finds the best way of doing a job; work measurement finds how long the job will take.

15.4 Employers want to meet the economic, technical, productivity, quality and other goals of the organization; employees want a job that is safe, satisfying and rewarding to meet their social and psychological needs.

15.5 Employers and employees.

15.6 No.

15.7 Because it affects the way operations are done – and hence the performance of the organization.

15.8 The physical environment, social environment and work methods.

15.9 Morale and motivation are improved by significant, identifiable and varied tasks, needing a variety of skills, and giving workers autonomy and feedback.

15.10 To find the time needed to do a job – its standard time.

15.11 Actual time is the time an operator actually takes to do the essential parts of the job; normal time is the time an operator would normally take to do the job if they worked at standard rate; standard time is the total time that should be allowed for a job, including allowances.

15.12 Using historical data, estimation or a time study.

15.13 The standard time.

Chapter 16

16.1 A self-contained piece of work with a clear start and finish aimed at making a unique product.

16.2 To plan, schedule and control the activities in a project – and make sure specifications are met within budget and time.

16.3 No.

16.4 Planning and execution.

16.5 Arrows show activities and nodes show the events at their start and finish.

16.6 A list of all activities in the project with their immediate predecessors. Durations, resources and other information can be added, but these are not essential for drawing the network.

16.7 Before an activity can start all preceding activities must be finished; the arrows simply show precedence and their length and orientation have no significance. There are also some secondary rules.

16.8 Uniqueness dummies make sure only two activities go between two nodes; logical dummies make sure the network shows the proper dependence.

16.9 The earliest time for an event is the latest time by which all preceding activities can be finished; the latest time for an event is the latest time that allows all following activities to be started on time.

16.10 The total amount the duration of the activity can expand without affecting the length of the project. It is the difference between the time available for an activity and the time actually used.

16.11 Zero.

16.12 The critical path is the chain of activities that set the length of the project. If any critical activity is extended or delayed the whole project is delayed.

16.13 CPM assumes activity durations are fixed; PERT assumes the activity durations follow a known distribution.

16.14 The rule of sixths uses three estimates of activity time to give the expected duration and variance; it is used in PERT networks.

16.15 The project duration is assumed to be Normally distributed with mean equal to the sum of the expected durations of the critical path, and variance equal to the sum of the variances.

16.16 The critical activities.

16.17 By the amount of the total float of activities on a parallel path.

16.18 By its total float.

16.19 The shortest time to finish an activity if more resources are used.

16.20 No.

16.21 They show clearly what stage each activity in a project should have reached at any time. This highlights any expediting, rescheduling and preparation needed.

16.22 By delaying non-critical activities to times when fewer resources are needed.

Chapter 17

17.1 All the physical items needed for making goods and services, including raw materials, components, sub-assemblies, parts, tools, consumables, services or any other types of item.

17.2 Logistics is responsible for the physical movement of all materials and products from initial suppliers through operations and on to final customers.

17.3 No.

17.4 Procurement or purchasing, traffic and transport, receiving, warehousing or stores, inventory control, material handling, shipping, distribution, location and communications.

17.5 To make sure that materials needed to support operations are available at the time they are needed.

17.6 Purchasing is concerned with the actual buying of materials; procurement is a broader term that includes a number of related activities.

17.7 The cycle starts with a person needing an item making a request for it, moves through the work done in the procurement area and suppliers, and finishes when the item is delivered to the person.

17.8 Procurement used to be a clerical job but is now seen as a profession. There are many changes that come with this adjustment.

17.9 Logistics is the overall function concerned with all movements of product; physical distribution is primarily concerned with movements out to customers; materials management is primarily concerned with movements in from suppliers.

17.10 Location, transport, inventory control, warehousing, communications, and so on.

17.11 Road, rail, air, water and pipeline.

Chapter 18

18.1 To act as a buffer between supply and demand.

18.2 A useful classification one has raw materials, work in progress, finished goods, spare parts and consumables.

18.3 Unit, reorder, holding and shortage costs.

18.4 Holding cost rises with higher stocks, while the others fall.

18.5 What items to stock, when to place orders, how much to order?

18.6 A single item is considered, demand is known exactly, demand is continuous and constant, costs are known exactly, replenishment is instantaneous, no shortages are allowed.

18.7 The order quantity that minimizes inventory costs, when some assumptions are made.

18.8 It reduces holding costs and increases all other costs.

18.9 The amount of an item that is in stock when it is time to place an order.

18.10 It is the lead time demand minus any stock already on order.

18.11 No; costs generally rise slowly around the economic order quantity.

18.12 It is the probability that a demand can be met from stock. This chapter has used cycle-service level, which is the probability that an item remains in stock during a stock cycle.

18.13 It reduces the probability of shortages and increases service levels.

18.14 By increasing the amount of safety stock.

18.15 Order quantity = target stock level − current stocks (− any orders outstanding).

18.16 For a periodic review system, as there is more uncertainty over a longer period.

18.17 A model where the item is only held in stock for a single period and is then scrapped.

18.18 It is the probability that at least n papers are sold.

18.19 If n is high enough for the inequality to become invalid each newspaper bought will give an expected loss.

18.20 They show the importance of items so that appropriate effort can be spent on controlling their stocks.

18.21 B items.

Chapter 19

19.1 Because they have long-term effects, are expensive, have serious consequences for mistakes, affect all operations, and so on.

19.2 No.

19.3 It can expand on the current site, open additional facilities, or close existing facilities and relocate.

19.4 No.

19.5 No; not necessarily as there can also be lower productivity and other high costs.

19.6 Culture, operation, type of organization.

19.7 No.

19.8 A feasible set approach compares a small number of feasible sites and chooses the best; infinite set approach uses geometric arguments to show where the best site would be if there were no restrictions on site availability.

19.9 Many costs could be included, but the most important are inward transport, outward transport and operating costs.

19.10 Inward transport moves materials in from suppliers; outward transport moves products out to customers.

19.11 They allow a range of factors, both quantitative and qualitative to be considered.

19.12 No.

19.13 Important factors might include population size and age, incomes, locations of hospitals and other doctors, public transport, roads, parking, security, location of other businesses such as pharmacies, and so on.

19.14 A measure for the centre of customer demand.

19.15 No.

Appendix

B Probabilities for the Normal distribution

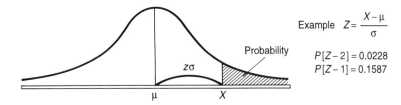

Example $Z = \dfrac{X - \mu}{\sigma}$

Probability

$P[Z - 2] = 0.0228$
$P[Z - 1] = 0.1587$

Normal deviate z	.00	.01	.02	.03	.04	.05	.06	.07	.08	.09
0.0	.5000	.4960	.4920	.4880	.4840	.4801	.4761	.4721	.4681	.4641
0.1	.4602	.4562	.4522	.4483	.4443	.4404	.4364	.4325	.4286	.4247
0.2	.4207	.4168	.4129	.4090	.4052	.4013	.3974	.3936	.3897	.3859
0.3	.3821	.3783	.3745	.3707	.3669	.3632	.3594	.3557	.3520	.3483
0.4	.3446	.3409	.3372	.3336	.3300	.3264	.3228	.3192	.3156	.3121
0.5	.3085	.3050	.3015	.2981	.2946	.2912	.2877	.2843	.2810	.2776
0.6	.2743	.2709	.2676	.2643	.2611	.2578	.2546	.2514	.2483	.2451
0.7	.2420	.2389	.2358	.2327	.2296	.2266	.2236	.2206	.2177	.2148
0.8	.2119	.2090	.2061	.2033	.2005	.1977	.1949	.1922	.1894	.1867
0.9	.1841	.1814	.1788	.1762	.1736	.1711	.1685	.1660	.1635	.1611
1.0	.1587	.1562	.1539	.1515	.1492	.1469	.1446	.1423	.1401	.1379
1.1	.1357	.1335	.1314	.1292	.1271	.1251	.1230	.1210	.1190	.1170
1.2	.1151	.1131	.1112	.1093	.1075	.1056	.1038	.1020	.1003	.0985
1.3	.0968	.0951	.0934	.0918	.0901	.0885	.0869	.0853	.0838	.0823
1.4	.0808	.0793	.0778	.0764	.0749	.0735	.0721	.0708	.0694	.0681
1.5	.0668	.0655	.0643	.0630	.0618	.0606	.0594	.0582	.0571	.0559
1.6	.0548	.0537	.0526	.0516	.0505	.0495	.0485	.0475	.0465	.0455
1.7	.0446	.0436	.0427	.0418	.0409	.0401	.0392	.0384	.0375	.0367
1.8	.0359	.0351	.0344	.0336	.0329	.0322	.0314	.0307	.0301	.0294
1.9	.0287	.0281	.0274	.0268	.0262	.0256	.0250	.0244	.0239	.0233
2.0	.0228	.0222	.0217	.0212	.0207	.0202	.0197	.0192	.0188	.0183
2.1	.0179	.0174	.0170	.0166	.0162	.0158	.0154	.0150	.0146	.0143
2.2	.0139	.0136	.0132	.0129	.0125	.0122	.0119	.0116	.0113	.0110
2.3	.0107	.0104	.0102	.0099	.0096	.0094	.0091	.0089	.0087	.0084
2.4	.0082	.0080	.0078	.0075	.0073	.0071	.0069	.0068	.0066	.0064
2.5	.0062	.0060	.0059	.0057	.0055	.0054	.0052	.0051	.0049	.0048
2.6	.0047	.0045	.0044	.0043	.0041	.0040	.0039	.0038	.0037	.0036
2.7	.0035	.0034	.0033	.0032	.0031	.0030	.0029	.0028	.0027	.0026
2.8	.0026	.0025	.0024	.0023	.0023	.0022	.0021	.0021	.0020	.0019
2.9	.0019	.0018	.0018	.0017	.0016	.0016	.0015	.0015	.0014	.0014
3.0	.0013	.0013	.0013	.0012	.0012	.0011	.0011	.0011	.0010	.0010

Index

Notes

Notes

Notes

Notes

Notes

Notes

Notes

Notes